Usability in Practice

How Companies Develop User-Friendly Products

Edited by
Michael E. Wiklund
American Institutes for Research
Lexington, Massachusetts

AP PROFESSIONAL
Boston San Diego New York
London Sydney Tokyo Toronto

This book is printed on acid-free paper. ∞

AP PROFESSIONAL
955 Massachusetts Avenue, Cambridge, MA 02139

An imprint of ACADEMIC PRESS, INC.
A Division of HARCOURT BRACE & COMPANY

United Kingdom Edition published by
ACADEMIC PRESS LIMITED
24–28 Oval Road, London NW1 7DX

ISBN 0-12-751250-0

Printed in the United States of America
94 95 96 97 98 IP 9 8 7 6 5 4 3 2 1

CONTENTS

Contents

Chapter 12   American Airlines   359
Janice S. James

Chapter 13   Usability Engineering at Dun & Bradstreet Software   389
Chauncey E. Wilson, Beth A. Loring,
Len Conte, and Karen Stanley

CONTRIBUTORS

Number in parentheses indicates page on which contributor's chapter begins.

Brenda J. Burkhart (489), Bellcore, 3 Corporate Place, Room PYA 2J-318, Piscataway, NJ 08854

Mary Beth Butler (293), Lotus Development Corporation, 1 Rogers Street, Cambridge, MA 02142

Stanley H. Caplan (21), Eastman Kodak Company, 20 Avenue E, Rochester, NY 14653-7008

Betsy Comstock (147), Digital Equipment Corporation, 146 Main Street, ML011-L12, Maynard, MA 01754-2571

Len Conte (389), Dun & Bradstreet Software, 550 Cochituate Road, MS 42D, Framingham, MA 01701

Mary Czerwinski (111), Compaq Computer Corporation, P.O. Box 692000, MS 100801, Houston, TX 77269-2000

Thomas Dayton (489), Bellcore, 3 Corporate Place, Room PYA 2J-318, Piscataway, NJ 08854

Mary Dieli (327), Microsoft Corporation, One Microsoft Way, Redmond, WA 98052-6399

Ken Dye (327), Microsoft Corporation, One Microsoft Way, Redmond, WA 98052-6399

Kate Ehrlich (293), Lotus Development Corporation, 1 Rogers Street, Cambridge, MA 02142

Liam Friedland (261), Borland International, 1800 Green Hills Road, Scotts Valley, CA 95067

Tom Gomoll (83), Apple Computer, Inc., MS 302-1HI, 20400 Stevens Creek Boulevard, Cupertino, CA 95014

Janice James (359), American Airlines, P.O. Box 61966, MD 4230, Dallas, TX 75261-9616

Robert J. Logan (59), Thomson Consumer Electronics, P.O. Box 1976, MS INH-405, Indianapolis, IN 4206-1976

Beth Loring (389), Dun & Bradstreet Software, MS 42D, 550 Cochituate Road, Framingham, MA 01701

Arnold M. Lund (457), Ameritech Services, Incorporated, 2000 W. Ameritech Center Drive, #2C46, Hoffman Estates, IL 60196-1025

Jay Lundell (195), Hewlett-Packard Corporation, MS 330, 8600 Soper Hill Road, Everett, WA 98205-1298

Marshall McClintock (327), Microsoft Corporation, One Microsoft Way, Redmond, WA 98052-6399

Michael F. Mohageg (227), Silicon Graphics, Inc., 2051 N. Shoreline Boulevard, MS 8V971, Mountain View, CA 94043-1398

Ron Perkins (427), Ziff Communications, 25 First Street, Cambridge, MA 02141

Cynthia Purvis (111), Compaq Computer Corporation, P.O. Box 692000, MS 100801, Houston, Texas 77269-2000

Thomas Rideout (195), Hewlett-Packard Corporation, MS 330, 8600 Soper Hill Road, Everett, WA 98205-1298

David Rollert (427), Ziff Communications, 25 First Street, Cambridge, Massachusetts 02141

Robert W. Root (489), Bellcore, 3 Corporate Place, Room PYA 2J-318, Piscataway, NJ 08854

Daniel Rosenberg (261), Borland International, 1800 Green Hills Road, Scotts Valley, California 95067

Aita Salasoo (489), Bellcore, 3 Corporate Place, Room PYA 2H-318, Piscataway, New Jersey 08854

Mark Simpson (327), Microsoft Corporation, One Microsoft Way, Redmond, WA 98052-6399

James F. Sorce (559), GTE Laboratories, MS 42D, 40 Sylvan Road, MS-38, Waltham, MA 02254

Karen Stanley (389), Dun & Bradstreet Software, 550 Cochituate Road, Framingham, MA 01701

Reynold P. Stimart (517), General Electric Information Services, 401 North Washington Street, Rockville, MD 20850

Robert A Virzi (559), GTE Laboratories, 40 Sylvan Road, MS-38, Waltham, MA 02254

Paul Weiler (111), Compaq Computer Corporation, P.O. Box 692000, MS 100801, Houston, TX 77269-2000

Ellen White (489), Bellcore, 3 Corporate Place, Room PYA 2H-318, Piscataway, NJ 08854

Anna M. Wichansky (227), Silicon Graphics, Inc., 2051 N. Shoreline Boulevard, MS 8V971, Mountain View, CA 94043-1398

Dennis Wixon (147), Digital Equipment Corporation, 110 Spitbrook Road, ZK02-1/N42, Nashua, NH 03062

Michael E. Wiklund, American Institutes for Research, 70 Westview Street, Lexington, MA 02173-3131

Chauncey Wilson (389), Dun & Bradstreet Software, MS 42D, 550 Cochituate Road, Framingham, MA 01701

Irene Wong (83), Apple Computer, Inc., 20400 Stevens Creek Boulevard, MS 302-1HI, Cupertino, CA 95014

CHAPTER 1

Introduction

Michael E. Wiklund
*Usability Engineering
Group
American Institutes for
Research*

Michael Wiklund directs the usability engineering group at American Institutes for Research, which delivers user interface education, research, design, and evaluation services to commercial and government clients. He has advised many companies on how to establish and maintain a successful usability program. His design portfolio includes numerous products for medical, scientific, business, and home use. Since 1987, he has been a visiting industry professor at Tufts University, where he teaches a project-oriented course—titled Applied Software User Interface Design. Since 1991, he has written a monthly column on usability engineering for Medical Device and Diagnostic Industry, a periodical read by approximately 40,000 product development professionals in the medical industry. He holds an M.S. degree in engineering design from Tufts University and is a licensed professional engineer (industrial engineering-human factors).

Let me introduce this book by celebrating the generous spirit of the people and organizations that have contributed to it. My goal was to pull together a set of case studies about establishing and nurturing a usability program within a product development organization. I reasoned that such cases would set a good example for others to follow, particularly those facing market pressures to reform their approach to user interface design. However, I was concerned that I would not be able to get enough companies to share such vital information about their product development process. As it turns out, my concern was unfounded.

Despite their heavy workloads, representatives from 17 major corporations were pleased to write chapters. I believe the forthcoming nature of their submissions demonstrates a collegial spirit found among people challenged to design usable products and their sense of a joint responsibility for making products serve human needs, not to mention the pride they take in their work. I owe them all a debt of gratitude for their contributions, which should have a lasting, positive impact on how product development organizations worldwide approach the task of user interface design. I also believe their contributions give people considering a career in usability a realistic sense for how things work in industry—warts and all. Furthermore, I think that the case studies on the implementation of usability programs and the tangible results (i.e. products that are capable of being used intuitively, correctly, and that users like) will captivate anyone concerned with design management and overall product quality issues (see Figure 1.)

Before commencing with the first case study, I would like to set the stage by explaining the organization of this book, commenting on the value companies place on usability and reflecting on the emergence of a usability movement in high-tech industries.

How This Book Is Organized

This book includes 17 chapters written by usability specialists from diverse product development organizations. In each chapter, the author or joint authors explain how their company develops usable products. Most start with a synopsis of their company's business, provide an overview of its usability program's origins and current status, present a product development case study that demonstrates the positive results of an investment in usability services, and summarize the lessons they have learned about implementing a successful program.

Each chapter is an independent work, written to promote a better understanding of the contributions usability can make to organizations and product designs. I did not especially encourage contributing authors from different companies to collaborate, although many are colleagues. Some authors recount the continuing struggle to introduce new methods into conservative organizations. Others describe how usability has become the hub of design activity in their company.

Readers do not need to study every chapter, nor read the chapters in order, to benefit from this book. Instead, they can pick and choose the chapters that seem most

Figure 1   Making technology as friendly as the family pet

Artist: Beth Anderson

relevant to their interests and needs. For example, those in the telecommunications industry might want to read the Ameritech, Bellcore, GE Information Services, or GTE Laboratories case studies. Similarly, readers in the consumer software business might want to review the lessons learned by Borland International, Lotus Development Corporation, or Microsoft Corporation. Although lessons on user-centered design appear to be no more dependent on industry sector than on corporate culture and usability program size and longevity.

Because the chapters ultimately needed to follow some sort of order, I grouped them by industry sector as follows:

- Consumer products
    Eastman Kodak Company
    Thomson Consumer Electronics

- Computer hardware and software
    Apple Computer, Incorporated
    Compaq Computer Corporation
    Digital Equipment Corporation
    Hewlett-Packard Company
    Silicon Graphics, Incorporated

- Consumer software
    Borland International
    Lotus Development Corporation
    Microsoft Corporation

- Online service and business software
    American Airlines, Incorporated
    Dun & Bradstreet Software Services, Incorporated
    Ziff Desktop Information

- Telecommunications hardware and software
    Ameritech
    Bellcore
    GE Information Services
    GTE Laboratories Incorporated

Arranging the chapters according to business sector seemed a simple and straightforward way to facilitate cross comparisons among companies that compete in the same or comparable markets. Clearly, I could have placed certain companies, such as Hewlett-Packard or Eastman Kodak, into two or more categories because of the breadth of their businesses. In such cases, I let the products featured in the associated case studies or the company's dominant business be my guide.

At the end of the book, I have provided a listing of resources for people just learning about usability or contemplating establishing a usability group. The resources include relevant books, periodicals, proceedings, newsletters, professional societies, academic programs, and usability consultant directories.

The Contributors: Authors and Companies

The authors who have contributed to the book are all active usability professionals. Many hold or have held leadership positions in the Human Factors and Ergonomics Society, the Usability Professionals Association, and the Association for Computing

Machinery's Special Interest Group on Computer and Human Interaction. Most have written extensively on the subject of usability process issues and applied user interface design. Several authors actually founded their company's usability program or currently manage portions of it. All care deeply about their mission to design usable products and help their companies win in the marketplace. All seem to thrive at usability challenges (both technical and organizational) and enjoy their work.

The computer and software industries are particularly well represented in this book, reflecting the fact that the usability movement has a solid footing there. However, several case studies focus on other product classes, such as communication and entertainment devices, which are not computers per se, even though they may incorporate microprocessor technology.

All the companies described here differ in important ways, despite a high-tech orientation. Some are multibillion dollar companies; others are smaller. Some develop products for industrial customers (e.g., for people managing communication networks); others make products for public consumption via retail avenues (e.g., a television set). Some companies have taken a systematic approach to usability for years, while others are just getting started. Some companies employ only a few people to work on usability problems (2-3); others have large departments devoted to usability (20 people or more). I consider this diversity useful, because readers are more likely to find examples of usability programs that have been established in companies and situations like their own.

Things to Keep in Mind

One of this book's strengths is that it presents 17 insider viewpoints on corporate design. Accordingly, readers get to hear the stories firsthand, with emphasis placed on those issues the authors feel most deeply about. For example, consumer software developers must be concerned not only with the impressions of their customers, but also of media reviewers who may use their products for only a short time then rate them against others. This is why the content and organization of each chapter varies somewhat, although I did ask authors to include certain baseline information, such as defining the composition of their staffs. However, authors had to weigh carefully what they could and could not reveal about their organizations and the products they produce. Generally, they have excluded proprietary information and obtained their organization's approval to publish their case study.

As a result of the necessity of obtaining approval, some authors may have hesitated to criticize their organization too harshly, even if there was due cause. To do so just would not have made sense for people who value their jobs and working relationships. Therefore, readers should assume that usability programs have a few more freckles and encounter a few more bumps on route to meeting their goals than reported here. Nonetheless, I feel the authors have been especially forthcoming in what they have revealed.

In addition, this book focuses primarily on success stories. I did not search out cases of program failure, even though several companies have invested heavily in usability only to later reduce their level of commitment because of limited resources or other reasons. I also concluded that inviting ex-employees to write postmortems about their past employers would have produced a particularly one-sided view of the subject.

One final point; usability practices are dynamic. They change year-to-year, if not month-to-month. People come and go, and the nature of the work evolves. Therefore, describing a usability practice is like taking a snapshot of a moving object (without panning). The only thing you can be sure of is that the state of the usability practice will be different almost immediately after the snapshot is taken. Accordingly, it is possible that some usability practices described here have doubled in size, radically change their services and delivery methods, or been abolished as part of a radical, cost-cutting maneuver. These are just the realities of working in the usability field.

Understanding Usability

Next, I would like to provide an orientation for readers who may be unfamiliar with *usability, an art and science that goes by many other names, including usability engineering, user-centered design, human factors engineering, human factors, engineering psychology*, and *ergonomics.* First, I offer a personal definition of *usability.* Then, I discuss the relationship of usability to product complexity and quality, the consequences of investing in usability versus being negligent, and finally, I describe the fundamental process that can translate an organization's intention to produce usable products into reality.

Defining *Usability*

An ordeal faced by most usability professionals is the need to constantly explain and justify what they do for a living. To outsiders, usability seems to be an obscure, somewhat mysterious, boutique design service. Even though usability has received positive exposure in the popular press, such as a major article in *The Atlantic*[1] and frequent articles in the *Wall Street Journal*,[2] many people still are unfamiliar with the concept. They know that products may be easy or hard to use, but are unaware that some people concentrate on usability as their profession. They do not understand that usability can be intentionally designed into a product; instead, they seem to think that if a product is easy to use, it is the result of a fortuitous but unpredictable set of circumstances. They are often surprised to learn that thousands of people have been working for decades (starting in earnest with work by the military in the 1940s) to expand the base of knowledge regarding people's interactions with technology and produce products that are more user friendly.

Nonetheless, more people learn the value of user-centered design each day. This may be because usability has become a heated battleground for software developers. Every week, the computer industry tabloids and magazines are chock-full of advertisements claiming the usability achievements of various companies' products. From the ads (see Figure 2), as well as more substantive discussions of usability in product reviews, people are coming to understand that usability is a key attribute of any product used by people. But, they still may be fuzzy on the basic concept of usability.

I think of usability as a cumulative attribute of a product. When a product development team designs a product, it tries to include the features people need to accomplish tasks, present those features in a manner that people intuitively grasp and find efficient to use in the long term. They also attempt to eliminate the potential for critical, design-induced mistakes and to include design qualities that make people feel good about using the product. Almost every aspect of a product's appearance, feature set, and interaction scheme (choreography, if you will) affects these goals. For example, if a control switch label is written in plain English and is large enough to be legible, usability increases. By comparison, if the label employs unfamiliar or ambiguous terminology or is too small to read, usability suffers. When designing a typical computer-based product, developing good labels may represent just one of hundreds or even thousands of design considerations. Total or overall usability depends on how well design teams handle all of these details.

If a product is to have a high level of usability, the product development team must approach the design of the user interface—the elements of the product that people interact with—at a broader conceptual level as well. Often, products noted for their usability may in fact be mechanically or electronically complex. This apparent paradox is often the result of good work by usability professionals, whose goal has been to evoke in users a simple mental model (framework) of how the product works and to protect them from having to learn unnecessary design details. For example, most people's mental model of a propeller airplane is simple: The engine turns the propeller, which pulls the craft through the air as it is supported by the lift developed by the wing. People do not need to know the details of aerodynamics and the specifics of how turboprop engines develop thrust to get the basic idea (see Figure 3).

Figure 2   Advertising excerpts

Lotus 1-2-3® Release 4 for Windows™

"In a recent usability study… Microsoft® Excel* users were asked to compare their spreadsheet to the new 1-2-3® Release 4 for Windows.™ They spent hours comparing the applications, performing everyday tasks like making charts, creating tables, printing reports. And when the test was done, four out of six Excel users had changed their minds–they preferred the new 1-2-3. We were flattered. But not suprised. After all, when we designed 1-2-3 Release 4 we talked to thousands of people just like those in the test–spreadsheet users of all levels. And we incorporated their suggestions into the new 1-2-3."

*Microsoft Excel Version 4.0   Advertisement in <u>PC Week</u>, November 22, 1993, p. 128.

Microsoft® Office Standard Edition

"The Microsoft Office couldn't have happened without a lot of concrete feedback from you. We've studied how you work and used your suggestions to develop great computing solutions. In our usability lab, 15 full-time scientists constantly watch how people use our products. In fact, we've tracked over 1.5 million user actions to understand just how you work with your computer. That's why Microsoft consistently pioneers better ways to work."

Advertisement in <u>PC Magazine</u>, November 9, 1993, p. 193.

Borland® Quattro® Pro 5.0 for Windows™

"The world's easiest Windows spreadsheet. Whether you're working alone on your spreadsheet or sharing data with a workgroup, only Quattro Pro puts everything you want under one roof. Complete on-line help and interactive tutors make Quattro Pro for Windows easy to learn. And Spreadsheet Notebooks make it easy to use."

Advertisement in <u>PC Magazine</u>, November 9, 1993, p. 6.

Figure 3   Getting the basic idea of flight

<u>Artist:</u> Benjamin Wiklund, 8 years old.

The same kinds of basic mental models can help people learn to use even more complex products, such as software used for three-dimensional modeling or interacting with direct broadcast satellite systems. Developing and successfully implementing simple models is one of the usability professional's most important talents.

Usability may also be thought of as a design philosophy that places users' needs high—if not first—on the list of design priorities. Companies are sometimes criticized for building products that are well suited to established manufacturing processes and marketing mechanisms, but do not meet users' needs squarely. This approach contrasts sharply with companies that are obsessed with understanding and meeting users' needs and adapting themselves—even reinventing themselves—to do so.

The Relationship of Usability to Quality

Not surprisingly, a philosophy favoring users' needs ties in closely with total quality management (TQM) goals.[3] Today, TQM is the vogue in product development organizations. According to the TQM dogma, organizations should bend over backward to understand their customers' needs so they will be in a better position to fulfill them. Clearly, a user-centered design process fits well with TQM initiatives, since the process emphasizes early and continual involvement of users in the design process.

Early involvement may mean bringing users into labs to work with existing products, conducting contextual inquiries (on-site interviews) with people as they use a product, or running a series of focus groups aimed at defining new product requirements and concepts. Further along in the design process, users may get involved in assessing alternative concept models and reviewing usability goals. When working models are available, users might "take them for a test drive" involving free exploration of product features and the performance of specified tasks.

When a company involves users to this degree, it is much less likely to mess up a design. And if the company does make mistakes, they will be apparent early in the design process when there is time to fix them or start again with a minimal waste of time and money. The result of the user-centered design process should be a higher quality product that provides a "glove fit" with users' needs.

When user interface designers hit the mark, it creates a terrific feeling for everyone involved. The product development team feels a tremendous sense of achievement, and users feel empowered by products that seem simple to use. It is this feeling that has driven the success of products such as Apple Computer's Macintosh® computer, the leading word processing applications, and the all-automatic, "idiot-proof" cameras. Designers and company executives feel good because such likable products can either boost sales or profit margins and build a reputation for design excellence. The user interface is an excellent place to focus quality improvement initiatives, because of its high visibility and the fact that so many users base their first and lasting impression of a product on the quality of its interface.

The Relationship of Usability to Complexity

The usability movement has been fueled indirectly by recent leaps in product complexity—what some people refer to as "creeping functionality." I link the "creep" among high-tech products to the ubiquitous microprocessor. In the past, adding functions to a product required a great deal of mechanical and electrical engineering. For example, if designers wanted to add a clock to an oven's control panel, they had to buy clock parts and bolt them into the faceplate of the oven. Today, the clock feature is a veritable freebie on more advanced ovens that employ a microprocessor and associated display to set the oven temperature, set the timer, and perform myriad other functions. The intoxicating effect of cheap-to-produce features has led to some clever (if frustrating for consumers) merchandising approaches (See Figure 4).

Figure 4   A stalwart consumer faces-off with consumer electronics (courtesy of American Institutes for Research)

Artist: Larry Hoffman

For example, in the case of modern, software-driven televisions, a low-end TV chassis may contain all of the features of a high-end one or at least have the processing power to deliver the full-feature set to the consumer. To differentiate a product in a line of similar products, companies simply enable the set of features necessary to be competitive at a given price point and disable the rest. By and large, advanced functions, such as a sleep timer, can be provided at little additional cost to the manufacturer.

However, few companies manage to overcome the tyranny of the usability-complexity trend shown in graph form in Figure 5. I developed this chart over several years by asking college students and people attending industry workshops to rate the usability and complexity of diverse products.

Figure 5 The general relationship between usability and complexity (dots represent products)

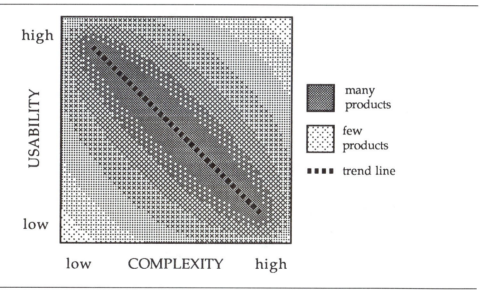

The usability-complexity trend suggests that usability diminishes as complexity increases. For instance, a pair of scissors is expected to be very simple and usable. In contrast, an older, computer-aided-design application running on a workstation is typically very complex and difficult to use. Fortunately for consumers, developers can buck the trend toward diminishing usability to some degree by investing in usability. Note that the graph includes products (represented as dots) that reside above the trend line, indicating that usability has held steady in the presence of increasing complexity. According to my own ratings, the aforementioned word processors and automatic cameras would fall in this area of the graph.

Without an investment in usability, it is tough to get into this rarefied domain. Usability platitudes and marketing hyperbole will not do the trick. For example, it is easy to say "we care about our customer" or "our products are user friendly," but such statements have a hollow ring to them. A user-centered design process provides the necessary substance.

Ramifications of Usability Excellence

In the 1990s, usability sells. At least this is the conclusion that emerges from an examination of product advertisements and the manner in which system developers market their wares to industrial users. It seems that everyone has become usability conscious. I credit the software industry for the increased awareness, because more than any other it has exposed consumers to usability engineered products. In the process, it has increased consumer intolerance for hard-to-use products.

As a result, usability has become a product differentiator. Given two products that offer the same functionality at about the same price point, customers will buy the one that is easier to use. This translates into bigger profits for the company that has paid more attention to user needs.

As a consumer and as a usability professional, I believe that usability actually will become less of a differentiator in the future, because most companies are investing in usability and ugly, disagreeable user interfaces have been vanquished. This has happened in large measure within sectors of the software industry. For example, Microsoft, Borland, and Lotus have waged a fierce battle marketing their so-called bundled software packages (Microsoft® Office™, Borland® Office™, and Lotus® SmartSuite™) on the basis of superior usability. In truth, all are pretty usable but, of course, all could be improved further since the perfect user interface has yet to be invented. If any of these three companies had not been invested in usability, it would be facing major problems competing in today's market.

As discussed in the literature, the positive ramifications of investing in usability extend beyond increased sales. The benefits include

- Reduced customer support and service costs,
- Avoidance of costly delays in the product development schedule in order to fix usability problems before going to market,[4]
- Reduced customer training costs,
- Simpler-to-prepare product documentation,
- Accurate, ready-to-use marketing claims based on tests.

Ramifications of Usability Negligence

Companies that defer their investment in usability run substantial risks in today's marketplace. Clearly, they risk losing in a product comparison based on usability. They also forego the benefits listed previously. However, for certain kinds of products, such as medical devices, the most substantial risk may be the least obvious one—the risk of a products liability suit.

Many accidents that lead to property loss or personal injury can be traced to design problems in the product's user interface. A recent book entitled *Set Phasers on Stun: And Other True Tales of Design, Technology, and Human Error* chronicles over a dozen cases implicating the user interface as the primary or contributing cause of serious accidents. When plaintiffs claim that a product defect has led to their loss or injury, as they frequently do, the burden of proof falls on the defendant (commonly the product developer) to justify the product design. In such cases, the ability to delineate a user-centered design process that draws on users and established human factors design principles (heuristics) to produce a design can be advantageous to the defense. Today, the absence of such a process may constitute negligence, severely increasing a manufacturer's exposure (see Figure 6.)

Figure 6 An absurd application of interactive voice response technology (reprinted by permission)

The Underlying Process

Having discussed briefly the possible motivations to establish a usability practice, let me review the underlying process. As previously mentioned, it is a process that involves early and continual involvement of users. Figure 7 provides a simplified view of the process. Close cousins of this process are described in several usability and human factors textbooks.[5]

Figure 7 A simplified view of the user-centered design process

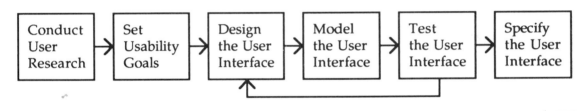

Conduct User Research

The user-centered design process typically begins by researching the users of the product under development. This activity may be limited to talking informally to a dozen or so people or may involve much more rigorous steps, such as conducting a series of focus groups, conducting a questionnaire survey, or observing and interviewing people as they use similar products. Some companies may also conduct usability tests of existing products (also called *benchmark tests*) to get a better sense for users' views and performance. Often, companies perform detailed analyses of user tasks as a basis for understanding control and display requirements or information flow (I/O) requirements. These activities all lead nicely into the next task: setting usability goals.

Set Usability Goals

The concept of setting a usability goal—taking a quantitative view of usability—is new to some. However, the exercise forces designers to think specifically about how users will react emotionally to a product and how well they will be able to perform tasks. For example, designers can set a numerical goal for how long it should take to add up a column of numbers on an computer-based spreadsheet (10 seconds), load a roll of film into a camera (20 seconds), clear a common jam in a photocopier (1 minute), or identify a frequent problem on a computer network (3 minutes). They can also set similar, numerical goals for the rate of users errors or the rate of success at a given task (1 error per 10 trials and 90% completion, respectively). Furthermore, designers can set goals for how high people will rate a product's intuitiveness or how enjoyable it is to use (an average rating of 5 or better on a 1-7 scale, 1 = poor, 7 = excellent).

The process is the same as setting a goal for the gross weight or power consumption of a portable computer, except that designers are preparing to measure usability. They can base goals on the performance of competing products, a company's current product, or on their best judgment of user's needs and the potential of new designs.

Design, Model, and Test the User Interface

Usability goals, coupled with the results of user studies, help designers formulate alternative concepts for the user interface. Many user interface design teams develop several alternative concepts in parallel, describing them in the form of interaction sequence diagrams, paper-based screenplays or electronic prototypes (for software), or physical mockups that people can actually touch (for hardware). Typically, the associated design effort is guided by a product-specific or corporate-specific set of design principles drawn from the human factors literature and experience.

Once there is something to show, users can get involved again by participating in focus group discussions of design alternatives or usability tests that provide feedback for designers. Normally, the feedback comes at two levels: opinions about the overall design and detailed suggestions for improving specific design elements. Interactive prototypes of varying degrees of realism also enable designers to observe usability problems at both a general and specific level. Designers can use this feedback as a basis for choosing a preferred conceptual model and associated solution and then refine it.

Usability specialists can also bring electronic prototypes (see Figure 8) or working models of near final designs together with potential users, either in laboratories or the field, to validate design features and detect any remaining usability problems that need to be fixed. Some user interface design teams extend the testing process to include field testing of production-line products as a means to document the benefits of a user-centered design process and prepare to design the new product's replacement.

Specify the User Interface

The usability endgame involves specifying the user interface so that it can be implemented properly by programmers, engineers, and the like. Depending on corporate documentation requirements, usability specialists may do any of the following: write detailed specifications, build a computer-based prototype or mockup that reflects final

Figure 8 Medium-fidelity prototype of a telephone (courtesy: American Institutes for Research)

design changes, create menu hierarchy maps or state diagrams that illustrate the user interface logic, or create templates and style guides to ensure the consistency and quality of future design changes.

Now that I have reviewed the user-centered design process, let me point out that every product development company puts its own spin on the process.

Joining the Movement

To complete my introduction, I would like to encourage companies that have not yet joined the usability movement to do so. My advice, based on many years of experience helping numerous clients make the transition to a user-centered design process, is to jump in—just as you would into a cold New England pond on the first hot day in June. At first, it may take some getting used to, but soon the shock will wear off and the experience will become quite refreshing (see Figure 9).

Figure 9 Jumping into user-centered design (courtesy: New Hampshire Office of Travel and Tourism Development)

Artist: David Brownell

Getting Wet

Many companies prefer to get wet by retaining the services of a well-regarded usability consultant—a conservative approach that may be expensive but enables managers to assess the impact on their organization before they make a full commitment. Another advantage to this approach is that it can be easier to let outsiders upset the status quo so that internal working relationships can be protected. For example, retaining a consultant to conduct a focus group with potential product users may disturb marketing staff members, who are used to controlling the flow of information from customers to design teams. Conducting a usability test of a prototype software application may make programmers feel judged. Yet, if a consultant conducts such activities in a nonthreatening manner and practices the politics of inclusion (i.e., consults with the vested parties to plan focus groups or a usability test, then inviles them to observe the sessions), good results should win people over, even the skeptics. Such demonstration projects provide just the kind of evidence needed to justify an in-house capability.

Finding a Leader

Usually, the next step is to hire a fairly senior individual with exceptional experience at related design challenges to assume the role of usability "guru" or "evangelist." Ideally, management will bring this person into the organization at a level high enough to garner respect from product development team leaders—a position equivalent to project team leaders, the technical communication manager, or the industrial design manager. Placing the usability specialist lower in the corporate hierarchy sends the wrong signal: that usability concerns are subordinate to other design and engineering concerns.

As readers will learn by reading the case studies, usability programs can take several directions once an organization finds a usability leader. Leaders usually start off with a mix of tactical and strategic activities, including running usability tests and conducting in-house training seminars on usability. Many feel a bit overwhelmed by the task of reforming their organization, but also thrive on the challenge—otherwise they would not have accepted the job. Almost all regard hiring a support staff as a primary goal, if not a condition of their own employment. My sense is that three people (a leader and two support people with formal usability training) is the minimum effective configuration for companies facing significant usability challenges. Nonetheless, some companies get by for a long time with a lone specialist who learns to get work done by drawing support from others that she or he has trained in the art and science of usability.

Assuring Long-Term Success

The long-term success of a usability program depends on many factors, but none as important as the quality of the usability leadership. Usability leaders face the difficult task of constantly selling and reselling usability to their organization because usability is ultimately a value that is added to a product but is not a functional necessity. This means they must serve not only as a design specialist, but also as an educator and promoter. Because their service is linked to many other product development activities (e.g., software, hardware, documentation, quality assurance, marketing, advertising), the work-coordination demands can be substantial. Then, there is the routine challenge of finding good support people and keeping them happy. Accordingly, companies should seek the highest caliber people to develop their usability program—people with capabilities equivalent to those who have contributed to this book.

Having Fun

My consulting experience and the case studies presented here convince me that designing a product that people will like and use effectively has to be fun, or you are doing something wrong. After all, usability specialists get to work on technical problems as well as with people. The work is intellectually demanding and also provides a creative outlet. Good results bring a lot of positive visibility from company insiders and the outside world. It is not as if usability people work on microscopic electronic parts buried inside of devices where they cannot be appreciated. We get to do the fun part, at least in our own minds.

But, there are ever-present threats to our good time. The fun drains away rapidly when usability specialists have to fight for respect, opportunity, and resources to do the job their employers hired them to do. Many usability specialists complain about the incessant need to sell usability, as if one were peddling snake oil. They also get frustrated when their role on a design effort is reduced to polishing up nearly finished designs, rather than getting involved earlier on when major user interface decisions are made. Also, many usability groups seem chronically understaffed and under-funded, which makes everything more of a struggle. Then usability specialists end up performing triage on the product line—helping the most needy products that are likely to make it to market, rather than aspiring to design excellence across the board.

Therefore, my closing advise to companies standing at the threshold of establishing a usability program is to make a full commitment. Hire good people, then give them the necessary power, resources, and respect to get the job done right.

Acknowledgments

I want to thank several people who have been important to the publishing of this book. First I thank my colleagues at American Institutes for Research (AIR), who encouraged me to move forward with this book project, helped put me in touch with a number of contributors, and gave me valuable feedback on the book's content. I thank Dr. Joseph Dumas, who has been my mentor for several years at AIR and has always been willing to cover my working drafts with red ink. I thank Professor John Kreifeldt (Tufts University) for getting me interested in human factors originally and supporting my professional development in many ways. I thank all of the contributing authors for their willingness to share their professional insights about establishing and nurturing a usability practice. I thank John Lehrer, who normally edits my magazine columns, for his comments on this chapter. I extend my appreciation to AP Professional's Jenifer Niles and Karen Pratt for their hard work and enthusiasm as we worked together to create this book. I thank my mother who gave me confidence at an early age to try new things—such as editing a book. Finally, I thank my wife, Pam, and children, Ben, Ali, and Tom, for their love and support while I worked on this book, taking over a corner of the kitchen table otherwise occupied by cans of Playdough and art projects.

References

1. J. Sedgwick, "The Complexity Problem," *The Atlantic* (March 1993), pp. 96-100.

2. Frequent articles appearing in the Marketplace section of *The Wall Street Journal*.

3. T. Berry, *Managing the Total Quality Transformation* (McGraw-Hill, 1990), New York.

4. C. Karat, "Cost Justifying Human Factors support on Software Development Projects," *Human Factors Bulletin*, Human Factors and Ergonomics Society, 35 (11), 1992:4.

5. J. Nielsen, *Usability Engineering* (Academic Press, Boston, 1993), pp. 72-114; D. Mayhew, *Principles and Guidelines in Software User Interface Design* (Prentice-Hall, Englewood Cliffs, NJ, 1992), pp. 578-598; J. Dumas and J. Redish, *A Practical Guide to Usability Testing* (Ablex Publishing Company, Norwood, NJ, 1993), pp. 1-83; D. Hix and R. Hartson, *Developing User Interfaces: Ensuring Usability Through Product and Process* (John Wiley and Sons, New York, 1993), pp. 95-116.

CHAPTER 2

Making Usability a Kodak Product Differentiator

Stanley H. Caplan
Eastman Kodak Company

Stanley Caplan has B.S. and M.S. degrees, both in Industrial Engineering from the University of Michigan, and attended the Human Factors in Technology program at the University of California at Berkeley. As an internal corporate consultant, he has performed and directed consumer research, product development, and job design activities. His experience encompasses consumer, commercial, and medical products, including Human Factors issues related to both hardware design and software interfaces.

Today's Human Factors function at Eastman Kodak Company draws its strength from the melding of about 25 people with varying backgrounds into a multidisciplinary internal consulting group. They provide usability engineering support for products ranging from cameras to copiers to blood analyzers and perform applied Human Factors research. It is a far different picture from Human Factors' beginnings in 1959 when it was dedicated to improving the job of employees performing heavy physical work. In the intervening years there have been many operational twists and organizational turns in the road. However, Human Factors has steadily expanded its influence on product development by broadening the base of products it supports and by increasingly becoming involved early in the development process.

This chapter begins by briefly describing how the practice of Human Factors has evolved during its 33-year existence at Kodak and profiling the type of issues that we address today. It is followed by a representation of a generic framework for a successful Human Factors program in a corporate environment. It describes basic functions that need to be performed, measures of success, and alternative organizational alignments.

The framework is the basis for the next section, which describes how those functions are delivered at Eastman Kodak Company. In the next to last section, two case studies illustrate the application of Human Factors at Kodak. The chapter concludes with a summary that shares lessons the author has learned from his Kodak experience.

Many terms can be found for the expertise applied to designing products that are easy to use in a productive and safe manner. Because that function is called *Human Factors* at Kodak, it is the term used in this chapter instead of others such as *ergonomics, cognitive engineering,* or *usability engineering*. Similarly, many expressions are generally employed to name the product feature that conveys ease of use. Advertisers especially like *user friendly* and *ergonomically designed*. In this chapter *usability* has been chosen to refer to a product attribute or the objective of a design effort. Another distinction that is made in the chapter is the difference between *client* and *customer*. Clients are the internal Kodak customers with whom we interact during the product development cycle. They include engineering, marketing, service, and management. Customers are people in the marketplace that directly use the product or make the decision to buy the product.

Evolution of Human Factors at Kodak

Today's expertise in product design Human Factors is built on the first decade of the group's work in occupational ergonomics. During that time, Kodak's ergonomists were concerned with workplace and job design involving

- Heavy effort such as lifting large, bulky objects and tending coal cars (Davis, Faulkner, and Miller, 1969).
- Visual demands such as inspection of moving webs of film and paper (Faulkner and Murphy, 1973).
- Design of manufacturing equipment such as control panels for slitters.
- The unusual demands presented by tasks that must be performed at extremely low light levels to avoid damaging light sensitive products.
- Analyses of error opportunities for manufacturing operations, including those relying heavily on the use of long alphanumeric strings for designating product components.
- Repetitive tasks such as camera assembly.

For the first decade, Kodak Human Factors was part of a large industrial engineering organization with dotted line accountability to the Medical department. This had come about because the Human Factors function was founded by Harry Davis, an industrial engineer, and Dr. Charles Miller, a company physician, who conceived the idea for a Kodak Human Factors function when collaborating on the evaluation and redesign of a stressful heavy job. In the late 1960s, leveraging our experience with demanding jobs and manufacturing equipment design, we began to work with product developers on the design of products. The first product study involved using EMG to evaluate alternative handle designs for our Super 8 mm movie cameras. Shortly after, while occupational ergonomics still constituted the majority of our work, the group was transferred to a newly formed corporate laboratory concerned with the health and safety of Kodak employees and customers. The breadth of experience in ergonomic job design gained from working in a large, multi plant industrial environment was captured in a two-volume book that has had extensive use in both academia and industry (Eastman Kodak Company, 1983, 1986).

In the latter 1970s, work in product design increased rapidly and eventually became a larger part of the group's effort. That led to spinning off the product design function into the Photographic Technology division, an advanced product development organization.

Product development work continued to expand in terms of both diversity of products supported and the depth of involvement. The biggest challenge was to get involved early in the development process. By the mid-1980s, we had helped design microfilm cameras, microfilm retrieval workstations, consumer cameras, photofinishing printers and related equipment, copiers, copier-duplicators, desktop and console blood analyzers, x-ray film processors, and information management workstations. We also helped resolve film design tradeoffs. At that time a major company reorganization occurred that divided it into individual, autonomous business units grouped according to types of product. Human Factors, like most support groups, was divided up and allocated to the businesses. One group was assigned to an advanced development group responsible for traditional photographic-type products related to the consumer imaging business. A second group was melded with industrial design, graphic design, and packaging engineering into a separate department responsible for supporting all commercial, industrial, and health-related businesses. Most of the products in these businesses were based on nontraditional technologies such as digital imaging, ink jet printing, and electrophotography.

In recent years, the company has gradually shifted away from narrow, vertically integrated product lines. This has been driven by the company's trend toward combining traditional and nontraditional Kodak technologies into hybrid products such as those comprising the KODAK Photo CD System, which have application in both consumer and commercial markets. This trend blurred the different product responsibility roles of the two Human Factors groups. More and more often, people from each group worked on the same hybrid project in order to apply all the requisite complementary skills and experience. As a result, the two groups have recently (during the course of writing this chapter) merged into a single organizational entity that can more effectively provide the right skills to projects and also achieve expanded personal growth opportunities within our profession. The type of Human Factors considerations encountered most frequently by people in the consolidated group include

Image quality evaluation.   Because Kodak is primarily an imaging company, improving image quality is the focus of many company units. The Human Factors group is concerned with the quality of hard images (comprised of prints and slides) and soft images appearing on displays. Prints, for instance, are judged on image characteristics and camera-film-user system performance as a function of usage circumstances. These are important for developing cameras, film, and paper that are effective under varying picture-taking conditions. We evaluate the quality of pictorial soft images and the legibility and readability of textual soft images to determine their acceptability against an established standard, the effect of imaging algorithms or the suitability of certain displays for use on products.

User-hardware interactions.   Design of control panels including selection, arrangement, and labeling of controls and displays for the large variety of Kodak equipment is a common activity and is invariably done in concert with industrial designers, graphic designers, electrical engineers, and mechanical engineers. Another of our major types of activities is designing for easy consumable changeover such as loading/unloading film and batteries in cameras, loading/unloading paper in copiers and photofinishing printers, changing toner in copiers, feeding paper into document scanners, and inserting chemistry slides into blood analyzers. We repeatedly encounter ergonomic considerations such as optimum forces for opening and latching covers and doors, easy jam clearance, location of input/output hoppers, and height of work surfaces. These issues occur in somewhat different ways on the diversity of products we support.

Operational logic.   Much of our equipment are so-called smart products, driven by embedded computers. Product developers look to Human Factors personnel to define the operational procedures and the display feedback that define the user interface for their products.

Labels and instructions.   Although our goal is to make the operation of a product functionally obvious, instruction labels are typically needed to supplement the operational logic. In conjunction with graphic designers who establish label appearance, we determine the need, content, and placement of labels.

Graphical user interfaces.   As electronic displays become more prevalent, especially on networked products, we have worked very closely with software developers to design graphical user-computer interfaces, especially in windowing environments. Applications have included information management systems, storage and retrieval of images from a picture database, and case management.

Except for its very early days, Human Factors has never been a free resource to its clients. We bill work to projects on an hourly basis and at a rate that reflects facilities, equipment, and supplies supporting the work. These include a print viewing room and a usability lab. The print viewing room is specially designed with neutral colors and lighting and contains a computer system that allows direct entry of print judging data. The usability lab is a specially built partitionable room with an observation room having a one-way mirror. Video and sound equipment are used to capture and mix multiple views of a test in progress. Editing equipment is employed after the test to select, rearrange, and annotate the videotape to create a summary of the test that highlights critical events, problems, and successes.

Framework of a Successful Usability Program

One way to look at a usability program is as a system of related functions or activities. Everything done as part of the program should be purposeful. A tool for that kind of analysis is the functional analysis systems technique (F.A.S.T.) diagram, which is a staple in the collection of techniques used by value engineers. The diagram is a structured method of function analysis that describes the functions of a system and how these functions are related. It is a logic flow telling *what* the system is, and *how* and *why* it works. Traditionally, F.A.S.T. diagrams have been used as a tool for improving a product or system design by either enhancing high value functions or eliminating low value functions. It can be applied to a complex system or a product as simple as a light bulb (Bytheway, 1971). It has also been used to look at an organization as a system and analyze its functions (Caplan, Rodgers, and Rosenfeld, 1991). In this section, the technique is used to generically describe a Human Factors function. Its application to Kodak is spelled out in a subsequent section describing specific company deliverables.

Figure 1 shows a functional analysis of a usability program. Each block in the figure describes a function in the program's operation. Each function is defined in a few words including an action verb and a noun. Read the diagram from left to right and ask the question "How?" of each function. The answer to the how question resides in those functions connected to (the right of) the function queried. Now, read the diagram from right to left and ask the question "Why?" of each function. The answer to the why question resides in those functions connected to (the left of) the function queried. For example, consider *Enhance Marketability*, function number 1, on the extreme left of the diagram. Going from left to right, ask how do you **enhance marketability**? The diagram provides the answers: *Ensure Customer Acceptance* of the product (function 2) and *Ensure Client Acceptance* of Human Factors (function 3). Continuing further, how do you **ensure customer acceptance** of the product (function 2)? The diagram responds with *Make Usability a Product Differentiator* (function 4). How do you **ensure client acceptance** (function 3)? *Make Usability a Product Differentiator* (function 4) and *Facilitate the Development Process* (function 5). Following function 5, the way to **facilitate the development process** is to *Ensure 1st Class Support* (function 6), *Effectively Manage Human Factors Resources* (function 7), and *Effectively Market Human Factors Services* (function 8).

Now reading the diagram from right to left, we ask of functions 6-8, why *Ensure 1st Class Support, Effectively Manage Human Factors Resources*, and *Effectively Market Human Factors Services?* The diagram answers to *Facilitate the Development Process* (function 5). For functions 2 and 3, ask why *Ensure Customer Acceptance* and *Ensure Client Acceptance?* The answer that satisfies both of these questions is function 1, to *Enhance Marketability* of products. By making sure functions are viable answers to the "how" and "why" questions, the logic flow is maintained.

As expected, the F.A.S.T. diagram shows that meeting the needs of both customers and clients is key to the success of any Human Factors usability program. Customers and clients are distinctly different people. Both are "customers" as the term is used in total quality management literature. However, customer as used here refers to either the end user or the purchase decision maker. They can be the same person such as the individual who buys a camera for personal use. They can also be the purchasing agent who decides which copier to buy and the operator who uses it. Client refers to the organization and individuals to whom Human Factors support is provided or who fund the support.

The highest level goal of virtually any usability effort must be to **enhance marketability** of products by **ensuring customer acceptance**. However, this cannot be done by the Human Factors group alone. Many other groups, such as marketing, systems engineering, industrial design, safety engineering, and product engineering, must also contribute. Likewise, **ensure client acceptance** as a goal is influenced by many factors outside the control of the Human Factors group. The product design community's perception of the importance of usability depends, for instance, on management's demonstrated commitment to it, how costs for Human Factors support are funded, and how Human Factors is organizationally aligned. While the three functions are important, they are outside the boundary of this analysis because they are mostly out of the control of a typical usability program.

The direct goals of a usability program are functions 4 and 5, *Make Usability a Product Differentiator* and *Facilitate the Development Process*. These are much more within program control. Their how functions, 6, 7, and 8, are quite broad but can be focused by continuing the F.A.S.T. diagram. How can you *Ensure 1st Class Support?*

Figure 1 F.A.S.T. diagram for a corporate usability program

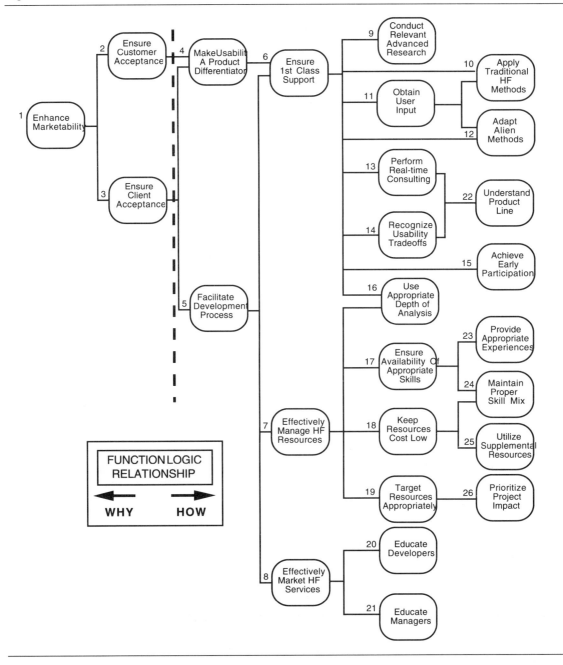

Conduct Relevant Advanced Research (f9).   As companies attempt to condense the product development cycle, there is inadequate time to pursue state-of-the-art user interface solutions during the cycle. That means to successfully integrate these solutions into a product, they must be explored and understood independently from specific product development projects and prior to their potential use on the projects. This is especially important for a company whose strategy is to be the leader in new product development. A usability research program is also important at follower companies, but its emphasis would be different. A typical approach might focus more on activities such as analyzing usability on existing competitive products and upgrading usability methodologies.

Apply Traditional Human Factors Methods (f10).   Within the large set of Human Factors methods there are usually several that can be appropriate for most problems. A major reason for using certain well-known Human Factors methods is to *Obtain User Input* (f11) that allows credible recommendations. Other methods for analyzing tasks and evaluating situations do not involve user input. Theoretically, a method should be used that gives a high level of confidence in its outcome. Practically, availability of time and money often dictate the method chosen.

Obtain User Input (f11).   This is, of course, a basic tenet of Human Factors. A "must" to doing this correctly is defining the right potential users—an especially difficult task when the business case or the requirements for the product have not effectively spelled it out. This can happen when a product is intended to be "all things to all people" or the product is not similar to one already on the market.

Adapt Alien Methods (f12).   Usability issues do not always lend themselves to traditional methods. Unique conditions such as the lack of a working model for usability testing require creative approaches to addressing usability issues. One approach is to apply some adaptation of methods from another discipline (Van Oech, 1990). Examples include borrowing focus group techniques from marketing and modifying them to collect quantitative usability and preference data and using value engineering tools, such as F.A.S.T. diagrams, to analyze functions of products and systems. As shown in Figure 1, some methods may be for the purpose of obtaining user input while other methods directly relate to ensuring first class support in a different way.

Perform Real-Time Consulting (f13).   Because so many usability issues arise during the development of a complex product, time and resource constraints make it impractical to study every one of them. Also, many issues may not be important enough to warrant usability testing, surveys, or field tests, especially if existing data from past studies can be adapted for the new situation. A lower level of confidence in the solution is acceptable in these cases. A good usability program has experienced people who can make reasoned, on-the-spot judgments about usability issues.

Recognize Usability Trade-Offs (f14).   Inevitably on a project, there are times when the best usability solution can be achieved only at the cost of added development effort, increased unit manufacturing or life-cycle cost, or a potential reduction in product reliability. Continually ignoring these considerations in the name of usability is not practical and jeopardizes the Human Factors engineer's rapport with the client. On the other hand, software developers, hardware designers, and the like sometimes magnify the obstacles to implementing usability features because they do not want to put forth extra effort.

Achieve Early Participation (f15).   The perpetual Human Factors lament. "We got involved after design decisions had been made, which prevented implementation of appropriate usability solutions." Early involvement across all products is difficult on a regular basis in a large company when the Human Factors group does not have adequate exposure to product development plans. Typically, early involvement will occur for a couple of product lines where repeat business over the years has evolved into a close relationship with the clients there. Companies having a prescribed corporate development process that drives all projects provide an opportunity for consistent early Human Factors involvement by formally including usability considerations in the first phases. Also, early involvement is likely at companies where senior executives have final product approval and usability is one of their criteria. This gives added importance and awareness of the Human Factors function to product developers. At NCR, for instance, there has been a long-standing program for high-level management review of their products' industrial design prior to release to market. Now, NCR is in the process of adding human-computer interface usability and mechanical design into that program. The intention is to allow management to review products from a perspective that integrates those three functions (Gary Wagner, private conversation).

Use Appropriate Depth of Analysis (f16).   It is important to give a reasoned solution based on an analysis effort that is commensurate with the importance of the issue, the time available to do it, and the money available to fund it. This is like walking a tightrope because it is often difficult to balance these factors and still be comfortable with the answer. Frequently performing studies, even when they are warranted from a usability viewpoint, can risk the perception of the Human Factors function being too "researchy" and affect credibility with uninformed clients over the long run. Also, use of the Human Factors resources for unnecessarily time-consuming analysis diverts those resources from areas of greater need in a resource limited situation.

Understand Product Line (f22).   Without knowledge of the product technology, the way it is marketed, and the ways customers use and can misuse the product, the Human Factors specialist will not be able to recognize how usability should be traded off against other legitimate product issues such as machine reliability or the need to match features on competitive products. Product knowledge helps make rational on-the-spot decisions required for real-time consulting.

Effectively Manage Human Factors Resources (f7).   This is a difficult challenge in companies that are working with reduced staffing levels as a result of downsizing. It requires a manager to encourage *Use Appropriate Depth of Analysis* (f16), *Ensure Availability of Appropriate Human Factors Skills* (f17), *Keep Resource Costs Low* (f18), and *Target Resources at Appropriate Projects* (f19). The F.A.S.T. diagram shows how they can be attempted.

Provide Appropriate Experiences (f23).   The type of growth experience provided to Human Factors individuals depends on the philosophy of the Human Factors management toward division of labor, i.e., specialist vs. generalist. Training, mentoring, and job assignments can be aimed at developing an in-depth expertise in one area, user-computer interface design, for instance, or can give exposure and on-the-job experience equally across several Human Factors areas. A practical approach that often prevails is one that builds on the inherent strengths of individuals for in-depth expertise and broadens it with experiences in other areas.

Maintain Proper Skill Mix (f24).   Through calculated hiring and by providing appropriate experiences, a group can be developed that, as a whole, has the set of in-depth skills necessary for the type of products supported. Of course, this skill set has to be updated to keep pace with technology and methodology changes.

Utilize Supplemental Resources (f25).   In most recent years, as companies have downsized, outsourcing and contracting have become a popular strategy to deal with high employment costs and uncertain demand. Human Factors groups have not escaped these policies. Student interns are another source of temporary help. Outside resources can be used to work under regular employees or can be assigned to independent projects. Whichever is done, care must be taken not to disturb long-term relationships with clients. External resources usually lack knowledge of company infrastructure or an understanding of the product line. However, they are a means of importing new ideas for both methodologies and solutions.

Prioritize Project Impact (f26).   It is difficult to say "no" to a request for Human Factors support on a project. However, limited in-house staffing may require it when considering priorities for committing resources. Setting priorities to projects requires judging their importance to the company and the potential impact the Human Factors function can have on them and is tempered by availability of appropriately skilled in-house Human Factors personnel, the practicality of using outside contractors or consultants, willingness of the developers to provide sufficient funding, and willingness of the developers to include Human Factors personnel as part of their team.

Measures of Success

At the highest level, survival of the Human Factors function is a measure of success, especially at companies in the throes of downsizing. More appropriate measures reflect acceptance of products in the marketplace and acceptance by clients of the Human Factors group as a full-fledged member of the product development team. The former can be determined through in-house usability testing studies, feedback from trade trials, independent consumer testing labs, and independent commercial product assessment services. Client acceptance, ultimately, is evident in repeat business; i.e., in a client organization that continues to rely on the Human Factors group whenever a new product begins development. A more direct evaluation of success with clients can be made by regularly surveying them through interview, questionnaire, etc. Other, less direct, measures may be possible, based on factors unique to specific organizational situations. Examples are year-to-year increases in funding commitments and increases in the number of different product lines supported.

Identifying possible success measures is easier than actually implementing them. Cost-benefit analyses are possible for certain usability cases such as user-computer interface projects (Mantei and Teorey, 1988). Quantitatively linking customers' usability ratings to their purchase decisions is another potentially useful approach (MacElroy, 1993). However, the potential benefits of quantitatively measuring success is usually not worth the cost to do it. Determining actual costs and benefits on a diverse project mix such as that described earlier in the case of Kodak would require data not regularly available. The effort to set up and track special data would be excessive, and the results would be unreliable. Also, when collecting subjective data, care must be taken to focus specifically on usability without confounding responses by attitudes toward other product attributes such as functionality, reliability, or input-output capability.

Does a Human Factors program always need quantitative or qualitative measures to justify its value year after year or on a specific project? How can management know the money it is spending on this function has some value? As it really happens, a Human Factors group at a large company will be required to periodically justify its contributions by "proving" that they are generating value. This invariably occurs in response to spontaneous management requests for support groups to give an accounting of their accomplishments. In my experience, a much more effective approach is proactively giving management periodic input of Human Factors' contributions to product development. A detailed project-by-project report or presentation may be appropriate for lower level management, but a brief accounting of major, discriminating usability accomplishments is probably more effective for upper management.

Organizational Alignment

Rational reasons for the organizational position of the Human Factors group involve organizational style of the rest of the company (e.g., centralized vs. decentralized), geographic location of clients, type of work performed, source of funding, size of the group, span of control considerations, and relationship with other support organizations. These considerations may be supplemented with political reasons influenced by power bases and individual preferences.

The best alignment of a Human Factors function is much easier to determine in a company with a narrow, well-defined product line than in a highly diversified company. For a large company such as Kodak, it is a challenge to achieve an alignment that puts the Human Factors function simultaneously close to customers and to developers of hardware, software, consumables, and systems for photographic, commercial, and medical products. Our discipline has always been difficult to "pigeonhole" because of its hybrid "psycho-engineering personality" and its applicability that cuts across lines of other traditional disciplines.

For a situation such as Kodak's, neither a totally centralized nor a totally decentralized Human Factors group is a good fit. A more effective approach for a group with a sufficiently large critical mass is to operate as a hybrid of a centralized and decentralized function as shown in Figure 2. It would consist of a central core of people who would do applied product research, maintain current knowledge of Human Factors methodologies and user interface technologies, and provide part-time support to small and unanticipated projects. Linked to this core would be additional Human Factors people who are colocated with developers on larger development projects and become knowledgeable about their product lines. If several larger projects are developing products in the same product line, one person may serve as a product line coordinator. A challenging, but important element of this arrangement is regular, reliable communication between the core and the colocated "linkers" so everyone maintains a feeling of belonging to an identifiable group and valuable knowledge transfer takes place. For example, the core people would advise the linkers about appropriate methodologies to use for a certain study, and the linkers would inform the core about customer needs so the appropriate research can be done.

This core-link hybrid type of group would be relatively independent of changes in the rest of the organization by being tied to projects, an entity that exists under all forms of organization. Its flexibility allows for putting the most resources on important projects, but still covering smaller ones as appropriate. Also, a group with this structure could more readily operate from any place in the company organization than a strictly centralized or decentralized group. A significant risk of the hybrid structure

Figure 2   Hybrid human factors organization in a large company

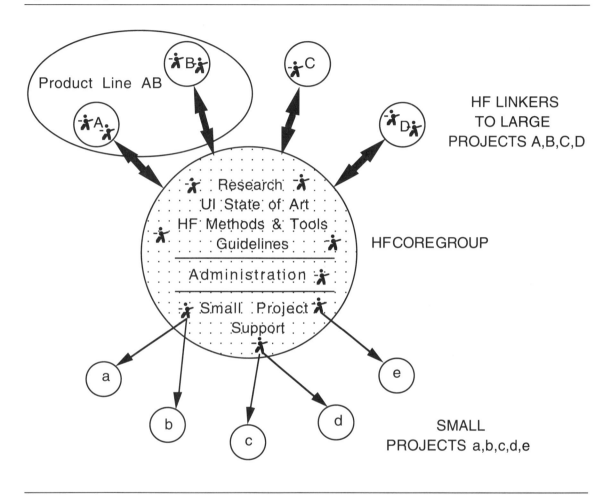

is that the colocated individuals will eventually develop a stronger allegiance with the client organization and possibly be absorbed by them to perform an independent Human Factors function. The resultant splintering of the Human Factors function would destroy synergy gained from being a consolidated entity. On the other hand, a close relationship with a client could result in a job transfer that offers the individual opportunities for personal growth into other areas.

Usability Program Deliverables at Kodak

This section discusses the deliverables associated with the lower level functions shown in the usability framework of Figure 1. The relationship is noted by annotating each type of deliverable by its associated function number. Included in the deliverables are both typical and unique ones that Kodak people have provided to individual product development projects. They are the tangibles clients expect from us during the development process and often appear as milestones on development schedules. Also described are global deliverables that transcend projects, such as those that involve disseminating Human Factors support to all parts of the company and managing Human Factors resources so the best personnel are available in both the short term and long run.

Provide 1st Class Human Factors Support

Usability studies, prototypes, documentation, and consultations are typical types of Human Factors deliverables to individual projects within Kodak. Because Kodak is an imaging company, evaluations of perceived image quality are another, unique type of deliverable.

Usability Performance and Preference Studies

The results of usability performance and preference studies are delivered in the form of written reports, presentations, or edited videotapes of study highlights. The appropriate form is determined by the nature of the study and the dispersion of the target audience. Usability and preference study deliverables are related to functions 10, 11, and 12 in Figure 1.

Because we test a diversity of products using prototypes, concept models, and functioning engineering models, many different kinds of tests are done. Some use traditional usability methods while others are adaptations of other methods. Often, special test plans are devised for the various usability issues that arise ranging from how people clean camera lenses to how they recover from a copier jam. Testing usually involves both performance and preference evaluations. However, we collect only preference data when testing nonfunctioning product concept models or when observation is not possible. For testing of broadly used products, representative users can often be found among the large employee population at Kodak or from temporary agencies. In contrast, we have had a market research firm or our own field people solicit subjects when studies required particular user populations such as radiology technicians, graphics arts specialists, photo researchers, art directors and other users of specialized computer applications.

Depending on the type of product, we either bring subjects to it or bring it to the subjects for testing. For example, subjects come to the usability lab for testing copiers, micrographic retrieval workstations, and x-ray processors that are too large to be easily moved from place to place. Designated tasks are performed such as those for testing a copier to determine how well subjects can set up the copier to run selected jobs, find and remove a jammed piece of paper, and load toner using an instruction label. Sometime, we run studies with the specific intent of evaluating instruction booklets (Faulkner and Caplan, 1977). In the case of small products, such as cameras, we can easily bring the product to the subjects. For in-company testing, we usually locate a convenient conference room near a large number of people to test film loading, battery loading, or camera holdability (Caplan, 1982). Some mall products are tested off company premises. KODAK Photo CD equipment, for instance, is tested in a home environment. Also, we give cameras to people to use around the home or on special occasions. Upon returning film and camera, they are interviewed or complete a questionnaire about their experience using the camera, especially concentrating on problems they encountered. The film is processed and we examine the prints to identify problems related to camera design. We also do external testing for special situations where subjects are not available locally.

We do other types of usability studies, too, but less frequently than those just described. We make customer visits to evaluate usability in context of the product's actual usage. Users operate the product in its typical application and explain what they are doing and where they have problems. Impromptu interviews are conducted to understand the causes and severity of the problems.

We have used psychophysical studies to determine user perceptions of image quality and preferences for product features. We used this method extensively early in the disc camera development program as part of a series of 63 different camera configuration studies. In one experiment, for instance, we used multidimensional scaling to analyze user preferences for seven camera configurations differing with respect to flash type, lens cover type, shutter release position, viewfinder position, and shape. Some of the results showed a strong dislike of pop-up flash and a split in preference for a lens cover vs. no lens cover (Caplan, 1982). Consequently, the first models in this camera line included versions with and without a lens cover, but none of them had a pop-up flash.

To diagnose certain kinds of design problems, we sometimes observe customers using our products in public but have no contact with them. This approach avoids the artificiality of the laboratory setting. In an early camera design study, an individual visited Niagara Falls to film 600 pictures of people taking photographs. The telephoto pictures showed how people hold the camera while taking a picture and how they carry it when not in use. From quantification of the various usage issues observed in this real situation, we gained important insights for camera design improvements. For example, we discovered some possible reasons for camera shake and implications for strap design. The potential for camera shake was apparent in the pictures of people holding purses or umbrellas on their arms as they attempted to hold the camera steady. Recently, we took the same approach using videotape to capture how people grip and carry cameras at Walt Disney World.

Expert evaluation is another type of study that does not involve the user. In this case, a Human Factors expert performs an in-depth analysis of a product's usability including all aspects of its operation and handling. This method is especially useful for assessing competitive products. We have done this locally and have traveled to other cities to do evaluations of newly released products. The advantage of expert evaluation is its relatively low cost, but it relies on the assumption that the Human Factors expert will accurately reflect the user's perception (Urban and Hauser, 1980).

Focus groups are a method this author has used in a variety of situations (Caplan, 1990). Usually I have conducted these groups to evaluate early product concepts, sometimes focusing on a small subset of usability issues and sometimes on the whole concept. Concepts have been represented by foam core models or working engineering prototypes. Unlike market research focus group studies, which can require many groups to get an adequate representation of participants, usability focus studies have required only a small number of groups to identify major usability issues with a product. For example, one group of x-ray technicians, evaluating a floor-standing medical product, strongly rejected a product concept configuration and suggested such improvements as a different location for the storage component and a different type of door for access to the loading area. The client, who observed the session, agreed the group's rationale was sound enough to warrant making changes in the design without running more groups.

Prototypes

Although sometimes an end in themselves, our prototypes are usually a deliverable at an intermediate product development milestone to serve as the object of testing or to replace a user interface specification document. We have also used them to convey a product concept, either for an existing product under development or for demonstrating the application of an advanced user interface technology to a class of products. In these ways, prototypes are deliverables related to functions 9, 10, and 16 in Figure 1. We have used many different kinds of prototypes depending on their purpose.

Soft prototypes are being used frequently to simulate physical control panels, touch screen applications, or other user-computer interfaces. When doing this, we collaborate closely with software developers and marketing planners. We always have primary responsibility for designing the interface, but our role in producing the prototype of that design is determined by circumstances of the development effort. We may prototype all, part, or none of it depending on the software tool used and the availability of a particular platform. For our first software prototyping effort in the early 1980s, we used the Dr. Halo paint package combined with a vast amount of C-code programming on a DOS-based platform. Now, we use many software and hardware platforms to accommodate the variety of user interface applications and development conditions we encounter. When it is practical to do so, we perform the prototyping on the same platform anticipated for the actual product. Using Dan Bricklin Demo and Hypercard on IBM and Mac platforms, respectively, we have prototyped control panels for copiers, printers, medical x-ray equipment, blood analyzers, and graphics arts machines. Graphical user interfaces have been prototyped on windows-based platforms for a variety of Photo CD workplaces and for special government applications. A specific case of a government application is described later in this chapter.

Hard prototypes in the form of foam core or polystyrene block models are used for demonstrating and evaluating physical concepts. On studies utilizing these kinds of prototypes, we collaborate closely with industrial designers to incorporate relevant functional and appearance features. Hard block models are especially suitable for small products. For example, we used hard block models for 35 mm camera studies and for the disc camera preference studies described in the previous section. Foam core, which is a layer of Styrofoam sandwiched between sheets of thick paper, is generally chosen to construct models of desktop and console size products such as printers and x-ray processors. We use engineering models for performance testing because their functionality makes them more suitable for that purpose.

Image Quality Studies

As part of our effort to design camera systems that are easy to use and give reliable results, we maintain a print evaluation program on a continuing basis. Initiated in 1976, this program was the backbone of our support for disc photography for which we had examined over 30,000 prints to identify picture taking situations and evaluate print quality against standards (Faulkner, 1982). On a print-by-print basis, examiners record situations such as the apparent occasion for the picture, the distance at which it was taken, the location, vertical vs horizontal orientation, the number of people or animals pictured, etc. Judges rate the quality of the print against standards for various system factors including those for users such as finger in front of lens, finger over flash, poor framing, poor focus, and under/overexposure. The observations are entered into a database along with the film and camera type used to take the prints. Data is analyzed to explore various design issues and conclusions are delivered to clients for improvement of existing products or for designing new trouble free camera-film-user systems. For the disc camera program, a set of system capability equations were derived from the data to formally relate camera design issues to frequency of usage under different picture taking conditions (Faulkner and Rice, 1982). A simple discovery from the data was that for certain camera models, finger over flash occurred three times as often when the camera was held vertically than when it was held horizontally while taking the picture. The exceptions were camera models having a lens cover or other protrusion that kept fingers away from the flash.

Soft image quality deliverables occur from a derivative of the ongoing print evaluation program and also result from individual studies using more traditional Human Factors techniques. These have included, for example, running tests of legibility performance and preference to find the best magnification and polarity for reading a projected microfilm image. Similarly, studies have been run to compare images viewed on different types of electronic displays (Cushman, 1992). The effects of image processing algorithms on perceived image quality has also been the subject of soft image quality deliverables (Cushman and Miller, 1988; Cushman et al., 1993).

In total, these deliverables are related to functions 10, 12, and 16 in Figure 1. Common Human Factors techniques have been used for soft image evaluation, but some of the print viewing techniques have been borrowed from quality control. In both cases, the analysis has been carried to a level needed to address the complex issues.

Documentation

Written reports, videos, and labels are forms of documentation alluded to elsewhere in the chapter. Another set of closely related documents that relate to functions 9 and 15 in Figure 1 are guidelines, design requirements, and design specifications. According to common definitions of these documents, they are listed here from general to most specific. In practice, the distinction, especially between the latter two, seems to get blurred.

We have often written design specifications to describe the operating logic of complex products. After an initial draft is established early in the development process, we continually update the document during the design process to keep track of decisions agreed to by the Human Factors group, software developers, and product planners. The document is a deliverable to the design community, but is also invaluable for technical writers who must produce a user's manual. Sometimes a specification for a single product evolves into a guideline document for a broader class of similar products. This has occurred for still imaging cameras, human-computer interfaces, and hardware interfaces. In a recent case, for example, guidelines originally developed for replacing consumables on a particular printer have been expanded to apply to all printers. It addresses effective design implementation for such things as detecting the need for consumable replacement/replenishment, finding and removing expired consumable components, packaging new components, and installing new consumables. Whether evolving from a product-specific document or originating as a product-class guideline, these documents are an effective way to transfer technology to the design community and are often requested by them.

Consultation

This deliverable, supporting functions 13 and 14 in Figure 1, is sometimes premeditated and is sometimes a shoot-from-the-hip, off-the-top-of-the-head, seat-of-the-pants, rule-of-thumb or some other type of experience-based anatomical recommendation given to the client. Clients like consultations because they are low cost (at the time) and yield immediate responses. When a consultation constitutes the initial contact with a new client, it often raises more questions than it answers and the client requests more support. Human Factors people who are colocated with clients encounter consultation requests frequently because clients take advantage of their presence. In some cases this kind of recommendation can be changed if later testing fails to verify its validity. In contrast, some recommendations, especially those made late in the development cycle, are "cast in concrete." Where they are not part of an ongoing involvement with the client, we try to limit consultations to less important issues and to situations where studies cannot be justified. Regardless of the circumstances, the importance of a usability issue is considered carefully when it affects cost, schedule, product reliability, appearance, or some other product attribute. To make these trade-offs, a thorough understanding of the product is necessary so we do not needlessly sacrifice usability , but also do not overvalue it.

Effectively Manage Human Factors Resources

The major reason behind the success of the Human Factors function at Kodak is that we have maintained a multidisciplinary group and delivered the right skills to the right projects at a reasonable cost to the client (functions 17, 18, 19). It starts with our thorough hiring process, which involves many people in the group. It extends to the way we deploy resources on projects and encourage cooperation and mutual support among group members.

Resource Deployment

Staffing and resource allocation is complicated because our Human Factors group has the characteristics of a job shop type of function. In other words, most requests for work arrive with little forewarning and require a plan for utilization of shared resources. Like Human Factors groups at many large companies, Kodak Human Factors resources operate at a high utilization level. Each new work input or loss of a resource is a perturbation to the system.

Our ability to commit resources is always affected by availability of appropriately skilled in-house Human Factors personnel, the practicality of using outside contractors or consultants, willingness of the program to provide sufficient funding, and willingness of the developers to accept us as an integral part of their team.

Occasionally, a new work request will arrive about the same time someone with the appropriate skills is just finishing his or her involvement in another project of a similar scope. Typically, however, there is little slack in the system and a "lesser of the evils" decision has to be made from the following alternatives.

- Switch someone off an existing product development project onto the new one. This risks alienating clients associated with the existing project.
- Stop or postpone work on Human Factors research projects so resources can be used to accommodate new requests.
- Hire contract or consultant labor.
- Utilize student interns. We have an ongoing program with Virginia Polytechnic Institute and State University (VPI)) that results in Ph.D. students spending semesters at Kodak working on projects of mutual benefit. We also sometimes use graduate level summer interns from schools such as State University of New York at Buffalo.
- Do not support new project (in reality, we find it very difficult to say "no" to a project).
- Understaff the project until more resources are available.
- Negotiate a later time to assign a resource and risk missing early involvement.

Our determination of the proper response to the request depends on the circumstances of the project. Requests are screened to evaluate what the client really wants, what phase of the product development cycle is currently underway, and whether we are likely to have an impact on the usability of the product. Requests can vary from "quickie" consultations to extensive projects. The consultations often turn into more extensive support. In general, project priorities fall into the following descending order:

- Projects at the beginning of their product development cycle.
- Projects in relatively early phases of development but that have not made irreversible product development decisions already precluding good usability solutions.
- Projects in latter phases of development that hold little promise of Human Factors impact, but on which our work can be applied to future products leveraged from the current one under development.
- Projects that give us the opportunity to get exposure to business units or product lines we have not previously supported.

To reduce some of the uncertainties of the job shop modus operandi we experience, a special arrangement was recently negotiated with a major client. Human Factors combined with closely related functions of industrial design, graphic design, and packaging engineering became a client center of excellence (COE) with a secondary reporting relationship to a client manager. A single representative of the COE was appointed who attends the manager's regular and special staff meetings along with his other subordinates. The appointed representative, a Human Factors person who also supports client development projects, serves as a liaison to all four groups to coordinate client support needs. The groups strive to provide a dedicated group of support people well-trained in their disciplines, knowledgeable about client customers and products, and physically located in the client's facilities. The client manager, in turn, buffers the variance in demand for our support by funding special studies that can be done as resources are available.

This relationship has been in effect for about three years and it has achieved many of the projected benefits. The liaison is keenly aware of current client plans for product development so that we can anticipate and plan support needs. Also, staffing can be coordinated across client projects. Finally, the arrangement has facilitated the opportunity for us to do a study that has resulted in improved product accessibility to special user populations. The result of all this is high credibility and a close, ongoing relationship with the client.

Build Long Term Group Strength

The strength of the Kodak Human Factors group comes from maintaining a mix of people with different, but complementary, backgrounds and giving them opportunities to grow. People with backgrounds in visual perception, cognitive psychology, industrial engineering, mechanical engineering, computer science, and photographic science address similar Human Factors issues on their various projects. Although the issues are similar, they manifest themselves in different ways across the broad spectrum of product types supported. The result is that individuals have an opportunity to grow through the variety of experiences they encounter as they work on more projects. Growth opportunities are enhanced by assigning an individual a "whole job" whenever possible. For instance, when a project involves both hardware and software issues, a single individual is responsible for both. We do not employ a strict division of labor along lines of different usability issues. Individuals build certain fortes from their own background and project experiences and then become resources to others in the group who are working on projects requiring that forte. People are not concerned that becoming an expert on certain issues will result in their being limited to working only on those issues.

Effectively Market Human Factors Services

No formal program exists to expand the coverage of Human Factors to new product areas within the company. We occasionally give Human Factors training courses, and when the opportunity arises, we give presentations to potential clients or do "loss leader" consultations, but in recent years, we have not spent overhead to aggressively pursue business. Human Factors is marketed to existing clients by each member of the group as they work on projects and build credibility. We sometimes apply a subtle form of marketing by involving developers in Human Factors studies and by distributing reports and memos to important people in the client community.

Measures of Success

For the most part, the success of the Human Factors group at Kodak can be measured only indirectly. Over the years, we have been increasingly getting involved in early project stages. Acceptance of Human Factors has recently been formalized by inclusion of usability considerations in the early phases of the corporate product development process.

As measured by the amount of recurring business, our client acceptance is high. It seems to be greatest among those clients who use us as a team partner. They tend to reemploy us project after project. The biggest challenge is getting that first project from a client unit and building credibility with them. Feedback from these and all clients is obtained on a regular basis by means of a questionnaire that asks for both ratings and open-ended responses. Low ratings or comments that indicate dissatisfaction are followed up by contacting the client and attempting to address his or her concerns. Success in incorporating usability into products is determined on those products that undergo user testing, but we have no broad-based program to obtain customer data that would pinpoint their perception of usability as distinct from other product features.

Case Studies

Two very different types of case studies are discussed to convey the variety of project types supported and the breadth of professional expertise resident in the Kodak Human Factors group. The first case study was chosen because, within a single product, almost all of the usability issues discussed earlier in this chapter—hardware, software, and instructional material—were encountered. The Human Factors client was the internal Kodak development team. The product is available in the marketplace for readers to explore in conjunction with the description of its development provided here. The second case study was chosen for its contrast to the first case study. It was done under contract with a government agency, and as such, the client and customer were the same—the Internal Revenue Service. It required an order of magnitude more Human Factors resources than the first case study, and its output is a graphical user interface prototype rather than a product for the marketplace.

KODAK CREATE-A-PRINT 35 mm Enlargement Center

This product, first introduced in the fall of 1988, is an image manipulation device developed to meet customer needs for enlargements that are cropped the way they want and for a shorter turnaround time of their enlargement order than the typical two weeks. The Create-A-Print 35 mm enlargement center, shown in Figure 3 and Color Plate I, is purchased or leased by retailers such as camera stores who position it for use by walk-up customers. The enlargement center enables the customer to do their own What-You-See-Is-What-You-Get (WYSIWYG) cropping and get a photographic print in less than five minutes. The customer inserts a 35 mm negative strip, views a frame from it on a screen, zooms and crops it to identify the part of the image to be enlarged, selects an enlargement size, and makes a print.

Retailers want a machine that is attractive to walk-in traffic and is not labor intensive. Therefore, Kodak's objective was to make a device usable by walk-up customers without assistance from the store clerk. This was characterized by the Human Factors' challenge to "make it like a soft drink machine in the middle of the desert" (David Aurelio, private communication). A Human Factors engineer was assigned to the project at its inception and participated as a full member of the design team, working throughout the development cycle with people from mechanical engineering, electrical engineering, software development, optics, equipment service, and industrial design. His expertise was applied to the design of hardware, user-control interface, and instructional material.

Hardware Usability

Like many of our equipment units that are used as a workplace, product configuration was an important enlargement center factor that involved many usability issues. Most of these issues were driven by anticipated retailer usage policy and presentation to customers. A vertical, rather than horizontal, orientation was selected because it required less valuable floor space and would be easier to place into an existing floor layout. This creates a standing workplace that is acceptable because customers are not required or expected to spend a long time at the machine. Anticipating that the unit might be placed against a wall, the center of the screen was positioned far enough from the side edge so that a customer would have room to stand squarely in front of the screen. The critical distance of 15 inches was determined anthropometrically from half of a 26-inch shoulder breadth plus 2 inches for elbow flex when using controls. The height of the screen was influenced by anthropometric eye-height considerations and the need for space to put the light path underneath it. A built-in workshelf provides room to lay out several film strips and to park personal items such as a purse or shopping bag. A trade-off between shelf size and footprint size was involved because they are directly correlated. A small light table for viewing a six-frame 35 mm negative film strip was incorporated into the shelf, and because the light table is always on when the machine is powered up, it is also a substitute for a separate power indicator. The light table was designed so that the film would have to be picked up on the edges to remove it from the flat surface. The film insertion slot is placed conveniently close to the light table so the film can be moved to it without a regrasp that could result in fingers touching the film surface. Another component whose location was carefully considered is the print exit. Its low height and vertical orientation conserve footprint. Its design features include easy grasp and face in delivery to provide print privacy.

The film gate was designed with many usability features. Either end of the film strip can be put in first because a DX barcode reader for sensing film type resides on both sides of the internal film track. If the film is inserted upside down, it ejects back to the user. When a strip is fed successfully, it starts the machine, eliminating the need for a separate start button.

Two tasks assigned to the retailer are paper loading and routine maintenance. Loading a 100 foot roll of paper into a cassette can be done in daylight. This was made possible by a new type of light-seal wrapping on the paper and a new clamshell design of the cassette that locks the roll into place when closed. Routine maintenance is required for the processing tank located in the bottom half of the machine. The tank rolls out on rails that fold up inside the machine behind the front panel when not in use. Access to the tank is through the front because, being the place where users stand, it is sure to be free of obstructions. The sides and back can be blocked by the counter or walls.

Figure 3   KODAK CREATE-A-PRINT 35 mm Enlargement Center

User-Control Interface

The user-control interface is composed of controls, display device, display content, and operational logic embedded in the software. The designers knew the control interface's appearance needed to be nonintimidating and its operation needed to be simple and fast to minimize customer queues and clerk intervention. As a result, the enlargement center contains only the most important features desired by customers, has limited capability for generating and displaying characters, and is operated using only a large, 2-inch trackball flanked by two knurled knobs and a selection button.

The Human Factors engineer rejected a proposed touchscreen for several reasons. Fingerprints on the screen surface would degrade the image of the negative on the screen and the perception of print quality. Also, it would disperse user control to two locations because some hard (off-screen) controls are also needed. A mouse was rejected in favor of the built-in trackball because it was felt the mouse would be subject to damage from dropping and could be easily stolen. Because users were not assumed to be computer literate, a mouse was not thought to be as intuitive as a trackball. The inherent slowness of accurately positioning a trackball was compensated for by designing large icon targets and a cursor easily seen against its background.

The screen is partitioned into two zones, a viewing zone and an icon zone. The viewing zone constitutes about 70% of the screen and shows an analog, positive image of the negative that has been captured by an internal video camera. Because about 6 seconds is required for the image of the entire film strip to begin appearing after the negative is inserted, a "countdown" clock rotates 90 degrees every second to assure the users that the delay does not mean their negative has disappeared into the machine. The strip is shown image by image as it moves into position so the customer will realize it was not altered, e.g., chopped, in the machine. Next to the image, in the second zone, are shown eight icons for selection of print size and orientation (landscape or portrait), for starting the print process, and for ejecting the film strip. The icons are continually present on the screen because software and hardware limitations precluded features such as progressive disclosure and character generation. Consideration was given to omitting the eject icon and automatically returning the film strip after a print is made. This would prevent users from forgetting to take their negatives with them when leaving the store. However, on the basis of usability studies (described later in this section) to determine the number of prints per negative and the number of negatives per trip made by users, it was decided to require a user action (select icon, press button) for ejecting their film strip. This avoided the need for most users to reinsert the film strip for each print. A similar user action is needed to make a print. Consideration was given to keying it off the size selection, but it was recognized that prints would sometimes be made prematurely before users were sure of their choice.

Instructional Material

Because of limitations mentioned earlier, an instruction label needed to be developed instead of on-screen instructions. The Human Factors engineer and the industrial designer worked closely to create and test iterative versions of labels. They coordinated their efforts by using a weekly schedule to complete an iteration a week for five weeks. Subjects were run on Fridays, results were analyzed and redesigns were done on Mondays and Tuesdays, and a new label was made and applied to the machine on Wednesdays and Thursdays.

The final instructions contain seven steps, each having a title and the required actions. Its usability was deemed acceptable as measured by the high percentage of people who could use the enlargement center without assistance during the in-house testing.

Support Process

David Aurelio supported development of the enlargement center in a way that is typical for a Kodak Human Factors Engineer who is a resource shared at the same time by several projects. During the course of development, he contributed an average of about one-fourth of his time supporting this particular project. He was part of the initial design team and continued his involvement until product launch. He ensured all usability issues were brought to the table, suggested resolutions to the issues, evaluated usability implications of proposed subsystem designs, made appropriate trade-offs where necessary, and prudently conducted usability studies. He did this through team and individual meetings and through practicing "design by walking around." Because he did not have a permanent office in the development area, he maintained visibility by frequently being present in the area and checking in with team members. Being there sparked spontaneous interactions about issues or to critique design ideas that would not have occurred otherwise.

Dave judiciously used traditional Human Factors literature, prior Kodak usability studies, and his own studies to develop data needed for his recommendations. For instance, he referred to anthropometric data to determine screen position and "knobs and dials" information to establish the appropriate gain ratio for the trackball and image manipulation knobs. Previous Kodak Human Factors studies for other projects revealed the kind of pictures people choose for enlargements and the extent to which they use zoom on a variety of different subject matter. Finally, Dave did a series of studies over a nine month period prior to product announcement to gain insight into how consumers approach, use features, and interact with the machine. The studies were done in a customer area of an in-house photo shop by observing people who walked up to use the enlargement center. The shop is available for use by any Kodak employee, but is physically located at a Kodak plant employing about 25,000 people. The building housing the shop also contains cafeterias, a gymnasium, and other employee-centered facilities that attract people from all over the plant. Although some customers noticed the observer, later analysis showed their behavior did not differ substantially from those that did not notice the observer. In the final study, subjects' video screens were recorded onto videotape for later analysis by transforming the enlargement center monitor's signals and channeling them directly to a VCR. In this way, no equipment was visible to the customers. Data collected included how many people were in the customer's party when they entered the shop, the number of people waiting in line, how many users sought clerk assistance and for how long, order characteristics (number of strips inserted, number of frames enlarged, number and size of prints), time on task for individual subtasks, total completion time, and reasons for making a replacement print when the first was unacceptable. The conclusions of the study were used to validate earlier usability design decisions and to help drive new design decisions.

Studies have also been done since the introduction of the Create-A-Print 35 mm enlargement center. These were primarily owner surveys done as part of research to explore various marketing issues, but include owner feedback on usability. In one study, all owners felt "the Create-A-Print center is easy for customers to operate," virtually all responded that customer and operator controls are good or effective, and a large majority felt the instructions on the machine and the manuals that come with it are good or useful.

Simulation of Tax Examiner Workstation

In this project, we produced a highly interactive prototype that simulated a future computer workstation of tax examiners at an Internal Revenue Service Center. The project supported the IRS's Tax Modernization Program, which is intended to reduce the handling of paper tax returns by providing image-based systems. To get the contract award, Stan Caplan prepared a formal proposal that described the process we would use, a schedule of work including project milestones, and the output we would deliver. The description provided in this section of the chapter emphasizes the process and the nature of the deliverables rather than specifics of the user interface.

The project's objective was to deliver, on time to the IRS, software code for a user-tested prototype, a written document defining in detail the prototype user-computer interface, and a videotape that featured the prototype to help visualize how work might be performed at an image-capable workstation. The prototype needed to embody a highly realistic representation of how images of tax return forms, taxpayer correspondence, and other information could be presented and manipulated. The Human Factors team of Christopher Koch, Walter Bubie, Kenneth Corl, Stan Caplan, James Wilson, and Richard Fox and the software development team of Charley Lightfoote, Steve Thillman, David Jones, and Frank Smith from our Commercial and Government Systems division worked closely with the IRS team in all phases of the project. The IRS was especially helpful to us for accomplishing knowledge transfer and arranging resources for information gathering, technical reviews, and usability testing. The development process involved five phases: human factors analysis, user interface design and prototyping, usability testing, user interface redesign and prototyping, and documentation.

Human Factors Analysis

This phase defined the scope of the prototype and the user interface design requirements. Our activities included

- Acquiring an understanding of the Tax System Modernization Program objectives and relevant service center functions. We accumulated information from public documents and service center visits where we observed existing computer-based and non-computer-based operations.

- Making assumptions about the future modernized tax system and its users that affect the user interface.

- Selecting a target service center function for analysis that was amenable to the necessary data collection, and could be accommodated within the contract time frame.

- Detailing the existing operations of the target function

- Defining functional requirements for the user interface of an image-capable workstation for that function.

User Interface Design and Prototyping

Our objective for this phase was to produce an interactive prototype with the required functionality and suitable for extensive testing. To achieve side-by-side two-page image display capability in a windowing environment, we elected to make a prototype of the design with TeleUSE, a user interface development tool now available from Alsys, on a Sun platform. This phase of the contract proceeded in two stages. In the first stage, we formulated several user interface design concepts based on different metaphors. Selected features from each of these were melded into one design concept that was prototyped in a scripted, noninteractive "electronic slide show" fashion. We then held a design review with the IRS, per our proposed schedule, to get feedback on this basic user interface concept. The second stage involved expanding the concept into an interactive prototype by

- Designing the details for appearance, navigation, interaction, and data presentation for a selected service center function.

- Scanning and tagging representations of tax returns, correspondence, and other related material that were the images and data to be worked on during testing.

- Prototyping of the design details.

- Writing code to create a database of images and data.

This phase consumed the most effort of any phase and required deliberate attention to effective methods for communicating design details from the Human Factors designers to the software developers. No single method was found that everyone could be comfortable with at all times. Methods used depended on the people involved, the type of information being communicated, and the time available. Special care was taken to avoid prototyping of the wrong thing because of a misunderstanding about the intended design. Hand sketches, computer-generated layouts, and handwritten descriptions, usually supplemented by verbal explanations, were typical. When certain design details were not adequately specified, software developers requested detail fill-in from the Human Factors specialists or provided it themselves. Throughout the process, Human Factors specialists and software developers coreviewed the prototyping in progress to ensure alignment of the design and prototype.

User Testing

Our user testing was conducted in the Kodak usability lab at the Elmgrove plant in Rochester. From a subject profile we prepared, the IRS identified potential future users of the modernized system employed at all 10 service centers. A schedule was established whereby pairs of individuals would arrive in Rochester late in the day, stay overnight at a local hotel, serve as subjects the next day, and return home that evening. This was done five days a week for several weeks. Each pair were either novice or experienced tax examiners from different service centers. The entire testing procedure required a full day and commenced with a brief orientation and training session. They then worked in pairs at the workstation, "thinking aloud" as they performed a predetermined set of tasks to practice all aspects of the simulated user interface. Testing concluded with a debriefing session consisting of a questionnaire and an interview. Task performance at the workstation was videotaped with separate cameras that simultaneously recorded the screen, keyboard and hands, and faces. IRS representatives observed the procedure from the control room of the usability lab and participated in the final debriefing.

User Interface Redesign and Prototyping

From results of the usability testing, we made improvements to the user interface design and incorporated them into the prototype. Needed improvements were identified by analyzing the observational data, "think aloud" protocols, questionnaire ratings and comments, and interviews from the testing. Further testing of the user interface was not done. From the enthusiastic reaction of the IRS users to doing their job this new way, the IRS contract team felt the prototype was successful and did not warrant further test iterations. The prototype code that existed at the end of this phase was one of the three contract deliverables.

Documentation

A second contract deliverable was a final report, written by the Human Factors team, which described the development procedure and design assumptions and

Figure 4 Example of screen for IRS workstation prototype

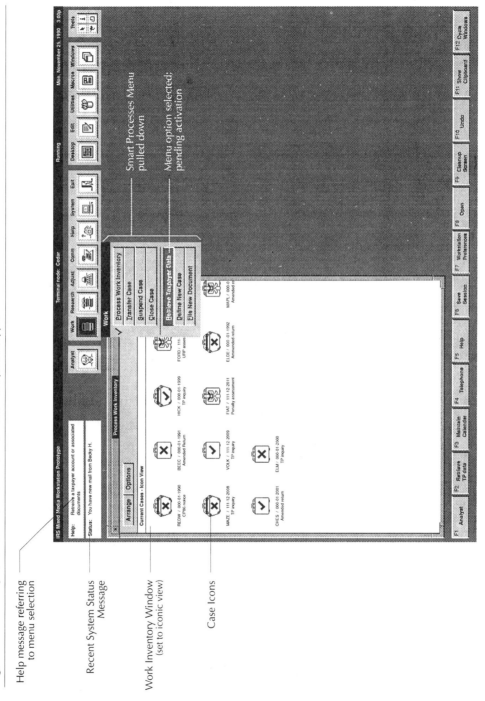

Help message referring to menu selection

Recent System Status Message

Work Inventory Window (set to iconic view)

Case Icons

This screen was first produced and published under United States government contract.

defined the details of the user interface design (Koch et al., 1990). The definition covered all elements of the interface including appearance, interaction, data presentation, and navigation paths. Also provided was a discussion of each function and its associated actions. Figure 4 shows one example of the many screen illustrations contained in the report.

The third deliverable was a professionally produced videotape showing how the user interface is used by tax examiners and comparing it to current methods.

Summary

Some authors cite both offensive and defensive reasons for applying Human Factors to the design and development of products; i.e., (1) to create a better product that more adequately fulfills user needs, and (2) to prevent losses from such occurrences as product recalls, excessive service calls, and poor product reviews (Cushman and Rosenberg, 1991). At Kodak, we apply Human Factors to achieve a competitive edge. With customers having many choices available when making purchases, we attempt to make usability an important factor that favorably differentiates our product offerings. We focus on both apparent usability and actual usability of products. Apparent usability is the ease of use that is perceived by a customer upon first looking at a product, but not using it. A control panel on a copier is an example of a component that conveys to a customer who will be in control—the machine or the user—when a copying job is to be done. The control panel effectively becomes the personality of the machine. Actual usability is the ease of use experienced during operation of the product. For novice users, actual usability is high when the product works the way they thought it would work. For power users, actual usability also means operations can be done productively.

Apparent and actual usability on a product are rarely achieved because of a major breakthrough. Rather, they result from the accumulation of many usability details that are addressed by our Human Factors people throughout the development cycle. In the end, the expense for Human Factors support invariably is a minuscule part of the overall product development cost. Figure 5 illustrates the consequences that can result from lack of attention to usability details or inadequate investment in Human Factors support.

Lessons Learned During Twenty-two Ergoyears

At this point, it is tempting to get philosophical and talk about lessons I have learned from the many and varied experiences I have enjoyed, my supportive and interesting colleagues over the years, and the sense of community I have felt as a member of the Human Factors profession. However, a quick second thought leads me to mention more practical lessons about usability testing, client relationships, and recognition for Human Factors work.

Now you see it, now you don't.   Understand how a product is marketed, especially how it might be demonstrated to the customer. Inclusion of a few "bells and whistles" may not add much to the actual usability, but may help salespeople highlight the apparent usability, thus making the product more marketable.

Divide and conquer.   In our usability lab, the off-line editing equipment resides in the control room. This creates a conflict when the control room is needed at the same time for running a usability test and for editing tapes from a prior test. It is more obvious to us now than when we built the lab in 1986 that a separate room should be provided for off-line editing. Another opportunity for improvement in a future lab upgrade is the sound situation. Both directionality of on-camera microphones and interference from air conditioning noise will require attention.

Figure 5   Example of user-hostile product resulting from inadequate Human Factors support during the development process

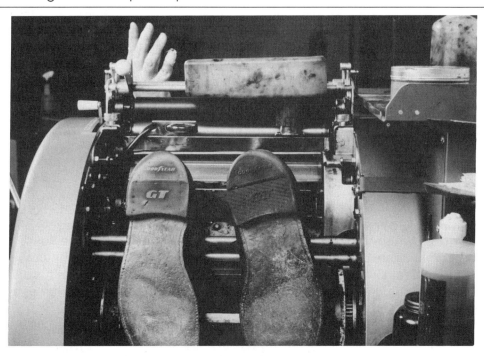

Here a test, there a test, everywhere a test, test.   Overtesting can hurt in the long run. Clients may avoid using Human Factors support if they perceive it will hold up the development process. It is important to be very judicious in deciding when to test and how to test. For many issues, a "quick and dirty" test may be sufficient. For example, when confronted with the need to specify how strong a fold-out shelf on a copier should be, the Human Factors engineer determined that a person leaning on the shelf was a likely scenario. In a short time he had collected data from having people lean on a scale placed on a shelf of the same height. Although not the usual kind of usability testing, its objective was the same as for any test—give timely input to development decisions that will result in usable products.

All aboard.   Take in clients as partners when planning and conducting usability testing. Involving them in the process gives them an understanding of testing and gets buy-in of the results. It may even be possible to use others in the client organization as subjects. On several of our studies, secretaries of client managers were used as subjects and this turned out to give Human Factors support high visibility.

No free lunch.   For a mature organization, billing out for the support time of a majority of resources is preferable to being a "free" service to clients. Some generic development or overhead funding is needed to do research in areas that cross client boundaries, but it should not overshadow the client supported work. Clients using some of their scarce funding for Human Factors support is a testament to the value they place on the function. It makes it easier to justify the existence of the function than when Human Factors is funded on the overhead line. It also gives the Human Factors function more visibility to clients and can strengthen ties with them. Because they are paying for the support, they will care about what they are getting and are likely to help make things happen. For an incubating Human Factors function, charging by the hour would not work as well. The function needs to be protected and nurtured until credibility can be built and a track record of successful support is achieved.

Out of sight, out of mind.   Colocating with a client is much more effective than residing in a central office, especially for an experienced Human Factors engineer. Sitting away from the client and waiting for him or her to call or attending meetings the client arranges proves that absence does not make the client's heart grow fonder. When colocated, the Human Factors individual is likely to be a full-fledged member of the design team and sometimes the client even may elevate Human Factors to full subsystem status. The spontaneous interactions fostered by colocation mean that many more usability details will be addressed.

Give them their due.   Many Human Factors professionals take great pride from seeing their thumbprint on products in the marketplace. Putting a lot of effort into the development of a product that, for whatever reason, does not make it to the marketplace can be very discouraging to the individual. It is important to give recognition for outstanding work regardless of whether or not the product goes to market.

Acknowledgments

People have always been the engine for the continued Human Factors effort at Kodak. In addition to our current group shown in Figure 6, about 150–200 people have passed through it. I am indebted to all of them for their competence, dedication, and cooperative spirit.

Figure 6   The Kodak Human Factors Group is comprised of professionals, technicians, and clerical staff. First row, left to right, are Novia Weiman, Helen Swede, Cathleen Daniels, Douglas Beaudet, Nancy Widger, Julia Cooke, Kathleen Donnelly. Second row, left to right, are Richard Pigion, Purnendu Ojha, David Aurelio, John Lacek, Deborah Howell, Walter Bubie, Jerald Muszak. Third row, left to right, are William Cushman, Stanley Caplan, David Mitropoulos-Rundus, Christopher Koch. Not pictured are Diane Bott, Joan Burkis, Shannon Casey, Jerome Flood, Jacqueline Gillis, Daniel Meyerhoefer, Rise Segur.

Mike Wiklund has been an "author's editor" and I thank him for anticipating my needs and encouraging me to make the chapter informative and enjoyable to read. I would also like to thank several others who took the time to review my first draft. Terry Faulkner, one of the earliest group members and now vice president and director of strategic and quality planning, helped me put the chapter into perspective and filled in missing pieces from those early years. From the Human Factors group, Bill Cushman, Purnendu Ojha, and Richard Pigion provided invaluable clarifications and Dave Aurelio articulately related his role in development of the Kodak Create-A-Print enlargement center. Kodak editors, Kay Servais and Carolyn Mauro translated the draft into understandable, properly punctuated English.

Finally, in order to be an "official" author, I should not fail to recognize the support of my family. My wife, Charlene, and daughters, Rachel and Johanna, gave me space to write the chapter by very patiently enduring my frequent absences from the mainstream of family activities.

References

Bytheway, Charles W. (1971). "The Creative Aspects of F.A.S.T. Diagramming," *Proceedings of the Society of American Value Engineers*, 4, Miami, pp. 301-319.

Caplan, Stanley H. (1975). "Guidelines for Reducing Human Errors in the Use of Coded Information," *Proceedings of the Human Factors Society, 19th Annual Meeting*. Reprinted in *Standards Engineering*, 28 (2), April 1976.

Caplan, Stanley H. (1990). "Using Focus Group Methodology for Ergonomic Design," *Ergonomics*, 33, (5, May).

Caplan, Stanley H. (1982). "Designing New Cameras for Improved Holdability," *Proceedings of the Human Factors Society, 26th Annual Meeting*.

Caplan, Stanley H., and Terrence W. Faulkner. (1982). "Camera Configuration and User Preference," *Proceedings of the Third National Symposium on Human Factors and Industrial Design in Consumer Products*, August.

Caplan, Stanley H., Suzanne Rodgers, and Harry Rosenfeld. (1991). "A Novel Approach to Clarifying Organizational Roles," *Proceedings of the Human Factors Society, 35th Annual Meeting*, September.

Cushman, William H. (1992). "Flat Panel Displays and the CRT: Contrast, Image Quality, and Usability," *Japan Display '92. Proceedings of the 12th International Display Research Conference*, Hiroshima, pp. 747-750.

Cushman, William H., M. Ghaderi, J. Divincenzo, and F. Samii. (1993). "Digital Image Quality for Text: Effects of Thresholding and Filtering," *SID International Symposium Digest of Technical Papers,* pp. 61-63. Society for Information Display, Playa Del Rey, CA.

Cushman, William H., and R. L. Miller. (1988). "Resolution and Gray-Scale Requirements for the Display of Legible Alphanumeric Characters," *SID International Symposium Digest of Technical Papers,* pp. 432-434. Society for Information Display, Playa Del Rey, CA.

Cushman, William H., and Daniel J. Rosenberg. (1991). *Human Factors in Product Design,* p. 4. Elsevier Science Publishers B.V., Amsterdam, The Netherlands.

Davis, Harry L., Terrence W. Faulkner, and Charles I. Miller, M.D. (1969). "Work Physiology," *Human Factors,* 11, (2), 157-166.

Eastman Kodak Company, Health, Safety and Human Factors Lab, Human Factors Section. (1983). *Ergonomic Design for People at Work,* Vol. 1. Van Nostrand Reinhold, New York, NY.

Eastman Kodak Company, Health, Safety and Human Factors Lab, Human Factors Section. (1986). *Ergonomic Design for People at Work,* Vol. 2. Van Nostrand Reinhold, New York, NY.

Faulkner, Terrence W. (1982). "Human Factors In Disc Photography," *Proceedings of the Third National Symposium on Human Factors and Industrial Design in Consumer Products.*

Faulkner, Terrence W., and Stanley H. Caplan. (1977). "Experimental Evaluation of KODAK EKTAPRINT Copier-Duplicator Instructions," *Proceedings of the Human Factors Society, 21st Annual Meeting.*

Faulkner, Terrence W., and Thomas J. Murphy. (1973). "Lighting for Difficult Visual Tasks," *Human Factors* 15, (2), 149-162.

Faulkner, Terrence W., and T. M. Rice. (1982). "Human Factors, Photographic Space, and Disc Photography," *Proceedings of the Human Factors Society, 26th Annual Meeting.*

Koch, Christopher G., Walter C. Bubie, and Kenneth Corl. (1990). *Mixed Media Workstation Prototype User Interface Definition.* Eastman Kodak Company, Contract No. TIR-89-0073, Internal Revenue Service.

Mantei, Marilyn M., and Toby J. Teorey. (1988). "Cost/Benefit Analysis for Incorporating Human Factors in the Software Lifecycle," *Communications of the ACM,* 31, (4, April), 428-439.

MacElroy, William. (1993). "Quantifying the Value of Usability," *Common Ground—The Newsletter of Usability Professionals, 3,* (3, September-October).

Urban, Glen L. and John R. Hauser. (1980). *Design and Marketing of New Products,* p. 375. Prentice-Hall, Englewood Cliffs, NJ.

Von Oech, Roger. (1990). *A Whack on the Side of the Head,* p. 104. Warner Books Inc., New York.

CHAPTER 3

Behavioral and Emotional Usability: Thomson Consumer Electronics

Robert J. Logan, Ph.D.

*Americas Design
Operations
Thomson Consumer
Electronics*

Dr. Logan has served as the manager of user interface design at Thomson Consumer Electronics since February 1992. Prior to joining Thomson Consumer Electronics, he was a human factors engineer at IBM in Poughkeepsie, NY, where he designed character based and graphical user interfaces for systems management software. While at IBM Poughkeepsie, Dr. Logan served as an adjunct faculty member at Marist College. Dr. Logan has also worked for IBM Owego, NY, as a human factors contractor for a Navy helicopter cockpit program. He holds a Ph.D. in Psychology from State University of New York at Binghamton. He is an officer of the Consumer Products Technical Group of the Human Factors and Ergonomics Society and a member of the Product Development and Management Association.

The formal usability program at Thomson Consumer Electronics (TCE) was started in February of 1992. Because this program is the first of its kind in the corporation, we created ourselves from scratch, and as such, are not encumbered with past organizational history or preconceived notions of responsibilities. We have adopted the basic usability concepts of early involvement, iterative design, and usability testing, but we have also begun to challenge and extend the traditional definition of usability and usability programs. This chapter reflects a snapshot of the development of our department, processes, and philosophy. In keeping with the general structure of this book, we will begin our chapter with an overview of Thomson Consumer Electronics' business followed by a description of our usability program, a case study, and conclude with a section on lessons learned. It should be noted that we assume that readers of this chapter are familiar with the basic concepts of usability and the appropriate processes.

Thomson Consumer Electronics' Business

Thomson Consumer Electronics is a multinational corporation that researches, designs, manufactures and sells consumer electronics products such as TVs, VCRs, camcorders, telephones, and portable audio systems. These products are marketed through a multibranded strategy divided across major geographic markets. In North and South America, TCE's brands include RCA, ProScan, and GE. In Europe, Asia, and Africa, TCE's brands include Thomson, Telefunken, Saba, Brandt, Ferguson, and Normende. In terms of overall color TV market share, TCE is number 4 worldwide, number 2 in Europe, and number 1 in America. To provide a sense of size of the TV market, a total of 23 million TVs are expected be sold in the United States in 1993. Moreover, TVs are present in 98% of the homes in the United States.

One significant trend in the consumer electronics industry, as well as several others, is the "digital revolution." The introduction of several key digital technologies such as HDTV, interactive TV, and the data highway are creating multiple new product opportunities that will dramatically change consumers' entertainment options. One example of this new opportunity is the RCA DSS digital satellite system, which is a joint development effort between Hughes Communications, Hubbard Broadcasting, and TCE. We will discuss this product in greater detail later in this chapter.

Thomson Consumer Electronics' Usability Engineering Program

Definition of Usability

A traditional definition of *usability* might cite successful attainment of some predefined goal by a majority of users within a specified period of time and a minimum number of errors. This type of definition, while rather cumbersome, is fairly traditional and necessary for many product environments, such as the military and process control. This definition reflects the functional heritage of the usability profession. In general, most attempts to improve usability have focused on work and productivity related products. As more consumer- and entertainment-oriented products receive usability attention, an expanded definition or alternative definition may be required. At TCE we are committed to going beyond, although what beyond is, is not completely clear. In this chapter, we will explore the development of TCE's new usability organization and our attempts to reexamine and expand the definition of *usability.*

Guiding Philosophy

At the core of our usability program is a concept called *mindesign.* At a linguistic level, mindesign is a play on the terms graphic design, industrial design, and software design. Instead of designing structural elements of a product, we are designing for the mind of the user and hence ease of use. At a conceptual level, mindesign represents a philosophy that reflects the need for integrated design of the total consumer experience from product and brand advertising, to point of purchase information, to packaging, to instruction books, and finally to actual product usage. This conceptual description sounds like systems design, and that is intentional. But the concept of mindesign is meant to incorporate more than functional system design.

Key to the mindesign concept is that usability has two elements, behavioral and emotional. Behavioral usability refers to the ability to complete some functional or goal directed task within a reasonable time. After all, if a product is not useful or is difficult to use, it will not meet the needs of the users and will most likely not be a success in the market. Emotional usability refers to the degree to which a product is desirable or serves a need(s) beyond the traditional functional objective. For example, there is nothing special about a T-shirt. If it has the appropriate number of holes in the appropriate positions and size, it will be functionally usable. Now consider a T-shirt that has a Nike logo on the front. The product takes on a whole new dimension. This new dimension relates to the emotional or humanistic elements of the product. The addition of the logo serves a need, or a user requirement in traditional usability terminology. In this example the need is one of communication or identification. Emotional user requirements can be as important as the behavioral user requirements for some product categories. Moreover, if these emotional elements are used appropriately, they can significantly improve product usability, not to mention competitive position in the marketplace.

Central to our concept of emotional usability are three related product attributes. First, products must be engaging. In other words, some products catch and hold one's attention better than others. If a product is engaging, consumers will be motivated to interact with the product. Second, products must foster a sense of discovery. Humans learn about the world through a process of continual exploration. Products designed to foster exploration will benefit by taking advantage of humans predisposition to learn through doing and finding new information. Third, products must eliminate fear. In most cases, fear of negative consequences decreases or eliminates behavior. While this can be adaptive in certain circumstances, it results in lost opportunities in others. A consumer who is afraid of breaking a product will be unlikely to explore the functional nuances.

Video games are a good example of products with emotional usability. For the most part, video games are fairly difficult to use and not particularly intuitive to the casual observer. However, users can and do become extremely proficient. One explanation is that these games have emotional usability. Generally the games are engaging due to the gaming concept or graphical treatment. Many games tend to foster discovery by requiring exploration to find clues or the "correct path." These games generally eliminate fear since the worst outcome is that either the user achieves a low score or the user restarts the game. Moreover, once a game has been played extensively it is no longer used since it is no longer novel (not engaging) and has become too easy (everything has been discovered).

It is our belief that a product designed with these three attributes will be intrinsically rewarding for humans to use and, if harnessed in the design of the product, can provide a powerful tool for enhancing overall system learnability and usability. We are currently exploring different levels of emotional usability. It may not always be necessary to have graphics and a video game type interface to have emotional usability.

Organization

Location in Organization

The TCE corporation is divided into three major organizations and multiple smaller organizations that all report to the chairman. Two of the three major organizations are sales and marketing. One sales and marketing organization services the Americas (North, South, and Latin) and Asian markets and the other services the European and African markets. The third major organization is operations, which includes product engineering, manufacturing, purchasing, and shipping (as examples). The remaining smaller global support organizations have a specific area of specialization. Americas design operations is one of these groups. Figure 1 illustrates the TCE organization from the user interface design department's perspective.

Figure 1 Americas design operations reports directly to the chairman, indicating the importance that TCE has placed on design.

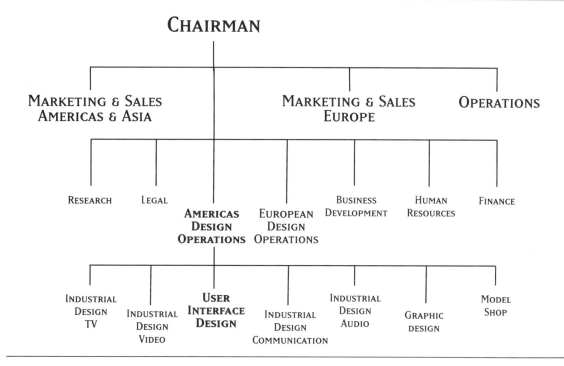

Usability issues are the responsibility of the user interface design department, which reports into Louis Lenzi, general manager of Americas design operations. However, each of the groups in the Americas design operations organization has the responsibility of fostering and ensuring product usability. User interface design in European and African products is in the process of being consolidated to a model similar to the Americas.

Usability Personnel

We created an eclectic usability team to address the emotional, behavioral, and technological aspects of our products. The team consists of a combination of traditional usability professionals and individuals recruited based on their technical excellence. There are currently 10 employees in our user interface design department, and we expect some moderate growth in 1994. In addition to the user interface design department there are five sister departments, composed of industrial and graphic designers, that contribute heavily to the design of the user interface.

The professional background of the user interface design department includes cognitive psychology, human factors, visual communications, graphic design, industrial design, electrical engineering, computer science, fine arts, literature analysis, journalism, anthropology, and education. This multidisciplinary team is the primary reason for our early success at TCE. First, each team member is armed with a different perspective and skill set that can be applied to design challenges. Second, the diversity of backgrounds allows us to "translate or interpret" our usability "lingo" to other organizations. This is particularly useful when trying to communicate the results of consumer research to other departments. Finally, our team can act in a checks-and-balances mode either within the design organization or in other parts of the company.

In addition to our internal personnel, we augment our skills, validate our designs, and seek stimulation from outside resources such as universities and consulting firms. For example, we sponsored design research programs with Ohio State University and Art Center School of Design. At Ohio State, an interdisciplinary class of students (with majors in industrial design, human factors, and marketing) researched, designed, and prepared prototypes of low cost video editing tools for the home. Students at Art Center researched, designed, and prepared prototypes of future home theaters that could be moved from one home to another. We sponsored applied cognitive psychology research at the State University of New York (SUNY) at Binghamton on the identification of appropriate labels for remote control buttons. Finally, we utilized the professional services of national and international consulting groups such as American Institute for Research, Doblin Group, Fitch Design, and Monterey Technologies on multiple design and usability programs. These external resources are key to our own technical vitality and represent valued partners in our product development process.

Responsibility

The usability team is responsible for the overall user interface design and usability of the TCE Americas TV (e.g., TVs, A/V receivers, HDTV, interactive TV, multimedia), video (e.g., VCRs, camcorders, laserdiscs), communications (e.g., phones, answering machines, two-way radios), and audio (e.g., personal audio, portable audio, clock radios) products. There are five major aspects of the user interface for these product categories (the importance of each varies with the product category):

1. On-screen displays. Menu systems for TVs and VCRs that are displayed on the monitor. Also includes LED and LCD displays on products such VCRs, phones, and audio products.
2. Hand units. Remote controls for home entertainment products and handsets for telephones.
3. Front panels. Buttons on the front of TVs, VCRs, telephones, etc.
4. Jack panels. Used to connect speakers and devices.
5. Instruction manuals. Every consumer device has some type of user instructions.

In addition to individual product design and usability, our user interface design department has the mission to develop cross-product consistency and a long-term vision based on consumer needs, life-style, and technology. Cross-product consistency is familiar territory for usability professionals. In our case this involves making all devices follow a consistent set of rules. For example, the main menu for a RCA TV should use the same navigation and structure as a RCA VCR. While this is common sense, the decentralized product structure that existed prior to the addition the usability group did not foster or enable such synergy. With this in mind, the user interface design department was created to work across all of the business units. The systems approach allows us to see the big picture that is sometimes missed by the individual product groups. This cross-product consistency has been the "low hanging fruit" for our department and has allowed us to make a significant contribution to the business quickly. We also have the more challenging mission to develop a long-term vision based on consumer needs, life-style, and technology for the new digital world of HDTV, interactive TV, and the data highway.

Process

As mentioned earlier, the usability program at TCE was started from scratch, so we had the opportunity to create a "textbook" type usability program and then improve from that point. In summary, we own the product user interface, have adopted a systems approach to product design and development, maintain early and continual involvement by users (through ethnographic research, market research, participatory design, and usability testing), utilize an endless iterative design process, are committed to all forms of rapid prototypes, and work with our after sales support organization to track consumer problems. Our only process problems to date are that we are a new department so (a) we do not have enough people, (b) some products that were started before we arrived, or just after, will not receive the full benefits of the usability process, and (c) it takes time to see the fruits of our labor in the marketplace.

Of the three "problems" it is fairly obvious that the last two will take care of themselves. The level of staffing is a more complex issue. On the one hand, we currently can not support all of TCE's programs. On the other hand, we do not want to grow too fast and loose the cohesion that has been fostered in our small, highly empowered team. A major advantage of a small team is that every member has the opportunity to see the whole picture. As the group gets bigger, communication becomes tougher, making it more difficult to work toward consistent products and a long-term vision. Our current plan is to grow slowly and rely on the abilities of a highly motivated staff and outside resources.

Figure 2   The majority of TCE's user interface design/usability work is completed in the early phases of the product cycle. Figure 2 shows a snapshot of these activities. The actual activities are adjusted on a program by program basis.

| | USER INTERFACE DESIGN RESPONSIBILITIES BY PHASE | | | |
TASK	PRE-DEVELOPMENT	CONCEPT	DESIGN	DEVELOPMENT
RESEARCH AND DESIGN	• ETHNOGRAPHIC AND BEHAVORIAL RESEARCH • IDENTIFY KEY UI TECHNOLOGY AND TRENDS • DEVELOP CONCEPTS • TEST CONCEPTS	• UI ARCHITECTURE • NAVIGATION AND HIERARCHY • CONSUMER TESTS • FEATURE REQUIREMENTS	• USABILITY TEST • CREATE DETAILED UI SPECIFICATION FOR ENGINEERING	• FINAL USABILITY TEST • ADDRESS DEVELOPMENT ISSUES
PROTOTYPES	• PROTOTYPE CONCEPTS • RESEARCH TECHNICAL FEASIBILITY	• LOW-FIDELITY PROTOTYPES OF HW AND SW • DETERMINE TECHNOLOGY REQUIREMENTS AND FEASIBILITY	• HIGH FIDELITY PROTOTYPES OF HW AND SW	• SUPPORT PRODUCT DEVELOPMENT • SUPPORT MARKETING AND SALES
VISUAL COMMUNICATION	• IDENTIFY GRAPHIC TRENDS • IDENTIFY NEW GRAPHIC TOOLS • DEVELOP GRAPHIC CONCEPTS	• GENERATE OVERALL GRAPHIC STRUCTURE • STORYBOARD UI • DEFINE KEY VISUAL ELEMENTS OF UI • INTEGRATE OSD VISUALS WITH IBs	• SPECIFY ALL GRAPHIC ELEMENTS • GENERATE BIT-MAPPED GRAPHICS • DEVELOP FONTS • CREATE ANIMATIONS	• FINE TUNE GRAPHICS
DOCUMENTATION	• IDENTIFY TRENDS IN INFORMATION DELIVERY TECHNIQUES • IDENTIFY NEW PUBLISHING TOOLS • GENERATE CONCEPTS	• GENERATE OVERALL IB OUTLINE, FORM, STRUCTURE, AND STYLE • TEST USABILITY OF IBs • GENERATE ON-SCREEN HELP AND QUICK REFERENCE INFO	• COMPLETE FIRST DRAFT OF IB • COMPLETE FIRST DRAFT OF HELP AND REFERENCE INFO	• BEGIN IB VARIATIONS FOR EACH MODEL OF LINE

One significant advantage we have had since the start of the program is the TCE development process. This process is based on four phases: (1) product concept, (2) product design, (3) product development, and (4) manufacturing. As you can see in Figure 2, a typical usability process can be plugged into this process. In fact, it was extremely easy to sell the usability process when it was explained in terms of the current TCE business model. We did find it necessary to add one additional phase that we call predevelopment. During this phase, we address issues that cannot be addressed in a timely or appropriate manner during the traditional fast paced product development process, in which speed and accuracy of decisions are critical. Predevelopment activities typically include ethnographic research on socio-behavioral trends, applied cognitive psychology research, and advanced concept development activities.

Summary of TCE's Americas Usability Program

To summarize, the usability program is new and still growing. We started the department by implementing the fundamental aspects of usability process, including early and continual focus on the consumer and maintaining an iterative design process that relies heavily on research and prototypes. From this baseline, we customized the department to meet the needs our consumers, business, and industry. Central to this customization is notion of mindesign and emotional usability, which we believe are essential for success in the consumer arena.

Case Study: RCA DSS Digital Satellite System

The RCA DSS Digital Satellite System is a major product development program for TCE and one in which commercial success is imperative (at the time of writing this chapter the product is not on the market). As a case study it is very interesting since it is the first major program that the TCE usability team participated in a significant manner during the development process. In addition, the program was already well underway when we arrived on the scene, so we had to hit a moving target. Finally, the nature of the product and several significant events during the design process served to define the personality and philosophy of the department as well as the company for the future.

Figure 3   The RCA DSS 18″ satellite dish, universal remote control, and set-top box represent the first of many pay-per-view and interactive TV systems that will be introduced in the 1990's.

Overview

The DSS System is a direct broadcast satellite system that delivers pay-per-view programming and approximately 200 channels of standard television programming to a consumers home through an 18″ satellite dish, integrated receiver/decoder (set-top box), and remote control (see Figure 3 and Color Plate II.) . The satellite network is owned by Hughes Communications and consists of two high power Ku-band satellites located in a geostationary position that provides complete coverage to the continental United States and parts of Canada and Mexico. Programming is provided by DirecTv (a Hughes subsidiary), United States Satellite Broadcasting Company (USSB is owned by Hubbard Broadcasting), and the National Rural Telecommunications Cooperative (NRTC). Programming is expected to include all of the major cable TV networks such as The Disney Channel, CNN, and ESPN. To assist consumers in finding a program that they want to view, the system includes an on-screen program guide that lists programs by time slot and allows the consumer to create custom searches. The consumer satellite dish, set-top box, and the remote control are designed, developed, manufactured, and distributed by Thomson Consumer Electronics under the RCA brand as well as OEM labels. The system is digital so the video signal will be S-VHS quality and the audio will be similar to that of compact disc recordings. For those of you who like technical details, the DSS System uses MPEG2 video compression. The initial retail price for the consumer components is $699; programming subscriptions and pay-per-view programs are extra.

The DSS Design Process

The design of the DSS user interface progressed through five phases. These phases reflect the development of the product but also illustrate the changing role and stature of the usability team in the product design process.

Phase 1: Getting Started

The first phase of the of the usability teams participation in the DSS program was predevelopment consumer research. This research focused on understanding consumers' home entertainment environment, their mind set with respect to consumer electronics products, their expectations of a DSS system, and identification of product design elements. The goal of this research was exploratory and intended to provide the design team (user interface, graphic, and industrial designers) with a high level conceptual model of consumers and their expectations of a new consumer electronics product. To assist us in our efforts, we enlisted the help of Fitch, Inc., of Worthington, Ohio.

To meet our research objectives, a TCE and Fitch team created an innovative consumer research program that relied heavily on participatory design techniques. Because this research was exploratory in nature and used nontraditional research techniques, we adopted a converging operations approach. This methodology allowed us to compare the results of several different techniques to identify underlying trends and expectations for the product personality. While the primary focus of this research was product form and aesthetics, we quickly realized that the conceptual information was invaluable to the broader issues surrounding the design of the user interface.

Overall, these techniques did not provide the traditional empirical data that a usability test would generate. It did generate information necessary to bring the designers' mental models into sync with the consumers' mental models. For example, a free association task generated strikingly different responses for TVs and computers. The term TV generated positive emotional associations such as "fun, relaxing, entertainment, family, and friends." The term computer generated less positive responses like; "yuck, work, hard, technology, and don't like." In addition, it was found that the TV and other entertainment products tended to be located in public spaces in the home and are used daily, whereas the computer was generally relegated to some remote location in the household and used relatively infrequently. This type of information was essential early in the design process. It was clear that we did not want the DSS product to be thought of as a computer (despite the fact that it has the functional complexity and computational power of one).

A second example of the importance of this type of early exploratory design comes from the design of the dish. The industrial designers at Fitch had created several innovated designs for the dish that were more sculptural in appearance than the traditional round form. The design team was very excited about the breakthrough designs. We had envisioned using the dish as an aesthetic element in a garden or as "yard art" (in a positive context). The consumer testing quickly changed our minds for both functional and emotional reasons. The design concepts were a little too "Buck Rogers-ish" for all but the early adopters (the first users-consumers of a new product or technology) and the early adopters had some concerns about the perceived quality of a satellite dish that did not look like a satellite dish. Even after we assured them that the "new" dish styles would work as well as a standard round dish, they remained unconvinced. So, at least for the first release we will have a "standard" round dish.

Phase 2: Catching a Moving Train

Armed with a list of consumer requirements, we had an image of what the product should be and were ready to implement our design. However, things are not always that simple. The usability team was new to TCE and was an unknown quantity. In addition, the DSS development schedule was extremely aggressive. Given these facts, the development community was reluctant to turn over the design of the user interface to our group. Their primary concerns were our ability to deliver a specification on time and with an appropriate level of information. As a compromise, due to pressure from upper management, the product developers agreed to jointly develop the user interface. A user interface work group was created with representatives from product management, engineering, and design to ensure that all needs and commitments were met. Smaller work groups were created to complete the actual design and development of the on-screen displays (OSDs) and remote controls. We will describe each of these in turn.

OSD Design

The original OSD design team of consisted of four people; two user interface designers and two product engineers. As mentioned earlier, the development schedule was extremely aggressive. During a three month period, we had to specify the menu navigation system, overall menu structure, and graphic primitives (the system has some bit mapped graphics capabilities).

The team of four met every- other- day for the three month period. Before each meeting we would identify an area of work, generate ideas (in teams of two), and then present our ideas during the meetings. The early meetings focused on high level rules of the user interface and the later meeting focused on the details. Along the way, we used a variety of prototyping tools, but the primary tools were paper and pencil and Visual Basic rapid prototypes. The meetings were tense at times, particularly in the beginning. Most of the early tension was due to the "new" process that was implemented and the joint ownership of the user interface. The product engineers were not used to working with usability professionals, and the usability professionals were eager to prove their worth. However, over time a mutual respect of the value of each members' professional skills was developed, and the only tension that remained was a healthy intellectual debate. As evidence, in the beginning of the process the development engineers insisted on writing the user interface specification. By the end of the process they indicated that they would rather have us write the specification since we were the "technical owners."

Overall, the design meetings were highly productive. We created an OSD system that is based on a simple interaction rule that is never broken. The rule is "point-and- select," which caters to the navigation requirements for the on-screen program guide and is easily learned by consumers (as demonstrated through testing; see later). We limited the number of on-screen structures to three major types—program guides, menus, and displays—thereby reducing the complexity of the system. We designed a system that does not look like a computer, avoiding the potential negative emotions noted in the consumer testing. Finally, we created a design that looks like a TV on the surface and does not confront "techno-phobic" users with detailed functions.

A sample program guide screen is shown in Figure 4. The body of the guide shows one half-hour time slot of programming. Consumers can move throughout the space using arrow on the remote control (see Figure 5). Users who want to view a current program, point to it and press the SELECT button on the remote. The program will be tuned. Consumers who select a program in the future, will be given a text based description of the program. To assist consumers in finding a program, the buttons along the bottom of the guide act as filters to provide a custom search strategy. Consumers who select Movies, will see a guide that contains all movies.

Figure 4   The RCA DSS program guide is designed with one rule for the consumer to remember: point and select.

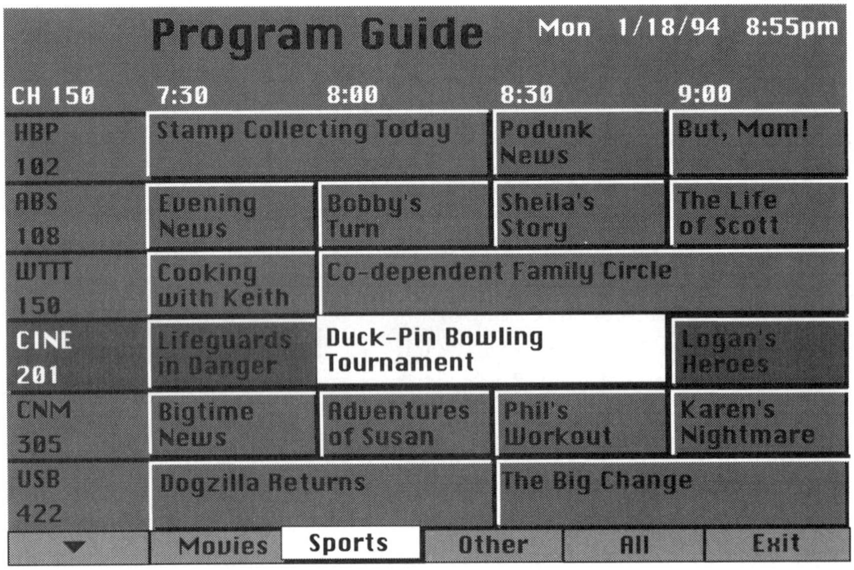

Program Guide			Mon 1/18/94 8:55pm
CH 150	**7:30** **8:00**	**8:30**	**9:00**
HBP **102**	Stamp Collecting Today	Podunk News	But, Mom!
ABS **108**	Evening News	Bobby's Turn	Sheila's Story	The Life of Scott
WTTT **150**	Cooking with Keith	Co-dependent Family Circle		
CINE **201**	Lifeguards in Danger	**Duck-Pin Bowling Tournament**		Logan's Heroes
CNM **305**	Bigtime News	Adventures of Susan	Phil's Workout	Karen's Nightmare
USB **422**	Dogzilla Returns		The Big Change	
▼	Movies **Sports**	Other	All	Exit

Figure 5   The RCA DSS remote control reinforces the fundamental user interface rule of point and select with four prominent navigation buttons.

Figure 6   A sample menu screen in the RCA DSS system.

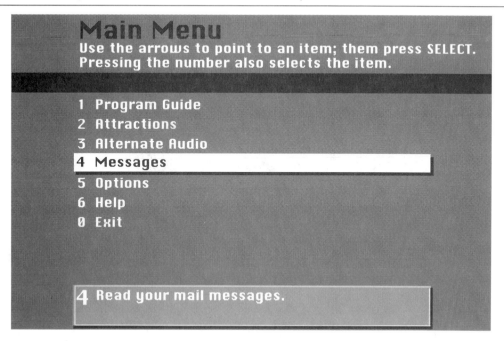

A sample menu screen is shown in Figure 6. The body of the menu shows the options available to consumers. Users navigate through the space by using the up and down arrow buttons on the remote. Each time they highlight a new choice, a description of that option appears at the bottom of the screen. Users can press the SELECT button on the remote to choose the currently highlighted item or press the number next the choice.

A sample display screen is shown in Figure 7. The body of the display shows the function to be performed on the screen. In this example, the screen allows the user to open his or her e-mail. As with the previous screens the users navigate the screen with the arrow buttons and press the SELECT button on the remote to make a choice.

Remote Control

The DSS remote control was collaboratively designed by an industrial designer and a user interface designer. There were three priorities for the design. First, the remote must reinforce the basic rule of "point-and-select" used in the OSDs. As can be seen in Figure 5, this was accomplished by placing the arrow keys and the SELECT button in prime real-estate and adding color coding. Second, the remote must look like a TV remote to reduce anxiety about the product. Notice that consumers can still change channels using the CHAN up-down keys, can still adjust the volume, and can still control their VCRs. Third, the remote must be consistent with other RCA brand remotes to maintain a family identity. To this end, we utilized the critically acclaimed and commercially successful remote shown in Figure 8 as the base and improved on it.

Figure 7   A sample display screen in the RCA DSS system.

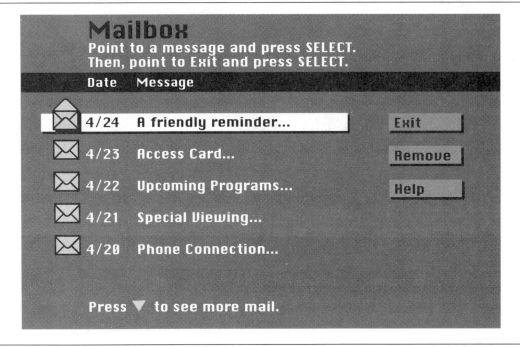

Usability Testing

During the design of the OSDs and remote we relied on an iterative process. Each iteration was based on a combination of informal usability tests, lessons learned from previous products, and heuristic rationalizations. Once the design stabilized, we created a fully functioning Visual Basic software prototype and solicited the service of Monterey Technologies, a full-service human factors consulting firm located in Cary, NC, to conduct a formal usability evaluation of the on-screen displays. We had become so "ego involved" with the product that we decided it was best to use an outside resource obtain an objective evaluation of the design.

Overall, participants were successful 72% of the time on the first attempt at a task. In addition, there was an extremely sharp learning curve. On the second attempt of similar tasks, success rate increased to 92%. These results were very encouraging since the product concept was brand new, the consumers were tested without the benefit of a real remote control (they had a simulation) or an owners manual, and the graphics were not the level that we expected in the product.

Figure 8   A traditional RCA TV remote control. This remote was a commercial success due to the color coding, shape coding, and functional groupings.

Phase 3: We're Going to Disney World!

Feeling pretty smug with ourselves about the success of the usability test we reviewed the program with our general manager, Lou Lenzi. During this review he had applauded the overall usability, but challenged our lackluster delivery of a standard "TV type interface" (e.g., white characters on blue screen). In our departments colloquialisms this was a "do over!" This also was a turning point for our the DSS product and the overall usability program at TCE. This is where we first encountered the need for "product emotional usability."

We had fallen into the tunnel vision of design that often occurs when the designer is also the usability person and passively accepts the prevailing system of constraints and schedule concerns. To break out of our design rut, we needed a method to question our basic assumptions and to get back in touch with what a consumer wants and needs in an interactive TV product like DSS. We decided we needed an off-site meeting to free ourselves from our current framework. This idea blossomed into a field research and brainstorming trip. We needed to immerse ourselves in a creative environment and observe a large demographic of consumers entertaining themselves. We considered traveling to LA, NYC, and Mall of Americas in Minneapolis.

Ultimately we decided on Walt Disney World in Orlando, Florida since it is the ultimate "consumer product." Disney is one of the few places in the world where one can observe a wide demographic, including infants to retirees, low income to wealthy, and any ethnic background you can imagine all entertaining-educating themselves and having fun doing it. We determined that by visiting Disney World we could invigorate our own creative processes and identify key product attributes that we could implement in our design. As a personal aside, one of the toughest things I have ever done in my career was to ask for permission to take a team of four designers to Disney World in November. Much to his credit, Lou Lenzi immediately saw the value of the research and approved the expense (and personally indicated relief that we did not choose Hawaii). Talk about empowerment!

During a four day period in November we spent 16 hour days alternating between observing the park's attendees interact with the exhibits and the park itself, analyzing other categories of successful consumer products, brainstorming, and designing a new DSS user interface. The research was extremely fruitful. One major finding was a result of a meta-analysis of why Disney World worked as a consumer product. We determined that Disney World (1) is engaging, (2) fosters a sense of discovery, and (3) eliminates fear. These are the three elements of our design philosophy that we discussed earlier. An additional key outcome was the identification of alternative user interface design concepts for the DSS system. However, the clock was ticking and the proposed changes were significant enough that they would cause a hit to the development schedule.

Phase 4: The Schedule, the Future

Given the fact that we were well passed the deadline for major design changes, we made cosmetic changes to the original design and created two (re)designs: a design for a second release of the product and a vision of where we need to be in the future (we are unable to discuss the content of these for proprietary reasons). The latter is perhaps the most important since fostered thinking outside the bounds of the current product. Basically, we identified the future technologies, services, and applications that we expected to be introduced with HDTV and interactive TV. We then identified potential user requirements. Based on these two areas of input we created a "user interface architecture" or a statement of where we need to be in the future. Once we had a vision of where we wanted or needed to be, all we needed to do was work backward to create the design of the second release of the DSS product. In retrospect, we should have begun the design of the user interface in this look-ahead mode.

Phase 5: Finishing Touches

At the time of writing this chapter, we are currently in the process of "putting the finishing touches" on the product. In addition to fine tuning the OSDs, we are actively writing the instruction books and creating a beta test plan for the actual DSS system before it is introduced into the market.

Instruction Book

The last major piece of the DSS user interface to be designed was the instruction book (IB). We started the design of the IBs with the assumption that people do not read users manuals and if they do, you only have a few minutes to demonstrate that the information is useful. In addition, we learned from our previous research that consumers tend to read the first couple of pages of an IB and then tend to randomly "flip through the book." With this mind set, we created a book that is based on conceptual information. The first several pages focus on the most important aspect of the user interface, the "point-and-select" rule, since we know from earlier usability test that consumers who understand this rule can use the product. We then explain the three types of screens and give a limited number of task-oriented examples. All of this is accomplished in 10 pages. The remaining 50 pages of the IB is a reference type document that the user does not need to read. This design is a major change from our more tradition task-oriented IBs, but early usability testing indicates that the technique is extremely successful.

Beta Test

At the time this chapter is being written, we are currently working on the DSS beta test plan. The beta test represents a great opportunity to gather "real data" and is perhaps the best usability test. The test will include 1000 households throughout the United States. Each family will be given a DSS system and free access to service. We will monitor system usage and periodically interview the consumers to identify usability issues. Depending on the nature and severity of any problems discovered, we will either fix them before product introduction or implement the improvements in the second release.

Summary of DSS Usability Program

Based on our usability test results, we are highly confident that we have designed a usable product that will please consumers, deliver unprecedented programming options, and provide excellent audio-video quality. The basic elements we described earlier—engaging user interface, fostering discovery, and eliminating fear—are present in the product and contribute to the overall usability of the product. The DSS system is also an example of systems design. DSS presents the consumer with a single message that is easy to learn and use, despite the fact the actual technology involved has the functional complexity and power of a computer. Look for the first product in early 1994 and with improved versions to follow. Finally, this project was perhaps the most important for our young user interface design department since it established our value to the development process and product design.

Lessons Learned

The Four Standards Are True

Most usability professionals would agree that for a group to be successful certain cornerstone elements must exist. First, it is important to have a commitment from executive management that usability is a necessary business priority. This point has been made repeatedly at all levels in the corporation. Most recently, our chairman, Alain Prestat, stated to a group of 400 senior managers in the Americas that user friendly designs are a key priority for TCE in 1994 and beyond. In addition, they must be willing to invest resources in the program and support the expert opinions of the group. Clearly the rapid growth of our group is evidence of TCE's commitment to usability. Second, usability activities must begin early in the process and continue throughout the product cycle. This includes "closing the loop" by tracking the product after introduction in the marketplace. Third, the design process must be iterative, and time must be included in the schedule for this iteration. Finally, a systems approach is essential. To be truly effective, a usability program must focus on all aspects of a product including hardware, software, and instruction manuals.

Direct Ownership of the User Interface Is Essential

At TCE we are responsible for creating the user interface specification for our products, which is used to implement the product by our development community. This form of direct ownership of the user interface places a usability team directly into the product development path. There are two benefits of this process. First, the usability group cannot be circumvented since they are in the critical path. Second, the usability group becomes directly accountable for the quality of the product. If a product is unusable, we only have ourselves to blame. The major risk of direct ownership is the potential loss of objectivity as the designer becomes the evaluator.

Must Utilize Effective Communication Techniques

It is essential that usability groups communicate effectively to other departments and management. In the TCE user interface design department we have adopted three initiatives to improve communications. First, we created a vision of where we want to be with our products and built a functioning prototype of this vision. We have found this to be the single most effective tool in to communicate what we want to do and why it is important. We have found on several occasions that the same idea receives dramatically different reception depending on whether it is a verbal concept or a functional prototype. Second, we focused on communicating what is important to the management team rather that what is important to usability professionals (save this for conferences or intradepartmental discussions). In our case, management cares about the quality of the product design and the level of customer acceptance. Managaers insist that we apply the best techniques available but are not interested in hearing the details of the cognitive psychology that was applied to the interface. Third, it is critical that we communicate clearly and repeatedly with the same message. With this in mind, we treat our presentations to management like an advertisement or commercial and present "info- bytes" that are easily internalized. To accomplish this, we limit our message to two or three key points and repeatedly present the message until we are sure that it has been absorbed. If necessary, we repeat the message over a number of months. When we hear managers or executive using the "info- bytes" when talking with others we move onto a new topic. Once you get the executive preaching usability, the rest of the organization starts to follow in suit, making our job easier.

Monitor the Checks and Balances

To ensure that we design and build the best possible products, we have adopted a checks and balances system. Internal to the user interface design department, we utilize internal reviews and consumer research. We also rely heavily on our sister departments of graphic and industrial design to participate actively in the design of the user interface. While the working relationship between these groups and usability can sometimes be strained by the competing desires for "form and function," ultimately our cooperation produces superior products. As usability professionals, we often forget that other aspects of the product are as important as ease of use, such as overall aesthetic appeal. For example, many of us pick our cars based on the appearance rather than the usability. Finally, we utilize external consultants and funded university programs as sources for "sanity checks" on our designs as well as injection of fresh ideas. At TCE we consider this type of "checks and balance" approach to product design to be key to our success.

Look Around, Backward, Forward, and at Your Shoelaces

It is extremely important that you spend time changing the level of focus and look at all sides of a problem. In other words, spend time looking at the big and little pictures. We believe four areas are important. First, it is important to spend time looking "around" at the existing competition and product environment to develop a frame of reference for product(s). Second, it is important to look "forward" to understand the consumer and technology trends that will affect product design decisions. Third, looking "backward" provides an opportunity to jettison the bad ideas and refine the good ones. Finally, it is essential that usability professionals spend time designing an actual product. We have termed this looking at your shoelaces because it forces you to focus on the details and nothing helps you understand a problem better than actually working through the nuances of a product. This also helps build credibility within an organization since you are seen working "in the trenches" rather than sitting in an "ivory tower."

Use the Best People

It sounds trite, but the quality of people on the usability team are the "make-or-break" aspect of a program. As mentioned earlier, we have created a multidisciplinary team to focus on usability. Each member has his or her own area of expertise, but also has additional competencies in other domains. It is our belief that usability professionals who work with consumer entertainment products have to be "Renaissance types" who understand the arts, sciences, and humanities.

Be Prepared to Take Risks

If usability was easy, every product would be usable. In order to make breakthroughs in product design and usability, it is necessary to take risks and challenge the standard assumptions. The best time to take these risks is in the beginning of new programs where there is time for mistakes and the bulk of the creative work is completed. They will not all be successes, but those who try a number of ideas will be rewarded with improved products. If these new procedures are used in conjunction with standard usability practices, product success is more likely.

Intangibles Make a Difference

There are always a number of things that are important but difficult to identify. If I had to speculate, I would guess that these intangibles ultimately relate to the work environment and the people in the environment. In our case, we are located in a design studio that tends to encourage creative thought. The studio is a large open space with a lot of visual (e.g., sketches, mock-ups, pictures, products), auditory (e.g., discussions, music, and general activity), and intellectual (e.g., work and non-work related) stimulation. The studio is stocked with the latest in technology and best tools available for all to use. When you combine this environment with a diverse, talented group of people, things just seem to happen. This is not to say that other environments would not work, rather for our particularly products and mix of people, this environment seems to be a key factor for success.

Conclusions

In the beginning of this chapter we expressed the need to go beyond the traditional definition of usability. Going beyond for TCE means creating a Renaissance style department in which the scientists, technologists, artists, and humanists collaborate during the design process to meet all of the users' requirements. It is our belief that for a technology to become truly useful to humans, the humanistic element of the products must be addressed as well as the technological and functional aspects. The net result of this new orientation are TCE products that have both behavioral and emotional usability. In other words, our products will be engaging, foster a sense of discovery, and eliminate fear. It is important to state that we do not expect all of the concepts that we discussed to translate to all industries. Clearly emotional usability is applicable for entertainment products such as consumer electronics, interactive TV, and multimedia. However, we also believe the concepts are important for certain work environments. After all, humans work better if they enjoy their job. Why not make their tools more enjoyable to use? As functionality and ease of use become standard across products, the companies that address the emotional elements of product use will differentiate themselves from the competition in the 1990s and beyond.

CHAPTER 4

User-Aided Design at Apple Computer

**Tom Gomoll and
Irene Wong**

Apple Computer

Tom Gomoll is the manager of user studies in Apple's personal computer business. When he joined Apple in 1988, Tom helped establish a formal usability engineering effort within the company by founding the user-aided design group. After managing that group for almost four years, he led the Macintosh human interface group, helping to establish user-centered design methodologies throughout Apple's software development organization. Prior to joining Apple, he worked as a writer at Oracle Corporation and also completed an internship in IBM's software human factors lab. He holds a B.A. in psychology from the University of Wisconsin—Eau Claire and an M.A. in professional writing from Carnegie Mellon University.

Irene Wong is the manager of user-aided design in the AppleSoft human interface design center. She played a major role in transforming the group from a usability program to a multidisciplinary human interface resource, providing scalable human interface support across hardware and software divisions. Before managing UAD, she worked as a usability specialist, making important contributions to the Macintosh PowerBook industrial design. She has a B.A. in psychology and Ph.D. in education, minor in anthropology, from Stanford University.

Apple Computer's Business

Apple Computer, Inc., develops and manufactures personal computing hardware and software. Located in Cupertino, California, Apple has grown to a company with net sales of $7.9 billion (fiscal year 1993) and approximately 12,000 employees worldwide. In the first half of calendar year 1992, Apple sold more personal computers than any other personal computer vendor (based on unit shipments as reported by InfoCorp, 1992).

Apple is firmly committed to a multibusiness strategy, focusing in four different development areas:

- Personal computer business
- AppleSoft
- Apple business systems (ABS)
- Personal interactive electronics (PIE)

The personal computer business is the cornerstone of Apple's multibusiness strategy. This business is responsible for developing personal computers and imaging products that are used by home consumers, educators and students, and business workers. Products developed by the personal computer business include the best-selling Macintosh® LC computers, the powerful Macintosh Quadra™ computers, the award-winning PowerBooks™, which set a new standard for notebook computing, and the affordable, high-performance LaserWriter® printers.

AppleSoft is responsible for creating innovative system software for Macintosh personal computers. System 7™, Apple's operating system for Macintosh, continues to provide easy-to-use, elegant solutions for users. QuickTime™, a system software extension, makes working with time-based media, such as sound, video, and animation, as easy as working with text and graphics.

Apple business systems recognizes that the client-server model of computing—networks of workstations and personal computers—is a faster, simpler, and more cost-effective way to manage the flow of information. To that end, ABS creates client-server systems that help people work together in new and better ways. ABS products include Apple Workgroup Servers, multivendor connectivity software, and network services software such as AppleShare and AppleTalk Remote Access.

The personal interactive electronics group is pursuing products to meet the needs of people entering the digital information age. PIE's strategy is to create intelligent, affordable, and portable products—called *personal digital assistants*, or PDAs—which are so compelling that they will change the way people access information, ideas, and images. The first Apple PDA is the Newton notepad, a product that integrates advanced hand-writing-recognition, communication, and data-management technologies.

Apple Computer's Usability Engineering Program

Early in 1988, Apple had no structured usability engineering program. However, the Apple culture supported and nurtured the idea of involving users in all phases of product design. The company was founded on the basic premise that personal computers can change the way people work, learn, play, and communicate. Given that fundamental premise, Apple engineers often stalked the halls, asking colleagues to try out their designs in an effort to identify flaws and pitfalls—flaws and pitfalls that would make the technology inaccessible to normal, nontechnical people. In fact, the Lisa interface— Apple's first graphical user interface and the foundation of the Macintosh interface— was designed by engineers who were very sensitive to users' needs. The engineering team bounced most design ideas off each other, not by asking each other "what do you think?" but rather by observing each other using the product. Their usability engineering process was informal, but certainly revolutionary at the time (1982). In short, Apple's "user-centered" attitude made it easy to establish a usability program.

In this chapter, we discuss how we established a more structured usability program within Apple, detailing our grassroots approach to usability, our proposals to upper management to enact the program, and our formation of a new usability group. Additionally, we outline the group's strategies, skills, and financial model and then provide a case study of how we integrated usability engineering into the Macintosh PowerBook product development cycle.

Establishing Usability at Apple: A Grassroots Effort

This section discusses our effort to incorporate usability testing as a part of Apple's product development process. Since no formal usability effort existed within Apple, we started from the bottom up; we conducted a test, presented the results, and made the argument for including usability in the engineering process.

Using the "Just Do It!" Approach to Usability

The roots of usability within Apple can be traced to concern about the usability of a product's documentation. In 1988, Apple released HyperCard, a new software product that delivered information in forms beyond traditional list and database report methods. In short, it gave users the power to dynamically link information and branch instantly to related facts. HyperCard was considered a breakthrough technology, but it was difficult to use.

To understand the usability of the HyperCard documentation, we decided to conduct a test of the *HyperCard User's Guide*. HyperCard 1.0 had already been released, and we wanted feedback to help revise the *User's Guide* for the next version of HyperCard. To collect feedback, we conducted an informal user observation; we asked users to complete a few tasks, referring to the book as necessary. From this study, we uncovered problems in the interface and problems in the documentation. To influence as many product changes as possible, we wrote a complete test report and created a highlight videotape illustrating common problems. We presented the tape to the development team, together with recommendations for improving the interface and book. The team embraced many of the recommendations and made important changes to the interface for the next release.

Winning Management's Support

After the success of the initial HyperCard usability study, we approached management requesting that usability be incorporated into the document design process at Apple. Following is the rationale we provided for a usability testing group:

1. *Why Test?*

   - *Testing helps us edit. Testing provides empirical evidence of where our documents work and where they fail with our users. This important link to our users is the most important benefit gained from testing.*

   - *Testing makes us better writers. By repeatedly exposing our writers to the kinds of problems users encounter when using our books, we teach writers to better anticipate users' needs. Writers exposed to test results over a period of time learn to write drafts that require less revision.*

   - *Testing helps us do research. Writers deal with questions about the relationship between our users and our books. Testing can address the issues we face and provide empirical data on which to base our decisions.*

   - *Testing helps us improve our products. When testing a book with a product, we also get valuable feedback on the design of the product. This feedback can be used to enhance product usability. (This is supported by responses from the HyperCard team, all of whom have asked to work with us to implement interface improvements suggested in the HyperCard test.)*

2. *Why Test In-House?*

   - *Our testers have a combination of skills that make them uniquely qualified to test Apple's documentation. By combining Apple writing experience with a human factors background, our testers are able to understand, record, and interpret the behavior of users in our tests.*

- *In-house testers have more opportunity to have an impact on our documents and products. Only someone familiar with the philosophy, style, and tone of our books will be able to communicate the results of the tests to the writers. Further, as staff members of a product team, in-house testers have more opportunity to drive interface improvements.*

- *Investing in our in-house expertise is investing in Apple. Investing in third party testers is an investment in a third party. We should take advantage of the opportunity to expand our own testing expertise.*

- *In-house testing is more cost effective. The HyperCard test cost roughly $5,000. Comparable tests using contractors have cost approximately $20,000. (These numbers are based on 1988 estimates.)*

Management responded by allocating one staff member (trained in writing and research) and money (approximately $50,000) to start a user testing function within the documentation group. After receiving this support, we designed a simple lab for conducting future studies. (We believed that a simple lab, with a few cameras, would more than adequately meet our needs; we were not concerned about using elaborate data collection tools or video equipment—we simply wanted a record of what we observed.) Figure 1 shows a schematic diagram of the lab.

Creating a Formal Usability Group

We built momentum for a formal group by conducting a user study that focused on all aspects of Apple's products: packaging, industrial design, interface design, and instructional design. In this study, we asked users to unpack, set up, and learn how to use a Macintosh II computer. We observed users in our new lab and made sure that key decision makers attended a few of the sessions. The result was a number of critical product improvements which helped us sell the long-term benefits of user testing.

After conducting the study, we produced a highlight videotape and presented it to product teams, managers, and executives throughout Apple. The videotape was so compelling—filled with clip- after- clip of users telling us how frustrated they were trying to connect cables, insert cards, and install system software—that we met with very little resistance over making changes to the product. Once we had gained mind share throughout Apple, we produced a one-page document outlining the benefits of user testing. This one-pager, reproduced in Figure 2, served as the catalyst for expanding usability within the Apple.

Showing the value associated with usability engineering was the first step toward establishing a usability group. To bolster our case, we gave concrete examples from

Figure 1   Apple Computer Usability Labs

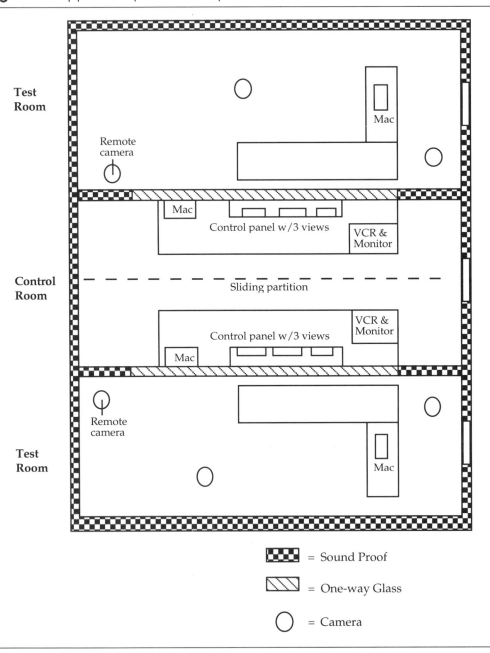

Figure 2 Benefits of user testing

The importance of user testing is clear. Testing helps us

- *Improve products: User testing provides the most graphic feedback about the difficulties users will have with a product. Designers can use this early feedback to make significant improvments to Apple products before they are released.*

- *Become better designers: By repeatedly exposing the designers who create Apple's products tot he problems users encounter, we help them anticipate users' needs. Over a period ot time, these designers learn to create products that are more sensitive to users' needs*

- *Improve the end user experience: By focusing moredirectly on the end user experience, Apple designs and creates products that are easier to assemble and use. This improvement translates into increased sales and customer satisfaction.*

Case Study

The Macintosh II open-the-box study resulted in many improvements to the product, including

- *Initialized hard disks and installed system software in the factory.*

- *Interface changes to system dialog boxes and the new Installer*

- *Innovative new packaging, which organizes the setup procedure*

- *The "Open Me First" booklet, which guides a user step-by-step through setting up a Macintosh*

This study helped save Apple money by reducing the number of pieces in the box and giving us a competitive edge over companies that require users to initialize their own hard disks and install their own system software. More important, by focusing on the end user experience, we are now producing a product that is easier to assemble and use and is therefore more attractive to our customers.

---

the Macintosh "open-the-box" study. Our next step was to present a coherent strategy for user testing within the documentation organization. Here is our executive summary from that strategy document:

> *This document presents a business strategy for Customer Communications' User Testing group. The importance of user testing is clear: it benefits Apple's users because they get a product that is better designed, better documented, and easier to use.*

The User Testing group will be staffed in two stages. For Fiscal Year 1989, the group should include two test designers and one coordinator. In Fiscal 1990, we should expand the testing group to include four test designers (two junior level) and one coordinator. Job descriptions for the user testing staff are found later in this document.

Because the testing group must grow at a controlled pace, it will not be able to take on every testing project proposed. In deciding what products are tested, managers from each of the groups will identify testing needs and present them to the test designers. The test designers will recommend testing schedules to their manager who in turn decides how testing resources will be allocated. The criteria for these decisions include the product's importance to Apple, the number of units sold, and the importance of the project as research.

Each user test follows a standard process that includes

1. *holding a testing launch meeting*

2. *writing a test plan*

3. *running pilot (preliminary) tests*

4. *running actual tests*

5. *interpreting data*

6. *writing a test report*

7. *presenting test results.*

For each test, the test designers will choose the testing method appropriate to the media and goals of the test. Examples of methods test designers might use include verbal protocols, constructive interaction, and focus groups.

In addition to user testing, the testing group will conduct market research. The market research effort will involve four distinct tasks: analyzing our audience, collecting existing research, presenting results, and conducting competitive analyses.

The User Testing group will conduct experiments to help answer basic questions about the relationship between users, instructional materials, and products.

Because we graphically illustrated the problems users encountered with Apple products and because we effectively evangelized the benefits associated with usability testing to upper-level executives, management signed up to support this strategy. To start the testing effort, we began by selecting a person to manage the group and by opening one job requisition for a usability specialist. At no time in this process did we have to conduct an elaborate cost/benefit analysis. Since Apple's culture supported user-centered design, we did not find it necessary to jump through hoops to establish the group.

The User-Aided Design Group

With support from management (John Sculley and his team) and a budget to grow, we formed a new usability engineering group. Our first two user tests—the HyperCard study and the "open-the-box" study—had one thing in common: both studies were completed after products had been released. We realized that many of the problems identified in those studies might have been avoided had we involved users earlier during the development process. Our goal for the new usability engineering team quickly became clear: conduct user studies throughout the product life cycle; simply stated, do "user-centered design."

Given our user-centered design directive and our desire to influence products throughout the cycle, we chose a name for the group that implied involving users during all phases of design: the user-aided design group (UAD). This chapter defines UAD's charter, discusses how we promote the group, outlines the skill set of the group, and provides a synopsis of the group's financial model.

Defining the Group's Charter

The user-aided design group started in the customer communications organization, the department responsible for creating and producing Apple's user instructional materials. Instructional designers have a unique sensibility for understanding users and tasks, so the it was natural for the writing group to nurture a usability testing team. As UAD conducted studies for customer communications, many of the product recommendations applied to other product components such as interface design, industrial design, product design, and packaging. We continued to uncover product problems only to find that there was never enough time in the schedule to make critical changes. Consequently, we argued that the best use of our usability resources would be to work more directly with the product teams, switching our focus slightly from documentation usability to total product usability. We needed to become involved earlier in the design and development process.

To achieve earlier involvement, UAD moved up one level in the organization and began reporting directly to the director of product marketing in the personal computer business. By elevating our position on the organizational chart, we made an important statement: usability was becoming more visible, more critical, in Apple's product development model. After making this key organizational shift, we drafted a broad charter for UAD:

Responsible for conducting the usability testing effort within the Personal Computer Business. This includes

- *implementing a cross-divisional usability effort to ensure that Apple's most critical products receive user testing support,*
- *evaluating Apple's industrial design, interface design, and instructional design to identify problems and improve Apple's ease- of- use,*
- *providing proactive environment for affecting important product changes, and*
- *promoting a "user-centered design" model across Apple's development organizations.*

Expanding our charter to focus on Apple's key products allowed us to drive user-centered design methodologies into the product development process.

Promoting the User-Aided Design Group

Early in UAD's history we developed a group logo (shown in Figure 3). Our goal was to create a very simple identity that would make it easy for clients in Apple to remember our work. The clean, user-centered logo design has proven to be a key to our success and recognizability: people know who we are and read our materials when they see the logo.

Figure 3   UAD logo

By far, our primary method of marketing our usability engineering service has been to take our results "on the road." To assure visibility, we produce high-quality videos, with narration and graphics, for those studies that affect a wide portion of the company. Then, we conduct a "road show." We send invitations at large and schedule time to talk at staff meetings, team meetings, and communications meetings. Our first highly visible study—the Macintosh II "open-the-box" study—has become part of Apple folklore. After five years, people still approach us with questions, comments, or criticism about that study.

We have not found it necessary to do an internal blitz outlining our services. We simply present our services to client groups in the context of user studies we have already conducted. Most groups are familiar with our work and contact us directly to work with them. The pitfall, of course, is that relationships are informal, based on personalities and random meetings. In the end, we will continue to drive user-centered design activities into the formal process by working with project leaders and total quality management representatives.

Hiring People with Multidisciplinary Skills

Given that the user-aided design group started in the user documentation department, it should come as no surprise that many of the usability specialists on the team we were able to complete a wide range of studies by working on many at one time. In addition, the consultant role allowed usability specialists to work on a wide variety of projects, something that was professionally desirable and motivating are formally trained in technical-professional writing. Usability specialists with background in writing and audience analysis come equipped with the sensitivities necessary to conduct valid, user-focused studies. As the role of usability specialists evolves into researcher, designer, and prototyper, we now find it critical to locate candidates with multidisciplinary skills. Specifically, we outline the following requirements when seeking qualified usability specialists:

- *B.S. or B.A. in psychology, cognitive science, or human factors (or equivalent experience). Masters or Ph.D. preferred.*
- *Extensive training in experimental design, human factors, ergonomics, and research methods and behavioral sciences.*
- *In-depth knowledge of interface design, industrial design, and instructional design.*
- *At least 2 years user testing experience .*
- *Market research experience desirable.*

Table 1 shows the general educational background and experience of the usability specialists who have worked in UAD over the past six years.

Changing the Financial Model

As a central resource for most of Apple, UAD's original funding model was structured to service the needs of our most critical internal clients. Funding came from the product marketing organization, with the understanding that the money belonged to Apple and would be allocated to work on the company's most important products.

Funding was split between permanent Apple employees and outside contractors and consultants. With only five people in the user-aided design group, obviously there were not enough resources to provide usability engineering support for the entire company. As we identified critical projects, we assigned internal resources based on availability and expertise. Generally, we allocated internal resources to work on the most important (read, visible) projects. All other requests were serviced by contractors and consultants.

We maintained a "pool" of money to be used on a quarterly basis for contractors and consultants. The pool was budgeted on an annual basis and the sum was determined by the number of key projects on the Apple project list, the need for usability engineering on those projects, and the historical record of money spent on contractors and consultants. This consultant model—shared dollars for critical projects—was very flexible in that it allowed us to conduct studies and research on a moment's notice without haggling over who pays for what and how much.

Table 1 UAD Group Background

Education	Experience
M.A., Writing/Psychology	2 years technical writing 5 years product usability
Ph.D., Education	4 years product usability
Ph.D., Psychology	3 years human interface/usability
M.A., Human Factors	15 years human interface/usability
M.A., American Studies	10 years journalist and technical writer 2 years product usability
M.A., Professional Writing	2 years human usability/interface
B.A., Professional Writing	3 years product usability/interface
B.A., Psychology	1 year usability coordinator
General Education	2 years usability coordinator

Further, the consultant model gave UAD the freedom to determine the scope and focus of our commitment to projects; consequently our roles were well-defined and

Although the consultant model had many benefits, it also had some drawbacks. As consultants, we were often outsiders on the product team, thereby missing out on some of the key interactions and decisions that were made during informal hallway discussions. (Being an outsider also offers advantages, however, such as maintaining objectivity in the face of extreme cost and schedule pressures.) Second, client groups did not routinely include usability engineering resources as a common element in their business planning; hence, it was more difficult to consistently integrate usability engineering into the product development cycle. Third, it was more difficult to track the costs associated with usability engineering because usability resources were not attached to specific projects. Our inability to track costs on a project-by-project basis also made it more difficult to provide a good business case for expanding the resources in the usability group. The need to develop a stronger business scenario developed from the evolving marketplace; as Apple's strategy increasingly focused on expanding market share while gross margins continued to drop, the company was forced to reduce operating expenses. One such way of cutting expenses is to reduce headcount, putting pressure on all functions to justify resources and expenditures.

Over the past year, we have seen this model change. As Apple faces more and more pressure to cut expenses, we have had to operate our business as an independent entity with accountability for the bottom line. The current model calls for us to work closely with cross-divisional clients, convince them of the need for usability engineering, and then convince them to pay for it. Not only do we ask them to pay for necessary contractor funds, but we also ask them to incorporate our headcount into their business plan. Although people within Apple fundamentally believe in user-centered design, it is possible that some teams may not be willing to pay for it in the face of time-to-market and cost pressures. So, it remains to be seen how many businesses within Apple will pay for usability engineering services, but all indications thus far point to very good success in adopting this new "business unit" model.

Managing and Distributing Resources

UAD generally dedicates staff to a single product area such as portable computers, desktop computers, software, and instructional design. To maintain a consistent usability engineering approach and to develop long-term relationships with teams, each staff member specializes on certain product lines.

In making the decisions about which projects to pursue and support, the usability specialists and manager use these criteria:

- the importance of the product to Apple's strategic success,
- the number of units sold or projected sales,
- the time remaining in the product schedule: is there time to incorporate the results from the study?
- the importance of the project as research for the department, division, or company.

In short, we get involved in as many projects as we can, given our resource constraints; however, usability engineering is still not a documented activity on Apple's formal product development chart. To this point, UAD has existed and grown by word of mouth and our ability to develop key relationships with specific teams or individuals.

Case Study: PowerBook 170

To illustrate the complexities and challenges of how a usability program integrates and hence contributes to product development, we will now examine the experience of UAD in Apple's first release of the PowerBooks in the early 1990s. The PowerBook is the first family of notebook computers in the industry that has successfully and gracefully delivered a built-in cursor control device. The innovative form factor supported comfortable use of the system anywhere and anytime.

This case study took place after UAD had gone through the early pioneering efforts of gaining official status as a usability group for instructional products. We have chosen this example because we can draw from hindsight to comment on our past actions and decisions. Furthermore, we can also describe the outcomes of our attempts to overcome the problems identified. The PowerBook episode highlighted the following aspects of usability engineering in action:

- How the usability group become involved
- The role of usability group in product development team
- Key strategies in design development

Gaining Entree

During the early phases of UAD's history, we had no formal process for integrating usability engineering into a project. We became involved through grassroot connections and word of mouth. Prior to the PowerBook collaboration, UAD had conducted a one-time validation usability study right before an earlier portable product shipped. Despite the brevity of our involvement and our inability to affect the design because of late involvement, the experience exposed us to the portables division. More important, the brief contact impressed on the product team the importance of including usability engineering early so that it could contribute to product development.

Faced with the challenge of creating an innovative laptop computer, a product marketer of PowerBook took the initiative to contact UAD. About six weeks after launching the PowerBook project, UAD started working with the key stakeholders on the usability effort—project leaders from product marketing, industrial design, mechanical and electrical engineering.

In hindsight, we find that the engineers and designers who bring us into projects are themselves responsible for fixing the usability problems that we unveil. Therefore the grassroots approach to gaining entree to projects is highly instrumental for promoting clients' willingness to change designs based on usability input. Nevertheless, it is not without shortcomings. First, grassroots channels are highly susceptible to turnover in personnel. Too much is left to chance and individuals' goodwill to ensure usability support where it is warranted. Second, usability champions who contact the usability group may represent only one of several stakeholders within a project. Besides lacking complete information that may have an impact on user experience, usability data may also risk being seen or used as a tool for advocates for certain ideas in a team to make a political statement. Third, the client may not always contact a usability group early enough to maximize the impact of usability engineering in a project. Last, the glaring lack of management initiative, often coupled with a lack of formal process for integrating usability in product development, can easily jeopardize usability efforts when time and financial resources are limited.

Since the PowerBook project, UAD had made good progress in closing the entree loop. Along with the grassroots channel, we have reenforced our efforts in soliciting high-profile projects from middle and upper management in the various divisions that we support..

Besides improving entree on a project-by-project basis, we have also focused on process change by working with the user experience architect's office headed by Donald Norman. The office spearheads efforts in devising immediate and long-term strategies for developing a coherent user experience across Apple's lines of products. We provided input for Don and his staff to establish entry points for usabilty and user-centered design efforts during product development.

Design Challenge

The design challenge in the PowerBook project was clear from product marketing data. To regain market share and emerge as a leader in the notebook market, Apple had to design a new line of portable computers to deliver the interface in a form factor that would support mobile computing anywhere, anytime. Furthermore, the weight and size of the products had to remain competitive vis-a-vis DOS-compatible laptop computers.

The strong emphasis of portability in mobile environments had important implications for the design language of the PowerBooks. First, it mandated the incorporation of a cursor control device into the unit. Second, with enhanced portability, we anticipated increased usage. Hence, comfortable use in both mobile and desktop environments also loomed as an important design goal.

In early kick-off meetings a few weeks before UAD's participation in the project, the engineering team started entertaining the concept of a central, frontal trackball-buttons arrangement as the built-in cursor control device. The idea allowed for easy, convenient access to cursor control without handedness bias. Furthermore, the space on either side of the trackball could be made big enough to provide comfortable palm rest surfaces and to house the battery and hard disk drive. Since the battery and hard disk are heavy, the forward center-of-gravity bias created would make it harder for the computer to slide toward the knees and off the lap than in designs with these components placed at the back. Although the design concept appeared sound, the team was eager to check its assumptions against reality by soliciting users' input to identify fruitful directions for implementation.

Scope of UAD's Involvement

In the PowerBook experience, the project team had by and large defined the parameters of UAD's involvement before they solicited our support. We were to focus primarily on the industrial design challenge of developing the new form form factor with special emphasis on the palm rest and central placement of the trackball and buttons.

In the actual involvement, the issues that our group investigated and went beyond the original order. Incidental data about other design elements, such as the keyboard, was inevitable because users interacted with a PowerBook as a system, not as discrete functional elements (e.g., the display, the keyboard, the trackball) as perceived in the organization of the project team. For example, though only the trackball was the focus of a user study, participants still had to type on the keyboard while using the trackball as they worked, say, in editing a memo.

In hindsight, we find that the scope of usability engineering in a project is influenced by, amid many things, two perceptions: the client's perception and the usability group's self-perception of its role and bandwidth for delivery. In the PowerBook project, many of the team members had never worked with a usability group before. Therefore, they relied on us to let them know what we could do for the team. At the time, UAD functioned primarily as a usability group that tested our clients' designs in a laboratory setting. Although the team found our involvement indispensable for working out the details of the form factor design, UAD missed many opportunities for usability engineering because of the way we perceived ourselves then.

Seeing ourselves as a "testing" group, we limited our impact to affecting products only after many conceptual parameters had been laid down. What if the assumptions were incorrect? We would be unable to change the fundamental problem. To avoid the pitfall, we now broaden usability engineering to include soliciting information to understand users' needs and tasks to inform the definition of product concept. This usability function is especially important when we have little or no information about the impact a new technology or product might have on how users interact with their environments and tasks.

Furthermore, perceiving ourselves as a "testing group" made us focus primarily on evaluating as opposed to delivering solutions. The skill set in the group also reflected heavy emphasis on research skills as opposed to design skills. Hence, we could at most recommend directions for improvement or contribute to solution brainstorming. We were not responsible for delivering the solutions ourselves. Although the PowerBook team was most receptive of our suggestions, not all engineering teams are. To increase the effectiveness of usability engineering affecting actual designs, UAD has extended its scope of involvement to include user studies *and* design and realigned our human resources to include skills in interaction design, visual design, and prototyping.

Another issue related to the scope of an usability effort is who does the scouting. In the PowerBook experience, the team defined the scope initially. Then it evolved over time with input from UAD. The gradually growing scope did not cause any problems because UAD had adequate resources to fund the entire usability effort including all the items added as the project progressed. However, as UAD moves from providing free support to a charge back model, who scopes the needs of a project becomes important. Project teams not sensitive to human interface concerns tend to underestimate the amount of work required to create a usable human interface. Hence, the resources they allocate may not be enough to do the job well. In our current operation, we have instituted within our group developing a usability engineering plan from the start. If, after the scouting effort, a client group still decided to keep the budget low, the client would have to make an informed trade-off. UAD would not be unreasonably burdened to deliver on a tall order with insufficient resources.

UAD's Role and Process

At the time of the PowerBook project, UAD operated as an external usability consultant group. We assigned usability specialists to projects for the duration of the usability effort. Primary contact with the team was limited to the key engineers and designers of the specific design elements in question. Communication to the entire team and beyond occurred mostly during dissemination of findings. As far as possible, we assigned the same specialists to a product division to maintain continuity and promote cross-pollination among related projects. In the PowerBook project, we adopted the same consultant model. Three persons from our group worked on the usability effort individually at different times during the project. To preserve continuity in communicating with our client, one person served as the key liaison.

We were the "users' voice" on the project team, walking the fine line between serving as team members and objective outsiders providing unbiased insights. As part of the engineering team, we were sensitive to the technical constraints that the design was under. However, our role as user advocate prevented the team from giving up too easily the quest for design alternatives that could better address users' needs.

Because including usability studies in product development was a new experience for most of the PowerBook team members, UAD had to provide a structure for scaffolding the collaboration. We had to let the team know how to work with us. First and foremost, we stressed the importance of avoiding the "toss-over-the-fence" syndrome, whereby designers design and usability specialists test. Rather than seeing designing and testing as two separate activities, we adopted the strategy of design for testing and testing to design, as succinctly summed up by the leading industrial designer on the team.

Based on users' feedback, usability specialists brainstormed for solutions and improvements with the engineering team. Moreover, UAD also furnished quick turn-around reviews for concept drawings and sketches of design ideas before investing resources in prototyping or conducting more user studies. After generating several potentially promising solutions, the industrial designers and mechanical engineers started prototyping for testing.

In addition to the cross-pollination in designing and prototyping, we also worked together closely in the user studies. Product marketing provided us with the customer profile for participant recruitment. The designers and engineers walked us through the rationale underlying the designs to help us understand their assumptions. We also asked them to express their hunches about what would work well and what problems they would anticipate in the study. Based on this input, UAD came up with a user study plan. Team members from the various disciplines helped review the test plans to make sure that the studies captured the critical issues in the design challenge. At the same time, UAD used the review opportunity to lay down the parameters of the studies, articulating to the client what questions could be answered from the results and what issues would go beyond the intent of the investigation. In this way, we promoted buy-in and created a common basis for interpreting the findings.

During data collection, the team members observed the participants in action behind a one-way mirror. Besides taking notes, they also jotted down questions that they had in response to what they saw in a session. Toward the end of the session, the usability specialist would gather the questions and pose them to the participant. Between sessions the dialog between UAD and the rest of the PowerBook team continued. An informal mind dump of the different issues emerged and some preliminary postulations for reasons underlying the problems were observed. For members who missed some of the sessions, we made videos of the test sessions easily available.

A couple of days after data collection and analysis, UAD discussed the findings with the team to avoid delay in the design process. Since we all had participated in the design, prototype, and evaluation, we could draw from a rich common knowledge base in addition to our diverse, multidisciplinary background in interpreting the results. UAD then generated a detailed report with design recommendations for improving the problems identified. Alternative interpretations that came out of the ongoing conversation with the rest of the team, provided they were sound, were also included in the report.

In hindsight, we find that, in the PowerBook project, UAD provided usability support as an outside consultant to the project. We did not colocate with the project team. Neither did we attend regularly team leader meetings at the project level. In contrast, our role was marked by deep but localized involvement. We collaborated closely mainly with a handful of key players involved in the development of the new central, frontal trackball and buttons.

The consultant model was efficient and effective for contributing usability feedback to the development of the form factor design because the scope and focus of the commitment was well-defined and confined. UAD members working on the project could simultaneously work on the PowerBook project and other projects without shortchanging the quality of our work. If we had colocated and assigned resources full time to the project, we would not have been able to handle the same number of projects during the same period.

Furthermore, by cycling several usability specialists through the same project during different phases, we were able to see the product through fresh eyes. Through this mechanism, we were better able to filter out researcher biases than we would have been had only one person shouldered the entire responsibility of conducting all the user studies in the project. The key was to have one single point of contact—a UAD liaison for the team. In this way we had continuity in communicating with the project team while avoiding losing objectivity in our usability effort.

Despite the advantages mentioned, the consultant model had its own drawbacks, too. The model limited our degree of integration into the project at large because of the limited contact with the people and information from the project team. Consequently, we were not best positioned to participate in design decision making, which often times occurred in private communication in cubicles and private offices rather than in formal meetings.

Whether the trade-offs between integration into a team versus efficiency in operating a usability group are worthwhile depends on the scope of the human interface challenge in a project. If the human computer interface is relatively simple, the consultant model will work well in general. On the contrary, if the design is highly innovative with a plethora of human interface issues and dependecies, the full-time colocation model will be more desirable. Hence it is important for the usability group to have the infrastructure to provide scalable services to its clients, varying the operation model to best meet the specific needs of a project.

Design for Testing in PowerBook Project

To portray the impact of usability in the PowerBook project, we have selected one facet out of the entire usability program of the project: the development of the central , frontal trackball and buttons design as an example to illustrate the key strategy in UAD's collaboration with hardware engineering: design for testing, testing to design.

Design for Testing

Testing to design or including usability feedback to guide design decisions during development as opposed to validating them after a design is completed is a well-understood concept among the majority of our clients. However, design for testing is an notion that still requires continuous evangelism, especially among hardware engineering teams.

In the development of hardware products, engineers build prototypes. The first prototypes are nonfunctional appearance models that highlight the aesthetics and industrial design of a product. Mechanical engineering prototypes, which come later, are functional but focus primarily on manufacturability. Often times these are the sorts of prototypes that engineering teams furnish for usability studies. Using engineering prototypes to explore human interface and usability issues is not ideal. The polished look of the appearance model tends to suggest that the fundamental design is completed. The refined look may steer user study participants toward reacting to the details of the implementation instead of the fundamental concepts underlying the interaction design. By the time functional models are ready, too many stakes are in the ground to make it cost effective to explore alternative directions in human interface design. In short, by the time we can user test the interaction with functional models, the form factor that supposedly should support the interaction is already frozen.

The design for testing approach resolves the problem by calling for building prototypes for exploring, postulating, and learning about the interaction first. Then the team can use the information to drive the industrial design of a product. Hence, in the early phase of development, we stress creating hardware-human interface prototypes. They maximize the integrity of the human-computer interaction at the cost of reduced fidelity in both appearance and robustness in implementation because of incomplete designs.

PowerBook Prototypes

In the first PowerBook study, it was premature to work out details in the industrial design without investigating the usability of the central cursor control concept. Figure 4 portrays the first prototype designed for user testing. It was crude and hardly came close to the actual shape and size of the final PowerBook design form factor. It was a mere shell with a keyboard, a trackball, and two buttons but without any electronics. Via cables long enough to allow participants to use the machine in various positions, each of these elements were tethered to a fully functional CPU external to the prototype.

Figure 4   First prototype

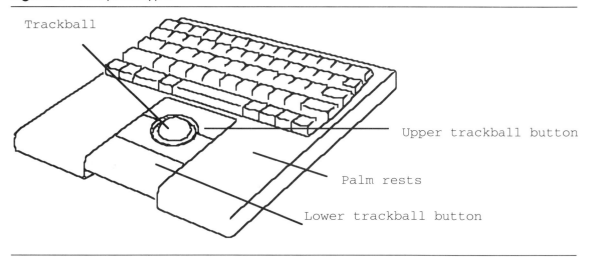

Despite its low fidelity, the prototype successfully represented in broad brush strokes the concept of a palmrest area on both sides of the cursor control device and central, frontal placement of the trackball and buttons, tentatively one above and one below the trackball. The armchair postulation underlying the two-button approach was that users would want to be able to control the trackball and buttons easily when their hands were on the home row or hovering over the keyboard. Having to reach all the way down to the button below the trackball would not be a graceful solution. Hence, the preliminary design included a button above the trackball that served the same functions as the one below. Users could then control the trackball with one thumb and the top button with the other. At the same time, the lower button would support a one-handed configuration, with the forefinger on the trackball and the thumb on the lower button.

By observing representative users work with the prototype, we learned that users found the form factor concept of a built-in trackball highly innovative. Because of the novelty in the approach, the top button was used less frequently than the bottom button because the two-thumb configuration postulated was not apparent or intuitive to participants. Even so, in the new design users did not have to move their hands as far before they could reach the cursor control device as they would in using the mouse.

We also learned that being able to move back and forth between the cursor control device and the keyboard without inadvertently pressing keys and buttons warranted more investigation. Moreover, the height of the palm rest emerged as a concern that might contribute to the comfort of use.

The subsequent rounds of user studies were targeted at the specific concerns identified as well as identifying new usability areas that the first study could not address. One important issue was the detailed design of the button configuration. At the early design phase, we needed feedback from users to help us select the most fruitful paths to pursue. Again, we used human interface prototypes to help us. Figure 5 shows four models that we studied.

The design team postulated different design considerations that might contribute to the ease and comfort of use of the cursor control device. These are listed in Table 2. The first column shows the design details considered. The second column lists all the options explored for each detail. The third indicates which among the four models exemplifies a specific design option.

Figure 5   Models studied   (Model A)

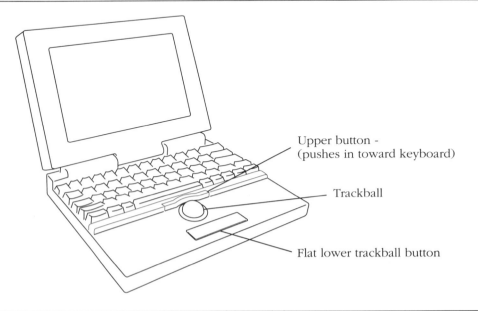

Figure 5 Models studied   (Model B)

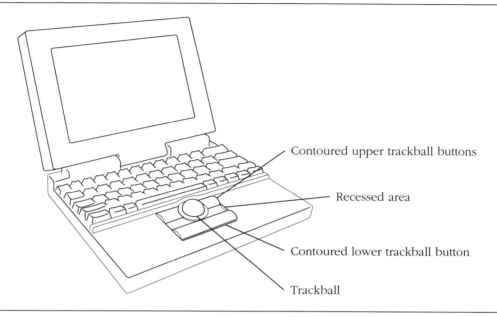

Contoured upper trackball buttons

Recessed area

Contoured lower trackball button

Trackball

Figure 5 Models studied   (Model C)

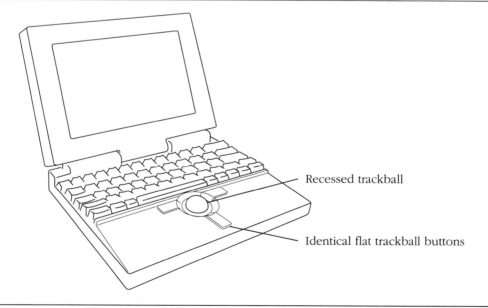

Recessed trackball

Identical flat trackball buttons

Figure 5   Models studied   (Model D)

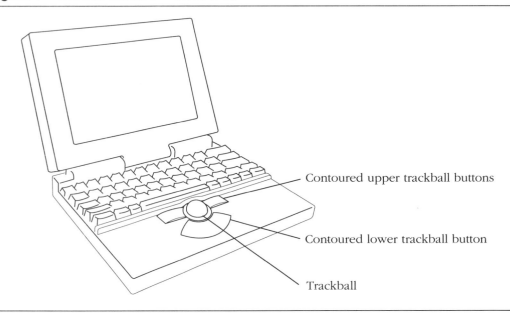

Contoured upper trackball buttons

Contoured lower trackball button

Trackball

We did not construct many prototypes modeling all the possible combinations of the factors in the table. Instead, relying on his design expertise, the industrial designer developed the four prototypes shown earlier. Each model embodied a version of how the various design considerations could be manipulated. For example, Model A has a single top button that presses in. It looks very different from the bottom button. The bottom button is large, rectangular with a flat surface. In contrast, Model B has two top buttons that again, look distinct from the bottom button. Instead of flat buttons, all the buttons are contoured. The shape and size of the bottom button are similar to those of Model A.

We did not intend any of the four models to be the ultimate design. Instead, each was merely a tool for exploring and learning. Certain concepts were exaggerated on purpose, such as contoured button surface in Model B to elicit responses. Then we conducted an observational study with potential customers and collected qualitative data to inform of our design decisions.

The results of the user studies directly affected the final design of the product as shown in Figure 6. We had one top button because two buttons tended to mislead users to think that the buttons might have difference functions. Moreover, the top was

Table 2 Design Considerations

Design Detail	Options	Model
Shapes for top buttons versus bottom buttons	Different designs for top and bottom buttons	A, B, D
	Same design for top and bottom buttons	C
Number of top buttons	1	A
	2	B, C, D
Mechanixm for accessing top button	Press in	A
	Press down	B, C, D
Size of bottom button	Big	A, B, D
	Small	C
Shape of bottom button	Curved	D
	Rectangular	A, B
Surface of buttons	Flat	A, C
	Contoured	B, D

button pressed down for it was more intuitive than pressing in. The bottom button big, curved and contoured to facilitate ease of access and also to provide tactile feedback for users regarding the location of their fingers without having to look at the unit.

In hindsight, the new form factor and the engineering effort were well received in the marketplace as well as in the design community. Within the first year of release, the PowerBook reached a billion dollars' worth of sales. The many design awards received included the IDSF Gold Award, ID Magazine Award, and the IF Award.

Figure 6   Final design

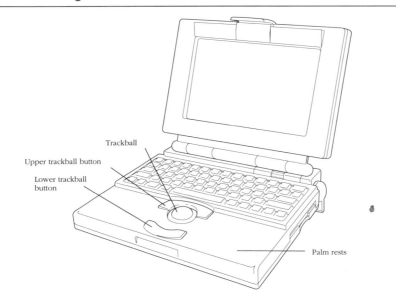

Epilogue

When this chapter was written, UAD underwent restructuring within the AppleSoft human interface design center. The charter of UAD today has been expanded beyond usability testing. In addition to user studies, UAD also furnishes interaction design, visual design, and prototyping support for human interface efforts in the AppleSoft division and Apple personal computer division. The services that we render are scalable along three dimensions to tailor to the specific needs of our clients.

First, we can provide single-skill support as well as combinations of multiple-skill support. For instance, when clients want to uncover problems of a product in the market to inform future products, they can come to us for a user study. In this case, we provide a single-skill service, namely, usability investigation in the users' natural environments of use. In constrast, a multiskill team with prototypes, user studies, interaction designs, and visual design skills can offer a more complete solution for addressing the human interface problems of a product still in development.

Second, we can also scale the duration of our involvement. Depending on the degree of innovation and complexity of a project, we can be involved as early as the conceptualization of the product, before the team defines the feature set. In other projects where the product concepts build on those of existing products, we can still make significant contribution as late as the pre-alpha stage. We strongly discourage teams to call on us when our input can no longer have any bearing on the design of products.

Third, the depth of our involvement in terms of our role and our deliverables are scalable, too. For human interface projects that are highly complex, we are part of the project team and are responsible for human interface design decisions. We encourage colocation with the rest of the team members to facilitate communication. In other projects where the human interface effort is less intense, we serve as external consultants who review projects at regular intervals.

We also adjust the scope of our deliverables primarily as attempts to work within our clients' budgets, since they have to fully finance our efforts. The deluxe package includes a detailed human interface engineering plan, storyboards, a variety of paper and interactive prototypes, human interface specifications and guidelines, and detailed usability reports with highlight videos of the test sessions. If a client has limited resources, we may advise substituting the detailed usability reports and video tapes with a discussion of quick findings with the team. The goal is to limit the influence of cost as a deterent for project teams to integrate human interface in their efforts.

Our initial experience operating under the new charter has been very encouraging. Our clients welcome our flexibility in helping them develop an optimal human interface package to suit their specific needs. The human interface engineers enjoy the change of rhythm in their work as they alternate between designing and conducting user studies. The broader charter that goes beyond usability support also provides more opportunities for professional development.

Acknowledgment

The authors would like to thank instructional products at Apple Computer, Inc., for the PowerBook illustrations used in the chapter.

CHAPTER 5

The Human Factors Group at Compaq Computer Corporation

**Cynthia J. Roe Purvis,
Mary Czerwinski, and
Paul Weiler**

Human Factors
Compaq Computer
Corporation

Cynthia Roe Purvis has managed the Human Factors Group at Compaq Computer Corporation for the past five years. Prior to joining Compaq, Cynthia managed the Human Factors Group in the Information Products Division of Xerox Corporation. She holds a Masters degree in applied experimental psychology-human factors from California State University, Northridge.

Mary Czerwinski has been involved in software user interface design since 1988. Prior to joining Compaq, she worked at Bellcore, Lockheed, the Johnson Space Center, then at Rice University as an adjunct professor of psychology. She received her Ph.D. in cognitive psychology from Indiana University at Bloomington.

During his three years with Compaq, Paul Weiler's focus was on the user interface aspects of software and controls, and automating the HF lab's data collection process. Prior to joining Compaq, Paul was an intern with IBM. He is currently completing his Ph.D. in experimental psychology from Colorado State University.

The purpose of this chapter is fourfold. It begins with a description of the original formation of the Human Factors Group at Compaq Computer Corporation, followed by a discussion of the group's current organization, domain and services. Next, we present a case study showing some of the research that helped define the Compaq Concerto™, the first pen-based notebook PC produced by Compaq. The chapter concludes with a review of several "lessons learned" while forming the group.

Compaq Overview

Compaq Computer Corporation, founded in 1982, designs, develops, manufactures, and markets a broad range of personal computers, including desktop personal computers, battery-powered notebook computers, and AC-powered portable computers. Compaq also produces servers for network environments. The company has approximately 10,000 full-time employees and sells and supports products in more than 100 countries. Annual revenues for Compaq in 1993 were over $7 billion.

Compaq is organized into three discrete business units: the Desktop Product Division, Portable Product Division, and System Product Division. All three are located at the main Compaq facility in Houston, Texas. The Human Factors (HF) Group provides product development teams within these divisions with information and recommendations that will improve the usability of their products, thereby helping our customers accomplish their tasks more effectively, efficiently, and comfortably.

Usability Engineering at Compaq

Increasingly posed with both hardware and software user interface design decisions, Systems Engineering championed the effort to form the Human Factors Group at Compaq in March 1989. The group is dedicated to helping Compaq product development teams make better educated decisions about user interface trade-offs. To help provide robust data supporting their user interface recommendations, the group strongly emphasizes human-computer interface (HCI) research. This research-oriented approach has existed from the very beginning of the group. During her original job interview, Cynthia Roe Purvis was clear that she would not accept the position as a single, "lone wolf" human factors professional (with no promise for additional staff until they "saw how things went"). Cynthia indicated that her acceptance of an offer was contingent upon Compaq funding a human factors laboratory and allowing her to hire at least three additional HF professionals. As an indication of their commitment to product usability, Compaq agreed, up front, to build the lab facility and staff several HF positions.

Hiring the Original HF Group

By late 1989 the core HF Group was in place. To assist with the hardware aspects of the HCI, we hired a human factors engineer whose experience and education focused on front-of-screen display image quality, keyboards, and cursor control devices. The second person hired had a B.A. in psychology and would support the group's research efforts. The third HF professional rounded out the group's talents with a rich background in the software and user documentation aspects of the human-computer interface.

To fill the two senior positions, we sought HF professionals with solid, graduate-level skills in design methodology. We also felt strongly that at least one individual should have a doctorate-level background in statistics. Since these people would be the first "disciples" of human factors within Compaq, interpersonal communication skills weighed heavily in the selection criteria. It was critical that these first HF professionals be able to interact effectively with many interdisciplinary teams.

HF Group as a Service Organization

From its inception, the group was set up as a service organization. Although it reports through Systems Engineering in the Desktop Division, the HF Group supports product development teams within all three divisions: Desktops, Portables, and Systems. Any individual or design team with a product-related HCI issue can request our services; no parochial priority is given to any one division. This centralized approach appears to function well. The demands of the various divisions come in waves. As a centralized organization, our resources (people, facilities, and equipment) can be shifted to meet these changing demands.

Compaq develops products through an interdisciplinary team approach. Given the number of hardware and software products under development at any given time, it is not practical for a member of the HF Group to attend all product team meetings. As a result, the group is set up to respond to the specific HCI needs of product teams on an "as needed" basis. To make this approach work, one of our initial tasks was to visit members of the engineering and marketing communities, introduce the HF Group, explain the services we provide, and encourage vigilance in recognizing HCI issues.

Marketing the HF Group

To educate the marketing and engineering communities about the new HF Group, we assembled a 35 mm slide presentation highlighting research that our members had conducted before joining Compaq. The presentation showed examples of usability laboratories in both university and corporate settings and demonstrated hardware and software research. HF Group members described to the project teams how usability testing might make their jobs easier—by using quantified user preference and performance data to help select or improve a project's user interface.

Although the HF Group could provide many other valuable skills and services, such as task analysis and user interface design, we initially emphasized our usability testing capabilities. We felt that this type of testing was something tangible that could be easily demonstrated in the slide show and a technique that teams could easily understand, concrete evidence of how HF could benefit the design process. Usability testing was used as a way to get the HF Group's "foot in the door." Judging by the group's acceptance into the engineering and marketing communities, this strategy seems to have worked quite well.

The HF Lab's Maiden Voyage

One of the group's first "customers" afforded an excellent opportunity to demonstrate the value of usability testing. In designing a new laptop PC, a product team was considering an innovative new cursor control device integrated directly into the PC's case. The team wanted to know how the new device would be perceived in comparison to the mouse. The team needed an answer in only a few short weeks. At that point, we had no video equipment, data collection tools, or a laboratory for that matter! We constructed a makeshift lab in the corner of a large storage room, hastily ordered a few pieces of video gear (shipped special delivery air freight!), and prepared to tackle our first research project.

Test subjects completed a set of target acquisition and text editing tasks using both a mouse and a prototype of the new device (tasks and test methods were modeled after Epps, 1986). Test sessions were videotaped and time stamped. The tapes were laboriously reviewed to calculate and record task times and error rates. The resulting data clearly showed the product team how the new device compared to the mouse in terms of both user preference and user performance.

The project's marketing manager used the results to support his recommendation to the corporate strategy team concerning the new cursor control device. This presentation provided an excellent avenue for many senior managers to hear about the Human Factors Group and to see a clear demonstration of how HF research could help teams make more educated decisions about user interface trade-offs. This study became the springboard for many more study requests.

Growth of the HF Group and the HF Lab

Awareness of the HF Group spread. It was not unusual in those first few years to get a phone call that went something like this, "Hi, you don't know me, but I've heard about your new group and the research you've been running. Can you help our product team address a user interface issue?"

The group's testing activities increased from 3 studies in 1989 to over 70 studies in 1993. Over 1000 subjects now participate in HF's lab and field research annually. The group has doubled in size to a staff of nine full-time professionals, with degrees ranging from B.A. to Ph.D. in such areas as human factors, applied experimental psychology, cognitive psychology, and industrial engineering. As was true in the original formation of the group, graduate research skills and intercommunication skills continued to be important selection criteria in hiring new HF professionals. In addition, as demand for assistance with software projects increased, skills in task analysis, graphical user interface (GUI) design, and software UI prototyping were sought.

A 4:3 ratio of graduate to undergraduate degreed members is maintained within the group. This ratio appears to maximize the talents of those with graduate degrees as well as keep the usability professionals challenged and busy. Those members with graduate degrees deal directly with the product design teams. Typically, each member may deal with three to five product teams at any given time. The support staff of usability professionals all hold undergraduate degrees in psychology or sociology and assist with the research.

The present HF facilities include three laboratories ranging in size from 250 to 400 square feet. The labs have ceiling-mounted video cameras as well as cameras mounted on tripods; all are equipped with auto focus zoom lenses and remotely controlled pan-tilt heads. A 225 square foot observation room with one-way mirrors overlooks two of the labs (see Figures 1 and 2). It is equipped with desktop PCs to run our DataLogger tool (described later in this chapter), video recorders, editing recorders, edit controllers, a digital mixer, and a character generator. Camcorders are used for field observations. As for audio equipment, the labs are equipped with speakers and wireless microphones for the test users, and the observation room is equipped with headsets for the HF testers. Up to 12 individual workstations can be run simultaneously.

The HF observation room (Figure 2 and Color Plate III) is used not only by the HF staff, but is also frequently visited by product team members who want to watch the research firsthand. Indeed we encourage developers to observe the subjects. Many an "HF skeptic" has been won over by witnessing the robustness of the group's research methods and data collection techniques, and above all, hearing and watching users firsthand.

Figure 1   Floor plan for the HF observation room and two of the HF Labs

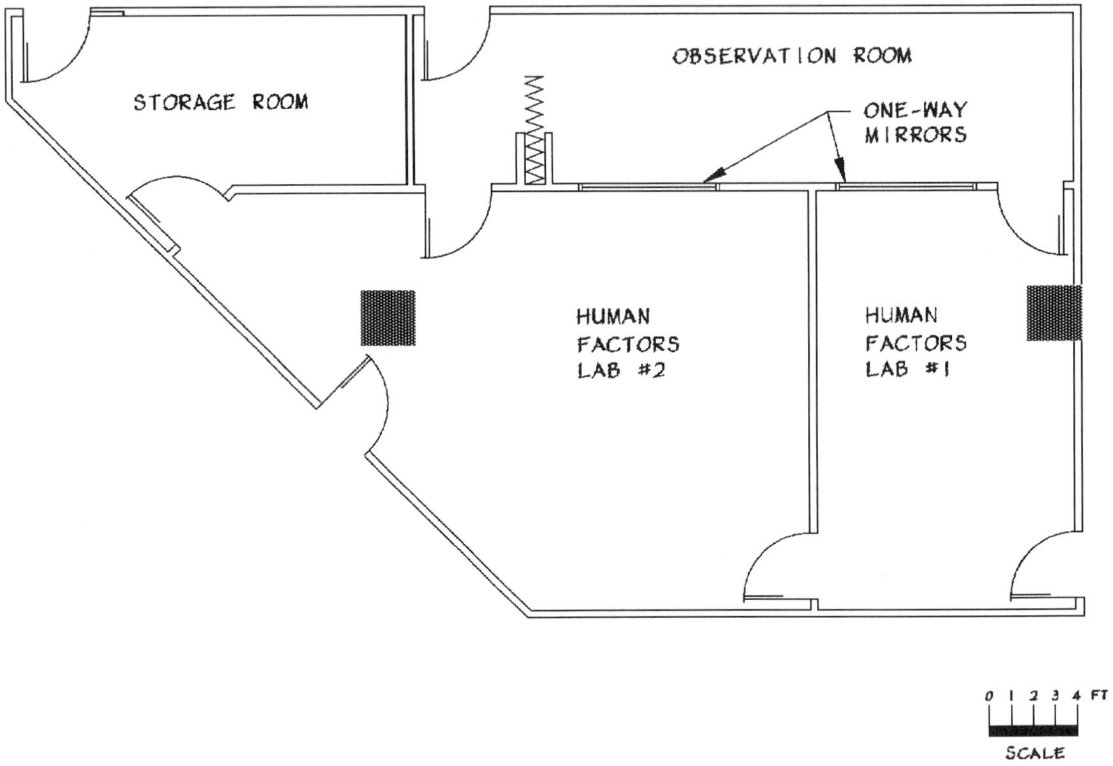

Services of the Human Factors Group Expand

In the beginning, the HF Group focused on research that could be conducted during the design phase of the product development cycle. As teams began to see the benefits of HF involvement, they tended to call earlier in the product development cycle. The corporate photographer was frequently asked to document the research that was being conducted. The 35 mm slide show was updated and expanded to promote a full host of user-centered design techniques. As more and more teams asked for our help, our group's range of services continued to expand.

Figure 2   HF observation room

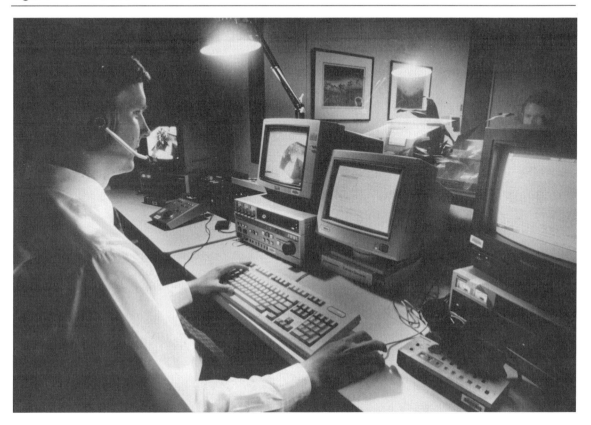

User Needs and Task Analysis

More teams began requesting field evaluations of users to help them determine the features and functions required for new products. Target users are observed and interviewed about their tasks, their environments, the efficiency of their current tools, their "time sinks" and "roadblocks," and any opportunities they could identify to improve their job efficiency and comfort. These analyses have been beneficial in completing the "circle" from the development and release of one product to the concept of the next product, and keep the teams focused on implementing products that truly meet users' needs.

Usability Goals Tables

Teams are encouraged by HF to build *usability goals tables* (see Nielson, 1993; Whiteside, Bennett and Holtzblatt, 1988) early in a product's design phase. Building these tables helps teams synthesize their expectations of a product's usability. The tables are composed of a list of usability attributes, methods by which these attributes can be measured (preference scales, error rates), and estimates of reasonable goals for each attribute: the minimally acceptable level, the planned level, and the best possible level. Figure 3 shows an example of one of our *usability goals tables*. This particular table was created for the installation process of a software utility. At first, the HF Group had to encourage teams to build these tables. Lately, however, the product teams themselves are initiating the process—a welcome sign of progress indeed!

User Interface Design

Rather than being limited to the role of usability tester, HF Group members are included in the early phases of both software and hardware user interface designs. And for software projects, HF is frequently relied upon to help prototype user interface approaches under discussion. Rather than just testing the designs at a distance, the HF representatives are considered an integral part of the design process—genuine team members.

Cognitive Modeling Tools in Software UI Design

As part of the HF Group's effort to design software user interfaces based on users' expectations of how the application should behave, the group began using cognitive modeling tools (e.g., Pathfinder, Schvaneveldt, 1990) to assist with this process. As an example of how these tools are used, consider the following hypothetical design scenario. During the conceptual design phase of a software application, the product team discusses ways in which the utility can be used, and the functions and features that they know will be included in the product. However, are not sure how to organize the functions to support the users' conceptual model. The human factors engineer can assist with this design puzzle by taking a list of the "concepts" (application features and functions) and having users sort these concepts into meaningful clusters or groups. For even more information about how to organize the concepts, the users can be asked to sort these groups into bigger groups, and so on. Finally, various scaling tools (like Pathfinder) can be used to produce a graphical view of the way users link thevarious concepts together and organize them in psychological space. This data can be used to organize the application's menu items, push buttons, and other UI controls.

Figure 3   A usability goals table

Usability Specification Table

Attribute	Measuring Concept			Measuring Method	Unacceptable Level	Minimum Level	Planned Level	Best Case Level
SOFTWARE INSTALLATION								
User's perception of install difficulty	Difficult	1 2 3 4 5 6 7	Easy	Average rating	<4.0	4.0 to 5.0	5.0 to 6.0	> 6.0
User satisfaction with install	Frustrating	1 2 3 4 5 6 7	Satisfying	Average rating	<4.0	4.0 to 5.0	5.0 to 6.0	> 6.0
Ease of locating information	Difficult	1 2 3 4 5 6 7	Easy	Average rating	<4.0	4.0 to 5.0	5.0 to 6.0	> 6.0
Terminology used	Unclear	1 2 3 4 5 6 7	Clear	Average rating	<4.0	4.0 to 5.0	5.0 to 6.0	> 6.0
Detail of help provided	Not Helpful	1 2 3 4 5 6 7	Helpful	Average rating	<4.0	4.0 to 5.0	5.0 to 6.0	> 6.0
DOCUMENTATION								
Documentation provided	Unclear	1 2 3 4 5 6 7	Clear	Average rating	<4.0	4.0 to 5.0	5.0 to 6.0	> 6.0
Ease of locating information	Difficult	1 2 3 4 5 6 7	Easy	Average rating	<4.0	4.0 to 5.0	5.0 to 6.0	> 6.0
Terminology used	Unclear	1 2 3 4 5 6 7	Clear	Average rating	<4.0	4.0 to 5.0	5.0 to 6.0	> 6.0
OVERALL								
User's level of confidence in ability to install and use utility	Not Confident	1 2 3 4 5 6 7	Confident	Average rating	<4.0	4.0 to 5.0	5.0 to 6.0	> 6.0
Time in error/Total time (%)		All tasks		Average percentage	>30%	30% to 20%	20% to 10%	<10%
Number of experimenter inverventions		All tasks		Average number of interventions per subject	>3.0	3.0 to 2.0	2.0 to 1.0	<1.0
Successfully install and use		All tasks		Percent of successes	N/A	N/A	100%	N/A

Out-of-the-Box-Studies

One very informative test we perform is called our *out-of-the-box* study, where we ask users to remove a product from its shipping carton, configure it, and perform various tasks. We have learned that users' first few minutes of exposure to a product can significantly contribute to their overall satisfaction, particularly with novice users. Videotapes of test participants clearly show areas where packing, location of manuals and accessories, and the overall setup process can be improved. Results of HF's first *out-of-the-box* study, which compared the unboxing process of one Compaq product to two well-known competitive products, was shown over fifteen times and seen by over one hundred people; yet another "spring board" for other research requests.

State-of-the-Union-Studies

HF's state-of-the-union research takes competitive hardware products, software products, or a combination of both, and pits them against each other. Subjects are asked to perform common sets of tasks on each product. Completion times, time in error, documented user interface issues, and user's preference ratings provide product teams with a good understanding of how products compare and how Compaq might make a newly developed product easier to use. These studies also provided robust data for setting up usability goals tables for new product designs.

Form Factor Studies

Industrial designers take advantage of HF's services early in the design process with *dueling prototype form factor* research. Their model shop provides prototypes of designs under consideration. Subjects are asked to simulate performing tasks using these models, e.g., standing and using a pen computer or typing on a notebook PC in a simulated airplane seat. Much can be learned about the comfort and ease-of-use of the different industrial design approaches before a dime is spent on the tools that would lock-in a design.

Field Studies

Armed with camcorder and DataLogger software installed on a notebook PC, the HF Group has moved out of the lab and into the field to test how well products perform in real-life situations. For example, a human factors engineer was present when the Library of Congress installed a network operating system on a Compaq ProSignia server. HF, along with documentation and marketing representatives, videotaped and observed the installation. After the installation, an interview session was held with the

Library of Congress network administrators to discuss documentation, usability, reliability, and performance issues with them, as well as to discover new ease-of-use directions and opportunities.

Human Factors Lab Tools

The increased demands for HF research, mandated that we automate our data collection tools in order to increase efficiency. Several new tools have reduced test preparation, data collection, and analysis time tremendously.

Tool for Logging Observational Data

We created the DataLogger software tool to help improve the data collection process beyond the use of pencil and paper and time-consuming videotape analysis. DataLogger's initial purpose was to record testing events, experimenter comments, and task times. However, it quickly grew to include the collection of subject errors and times, the number of experimenter interventions, how and what documentation was used, and the completion of task milestones (see Figures 4 and 5). Further enhancements included the addition of two analysis capabilities. First, a summary table including task and error times, their relative percentages, and total number of interventions are computed for the subjects in a study. Second, by linking to Microsoft Excel through Windows Dynamic Data Exchange (DDE), we produce a task time and time-in-error graph that can be included directly in the final report.

Paul created the core DataLogger tool over a two week period using Asymetrix ToolBook. Enhancements have been added over the course of a year as new features were desired. Overall, the tool has decreased the group's time spent in data analysis, especially in the area of computing task and error times. DataLogger has also afforded us more accurate data collection during field studies via its time stamping and summary capabilities. Future enhancements include the ability to interface with video recorders to mark key usability events and expedite the location of the segments after testing.

Tools for Cursor Control Device Research

To enhance the collection of data for cursor control devices (mouse, trackball, etc.), we developed a suite of software tools which exercise a subject's aptness with a cursor control device on the most basic level: acquiring targets, selection, insertion, and manipulation. The tools were developed using Asymetrix ToolBook and provide HF with a wealth of objective performance measures for use in analysis.

Figure 4   DataLogger tool

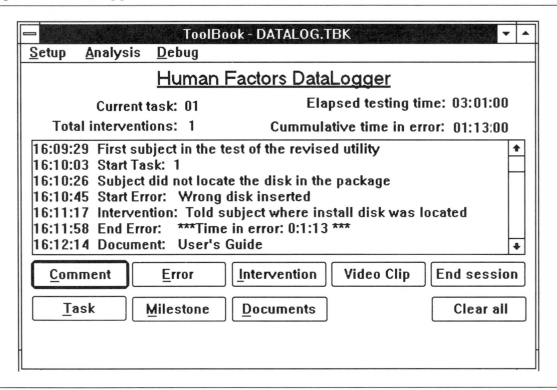

The *target acquisition* tool was based on Epps (1986) research and presents users with target squares of varying size (.13, .27, .54, 1.07, and 2.14 cm) and distance from the starting point (2, 4, 8, and 16 cm). A user presses the start button, moves the pointer to the target, then "acquires" the target with a single click (See Figure 6). The size and distance of the targets are recorded along with the time required to complete the movement and the number of errors in acquiring the target.

A *text typing* tool was created to test users abilities to move from the keyboard to a cursor control device, acquire a textual target, select it with a double-click, then move back to the keyboard and type. Users press the start button to begin timing and then select each number target by double-clicking on a number. Next, the user changes the number to the corresponding word and then moves on to the next number. This process is repeated for each of the 10 targets in order (See Figure 7). The time to modify all ten targets as well as the number of single and double-clicks are recorded for analysis.

Figure 5   Session summary data from DataLogger

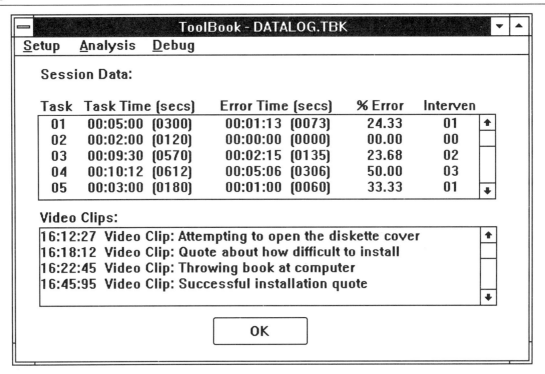

A _box move and stretch_ tool was created to test users abilities to select, move, and size graphical shapes. Users press the start button and then select and move one of the four boxes by clicking and dragging it to the target area. The box is then sized by clicking and dragging the corner handles until the box is aligned inside the two boundaries of the target area (See Figure 8). This process is repeated for each of the four boxes and then the Finish button is pressed to stop timing.

Figure 6   Example of a target acquisition task

Figure 7   Example of a text typing task

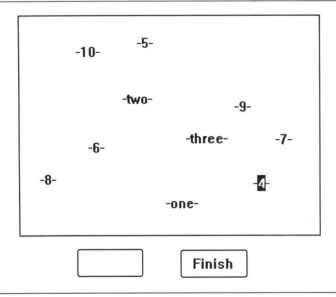

Figure 8   Example of a box stretch task

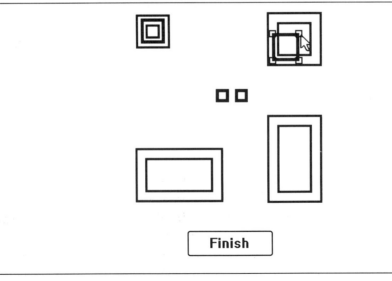

Tool for Front-of-Screen Display Image Quality Research

Using Tinker Passages (Tinker, 1963), another tool was developed for front-of-screen display image quality research. Tinker Passages contain a single word that does not make sense with the rest of the passage. For example:

> On his way to work one morning,
> Mr. Smith slipped on the ice and broke his
> leg. Several months went by before he
> was completely well and could see again.

The word *see* does not make sense for the given passage.

Subjects are asked to click the left mouse button to view a passage in one of the display's four corners or the center of the display. Subjects then click the left button again when they have identified the inappropriate word and are then prompted to enter it. The time to identify the word, the inappropriate word itself, the one entered by the subject, and the result of a comparison between the two words are then written to a file for later analysis.

Tool for Keyboard Research

To expedite the analysis of user performance data in keyboard research, another internal tool was developed. The *typing error analyzer* (TEA), created using Microsoft Visual Basic, helps us count typing errors and categorize them among 30+ error types.

Files containing passages typed by subjects are compared with error-free files of the same passage. TEA locates differences and, in some simple cases, is able to automatically categorize the error. For example *dg* rather than *dog* would be categorized as an alphanumeric omission error. In cases where TEA cannot automatically determine the error category, it displays the offending string, the correct one, and a list of error categories. The HF professional running TEA can categorize the error, and then continue with the comparison scan. The TEA output file can be ported directly into SAS for data analysis.

Prior to the TEA tool, the manual error analysis for a single keyboard study (up to 200 files) would take weeks to complete. With the development of TEA, these files can be analyzed in a matter of days.

Case Study: Compaq Concerto™

To demonstrate the types of research conducted by the HF Group, a sampling of the studies conducted for the Concerto Team will be described. The Compaq Concerto, shown in Figure 9, is an i486-based pen-enabled notebook computer which offers an innovative design that adapts to many different environments. When users are in a limited work area, it can be as compact as a traditional notebook PC. When one has a little more room in which to work, the keyboard can be detached. Alternately, the keyboard can be removed, leaving Concerto's pen to serve as the sole input device.

The Human Factors Group conducted over 20 studies to assist the Concerto Team with the design of the user interface. A sampling of this research is described covering both hardware and software components of the system. Studies evaluating the Compaq Concerto form factor (shape and design) will be discussed, as well as research involving the "touch and feel" of the keyboard, pen, and writing surface. In terms of software research, several utilities that assist Compaq Concerto users with system setup and security will be summarized.

Notebook PC Form Factor Research

Early in the design phase, the product team asked HF to evaluate the usability of two new notebook PC "form factors" under consideration for the next generation of Compaq notebook products. To begin the process, HF asked the team to create a usability goals table to help quantify their usability expectations. Through a brainstorm and list-reduction process, the team decided on a list of "usability attributes" that were important for the success of a new notebook form factor. For example, they wanted the new design to be perceived as innovative and contemporary, and they wanted the keyboard positioning and angles to be perceived as flexible and comfortable. The team agreed on 10 attributes that it wanted the study to measure:

1. Perception of the shape and design
2. Ease of set up and close up
3. Perceived size
4. Perceived weight
5. Keyboard position and angle
6. Display position and angle
7. Stability of the keyboard and the unit as a whole
8. Overall acceptability
9. Ease of transporting the unit
10. Connector accessibility

Having agreed on these attributes, the team then decided what type of rating scales would best serve to measure its "goodness." Finally, the team quantified their expectations by setting three goal levels: a "best possible" level (which might be reached if an aspect of the form factor was extremely well perceived), a more reasonable "planned" level, and a "minimally acceptable" level.

Figure 9   The Compaq Concerto™ notebook PC

Thirty users, mainly those adept at using notebook or laptop PCs, participated in this study. The team was well aware that the perceived usability of a notebook PC could be affected by the environment in which it was being used. For this reason, the team requested that the test PC models be used in three types of work environments: desktop, airplane tray, and laptop. A 29″ high work table and ergonomic chair were used for the desktop environment. A chair with four legs (without rollers) was used for the laptop environment.

To create the simulated airplane seat and tray table, the Industrial Design Group modeled a tourist-class airline tray table along with the back of a reclined seat (assuming the passenger in the preceding row was fully reclined). Measurements for this model were obtained from an airplane seat manufacturer. To complete the airplane tray environment, an ergonomic chair was fixed in position and height to simulate the user's airplane seat. During the study, several participants who regularly use their notebook PCs on airplanes expressed that this simulated seat and tray table (shown in Figure 10) was indeed representative of those found on airplanes.

Figure 10   User typing on a Concerto prototype in a simulated airplane seat

Procedure

At the beginning of a session, each subject was informed that he or she would be evaluating three different notebook computer designs (the two new prototype designs and a Compaq LTE Lite notebook PC used as a benchmark). He or she was told that the computers were nonfunctioning models with mechanically working keyboards. Each PC was used by each participant in the three environments (desktop, airplane tray, and laptop).

Each user started in the desktop environment. The user was instructed to carry the first model to the work table, adjust the ergonomic chair until he or she was comfortable, then open the unit. In this environment (and only in this environment) the user was instructed to connect a printer and mouse cable to the PC. Once the PC was set up, the user was instructed to type a passage of text provided on a typing stand. Afterward, users were instructed to detach the cables, close the model, and complete a questionnaire.

Each participant then carried the closed unit to the airplane tray environment, set up the model on the simulated tray table, and typed a second passage. When the user finished typing, the model was closed, a questionnaire was completed, then the unit was carried to the last environment. In the laptop environment, each user sat in a chair, set up the model on his or her lap, and typed a third passage. (At the time of this study, it was not known that the final product, Concerto, would be pen enabled. As result, the tasks performed in this research used only the keyboard for input. Studies involving penning tasks were run later in the development cycle.)

After using a model in all three environments, the user filled out an overall questionnaire that included a final 80-point interest-in-use rating scale. After a short break, the process was repeated with another model. The order of model presentation was determined using a Latin-square design to balance possible order effects. The order of the environments was kept constant (because it was felt that the order desktop, airplane tray, then laptop best reflected the order in which a notebook PC might be used). After the process was completed with all three models, the user was interviewed, and of course, thanked for his or her participation.

Analysis

Individual analysis of variance (ANOVA) procedures were performed on the preference rating scales to identify any statistically significant differences (i.e., $p < .05$). The overall 7-point rating scale and the 80-point interest-in-use scale that were administered only once per form factor (after the form factor had been used in all three environments) and were analyzed as a one-way, within-subject design (one independent variable of form factor, three levels). The other rating scales, which were administered after each environment, were analyzed as a two-way, within-subject design (independent variables of environment, three levels, and form factor, three levels).

Results

Results showed the Concerto Team how each of the two new form factors met its predetermined usability goals in each of the three environments. Statistical analysis of the preference ratings, detailed lists of observed user interface issues, and an edited videotape showing users in each of the three environments assisted the team in deciding its form factor direction and helped the industrial designers and engineers understand where they needed to focus their efforts. Additional form factor research was later run asking users to simulate the use of the pen in several standing and seated positions. Each iteration of form factor research provided the team with detailed data about which aspects of the design were well received and which needed refinement.

Pen Form Factor Research

To assist the team with the design of the stylus, a series of pen form factor (shape) studies were conducted. The main objective of the first study was to identify two or three top candidate shapes to be used in further testing. A secondary objective was to determine how well the candidate models compared with three existing, competitive pen form factors. User preference data was collected from a total of 50 participants regarding the shape and "feel" of 22 candidate form factors. Special effort was made to gather input from a variety of users, e.g., males and females, left-handed and right-handed, as well as users representing a wide range in hand size.

Procedure

Fourteen nonfunctioning pen models were constructed and provided by the Industrial Design Group, along with five standard writing pens, three mechanical pencils, and three functioning competitor models. All nonfunctioning models were painted the same metallic gray color. A wide variety of sizes and designs were included, ranging from the conventional to nonconventional. After having their hands measured for breadth and length, each subject was shown the 25 pen models and asked to select a group of 8 "semi-finalists," concentrating only on the shape and feel of the pen models and ignoring weight, pen color, and the presence of button or clip attachments. To assist them in the decision process, participants were given a sheet containing five numerals, a word in cursive writing, a printed word, an editing "gesture" (representing a delete function), and a circle. Each subject was instruct to "go through the motions" of copying or writing each item using each of the pen models while focusing on their shape and feel. In addition, they were told to keep the tips of the pens above the paper, so their decision would not be influenced by the feel of the pens on paper.

Upon selecting the group of eight semi-finalists, each subject was then required to select three finalists, rank them according to preference, and provide interest-in-use ratings. The interest-in-use ratings were performed on a scale from 1 to 10, where 1 indicated a low interest and 10 indicated a high interest. At this time, verbal statements were recorded from participants regarding their "likes" and "dislikes" for the three finalists as well as the general criteria used in their selection process.

For the final comparative measure, participants were required to physically place their three finalists and the three competitive benchmarks along a scale marked on a 60" table. One end of the table was marked with a sign "worst possible shape," while the other end was marked "best possible shape" (in essence, a 60-point rating scale). Distances were recorded which reflected the relative standing of the candidate and competitive pen models in terms of overall preference for shape.

Results

Results of this first pen form factor study showed the industrial designers and engineers which pen shapes and designs were preferred by users. These preferred shapes were then refined for the next iteration of testing.

Pen Tip-to-Surface Research

A series of studies was conducted to help the Concerto Team select pen tip and writing surface materials. Thirty to 40 PC users participated in each iteration of this research. The main goal of the first study was to collect initial information on user preferences for annotation and pen input with candidate pen tip and surface combinations. As a comparative benchmark, user preferences were also collected for pen tip materials from known competitors. A secondary goal of this first study was to examine the durability of the candidate pen tip materials when used on various writing surface materials.

Procedure

In the first pen tip-to-surface study, user preference data was collected from 15 men and 15 women (20 right-handers and 10 left-handers) regarding the general "feel" of three candidate pen tip materials in contact with six different writing surface materials (four types of glass and two types of plastic). In addition, pens from three known competitors were included.

Participants were scheduled for a 45 minute test session. Each subject was presented with the six candidate writing surfaces and six pen tip materials. Starting with the first pen tip material, subjects were asked to indicate which surfaces they found acceptable or preferable and which they did not prefer with that pen tip. To assist them in this decision process, participants were instructed to repeatedly perform a simple annotation task by tracing the figures and items on a simple task sheet that had been placed under each of the writing surfaces.

The annotation-tracing task consisted of the following items: (1) a set of three vertical "pull down" lines, (2) a set of four continuous "loops," (3) the numerals 1 through 4, (4) the word ROPE in block capital letters, (5) a large right triangle, (6) a set of six dots, and (7) a designated rectangular area for users to write their signature.

Upon selecting the surfaces they found acceptable, the subjects were then required to rank the surfaces according to preferences, e.g., how unnatural or natural the writing surfaces felt, how rough or slippery the surfaces felt, how much they liked or disliked the surfaces. Last, verbal statements were recorded from participants regarding their "likes" and "dislikes" for each writing surface with the first pen tip material. This same cycle was repeated until each participant had evaluated all six writing surfaces using each of the six pen tip materials. The order of presentation for the pen tips was counterbalanced to reduce any systematic order effects.

After evaluating all pen tip and surface writing surfaces, subjects participated in a short interview session in which they could discuss their opinions about each of the writing surfaces and pen tip materials as well as the general criteria used in their decision process.

Results

Results showed the Concerto Team the combinations of pen tips and writing surfaces that were perceived favorably and how the candidate pen tip materials compared to the competitive benchmarks. Results also indicated which writing surfaces could be dropped from consideration due to poor user acceptance ratings or scratches and obvious signs of wear with minimal use. Later studies helped the team to continue to narrow the field of choices and refine the materials selected for the final product.

Keyboard Touch and Feel Research

To help select a keyboard technology, a series of studies beginning in 1991 were conducted evaluating various key switches being considered by engineers. Approximately 30 PC users participated in each study. Five notebook keyboards were included in each study, including the Compaq LTE Lite notebook keyboard as a benchmark.

Performance and Preference Measures

User performance data included typing speed (words per minute) and typing error rates. Errors were assigned to one of 30+ categorizes. For example, for the word *father*, the following errors would be categorized as follows:

faoher—wrong letter
fathher—double strike
faher—omission, alphanumeric
fAther—caps added
fahter—out of order
fat her—commission, space

User preference data was collected using more than 30 rating scales designed to address overall impressions and "touch and feel" characteristics of the keyboards. Seven-point and nine-point bipolar rating scales were used along with a comparative "report card" scale ranging from A+ to F, on which users "graded" the keyboards in terms of overall preference. In addition, a comparative interest-in-use rating scale was used, on which users indicated their interest in using each of the five keyboards along an 80-point scale ranging from "definitely not interested" to "extremely interested."

Procedure

Operators were required to perform a series of timed typing tasks on each of the five keyboards. For each typing task, operators typed from prepared text and were instructed when to start and stop typing. After the task, each operator completed the series of rating scales, took a break, and was assigned a new keyboard. This procedure continued until each operator had typed on and evaluated each of the five keyboards. After evaluating the fifth keyboard, each operator completed the comparative interest-in-use ratings. The order of keyboard and typing task presentation was structured using a Latin-square design to balance possible order effects. Individual discussion interviews, designed to gain a further understanding of the user's preferences and opinions, were conducted with each test operator at the conclusion of the test session.

Analysis

The *typing error analyzer* tool was used to calculate typing speed and error rates. Individual analysis of variance (ANOVA) procedures were performed on the typing speed data and each of the 30+ error categories to identify any statistically significant differences in typing performance among the five keyboards (error data was expressed in terms of a percentage score: frequency of a particular error type over total number of characters typed). Individual ANOVA procedures were also performed on each of the rating scales to identify any statistically significant differences in preferences among the five keyboards

Results

Results showed how each keyboard compared to the Compaq LTE Lite benchmark in terms of user preference and user performance (typing speed and error rates). The analysis of the preference scales provided detailed information about how each keyboard was perceived. For example, in comparison to the benchmark, users in the first study perceived that one of the candidate keyboards was difficult to get used to, was more fatiguing, had a less acceptable key action, had shorter and less acceptable key travel, etc. Performance results for the same candidate keyboard showed that, in comparison to their performance on the benchmark, users were typing slower and making more alphanumeric omission errors. Through a series of these keyboard studies, the team was able to select a key switch technology that they felt would be well received by Concerto users.

Control Points™ Research

As part of the ongoing form factor research for Compaq Concerto, HF was asked to evaluate several different versions of control points that were to be ingrained into the computer's bezel. These control points would be pen-sensitive indentations in the hardware of the computer that would invoke a software "pop-up" icon which allows the subject to control frequently needed functions such as display contrast and battery gauge. For instance, if a subject wished to change the volume of the speaker, a control point would be tapped with the pen, and a software icon would come up showing the current volume level and would allow the level to be changed.

Procedure

Subjects were asked to perform several tasks using paper and software prototypes of the control points and their pop-up icons. They were asked to identify the pop-up icons (provide labels for them), perform matching tasks with the icons and their proposed labels, and provide subjective ratings on the match of the icon and its label. They were also asked to perform contextual usage exercises using prototypes of the control points and pop-up software icons. Contextual usage exercises are tasks that users are asked to perform using a prototype of the model as they would in their work environment, with the HF professional noting any usability issues along the way.

Results

Identification and matching results collected from the labeling exercise with the icons (percent correct scores) were used to determine the most intuitive labels for those icons. An ANOVA indicated that there were significant differences across the various candidate icons for each of the control point concepts, and the most intuitive control point label and icon pair was identified from this data. It was also noted during the contextual usage part of the experiment, that subjects' preferences for various icons and their labels changed when using the keyboard as the input device instead of the pen. Based on these results, an icon group was developed that supported subjects' expectations about how to use the control points and their pop-up icons with or without keyboard interaction. It was also demonstrated that users expected the screen to be sensitive to pen interaction for these icons during the contextual usage exercises. Engineering and the Industrial Design Group worked together to implement these changes and add the new functionality.

Password Verification Research

One of the security management features included on Concerto is an option allowing users to set a personal identification number (PIN), such as those used with automated teller machine (ATM) cards. HF was asked to help design the pen-enabled keypad that would be displayed when users needed to enter their PIN. HF tested four different candidate versions of the PIN "pop-up icon" for the unit. The four versions of the pop-up icon tested included the use of a backspace key after PIN entry, as well as auditory feedback, use of a backspace key without auditory feedback, or the use of a clear key (in lieu of the backspace key) with and without auditory feedback. The clear key would erase the entire sequence of PIN entries after a mistake, while the backspace key erased merely the last number entered.

Procedure

Thirty-one subjects were included in the study. Subjects' experience levels ranged from very novice to very expert (five user groups were targeted and identified during the subject selection stage). Subjects performed pen-based tasks including the entry of correct and incorrect PINs on each of the four icon versions; the order each subject saw each icon version was counterbalanced. Subjects provided overall preference data for the icons and subjective ratings on the usability of each icon version. Users' task and error times, as well as human factors issues observed during PIN entry, were also collected.

Results

A 5×4 (experience of user group by PIN icon version) ANOVA was used to analyze the subjective ratings in order to determine each PIN version's relative ease-of-use. No significant differences were observed across user groups, and a PIN version that included a backspace key in the upper right-hand corner and auditory feedback was significantly preferred (via post-hoc analyses) out of the four icon versions. User interface issues and other data collected demonstrated that more enhanced feedback (e.g., stronger 3-D depression of the icon buttons during PIN entry, and louder auditory feedback) was needed during correct and incorrect PIN entry. These changes were implemented for a usable PIN entry user interface design.

Welcome Center and Control Center Research

Compaq offers many useful software utilities, applications, and online users' guides to help Compaq customers understand and maximize the use of their PCs. However, HF research indicated that many users were not aware of the existence of these software utilities, or were unable to invoke the software from their GUI environment. As a result, HF was asked to participate on a team to improve the accessibility, organization, and ease-of-use of the software applications provided by Compaq. The research described in this section focuses on how HF helped the team address the organization and accessibility issue. The following section provides an example of how the user interface design of one utility, Computer Setup, was improved.

To begin the design process addressing the organization and accessibility issue, HF performed a cognitive analysis of the way PC users organize the information and utilities provided on Compaq systems. The goal of this research was to try to use the results of a cognitive modeling tool to design a graphical user interface (GUI) that organized Compaq and third-party utilities and made them easier to find and use.

Procedure

The information that test subjects organized included utilities and applications offered by Compaq and those available through Microsoft Windows Program Manager. The analysis involved subjects coming into the lab and reviewing index cards with program or utility names and definitions written on them. Users then organized these cards into piles of applications and utilities that seemed to belong together in the same group. Also, hierarchical information about how to organize the applications and utilities was collected, by having the users place similar piles of cards into small envelopes, and then placing related small envelopes into larger envelopes. Five different user groups, ranging in expertise from no computer or mouse experience to highly experienced, were run through the study, for a total of 41 subjects.

Results

The Pathfinder cognitive modeling tool was used to get a two-dimensional spatial layout of the applications and utilities and to demonstrate graphically how users view the relationships and organization of the applications. The average resultant categorization scheme was chosen for implementation into a graphical user interface that organized the applications and utilities.

Iterative GUI Design and Test

The next phase of this research involved designing an easy-to-use graphical user interface based on the results of the Pathfinder analysis. Before we could proceed, however, we had to choose a visual metaphor in which to present our applications and utilities. Team members from HF, marketing, and graphics design worked together on several different metaphors. Early concept studies using paper and pencil artistic renderings of the metaphor allowed us to hone in on a "big button" metaphor for the user interface. Essentially, each of the higher level categories that fell out of the sorting study was implemented as a "big button" on the user interface. HF testing with both computer experts and novices demonstrated that the button metaphor was intuitive, even for first-time computer users. Several iterative design and test periods ensued, in which decisions to add a message line, multiple paths to the same utility, and double-click-single-click equivalence were made. The decisions were based on users' subjective and objective behaviors upon using the utility to perform real-world tasks. Five iterative test sessions were conducted prior to the release of the software. Figure 11 shows the graphical user interface (the Control Center) that was implemented based on this research. Two other screens following this metaphor, the Welcome Center and the Learning Center, were also designed.

Computer Setup Utility Research

As part the efforts to make Compaq PCs easier to set up and use, a new Windows-based utility was created to provide users with easy to access information about their system (See Figure 12). In addition, the utility provides users a quick and efficient means of making changes to the system settings without having to stop what they are presently doing.

Categories of system information were created with two principles in mind: (1) users should be able to get an overview of major system information in one place, and (2) novice and advanced users require different levels of information and should there fore be separated in some fashion. An initial prototype of the interface was developed and refined by a design team and then tested for the goodness of concept. Users were

Figure 11 Compaq Control Center

asked to locate various pieces of information about the system by using the prototype. User reactions were very positive and encouraging about the utility's design and functionality.

Two additional iterations of testing, using preliminary, then fully functional versions of the software confirmed the benefits of the utility. The second iteration had users performing the same tasks as in the first study plus additional tasks, including changing system settings. Again the utility was very favorably rated and users were able to locate information quickly and easily. The third iteration of testing was conducted at Innovate '93, an industry-wide technical conference sponsored by Compaq. Users from around the world participated in a walk-up test using the fully functioning hardware and software. All subjects used a pen to complete the same tasks as in the second study. Once again, the utility was favorable rated and users were very productive with the pen.

Figure 12   Compaq Computer Setup

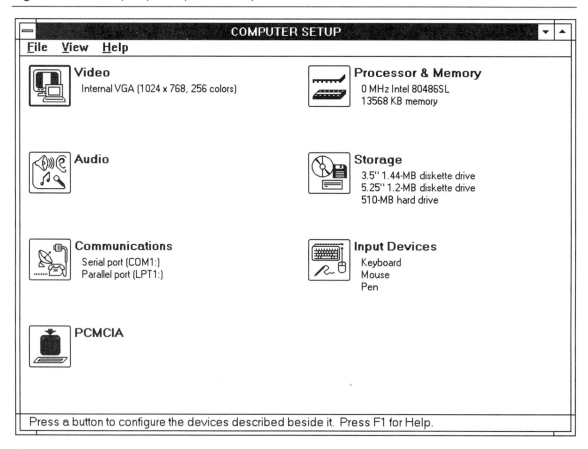

References to HF Testing in Marketing Literature

In the final stages of Concerto's development, when the advertising and marketing literature was being written, the human factors research that had played a part in the design was reviewed once more. It was indeed very rewarding for us to see references to our research in the ensuing Concerto product literature, e.g., "After endless hours of customer research and human factors testing, Compaq is delivering the product that . . . gets you what you need most, when you need it most—regardless of your working environment . . . it gives you the ability to work more ways, more comfortably than any other notebook you've seen."

The features and benefits brochure goes on to specifically mention several HF studies; for example, "Another key element in a natural pen design was to ensure that when used to contact the display, the feeling is similar to that of pen and paper. Many glass surfaces and tip materials were tested to make sure that the pen didn't slip, the contact wasn't too harsh, and the pen strokes weren't too broad or narrow. The resulting display includes an etched glass surface which most accurately duplicates the actual feeling of pen and paper." The brochure concludes with, "To truly appreciate the usability of Concerto, you'll have to try it like the participants in our human factors testing did. Once you get your hands on it, you'll see how it can make you more comfortable and more productive."

And the testing continues. Compaq Concerto was announced while we were writing this chapter. We are now planning follow-up research with some of our first customers to determine what ease-of-use opportunities exist for the next generation of Compaq pen-enabled PCs.

Lessons Learned

Built from a Foundation of Research

In retrospect, the terms that Cynthia laid out in her original interview appear to have played a critical role for the eventual success of the group. Cynthia insisted upon support for building a laboratory and a core staff. This original group and laboratory enabled the first pieces of research to be conducted in a timely manner. It was upon this original research that the reputation of the group was built. Had Cynthia agreed to be a "one person band" and "see how things went" before receiving additional commitments to staff and lab resources, it is unlikely that the group could have had the same success.

The decision to honor graduate-level skills in research methodology and statistics during the hiring process also appears to have paid off. These skills significantly contributed to the quality of the group's research. And it was upon this robust research that the group was able to grow (eventually double in size), gain increased visibility, and most important, affect the human-computer interface of products produced by Compaq.

Moreover, the decision to honor interpersonal communication skills during the hiring process also appears to have paid off. With the excellent combination of good research skills along with negotiation techniques, the HF Group was able to show teams how their user interface designs could be improved. It was believed from the start that even the most brilliant user interface ideas could be instantly crippled if they were not effectively communicated and negotiated. Interviews for new members of the HF Group continue to focus on finding individuals with solid "people skills," those who can effectively function within interdisciplinary teams and gently persuade the inevitable "HF skeptics."

Management Support

The HF Group has strong support from the senior management of Systems Engineering, to which it reports. This support has played an invaluable role in the group's growth. Not only did senior managers support the growing needs for increased personnel and lab resources, they also helped elevate critical user interface recommendations.

Normally, test results are presented directly to the person or team requesting HF's assistance. On rare occasions, however, critical usability issues may need to be quickly elevated to the corporation's senior staff. Fortunately, this does not occur very often; however, when it does, management is ready to listen and quickly elevate the findings as necessary to the senior staff. We firmly believe that senior managers listen and respond because the HF group has worked hard to maintain a high quality of research, worthy of management's trust.

Involving Product Teams in the Design of HF Research

The HF Group learned, over time, how important it is to closely involve product teams in the design of HF research. When study results were not positive, some team members preferred to focus their energy on criticizing the test methodology, rather than considering the possibility that the data was valid. We found, however, that when product teams are included in designing the test methodology, this skepticism could be avoided altogether.

Usability goals tables help tremendously in this regard. Through them, a team can synthesize and clarify its expectations, understand which product attributes are important, and devise a plan to measure them. When the study is completed and the data presented to the team, the presentation begins with the *usability goals table* to remind the team of the goals that it helped to set. The presentation always concludes with a summary of how each of the goals was (or was not) met.

Task and users' needs analyses and *state of the union* studies also help in this regard. When the team is provided with robust information about how well users' needs are being met with products currently on the market, its ability to determine important usability attributes and set realistic usability goals is enhanced greatly.

Compromises in the Test Methodology

Having four to six weeks to design, run, and analyze a study is considered a luxury in the applied setting at Compaq. The HF Group certainly never gets to run that ideal full factorial design; schedules and deadlines constantly force compromises in test methodologies. However, the group tries to understand when cuts in the test design can be made and at what point further compromise cannot be made.

The group has learned that test methods can be overly compromised. Team members may say, "Please, can't you just run a quick study to get us some data by Friday? We understand that it's not much time and we understand that it will have to be 'quick and dirty'." However, when the results turn out not to their liking, those same team members will be the most vocal about criticizing the test methods and questioning the validity of the results. Ironically, the HF Group has had several teams come back with, "If we give you another day, can you run another study?" Not only is the robustness of the data sacrificed in these situations, HF professionals are left with an uncomfortable sense of having done a mediocre job. Nobody wins.

So the HF Group has learned to set limits on how far they are willing to compromise their research. And the group's members have learned some techniques to help determine where compromises can be made. With each study, the human factors engineer tries to focus on the most important factors. When a product team first approaches the group with an issue, before telling the team that it cannot be done in the amount of time that is allotted, HF has them list all the factors (with all the levels of each factor) that it might want covered. HF will draw out the team's expectations, and then show it how the desired 3 x 6 x 3 design with six users per cell will take four months to run (considered an inordinate amount of time in the fast-paced product development cycle at Compaq)! The team quickly sees the dilemma and then, as a team, decides which factors are truly the most important to focus on first. Perhaps a series of studies can be planned, where the team agrees to take them one at a time and reconvene to determine whether the entire series is necessary. Often, the first study in the series is sufficient to allow the team to make its user interface trade-offs.

Edited Videotapes

Edited videotapes have proven to be one of the most persuasive communication tools that HF has discovered to date. User interface issues lists, charts showing statistically significant user preference differences and error rates do not "hold a candle" to a 10-20 minute edited videotape showing struggling, frustrated users trying to complete a task! Users discussing their impressions after they have completed a usability study holds much more power than a human factors professional expressing the same views.

Because the tapes are often shared among product team members and subsequently viewed without a human factors person present, HF tries to make them self-explanatory. Opening title screens and voiceovers describe the goals and the design of the research and experience of the subjects. The majority of a tape will describe the top user interface issues observed. Each of these issues is introduced with a title screen (created with the character generator) and a voiceover. The introduction is then followed with clips that demonstrate the issue, e.g., clips of two or three test participants struggling at the same place in the user interface. After the top issues are summarized, the end of the videotape usually includes clips from the debriefing interviews that summarize the "bottom line."

Edited videotapes not only provide a powerful communication tool, they often help HF reach a larger audience. Inevitably, clips of struggling users can be painfully funny to watch. News of the videotapes spreads, and often HF is asked to report on a study and show a tape to numerous teams. This can not only increase the impact of a particular study's findings, but also helps to "spread the word" about the Group and keep teams informed about HF services.

Weekly Status Reports

The Human Factors weekly status reports play a significant role in keeping people informed about the HF Group and also help the group grow. The reports were initially meant to keep HF's management informed of ongoing design and research activities. Weekly, each HF Group member sends Cynthia an update on his or her previous week's activities and goals for the coming week. Cynthia then consolidates their reports into one to three pages. As people learned about these weekly reports, they asked to be added to the electronic distribution list. The report keeps members of engineering and marketing aware of HF's services and keeps them up to date on HF's current efforts. The reports provide a certain amount of evangelism throughout the three product divisions and are now distributed internationally to over 50 Compaq employees.

Aside from providing an excellent communications tool, the reports have proven to be an invaluable tracking mechanism. They can be used to quickly assemble quarterly accomplishments. Furthermore, when a product team is preparing the "ease-of-use" sections of its advertising and product literature, a summary of the HF design and research activities conducted for that particular product can be assembled quickly.

HF Research Tracking Board

Given the volume of research we conduct, a tracking board has proven invaluable in organizing the group and recognizing resource priorities. A 5' x 4' magnetized white board is divided into a grid. Each column represents a work week (about 15 weeks are shown at once), while each row indicates a study to be performed. Colored magnets represent time set aside for test preparation, data collection (in the lab or in the field), and data analysis.

Every Monday, the HF Group meets to review the board. New studies are added in the general vicinity of when the study might be conducted. This meeting time allows the group members to stay in touch with each other and hear about the user interface designs under development by the product teams and usability research that is planned. This time is spent juggling priorities, assigning human factors engineers to product teams and usability professionals to each piece of research, and finalizing lab resource requirements for each study.

One-on-One Meetings

Interpersonal conflicts can be the most serious threat to the effectiveness, or even survival, of any group. As a result, HF honors the importance of the group's personal dynamics. We strive to maintain a sense of "community" in the group, communicating with authenticity, dealing with difficult issues, bridging differences with integrity. An excellent reference for this "community building" approach is provided by M. Scott Peck in *A World Waiting to Be Born: Civility Rediscovered*, 1993.

To help nurture this sense of community, each member of the group meets with the HF manager for an hour each week. When a human factors engineer and a usability professional collaborate on a particular piece of research, they too set aside time each week to talk. These "one-on-ones" provide a dedicated time where designs and research can be reviewed and feelings can be expressed. It is a time in which a two-way relationship of trust can be built between members of the group. Through these one-on-ones, "people challenges" and issues appear to surface and get resolved much earlier than they otherwise would if members were meeting on a more informal basis.

Freedom to Grow, Kaisen

Kaisen is a Japanese term. It refers to a state of acceptance that there is always room for improvement and that improvement does not only occur in large, revolutionary waves but may occur equally, or more powerfully, in small, incremental steps. A *kaisen* state of mind is constantly vigilante to seeking out opportunities for small refinement. The HF group strives to keep this state of mind. For example, the group has not locked itself into "cookbook" approaches to design and research. Each member of the group is encouraged to try new approaches and to suggest new ideas. And time is set aside for the group to meet as a whole, to share ideas, and to brainstorm new opportunities for improvement.

In Conclusion

Over the past five years, the Human Factors Group has been asked to assist with almost every aspect of Compaq products that users touch, see, or hear—from keyboard "touch and feel" to portable keyboard layouts; from integrated cursor control devices to front-of-screen image quality of displays; from printer control panel design to digitized voice error messages used by sophisticated diagnostics tools; from the recognizability of icons to intelligent configuration software; from the servicability of CPU components to the GUI design of security management software utilities. We appear to have successfully "spread the word" about the HF services; i.e., there is currently no need for our group to seek out "new business" because so many teams are "knocking" at our door. Not only has the group been able to assist with a myriad of hardware and software user interface issues, teams are asking for the group's assistance earlier and earlier in the design process. Moreover, the group is now participating on strategic teams, who are asking what "ease-of-use" opportunities should receive research and development focus for products of the future.

References

Epps, Brian. (1986). "A Comparison of Cursor Control Devices on Target Acquisition, Text Editing, and Graphics Tasks" Doctoral dissertation, Virginia Polytechnic Institute and State University. *UMI Dissertation Services*, Ann Arbor, MI.

Nielsen, Jakob. (1993). *Usability Engineering*. Academic Press, Boston.

Peck, M. Scott. (1993). *A World Waiting to Be Born: Civility Rediscovered*. Bantam Books, New York.

Schvaneveldt, R. (ed.). (1990). *Pathfinder Associative Networks: Studies in Knowledge Organization.* Ablex, Norwood, NJ.

Tinker, M.A. *Legibility of print.* Ames: Iowa State University Press, 1963.

Whiteside, J., Bennett, J., and Holtzblatt, K. (1988). "Usability Engineering: Our Experience and Evolution," in M. Helander (ed.). *Handbook of Human Computer Interaction*, North Holland, New York.

CHAPTER 6

Evolution of Usability at Digital Equipment Corporation

**Dennis R. Wixon and
Elizabeth M. Comstock**

*Digital Equipment
Corporation*

Dennis Wixon is a usability principal engineer in the Usability Expertise Center at Digital Equipment Corporation in Nashua, New Hampshire. His current work includes program management for Contextual Inquiry, development of design review processes, and design of user interfaces. Dennis has worked at Digital since 1981 when he joined the Software Usability Engineering group. He received a Ph.D. in social psychology from Clark University in 1981 and taught experimental psychology, graduate statistics, and introduction to programming at Clark University and Holy Cross College.

Betsy Comstock is a usability consultant engineer in the Usability Expertise Center at Digital Equipment Corporation in Littleton, Massachusetts. Her work focuses on developing distributed network resources that are easily managed and easily available to users. She has been working on the usability of computer systems at Digital since 1981, when she joined the Corporate Human Factors Group. She has consulted with the U.S. Army Natick Research and Development Laboratories and with Abt Associates Inc. Betsy received a Ph.D. in experimental psychology from the University of Massachusetts in 1975 and taught psychology at Bucknell University.

Usability in Practice

Organizational Overview

Overview of Digital

Digital Equipment Corporation™ is a large, international corporation with a rich and varied history. Founded in 1957, it introduced some of the first interactive and distributed computer systems. After early success in developing low-cost interactive systems for the scientific and technical markets, Digital expanded its offerings, developed a highly successful line of peripherals such as terminals and printers, introduced the VAX™ family of computers, and pioneered network-distributed computing.

Today, with a Fortune 500 rank of 28, Digital is one of the largest corporations in the United States. Revenues for fiscal year 1993 were $14.37 billion, and employment stood at 94,000. An international corporation with over 800 facilities in more than 100 countries, Digital provides computer hardware, software, and integrated system services in areas ranging from large mainframe super computers to desktop components such as printers and personal computers. Digital produces applications in areas such as transaction processing, data management, telecommunications, finance, real-time data acquisition and control, vector processing, education, publishing, manufacturing, software-development, and health care.

Digital's size and diversity have influenced the ways that we, as usability professionals, do our jobs. There are hundreds of organizations in Digital that develop products, processes, and services. All of them need usability support, but each has its own mini-culture that usability professionals need to understand. Specific usability needs and opportunities are different in different development organizations. In adapting to the diversity among development organizations, we have developed and refined a large number of methods and techniques. Some of these will be described in the following sections on usability services and the case studies.

Our experience suggests that Digital's management is less hierarchical and its development practices less standardized than other environments in which usability professionals might work. At Digital, line managers have a high degree of autonomy. Direction from top management has been embodied in simple principles such as "The customer should be the focus of all we do." There have been few standardized policies and procedures. For usability professionals, the impact has been that there is no uniform process to enforce usability practices across the corporation. Instead, we need to sell our work on the basis of its benefits to each development effort.

Digital continues to develop leadership products and to build on its technological strengths. But, faced with increasingly competitive markets and a general revolution in information technology, Digital has been undergoing major changes during the last few years. The corporation is becoming more customer-centered and is adopting more uniform development practices. These changes signal an increased emphasis on usability and an increased regularity in the ways that usability work will be included in product development.

A Brief History of Usability in Digital

Usability work at Digital began in 1979. Among the first usability professionals at Digital were Charles Abernethy (Abernethy, 1981), John Whiteside (Whiteside et al., 1982), and Harry Hersh (Hersh, 1982). There were two major usability groups providing a wide variety of usability services throughout the corporation. One, the Corporate Human Factors Group, began as part of the Industrial Design Group. The other, the Software Usability Engineering Group, was part of Software Engineering. There were also a number of usability professionals reporting to specific product development or service organizations, such as workstation development, field service, or corporate research.

This division of usability professionals arose partly because human factors and usability were relatively new disciplines; no top management said, "This is where usability professionals belong in Digital." Line managers who first recognized the value of usability hired usability professionals within their organizations. However, as Digital's usability community developed, most of its members saw that the division into separate groups was not optimal. Differences between the groups in funding models, geographical and organizational location, and philosophy tended to foster divisiveness. Each group tended to think that it knew "the right way" to do usability work (and perhaps that others did not). The division into separate groups decreased sharing of knowledge and inhibited cooperative work.

Creating the Usability Expertise Center

By 1992, members of both usability groups recognized the limitations in our separate organizations and decided to work toward merging. A small team of usability professionals began considering reorganization options and soliciting high-level management support. One organization we investigated was Digital's Information Design and Consulting (IDC) group, a broad engineering services organization that provides information products, documentation, training, and design consultation throughout the corporation. We discovered that IDC had placed usability at the center of its long-term strategy and had decided to consolidate the usability specialists currently in its organization. Working as a task force of usability professionals and IDC representatives, we weighed many organizational characteristics, developed a long-term strategy, and decided to propose merging most of the usability professionals in Digital into a single organization within IDC. Our proposal was accepted by the senior managers of both our organizations and IDC, and we merged in the spring of 1993.

Now we are a diverse organization called the Usability Expertise Center (UEC), part of IDC. We share knowledge, group policies, and strategies. Our 20 members have varied backgrounds and skills, including user interface design, psychology, human factors, graphic design, software and hardware engineering, ethnography, and technical communication. In some cases, we supplement our staff with consultants, especially if we lack expertise in a particular subject matter or if we lack the resources to support a particular project. It is also important to point out that we are not the only people working to bring usability to Digital's products and services. Most product development groups routinely employ a wide variety of methods to ensure that their products are usable. These methods include Contextual Inquiry (described later under Case Study 2), Quality Factor Deployment (King, 1989), documentation usability testing (Raven and Beabes, 1992; Flanders and Raven, 1993) and participatory design (Good, 1992).

Space and Tools for Usability Work

Our offices are geographically dispersed in groups of two to eight, because we find it works best for usability professionals to be located in the same building or set of buildings as the development teams they support. However, these teams are more widely dispersed than we are, so most of our members spend a portion of each week working at sites other than their "home base." We also frequently travel to Digital customer sites.

To support our work, we have several VHS and 8mm portable video cameras, tape recorders, and laptops. We use a variety of standard and specialized tools for logging and analyzing keystrokes, preparing prototypes, and data analysis.

We support two usability labs. One is a large (approximately 20 feet by 40 feet) multipurpose room with one wall-mounted video camera and one video camera on a movable tripod. Both cameras pan and zoom. On one side of the room is the video-operator's console. The lab has no one-way mirrors or special sound equipment. We use this lab for usability tests ranging from keyboard testing to installation testing of large systems. We rearrange the furniture in the room to simulate a customer environment for the product set we are testing. There is ample space in the lab for observers. We have found that it is rarely necessary to isolate participants in usability studies. One exception is keyboard testing, where speed and accuracy are crucial measures. But in usability tests like those described in the first case study, enrolling both the observers and the participants as coinvestigators has worked extremely well. We instruct observers in how to take notes and what to say and *not* say to the participants.

We have found that these observers remain interested and attentive longer than those who watch from behind one-way windows. Participants understand that they are doing something useful and important because they can see observers taking notes and listening attentively to what they say.

The second lab is a small set of two rooms separated by a one-way mirror. It contains an audio patch panel, Ethernet drops, and video recording and editing facilities. This lab is most effective for usability tests in which a single user sits at a workstation throughout the test session or when a test requires a controlled environment.

We now conduct much of our work in less formal, more authentic locations, such as users' offices, trade show floors, and customer sites. We also have two office cubicles reserved as an "unlab" for usability awareness activities and demonstrations.

Usability services

The 1993 description of our usability consulting services includes the 21 categories shown in Table 1. Our services did not emerge all at once. Since 1979, the specific methods evolved and changed, and the list of services grew. While the general goal of building usable products has remained the same, the practices and techniques have expanded dramatically as we learned to work more effectively within Digital's development processes. We learned to tailor our methods to the needs of each client product development group, and we developed hybrid methods and new methods suited to each stage in the product development process.

Funding Usability Work

The specific services delivered to our clients are determined through a proposal writing cycle. The usability professional and a business manager from our parent organization meet with the client to agree on the usability services and the budget. We work primarily with clients inside Digital, but we also offer services (such as courses and consulting on topics on which we have particular expertise) to customers outside Digital.

Currently, the Usability Expertise Center operates according to two funding models. In the *consulting model*, usability work is paid for by a product development group. Usability professionals contract with product development groups to deliver a tailored set of services and results. This model works well when the goal is usability of a specific product set, such as a family of hardware or software products. It does not work as well for strategic work, such as developing new methodologies or contributing to international usability standards. Such work is usually cross-product or on topics not resident within a specific product development group. For such strategic

Table 1   Services of Digital's Usability Expertise Center

Usability Services	Description
Customer data collection and analysis	Applying techniques such as Contextual Inquiry, questionnaires, telephone surveys, and focus groups
Work flow and task analysis	Assessing the work people do, and the physical and technical environments in which they work
Competitive analysis and technology reviews	Assessing the quality and competitiveness of Digital products, with respect to usability
User interface specifications	Defining detailed requirements for hardware and software user interfaces
Usability goal definition	Setting goals for product usability
User interface prototypes	Building paper-, software-, or hardware-based drafts of user interface designs
Iterative design and review	Designing, evaluating, and redesigning hardware, software, and documentation user interfaces
User interface walk-throughs and test drives	Informally evaluating early product designs
Observational evaluations	Conducting usability tests, such as Day-One Tests, of products under development
Guidelines, standards, and specifications reviews	Evaluating products for compliance with guidelines, standards, and specifications
Creation of standards and guidelines	Creating, managing, and contributing to corporate, national, and international standards and guidelines related to ergonomics and usability
Productivity and performance testing	Quantitative evaluation of user performance based on measures such as speed, accuracy, and errors
Post implementation and post ship studies	Field evaluation of products for user satisfaction and performance
Usability awareness activities	Team-oriented usability activities, such as School of Marketing, that increase appreciation of the importance of usability
Usability courses and training	Classroom training in Contextual Inquiry, usability methods, documentation usability, user interface design, Vector Comparative Analysis, and assistive technologies
Usability mentoring	Helping individual development team members apply usability methods in their work

Table 1 Services of Digital's Usability Expertise Center (Continued)

Usability Services	Description
Assistive technologies consulting	Making products accessible to persons with disabilities
Internationalization consulting	Designing products and services that meet internationalization standards
Corporate identity development	Enhancing product image, consistency, and marketability
Engineering process consulting	Implementing programs such as "voice of the customer" and participatory design, and integrating them into the overall product development process
Strategic program consulting	Consulting on cross-organizational strategic usability issues

work we use a second funding model, called the *central model*, in which funding comes from a central organization such as research or standards or from corporate advanced development funds. The central funding model does not work as well for product development efforts because any individual product development group may not receive the usability services it deems important for its product. Today, we consciously balance both funding models (for further discussion of these funding issues, see Rohn and Braun, 1993; Shackel, 1992).

Incorporating Usability into the Development Process

Product development groups and their individual developers differ widely in their understanding of usability methods and results. Clients working with us for the first time often come late in the development process seeking help with a usability problem. Over time they learn the need to incorporate usability as part of the overall development process. Some clients alter their development process to incorporate usability, while others expect usability to be done as part of the process they are already using. A few clients approach interface designers seeking "usability approval" for designs that already exist.

While it might seem tempting to specify an ideal usability process and require clients to match that process, such an approach is not practical, is not in the best interests of the corporation, and does not match our belief that there is no "best" way to achieve usability. No single process accommodates the different cultures, knowledge, and development constraints. If we were to enforce one process for all clients, developers would simply ignore us. Instead, we assess each development scenario individually and offer a tailored set of methods. In accommodating our methods to clients' needs and processes, we can have some impact on the current project and open the possibility for more impact in future projects. Such challenges have led us to develop new methods, which have then been applied to other projects.

We have come to appreciate the demands on development organizations. These demands include compliance with industry standards, extremely short development schedules, small profit margins, and rapid high-volume manufacturing. Therefore, we now make simpler presentations and more specific recommendations. In some cases, we simply show a videotape of users working with a system to illustrate the issues and motivate the team to make changes. We use software prototypes as user interface specifications and designs.

We now recognize that incorporating usability into products involves getting the development team to appreciate the experience of another person. Therefore, we have moved from more objective methods toward participatory design techniques. In general, we see our methods as fitting along a continuum that moves from discovery to decision to design and finally to evaluation (see Figure 1), with information flowing into each stage and feedback relating to the previous stage. This continuum matches the progression involved in developing a product.

Figure 1   Continuum for the Development Process

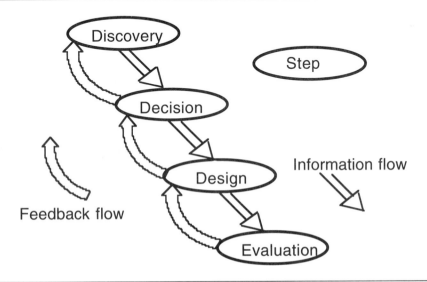

Methods such as usability testing tend to be best suited to the evaluation stages in product development. They answer questions such as, "Is this product usable enough? If not, how can we fix the 'usability bugs'?" Experiments or comparative studies are best suited to making very narrow decisions about incorporating one or another feature into a particular product, for example, "Should menus be deep or shallow?" or "Is product X more usable than product Y?" The two case studies discussed in the following pages point out that, as we gained more experience, we developed and employed new methods that were more suited to the discovery and early design stages. These methods help answer questions such as, "How can we make the next generation of products better match the way people do their work?" or "How can we change the engineering process to result in more usable products?"

Developing Products and Processes—Two Case Studies

We sometimes describe usability work as contributing to Digital in two important but different ways: product development and process development. The broad goal for both is to produce highly usable products. However, since product development and process development differ broadly in the characteristics of the work, we discuss two case studies. The first case study describes usability work during the development of a family of products. The second case study describes the development of a new usability methodology and its establishment as an integral part of the development process. Both illustrate the transition in our work from the emphasis on evaluation to the emphasis on design and discovery. Together, these two case studies provide a more complete picture of our ongoing usability efforts at Digital.

Case Study 1: Developing Usability in a Family of Products

This section describes the contributions of usability professionals in the development of five families of Digital computer systems: Micro/PDP-11™, MicroVAX II™, MicroVAX™ 3000, VAX 4000, and DEC™ 4000 AXP™. These computer systems were developed at Digital between 1981 and 1992. They differ dramatically from each other in power, speed, and architecture (PDP-11™ to VAX to Alpha AXP™). However, they are grouped here because they share many characteristics:

- They are workgroup computers that typically provide computing resources to groups of people, not individuals.

- They are usually located in open office areas, not individual offices or computer rooms.
- They reside in "desk-side" enclosures, not in desk-top enclosures, large mainframes, or racks.
- They include in the same enclosure the CPU, storage devices, and a variety of backplane modules and I/O connections.

Some aspects of our work on these systems are described in two papers (Comstock, 1983; Comstock and Clemens, 1987).

As our work progressed from Micro/PDP-11 through DEC 4000 AXP, we applied lessons learned from one family of computer products to the next family. We learned how to bring usability into complex system design. We refined standard methods and developed new methods. We found ways to enhance the engineering and management processes to increase our effectiveness, and we took on larger responsibilities in order to ensure usability.

We would like to share some of the lessons, anecdotes, and solutions. This case study discusses labeling, user interface consistency, unpacking and moving, computer manuals, and the design of the installation process. We will focus on the practical realities, complexities, and design trade-offs that characterize the work of applying usability.

Bringing Usability into Complex System Design

What is it like to bring usability into the development of workgroup systems? Complex. The work is complex not only because the products and their uses are complex but also because the development process itself is complex. The development of a new computer system involves many disciplines. Therefore, development teams are large, have diverse goals related to their members' specific responsibilities, and have complex, interdependent schedules and constraints. Working with these teams demands communication and networking skills adapted to the team's culture. Moreover, these development teams may have only a vague idea of the roles that usability professionals might play during development. Usability professionals need to work closely with different team members whose work may have profound implications for the resulting product's usability.

Throughout the development of the Micro/PDP-11, MicroVAX II, MicroVAX 3000, VAX 4000, and DEC 4000 AXP, one usability person (or occasionally two) worked as a member of the development team. The work ranged from approximately quarter-time to full-time for one person, depending on whether time-consuming activities, such as usability testing, were being conducted. Other members of the development team included

- Field service engineers
- Firmware and software engineers
- Graphic designers
- Industrial designers
- Manufacturing planners
- Marketing representatives
- Mechanical and electrical engineers
- Packaging engineers
- Product managers
- Qualification and quality assurance representatives
- Safety and regulatory engineers
- Technical writers, illustrators, and editors

Usability professionals worked throughout the development of these five computer systems. We conducted usability tests early in development, and always took a "whole systems" approach, considering it our responsibility to ensure usability in everything that the user experienced.

Labeling with Words or Symbols

One challenge in designing a hardware user interface is labeling the components. The hardware user interface includes any aspect of the hardware that a user operates or interprets as part of performing any task with the system. The primary components of the hardware user interface for these workgroup computers are the connectors, fasteners, switches, indicators, and their labeling. Like any good user interface, the hardware user interface should be consistent, easy for users to interpret and operate, and error resistant. Guidebooks such as Van Cott and Kinkade (1972) and Woodson (1981) offer a great deal of good advice. We made frequent use of this kind of advice to help guide the design of the "knob-ology" aspects of the user interfaces for the workgroup systems.

Nevertheless, the hardware user interface design proved to be one of the most demanding and interesting usability problems. Should components be labeled with words? Or should they be labeled with international symbols, such as those specified by IEC (International Electromechanical Commission), ISO (International Organization for Standardization), or DIN (German Standards Institute)? See Figure 2 for examples of symbols sometimes used on computer products.

Figure 2   Examples of International Symbols for Computer Functions. The symbols stand for 1. Brightness, 2. Contrast, 3. Off, 4. On, 5. Write, 6. Write Protect, 7. On Line, 8. Ready, 9. Halt, and 10. Restart.

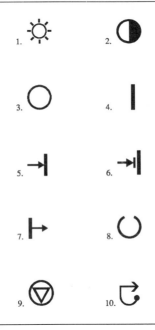

During product development at Digital, powerful practical constraints and cost considerations favor the use of symbols over words to label controls and indicators. Digital is an international corporation and a given product might be shipped anywhere in the world. If labeling were in words, then labels would need to be translated and printed in multiple languages. Producing multiple-language labels could be extremely expensive and difficult to implement. International symbols seemed a more practical solution because they would not be language or country specific, would need no translation, would afford a more aesthetically pleasing design, and would fit more easily onto small computer control panels. For example, the control panel for the Micro/PDP-11 was about 2 inches by 3 inches, yet needed six switches and two lights.

However, during the development of the Micro/PDP-11 and MicroVAX II, usability review identified several problems with using only symbols to label all of the user interface components. Not all of the symbols were understood by computer users. Symbol usage throughout the computer industry was inconsistent. Many of the functions that needed to be labeled were for fairly abstract concepts such as "halt," "reset," "write protect," "on line," and "ready."

Consider the symbols shown in Figure 2. The symbols numbered 1, 2, 3, and 4 represent "brightness," "contrast," "off," and "on." They are frequently used on consumer products, are becoming widely recognized by computer users, and represent fairly concrete functions. Symbols 5 and 6 are not well recognized and the functions they represent do not have immediately obvious results. However, when people are told that these two symbols label the positions of a switch that "write enable" or "write protect" a disk, then they almost always correctly identify which symbol stands for which position. Symbols 7, 8, 9, and 10 are more abstract, are not as well understood by people, and can have undesirable consequences if misinterpreted. They are the symbols for "on line," "ready," "halt," and "reset." Pressing "reset" when you intend to simply halt the CPU or turning off the "on line" switch when you intend to write protect a disk can be serious mistakes resulting in the loss of users' data.

For a brief period in 1983, usability professionals advocated consistent labeling with text to make the hardware user interface as understandable as possible. However, it became clear during design meetings that this position would lose; the design was leaning toward the use of international symbols throughout. Other members of the development team dismissed usability concerns with phrases such as, "Well, the users will just have to learn what the symbols mean." They suggested a variety of solutions such as special cue cards for operators. Another set of developers believed that most computer operators spoke English, and they proposed that we label the controls in English only.

Usability professionals proposed a compromise solution that then became the standard for the Micro/PDP-11 and MicroVAX computer systems. We sacrificed consistency for the sake of usability where it mattered most. We argued that text was essential only where three conditions were true:

- No well-understood symbol was available.
- The function was abstract (for example, "reset").
- The consequences of misinterpretation were severe (for example, loss of data).

When we applied these criteria, we judged symbols to be appropriate for labeling most aspects of the hardware user interface. We labeled all cable sockets with symbols because in Digital systems sockets accept only the appropriate cable connectors. We labeled power switches with symbols because the symbols O and I were becoming generally accepted. The design team eliminated the need for labeling some switches by changing the design; for example, instead of labeling a switch with positions for Thinwire and standard Ethernet, they positioned the switch between the two connectors and made it slide toward the desired connector. We left indicator lights unlabeled if their meaning was an expected "on," "functioning," or "available." As far as the claim that all operators spoke English was concerned, we argued that even if it happened to be true currently, it was certainly *not* a very sensible long-term requirement if Digital expected to move into new markets.

On the Micro/PDP-11 and MicroVAX II systems, according to these criteria, the six front panel switches and indicator lights were the only ones requiring language-specific labeling. We proposed to the design team that machines be manufactured with English-language labeling in place (because that represents the majority case) but that we also supply a single sheet containing labels in all required languages. We then calculated that the increased cost of providing a label with every system was $7.75. The development team decided that the increased cost was justified for the sake of usability and customer satisfaction.

During the process of developing labeling strategies for workgroup machines, we learned two important lessons that apply generally across most aspects of system development.

First, design all interacting aspects of a system together. Even a computer system's labeling strategy should be designed as an integral part of the overall system design. This may sound simple, but in our experience, aspects of a system such as labeling are often considered add-on features to be done late in the development process. This often results in expensive, awkward, or unusable solutions. In the case of the labeling strategy for the Micro/PDP-11, the controls, indicators, and printed circuit board were designed before the details of the labeling strategy had been determined. The resulting label solution was expensive because it required individual cut-outs around each of six switches and two indicator lights. Designing the labeling solution early is much more cost-effective. In the DEC 4000 AXP and follow-on systems, any labeling is designed so that cut-outs around switches are not required. Moreover, it is now appropriate to consider labeling with symbols, since there are fewer controls on the product (usually only *reset* and maybe *halt*) and symbols for computer functions are coming into common use.

Second, be willing to work within constraints that you cannot change to find an acceptable solution. In the labeling example cited here, the constraints came from corporate strengths, such as manufacturing efficiency and worldwide distribution of products. Recognizing which constraints can be changed and which cannot often requires trying to change some of the constraints. Changing constraints requires good negotiation and teamwork skills.

Using Principles to Achieve User Interface Consistency

Designing a hardware user interface is particularly challenging on workgroup computer systems because the systems are made up of components developed by a large number of different engineering groups. For example, the enclosure, the CPU, and the power supply components all may be developed by separate groups. In addition, these systems can house a large number of "mix and match" components, such as diskette drives, optical disk readers, and backplane modules for specific purposes; these are developed in different parts of the corporation and by other manufacturers. With all these components, how can a consistent hardware user interface result?

The problem has not been completely solved, but the approach taken with the DEC 4000 AXP came closer to a consistent hardware user interface than has been true with any previous system. Working with a cross-disciplinary team of product developers, we wrote a hardware user interface specification as part of the early product specification phase. The effort began by laying out the three guiding principles on which the interface design was based:

- Keep physical interaction with the hardware to a minimum. Almost all interaction with the system hardware is accomplished from the console terminal. The switches and indicators provided on the DEC 4000 AXP system hardware are only those needed to support actions that must be performed at the computer's main hardware unit. For example, status lights indicate whether an entire field-replaceable unit is functioning properly, not whether a smaller part of the system is functioning properly.

- Follow Futurebus+ user interface conventions. Futurebus+ is a major component of the DEC 4000 AXP system. It has a simple, two-indicator user interface defined by an IEEE standard (*Futurebus+ Physical Layer and Profile Specification, P896.2*). Futurebus+ conventions provided the basis for a consistent user interface across all major system components. For example, wherever possible throughout the DEC 4000 AXP, green LEDs were used to signify normal operation or "run," and yellow LEDs were used to signify abnormal states or "fault."

- Make connectors, indicators, and switches international and simple to interpret. For the reasons described earlier, the halt and reset switches were labeled in English, and multilanguage label sheets were provided. All other labeling of connectors, indicators, and set-up switches used international symbols in accordance with internal Digital standards (which are based on industry standards).

The hardware user interface specification covered all switches, indicators, connectors, and labels on any component that was being newly engineered for DEC 4000

AXP. It factored in all known outside components, such as tape and disk drives, and strove for consistency across all components. The user interface specification became a chapter in the complete system specification and was used to guide the design of the hardware user interface throughout development.

Designing for Easy Unpacking

One of the most surprisingly enjoyable parts of working on hardware usability is ensuring that recipients can safely and easily unpack their new computer. When we first began working on shipping containers and the unpacking process, a common unpacking technique for heavy computers was referred to as "four men and a boy." This meant that the only way to remove the system from its shipping pallet was for four men to lift the unit and a boy to slide out the pallet before the four men carefully lowered the computer to the floor.

The Micro/PDP-11 is a good example of a product whose design did not facilitate easy unpacking. The computer weighed approximately 70 pounds; it was 24.5 inches tall and only 6 inches wide. It had front and rear snap-on panels that were relatively fragile. Therefore, to keep the box stable and to protect the front and rear panels during shipping, the packaging engineer designed a shipping container that required the unit to be placed on its side, encased in a corrugated sleeve. Then, to help people unpack it, we developed unpacking illustrations that showed people how to tip the box on its side and remove the packing materials, and presto, the unit itself was in its upright position (see Figure 3).

This may have been a fine idea for protecting the computer system during shipment, but during usability testing, we observed big problems with unpacking. Unpackers did not always identify which side was the correct side—they tended to tip the box to the wrong side, thereby ending up with their computer sitting exactly upside down. We tried to fix this problem with more specific arrows and clearer illustrations, but with limited success, because some unpackers never looked at the unpacking illustrations. No matter how large, clear, and carefully placed the unpacking illustrations were, they did not always work.

We observed three general types of behavior during unpacking tests:

- Some unpackers studied the illustrations carefully and tried to follow them. These seemed to be a clear minority.

- Some unpackers took a general glance at the illustrations to get the "gist" of the unpacking and then proceeded without trying to discern exact details.

- Significant numbers of unpackers ignored the illustrations completely. They tended to cut the bands and start lifting the contents straight out of the box.

Figure 3 Unpacking Illustrations for the Micro/PDP-11

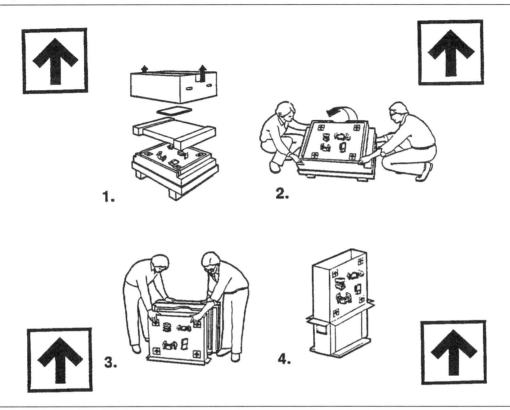

Readers might wonder why we did not add words to make the unpacking instructions clearer. The reason is the same as was discussed for product labeling previously. At Digital, no words are used in unpacking illustrations printed on the outside of a shipping container because a Digital system may be shipped to any location in the world. The cost of printing and coordinating use of language-specific unpacking instructions is prohibitive. This constraint certainly increases the design challenge, because even international packaging symbols are not always interpreted properly. For example, one packaging symbol is a square with an arrow inside, intended to indicate "this way *up*," as shown at each corner of the unpacking illustrations in Figure 3. In one unpacking test we performed with these international symbols, a package handler looked at a box sitting with the arrow symbol pointing down. When asked, this package handler said he thought it must mean, "this way *down*," because that was the way the box was sitting.

The experience with the Micro/PDP-11 shipping container taught us two general lessons. First, design products with their shipping and handling in mind. Making a fragile or unstable product easy to unpack may be impossible. Second, design shipping containers that build on people's knowledge of how to unpack things. We came to understand that people have a strong sense that they know how to handle and unpack boxes—they have been unpacking things for most of their lives. Unpacking should require as few special steps as possible.

Figure 4   Unpacking Illustrations for the MicroVAX II

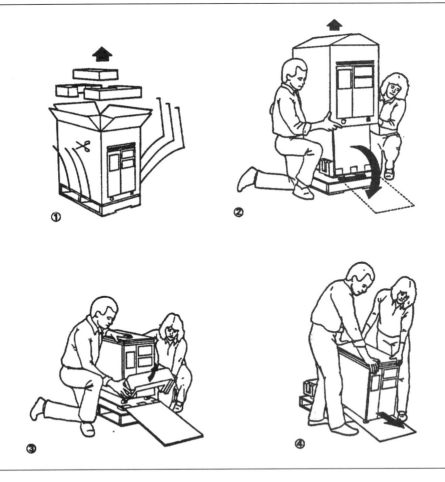

A much improved packaging scheme was developed for the MicroVAX products (see Figure 4) and used for the VAX 4000 and the DEC 4000 AXP, with alterations to accommodate their different sizes and weights. The systems are designed with casters or wheels and more rugged panels. Unpackers open the shipping container "like a regular box," remove the top contents and the corrugated sleeve, and then roll the system down the ramp off the shipping pallet.

Answering Immediate Design Questions

Sometimes usability professionals must conduct quick, unplanned usability studies to answer immediate design questions. For example, the DEC 4000 AXP is the heaviest "pedestal" system Digital has developed (about 250 pounds), and there were many concerns about whether it could be supported on its casters and moved effectively. It also requires a large volume of moving air to cool it, and the design incorporated louvers along the top front edge. We were concerned that people unpacking or moving the system might put their fingers into the louvers and use them as handholds to help maneuver the unit around corners or over cables or door sills. We received skeptical glances when we suggested this potential problem to others on the development team. It would be silly for someone to put their hands into the louvers—after all, the designers never used the louvers in this way themselves.

Our answer was to conduct a simple unpacking test with a mock-up of the system enclosure. We added lead weights to the frame to approximate the final machine weight and asked six pairs of unpackers to roll the unit down its ramps off the shipping pallet, move it over a cable on the floor, and turn it around into final position next to a wall. Figure 5 shows a collection of scenes from the videotaped sessions. By the end of the six test sessions, the louvers and top of the machine were thoroughly broken, and the engineers were convinced that the louvers needed to be significantly stronger.

Developing Easy-to-Use Instructions

The computer manuals that come with hardware systems are important to overall system usability. They help users get their jobs done and to perform tasks such as installation, operation, and repair. The biggest usability challenges are to make the manuals clear and to help users find and navigate quickly through the information they need.

Figure 5   Moving a Prototype DEC 4000 AXP

Developing clear step-by-step instructions is a skill most members of the information team (technical writers, editors, and illustrators) have developed extremely well. Usability testing is frequently a routine part of information development at Digital, and it is often an excellent tool to help "debug" the sequence of steps, the text and word usage, and the illustrations. Two examples illustrate some of the interesting findings that can arise from documentation usability testing.

We once tested the usability of a set of repair procedures that users might try on their own before calling Digital for repair service. Each procedure that involved opening up the machine began with a warning surrounded by a box, similar to those shown on the left in Figure 6. During usability testing of these repair procedures, we observed person after person skip the box with the important warning, go straight to step 1, and remove the cover without turning off the power. We were able to eliminate this dangerous behavior by incorporating the warning into the steps of the procedure, as shown on the right side of Figure 6.

Figure 6 Two examples of initial instructions. Note that those on the left did not work as well as those on the right.

Warning:
Before beginning this procedure, set the power switch to O (Off) and unplug the power cord from the wall socket.

1. Remove the top cover . . .

1. Set the power switch to O (Off).

2. Unplug the power cord from the wall socket.

3. Remove the top cover . . .

Even manuals written with very clear step-by-step instructions may make the overview of a procedure look too much like the procedure itself. In our usability testing, we have frequently seen chapters begin with a prominent bulleted list of what the chapter will guide the user to do. But the bulleted list looks so much like actual steps that users often begin struggling to perform them. Those users are surprised when they finally turn the page and see the details of how to perform step 1.

Another example of usability contributions to documentation occurred with the DEC 4000 AXP. While the design was just sheet-metal mock-ups, usability professionals worked with the technical information team to test the mock-ups. We had no documentation, no labeling, not even any outer panels on the product. Nevertheless, we brought service engineers to the development lab and asked them to explore what they saw and tell us what they could identify and what looked confusing to them. We also asked them to take the system apart as if they were replacing a failed component and tell us their impressions as they went along. One result of these early "mock-up test drives" was the beginning of the terminology list used later in the system documentation. Editors and writers who attended the sessions noted the words that service engineers used when they described the product. For example, "This looks like it must be the backplane." So it was called *backplane* in the later documentation, even though technically it might have been more correct to call it the *center plane.*

Conducting Day-One Tests

At the time of the MicroPDP-11, hardware development organizations believed that "installation" included all the steps from receipt of the hardware to turning on power and performing basic hardware diagnostics. They usually did not consider software installation to be part of the same installation sequence. This was because different organizations did software development, customers who bought a particular hardware system might want completely different software, and the hardware and software were installed by different teams of field support people. As multiuser computers became simpler, this split between hardware and software installation became less meaningful. Customers began to consider an installation incomplete until their application was running and the system was performing as intended.

At the same time, there was a major push in Digital to simplify the installation of computer systems. It was much less expensive to send just one service engineer to install a system than to send a team of two or more. Moreover, some customers wanted to save time and expense by doing the entire hardware and software installation themselves. Therefore, usability professionals, technical communicators, product managers, and developers began working on simplifying the process of installation. We found that we needed to improve things like shipping paperwork, arrangement of the contents of a shipping container, unpacking procedures, software installation and configuration, software licensing, network connections, and initial system use.

To understand and improve the whole set of activities termed *installation*, we developed a method we called *Day-One Testing*. Day-One Testing is a form of usability testing that mimics all the activities that users or field service engineers must perform to bring a system from sealed shipping containers to functioning applications. We bring participants to the lab, which we have set up to look like an ordinary office at a typical company. We ask participants to assume that they are new employees who have been hired to install and manage the new computer system. We set the stage more fully by giving them a "letter from the boss," who regrets that she cannot be there to welcome them that day but wants them to know a few things before they start. The letter then indicates that the new system from Digital has just arrived and gives a few necessary pieces of information, such as where the new system should be located and what it is expected to do.

Typically, we ask pairs of participants to work together because they feel more comfortable and naturally talk with each other as they work, thus making the observers' job easier. With the participants' permission, we videotape the sessions. There is usually no one-way mirror for Day-One Testing. Participants know they are being watched, and we have found that it is more comfortable for the participants to be able to see the observers taking notes and to speak directly to them to ensure that important information is captured. There is an extra requirement to train the observers to refrain from talking or giving hints, to take notes about everything they observe, to remain interested in the product's performance, and not to jump to premature conclusions about quick fixes. Observers then participate with the usability professionals in summarizing the results and recommendations.

Day-One Testing must be done early enough in the development process that results can be incorporated into the design. Therefore, we typically use draft manuals, shipping containers with first-draft unpacking illustrations pasted on the side, and hardware that functions only partially. Day-One Testing is sometimes difficult to arrange. We often joke that the process of setting up for a Day-One Test is like a scavenger hunt, because we have to collect or mock up all the system components to simulate arrival at a customer site. We have found that participants are surprisingly tolerant of the mock-ups. With a little ingenuity, it is possible to conduct a full Day-One Test with completely nonfunctional hardware. One technique we call the "horse-blanket" method. The participants install the nonfunctional hardware as if it worked. When they start to turn it on, we remove the "horse blanket" (or other suitable covering) from a system running prototype software and ask the participants to continue as if this new system were the piece they just installed.

Setting Usability Goals

One of the strongest lessons we learned from our focus on the ease of installing complex computer systems is the power of setting goals. Criteria for success help to define the work to be done.

Setting goals about installation instructions helped us move to easier installation of computer systems. As Rubinstein and Hersh (1984) have pointed out, a powerful form of setting goals is to "write the user's guide first." When the MicroVAX II was being designed, a typical hardware installation guide was about 30 or 40 pages long. There was general agreement among design team members who were trying to simplify installation that an ideal installation manual would take about seven or eight pages to cover everything from unpacking through system prompt. Some developers thought we should just tell the technical information team to make the manual simpler. But the information team members correctly maintained that a prerequisite to a simpler installation manual was a computer that was simpler to install. So, the technical information team, product manager, and usability professional generated a model manual that was exactly seven pages long, mostly illustrations. This manual served to make it obvious to all developers what needed to be true of the computer system itself if the goal of simple installation was to be achieved. There could be no setting of tiny DIP switches or choosing between 120 and 240 volt power settings, because each would "waste" at least a page to describe. There could be no duplication of information available elsewhere; for example, we would need to rely on the manual shipped with the video terminal for its complete installation. And the system would need to be robust enough and smart enough to come up properly without needing to set firmware parameters or perform hardware diagnostic routines.

It would be terrific to report that the final MicroVAX II installation manual was seven pages long, but the truth is that it was not. The actual installation instructions were somewhat simpler, but still required 30 pages and lots of words. Why? Too many changes in development, technology, product strategy, and Digital manufacturing and distribution would be required. For example, we wanted to eliminate the step of asking the installer to set the voltage select switch. However, because of Digital's worldwide distribution processes and available power supply technology, it would have been prohibitively expensive to make this happen. Now we use power supplies that automatically sense the proper voltage, so the step is not present in today's installation manuals.

In sum, it required several generations of products to simplify some of the complexities in the installation process. It was not until the DEC 4000 AXP, which has a simple fold-out installation card, that we achieved installation instructions for this class of workgroup machines that matched the model manual in simplicity. Nevertheless, the spirit of the model manual set a standard. It ushered in a new simplicity to installation by demonstrating what needed to be true of the system in order to support simpler installation.

Another good example of goals driving simpler installation occurred with the DEC 4000 AXP. After studying competitors' installation processes and Digital's business needs, the product manager and technical communication team set a goal of "1 hour from boxes to $." This meant a total time of 1 hour to unpack, install all the hardware, and bring up the OpenVMS operating system (whose system prompt is a $). Again, it became obvious that to achieve this goal, the computer system, the manufacturing process, and the installation process all needed to be designed to achieve ease of installation. For example, we improved the unpacking by better organizing the contents of the shipping container. We created what we dubbed the "day-one box" and the "day-two box." In the day-one box were all the items essential for the installation, such as the console terminal cable, the power cord, and the owner's guide. In the day-two box were all the items essential to ship, but which were not needed until later and which made the installation more complex if they got mixed up with the day-one items. These included things like loop-back test connectors, blank media, tape cleaning kits, and extra labels. The 1-hour goal also made it obvious that the system must ship with its disks already configured and its software already installed. In the final round of usability testing, full installations required an average of 53 minutes for pairs of first-time installers. The range was 48 to 65 minutes.

Using Methods Effectively

Not all methods that yield accurate data have equal power to bring usability into product development. Two of the characteristics of effective usability methods are whole-system testing and face validity.

We learned the importance of whole-system testing during the usability work on installation. We began doing Day-One Testing to improve the ease of installation of Digital's products. However, we quickly realized that a great deal more was occurring. The usability lab is often the first place that *all* the components of a system come together as they will at a customer site. The biggest usability problems usually occur at the interfaces between system components, where individual developers' responsibilities failed to overlap smoothly. After difficult installation sessions, we often overheard developers closing the gaps between their areas. For example, if a cable were missing from the shipment, we might have heard, "But I thought the cable was going to be shipped with the system!" "Oh. I thought the cable would be shipped with the expansion box." Whole-system testing brings a great deal of leverage to the usability testing function, because we are in a position to discover problems that otherwise would not be seen until the product arrives at the customer's site.

Effective usability methods must also have face validity—the perception by developers that a usability method fairly measures what it is supposed to measure. In a development group, design decisions are often made by consensus, and test results are only as good as their power to convince developers to make appropriate design decisions. If usability professionals push a method that team members do not trust, then the results are typically not believed and not incorporated into the design.

Day-One testing is a good example of a method with excellent face validity. Everything in the test environment simulates a customer environment almost exactly, and developers believe that any problems discovered must be corrected. An example of a test method that yielded excellent usability data, but which had poor face validity and was not overall very successful, we called *no docs* testing. The procedure is to test a product without giving the user the benefit of any manuals or online information. Results show how "robust" the product usability is, what aspects of the product are obvious without added instructions, what users' natural approach to the product is, what things they try to do first, what causes particular difficulty, and so on. Nevertheless, the method does not have sufficient face validity. Developers typically reject data from this kind of usability testing with arguments such as, "But users *should* always have the manual available. Testing without the manual is not valid." Therefore, we use this method very sparingly, only when it is clear why no manual is provided, such as in the development of product terminology.

Extending Usability into Development Practices

Usability work can improve more than specific products; it can also improve product development and management practices. The usability work on easy installation has been instrumental in changing management and product development processes at Digital in two major and very different ways.

First, the work on simplification of the installation process has been summarized in an internal Digital standard called *Customer Installability: Product Requirements*. This document, which is owned and maintained by a member of the Usability Expertise Center, specifies what must be true of all Digital customer-installable hardware and software products worldwide. For products not intended to be installed by customers, the standard serves as a guideline to help achieve ease of installation.

Second, a new method was born to increase awareness of the importance of usability. During Day-One Testing of the MicroVAX and VAX 4000 products, we were asked by engineering teams to include particular high-level Digital managers as participants in the Day-One Test sessions. At first, our inclination was to protest that, "They are not members of the target audience for the installation of this product." But we came to see that the purpose of usability testing is not always to improve a product design. Sometimes what needs to be improved are the development processes and priorities set in an organization. The managers are in the best position to effect change in these processes and priorities. Therefore, it is extremely valuable to give them an experience that raises their awareness of the usability of the products for which they are responsible.

We now use a method called *School of Marketing* to give high-level managers and developers a firsthand experience using Digital products to solve a representative customer problem. The name was first used by Ken Olsen, the founder of Digital, who set up similar exercises for his top managers, believing that the best marketing education occurs when people "walk in the shoes of the customer." We run School of Marketing sessions very similarly to usability test sessions, with the following exceptions: participants are not representative members of the user population, the products included in the session are already being shipped or close to being shipped, and the focus is on learning by the participants, not on fixing any particular product.

The process of setting up and conducting a School of Marketing exercise is often very difficult. Consensus must be built among product developers, who want their products to be represented fairly and to look good. Results must be treated especially carefully to avoid confusion with usability testing. But the results of School of Marketing sessions can be dramatic. Frequently, participants request further usability work for their own product development organization. Some participants have launched new programs to incorporate usability throughout their group's development process. And the sessions are extremely memorable for the participants; we have heard anecdotes from these sessions related passionately in conversations. For example, nearly two years later, we heard one manager describing how in her School of Marketing session she typed INSTALL instead of the VMS command INSTAL and how difficult it was to discover that a correct command was a misspelled word.

Case Study 2: Establishing Contextual Inquiry as Part of Development Practice

In contrast to the first case study, the second case study focuses on the creation and integration of a usability method into Digital's development processes. We believe that in addition to improving the design of products, usability professionals need to influence the development process. In the first case study we pointed out how lessons learned on single products were incorporated into large-scale programs. We also discussed methods, such as the School of Marketing, that were designed not only to produce changes in a product but also changes in the thinking of development managers. The second case study chronicles our efforts to systematize a discovery-oriented methodology called *Contextual Inquiry* into Digital's culture.

In this section, we describe the environment in which Contextual Inquiry developed and why we saw it as filling a fundamental need. Then, we briefly define Contextual Inquiry and describe its three fundamental principles with examples from development efforts. We then discuss the origin and evolution of our Contextual Inquiry training program. Finally we briefly illustrate the incorporation of Contextual Inquiry into our general development processes.

Developing a Holistic View of Usability

We did not seek out a new method for the sake of change. Rather, around 1987, we saw some of the limitations in our current approaches to usability. At that time, our approach was characterized by defining and setting usability goals with a product development team, followed by testing early versions of the product against these goals in a lab. We would then report to the development team the problems that users experienced and the overall performance of the system in relation to the goals and metrics we had jointly set. We called this approach *usability engineering* (Good *et al.*, 1986), and it is currently well described in Chapter 4 of Jakob Neilsen's usability engineering book (Nielsen, 1993). This was one of the most effective approaches we had used to date. We worked with development teams to set the specific usability metrics for each product. In terms of those metrics, we were producing measurable usability improvements of approximately 30% (Whiteside, Bennett, and Holtzblatt, 1988). However, we were beginning to have doubts about our effectiveness in a broader product context.

Specifically, products that we had viewed as usability successes were not succeeding in the marketplace. We recognized that the usability tasks and metrics that we were developing with design teams were too narrow and did not reflect complete customer needs. For example, we were able to greatly improve window-related operations in a particular workstation interface. However, the interface was not a true direct manipulation environment and was not competitive. Our reflection on the overall failure of this product in the face of what we had viewed as a most successful usability effort led us to question our basic approach of defining usability in terms of operational measures.

At this point, we began to see usability more holistically. We realized that the success of usability tests of the type we had been conducting rested on the relevance of the task to actual customer needs. We saw that in addition to usability (i.e., how the product is used), we needed to consider the usefulness (i.e., what the product can do; Gould, Boies, and Lewis, 1991). In fact, we came to believe that an effective approach to usability required a much broader understanding of the customers' work and environment than our laboratory-based tests were providing. We realized that the effectiveness of usability engineering and product design rested on this broader understanding. Thus, we began searching for methods that would produce a more holistic understanding of customer work in its environment. As a result, we developed Contextual Inquiry.

Contextual Inquiry is an interpretive field-research approach encompassing a number of specific techniques. We see it as rooted in an overall philosophical approach that looks at systems holistically, takes an integrated approach to the development of understanding, and reflects a bent toward discovery as compared to evaluation, validation, or confirmation. We see it as part of a family of methods that adopt a modern stance with respect to the possibility of knowledge—understanding cannot be split from the methods that are used to gather that understanding. In other words, Contextual Inquiry is one way to "know the user"; how you go about knowing determines in part what you can learn.

Three concepts provide the framework for the practice and theory of Contextual Inquiry: *context*, *partnership*, and *focus*. In the sections that follow, we discuss each concept and illustrate how it has been applied in actual design examples.

Seeing Work in Its Natural Context

We believe that understanding the *context* of work is a prerequisite for effective design. Simply seeing work in its natural environment has broadened the horizons of a number of development teams. For example, one team was developing process control software. They needed to alert the operator's attention to any aspect of the process that was out of bounds and thought a flashing red warning would work well. It certainly was salient to a designer working at a single workstation. However, when the design team visited a customer, they found that operators worked in front of a bank of 16 screens. Amid all this visual clutter, a single flashing message was lost.

In another case, a design team was working on a network diagnostic system for a nationwide communications company. The development team assumed that the appropriate display for such a network would be a nationwide map showing the network connections throughout the United States. When they observed work in the customer's context, they found that the network company organizes their network according to customer accounts. It was much more important for them to know *who* was experiencing network problems than *where* those problems were occurring, because the first stage of dealing with a network problem is to contact the customer. Often problems were resolved with this initial contact. This organization of the user interface in terms of *who* instead of *where* came as a surprise to the development team, but it was absolutely necessary as a first step in design.

Philosophically, context implies that the meaning of things is embedded in the environment in which they exist. Within this framework, understanding what words mean involves understanding the culture and environment into which they are woven. For example, one customer said, "I need to share data with my colleagues." The sales team and engineers took *sharing data* to mean "I need to be able to ship a file from one workstation to another easily and reliably." The customer certainly meant that they need a reliable network, but also they meant considerably more. To them *sharing data* meant being able to exchange data between spreadsheets of different vendors without losing information. Understanding the deeper meaning of *sharing data* entails understanding words in context.

Simply visiting customers is not sufficient to understand their context. The request to share data was made at a customer site but was misinterpreted by members of the sales team. Although sales teams and engineers visit customers on a regular basis. They often talk to customers outside their work context—in a well-appointed conference room or over an elegant dinner. In contrast, by looking at actual work or reviewing real case studies, engineers and designers learn to appreciate the "web of meaning" in which customer requests are embedded.

When it is not possible to study work in its full context, there are a number of ways to "reproduce" the customers' context. To study processes that take place over time we use a method called an artifact walk-through. This process produces a map of a customer's work flow and environment by conducting a review of a specific case. We use artifacts such as memos, forms, and reports to ground the review of that case. We recruit a team from the customer's site and review the case from multiple perspectives. A map of the case is produced during the review as a concrete representation of events, actions, and decisions in the case.

Thus, while it is expensive to send development teams to see their customers' work environments, we see it as a critical aspect of development. To gain insights into customers' work and to appreciate their insight, we need to study that work in context.

Forming Partnerships with Users

The second major concept in Contextual Inquiry is *partnership*. Unfortunately, many of our methods for understanding customers involve no mutual participation and coownership between the designer and the user or customer. Characterizing users by education level, familiarity with computers, or work motivation, while possibly important for design, represents a detached and abstracted way of understanding people. In contrast, Contextual Inquiry begins with the premise that users are expert at their work (Figure 7). The design of systems starts with an understanding of that work and ends with technological artifacts that support that work and its goals.

Development teams have made a number of discoveries by treating customers as partners. In a recent example, a user being interviewed about debugging said that he wanted "aliasing" in his tools. The interviewer (a software engineer) "knew" what aliasing meant but decided to ask the user what was meant by aliasing. The user then proceeded to describe not only aliasing but also customization of the existing interface, the ability to extend the system by teaching it command sequences, and several other important features. Treating the user as a partner in the investigation was critical to uncovering these insights.

Figure 7   Conducting a Contextual Interview

In another example, a hardware design team was interviewing its "customers"—the workers at an assembly plant. As part of establishing partnership, the interviewers showed examples of their own work, such as component packaging. In this way, they created an opening for the assemblers to discuss their work as equals. The result of these visits was not only richer data but also an enthusiasm on the part of the manufacturing organization for more such visits. Initial concerns over whether assemblers would have anything to say were dispelled.

Some teams make partnership an aspect of their full development process. For example, TeamLinks™ (a client-server tool providing services such as e-mail, file sharing, and workflow managment to workgroups) for the Macintosh™ established an ongoing partnership with a carefully chosen group of customers. These customers participated in initial requirements gathering and rating, in an iterative series of user interface and functionality prototypes throughout development, and in final field test. The result was not only a product that was well received by customers but also a product whose development schedule was shortened through effective rating of features, which used familiar metaphors to introduce concepts and had a consistent and effective interface (Huntwork *et al.*, 1993).

Customers and users like to be interviewed as partners. They appreciate the opportunity to have input into the product development and to be treated as equals and listened to during the interview. Once they have experienced a contextual interview, they tend to be enthusiastic supporters of the process. For example, upon seeing the suggestions from an interview incorporated into the product, a TeamLinks participant said, "Boy you are really listening to us."

This concept of partnership serves a philosophical-political purpose: to give users and customers control of their work, even while supplying them with tools that transform it. It also changes the way researchers, engineers, and designers interact with customers. Interviews do not follow a detailed script, and interviewees can change the direction of an interview based on their work experience.

Empowering users and interviewees to direct the flow of an interaction is countercultural. Both journalists and social scientists often pride themselves on taking an objective approach, controlling the interview, and following their script. Similarly, a maxim in court proceedings is "don't ask a question unless you already know the answer." In contrast to the objective approach, in Contextual Inquiry interviewers learn from their partnership with users.

Focusing Data Gathering

Finally, *focus* introduces the idea that data gathering must have a considered and explicit goal. This goal is dependent on the design team's current understanding that a design team has of their clients and the teams information needs. Focus means that design team members need to make their assumptions and prejudices explicit and shared within the team. It also means that they must be prepared to change these assumptions and beliefs in the face of conflicting evidence from customers. Finally, from a practical perspective, it sets the boundaries on an interaction with customers or users and determines the processes used.

For example, with one focus we may visit a customer to learn about the use of a tool—how it supports work or gets in the way. With another focus, we may visit a customer to understand the factors involved and the process used in making a purchasing decision. In each case, we talk to different people and use a different process.

Focus evolves throughout the development process. For example, in the TeamLinks for Macintosh example, the team began with a broad focus of understanding customer needs. To its surprise, specific features of the product were overshadowed by customer concerns about how the product would fit into the existing work environment. In addition, the focus of these early inquiries differed depending what type of customer the development team was talking to. For information services managers the focus was on their office strategy; for end users the focus was on how people worked as a team sharing data and communicating with each other. Later the focus became more specific, and we studied particular business practices using our artifact walk-through technique to provide the basis for prototypes. Finally, as development progressed, the focus changed to the look and feel of the user interface, which was explored through a series of prototypes. In another example, in the early stages of our work with DEC RALLY™ (a fourth-generation product development environment), we began with a very broad focus of understanding work with the current product. This broad focus uncovered the importance of displaying long variable names. While the problem had been noted by the development group, its significance was not appreciated until we showed a video of customers experiencing the problem and explaining how they could not use the typical work-around (shorten the variable names). (These examples are described in greater detail in Huntwork *et al.*, 1993, and Wixon and Jones, 1994.)

From a philosophical perspective, *focus* emphasizes the need for clarity, explicitness, and openness in the design process. It suggests that there is a relation between the breadth of focus and the ability to discover new things. The less restrictive our search, the more likely we are to learn unexpected things. We believe that our usability methods can be ordered according the breadth of their focus. Early experimental work had a very narrow focus, which was testing a hypothesis about some particular feature. Usability engineering work had a broader focus of uncovering the problems users had in completing a specific task. Finally, in Contextual Inquiry, the role of focus is recognized explicitly, and we urge teams to set a broad focus to make space for discovering what user work is really like.

Collecting and Analyzing Contextual Inquiry Data

In general, Contextual Inquiry interviews of users take place while they work and last between 1.5 and 2 hours. We urge interviewers to work in pairs. Each member of a pair has a different role: one is the primary interviewer and the other takes notes. Pairing provides a basis for sharing the information teams gather. We also urge teams to visit as many sites as possible and to maximize the diversity of the sites they visit.

In practice, the number of sites visited typically ranges from three to ten. The number of interviews conducted has been as few as 5 and as many as 110.

The raw data from a Contextual Inquiry consist of videotapes, transcribed audio-tapes, or notes. We use a variety of methods in analyzing these data. Sometimes results are directly incorporated into products. It can be enough simply to show the development team a videotape of a user struggling with a system. In other cases, the analysis of the data is much more formal. For example, a team may use the data from a Contextual Inquiry to provide input into a Quality Function Deployment planning matrix. In this case, the team uses a bottom-up process to group the data into a hierarchical structure reflecting customer needs. This structure then serves as one axis of the QFD planning matrix (Cohen, 1988; Zultner, 1993). This planning matrix will help the team make decisions about which customer needs to address and what features could address these needs. If the team is ready to begin product design, they may use the data from a Contextual Inquiry to construct a model of user work.

Developing the Contextual Inquiry Course

In 1987, there were four or five usability professionals actually conducting contextual interviews. We operated as consultants conducting studies for client product groups. Both we and our clients saw a need to extend the practice of Contextual Inquiry beyond this small number of practitioners.

We came to believe that many products and systems could benefit from conducting a Contextual Inquiry. However, as long as we operated on a consulting basis, the application of this method was limited in several ways. First, we were providing development teams with only a copy of the customer and user experience. We were acting as filters—picking sections of videotape to show, organizing our reports in terms of problems or requests, and generally digesting and synthesizing the data. We concluded it would be better if we could get the development teams themselves to directly experience their customers' work. Not only would the results be more compelling, but they would also be richer and more diverse. Because developers often had a better feeling for what could be done with the technology, they would see more possibilities in the work situation. Second, we knew that there would be a only limited number of us in comparison to the number of development efforts that could benefit from such an approach. We concluded that if we could adequately train engineers, product managers, and information providers to do Contextual Inquiry, we could greatly broaden its range of application and enrich the results for each group.

At the same, time a number of groups were asking if they could learn to do Contextual Inquiry. For example, quality organizations in Digital had existed for a number of years and had brought valuable technologies such as code inspections and Quality Factor Deployment (QFD) into Digital. They contributed to the development of Contextual Inquiry and saw its broader application to an overall development process. In addition, teams with whom we had worked expressed an interest in having their engineers and information providers learn the methodology. In response to these needs, we developed a Contextual Inquiry course.

Development of the training began with a commitment to both teach the concepts of Contextual Inquiry and to provide users with the experience of doing an interview and organizing the data from that interview. By providing both theory and practice, students would be able to adapt Contextual Inquiry methods to the specific needs of their development project. At the same time, the course included a number of concepts borrowed from usability engineering, usability in general, and a broader philosophical perspective provided by the work of people like Pelle Ehn (1988) and Kim Masden (Kensing and Masden, 1991). The course was also influenced by the experience of the team as consultants in user interface design; thus many of its examples and concepts were drawn from experience. We also wanted to keep the course relatively short; thus, we developed a one-day course.

Demand for the course grew to the point where dozens of courses were being taught each year. The practitioners who were teaching the course felt overwhelmed with the demand. One of the initial developers and the instructor who had taught the most courses developed a "train-the-trainer" curriculum to develop a set of certified trainers and practitioners. Since then, six instructors have been certified both in the United States and Europe. Consistent with the overall approach of Contextual Inquiry, certification involves both learning to teach the course materials and conducting and managing a project that uses Contextual Inquiry. This certification processes provides the instructors with a firsthand experience of the method and with a set of examples that go beyond those provided in the instructor notes for the course.

While Contextual Inquiry had been successfully applied by usability professionals and people with a background in field research, it was not clear how well it would transfer to people with different backgrounds. We felt that it was necessary to monitor the effectiveness of the Contextual Inquiry training in three ways:

- We surveyed each class immediately after the training to determine their reaction to the course.

- We informally kept track of teams and how Contextual Inquiry had worked for them.

- We surveyed the course participants systematically each year to assess if they had put their training to use and how effective it was.

Improving the Contextual Inquiry Course

Hearing the Anecdotes

While a number of teams were reporting success in conducting Contextual Inquiries, there were also a number of disturbing reports coming back. In one case, an engineer conducting an inquiry left the participant alone with the system while he went off to take a shower. He returned and ate breakfast in the her presence while she was working, ignoring broad hints from the participant such as "a cup of coffee would sure taste good now." Clearly, there was no partnership in this interview. We also heard reports that engineers were saying "We can't talk during a contextual interview." The course materials emphasized the importance of not "explaining" the system to the participant, but we had never intended to say that the interviewer should be totally silent. Clearly, certain distinctions and concepts were not getting across in our course materials.

Another series of anecdotes came from an external consultant's evaluation of one team's product development efforts. The evaluation pointed out several ways in which Contextual Inquiry failed for this team.

- The focus for the team was very broad and somewhat unclear. Without a clearly stated focus that the group shared, the quality of the data varied considerably from interview to interview.

- The team collected data that was seen as irrelevant to this particular project.

- Partnership was not established with some participants. Specifically, interviewers did not explain that interviews would be done as the participants worked. As a result, a number of interviews were simply broad discussions of features that the customer liked and disliked in the current product. The critical aspect of Contextual Inquiry of having the customer do real work and illustrating their requests while working on the system was missing in these cases.

We also found that some groups were setting a focus that was too narrow and not constructed in a way that would uncover useful information. In these cases, the focus was a list of specific questions, which would serve as a detailed script for a traditional interview. In addition, often the questions asked a participant for an abstract conclusion about an aspect of the product. For example one question was, "How did you like the documentation for product X?" This was not what we meant by a focus. A list of specific evaluative questions sacrifices partnership because it makes the participant the subject of an interrogation controlled by the interviewer. Thus, the interviewee cannot be a coparticipant helping to set the direction of the interview within a framework provided by the interviewer.

At the same time, evaluative questions ask interviewees to draw abstract conclusions using scales that are unspoken and unknown to the interviewer. The question, "How did you like the documentation?" may generate the answer "I like it," but it may not be clear what the participant is using as a basis for evaluation; for example, "The documentation is great—carrying it around is good exercise" or "It looks attractive." Even if the interviewee states a reason for liking the documentation such as "It has a good index," it is still not clear what makes the index good. Questions more consistent with the thrust of Contextual Inquiry would be: "How did you learn to use the system?" "Where do you go for information?" "Can you show me a typical example of when you would look for information?" These represent a focus on providing information combined with a commitment to learn how the participant seeks such information.

Finally, during the course, students had asked about how to study work that took place over a period of time, involved a group of people, or could not be interrupted by questions. Students had also asked about how to apply the interview method when new technology that had never been seen before was involved. To address each of these concerns, we developed a range of methods (post observation inquiry, artifact walk-though, future scenario, and prototype testing), but we had not yet fully incorporated them into the course.

Conducting Systematic Surveys

We conducted surveys after each course and a set of surveys a year later. In surveys that followed the course, students filled in a number of scaled questions concerning the quality of the materials, the delivery and knowledge of the instructor, whether they would recommend the course to others, and so on. There were also some open-ended questions: "What did you like most about the course?" and "Where would you suggest improvements?" Results from the postcourse survey were generally positive. (We report question, median response, and percentages in the left three columns of Table 2.)

The open-ended questions produced a number of positive statements, such as

- (the materials for the exercises were) "inspired, perfect"
- "an excellent tool for gathering and sorting customer information"
- "It presents an approach for gathering and analyzing customer information that should help solve problems I've seen in trying to gather and analyze customer data"
- "solidifies understanding of the listening process"
- "I learned a lot about the actual techniques"
- "good use of examples"

- "clear and concise format"
- "I liked the exercises and the interactiveness during the lecture part"
- "very informative and fun"
- "kept my attention and penetrated"
- "I would not change anything"
- "Delivery was clear and concise"

Table 2   Contextual Inquiry Course Survey Results

Question	Median Response	Percent of Responses in Previous Course	Percent of Responses in Revised Course
How well organized were the course materials?	Well organized	43%	57%
How would you rate the instructor's knowledge of the materials?	Very good	42%	77%
What did you think of the course length?	Just long enough	63%	78%
Will you recommend this course to others?	Yes	80%	91%

There were also a number of changes suggested. For example, a number of people felt that the course was too conceptual and that there were not enough practical exercises. As one student put it, "Skip the commercial, and show me how to do it." Other students found that sections that briefly described related methods (such as QFD) were not useful. The general sentiment was that we should include enough material to do these methods justice or leave them out entirely.

In addition to the surveys immediately after the course, we conducted a yearly follow-up survey with people who had taken the course to find if they had put the methods into practice and, if not, what had stood in their way. We found that about

45% of those responding actually used Contextual Inquiry. A number of factors beyond our control, such as a lack of management support or funding or not working on product definition, were reasons for not conducting Contextual Inquiry. However, there were also factors we could address. For example, almost a third of those responding found the class "insufficient preparation for conducting a Contextual Inquiry." They had trouble setting a focus, and they asked for additional help in planning a Contextual Inquiry, interpreting and synthesizing data, and applying Contextual Inquiry more broadly to areas like process design.

Developing a New Course

Taking all this information into account, we decided that we needed to revise the course and that we had to strike a delicate balance between preserving the strengths of the initial course and addressing the problems we had uncovered. To do so we used a QFD like process to rank our goals for changes to the course; in priority order they were

- Increase the proportion of students who use Contextual Inquiry after taking the course.
- Eliminate the complaint that there is too much conceptual material.
- Provide more skill training.
- Eliminate complaints about insufficient coverage of other methods.
- Eliminate the perception that this is "just common sense."
- Provide a better understanding of the application of new methods such as artifact walk-through.

We then evaluated the extent to which a number of changes would fulfill these goals and decided that the following changes had the highest leverage:

- Expand the discussion of other methods like artifact walk-through.
- Add a section on setting a focus.
- Eliminate much of the material about generic usability issues (this would also broaden the scope of the course).
- Eliminate sections describing related methods while expanding sections that dealt with the "flow" of Contextual Inquiry data into these methods.

We then revised the course and evaluated the effectiveness of the new course.

At the time of this writing, the new course is less than one year old and so we have only course evaluations and anecdotes to report. However, the response has been positive. The results from the evaluations are presented in Table 2 (the left two columns reflect questions and median response, the third column reflects evaluations from the previous response, and the right column reflects evaluations for the revised course.)

The qualitative responses to our questions also indicate that we have eliminated some of the chronic complaints with the course. Finally, our anecdotes are also more positive. Students report that they have successfully used the method in their projects. We have not heard that the previous problems (such as too broad or too narrow focus for studies) are still occurring.

Using Contextual Inquiry in Development

Contextual Inquiry has been widely adopted in Digital. It has been applied to software, hardware, documentation, and internal processes and procedures. A number of groups have not only used the methods, but have developed supporting materials and extended the approach. We will present a few of the examples.

Over the life of the course we have trained over 1000 people. We conduct more than 12 classes a year, with most of those for intact teams (the entire class is from a single team). We prefer to teach intact teams because we believe that training all the members of a team increases the likelihood that the team will actually use the method. We often train groups "just in time," that is within a week of their upcoming customer visit. We have also developed variants of the course to meet the needs of specific teams. At the same time we have begun to offer the Contextual Inquiry course to Digital customers.

A number of parallel developments have contributed to the effectiveness of Contextual Inquiry. First, several Digital groups have implemented ongoing programs of customer visits. For example, the OpenVMS™ group regularly visits customer sites and reports to other group members on their experiences. It has developed a customer visits guide that gives a step-by-step approach to getting the most out of their customer visits. The group's approach builds on their background in Contextual Inquiry but has elaborated and extended it beyond its roots. Their document, *Customer Visits Guide*, describes not only how to plan and conduct a customer visit but also how to interview and analyze data from a Contextual Inquiry perspective. It has conducted a series of visits throughout the development cycle. These visits have involved both requirements gathering and prototype testing. In the course of these visits customer feedback has given the group cause to rethink its previous plans and assumptions. It is planning on continuing these contacts. It views this as a form of continuous field testing.

Similarly, groups whose charter includes fostering software quality have incorporated Contextual Inquiry into their practice. They have developed courses such as

Voice of the Customer that introduce many of the principles and practices of Contextual Inquiry. They have also contributed many examples to our collection of case studies.

Responses to Contextual Inquiry from both development groups and customers have been positive. Specifically, managers have told us that debriefing within the team after visits generated dozens of solutions and ideas. They have also pointed out that the experience of doing a Contextual Inquiry project together gave the engineers a broader picture and produced an "esprit de corps." In other cases, the findings from Contextual Inquiry have helped to redirect product development efforts, reducing time to profit and increasing customer satisfaction. In the specific case of TeamLinks for the Macintosh the development manager said: "Without this approach we would have spent 18 months and $2 million to build an uncompetitive product."

In contrast to this disaster scenario, the responses by customers to the actual TeamLinks for Macintosh product are very positive, for example:

- "I thoroughly enjoyed testing the product. I am definitely going to buy it." (major government contractor)
- "It looks like a winner." (large pharmaceutical company)
- "Easy to use, our whole branch will want this; it is exactly what I've imagined and desired for months." (agency of the United States government)

Beyond its direct influence on products, Contextual Inquiry has influenced a number of other methods. Even simple and inexpensive approaches such as telephone surveys tend to have more open-ended questions and allow for more participant direction. Similarly, Contextual Inquiry has been combined with methods such as QFD, Vector Comparative Analysis (Raven and Wixon, 1992; a method for evaluating competitive products), and using prototypes to produce hybrid methods that are stronger than their parents. In fact, Contextual Inquiry has been incorporated into the recently developed and recommended process for software development.

Contextual Inquiry has also been applied beyond its initial scope of product development. It has been used to study the sales process and internal support functions. One of our largest Contextual Inquiry projects is currently taking place in personnel, where 36 investigators interviewed over 50 managers with respect to Digital's personnel services. The department will be producing people process models for a number of personnel functions and use information from Contextual Inquiry interviews to redesign people support services from the point of view of the manager.

We have found that by sharing some methods we can greatly increase our effectiveness. However, the effectiveness of such sharing depends on the careful monitoring of the lessons taken away by development teams and their effectiveness in applying them. The effectiveness of sharing a method also depends on the method itself. For example we developed a highly rated course on usability engineering and supplemented it with a handbook. But, we found that usability engineering was not widely practiced outside the group of usability practitioners. While we cannot be sure of the reason, one possibility is that usability engineering is a highly refined method that requires some special background (such as experimental design) and has a precise focus of application (improving usability of products). In contrast, Contextual Inquiry applies more broadly and is easier to adopt because it is closely related to values held by teams (understand your customers) and it is based on more easily understood skills (conducting an open-ended interview).

Finally to ensure ongoing support for the growing community of Contextual Inquiry course instructors and partictioners, we implemented an electronic conference and bimonthly Contextual Inquiry forum meetings. The forum is the core group that planned the revisions of the course and continues to be a source for development of new methods within the Contextual Inquiry framework.

Lessons We Learned

In addition to the specific lessons described in each of the case studies, our experience with workgroup computers and Contextual Inquiry led us to the following recommendations:

- Use multiple methods, hybridize them, and invent new ones to get the usability work done.
- Use a convincing method rather than the "right" method.
- Study work in context, and design and test together all interacting aspects of a whole system.
- Recognize which product development constraints can be changed and which cannot. Work within constraints that cannot be changed to find an acceptable solution.
- Develop good negotiation and teamwork skills for working with large, complex, and diverse development organizations.
- Employ simple and straightforward system usability goals.
- Treat users as partners in design.
- Work to improve processes and priorities, not just products.
- Spread appropriate methods through effective training programs.

Our experience at Digital suggests that usability work in a corporation changes along several dimensions as it matures. At the beginning, when usability is novel and needs to be sold to developers, usability professionals tend to focus on a relatively limited set of methods, such as giving expert advice to product developers and conducting usability studies. The work draws on its academic roots. Success depends on things like prestige, visibility in the corporation, and high-level sponsorship.

As usability professionals become more experienced with the specific corporate cultures in which they are working, they expand their methods, apply them more effectively, develop new and hybrid methods, and tune their work to ensure that it is as effective as possible. They share their methods widely. Basic usability work is likely to be done by developers in a wide range of professions, not just usability professionals.

In general, we have seen a strong tendency for our methods and contributions to move toward the early stages of the development process, thus moving us more to discovery and decision as compared to evaluation. One reason for this is that the early stages of development are where one can get the best leverage because other types of work (such as decision, design, and analysis) rest on the foundation of understanding created at the discovery stage.

Products will come and go, design methods will evolve, and tools will improve. We expect that, as technology and corporations change, so also will the professional practice of usability. Usability methodologies will become more tightly integrated with the development process and will benefit from cross-fertilization from other fields (such as art and anthropology). We also anticipate breakthroughs in user interface technology. All these trends will challenge usability professionals as they design tomorrow's products and processes.

Acknowledgments

The success of usability at Digital is due to the work of many people. We would like to gratefully acknowledge some of the work that has contributed to the material discussed in this chapter.

Case Study 1 represents the work of Betsy Comstock and many others. Charlie Abernethy, Stew Beckley, Anne Clemens, Nancy Clark Dorsey, Diane Hodes, Linda Hoffberg, Stacie Krafczek, Bob Morse, Jon Mysel, Jackie Schrier, and Sarah Webber conducted Day-One Tests or contributed to the development of the method. Debbie Falck, Diane Hodes, Linda Jaynes, and Anne Parshall provided insights that supported the work with symbols. Maria Falkner, Bob Hanson, Marcus Koepke, Karen Korellis, and Stuart Morgan were among the gifted industrial designers whose contributions were essential to the usability of the workgroup computers discussed here. The hardware user interface for DEC 4000 AXP could not have been successful without the contributions of Brad Chapin, Mike Collins, Ernie Crocker, Judy Hall, Karen Korellis, Len Kreidermacher, and Dave Symmes. Nan Bulger, Brian McBride, and Dave Porter worked hard to maximize usability in their shipping container designs. Jackie Schrier's ideas led to the discussion of face validity. Mike Miller conducted the study of the ease of moving the DEC 4000 AXP. Rich Clayton conducted the DEC 4000 AXP mock-up testing. Stew Beckley, Pat Billingsley, Anne Clemens, Peter Conklin, Debbie Falck, Judy Hall, Mary Utt, and many technical writers, editors, and illustrators made major contributions to the work described here. Nan Bulger, Mary Ellen Connell, Judy Hall, Susan Marsh, Kathe Rhoades, Joyce Snow, Rich Trubey, and Bob Young were instrumental in achieving the installation goals for the DEC 4000 AXP. Bill Bazemore ensured that the Digital standard on customer installation was written and maintained. Peter Conklin, Rich Clayton, Cristina Davy, Ralph Dormitzer, Nancy Clark Dorsey, Judy Hall, and Jean Sifleet supported the development of the School of Marketing techniques.

Many people have contributed to the development and growth of Contextual Inquiry at Digital. John Whiteside provided inspiration and support for the original development of Contextual Inquiry. Karen Holtzblatt developed the concepts of Contextual Inquiry. She, Sandy Jones, and Steve Knox developed the initial Contextual Inquiry course with ideas from Lou Cohen and Russ Doane. A course for the ACM SIGCHI conference was developed by Karen Holtzblatt, Sandy Jones, Dennis Wixon, and John Bennett. Sandy Jones developed the Contextual Inquiry certification process and has trained hundreds of people inside Digital. Dennis Wixon, Minette Beabes, and Mary Beth Raven developed the revised version of the course with help from Russ Doane, Pat Lastella, Kelly Klein, Inka Rimpler, and Anne Smith Duncan. Rande Neukam suggested the artifact walk-through approach. Micheal Good has contributed numerous ideas from the domain of participatory design. A number of people have contributed case studies, new techniques, ideas, materials, and offered advice for the Contextual Inquiry program over the years, including Michelle Ackerman, Bob Buckland, Russ Doane, Steve Knox, Anthony Hutchings, Minette Beabes, Chauncey Wilson, Thomas Spine, and Suzy Cane. Chet Mitchell directed the personnel study. Anne Parshall has done some of the most extensive field work at Digital. Doug Muzzey managed the TeamLinks effort and Paul Huntwork directed several process related aspects of that work. Chris Pietras planned, managed and conducted the customer-related work in TeamLinks; she also ran the prototyping effort and directed the design work. Susan George and Connie Pawelczak directed the voice of the customer work in OpenVMS. Linda Alexander, Pam Ellis, Suzy Kane,

John Smart, Minette Beabes, Jon Rochester, Merle Roesler, Ann Dibona, John Knowles, Stephen Ralls, and Jim McAlesse developed the *Customer Visits Guide.* The Contextual Inquiry program has been supported by Digital Equipment Corporation.

In addition, we gratefully acknowledge the contributions of all the volunteers who have participated in our usability studies, all the students and practitioners of contextual inquiry, and all the generous supporters of usability throughout Digital.

We also gratefully acknowledge the following people who reviewed drafts of this chapter: Minette Beabes, Jo Ann Bennett, Stew Beckley, Michelle Chambers, Anne Smith Duncan, Alicia Flanders, Rick Frankosky, Bob Johnson, Suzy Kane, Brian McBride, Doug Muzzey, Anne Parshall, Lynda Petralia, Chris Pietras, Mary Beth Raven, Susan Schultz, Leo Treiggari, Mary Utt, Doug Muzzey, and Sarah Webber. Finally, we thank Charles Frean for video post-production and design.

Digital Equipment Corporation, Digital, DEC, VAX, Micro/PDP-11, PDP-11, MicroVAX, MicroVAX II, AXP, Alpha AXP, TeamLinks, DEC RALLY, and OpenVMS are trademarks of Digital Equipment Corporation.

Macintosh is a trademark of Apple Computer Corporation.

References

Abernethy, C. N. (1981). "Integrating Human Factors and Industrial Design, Integration at a Practical Level—A Panel Discussion," *Proc. Human Factors Society 25th Annual Meeting*, Rochester, NY, p. 117.

Comstock, E. M. (1983). "Customer Installability of Computer Products," *Proc. Human Factors Society 27th Annual Meeting*, Norfolk, VA, pp. 501-504.

Comstock, E. M., and Clemens, E. A. (1987). "Perceptions of Computer Manuals: A View from the Field," *Proc. Human Factors Society 31st Annual Meeting*, New York, pp. 139-143.

Cohen, L. (1988). "Quality Function Deployment: An Application Perspective from Digital Equipment Corporation," *National Productivity Review 7* (3), 197-208.

Ehn, P. (1988). *Work Oriented Design of Computer Artifacts.* Arbetlivscentrum, Stockholm (available from Lawerence Earlbaum Associates, Hillsdale, NJ).

Flanders, A., and Raven, M. E. (1993). "Managing for Usability," *Proc. InterChange Technical Writing Conf.*, Lowell, MA, pp. 65-67.

Good, M. (1992). "Participatory Design of a Portable Torque-Feedback Device," *Proc. ACM CHI'92 Conf.,* Monterey, CA, pp. 439-446.

Good, M., Spine, T., Whiteside, J., and George, P. (1986). "User-Derived Impact Analysis as a Tool for Usability Engineering," *Proc. ACM CHI'86 Conf.,* Boston, pp. 241-246.

Gould, J., Boies, S., and Lewis, C. (1991). "Making Usable, Useful, Productivity-Enhancing Computer Applications," *Communications of the ACM, 34* (1, January), 75-85.

Hersh, H. (1982). "Electronic Mail Usage Analysis," *Proc. Human Factors in Computer Systems,* Gaithersberg, MD, pp. 278-280.

Holtzblatt, K., and Jones, S. (1993). "Contextual Inquiry: A Participatory Technique for System Design," in D. Schuler and A. Namioka (eds.), *Participatory Design: Principles and Practice.* Lawrence Earlbaum, Hillsdale, NJ.

Huntwork, P., Muzzey, D., Pietras, C., and Wixon, D. (1993). "Changing the Rules: A Pragmatic Approach to Product Development," *Digital Technical Journal 5 (4),* Fall '93, 18–35.

Kensing, F., and Madsen, K. H. (1991). "Generating Visions: Future Workshops and Metaphorical Design, in J. Greenbaum and M. Kyng (eds.), *Design at Work.* Lawrence Earlbaum, Hillsdale, NJ.

King, B. (1989). *Better Designs in Half the Time: Implementing QFD in America.* Goal, QPC, Meuthen, Boston.

Neilsen, J. (1993). *Usability Engineering,* Academic Press, Boston.

Raven, M. E., and Wixon, D. (1992). "Total Quality Management with Vector Comparative Analysis," *Proc. 1992 IEEE Int. Professional Communication Conf.,* Santa Fe, NM, pp. 442-444.

Raven, M. E., and Beabes, M. A. (1992). "Redesigning a Help Menu Based on Usabiliy Testing," *Proc. 39th Int. Technical Communication Conf.,* Atlanta, pp. 159-162.

Rohn, J., and Braun, S., (1993). "Structuring Usability Within Organizations," *Usability Professionals Association Conf. '93,* Redmond, WA.

Rubinstein, R., and Hersh, H. (1984). *"The Human Factor: Designing Computer Systems for People.* Digital Press, Burlington, MA.

Shackel, B. (1992). "HUSAT—Twenty-one Years of HCI the Human Sciences and Advanced Technology Research Institute," *Proc. ACM CHI'92,* Monterey, CA, pp. 281-282.

Suchman, L. (1987). *Plans and Situated Actions: The Problem of Human-Machine Communication.* Cambridge University Press, New York.

Van Cott, H. P., and Kinkade, R. G. (eds.). (1972). *Human Engineering Guide to Equipment Design.* U.S. Government Printing Office, Washington, DC.

Whiteside, J., Archer, N., Wixon, D., and Good, M. (1982). "How Do People Really Use Text Editors?" *Proc. Conf. on Office Information Systems,* Philadelphia, pp. 29-41.

Whiteside, J., Bennett, J., and Holtzblatt, K. (1988). "Usability Engineering: Our Experience and Evolution," in M. Helander (ed.), *Handbook of Human Comptuer Interaction,* pp. 791-817, North Holland, New York.

Wixon, D., Holtzblatt, K., and Knox, S. (1990). "Contextual Design: An Emergent View of System Design," *Proc ACM CHI' 90 Proc.,* Seattle , WA, pp. 329-336.

Wixon, D., and Jones, S. (1994). "Usability for Fun and Profit," in P. Polson and C. Lewis (eds.), *Human Computer Interface Design: Success Cases, Emerging Methods, and Real World Context.* Forthcoming, Morgan Kaufman.

Woodson, W. E. (1981). *Human Factors Design Handbook,* McGraw-Hill Book Company, New York.

Zultner, R. E. (1993). "TQM for Technical Teams," *Communications of the ACM 36* (10, October), 79-91.

CHAPTER 7

Hewlett-Packard's Usability Engineering Program

Tom Rideout
Jay Lundell
Hewlett-Packard

Tom Rideout is the Corporate Usability Engineering Program Manager at Hewlett-Packard. He works across HP businesses to develop and improve usability engineering programs. His previous positions at HP were in managing human factors functions for HP test and measurement products and in office automation software. He received his Ph.D. in applied cognitive psychology from the University of Washington.

Jay Lundell is the lead human factors architect at Hewlett-Packard for the Common Desktop Environment. Jay has previously worked on the HP Visual User Environment (VUE) and various system administration programs and multimedia and collaboration software packages. Previous to his work at Hewlett-Packard in Corvallis he managed the human factors group at Hewlett-Packard's Fort Collins site. Jay received his Ph.D. in cognitive psychology from the University of Washington.

Introduction: Diverse Approaches to Usability Engineering

Flexibility is critical to successful usability engineering in Hewlett-Packard. For us, the most effective way to implement user-centered design has been to adapt usability engineering resources and methods to individual businesses. There are several reasons that one size would not fit all, including different product types, business needs, levels of understanding about usability engineering, work environments, and availability. Our task is to understand the circumstances within each organization so that we use methods that will provide sustainable improvements.

Diverse Product Types

Hewlett-Packard enjoys a very broad set of product lines including calculators, computers, software, medical equipment, test and measurement equipment, scientific instruments, and peripherals. This means we have virtually every imaginable type of usability engineering challenge in both physical and cognitive ergonomics. The breadth of methods that we use is partly a result of this product diversity and the different businesses and cultures associated with different product lines.

HP OmniBook

The HP OmniBook, pictured in Figure 1, required innovative design work to deliver a usable system in an ultra-light, extra-long battery-life package. The usability engineering effort on this product was a cross functional effort spearheaded by Paul Sorenson (Human Factors Engineer) and Mike Derocher (Industrial Designer), who worked as integral parts of a multidisciplinary development team. They focused their efforts on a pop-out mouse, the keyboard, and the display. The mouse pops out from a hidden storage panel.

Mouse

This team's objectives for the mobile mouse were to provide customers with instant productivity, with a comfortable built-in design. The team applied usability engineering methods from early foam-core studies, through two full iterations of testing with users from outside the division developing the product. The resulting slant-up design resulted in user performance equal to or better than the most commonly used alternative portable pointing devices.

Figure 1   HP OmniBook

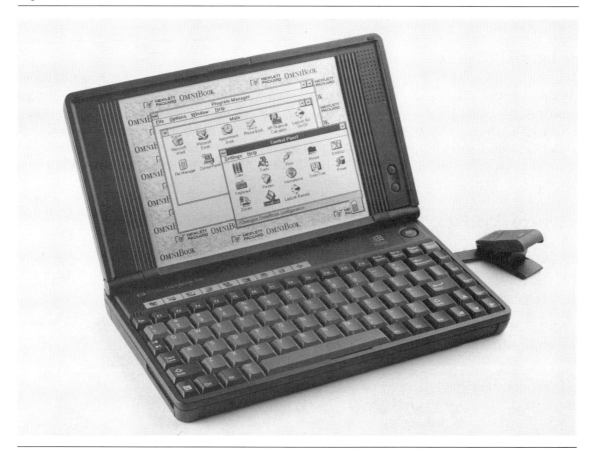

Keyboard

The team's objective for the keyboard was to produce the smallest, most portable product possible that users would perceive as equivalent to a full-size keyboard. The Human Factors Engineer tested 90%-size models and full-size models. The results showed that users consistently and strongly preferred the full-sized keyboard. We changed to a full-size design as a result of this work.

Display

The team responded to undesirable visual effects from the LCD display when they used 50 Hz European power supplies. The Human Factors Engineer worked closely with R&D engineers to identify and implement solutions. The Industrial Design and

Human Factors group built a lighting-environment simulator and developed standard methods for display evaluation for real-world lighting conditions for this and future products.

HP DeskJet 1200C™

The HP DeskJet 1200CTM color printer, pictured in Figure 2, represented an entirely different set of design challenges. It has a front panel, rather than a keyboard, and requires user interaction with print media (e.g., paper) and print cartridges. Steve Breidenbach led the usability engineering effort on this product. He joined the organization shortly before the initial prototypes for the product were built. Since there were several prototype cycles planned, he took the strategy of providing consulting followed by iterative prototype-test-refinement loops.

As with the OmniBook project, the human factors engineer became an integral part of a multidisciplinary development team. He encouraged broad participation in usability

Figure 2   HP DeskJet 1200C™ Printer

engineering with open invitations to test sessions and individual follow-up discussions on design improvements. The learning products staff assisted in the conduct of the test sessions and provided prototype instructions for the tasks addressed in the testing. The team focused on the usability of input media tray (paper tray), envelope feeding, print cartridge loading, and multilingual instructions. In all, the team completed six product usability tests prior to shipment.

Input Media Handling

The usability testing demonstrated that the team had significantly improved media tray installation as result of the work. In addition, the team made it easier to load media (e.g., paper and transparencies) correctly by adding side rails to provide good visual cues for media quantity and by designing effective icons to aid users in correctly orienting the media in the tray.

Envelope Feeding

The team added an angled width-adjustment guide and icons that made it easier to load envelopes in the manual feed slot at the top of the printer.

Print Cartridge Loading

The team designed and tested a new graphics-only pull tab to make the task of identifying and removing the protective tape from print cartridges easier for users. The team also designed and tested a new graphics-only instruction label that it added to the printer to improve user print cartridge loading performance.

Multilingual Instructions

The final usability test focused on the effectiveness of instructions provided in languages other than English. Users attempted to complete a set of key tasks using documents in their native language. As a result, the team was able to make several language-specific improvements to the documents.

HP Visual User Environment (VUE) 3.0

The HP OmniBook and HP DeskJet 1200CTM presented significant challenges in the definition and physical design of a product. HP VUE 3.0 (Figure 3) represented an entirely different challenge since, as a software product, it has *no* hardware. The details of the work, led by Jay Lundell, in defining and designing this product are described as a case study in the second half of this chapter.

Figure 3   HP VUE 3.0

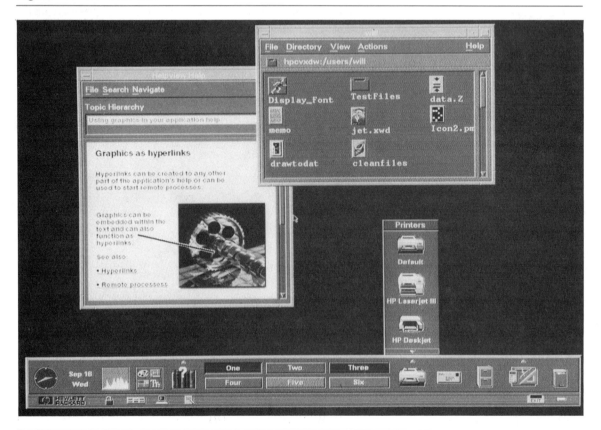

Diverse Business Needs

Our business needs for usability engineering vary from reducing costs and increasing product revenue, to no business need at all.

Cost Reduction.   Some organizations minimize costs with usability engineering. They achieve financial returns by decreasing direct costs such as support calls or by increasing productivity in product development and sales. They carefully analyze costs and systematically deploy usability engineering methods to reduce them. These motivations are primarily internal: customers usually benefit as a side effect since cost-saving strategies often improve the final design (e.g., easier to install and configure products).

Increased Product Revenue. Most of our businesses apply usability engineering to increase product revenue by increasing initial sales or customer loyalty. These organizations can apply usability engineering to increase customer productivity and satisfaction. This is a sound business proposition if cost of ownership and satisfaction in using the products are important in the market. This business need is entirely customer driven and bounded only by internal constraints such as cost and time to market.

No Business Need. For other organizations, there simply is no reasonable business proposition to make any explicit investment in usability engineering. This is a reasonable conclusion if significant cost savings or increased product revenue is not achievable.

To succeed in this diverse environment, we do not assume that a single process will be appropriate for all businesses. Instead, we attempt to understand the business opportunities and then determine whether we can adapt appropriate usability engineering methods to the situation. This means understanding the current level of knowledge and awareness of usability engineering and understanding the characteristics of each of our work environments.

Diverse Levels of Usability Engineering Knowledge and Awareness

From one organization to another we have enormous variation in the awareness and understanding of usability engineering. Some are very sophisticated. These have had the benefit of excellent human factors and ergonomics professionals who have worked on product development and communicated best practices.

A few organizations have absolutely no exposure to professional usability engineering and may have no concept of whether product usability is relevant to their business success. Often, these organizations confuse product usability with the appearance of a user interface or the mechanical interactions associated with the surface structure of the product. More often, it is something that they just do not think about. These organizations are more likely to find fault with their sales force being able to articulate the value of a product or with their technical communications staff being able to succinctly characterize how to use a product. The causes of these difficulties, such as unnecessary product complexity, may simply not be visible to these organizations.

Diverse Work Environments

Work environments also vary considerably from one organization to another in Hewlett-Packard. The work environment determines what sort of approaches can succeed in the short term. A very strong product marketing group can characterize users, their needs, and translate this information into lists of planned product features. The same department in another organization might only introduce and sell products rather than help define them. Different tactics are necessary to improve product usability in these different work environments.

Systems engineering work (e.g., using user interface guidelines across products) may not be feasible in an environment with very independent project teams. They may build related products, but may be motivated to leverage between products only to the extent that it helps them finish their own product sooner. Systems engineering can thrive in organizations that systematically build product families to optimize business results across project teams. They are motivated to build things that can be leveraged.

The following sections describe different approaches that we have taken to usability engineering at Hewlett-Packard. The models characterize the dynamics of usability engineering programs when there is an opportunity to contribute to business success. In practice, we do not use these models as described, rather, we combine elements of each and change them, based on our needs. They are organized by the presence or absence of specialized help in usability engineering. In this area, as with others in Hewlett-Packard, people are our most important asset.

No Specialized Help

Organizations without specialized help usually start out by raising the level of knowledge and awareness of key issues in usability engineering. We deliver classes for this purpose that range from introductory overviews to in-depth courses on specific methods (e.g., task analysis). This is a temporary approach for these organizations. They usually go one of two ways if they choose to pursue usability engineering after initial training:

- *Obtain consulting from internal or external human factors professionals.* Organizations do this to translate interest in the general area into results on a specific project. The level of success depends on the consultant and how committed the HP organization is to making a difference. Hands-on consulting doubles as training. Successful organizations continue to use consultants or hire internal specialists for the work (later sections describe these situations).

- *Make product usability the job of existing staff in addition to their current job responsibilities.* This is appealing to organizations with stable or declining businesses that are extremely cost conscious and motivated to minimize the apparent risk of any investment. Usually people that add usability engineering to their job description have jobs in which success is limited by poor product usability (e.g., technical support, technical communications). These people invariably seek additional training and help as they begin.

Pros.   These are low-cost, low-risk ways to introduce usability engineering. They require no long-term investment and do not threaten the existing work group structure. The organization can use consultants to extend their initial learning without taking on long-term employment responsibilities.

Cons.   Without additional steps, the approach does not provide sustainable improvements to usability engineering processes. The consulting avenue is only a temporary solution if there is an ongoing business need. Training existing staff is also limiting:

- There is very little at stake for in-house staff members who are asked to address usability. They usually have another job as their "primary" job. Their success almost always depends on successfully meeting the demands of their primary job. They stand to gain only "bonus points" for succeeding in usability engineering. When they experience a time crunch, they revert back to their primary jobs.

- It is very difficult for existing staff members to develop competence in usability engineering on the job, much less be aware of what they know and what they do not. We have had most success sending people to condensed degree programs (e.g., Virginia Polytechnic Institute) rather than short courses if they are to provide professional support.

- This situation often evolves to multiple people providing fractions of time while they are "in training." The net effect is that these organizations spend the equivalent of one or more people-years on usability engineering, without having staffed the position with a trained, experienced person with demonstrated success. This maximizes the long-term payroll and training costs associated with the function, while minimizing long-term effectiveness.

Lone Rangers

We use experienced individual Human Factors specialists to address usability issues across the range of an organization's projects, as with each of the example products described in the first section. The in-house specialist ensures the availability of state-of-the-art methods and knowledge. The primary challenge created by this model is to get maximum leverage from someone who is spread too thin. This creates the potential for burning out your specialist. In addition, product teams may lose the sense that the specialist is a team member if the specialist works on more than three projects at once.

The Champion Model

One solution is for the specialist to work primarily as a coach to other people. Each project appoints a usability "champion," who is responsible for product usability on that project. The responsibility of the specialist is to work with each of the champions to ensure that they are successful. Mrazek and Rafeld (1992) provide a more complete description of this approach.

Pros.   The champion model can provide sustainable improvements to an organization's usability engineering processes.

- It ensures the availability of specialized expertise from someone who understands the ongoing business issues and development environment.

- It is well suited to work environments in which product teams work very independently from one another. The person responsible for product usability is a full time member of the product team.

- It requires only one on-site professional, in most instances, while providing activity on a broad set of products.

Cons.   The champion model is only as effective as the expertise and availability of champions.

- The stability of this approach is greater than the no-specialist scenario, but still has its risks. The specialist invests time and resources in training and coaching champions that may change projects or responsibilities at any time. One organization that used five *full-time* champions on a key program, lost all of them in less than a year to reorganization and changes in work assignments.

- Champions typically take on usability in addition to their "primary" job. Their success almost always depends on meeting the demands of their primary job. When they experience a time crunch, they revert back to their primary jobs. If champions take on usability as a full-time job, they are less effective and require more training than an experienced specialist.

- Some organizations need more advanced methods (e.g., quantitative benchmarking) than can be coached effectively.

- The usability specialist is isolated and has limited opportunity to ask questions, share insights, and get ideas and feedback from colleagues. This is not an optimum placement for a recent graduate. It also creates some difficulties for experienced specialists in maintaining or developing new skills and advanced methods.

The Hybrid Model

The hybrid model is a variant of the champion model in which the specialist works with either formal or informal champions on projects, but is also responsible for the direct conduct of more specialized activities, such as quantitative evaluations, attitude scaling, or competitive benchmark comparisons. Typically, the specialist is an integral part of one to three product teams and enlists the help and involvement of others whenever possible. It is the specialist's responsibility to determine what needs to be done for products and ensure that it gets done. The hybrid model is the closest fit to the usability engineering programs described in the first section. Two of the three Human Factors Engineers involved in those projects had previously worked in "traditional" Human Factors groups in HP.

Pros. The hybrid model can provide sustainable improvements to an organization's usability engineering processes.

- This method ensures the availability of specialized expertise from someone who understands the ongoing business issues and development environment.

- It can be adapted to work well in "systems"-oriented work environments or places in which product teams work very independently from one another. In the systems environment, the specialist typically takes on mostly systems engineering work while coaching others on specific projects.

- It provides flexibility for the specialist to do the work directly, with help, or through others depending on what makes sense.

Cons. The hybrid model has the disadvantages associated with champions, to the extent that they are used, although it is more stable, and better for handling methods that are hard to coach. The approach can cover fewer products than the champion model, but with greater flexibility and expertise.

"Traditional" Human Factors Group

HP has multiple groups of human factors professionals that are responsible for usability engineering work. They provide advanced quantitative methods, training, and coaching. They provide a professional environment in which specialists can learn from, and rely on, each others' expertise. The groups also can provide a modest career path for people who wish to stay focused on usability engineering. These groups can be good professional development environments for recent graduates. However, they can differ greatly in their basic approach to addressing product usability. The following sections contrast two approaches for traditional groups.

Service Provider Model

In the service provider model, human factors groups are independent organizations that support a variety of products or even diverse organizations. They function as "information brokers," people whose primary responsibility is to supply information to cross-functional product teams. What distinguishes these groups is that they are not an integral part of the development organizations they support. The organization may consider them indispensable, but they operate as internal consultants rather than as any other member of the development team. They step in at the request of the organizations they support, or through a negotiated support agreement. They "own" only the information they provide or, in some cases, usability processes and measurement. They rarely have responsibility and authority over the usability of the end product. If they support very large organizations, they may represent a collection of "lone rangers."

Pros. The service provider model permits sustainable improvements in usability engineering processes and makes specialized expertise in usability engineering available to product teams.

- This approach allows for flexible staffing. Product teams can staff their projects using fractions of people's time rather than forcing an "all or none" hiring decision and still get top-notch help. Specialists can move from product to product based on peak demand and smooth out the peaks and valleys associated with individual projects.
- It provides stability to the human factors engineers since they are not tied to the success of any one project, but a group of projects or organizations.
- It assists the development of some specialists by exposing them to more varied product types than would be possible otherwise.

- Services can be provided to individual project, or component teams in independent work environments, or to systems teams in a system environment, depending on interest and need.

Cons. Most disadvantages of the service provider model arise from the independence of the organization from the product development team. These disadvantages are manageable to some degree; however, they *do* require managing.

- The product team may see the specialist as an outsider because he or she is are a part of an entirely separate organization; this limits the specialists' effectiveness (Lundell and Notess, 1991). Attending team meetings and developing professional relationships can help reduce the problem.

- Information brokers often have no "overriding" charter. The job is to provide the information and methods that people ask for rather than to articulate and meet specific business goals. They rarely have the authority to ensure that action is taken where it is warranted nor are they accountable for the consequences of action or inaction.

- People working in this model can burn out if they work at the peak levels of demand within projects. Within a product team, there may be intense flurries of effort to meet deadlines. Less demanding times often follow. The specialist who attempts to optimize effectiveness by going from one frenzied team to the next joins the ranks of the perpetually exasperated.

- With an eye to avoiding risk, this model can allow organizations to "dabble" in usability engineering forever. They may continually try a little at minimal cost to "see what happens" versus investing to accomplish an agreed upon business goal. Dabbling is seductively low risk, but ultimately has correspondingly low benefit since gains are opportunistic rather than part of a coherent business strategy.

Systems Engineering Model

In this approach, the Human Factors Engineers are an integral part of the organization whose products they work on. They are organized in a group, but as individuals are members of one to three product teams. They have responsibility and authority for decisions in product definition, design, and testing that primarily affect the usability of the product. They are accountable for achieving the business returns planned from product usability, whether these are measurable through reduced support costs or users' perception of product usability. They typically focus their efforts on system-level issues in product definition and design to maximize their contribution and advise product team members on component issues as time permits.

Pros.   The systems engineering model permits sustainable improvements in usability engineering processes and makes specialized expertise available to product teams. This approach has unique advantages that derive from integrating usability engineering activity with the product development organization.

- The Human Factors Engineers are clearly part of the product development team(s). This helps communication and teamwork.

- The responsibility and authority of the group are clearly defined. This simplifies decision making and ensures that the people closest to the problems make prompt decisions. Accountability for results maintains focus on business success.

- It requires a relatively long-term commitment to use usability engineering to business advantage. This means members of these groups, and their managers, tend to focus on getting work done rather than on getting funding.

- There is relatively good continuity of work assignments. That is, the same person(s) work on a product(s) over an extended period of time. This fosters organizational learning that would be difficult otherwise.

Cons.   The systems engineering model is applicable only to organizations that use an interdisciplinary design approach that emphasizes leverage among products. At a minimum, this means that the organization has adequate size and business needs to justify this sort of organization. Other disadvantages come from the organizational link required by the model.

- The group is only as stable as the organization of which it is a part. As product lines come and go, it may be very difficult to leave a highly tuned work group intact. We can mitigate this by mixing contract with full-time work, but we must manage it as a potential problem.

- If this sort of organization starts up in a business for which it is not a natural fit, there is likely to be a difficult break-in period. During this time, the focus on systems engineering and matching responsibility and authority will require consistent support.

Summary of Basic Approaches

The diversity of Hewlett-Packard's business requires that we are very flexible in usability engineering. The preceding approaches illustrate a variety of ways we go about setting up usability engineering, each with its own merits. None of the methods is sacred. None does a good job of characterizing any one of our organizations. In almost all cases we draw from the different techniques based on our business needs and adapt them as our needs change over time.

The same holds for the physical facilities and tools that we use. For one organization, a traditional in-house human factors laboratory is critical to provide quick, objective data on prototypes or competitive products. For other organizations, in-house labs make no sense at all. Consider our customers who use digital signal analyzers to do "modal analysis" to determine the physical properties of commercial jet wings. These folks are tough to book for an in-house test session; it is also hard for them to bring a sample of their work with them. Organizations in this business area tend to rely on field research at customer sites.

The following case study is typical in that it describes how we combine and modify elements from each of these approaches to address the specific needs and culture of one of our development organizations. Other elements of successful programs have included highly skilled people, an understanding of business purpose, a focus on users and tasks, and expanding existing processes to include usability engineering.

Case Study of HP VUE 3.0—Overview

In this section, we describe how we actually used these approaches on HP VUE 3.0. This project was not a typical Hewlett-Packard project; there is no such thing. However, it does illuminate how we opportunistically tailor usability processes and approaches to the needs of a particular project to increase the efficiency and effectiveness of scarce usability engineering resources.

Project Background—HP VUE 2.0

HP VUE 2.0 was a graphical "desktop" application environment (Figure 4) for the Hewlett-Packard UNIX™ (HP-UX™) workstations that preceded HP VUE 3.0. It provided file management, session management, and a common user-interface approach for applications written for the environment. The user-centered design approach used in this project was a service provider model in which the services were provided from a remote location. The HP VUE 2.0 group, which was based in Corvallis, Oregon, contracted a HP human factors professional based in Fort Collins, Colorado, to provide the equivalent of one-half of his time to work on the project. The human factors engineer (HFE) started by providing a two-day course in user-centered design to the majority of the software engineers working on the project and thereafter provided consulting and usability testing throughout the project. Although successful in many ways, this caused some problems:

Figure 4   HP VUE 2.0

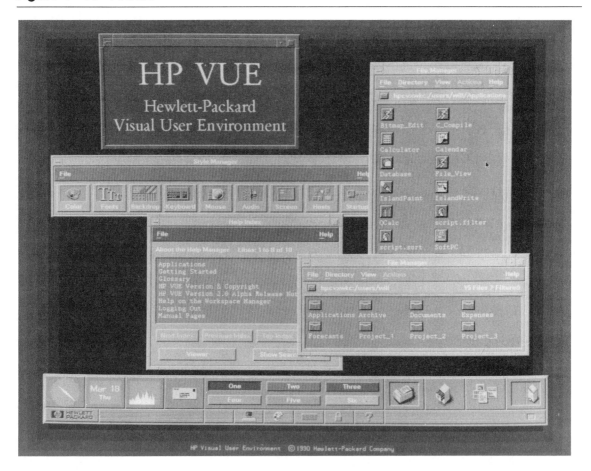

- The HFE was an "outsider" because of his part-time status and remote location. Not only was it difficult to engage with developers, it was difficult to work effectively with other team members who had overlapping usability concerns, such as the visual design, marketing, documentation, and support groups.

- Ongoing, one-on-one consulting was difficult across geographic areas. The primary approach that the HFE adopted was to react to proposed designs rather than to participate in and lead the user interface design work.

- The HFE was not able to reinforce the lessons that the product team learned in training through close follow up contact. As a result, there were few "usability champions" to help; this compromised the effectiveness of the training.

- The management team "felt good" about having a half-time HFE on the project. As a result, it did not make any additional investments in usability engineering that would have helped.

- The HFE divided his time among multiple projects. It was hard to maintain the focus required for this project with only half of his time available. The project itself was divided into multiple components that were managed across three development teams, which added to the complexity of working with the teams.

In spite of these problems, HP VUE 2.0 users responded favorably to the usability of the product. Competitive usability tests showed that the software performed well against other UNIX™ desktop applications. We attributed this more to the lack of competitive graphic UNIX™ desktop applications at that time, than to outstanding design on this particular release.

Work Environment—HP VUE 3.0

As the HP VUE 3.0 project got underway, the project management decided that product usability was a primary objective. The managers reached this decision using information from a variety of sources: ease of use objectives provided by top management, market data that indicated that improved ease of use could significantly improve market share, and from the perception that the usability engineering efforts of HP VUE 2.0 had been valuable. As a first step, the Corvallis group hired the HFE from Ft. Collins and moved him to Corvallis. The HFE joined the software R&D group to work full-time on HP VUE 3.0 (Figure 5 and Color Plate IV). The project immediately took on more of the characteristics of a hybrid lone ranger model.

The hybrid model was appropriate for the HP VUE 3.0 project. It required a systems approach in which the HFE could work on the architecture, establish usability engineering processes to be integrated into the existing product life cycle, and coach usability champions on individual components.

The HP VUE 3.0 team was a relatively small group consisting of R&D, a Marketing group, a Support group, Documentation, and Quality. The R&D group had a strong culture, and was known to be both innovative and independent. The Marketing Department had a reputation for working well with the R&D group to communicate customer needs and requirements. The Documentation group was beginning to form well-managed processes for providing on-line as well as hard-copy documentation and had begun to form a task-oriented model for documentation design.

Figure 5   HP VUE 3.0

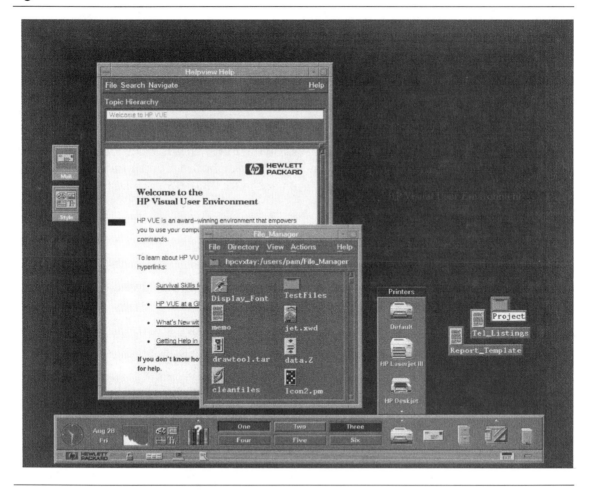

The HFE reported to the Quality Department, which was part of the R&D group. The Quality Department had just revised the division's software life cycle, and this life cycle was ready to test on the HP VUE 3.0 project. In short, many processes were already in place and gaining momentum as the project got underway. In this environment, the HFE received a fair degree of support; however, it was apparent that the success of the project would depend not only on establishing new usability processes, but on leveraging existing processes. It would have been unproductive to try to change such a culturally strong organization overnight.

Investigation—HP VUE 3.0

The Marketing and R&D teams identified the expected financial returns from product usability and took a lead in understanding the target customers. They also took a lead in identifying product requirements from informal customer feedback. In addition, the Quality and Marketing departments proposed using a more rigorous process for customer feedback called *Quality Function Deployment* (QFD) as a first step in the investigation.

"Standard" QFD is used to systematically collect, analyze, and rank customer requirements. The requirements are mapped to functional specifications that map to detailed features of the product, that, in turn, map to user interface components, and so forth. The essential character of QFD is that customer requirements propagate down through the final details of product development. QFD lends itself very well to established user-centered design processes.

We made the following modifications to the standard QFD process:

- We used QFD to establish key supported tasks in addition to user requirements.
- The HFE participated in over 30 customer visits, as did members of the R&D team, to facilitate direct understanding of usability needs and ensure objectivity and consensus on the results.
- We followed initial QFD visits with user interface review sessions to verify customer requirements (described later in the User Interface Design Follow Up section).
- We directed user testing of key supported tasks from the QFD process as further validation of the product design (described in the Testing—HP VUE 3.0 section).

Thus, the HFE applied his expertise to a usability related process to leverage a preexisting commitment from the team. The result was synergy between usability engineering and the QFD process.

We also established a process to determine the order in which we would fix usability defects. A team consisting of representatives from all relevant groups assembled a list of usability defects that existed from HP VUE 2.0 (see Figure 6).

Figure 6   Example of usability defects from HP VUE 2.0

Component	Usability defect description	Severity level	Eng effort	Fix priority
File Manager	Can't place files in arbitrary locations.	83	high	1
File Manager	Navigation to other directories is difficult.	74	medium	2
File Manager	Can't directly rename file/directory.	65	med-high	3

We instructed each member to rate the severity of each defect on a scale of 0–100, without regard for how we would fix the defect. We jointly reached a consensus on items for which the ratings were highly variable. We then went through each of them with the engineer responsible for fixing the defect, discussed solutions, and assessed the engineering effort. We placed all of the results into a table and assigned a priority for fixing the defects by considering the severity level of each and the engineering effort required. Finally, we established cut lines for which solutions we would implement.

This process had an additional benefit—it turned the participants into usability champions for product defects. The participants became knowledgeable of the scope of usability defects in the product and became active in ensuring that we fixed these defects.

Product Design Using Key Supported Tasks—HP VUE 3.0

The HFE combined QFD data collection and task-oriented work on documentation to develop key supported tasks for the entire product. This worked well because it leveraged two existing, well-accepted process. The key supported tasks were the focal point of the user-centered design efforts for HP VUE 3.0 and provided a common design and testing framework. We developed an extensive list of these tasks for each of the HP VUE components.

We then categorized each task by

- The user types that do the task (i.e., typical, advanced, system administrator).
- The frequency with which users would perform the task.

We used the key supported tasks in various roles throughout the product life cycle. For example, the development team used these tasks to define the external specifications for each of the HP VUE components. They documented the user interface by describing the steps to perform these tasks. This forced developers to focus continually on the user's tasks while designing the user interface. This prevented technological considerations from interfering with the user interface development and prevented drift from the product definition (see Figure 7).

Figure 7 Example of how key supported tasks were used in the HP VUE 3.0 specification

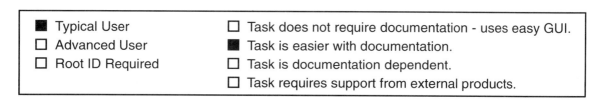

The documentation team used the tasks to organize the hard copy and on-line documentation. They used the task categories to help determine the style and depth of the writing for each task, e.g., documenting a task that required users to edit system files required more depth than documenting a task supported by an intuitive graphic user interface.

The HFE also used the tasks as the pool from which to conduct user testing on the product. The user profiles and task categories helped the HFE define the types of users to recruit for testing. Tasks that the team rated as frequently done by users or most critical we gave precedence for user testing.

User Interface Design Follow Up

Once the user interface was underway, we wanted to verify that the design solutions would actually meet customer requirements. The team took pains to accurately record these requirements on the QFD visits, but we still were left to speculate on some customer needs based on a few customer statements. We were not confident that we had arrived at a reasonable user interface design solution.

Other factors also drove the inclusion of product features, such as the desire to provide some support for multimedia and object orientation. We wanted to be sure that features that we included for strategic purposes but that customers did not specifically request were valued appropriately. Because of our resource limits (we had used most of our travel budget on the initial QFD visits), we used multiple low-cost methods to follow up on designs.

Review Sessions

We identified a subset of the original QFD customers to visit again. We chose these customers mainly because they were close to us, and to approximate a representative cross section of our original customer list, we included about 20% of the customers from our original customer visits. We then made a videotape that depicted user scenarios with the HP VUE 3.0 design prototypes. This was much easier way to get feedback than to demonstrate the actual software. It did not require us to tote around a HP workstation or wrestle with software installation on a customer's machine. At each site, we played the videotape, described each scenario, and asked a series of predetermined questions about each component. The data we collected from this exercise were invaluable. We found out very early where the product did not meet customer needs. We dropped several features from the design when customers told us they did not need them. This saved the project many engineering months by eliminating planned development time.

Telephone Interviews

We interviewed selected customers by telephone to ask specific follow-up questions. For example, a few customers expressed concern about security. After designing a few possible solutions to the problem, we faxed a description of the designs to the customers and interviewed them over the phone for their opinion of which was best and why.

Prototype Testing

We conducted usability prototype testing on issues that we felt we could not address solely through customer opinions. These were issues that addressed the implementation of the design rather than the requirements. The issues included performance and learnability of key supported tasks. We used customer profile data from the QFD analysis to recruit users for the test to ensure the validity of the testing.

"User Experts"

The team often deferred to "user experts" on questions that they could not resolve with the first three methods. The user experts were a handful of people who had participated on all of the customer visits or performed the analysis for the QFD data.

Testing—HP VUE 3.0

Because the HP VUE 3.0 program was so large (it was made up of 10 major projects with a total of 218 key supported tasks), it was not possible to cover all aspects of VUE

3.0 through human factors testing alone. Furthermore, the HFE was consumed with the myriad day-to-day design and architectural issues. Therefore, for ongoing validation, we invested in some human factors testing and supplemented this with a variety of other approaches to ensure usability.

Heuristic Evaluation

We established a dialog review committee that was responsible for consistency across components. The committee was a cross-functional team that included two other participants from R&D, one from marketing, one from documentation, and one from support. The HFE wrote up a list of HP VUE 3.0 usability principles and user interface design rules for the committee to review. Each person evaluated all of the HP VUE dialogs, help messages, menu bars, and error messages for consistency and compliance. We then compiled the list of problem areas and met to agree on solutions. The committee gave this information to the component owners who were responsible for fixing their parts. This is very similar to the heuristic evaluation technique described by Nielsen and Molich (1990).

This committee was very effective in finding problem areas and inconsistencies. The number of inconsistencies that we found surprised us, since the same group designed all of the software using the Motif user interface library, and the team had easy access to the daily running version of the code. However, engineers tend to focus on their own component during the critical development period, and the Motif guidelines allow for enough flexibility that it is easy to design interfaces that are quite different from each other. Moreover, it is easy to miss inconsistencies in design unless you are specifically looking for them.

Aside from finding inconsistencies, the dialog review committee effectively made positive changes in usability processes because

- Each project area had a representative that provided a unique perspective. For example, the support engineer pointed out error messages that resulted in significant support calls with HP VUE 2.0. The committee recommended extensive changes and additional on-line help for these trouble areas.

- The committee was highly visible and garnered strong support from management. Several of the members were lead architects for the project and their opinions were highly regarded.

- The redundant review process captured many more problems than could have been captured via human factors testing alone or a single expert evaluator. This has been demonstrated empirically (Jeffries, Miller, Wharton, and Uyeda, 1991).

Internal Alpha Release Testing

One advantage of being in a large high technology company is that a product group may have access to a large base of internal users that are similar to "real" users. These users are very easy to access if the company has an extensive wide area network. This was the case for HP VUE 3.0. We deposited the alpha version of HP VUE 3.0 in a location that others could easily access and broadcast its availability through an internal electronic bulletin board system. We asked anyone installing the software to fill out a questionnaire with his or her name, address, job description, work environment, etc. We asked these users if they would be willing to respond to some questions after a short evaluation period. Most replied that they would. This was a very low-cost method to obtain relatively accurate feedback from users doing real work.

A potential problem, of course, is that the internal users might not have accurately reflected the actual target customers for the product. Another problem was that we could introduce bias by using internal HP employees. To solve the first problem we compared the users' job descriptions and work environments with profiles obtained from actual customers in one of our annual surveys. We found that we could obtain very similar population characteristics by removing software programmers who were very familiar with HP VUE 2.0 or HP VUE 2.0 based technology such as Motif. For the second problem, it has been our experience that internal HP employees do provide biased product feedback—they are quite analytical, critical, and vocal when it comes to evaluating internal products compared to our customers. Since we restricted the data to identify problem areas (and not, for example, to compare with data on competitive products), we were confident that the data were accurate and useful.

Human Factors Testing

The HFE conducted three human factors tests at the Corvallis site in the alpha phase of HP VUE 3.0. These tests assessed the most critical of the key supported tasks. We defined as critical those tasks that met either or both of the following criteria:

- Tasks directly related to the attainment of usability objectives
- Important tasks that could benefit most from early feedback or iterative design, based on the information available at that point in the project.

These tests followed a standard approach. The HFE sent out early drafts of the test plan for review, and modified the plan accordingly. During testing the HFE collected time and error data as well as user comments and subjective ratings. The HFE then published test reports that listed the usability problems, estimated severity levels for those problems, and recommended design changes that would fix the problems. In addition, we contracted the human factors group in Fort Collins to conduct testing on some of the more stable key supported tasks. Using a remote site for this testing worked well since the implementations were relatively standard and stable (e.g., renaming a file by click-and-type).

Usability and Process Metrics—HP VUE 3.0

At the very beginning of the project, we had worked together to identify usability objectives. The team used a format in which each objective had one or more strategies for attaining the objective. Each of the strategies had an owner and one or more measures and targets. We established minimum acceptable measures as well as target measures for each strategy. An example of this format is illustrated in Figure 8.

Figure 8 Objective format used on the HP VUE 3.0 project

No.	Objective	No.	Action Plan	Owner	Measures/Targets
1.	Improve the ease with which users can set up and tailor their workstation environment to maximize productifity and satisfaction.	1.1	Improve ease with which end users can perform object management and organization tasks.	File mgr team	a. Human Factors test using key supported file manager and desktop tasks. **Min** - 60% success rate **Target** - 80% success rate b. Fix all "must" file mgr usability defects.
		1.2	Improve ease with which end users can customize the appearance and behavior of the VUE environment for maximum productivity.	File mgr, Style, and WS mgr teams	a. Human Factors test using key supported customization and action and filetype tasks. **Min** - 50% success rate **Target** - 75% success rate b. Customer survey **Min** - 50% of all users have customized or know how to customize their VUE environment. **Target** - 70% of all users . . .
		1.3	Ensure compliance with the Motif Style Guide.	Lundell	Achieve checklist compliance with 1.1 Motif checklist.

We chose metrics based on the strategies that we used to achieve the objectives. For example, some metrics depended on the results of post release customer surveys and were impossible to assess until long after the project was complete. Other metrics were simple "checklist" items that we could use right away against the external specification—long before coding had begun. Human factors testing falls in the middle of these two extremes. We tried to assign both short-term and long-term metrics for each major objective. The short-term metric we used during product development as a way to assess whether we were progressing toward our objective. We used the long-term metric to directly measure whether we had achieved our objective (external validation) and as a baseline for the next release of the product.

We also hired the Fort Collins human factors group to conduct an extensive usability benchmark test after we released the product. Although this type of testing can require a great deal of time and expertise, an outside human factors group can do it as long as the tasks are well defined and the software and documentation are complete. Contracting this work to another group was cost effective. It allowed the HFE to work in parallel, devoting time to design activities that required much more detailed knowledge of the product and organizational objectives.

In addition to assessing the actual usability of the product, we wanted to directly assess the utility of the processes we had established during the project. We used two measures: the data obtained from a project post mortem survey and a QFD requirements correlation metric.

Project Post Mortem Survey

The project post mortem survey is a standard process in this organization's lab. Every project member fills out a survey that covers all aspects of the project, including product objectives, staffing, design, testing, and verification. We enlarged on this established process to include questions on the QFD process and the usability activities. All respondents rated the project on a 5-point scale (very poor to very good) on dimensions such as "effectiveness of human factors testing" and "ability to incorporate human factors input." These ratings were very positive and have served to establish baseline metrics for improvement in the future, as well as to encourage further investment in human factors activities on future projects.

QFD Requirements Correlation Metric

There were 404 customer requirements obtained from the QFD customer requirements, each of which received a rating value from 0 to 9, depending on how strongly each requirement related to the needs of each customer segment (see Lundell and Williams, 1993, for more detail). The project team devoted a great deal of time and effort toward ranking the requirements and designing the product to meet those requirements. The question, then, was; How well had we met those requirements? Although we knew that customers would ultimately answer that question, we thought it would be useful to conduct our own self-evaluation of the project.

The HFE distributed a list of the top 100 customer requirements to key project personnel. The HFE asked them to rate HP VUE 3.0 against each of the requirements on a rating scale of 0-9, where 0 meant that HP VUE 3.0 did not meet the requirement at all and 9 meant that HP VUE 3.0 totally met the requirement. The HFE then correlated these ratings against the original importance ratings assigned to the customer requirements. This correlation score is a measure of how well we felt we met the customer requirements overall and can be used as an estimate of the effectiveness of the QFD process.

We also constructed two lists from this data. The first list was the list of "Top Hits for HP VUE 3.0." This list contained about 30 requirements that customers rated as important and that we gave high scores in our self-assessment. The second list was the list of "Top Misses for HP VUE 3.0" and contained about 30 requirements that customers also rated as most important, but that we gave low scores in our self-assessment. We used this list, along with a list of unresolved usability defects, as the starting point for the follow on product to HP VUE 3.0. We found three systematic differences among the lists. First, the "Top Hits" were well-understood customer requirements that we could meet unambiguously, e.g., "The on-line help displays graphics." Second, some of the "Top Misses" required a systems approach that was not completely within the team's control, e.g., "HP VUE has good performance in minimum RAM configuration" would have required coordination from multiple software and hardware providers in our business area. Third, another group of "Top Misses" were items for which the team had not reached consensus.

Case Study Summary

In summary, the HP VUE 3.0 project successfully made substantial improvements in user-centered design. In spite of a very aggressive schedule and limited human factors resources, considerable usability engineering work took place. We were able to lay a foundation for implementing sustainable usability engineering processes. Management support was instrumental to this success, both in terms of the initial allocation of human resources and in terms of continually stressing its importance throughout the HP VUE 3.0 development cycle.

Lessons Learned

Flexibility

Flexibility in choosing and applying organizational and technical models has been one element of our successes. We have learned that a "universal" program for a company as diverse and dynamic as HP is not the right answer. The opportunistic approaches described in the case study were useful to introduce novel user-centered design techniques. However, we continue to adapt our approaches and methods to maintain and improve usability engineering in a rapidly changing environment. Our organizations must be able to quickly assimilate new techniques into their development cycles. It works best when we have methods on the shelf, ready to be quickly adapted to emerging needs. This means documenting the procedures and formally validating them as standard practice.

People

Experienced Professionals

A common element of successful usability engineering programs for HP has been the direct involvement of highly skilled, experienced human factors professionals. Although they are quick to use low-tech quick and dirty methods when appropriate, they also know what risks they are taking and when sophisticated hi-tech methods are the right choice. They can tell the difference between new methods with new contributions and repackaged leftovers that have hit the conference circuit for commercial benefit and individual notoriety.

Broad Involvement with Ownership

Our successful programs have treated usability engineering as a cross-functional process that requires active participation from every department involved in product definition and design. The teams for the HP OmniBook, HP DeskJet 1200C^{TM}, and HP VUE 3.0 emphasized cross-functional participation and concluded that it was an essential ingredient to their success. We have also found that broad involvement is most effective when complemented with ownership—someone's primary job responsibility is to own the process, specialized methods, and result. A shared business purpose provides a unifying focus for these diverse teams.

Business Purpose

Members of our successful usability engineering programs can articulate the business value that they provide. That is, they know whether they are attempting to save money through reducing support calls related to installation and configuration or whether they are increasing market penetration by giving our sales force a justifiable claim to superior user productivity as compared to our competitors.

We have heard proposals that the service model supports a business focus because of objectivity inherent in working in an organization independent of specific project teams. However, all organizations are subject to pressures of one variety or another that influence the way in which they do their work, whether it is pressure for funding, obtaining the satisfaction of "clients," or schedule pressure. Our experience has been that what determines whether data are collected and reported effectively is the competence of the human factors professional and a work environment that rewards optimizing product usability and associated investments. Arranging funding from relatively high levels of the organization or ensuring that the usability engineering function is directly accountable to functional management (e.g., R&D, Marketing) maintains focus on business success, rather than the pressures of a particular department. This is important, since so much of this work is "white space" work—pulling together information and interests from a variety of internal and external sources. The actions taken often represent trade-offs in quality and effort that have differing effects on different parts of the organization.

Focus on Users, Their Goals, and Their Tasks

Usability engineering is all about making users more productive and satisfied using our products. It is no surprise that focusing on users and their work is a requirement for successful programs. People in successful programs know who the target users are, what they are trying to do, and how we are going to help them get it done. The HP VUE 3.0 team collected this information from diverse sources and used it extensively (see Figure 9).

Take a "Piggyback" Ride on Accepted Processes

The technique of "piggybacking" usability processes onto existing processes is valuable for us. Product life cycles, defect tracking systems, objective setting, customer visits, and customer response card systems are all examples of well-accepted processes that we have expanded to include usability engineering. Building innovations onto existing processes minimizes resistance to change. It also allows teams to use the innovations faster, since they are in a familiar framework. More detailed descriptions of some of these examples are available in other publications (Rideout, Uyeda, and Williams, 1989; Rideout, 1992).

Figure 9   Sources for key supported tasks and their uses

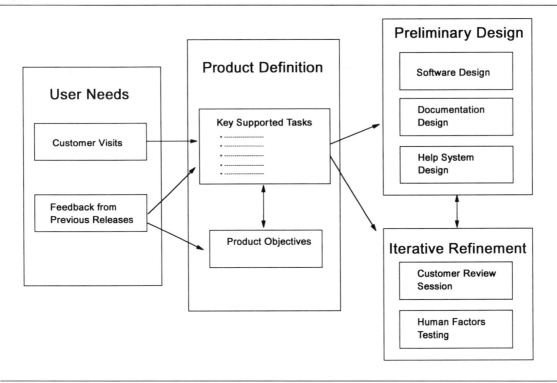

References

Jeffries, R., Miller, J. R., Wharton, C., and Uyeda, K. M. (1991). "User Interface Evaluation in the Real World: A Comparison of Four Techniques," *Proc. ACM CHI '91 Conf.*, New Orleans, pp. 119-124.

Lundell, J., and Notess, M. (1991). "Human Factors in Software Development: Models, Techniques, and Outcomes," *Proc. ACM CHI '91 Conf.*, New Orleans, pp. 145-151.

Lundell, J., and Williams, D. (1993). "Integrating Human factors into Software Development: A Case Study," *Proc. Fifth Int. Conf. on Human-Computer Interaction* (HCI International '93), Orlando, FL, 1, pp. 404-409.

Mrazek, M., and Rafeld, M. (1992). "Integrating Human Factors on a Large Scale: "'product Usability Champions,'" *Proc. ACM CHI '92 Conf.*, Monterey, CA, pp. 565-570.

Nielsen, J. (1993). Usability Engineering. Academic Press, Boston.

Nielsen, J., and Molich, R. (1990). "Heuristic Evaluation of User Interfaces," Proc. *ACM CHI '90 Conf.*, Seattle, WA, pp. 249-256.

Rideout, T. B. (1991). "Changing Your Methods from the Inside," *IEEE Software*, 8, (3, May), 99, 100, 111.

Rideout, T. B., Uyeda, K. M., and Williams, E. L. (1989). "Evolving the Software Usability Engineering Process at Hewlett-Packard," *Proc. 1989 IEEE Int. Conf. on Systems, Man, and Cybernetics*, 1 (November), pp. 229-234.

CHAPTER 8

Usability in 3D: Silicon Graphics, Inc.

Anna M. Wichansky
*Computer Systems Group
Silicon Graphics, Inc.*

Michael F. Mohageg
*Visual Magic Division
Silicon Graphics, Inc.*

Anna Wichansky founded and managed the Human Factors Group (later Customer Research and Usability) at Silicon Graphics for three years. She has 15 years experience applying her behavioral science and engineering design expertise to human factors problems in computer systems, transportation, telecommunications, entertainment and consumer products. She received the A.B. in psychology from Radcliffe College, and M.S. and Ph.D in psychology concentrating in human factors from Tufts University. She was twice elected an officer of the Human Factors Society.

Mike Mohageg received his M.S. and Ph.D. degrees in industrial engineering and operations research from Virginia Polytechnic Institute and State University. He joined the Silicon Graphics Usability Group in 1991 as a member of the technical staff and has been involved in projects ranging from system hardware usability to multimedia authoring applications. His expertise includes hypertext, multimedia user interfaces, and input devices.

This chapter is about the usability program at Silicon Graphics, Inc., a high technology Silicon Valley computer company. It describes how we started and how we were successful in making 3D computing more usable. The momentum of growth and change at Silicon Graphics since 1990 and its distinctive corporate culture have been overwhelming forces driving our work and shaping our organization. Therefore, we have described quite candidly how we encountered obstacles, adapted to them, and embraced change as our friend, which is an important key to survival in the high technology world.

Silicon Graphics' Business

Silicon Graphics, Inc., is the world's leading supplier of visual computing systems. The company was founded in 1982 and has pioneered the development of color three-dimensional (3D) computing. Its product offerings include RISC workstations, servers, and supercomputers. Currently 61% of its $1 billion annual revenue comes from its low-end products (Indy™, IRIS Indigo®, Indigo2®, and Magnum® workstations and servers) and 39% from its high-end products (Challenge™, Onyx™, and Millennium® systems). Roughly half the products are sold outside North America.[1]

Silicon Graphics also provides the IRIX operating system, client-server software, and other software development and end-user computing tools to bring its visual computing capabilities to its customers. The primary applications for these systems are technical, scientific, and more recently multimedia software. The traditional markets for these products have been mechanical engineering, computational chemistry, molecular modeling, earth sciences, and visual simulation. These are rapidly expanding to include engineering and graphics design, computer-aided software development, medical, and entertainment.

Silicon Graphics' success depends upon "[its] ability to introduce leading edge products at a rapid pace, while minimizing any disruption to [its] business."[2] The company merged with MIPS Computer Systems in 1992 to ensure the continuing development of ever-more-powerful microprocessors, which will propel Silicon Graphics' 3D and multimedia capabilities into computer and consumer products. This strategy has allowed Silicon Graphics to participate in exciting joint ventures,

---

[1] Figures taken from Silicon Graphics 1993 Annual Report.

[2] Silicon Graphics 1993 Annual Report, p. 3.

including the digitization of the film industry with partner Eastman Kodak and inter-active television with Time Warner Cable. Growth also depends upon proliferation of its technologies into an expanding range of applications, demanding lower cost work-stations, easier-to-use, more fully functional software, and open, flexible client-server networking capabilities. Recently, a major goal was achieved with the introduction of Indy, a multimedia workstation priced competitively to a high-performance personal computer. The Indigo Magic™ software end-user environment for the Indy provides point-and-click ease of use to all major IRIX operating system functions, system administration utilities, and end-user applications for imaging, sound, and video.

On February 22, 1993, President Clinton and Vice-President Gore visited Silicon Graphics and pronounced the company a role model for innovation in American cor-porations.[3] The company has approximately 3800 employees worldwide, including manufacturing sites in Mountain View, California; Neuchatel, Switzerland; and Kawasaki, Japan. The corporate culture is results driven, team oriented, and funloving.

Silicon Graphics' Usability Program

From Humble Beginnings . . .

Anna Writes:

Toward the end of the 1980s, Silicon Graphics recognized that to grow as a company and become a competitive force in the workstation market, it would have to achieve high-volume sales. While the company had established a worldwide reputation for its leading edge 3D graphics technology, "Silicon Graphics" was not exactly a household word for 3D. The mission to bring 3D to all computer markets was hindered in part because the products were not easy to use.

The typical scenario in early 3D computing was that some technical or scientific guru would determine that he wanted to visualize his data in 3D. A supercomputer would be ordered, sometimes costing several hundred thousand dollars, installed and cared for by the vendor, and a programmer would be hired to "use" it. The guru would direct the programmer as to what the application should do, and the machine

---

[3] The President's opening remarks included the following statements: "I wanted to come [because] I think the gov-ernment ought to work like you do ... America's biggest problem is that for too many people, change is an enemy, not a friend ... One reason you're all so happy is you found a way to make change your friend ... " (*Microtimes*, April 5, 1993, p. 32).

would sit in the corner, being admired for the pretty pictures it could produce in the skilled hands of the programmer. Then the staff members would go back to their desks and do "real work" on their personal computers or some other less glamorous, more practical workstation.

Silicon Graphics was determined to change its image of being a special-purpose, one-per-customer-site system by developing a low-cost 3D workstation as easy to use as a personal computer. The product they set out to design was dubbed the Personal IRIS.

In 1987, the company hired Amy Smith to start a Product Usability Group, a move supported by Marketing. She developed detailed plans to improve the usability of the products. The group included technical writers producing end-user and developer documentation. However, they also interviewed customers for feedback on usability issues and performed usability testing in a conference room using early mock-ups of new products. They invited product developers, marketers, and company executives to participate as subjects in their tests or to take home the VHS videotapes of their colleagues trying to use the system under construction.

This made a big impression on engineering and management. Attendance was so good at the testing, that the testers were practically squeezed out of the observation space. Also, people began to realize that the products were not so easy to use and that some fairly straightforward fixes could be applied to make them better. For instance, they began to pay attention to the design of peripherals and components that would install easily, since this was the first customer-installable Silicon Graphics machine. Product designers realized that closure mechanisms, forces, and other aspects of the hardware packaging would need some "adjustment" for personal computer users. If they weren't successful, it would cost the company money in customer support to answer hot-line calls or visit the customer to install or upgrade a volume product. Software developers realized that end-users would need a simplified interface to IRIX (essentially a Unix operating system), which would be easy to understand, as well as graphical and colorful. Additional information had to be provided beyond standard Unix error messages, which were notoriously "unfriendly" (my favorite is "Fatal error: System panic"). They began to devote some effort to providing a logical consistent interface for basic file management and system administration tasks.

The Product Usability staff did a great deal to introduce Silicon Graphics to functional usability engineering processes. They got people interested and involved, without making them defensive. Their usability efforts were recognized as valuable and credible. They established the first test suite and created a demand for (a lot) more than they could initially handle. This laid the groundwork for a more formal human factors effort.

Building an Infrastructure for a Larger Effort

Hiring the Manager

At the time the company began interviewing for a human factors manager, the writers were having trouble meeting the demand for usability services with the existing staff and facility. Usability opportunities in the early product design cycle were not being addressed as the company grew and new product development expanded. It was time to introduce additional aspects of the usability engineering process that would allow more problems to be anticipated before the product was designed.

The company was looking for a manager with a significant track record for improving the usability of products. It was important to add some breadth of experience to the current team, including application of usability engineering techniques to displays, software, and input devices as well as documentation. In order to cover the potential scope of Silicon Graphics products, they realized the need for knowledge of ergonomics, anthropometry, standards, and biomechanics, as well as skills in user interface design and testing. This background would enable broader and deeper coverage of usability issues. The Human Factors Group was initially organized with the two documentation groups under the Product Usability Manager, who reported to the Vice President of Marketing.

Scoping the Work

Upon starting the program, it was important to assess the status of projects in progress and determine the relevant players in the company who would be the primary contacts of the usability group. At the time, there were three product divisions, and my Marketing VP had given me clear orders to support our home division, Entry Systems Division, as a top priority. I had a staff of one highly competent electrical engineer with a customer support background, who was familiar with the company culture and products. She had set up the first test suite and performed much of the testing. My first objective was to try to make order out of chaos. Later I would learn to embrace the chaos as an essential ingredient of Silicon Graphics' success.

I met with everyone. The manufacturing technicians on the assembly line had noticed certain usability problems as they put together the products to ship. The engineers and marketers (also engineers), their managers, and directors had widely diverse expectations of my role and what my group would be doing, including manual writing, quality conformance testing, and customer demonstrations.

The company executives wanted to know how much it was going to cost and how long it would take to get the "usability thing" in gear. They were optimistic but impatient for results; they saw budget being spent on something that they did not fully understand, and became skeptical when the products didn't improve in six weeks or even a full quarter. (This was due partly to the fact that the earlier usability efforts were done "on a shoestring" and the costs hidden in the documentation budget.) Meanwhile, my Marketing VP reminded me that "you can always tell the pioneers by the arrows in their chests," convincing me not to be overwhelmed by the mountain of requests and skepticism about the process we were trying to instill. It was encouraging for an executive to grasp the fact that the "usability thing" would take time to work, at least a product lifecycle, and that it would not be a good idea to spend all of our resources making short-term fixes to current products.

The requests from Engineering were highly varied, requiring work from the highest level of planning to the lowest level of product detail. They included everything from figuring out how high a desktop computer should be to setting forth the usability goals and objectives for an entire new line of computers. By far the most unique and specific requests came from Manufacturing, including design of ergonomic shipping cartons, ergonomic grounding straps, and ergonomic SIMM (memory module) sockets.

On the software side, we were also getting requests from all over the company. Some were for a complete usability program or for testing a product they had already developed but not released. Others were highly specific; for example, the wording of an error message or the color of an icon. And the technical writers still wanted their books tested. (I mean all the books, including the developer documentation, which was about 50,000 pages!)

Also, in a scenario familiar to so many in the human factors profession, we started with no known budget, no assigned space to expand the lab, and no firm headcount commitment for staffing. The first year was, needless to say, very challenging.

However, my manager and I had a plan. We figured with about three staff people—one for hardware, one for software, and one for documentation—we could start to cover the territory. Also, we had scouted out a site in our building with high walls and doors that would make a larger lab (most of us work in open cubicles). I had days to put together a budget for the department, since I was hired three weeks before the start of the new fiscal year. Mostly I relied upon vendors I had worked with in previous labs and the Human Factors Society salary surveys to develop this. In true Silicon Graphics fashion, the usability effort was flying by the seat of its pants and bringing facilities, staffing, and finance along for the ride!

Designing a Lab We Could Grow Into

The lab layout we designed is shown in Figure 1. The lab is approximately 900 square feet and is divided into five rooms. There are two two-room subject-tester suites. The subject and tester rooms are separated by one-way mirrors. There is a large, conference-style observation room in which observers can watch events in the subject rooms on a wide-screen television monitor. At least two views of the subject rooms are combined on a single video monitor, usually the subject and her computer screen, shown as a smaller picture within a larger picture.

Figure 1   Floor plan of Silicon Graphics Human Factors Lab

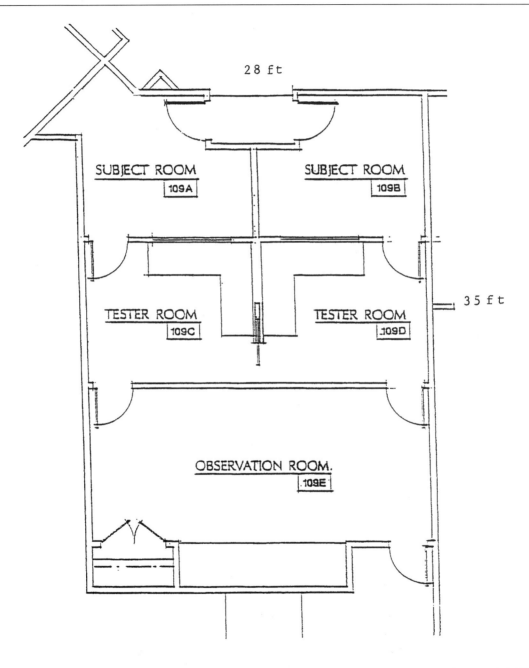

We learned a lot from the first test suite that was built in the former storage space, and this helped us to develop requirements for a larger facility. We wanted a lab located in the same building as our group and the engineers, because we often moved equipment from offices to the lab. We wanted it located close to the lobby so subjects would not have to see our whole development effort on the way to the test! Because there were now two of us trying to test and we were already bumping into each other trying to schedule the lab, we decided a minimum of two subject-tester suites would be required. We also wanted a comfortable facility for the engineers and others to watch the testing, but we did not want them sitting on top of us! Therefore, we built an observation room, where they could watch testing from either room on large screen monitors. Also, it was easier to take notes because it was well-lit, in contrast to the dark tester rooms next to the one-way mirrors. Up to fifteen developers have watched at one time. They appreciated this space because they could "express themselves" and "escape" easily without disturbing the subjects. We asked that each room in the new lab have its own thermostat and ventilation, so testers and subjects could "keep cool" during the tests. We furnished the lab with the most adjustable ergonomic furniture we could find, so that backaches and neckaches would not influence subjects' ratings of our products.

Because Silicon Graphics was growing so rapidly, we decided to scale the lab facility so that eventually the lab could accommodate usability testing for the rest of the company. Our management was aware of the multidivisional need for services and felt it was prudent to plan so that we would need no more than one lab on the Mountain View campus. This led us to include heavy duty power requirements for supercomputers and sufficient networking capabilities to accommodate many machines. We also put a pocket door between the two experimenter cubicles, so that one tester could run two subjects at a time in cooperative work testing.

An equipment list for the lab is shown in Figure 2. Initially, one side of the lab was designated the hardware side and the other the software side. The hardware lab contained two camcorders, which were used on tripods to position around people doing physical hardware tasks such as installation. The software side contained a wall-mounted camera trained on the subject and a VideoCreator™, which is a scan converter sending RGB signals from the computer directly to a VCR to record the screen images. This eliminated the need for a camera behind the subject's head and has been extremely useful. As the group's activities evolved more toward software testing, the equipment on the hardware side was upgraded to provide better capability for capturing the screen graphics and video as well.

Figure 2 Equipment list for Silicon Graphics Human Factors Lab

2 professional quality SVHS video recorders
2 professional qualilty color SVHS-compatible video cameras with wallmount brackets
2 camera remote control units
2 SVHS camcorders with tripods
1 SVHS editting console
1 digital audio/video mixer
4 12 in. color monitors
2 32 in. color monitors
1 consumer quality SVHS video recorder
2 Silicon Graphics VideoCreator™ scan converters
1 Silicon Graphics 4D25 Personal Iris™
1 Silicon Graphics Iris Indigo™
1 Silicon Graphics Indigo2™
1 Silicon Graphics Iris Indigo Elan™
1 Silicon Graphics Indy™
1 Apple Macintosh II/System 7.0™
1 386/Windows™ personal computer

2 adjustable workstation tables
8 adjustable ergonomic chairs
2 equipment side tables
2 built-in corner unit work surfaces with adjustable keyboard trays
2 4 ft. x 6 ft. one-way mirrors
1 10 ft. oblong conference table
12 ergonomic swivel conference chairs

One tester suite is equipped with SVHS source and record VCRs for editing and a simple but professional quality editing console. A mixer has been added to provide the picture-in-a-picture capability and simplify editing. The editing equipment has seen light use. Much of the editing setup doubles as recording equipment, and it needs to be reconfigured everytime we edit a tape. This was inconvenient and we often resorted to queuing up segments of video on source tapes for the engineers to watch.

There are trade-offs between having professional quality video equipment in the lab and consumer quality equipment in other places, where the audience would watch the tapes. For instance, it was a problem recording in SVHS format, which was required for graphics quality, and not having a VHS tape immediately available after the test for the developers. In a new facility, called the Living Room, that built for the Time Warner interactive television project, we decided to use Hi-8 to VHS formats, so we could always have a VHS tape "to go" at the end of any testing session.

Some of us use commercially available data logging software that runs on a PC. The rest use paper-and-pencil logs of subject task times, errors, and other data. In general, the PC-based tools provide a better organized data log, which is easier to read after the test. The paper-and-pencil logs are more flexible and may be more suitable for pilot testing. We acquired commercially available data analysis software early on. In general, because small numbers of subjects are run in iterative test scenarios, where a lot of verbal data is collected, on-line statistical analysis are not usually necessary.

Hiring Staff Members

Although the group was started with technical writers and a customer support engineer as part of the staff, we found over time that the usability issues the company was facing required more than the usability testing expertise that these staff members had developed on the job. There was a strong need for methods that could be used earlier in the product development process and specific types of knowledge that could be more properly described as human factors engineering and user interface design. Eventually, given our marketing organization, we also found the need for market research expertise to help us collect early data on user requirements and customer satisfaction with our released products' usability.

The first order of business was to hire the three people to work on the usability of end-user software, end-user hardware, and developer software. We hired individuals with three to five years experience in a nonacademic setting applying the human factors discipline, and Ph.D degrees in human factors from universities noted for their programs, and certified by the Human Factors Society. All staff members had experience working on a variety of hardware and software products, since versatility and flexibility were considered key requirements for success. We stressed a quantitative background in behavioral data collection methods, knowledge of human factors standards and principles, and expertise in human-computer interaction, anthropometry, and biomechanics (important for hardware). We also looked for in-depth specialization in areas such as on-line documentation, programmer interface, displays, input devices, user interface design and prototyping. These skill sets have served us well in contributing to the usability of Silicon Graphics' products.

Because we started out with a small staff, we hired free-lance contractors to supplement our effort as project load demanded. We typically had the staff working on three or more projects at a time; when the load exceeded that, we hired some short-term help. The contracts would often last 6-12 months. All contractors had at least a master's degree in a human factors-related discipline (psychology, industrial engineering, computer science), plus several years of experience working in the field. Our contractors were typically given offices with the rest of the group and used our lab facilities. Thus far we hired two contractors to permanent staff positions.

Occasionally we had a special need for a survey, focus groups, a video production, or other project that required the use of outside consulting firms, which we also readily employed to support our efforts. We developed some excellent relationships with local small businesses for these purposes.

Organizing Our Mission

Our mission was to provide customer research and usability consulting services to improve the competitive value of Silicon Graphics' products. Our primary services included customer research (focus groups, surveys, conjoint analysis); user interface design consulting (as opposed to design itself, which was performed in Engineering); product design consulting (Product Design being an Engineering function); usability testing; and marketing support (competitive analysis, customer visits, customer demonstrations, and public relations). Until mid-1993, the group was organized functionally according to Figure 3.

Figure 3   Organization of Silicon Graphics' Customer Research and Usability Group

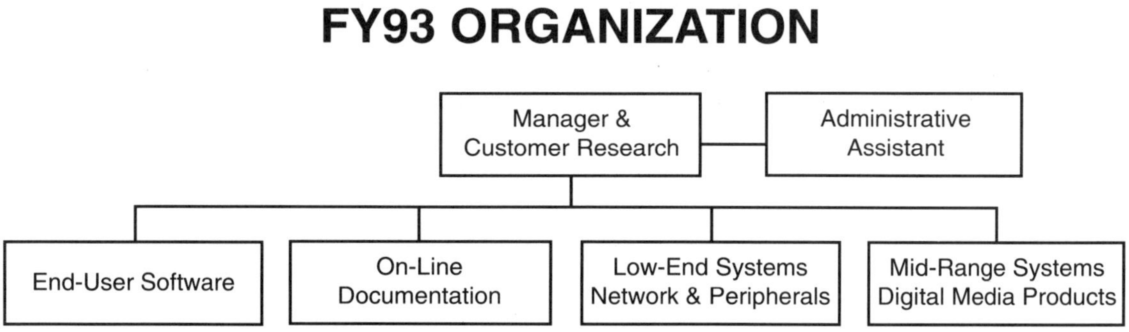

FY93 ORGANIZATION

```
              ┌──────────────────┐       ┌──────────────────┐
              │   Manager &      │───────│  Administrative  │
              │ Customer Research│       │    Assistant     │
              └──────────────────┘       └──────────────────┘
                        │
      ┌──────────┬──────┴──────┬────────────────┐
┌───────────┐ ┌───────────┐ ┌───────────────┐ ┌──────────────────┐
│ End-User  │ │ On-Line   │ │ Low-End Systems│ │ Mid-Range Systems │
│ Software  │ │Documentation│ │Network & Peripherals│ │Digital Media Products│
└───────────┘ └───────────┘ └───────────────┘ └──────────────────┘
```

Of course, in a company like Silicon Graphics, whose own mission is always growing and changing, one might expect a lot of variation in the organization of a service group like ours. At any given point in time, our objectives revolved around the products under development, which were driven by the downsizing and cost-reduction of our hardware and the integration of multimedia capabilities into our systems. The group resided in a hardware division for the first two years and a software division for the third year, with multiple upper management changes and a major corporate reorganization following the MIPS merger. Under the Marketing umbrella, we maintained a process-driven orientation that was flexible enough for us to work on most any product. Currently, the group reports to Engineering and anticipates a more direct role in user interface design.

Running the Program: "Thriving on Chaos . . ."

Fitting into the Spirit of Silicon Graphics

The Spirit of Silicon Graphics is the company credo (see inset). It provides insight into what employees will face as they attempt to thrive on the chaos rampant in today's high tech companies. A popular Silicon Valley bumper sticker asks, "Are we having fun yet . . .?" At Silicon Graphics, the culture *demands* that we have fun while we work!

Silicon Graphics
Computer Systems

THE SPIRIT OF SGI

We who ...
Are open and receptive,
hear and understand,
Talk straight and honest,
are heard and understood.

We who ...
Are full of enthusiasm and fun,
watch it spillover and catch on.
Respect, trust and support,
are lifted above our squabbles.

We who ...
Seek solutions rather than blame,
fuel and sustain our growth.
Empower others and delegate,
find our scope increased.

We who ...
Set objectives and propogate them,
find our objectives met.
Encourage creativity, see results
beyond our expectations.

The flip side finds employees working long hours on short-staffed projects. The company has succeeded against the odds of bigger, richer competitors who can invest more resources in new product R&D; smaller, faster competitors who can get to the market earlier; and the constant pressure of Wall Street analysts who set their own expectations for company growth, driving schedules and costs ever downward. Because of rapid growth, many employees are new, bringing with them processes from other companies which the rest have never seen before. This is often good, because it improves the way we do things; on the other hand, we rarely do anything the same way twice.

Usability engineering is a process-driven discipline. We have certain methods that we prefer to execute at particular times in the product development cycle, assuming there is some kind of standard cycle and we can determine what that cycle is. We like to get in early on the process, assuming we can identify when the requirements planning started; and we like to iterate our design and testing to get it just right, assuming there will be time to do it more than just once.

In our experience at Silicon Graphics, all of these assumptions have been violated at one time or another. The company often uses different cycles to develop different products, even products of the same type such as hardware systems. There is no corporate mandate for the steps the developers should follow; they are encouraged to be flexible, depending upon the purpose of the product. Product planning may start at the beginning of the product development cycle. More often, it happens toward the middle, with the product already cooking for a few months in the heads of a couple of engineers before upper management blesses the idea with project status and resources. And depending upon the competition, the need to ship products to meet financial objectives, and other constraints, there may be one chance to design and code or build a product. As the human factors person, you hope you are right the first time, because there might not be a second chance! (Well, maybe in software, where there's a second release.)

Further, Silicon Graphics is very results driven. The engineers do not necessarily want a *process* for designing comprehensible icons; they want the icons themselves. Our greatest successes as a usability team were in the areas where we could rapidly produce some aspect of the product itself.

The keys to success in this type of environment were to have excellent working relationships with engineering, communicate informally as much as possible (particularly at lunch, on the soccer field, or over the cubicle wall), and be fast on your feet about making your inputs. We could not investigate every issue as thoroughly as we would have done in graduate school. However, given a collective experience of 40-50 years applying human factors, we often improved the quality of products by contributing our best guesses as well as our hard data to the product development effort.

User Interface Design at Silicon Graphics

Until mid-1993, most user interfaces (UIs) were designed by Engineering. The Usability group was in marketing, and our contributions typically came later in the development cycle. These contributions included usability reviews of semifunctional alpha software, usability walkthroughs (with emphasis on providing proper functionality), usability testing, and some UI design.

Due to the large number of projects we were supporting and the tight development schedules, it was often difficult to do early prototyping or test design alternatives. Therefore, some of our biggest successes came in the second release of a product.

In mid-1993, the group was moved to Engineering and placed under a new manager, Bob Vallone. The new goal is to centralize and integrate usability and UI design expertise in one group that is jointly responsible with Engineering for product user interfaces. The UI designer is now part of the usability group and additional UI designers have joined the group. Additionally, the new group manager is working to reduce the number of projects supported in order to increase the intensity of involvement early and throughout the development cycle. The current model emphasizes *collaboration* (among UI designers, usability professionals, engineers, writers, and marketers) and *iteration* (mock-ups, low fidelity prototypes and interactive usability evaluations, followed by usability testing and field studies at customer sites later in the lifecycle).

Adapting standard methods

Given the preceding environment, many of the methods we were traditionally taught in graduate school did not apply very well in toto to usability engineering at Silicon Graphics. However, almost all can be adapted to be useful in this setting. Some work better than others, and those will be described.

User requirements often involve an extensive review of the literature, application of existing standards, and task analysis or systems engineering studies to generate proper descriptions of users, their jobs, and other characteristics in order to specify a new product. We often generated requirements based on experience and test results with the previous generation product, since the user base was fairly stable (it often expanded but still included past audiences). Interviews with country marketing managers helped us focus on ergonomic requirements that were critical to international sales.

Because the product development cycle was so fast, it became imperative to find a way to provide feedback on products *before* they could be tested with users in the lab. Shortly after we started the group, we became heavily reliant on Jakob Nielsen's *heuristic evaluation* method (Nielsen, 1989, 1990). This has become a standard part of our process, its success limited only by the availability of non-usability staff to participate in the reviews. We extended this technique to help us perform usability reviews of hardware, including specification drawings, foam mock-ups, and prototype components and packaging, using a team of two to three human factors staff personnel plus product designers and technical writers.

Prototyping is a common activity performed by usability groups, and it has been proven highly successful in reducing total time to code and improving the quality of the final product (Jones, 1978). Although it was always a goal of the usability group to perform rapid on-line prototyping, it was difficult to find a tool that would run on the IRIX operating system, which successfully represented Silicon Graphics' unique 3D graphics capabilities, and was easy for us to learn and use in the context of our development effort. We have successfully used bx, a Motif-style builder tool, to complete early interaction model prototypes of Indigo Magic for focus group evaluation.

Our greatest adaptation of methods came in the area of *usability testing*. We performed a very wide variety of tests, from "before and after" testing to compare product versions, to just-in-time (JIT) usability testing, to answer an urgent question. Probably our most formal and well-constructed test was performed on the IRIS Insight™ on-line documentation (Mohageg and Davilla, 1992). This involved a series of tests that gave feedback to Engineering on the user interface for a hypertext on-line documentation system and provided comparisons with reading text documentation. Substantial improvements in user performance over the alpha software were realized in search time for topics and a reduction in user errors. Reading speeds were comparable to that of paper documentation, which is a tremendous accomplishment for an on-line user interface.

We performed a JIT test when Silicon Graphics was about to ship an audio upgrade to its Personal IRIS 4D30 Series workstations. There were serious questions posed by manufacturing about the customer installability of the audio board. Thanks to the teamwork of a well-oiled "usability machine," which included our colleagues in Documentation, we were able to answer the question empirically in only one and a half days! Five of us worked together to recruit and test 12 subjects on the installation procedure. Our administrator worked with an employment agency to recruit and schedule subjects. We were fortunate in that the test and data collection materials were already designed for an earlier system. We had two testers, one in each identically configured test suite, running subjects simultaneously from 8:00 AM to 6:00 PM the same day. One documentation manager greeted subjects and administered pre- and post-test questionnaires. A fourth person set up data collection file templates on the computer, entered the data immediately after each subject was run, and ran the statistical analysis at 6:00, when all data collection was complete. We generated several slides summarizing the results and presented them to Manufacturing and Engineering bright and early the next morning! A decision was made by 11:00 AM to change a part and ship the product.

One of the most effective metrics we have found in convincing Engineering to make changes has been the number of subject calls to the "hot line." In each test, we simulate the company's customer phone support service. Since we know the cost to Silicon Graphics of one of these calls and we can observe how many calls were made per subject in a test, we can calculate the cost to the company of any particular usability problem over the projected unit sales, until the problem is fixed. With volume sales as a goal, this is usually a large number, and provides incentive to fix the problem as quickly as possible.

While JIT testing is not that common, it is usual to test small numbers of subjects, have the engineers watch (and sometimes run up and down the stairs to change things on the fly), and perform several iterations of the design-test cycle. The experimental designs are often within-subjects, with subjects evaluating one or more alternative product designs. The types of subjects have evolved from internal employees to external temporary agency workers, depending upon time and budget.

Focus groups and other entirely subjective data collection methods require special recruitment techniques, often with high monetary incentives, to get outside subjects who are considered valid by the marketing and development team. This has been done for us by a market research firm, which uses zip codes and keyed mailing lists to find candidates and performs a careful telephone screening to make sure they match our customer profile before sending them to us.

Public Relations and Other Side Effects

In addition to our product development support activities, there are internal and external responsibilities required for being a good citizen if you are running a usability lab in Silicon Valley. The first is to give lab demonstrations to groups of schoolchildren in the Bay Area, who are routinely invited to Silicon Graphics on their field trips. This has been a fun and rewarding experience for many of us, to explain human factors for the first time to kids who may someday join us as colleagues. We have also spent time with other high tech companies in the Valley and as far away as the United Kingdom, who have come to see the lab in anticipation of building their own facility.

One of the most interesting (and stressful) demos was requested by our Investor Relations department, which called late on a Thursday night to say that an analyst from a big investment bank in New York was coming on Friday, to see how "user friendly" the products were, since our strategy was based upon selling volume. Could we set up a usability test for him?

Luckily, our IRIS Indigo had been tested inside and out (over 200 subjects had participated in iterative testing in the course of its development). We were able to get a new unit directly off the manufacturing line on Friday morning, cut the shrink wrap, and set it up to make sure it would function. We then carefully repackaged and sealed it in anticipation of the analyst's visit. He arrived about 4:00 on Friday, with great enthusiasm unpacked and set up the Indigo, "bounced the Jello" (that's a demo), and was on his way. His time: 9 minutes, 49 seconds, beating the average user time of 11 minutes! He returned to New York a happy man, and our Marketing vice-president emitted a great cheer of joy (which drowned out our sighs of relief) upon hearing the results. (Contrary to the rumor that went around, the lab did not appear on *Wall Street Week* that night.)

The lab has also been used routinely in customer visits, to impress them with Silicon Graphics' commitment to product usability. It was an important factor in Silicon Graphics' recent deal with Time Warner to develop an interactive cable television system. Time Warner executives toured the lab and were impressed with the resources and attention paid to usability, which would be critical in producing an entertainment system.

In return for all their good help on the lab, Facilities and Human Resources pressed us into service when it came time for Silicon Graphics to set up a repetitive strain injury (RSI) prevention program. We were happy to oblige; it was the start of a much bigger effort and the eventual hiring of a Safety and Environmental Manager with ergonomic expertise outside the Usability Group.

Maintenance: How to Take a Licking and Keep on Ticking

Our group met on a regular basis (every two weeks for one and a half hours) to coordinate testing schedules and discuss what was going on in the group and how we could work on common problems. It was very important to members of the group to have other individuals with common backgrounds with whom they could discuss projects, methods, and obstacles. This is an important morale boosting benefit of having a Usability Group (many) rather than a Usability Engineer (one).

Some groups running labs assign the responsibility of lab administrator to one individual. This strategy can really bring the lab operation to its knees if the administrator is unavailable! For this reason, we all took turns doing some lab administration. This also gave new members of the group the opportunity to design changes into the lab, which kept the lab current and flexible to adapt to the latest agenda of the company.

Many of the methods and techniques just described are illustrated in the description of how Showcase 3D, an end-user 3D graphics product, was developed. This is a particularly good example of a "conversion" of Engineers into usability believers and the complexities that 3D software can present to an "average" user, who may have experience only with 2D computing. Note that this particular case is a "typical," rather than "prototypical," example of an industrial project. While the Usability group constantly strives toward involvement throughout the product development cycle, this ideal situation is difficult to find due to the scheduling and staffing constraints of most projects. See Mohageg and Davilla (1992) for a description of a project with a more "ideal" usability case study.

Showcase 3D—A Case Study

Background

Mike writes:

This case study describes the usability work for a three-dimensional drawing and modeling environment included in an end-user multimedia presentation and drawing package called Showcase 3.0. Showcase is bundled with Silicon Graphics workstations. Earlier versions of Showcase provided users the ability to create full-color documents incorporating sound, video (live or digitized), images, and a wide variety of two-dimensional graphics. Additionally, the application literally "showcased" many of the digital media capabilities of Silicon Graphics workstations. However, a significant piece of the Silicon Graphics computational prowess was missing from earlier versions: truly interactive 3D graphics and modeling. Therefore, a significant feature enhancement in Showcase 3.0 was to include interactive and usable 3D graphics.

A team of developers from the IRIS Inventor group, a toolkit for developing real-time, interactive 3D modeling capabilities (Strauss and Carey, 1992; Wernecke, 1993), was assigned to design and deliver the 3D environment within Showcase. While the task of designing 3D modeling environments was not new to the 3D team, the target audience was. The 3D team had provided their toolkit (and applications based on the toolkit) to users who were experienced programmers and familiar with 3D modeling (or familiar enough to use it in their applications). Including 3D in a "low-end" presentation package was going to expose 3D to a very heterogeneous user base with varying levels of experience and knowledge in 3D environments. Thus, it seemed imperative that usability be involved in the design and evaluation processes.

There were three main goals for the 3D environment. First, we wanted to provide an environment that novice and intermittent 3D users could understand and use. Second, we needed to provide the basic necessities for creating, importing, and viewing 3D graphics and models. A high degree of interactivity and naturalness were key. Finally, we had an ulterior motive of laying the building blocks and UI foundation for a stand-alone 3D drawing and modeling application. We envisioned such an application would eventually emerge from this work.

Attitude and Approach of the Team

The attitude of the 3D development team was mixed. Some believed that if they were thoughtful and careful in designing the user interface, the end user would have no problems using the product. This expectation is common among developers and seems to transcend both hardware and software projects. Others in the team were genuinely looking forward to the usability feedback. Afterall, history has shown even the best and most ingenious user interfaces can benefit significantly from usability evaluations. Feedback from the targeted user population has always yielded a measurably better product. For instance, we were able to measure a 60% task time reduction and an 18% accuracy improvement after feedback from usability testing had been folded into an on-line documentation system (Mohageg and Davilla, 1992).

After lengthy discussions, the usability manager convinced the 3D team's manager to allow a usability review of the product and perhaps a usability test, if deemed necessary. The Showcase 3D development team was unsure of how usability feedback would help because they had never worked with us before. They expected feedback on fairly low-level issues such as layout, menu names, and icon positioning and design. Additionally, the 3D team believed the usability evaluations would confirm the ease-of-use of their designs.

The product was in the middle stages of the development cycle. However, while a good deal of the functionality had been implemented there was still ample opportunity to enhance existing features and add new ones. This flexibility was due to Showcase 3D being written using a toolkit that allowed for speedy changes to the UI.

Selecting the Appropriate Methods

Since a considerable portion of the coding had been completed early usability input methods (e.g., requirements document) would have simply set back the development. We decided a usability review, followed by a usability test, would be most appropriate. A review would identify potential usability problems for novice and intermittent users and had two additional objectives:

1. show that the usability group could provide useful feedback from a perspective different than that of the developers,
2. suggest solutions to problems that they would implement or challenge.

In the second case, I hoped the design recommendations would be compelling enough to convince any skeptical developers of the need for usability testing.

The Usability Review

I obtained a copy of the latest prototype version of Showcase 3D and conducted the review on the lowest end Silicon Graphics' machine at the time: an IRIS Indigo™, with a MIPS R3000 CPU, standard 8-bit graphics, and a 1024×768 resolution monitor. The Indigo in this specific configuration was used since it was the likely workstation of our customers for low-end products.

The design review was critical for establishing credibility with the 3D team. It provided an opportunity to show that we had more to contribute than feedback on icon design, layout, and menu names. The information generated would address user expectations and needs based on our understanding of the intended tasks and users' knowledge of 3D (which I assumed to be minimal). A total of 17 issues were identified in the review, ranging from functional inconsistencies to enhancing existing functionality to including new, vital functionality.

Functional Inconsistencies

Immediately the review identified inconsistencies with the 2D portion of Showcase. Methods for selecting objects, cut/copy/paste, deleting objects, and some menu terminology were found to be different. The methods for performing these tasks in 2D were also very easy and usable, therefore making these items more consistent with Showcase 2D would solve the problems.

These low-level items were fairly straightforward and certainly did not require a usability professional to discover them. The 3D team quickly implemented the suggested changes.

Alteration of Existing Functionality

User Model—Scene vs. Camera Manipulation

Alterations to existing functionality were proposed to facilitate the users' ability to formulate a mental model of the operation of Showcase 3D. There was a big difference between the developers' model of how 3D "should" work and the mental model users' were likely to adopt. The developers had used a model that treats a 3D scene as a stationary entity. The mouse is then used to move a camera around the scene. Users see the view from this camera. For instance, a user who moves the mouse to the right is moving the camera to the right. Objects will appear to move, but only due to the change in position of the camera.

In contrast, I believed users would view the scene and its contents as objects that were being manipulated by the mouse (based on users' experience with 2D graphics). Cameras per se would have no relevance in this model. Also, it seemed this scene manipulation model *should* be promoted since it was a natural extension of users' model of 2D operations, where users directly manipulate the object(s) of interest. I pushed to have the latter model reflected in all existing operations. The 3D team suspected this view was representative of low-end product users and agreed to alter appropriate portions of functionality to reflect the scene manipulation model.

For instance, the 3D team had designed translation along the z-axis (into and out of the display) such that moving the mouse forward (away from user) brought objects closer while moving the mouse backward (toward user) pushed objects away. This operation was logical if the mouse were controlling the camera position. However, it was inconsistent with a model where the mouse controlled the scene; moving the mouse forward needed to "push" the objects away and "pull" the object close when moving the mouse backward.

Recommendations for New Functionality

Orientation

The most critical new functionality proposed was a method to help users maintain a sense of orientation. With the existing design, there were no cues concerning the orientation of the scene nor the relative positions of objects in it. For instance, from looking at the 3D scene in Figure 4, it is impossible to determine which object is closer or if the scene has been rotated from the original position. From a usability perspective orientation was critical, especially for users who had rarely interacted with 3D drawing environments.

Based on the work of Herndon, Zeleznik, Robbins, Conner, Snibbe, and van Dam (1992), we hypothesized that a walled background which would "house" the 3D objects could allow users to see the location of objects and the orientation of the scene. Potentially we could cast a constant shadow of objects to provide information concerning their positions. Shadows will be discussed in detail in the Design Solutions section.

However, the 3D team was uncertain as to the true need for elaborate orientation and scene rotation mechanisms. The additional work required was significant, and they were not 100% convinced that the proposed solutions would solve the problems. We agreed to pay close attention to these issues in the usability test without changing the current design.

The Usability Test

Tasks

Initially, I generated a list of issues to be tested. I reviewed this list with the 3D team to make certain we all believed the same issues to be worthy of testing. Of particular interest were drawing functions, manipulation tasks (e.g., moving, scaling, rotating), and orientation feedback. I then developed tasks to evaluate the issues of interest. Finally, the developers performed the tasks with the prototype software to ensure they were satisfied with the task scenarios.

Participants

Ten Silicon Graphics employees participated in the study. Half the participants were experienced and knowledgeable users of various CAD packages or 3D modeling applications. The second half of subjects had never used three-dimensional graphics or modeling applications.

Figure 4   A 3D scene from the early prototype. The cone is closer in space than the box. The outline around the box is a manipulation box that appeared around any selected object. (See Color Plate Va.)

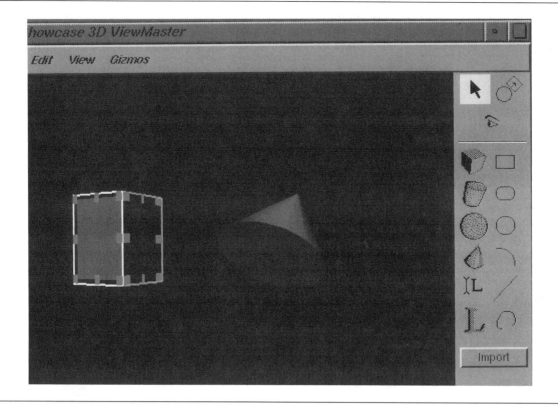

Some usability groups are reluctant to use company internal subjects. We have found our employees to be more demanding of our products than even "real" customers. Therefore, we feel comfortable using internal participants when necessary. However, there is considerable face validity in using a representative sample of "real" customers; these subjects should be used when time and cost resources allow.

Procedure

All participants performed five tasks in random order. The tasks required 12 to 20 minutes each. I used time as the key performance measure and recorded errors in a binary fashion: tasks were performed either correctly or incorrectly. Errors were difficult to track since there were no quantifiable degrees of task success. A seven-point Likert scale with positive and negative anchors was used to collect opinions concerning various tasks and features.

A scan converter generated NTSC video from the test machine; this video signal and that from a camera focused on the participant were fed to two monitors in an observation area. The developers attended the test sessions and observed participants using the software.

Results

The test yielded 12 problem areas including issues such as orientation, system modality, and object rotation. This section will discuss findings related to the user orientation problems only.

Orientation

Novice users, in particular, had difficulty determining the location of objects in space and their location in relation to one another. Many also needed assistance in grasping the concept that the environment they were using was literally a space and not a flat surface. For instance, in a sample 3D scene, two identical cylindrical objects were placed in space. One object was closer to the user than the other. The user would rotate the scene about and observe the "physical" distance between the objects. Yet, in attempting to draw a replica of the objects, users would draw one cylinder (usually the one closest in space), make a copy, then reduce the height of the copy! Reducing the height of the copy made their drawing look identical to the sample, but the objects were side by side rather than separated along the z-axis. It was clear that novice users were having difficulty grasping the concepts of 3D, and there were no mechanisms available to facilitate the learning.

Scene Rotation

Users could rotate a scene by entering a rotate "mode" (by clicking on the eye icon in Figure 4). In this mode, as the user moved the mouse in various directions, he or she was actually moving the scene in free, three-dimensional (x-, y-, and z-axes) scene rotation. Testing found that users had a strong desire for the inclusion of constrained rotation that would allow rotation along a specific plane. For instance, most needed the ability to rotate the scene radially without any up-down (y-axis) displacement. In addition to providing easy movements, constrained rotation would allow users to easily return the scene to its original position. This task was often cumbersome with free rotation. Also, most users wanted to perform free and constrained rotation without having to enter a mode.

Moving vs. Scaling

All the selected objects in the scene were surrounded by a 3D manipulation box. The cone in Figure 4 is selected and shows its manipulation box. Grabbing a manipulation box on any side would move the object in that plane. For instance, clicking on the front plane would allow up-down and left-right movement. Clicking on the top would allow left-right and forward-backward movement. Users had no problems in using this object movement scheme. However, they found it very difficult to decipher the location of the object they were moving in relation to a stationary object. Due to lack of position feedback, it was often unclear whether the two object were at roughly the same z-axis position, for instance.

To exacerbate matters, the behavior of an important scaling operation also created object position ambiguities. As seen in Figure 4, there are green handles along the edges of manipulation boxes. Users could click and drag these handles to change the size characteristics (scale) of objects; much the same as in 2D graphics. The problematic operation was in manipulating corner handles. The corner handles would perform uniform scaling; therefore, the object would appear uniformly larger or smaller in all dimensions during the resizing operation. The problem in allowing this operation was that users became quickly confused as to whether they were actually resizing an object or moving it along the z-axis instead. The visual appearance and feedback was identical for a uniformly enlarging or reducing object and one being moved toward or away from the user.

Design Solutions

While a number of usability issues were identified and addressed, only the design solutions to user orientation and related topics will be presented. The designs discussed below were a collaborative effort and required much iteration; please see the acknowledgments section for a list of the contributors.

Goals

Our goal was to provide cues concerning scene orientation and the position of objects within the scene. Additionally, we wanted to allow for mode-free constrained and free rotation of the scene.

Walls

We created walls to illustrate the sides, floor, and ceiling of the 3D space as seen from the users vantage point (Figure 5). The concept was that users would be able to immediately grasp the three-dimensional nature of the space they were viewing. The testing showed that novice users had been inconsistent in adopting a 3D view of the scene. Simply providing walls that defined a space reiterated the 3D nature of the scene at all times.

However, we needed to make special provisions for the walls. Normally walls imply a fixed space, as in a room or a box. The 3D scene had to be limitless to accommodate

Figure 5 A 3D scene from the finished product. The concept of "space" is immediately visible. Also, as can be detected by looking at the shadows, the box is closer in space than the cone. The top of the scene is blue and the bottom is brown. These colors are maintained despite any scene rotations so users can quickly identify the "true" top and bottom of their scene. (See Color Plate Vb.)

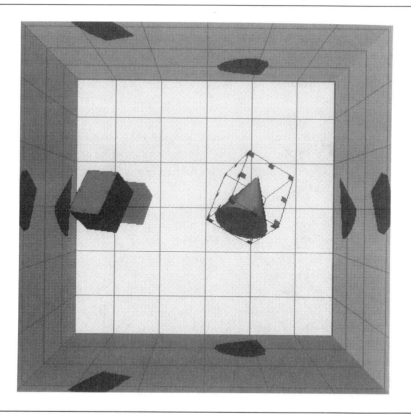

both small and large drawing spaces. Therefore, we made the walls adjustable. Walls and the floor would automatically move to accommodate a users scene requirements. For instance, if a user moved an object until it came in "contact" with a wall, the wall would simply move away in the direction the user was moving the object. Other walls would automatically adjust to keep pace with the moving wall. In this fashion, the user always had a base level of orientation concerning the scene.

This moving wall approach could not be applied uniformly. The scene would have been a constantly changing kaleidoscope if we were to change the walls any time users made alterations. The approach we adopted was to alter wall position only when the scene needed to enlarge. If users moved objects toward the center of the scene there was no wall movement. This design provided predictable wall changes and scene stability. If they desired, users could resize the walls to their current scene at any time by executing a menu command. This command was especially useful for reducing the size of an unnecessarily large scene.

The walls became the basis for much of the orientation feedback concerning the scene, the objects within the scene, and the position of objects in relation to one another. The walls even became the doorway to mode-free scene rotation. Each of these will be discussed.

Scene Rotation and Orientation

Constrained Rotation

Mode-free, constrained scene rotation was a critical need; testing illustrated that it was even more critical than free rotation. Therefore, we integrated constrained rotation directly into the walls. Without changing modes, users could click anywhere on a wall and the entire scene would rotate parallel to that wall (or plane). For example, in Figure 5, clicking on the floor and moving the mouse to the left would rotate the entire scene radially from left to right with no up-down (y-axis) displacement. Clicking on the back wall and moving the mouse to the right would rotate the scene clockwise with no backward-forward (z-axis) displacement. Figure 6 shows a scene rotated roughly 45° radially by rotating the floor of the scene.

Proper feedback was provided before, during, and after scene rotation. When the user clicked on a wall, the axis of rotation for that wall would appear, as would a large arrow showing the plane and direction of rotation. Both these UI components were visible during rotation as well. Since the walls were an integrated component of the scene, the walls themselves would rotate along with the objects in the scene. Thus, the direction, speed, and amount of rotation was clearly observable. Finally, when rotation was completed the position of the walls provided immediate feedback as to the orientation and position of the scene (Figure 6). The user could return to this scene at any time and immediately understand the orientation.

Figure 6   A 3D scene rotated 45 degrees. The locations of the walls show users that the scene has been rotated from the original position. The shadows continue to provide object location information as the scene rotates. (See Color Plate Vc.)

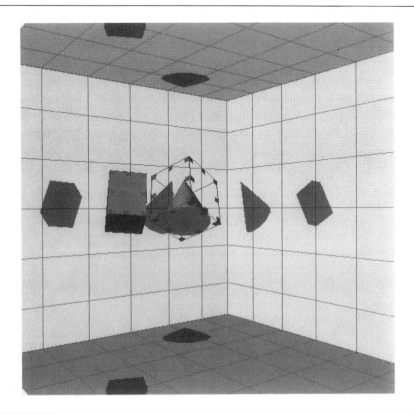

Free Rotation

Unfortunately, we were unable to allow modeless free rotation. Most prototype schemes created more confusion than utility. The final design required users to click on an icon to enter a free rotation mode similar to that described earlier (with a virtual trackball). Nonetheless, we were content in knowing we had provided mode-free constrained rotation, which was more critical than free rotation for novice and intermittent users.

Object Position

The best method for showing object position was to cast shadows on all visible walls (Herndon et al., 1992). However, casting a shadow for all objects simultaneously and

constantly re-calculating shadow positions as the scene rotated was highly CPU intensive. Our solution was to cast a shadow for selected objects only. The solution worked
well. For instance, in Figure 4 the user had no concept of where the selected objects
were in relation to one another. In Figure 5, the shadows of the selected objects immediately convey significantly more information concerning the position of objects compared to each other and to their environment.

We built extra capabilities into the shadows. For instance, we found moving an object
in a scene crowded with other objects could be difficult because accessing the desired
side of the object's manipulation box was problematic. As a result, we allowed users to
move shadows in order to move objects. If a user moved a shadow appearing on the
floor (or wall), the object was moved parallel to the floor (or wall). This feature allowed
for moving objects (in any orientation) with no dependencies on the manipulation box.

Other Enhancements

Another enhancement to help orientation was to alter the functionality of the corner
scaling handle to perform nonuniform (instead of uniform) scaling. Combined
with the shadows feedback, the user could immediately determine the nature of the
manipulation.

Lessons Learned

Usability

The combination of usability review and usability testing yielded excellent results. We
were able to use the review as a springboard for recommending that testing occur.
Additionally, the review allowed for a test focused on issues that both usability and
the development team agreed were of interest. However, key in performing evaluation is the usability person's ability to learn about the topic as quickly and thoroughly
as possible. The implication is that usability professionals must have the breadth of
experience to allow for fast learning of key concepts and models in the UI (of own or
competitive products). It is also critical to learn and adopt the vocabulary of the application domain to the extent possible; doing so will allow the usability professional to
"talk the developers language" and get points across.

Simultaneously, the usability person must be able to set aside his or her experience
and the ability to grasp concepts quickly. Essentially, the person should be able to simulate the thoughts and knowledge of the targeted customer base. Failure to adopt the
user's point of view in usability evaluations will yield feedback restricted chiefly to
lower level items (e.g., layout) and many important problems (e.g., missing functionality) may be overlooked.

3D Team

The usability review provided the 3D team with more feedback than anticipated concerning many of its key assumptions. The review illustrated the necessity for user testing, especially on the issues of orientation, object manipulation, and general interaction with 3D scenes. The testing was a tremendous learning opportunity for the developers. The entire team observed the testing and watched as subjects struggled with various functions (or lack of them). The testing clearly convinced the developers that some of their assumptions would not hold for this new user population of 3D novices.

Finally, the developers clearly understood the importance and utility of user feedback and usability input. Much of the concern I had expressed during the usability review was confirmed in the testing. These confirmations created a new degree of credibility for usability among these developers.

Summary: Success Strategies for Usability in High-Tech

1. Build the Best Lab You Can Afford

Scope for the future if possible, when your usability efforts will expand. Consider how many people will ultimately be using the lab, and the range of products you might be asked to test. Our lab has become a showplace for the company where Sales and Marketing representatives like to bring customers, and a multi-use facility with constant traffic.

2. Hire the Most Qualified People You Can Find

This adds credibility to the program and creates a collective resource of experience to draw upon as you solve a diversified range of usability problems. The individuals you hire should also provide access to a network of professionals outside your company with more specialized expertise if your project needs it.

3. Be Sensitive to the Corporate Culture

If the culture is very informal, strip away the formalisms of your discipline. It was more important to provide content rather than process and be part of the team rather than be an isloated expert at Silicon Graphics.

4. Adapt the Organization of the Group to Corporate Change

With the mergers and restructuring of corporations today, this may require expanding, splitting, or otherwise rethinking the structure of the group to better serve the needs of the company. Corporate change may create opportunities for usability to infiltrate new projects and new parts of the company business. It may also require retraining or hiring individuals with different types of expertise.

5. Use Data or Feedback from "Real Users" Performing "Real Tasks"

Credibility is an issue here. If the subjects' characteristics do not ring true to the developers, they will not believe your study's results. Developers and marketers should have a say in the recruitment requirements for subjects. The usability engineer may help to forge a common understanding of the target user's characteristics. In general, it is not advisable to test other members of the project team, and it may not be acceptable to test other company employees, depending upon what types of judgments they will be making in the test. The validity of the test data may be jeopardized by recruiting employee subjects who are possibly biased for or against the company, even if they meet other subject requirements.

Similarly, the tasks subjects perform must test the issues of concern, while still being representative of the work a user may do with the product. The development team must accept the tasks as being valid prior to the test. If possible, the team should perform the tasks before the test to make certain they are acceptable.

6. Have Developers Watch People Using the Product

Seeing is believing. This can be done live, or *post hoc* via video recordings. It will be easier to convince them to make changes if they have seen users stumble with their own eyes; in fact it may take little or no convincing at all! Developers and UI designers (who may be the usability person as well) see usability problems as they happen and documentation writers find glitches in their documentation or find a better method of explaining UI components. In our experience, live viewing often seems more compelling than video tapes or the usability professional's recommendations.

7. Provide Design Alternatives for Product Feature Problems

In addition to showing flaws, be familiar enough with the product and the goals developers are trying to achieve to suggest some design alternatives which might work. This requires submerging oneself at a detailed level in the design (see 8 below). Often developers will do one of three things with this information: adopt the recommendation completely, reject the recommendation but provide an alternative of their own, or build upon the design you have proposed to improve it or make it feasible. In any case, the product is improved.

8. Walk a Mile in the Developer's Shoes ("Get down in the trenches...")

This requires immersing oneself in the details of the design, and empathizing with and solving the developer's problems. Most developers want to create usable products; however, there are many obstacles in today's development environments, such as intractable user interface toolkits, time limitations, staffing limitations, performance hits, etc. Apply your knowledge of software development or product design to help the developer find a solution or compromise which improves the usability of the product without jeopardizing the schedule, cost, performance, or other aspects of product success which are often traded off with usability. This may require extra homework for the usability engineer, which is often well worth it in terms of good relationships with developers and product successes.

9. Pick Your Battles Carefully

Decide for which issues you are willing to "go to the mat", and which are secondary. The primary issues should be those that affect the largest numbers of users, or that cause the worst usability problems (e.g., crashing the system, physical injury). Prioritizing these issues will result in less resistance when a truly critical problem comes along; the developers will know the Usability Group is not "crying wolf" over an insignificant problem if they have observed a range of prioritized responses in the past.

10. Show Respect for Developer's Work

When providing feedback, include the positive results, preferably first. Let them know what the customers can use and appreciate. Then approach the problems in a prioritized way (see #9). Give them feedback when they make progress, and spend the time with them to work through problems if necessary. Finally, celebrate your breakthroughs and successes together!

Future Directions

Anna has transferred from the Visual Magic Division Usability Group to the Computer Systems Group. She is a member of the Time Warner Project team where she manages the development of input devices for interactive television. She has also designed a facility called The Living Room, which is a new usability testing lab simulating a home environment where viewers can watch television.

Mike continues to be part of the Usability Group, which has moved to the Engineering Department of the Visual Magic Division and is now managed by Bob Vallone. He is continuing his usability work with multimedia user interfaces, and 3D input devices.

Acknowledgments

Howard Look, David Mott, Alain Dumesny, and Rikk Carey (from the Inventor Toolkit Group), and Debbie Myers (from End-User Publications) contributed significantly to the design solutions described for Showcase 3D. Special thanks to Howard Look and David Mott for also implementing most of these design concepts using the Inventor Toolkit. We appreciate the time and interest of Amy Smith and Bob Vallone, past and current Usability managers at Silicon Graphics, in reviewing this manuscript.

References

Herndon, K.P., Zeleznik, R.C., Robbins, D.C., Conner, D.B., Snibbe, S.S., and van Dam, A. (1992) "Interactive shadows." pp. 1–6. In *Proceedings of the Fifth Annual Symposium on User Interface Software and Technology.* Association for Computing Machinery.

Jones, T.C. (1978) "Measuring program quality and productivity." *IBM System Journal* 17 (1), pp. 78–86.

Meeks, B.N., (1993) "Silicon Graphics: The Presidential Visit." *Microtimes,* p. 32, April 5.

Mohageg, M.F. and Davilla, D.M. (1992) *Hypertext vs. paper for system documentation: An empirical Comparison.* Mountain View, CA: Silicon Graphics Computer Systems, Customer Research and Usability Group.

Nielsen, J. (1989) "Usability engineering at a discount", pp. 394–401, in Salvendy, G. and Smith, M.J. (eds), *Designing and Using Human-Computer Interfaces and Knowledge Based Systems.* Elsevier Science Publishers, Amsterdam.

Nielsen, J. and Molich, R. (1990) "Heuristic evaluation of user interfaces." *CHI'90 Proceedings.* pp. 249–256. ACM Press, April.

Silicon Graphics, Inc. *1993 Annual Report.* Silicon Graphics, 2011 N. Shorline Blvd., Mountain View, CA 94040 USA.

Strauss, P.S. and Carey, R. (1992) "An object-oriented 3D graphics tooklit." *SIGGRAPH '92 Conference Proceedings,* pp. 341–349, Association for Computing Machinery.

Warnecke, J. (1993) *The Inventor Mentor:* Addison-Wesley Publishing Co., Reading, Massachusetts.

CHAPTER 9

Usability at Borland; Building Best of Breed Products

Daniel Rosenberg and Liam Friedland

Borland International

Liam Friedland   Daniel Rosenberg

Daniel Rosenberg is currently the user interface architect for Borland International. He (and his design staff) provide UI and graphic design support for Borland computer language, applications and database products running under several different operating systems. He is also responsible for coordinating cross-product UI consistency and usability testing within Borland. He represents Borland at industry, press, and international standards meetings related to user interface design. His first book, Human Factors in Product Design *(Elsevier Press, 1991), is used as a textbook in universities throughout the world. In addition he has written articles in a variety of journals including* Human Factors and Innovation *magazine. He is also a contributing author in the* Handbook of Human-Computer Interaction *(1988) and* Coordinating User Interfaces for Consistency *(1989). He holds both BS and MS degrees in engineering from Tufts University.*

Liam Friedland is a graphical user interface designer at Borland International and a staff member of the user interface design group. He is responsible for supporting the user interface design of Borland application products. He was responsible for the user interface design and usability testing of the case study presented in this chapter. He holds a BS degree in industrial design from San Jose State University.

Borland's Products and Organization

Borland International is a leading vendor of personal computer software. The company employs approximately 2000 people worldwide. In addition, the company develops client-server software hosted on a variety of workstation computers running several different operating systems. Borland sells approximately 20 separate software products both through direct sales and through distributors via the retail channel. All products are available on an international basis, usually in up to 15 separate languages. On occasion Borland software is sold bundled with computer hardware. These range from add-on board manufacturers to completely configured personal computers with the software preinstalled before shipment. Borland also sells software suite products that contain a set of products in a single package, such as the Borland Office, which is jointly developed with WordPerfect Corporation.

The Borland Organization

Product engineering (R&D) at Borland is structured along individual product lines. A small team of engineers is responsible for the design and implementation of each product. The marketing, quality assurance, technical support and publication functions are all centralized departments working across the various product lines with individual team members assigned to a given product for the duration of at least one release cycle.

The user interface design department is also a centralized resource within the company reporting directly to the vice president of engineering. The business model for usability engineering at Borland is to have a central group responsible for the UI design, prototyping, specification, and testing of all products, while at the same time involving almost everyone in the company in the usability testing and assessment process.

The primary rational for centralizing the user interface design function at Borland is that it is easier to manage cross-product UI consistency issues by having a small group of designers responsible for the design of all products. Design decisions can be made quickly and with effective knowledge of the overall business plan while at the same time the overall quality of design work is much higher. Other companies have invested in creating lengthy style guides and specification documents that programming teams are asked to follow. This approach has significant drawbacks. It requires an extensive maintenance effort to keep the style guide current and a lot of policing of the specification to make engineers follow it. In addition style guides tend to stifle innovation and never really cover the truly difficult issues in UI design. Borland has never taken this approach.

Borland Products

Borland has one of the broadest product families of any software vendor. Its products must be designed for power, interoperability, and ease of use at the same time. In addition, a wide range of users with varying skill levels must be able to use the same product. The major product lines and a summary of typical users is contained in Table 1.

Table 1   Borland's Primary Product Lines

Category	Product	Typical Users
Applications	Quattro Pro for Windows Quattro Pro for DOS	First time spreadsheet users, experienced financial analysts, database access and application developers
Languages	Borland Pascal (DOS and Windows) Borland C++ (DOS and Windows) Borland C++ (OS/2)	Educational market, universities, amateur and professional programmers, systems and network programmers
Database	Paradox (DOS and Windows) dBase (DOS and Windows)	Third party developers, database specialists, casual users and users of custom developed database applications
Server	Interbase (UNIX, NT, and NLM)	Medium and large scale systems development, transaction processing, client-server systems

As shown in Table 1, Borland's products span a wide range of product categories and users. Borland C++ and Borland Pascal are commonly used in universities throughout the world to teach programming. At the same time the majority of commercial PC software for both the Windows and DOS platforms is written using Borland C++. Spanning the range from novice to professional users creates a number of unique usability challenges. On occasion, product lines can be divided into standard and professional editions to minimize the complexity for new users. However, this alone does not address the user's needs as they grow into the more powerful version. Designing a scalable user interface model where the product's functionality is progressively revealed, as the user needs it, is key to the success of these types of products. Building products with an elegantly layered user interface can be accomplished only through a formal usability engineering process.

Similarly, Quattro Pro, Borland's spreadsheet product line is sold to a very wide range of users. It is packaged in standard and workgroup editions. The standard edition is used in the home computer market for personal financial management and by business school students learning financial analysis. The workgroup edition is most often found at the professional end of the market. It is used by knowledge workers and analysts that need access to corporate databases, numerical and data manipulation tools, statistical modeling tools, and the ability to interactively publish and subscribe data among their coworkers. Quattro Pro is also used to create entire applications with its built in user interface construction environment and extensive macro programming language at major accounting firms such as Price Waterhouse.

Database products like Paradox and dBase also pose challenging usability problems. PC database products are used by professional developers to program custom applications. They are also used by casual users that want to work with data interactively on an ad hoc basis. In large corporations there is a mix of ad hoc usage and custom designed database applications. In addition, products like dBase and Paradox are often used as the sole software product to manage small businesses.

The Goal of the Usability Engineering Program

Borland's usability engineering program is structured specifically to deal with the challenge of making high performance, fully featured products accessible to the average user. In particular, the user interface design process focuses on layering the product functionality so that users can grow into the products without being overwhelmed initially. This includes not only designing and testing the user interface of the basic product but also designing extensive built-in support and training features so that users can comfortably learn and explore the product as their needs and experience level grows. The case study described later in this chapter documents the usability engineering program for the interactive tutorials, and object help features introduced in Quattro Pro 5.0 for Windows.

Why Usability Is Important to Borland

Usability is a key component in the success of Borland products. There is a direct relationship between product usability and corporate profitability. Three dimensions exist to this relationship:

- Corporate evaluation and acceptance process,
- Trade press reviews,
- Cost of product technical support.

Each of these areas will be discussed.

Consumers of PC software, particularly on graphical user interface platforms such as Microsoft Windows and OS/2 have very high expectations for product quality and reliability. PC software is a mature business, now over a decade old. People's expectations are high because they rely on these software products for the livelihood. They purchase software to help them perform their work, not because they like computers. In addition, the computer press serves as a watchdog to contrast and compare among the products constantly publishing information about product quality and suitability to the general public.

In addition, most large corporations perform detailed review and analyses of software before choosing a product as their "corporate standard." One of the main concerns within MIS departments responsible for internal support and deployment of PC software is the training cost associated with each new product. The relationship between product usability and training costs has been documented by Nielsen (1993). Obviously, the better the user interface, the lower the training cost per user and the greater the probability that your product will be purchased as the corporate standard.

Product sales, particularly through the retail channel, are effected by product reviews in the trade press. Most PC-oriented computer magazines consider ease of use a key factor in their product review criteria. In some cases trade magazines (for example PC/Computing) have their own in-house usability testing laboratory. These facilities are used to test typical users' abilities to install and use a product. The results weigh heavily in the outcome of the reviews. Positive reviews and "best of breed" awards have a significant effect on product sales, with many magazines giving out official seals of approval as shown Figure 1. They provide the equivalent of millions of dollars of advertising, which many small companies cannot afford.

Even after a software product has been sold, usability continues to effect corporate profitability for the vendor. Borland, like most PC software companies, provides free technical support for the first 90 days after a product sale on most products. Providing this technical support is costly. Within the industry a typical technical support call costs between $15 and $30 to service. This figure varies with both the complexity of the product being supported and the cost structure of the business. However, it does not necessarily vary with the cost of the product or the products profit margin.

The support phone lines must be staffed by skilled technicians knowledgeable in both the product and the software platform it is running on. Price wars as well as the general trend toward lower retail pricing for PC software introduces a new risk for the software industry. A poorly designed user interface could erode a companies profit margin due to increased technical support costs. With full featured spreadsheet and database products selling in the $99 to $150 price range it only takes a few calls per customer before you have actually lost money by selling the product to that particular customer.

Figure 1   Example of how magazine awards are used as built in advertising on product packaging

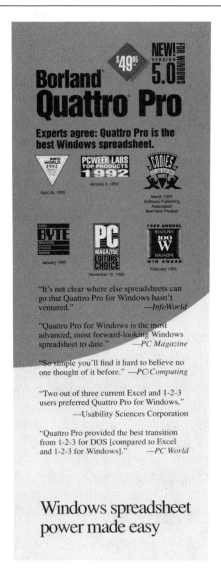

For example, operating system products such as MS Windows or IBM OS/2 while not expensive to purchase are very complex and generate a high volume of technical support calls. This is probably the main reason that Microsoft switched to a 900 number for paid support for the Windows product line.

Borland's Usability Engineering Program

Borland's usability engineering program has three specific goals:

- To build "best of breed" products that are both powerful and usable,
- To increase the profitability of the company through good UI design,
- To make usability an endemic part of the Borland development culture.

Achieving these goals requires managing both the product design process and the people involved in it. A concerted effort is required to collect feedback from existing users as well as potential new users. Both formal usability testing and heuristic methods must be applied throughout the development cycle. This section describes how the usability engineering program at Borland originated, operates, how it is staffed, and the kinds of activities that it is involved in.

History of the Borland UI Design Group

The usability engineering program at Borland was started as part of a corporate technology development center in 1990. The technology development group has expanded into other areas as well but the user interface group is no longer part of it. Originally Borland formed the technology development center to design and manage technologies that were shared across multiple product lines. There were several other departments in the original center, focusing on multimedia tools, application scripting languages, and computer-based training technology.

The user interface group currently reports to the executive vice president for product development the chief technical officer for the company. This organizational change was made because of the critical impact that usability has on product success and the belief that usability engineering decisions required executive level attention and enforcement. It also allows the group to report to a "neutral party" should the need for escalating design decisions and issues arise.

Staffing

On a day-to-day basis Borland R&D technical direction is provided by small groups of "architects" and the engineering vice president. The architects are senior level engineers with expertise and responsibility in specific areas, for example database engine design and C++ language definition. Technical direction for the user interface area is managed the same way as these other technical areas.

The usability engineering process is controlled by the user interface architect. This includes everything from conceptual design though final usability testing. There are no standards committees for UI issues, and it is not a democratic process. Borland senior management is deeply involved in assessing product usability and plays an active role in making design changes and soliciting feedback from both customers and the press. Borland's CEO, Philippe Kahn, is in effect an adjunct member of the user interface design department. As usual, the CEO has the last word on usability issues and everything else. If management is not satisfied with the product's user interface design or the product does not meet its usability objectives (developed as part of the initial product plan), it goes back to the drawing board for a design overhaul.

In addition to the architect, the usability engineering group has a professional staff of four full-time employees. Three of these employees are graphic or industrial designers. The fourth team member is a human factors psychologist responsible for overseeing usability testing of both Borland and competitive products as well as managing the day-to-day operation of the usability testing laboratory. UI design quality and cross-product consistency is maintained by having the same small group of individuals design all products, not by providing massive specifications and guidelines that programmers are expected to read and follow.

Borland has adopted a somewhat uncommon approach to staffing the usability laboratory—the use of virtual staff. This approach has some singular advantages. First, it allows for rapid increase and decrease in staff size to match demand. Second, it makes available to the lab manager a number of people who are expert in the product domain, often a weak area in traditional human factors staffing.

The usability laboratory technicians are drawn from a large pool of A technicians who rotate through a series of laboratories at the company. Getting the participation of the technicians to watch users experience both successes and failures when using products provides them with a greater sensitivity to the importance of good design and to the factors that differentiate between good and bad design.

Members of the publications and QA teams are also part of the virtual team. The editors responsible for documentation are product domain experts and have been found to be very good at creating representative task scenarios with which to test various levels of user expertise. In addition, they often have insight into the sources of user difficulty that only domain experts could have (i.e., discriminating between the user having problems due to not understanding the product, problems in the interface itself, or to negative transfer of training from previous products). Technical editors are already used to adopting a user-centered approach, and watching user difficulties enhances their sensitivities to those product areas that might need special attention in documentation or on-line help text. Hence both functional areas synergistically help each other in the usability engineering mission. The QA engineers are often sensitive to platform design standards and to internal product consistency and add assessment in those areas. In addition, their participation gives them customer interaction that they would not normally have.

Members of the marketing staff are also used to help define the characteristics of various market segments, so that subject selection can be based on those segments. They provide information about how products are used and about customer expectations in a number of areas. In addition, they help define which features of competitive products should serve as benchmarks, so that usability testing can tell us how well we have done. These benchmarks are generally used as a measure of design objectives, instead of more traditionally derived usability goals, because software sales are market driven, and customers have become sensitive to buying products that are considered "best" in specified areas.

In addition each product or project has one software engineer responsible for the implementation of the user interface code. This makes it possible for a small centralized group to support a large number of products. It also makes it possible to address cross-product consistency issues without involving hundreds of people.

This "grassroots" involvement approach coupled with a dedicated team of UI designers seems to work well at Borland. It gives a small group of user interface specialists control over the design of all product-user interfaces. At the same time, it provides the leverage and organizational structure to gather data, make decisions and get ideas implemented. While this organizational model works well for Borland, it might not work as well in other corporations with more formal corporate cultures.

Physical Facilities

The user interface group at Borland is located in a suite of offices in the middle of the engineering organizations office space on the third floor of Borland's' campus complex. This location was intentionally chosen to give the user interface design group good access to all the programming teams. It also makes it easy for project managers and programmers to just drop in and see what is going on not only on their own projects but on other products as well as they move through the building. The usability testing laboratory is located on the floor below the office suite. It is composed of a cluster of four rooms. The floor plan for the laboratory is shown in Figure 2.

Borland's usability laboratory has a typical design for a laboratory of this type. It is similar to the other testing facilities described in this book. The laboratory suite is built around a central control room, which houses all of the video recorders and data logging equipment, a video editing panel, and storage space for supplies. Two separate test rooms are attached to the control room. Each test room has video cameras, networking, and a PC with a video capture board that feeds directly into the video editing bank in the control room. A one-way glass mirror separates the testing rooms from the control room. All the rooms are connected via an intercom.

The fourth room in the laboratory suite is a conference room, which is also wired for video playback and recording. This room is used to watch usability tests as they are conducted and to hold debriefing sessions with project managers after a round of usability tests are completed. The conference room is also used to hold focus groups that are often brought in to evaluate product prototypes and new product concepts that are not quite ready for formal usability testing.

The usability laboratory is situated across from the corporate library directly above the main lobby entrance to the building. This allows easy and secure access to the laboratory without walking through any of the engineering areas in the building. The library area is used as staging location for subjects waiting to participate in usability tests. The current Borland usability laboratory was constructed as part of the new Borland campus complex that opened in the fall of 1993. This was a major advantage because it was planned into the design of the campus years in advance. Fortunately choosing the best location and layout was not constrained by the design of an existing building.

Information Infrastructure

Although Borland has a state-of-the-art usability testing facility, in many ways the software tools used to manage the software engineering process are the most important element in insuring product usability.

Three common software tools play a role in managing product usability. While these tools are also used for other more general engineering purposes, they have been enhanced to handle usability information management as well. These tools are

- The corporate bug tracking system (BTS) database,
- The software version control system (VCS),
- The field-technical support database.

The BTS is the backbone of the information infrastructure for managing the entire software engineering process. It is a network-hosted Paradox application that tracks open, pending, and closed bugs associated with every product under development. The BTS system is entirely on-line, it does not exist in any paper format. All bugs, including user interface ones are categorized by both severity and priority. UI bugs can have the maximum severity rating (usually for design problems) and become "show stoppers" that must be fixed before the product can be shipped.

Figure 2   Floor plan of usability lab in Borland's new campus

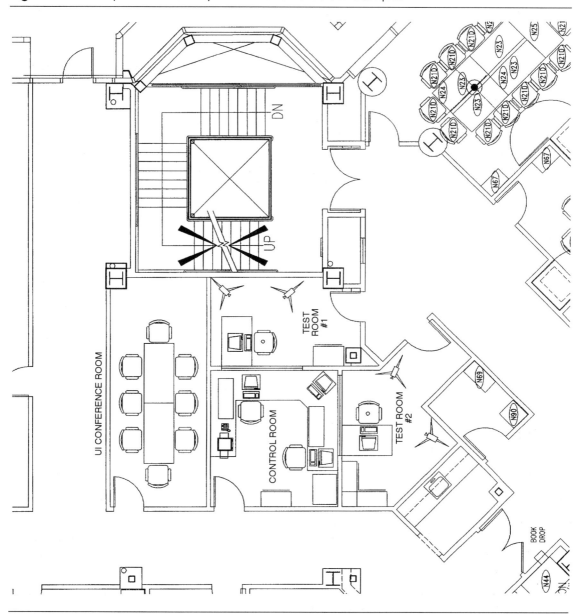

User interface problems and suggestions are generally entered into the BTS by members of the product QA team, the product documentation team or as a result of usability testing. These bugs are assigned by the project BTS administrator to a specific member of the UI group or sometimes the project manager. Regardless of to whom the bug is assigned, the information is available to the UI architect. A UI group member assigned a bug to fix may directly change the product by altering the user interface resources files for icons, menus, or dialog boxes or may work with a programmer directly to rectify the problem if it is deeper in the product code. Often he or she will design and construct several prototypes to test out a new design before changing the code.

In addition employees working on unrelated projects are also encouraged to use products at the alpha and beta level and to enter their "suggestion" bugs into the BTS. Borland has a history of paying a cash bonus per bug to employees for bugs entered on a product they are not officially working on. This cash incentive ranges from $50 to $500, based on the severity of the bug and really encourages people to try out products and make unique and thoughtful suggestions for its improvement.

Although user interface "bugs" can be assigned to either the project manager or a member of the user interface design group, major cross-product usability and consistency bugs are assigned to the corporate user interface architect. The most important benefit of using the BTS to track usability issues is that information does not get lost in the process. At any point in time you can tell who is assigned to resolve a particular design issue. A second advantage of using the BTS as a usability management tool is that the tool is in use on a daily basis within the engineering organization so that people are prone to use it. Figure 3 shows a sample screen from the BTS describing a bug that was assigned to one of the authors to fix in a software module.

The second tool that is important to the usability engineering process is the version control system. Version control systems are used in software development to manage access to source code and resource files for a project while it is under development. The goal of a VCS is to make sure that two (or more) people are not working on the same code at same time overwriting each other's changes. The user interface group creates and manages most of the user interface resource files for icons, dialog boxes, and other graphic elements in each product. These resource files need to be under formal engineering change control and this service is provided by the VCS.

The last tool that is important in the usability engineering process is the technical support tracking system. This is a separate network database application designed to track problems and suggestions that customers identify when they call in for assistance. In addition, customer comments logged on Borland hosted bulletin boards and forums on CompuServe are also entered into this system. Both the user interface group as well as project management continuously monitor this system. Suggestions that come in through this system are reviewed before starting design work on a new release. They are also used to identify problem areas to perform formal usability testing on.

Figure 3   Sample BTS screen showing a UI bug assigned to the author

```
Viewing Bug Descriptions, [F10]-Menu                    Record: 39 of 67
[Alt-F1]-Keystroke Help, [+/-]-Scroll Steps, [Ins]-Resolution Information
                         Bug Description
                                              IBR #: AD_ ◄27297
          Product: Advisor                   Status: Pending
     Program Area: Advisor                Resolution: Fixed
          Keyword: Font                  Verification: Verified
    Cat/Priority: D / 2                    Programmer: Dan Rosenberg

        Found by: Steve Fontenot      Group: QA        Date: 7/01/93
    Submitted by: Steve Fontenot  How Found: HOC    Build #: N/A
     Attachments: None                 Flag: No   Version #: Non-Ship

Brief Desc: The error message that comes up when attempting to change the sub-
            title via the advisor needs to be changed. It currently reads
            "The currently selected object(s) do not contain a text font
            property." This is not true and should be changed to something
Steps to Reproduce:
      1 like "The advisor is unable to change the font property in the
      2 current context." or something like that.
      3 /* Also need to change help screen/link to something else */
      4 a1..b2:1..4    <Select>
      5 Graph|New|<Ok>
      6 Graph|Titles|[Sub = Sub-title]|<Ok>
      7 <Select sub-title>
```

Managing Usability During the Product Development

Software development like most engineering processes proceeds in stages of development, from design to implementation and then to testing. The process is iterative. For example, testing on the first modules of the product may begin before the design is complete on other modules. The following section describes the focus of the usability engineering program during the various stages of development.

Product Planning and Initial Design

During the early phase of product development the usability engineering process at Borland focuses on three specific goals:

- Collecting and analyzing feedback from users and reviewer,
- Designing and implementing prototypes,
- Verifying that the design concept works.

For both new products and upgrade releases of existing products it is necessary to survey customers and reviewers opinions about the design of our products as well as the design of competitive products. A great deal of this information flows directly into the company through the technical support tracking system and product reviews published in the trade press. Major corporate customers that serve as beta test sites are also large contributors of ideas for new features, design changes, and new products.

However it is still necessary to solicit ideas and get feedback on where a particular product category should evolve and what user needs remain unaddressed by existing products. This information gathering process is never complete but at some point you take the information that you have and start to design a new product.

The design process then shifts to building user interface prototypes using a collection of off-the-shelf and internally developed tools. These prototypes are used in focus groups to solicit feedback and verify that the information collected earlier has been interpreted correctly. Usually these prototypes are shown to customers and user groups under a nondisclosure agreement. At the same time the product engineering team is studying the feasibility of new features and contributing to the overall design of the prototype.

It is normal to go through a dozen or more iterations of the user interface prototype, often building prototypes of several different ideas in parallel. During the early phase the prototype is used repeatedly in focus groups with customers to determine if the overall design is understandable and if the product feature set will match the user's perceived requirements.

When the prototype is complete it becomes the living specification for the overall product user interface. The prototype is always complete enough to demonstrate the overall user model for the product but does not detail every dialog box or control in the product. The prototype itself is often placed under version control.

Product Implementation Phase

During the early implementation phase, the user interface group concentrates on creating all the various UI resource files for dialog boxes, icons, and other graphic elements. The menu tree for the UI is finalized by the end of this phase.

During this phase, the detailed design of the product as well as the user interface is completed. Typically this includes every menu, icon, dialog box, and property inspector panel, many of which are never developed in the context of the UI prototype. As each element is designed and implemented it is subjected to internal review and testing. This in turn starts to generate user interface feedback and comments in the BTS system described earlier.

Formal usability testing is performed at various stages of development and those results are then fed back into the design process and changes are made. During this phase usability testing will focus on large issues such as navigation through the product, layering of the functionality and the grouping of features. Smaller details such as the design of individual icons are usually left until the basic design is proven.

Product Completion Phase

The product completion phase usually begins with the final round of usability testing. At this stage the product features are completely implemented. Data from this last usability test, in conjunction with information logged in the BTS database, is used to determine the final user interface changes in the product. Once this last round of changes is complete the user interface design of the product is frozen. This is required to allow ample time for the documentation to be written and the entire product to be tested. At this point in the development process it is very expensive to make changes to the design and the user interface group usually moves its focus of attention to other products.

Usability testing may continue during this phase, but it is often shifted outside the company to independent consulting laboratories. This last round of usability testing is usually done in conjunction with competitive products. The information that it generates is used primarily by marketing to position and promote the product. On occasion, if the results of an independently conducted test indicate a products ease of use is significantly better than the competition, this data will be used as the basis of an advertising campaign. An example of an advertisement using the usability theme is shown in Figure 4.

Figure 4   Sample advertisement designed around the usability theme

Figure 5   Sample Quattro Pro 5.0 for Windows packaging incorporating the usability theme

Figure 5 shows the packaging design for the latest version of Quattro Pro for Windows. This box aggressively asserts that it is easier to use than the competition, a claim based on the results of independent testing. Marketing usability is also part of the usability engineering process. Another example of this approach was Microsoft's advertising campaign for Word for Windows 2.0 that focused on attacking the competition based on ease of use claims.

Case Study: Quattro Pro 5.0 for Windows—User Interface Development for Computer-Based Tutorials at Borland International

Overview

Quattro Pro for Windows is Borland's spreadsheet product for Microsoft Windows. It is used primarily for financial management and analysis. Its built-in graphic capabilities allow users to visually display their data in colorful graphs and charts. Quattro Pro also features tools that access databases and do statistical modeling. The

Workgroup edition of Quattro Pro features a publish and subscribe protocol that permits users to share information. The user interface construction environment and an extensive macro programming language allow construction of entire applications. This case study describes the design, development and user testing of computer-based tutorials in the second version of Quattro Pro for Windows.

Several distinct requirements for the design and usability of the user interface of the computer-based tutorials (CBT) were added to Quattro Pro for Windows in its second release:

- Provide access to a powerful, feature rich product with a large amount of user interface,
- Provide users with a more interactive product learning experience than competitive products,
- Reduce end user training costs,
- Reduce product support cost and cost of goods.

Each of these elements will be discussed.

Borland products offer a large amount of power and functionality to their users. Consequently, the amount of user interface accompanying this functionality is also large. Typically, Borland has offered paper-based tutorials and extensive documentation to its users as a means to learn how a product works, its features, and the functionality that it offers. CBT provides a way to demonstrate these features and functionality with the users' own data. With CBT, the breadth of the user interface can be explored progressively at the user's own pace.

When using paper-based tutorials, users must divide their attention between a printed manual and the product on screen. Instructions must be mapped conceptually by users to what they will see on screen. CBT sidesteps these factors by placing an interactive tutorial alongside the product users are attempting to learn. Text, illustration graphics, and the user interface itself can be used to demonstrate actions that would normally be described textually in a printed tutorial. Making product learning an integral part of the product provides the benefits of on-screen display of information while eliminating steps users must go through with paper-based tutorials.

Reducing the steps that users go through to learn and understand a product's functionality can lead to a reduction in training costs for an organization that purchases software with CBT.

Switching from paper-based tutorials to CBT, Borland has experienced a reduction in its operational costs in two areas; documentation and technical support. The on-line tutorial has eliminated tutorial printing expenses entirely. Technical support calls have been reduced due to the inclusion of tutorials that address the most frequent questions customers have about how to use the product.

Research and Analysis

The first release of Quattro Pro for Windows utilized two on-line mechanisms to assist users in learning the product. These were an active status line and a traditional Windows help file. The active status line displays the name of a toolbar button or menu item when the mouse cursor is placed over them. This status line functions simply as a label, helping users to identify what toolbar button or menu command the mouse is currently on. The standard Windows help system (WinHelp) is an on-line help system provided for all applications running on MS Windows. WinHelp is a hypertext based help system that allows users to browse through a variety of topics pertaining to an application's interface and functionality. Invoking WinHelp usually requires users to navigate a maze of content topics before actually getting to the topic of interest. Input from users and Borland product marketing helped determine that an intermediate level of information ought to be available to users to provide more detail than the status line, but without the necessity of invoking WinHelp.

The design process began with a review of other on-line tutorial systems. At the time, there were no truly interactive systems that worked with a users' own data. Tutorials either took the form of a slide show where users jumped from one screen to the next, or else presented a do-the-task-for-me-but-don't-tell-me-what's-going-on approach. A review of the human factors literature revealed little research of practical applicability. Macintosh-based tutorials were influential in regard to content development. They had a nice mix of text and graphics that was admired by the content development team.

Analysis of how users could teach themselves about a product led to two different design solutions. Both of these were layered into the product between the user interface and WinHelp. The first can be characterized as providing users with a tip or hint about the user interface. This would take the form of a simple cue to enable them to find out quickly what a user interface element was for. The second solution concerns learning about how a larger chunk of functionality works. This was to be done interactively via lessons where users would be guided through the necessary steps to complete an operation.

The two parallel design solutions proposed were

- Object Help™,
- Interactive tutors (CBT).

Both of these are described in detail in the following section.

Detailed Design

Although design and usability testing were intermixed throughout the development process, the approaches we took for testing the various designs are described separately in a later section of this chapter.

ObjectHelp Design

We started the design process on ObjectHelp with a fairly clear idea of the direction in which to proceed. Examination of the Macintosh Bubble Help system yielded several important ideas. The first was that pointing at an interface object and giving a short description of it was an ideal way to help users understand the product. However, the modality of Bubble Help was found to be much too intrusive. Bubble Help is either always on or always off. Users we surveyed found it quite irritating to have text bubbles popping-up at every mouse click. A different strategy was applied for ObjectHelp, whereby pop-up help would be made available on a per object basis only when the user needed it.

From these conclusions, sketching of different screen layouts began for the ObjectHelp window utilizing pencil and paper (Figure 6). A variety of appearances and pointer devices as well as square, round, and other window shapes were tried out in this early phase. Pointers to the object varied from squiggley lines to arrows. These sketches were used to evaluate which ideas provided the best appearance for layering into the user interface and which ones would be the easiest to implement.

After selecting several concepts for further development, paint packages and prototyping tools helped to simulate appearance and behavior. Prototypes featuring modeless or sticky window behavior where users could pin down the ObjectHelp window provided a way to see how the windows would look when sitting on top of the application user interface (Figure 7). One of the major considerations for the design team was that they be easy to read as well as distinguishable from the application user interface.

Demonstrating the prototypes throughout the company provided input from a variety of sources, including product marketing and management, quality assurance, technical support, and upper management. The look of the designs as well as the functionality changed as a result of this feedback. Initial designs included buttons on the ObjectHelp window that could link it to WinHelp, an object's property inspector, and the CBT system. These ideas did not make it into the subsequent design phase. It was discovered that this approach complicated the user interface too much, overloading what needed to be a very simple and direct interaction. The link into WinHelp did remain in the final design as it provided an excellent indexing mechanism into that system. Colors, fonts, and pointer shapes also changed based on feedback from these various groups.

In the final shipping version (Figure 8), ObjectHelp is invoked by pointing the mouse cursor at a UI object and clicking the right mouse button while simultaneously pushing the Control key on the keyboard. It features a small, pop-up window with a textual description about an object and a pointer from the corner of the window to the object. The ObjectHelp window also has a small button near its lower edge with the word Help on it. Users have two options once they invoke ObjectHelp. Clicking anywhere in

Figure 6   Early sketches of ObjectHelp concepts

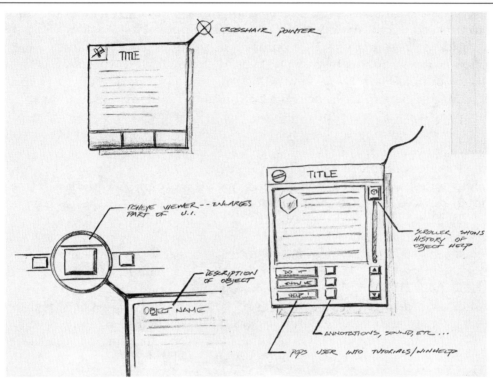

the interface or on the ObjectHelp window itself will eliminate ObjectHelp. Clicking on the Help button dismisses ObjectHelp while invoking WinHelp and the help topic for the selected object. The final design uses a pointer that is similar to the call-outs in the CBT system; however the colors used for ObjectHelp make it appear as if it were an integral part of the application.

CBT Design (Interactive Tutors)

Following analysis of the competition, an iterative design sketching phase began to explore various ideas and approaches for navigation via quick pencil and paper sketches. This process utilized various metaphors and physical analogies in an effort to synthesize new ideas and directions for navigation. Some of these possibilities included an InfoStick (see Figure 9), posters, billboards, a jukebox metaphor, televisions,

Figure 7   Electronic sketches of initial ObjectHelp design proposals

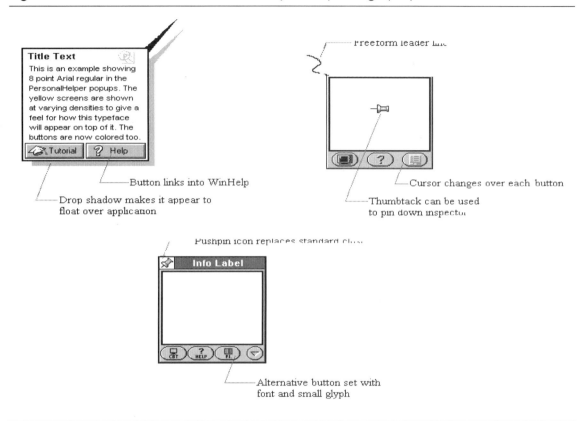

and many others. These sketches describe the visual appearance as well as any written thoughts on interaction and serve as documentation of the creative process as the design evolves. They are also used as a presentation tool for showing ideas to other members of the development team. After documenting approximately fifteen separate approaches to the tutorial user interface, the engineering team met for review and discussion of the ideas. Several of these ideas were selected for further exploration and detailed design.

Visual exploration of the most promising concepts was done using paint packages for pixel development and simple prototyping tools such as Asymetrix Toolbook to simulate behavior (Figure 10). This type of concept development process provides more elaborate simulation and detailing of the design than is possible on paper. Using this

Figure 8   Final user interface design for ObjectHelp feature

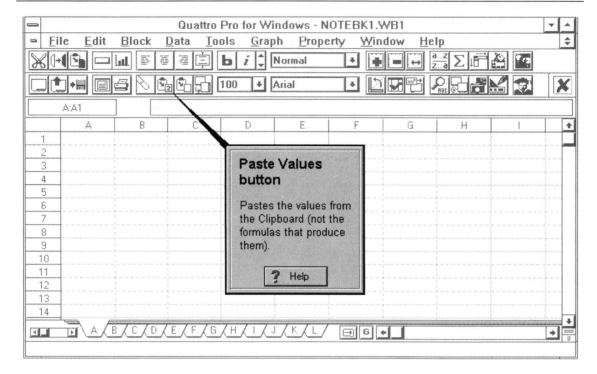

approach allows other team members and the designers to see exactly how an idea might look and behave on screen when in use. It also permits a fast turnaround time on the simulations without the need to write any code. This is advantageous because it allows the engineering team to proceed with the behind-the-scenes coding necessary to make the system run, without having to worry about the details required to build the user interface.

Demonstrating the various concepts to groups throughout the company provided enough feedback to confirm that the best approach for CBT was one where text, conceptual illustrations, and the CBT navigation controls were placed together in a single window. This window would be fairly small and unobtrusive and would "float" in the lower right corner of users' screens. In addition to the CBT window, pointers were used as call-outs to highlight specific elements of the product user interface, in effect using the application itself as an explanatory illustration.

Figure 9   Early paper sketches of user model of interactive tutors

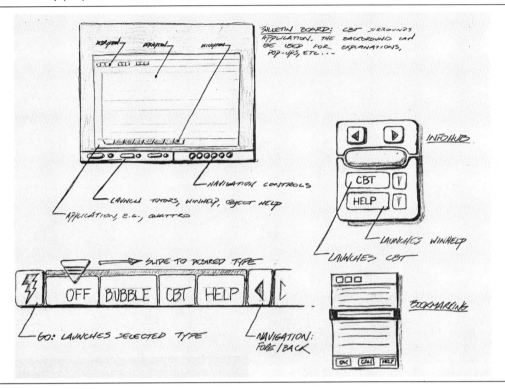

Even though the window layout and navigational approach had been resolved, detail work on the exact look of the CBT screens and buttons was still in progress. Initially, several controls in addition to the navigational buttons appeared in the CBT window design. These included a progress indicator pop-up, an index button, and a button to invoke WinHelp. In the end, simplicity ruled as the best design approach. Only three essential controls appeared on the tutorial window: move forward, move backward, and cancel the tutorial. A percent completed progress indicator is used to inform users how much of the tutorial they had finished completed the UI design. With final detailing of the buttons complete, a traffic light color metaphor was selected for use on the buttons: red for cancel or stop the tutorial and green for forward and backward to indicate movement. A very light wash of yellow fills the CBT window in order to visually distinguish it from the application and also as a visual reference to the ubiquitous post-it note found tacked up on computer monitors everywhere (Figure 11 and Color Plate VI).

Figure 10   Sample prototypes early in the CBT development cycle

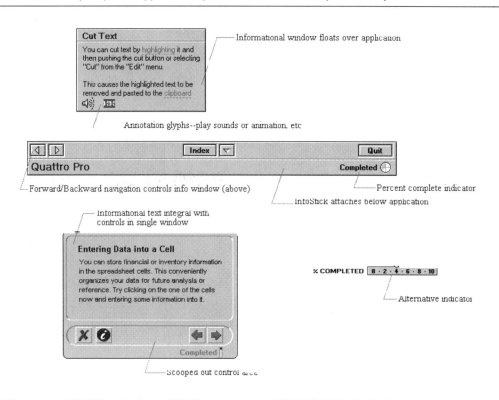

CBT teaches users how to accomplish specific tasks with the software application they are using. It can work either with the user's own data or with sample data provided with the application. This permits users to be productive while simultaneously learning to use the product. The advantage to this solution is fairly clear. Most tutorial systems are essentially interactive slide shows that move forward or backward through a fixed presentation. With this type of slide show presentation, users usually are not even looking at the actual product, but rather a screen shot of the product. In contrast, Borland's CBT system works in parallel with the product user interface. Users learn by doing, not by watching. The CBT system guides users through a series of tasks (creating a graph in a spreadsheet for example) by prompting them for input and checking for errors using text, graphics, animation and pointers layered on top of the application interface. Most important it works with a user's data.

Figure 11   Finalized CBT design for Interactive tutorial feature

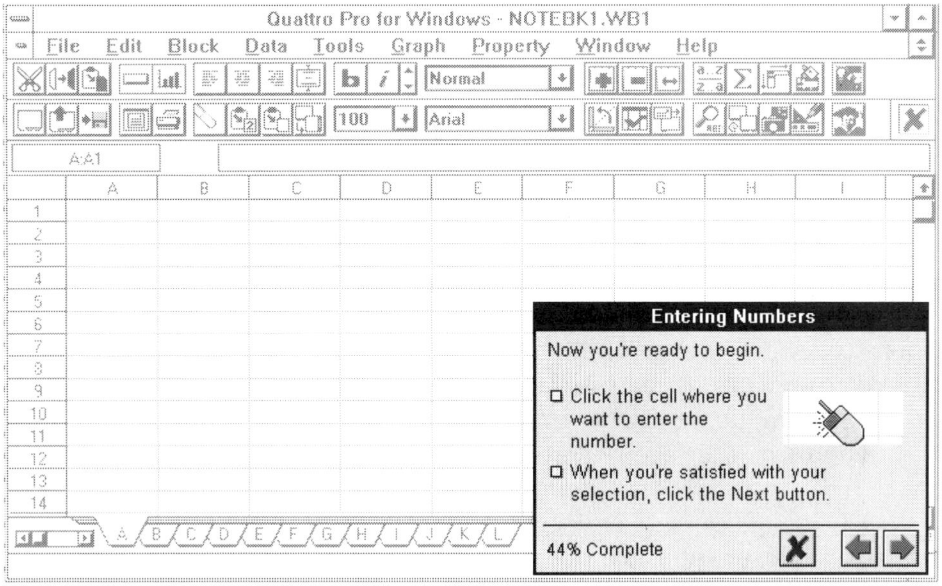

Tutorial Content Design

Tutorial lesson content development was handled by a team of content authors and not directly as part of the user interface design for CBT. Development of the CBT navigational model also included a topic catalog from which users could select the tutor they wish to use. When CBT is first started, the user is presented with this table of contents, listing the tutorial topics for the application. Graphing, entering data, modifying notebooks, printing, and an introduction to the product are examples of the topics included in Quattro Pro's CBT. A mouse click on a particular topic title starts the tutorial for it. The first screen of the tutorial is a brief summary of the lesson accompanied by an illustration that graphically portrays the task the user will be performing. Users can run the lesson by clicking on the forward button, or they can click the cancel button and return to the contents screen. If they run the lesson, the following screen allows them to choose whether they would like to use their own data or example data. The final screen at the end of a tutorial is a mini table of contents with lessons related to the one just completed. Users can either study a related topic or return to the main table of contents. From the main contents screen the user can pick another topic by clicking on its title or leave the tutorial system entirely by clicking on the cancel button.

The management teams from technical support, product marketing, engineering, and the CBT content development team developed three criteria for selection of CBT topics:

1. Provide users with the basic information needed to learn the product model.
2. Document areas that generate a high percentage of support calls.
3. Cover topics that were traditionally addressed in the paper tutorials

After selecting the topics for each lesson, the lesson content was developed in story-board form by a multidisciplinary team. This group consists of writers, scripters, a user interface designer, and members of the CBT engineering team. The writers are responsible for determining how the steps of a task can be explained to users. Their other responsibility is to determine what actions in the application users can or cannot take as they move through a tutorial. The scripter blocks or permits user actions within an application, using a scripting language that enables or disables functionality as required. The user interface designer's role is to examine the written content and determine where conceptual illustrations can aid understanding or replace text entirely.

Additionally the user interface designer works with the writers to storyboard user interactions for tutorial navigation. Placement of illustrations in the CBT window, organization of type, and bulleting are also tasks with which the designer is involved. The designer and writers work closely together to craft the look and the explanations that form the lessons. The CBT engineers work to extend and enhance CBT functionality as new ideas for interaction strategies and visual appearances are devised. Throughout the content development process, ideas are constantly being reviewed and refined. This is done on an informal basis by having all members of the team review tutorial content and keep notes on areas they feel are confusing, or difficult to navigate. Proceeding in this way allows quite a bit of refinement to occur before the tutorials are ever seen and tested with their intended users.

Usability Testing

There were several components to the user testing of CBT:

- Testing tutorial content,
- Testing the navigation model,
- Testing window layout.

Tutorial content refers to the text and illustrations the users see as they proceed through a tutorial lesson. The tutorial content embodies all the instructions and information users need to complete a tutorial lesson. The *navigation model* refers to the way users access the CBT system, how they enter and exit each tutorial lesson, and how they move through a lesson. *Window layouts* are the arrangement of the tutorial windows on screen; in particular, how they are placed in relation to the Quattro Pro for Windows application itself.

A combination of heuristic analysis and traditional user testing assisted in the evaluation of these three components. Heuristic analysis refers to analyzing a product's user interface by having people sit down and use the product while keeping notes on where usability problems exist. Decisions pertaining to navigational and window layout were primarily dealt with heuristically, by having a variety of people throughout the organization review and evaluate the design proposals. Operating in this fashion afforded rapid feedback about the various design proposals and the ability to quickly modify and adjust designs then redistribute the revised mockups for further evaluation. The results of the feedback produced a design that appeared to meet all the needs of the CBT content development team. Review of tutorial content and modifications occurred periodically throughout development whenever deemed appropriate by the content development team.

User testing of CBT focused primarily on assuring that lesson content was easy for users to understand. Videotape and extensive note taking helped to document the areas where users were having problems with descriptions and illustrations. Additionally, the navigation model and window layouts had to be reviewed to ascertain that they were easy to understand, too. As a component of this testing the colors selected for screens and buttons, as well as the button glyphs themselves also went through a review by users. Table 2 shows the total percentages of testing done heuristically and through formal user testing for the three components.

Table 2   Percentage of testing performed heuristically vs. testing performed formally in the usability lab

	Heuristic Test	**Formal Test**
Content	35%	65%
Navigation	85%	15%
Layout	80%	20%

The following section describes the testing methods utilized to evaluate CBT lesson content, navigation model, and window layouts. As mentioned earlier, the focus of user testing for CBT was on lesson content; however, navigation and window layouts also went through testing. The primary concern was that text and illustrations convey the appropriate amount of detail to allow users to accomplish the tasks in the tutorial quickly and easily. Data was collected about where text or an illustration were either misleading or needed embellishment in order to clarify a point or an instruction. Careful observation of users' interactions with the tutors helped determine whether they had difficulties with the presentation of information on the screen or navigation through the tutorials. Another factor considered was whether users understood that they could use their own data or if they thought only sample data could be used. This point strongly differentiated Borland's tutorial technology from those of our competitors.

Twelve people in total went through user testing. Eight of the twelve people tested were from outside of Borland. Two types of users participated in the testing:

- Windows users with little or no spreadsheet experience,
- Macintosh users with little or no spreadsheet experience.

Users with no spreadsheet experience were representative of many new users who lack understanding of basic spreadsheet concepts and operations. Windows users helped to ascertain whether the designs met their expectations of Windows. Macintosh users typically expect a high degree of ease of use from computer systems. New computer users were purposely avoided as test subjects. We did not want the lack of basic computer familiarity to factor into users' evaluations of the tutorials.

The tests consisted of having each user study and complete five lessons. Upon completion, each had to perform the task just studied without consulting the tutorial if possible. Thinking out loud during the tests was strongly encouraged so that users' thoughts could be recorded should they have conceptual or navigational problems. After finishing a lesson, users filled out a questionnaire of subjective ratings about the lesson. Reviewing the lesson while completing the questionnaires helped users remind themselves what particular areas had been difficult to understand. Once a sequence of tutorials had been completed, users were given a survey in which to subjectively rate the group of tutorials and their effectiveness as a whole. A post test interview allowed users to further articulate any other thoughts they had on tutorial design. If a written comment indicated some type of difficulty, it was explored in more detail during this phase of the test. Questions about how to resolve the problem areas they encountered—such as "How would you improve that illustration?" or "Why isn't that description clear?"—also helped to gain more information about why something was difficult to understand.

Although users were timed on how long it took them to complete each lesson, this criterion was not used in evaluating tutorial effectiveness. The reason for this was that all of the users had little or no spreadsheet experience and were, therefore, completely new to the material being presented. As expected, users' approaches to learning varied widely. Some were able to complete tasks very quickly by browsing the information for the gist of an idea and then proceeding with the task, while others took time to ponder and study the material more thoroughly before taking any action. Users rated the time it took them to complete a task from a subjective standpoint. A question in each post tutorial survey read: The speed with which I was able to complete this tutorial was Slow, Moderate, Fast. An area was left below this question for an explanation in the case that they found it slow to use. Users rated the completion of the tutorials as fast to moderate. No users rated the tutorials as being slow to use.

After completing user testing, a comprehensive list of problems encountered during the tests was drawn up. Users' difficulties with the lessons fell into the following categories:

- Conceptual text,
- Instructional text,
- Illustrations.

Conceptual text refers to the underlying ideas of each tutorial, i.e., what we wanted the user to understand as a result of completing the tutorial. *Instructional text* is the information given to users to guide them through the actual mechanics of completing a lesson. This could include directions to make a menu pick or press the forward button of the tutorial. Problems with illustrations occur wherever pictures accompanying text do not show a concept particularly well or wherever an illustration ought to be included with text or instead of text but is not. The content development team reviewed this list as well as the proposals for solutions provided by the users themselves. The team ranked the items on the list with the most detrimental problems taking the highest priority. Working collaboratively, the team addressed each issue in an effort to generate as many different solutions as possible. In some cases, users' recommendations offered the best solutions and became part of the final lesson design. Through a series of meetings, the content team adjusted the text and illustrations for all significant problems in the lessons. Once all the issues had been resolved, the team incorporated the reworked text, illustrations, and accompanying scripts into the lessons. A final review by editors and other members of the Borland technical writing community provided a final check on clarity and grammar.

As mentioned previously, there were also concerns about the problems that users might encounter with window layout and navigation. The final questionnaire queried users about specific elements of the window layout and navigation. This was followed up by questioning during the posttest interview with the CBT panel on screen. Users were asked about the colors, window's layouts, button symbols, and the simplicity of moving through the tutorials. From this evaluation it became clear that these issues had been dealt with effectively through the heuristic analysis and iterative design process earlier in the development cycle. Users found tutorial navigation straightforward and uncomplicated. In addition, screen layout issues had been resolved except in one instance where the tutorial window was overlapping an area of the screen that users needed to see in order to complete the lesson.

Summary of Case Study

The organizational structure within Borland played an important role in helping to determine the outcome of the CBT-user interface. People from a wide variety of groups enthusiastically participated in reviewing the user interfaces and contributed ideas to improving the designs. Drawing from the strengths of these different viewpoints yielded more robust interfaces requiring only slight revisions as product engineering proceeded. User testing of these interfaces confirmed that they were simple and flexible enough to provide users with the functionality and navigation they needed.

Our usability lab was another important component in testing of the CBT content. The ability to bring users from outside of the organization into the testing facility and record the problems they encountered using CBT was vital in adjusting lesson content. This permitted revision of the lessons with actual data about where users were having problems.

Through a combination of concept development, prototyping, heuristic analysis, and user testing, Borland was able to design and implement its interactive CBT system. Designing the interface before the product was built allowed us to explore a wide variety of solutions cheaply and efficiently. Heuristic analysis provided enough feedback of the conceptual designs to allow us to proceed with development without necessitating formal usability testing right away. User testing of the product pointed out many areas in the lesson content that needed adjustment while confirming that the user interface was simple and effective.

Lessons Learned

The key lesson learned at Borland is that to build truly usable products efficiently the usability engineering process has to blend directly into the corporate culture. The PC software industry may be somewhat unique in that the marketplace demands usability and failure to deliver it can be fatal. Usability is not an optional feature in this market.

The active ingredients that have evolved in the Borland culture to integrate the usability engineering process are

- Management support through active involvement,
- Grassroots participation by everyone in the company,
- A centralized UI design architect to control the process,
- Using existing tracking tools that engineers are familiar with.

Borland's management truly believes that usability is important and that just talking about it is not enough. The executives use the products, demonstrate them to the press and users groups, and then document the feedback afterward so it can be addressed and design changes can be made in response to it. For example Borland's CEO frequently sends lengthy e-mail messages to both the UI architect and product managers documenting not only his impressions of the product but also those of customers that he meets with.

There are also no artificially induced budget constraints on the UI group. It is always assumed that the value of the good design far outweighs the cost of running the group as a centralized part of the organization. No charge-back mechanisms or other "funny money" schemes hinder the effective deployment of the group's talent.

At the grassroots level, all employees have to believe that they are empowered to contribute to the usability process and be encouraged to do so. Providing cash incentives works very well in this case not only because it motivates people but because it proves that the company really believes its important. Having the QA engineers and technicians trained and working shifts in the usability lab also helps make the process tangible and effective.

Having a centralized UI design architect with the authority, design skills, and negotiating technique to manage the process in the same fashion as other respected technical areas in the company are managed gives the whole process credibility. In addition, allowing the user interface department to perform the actual resource file (and sometimes code) implementation makes life easier for the product development teams, so they are willing to give up some control in return. Best of all, having a centralized UI group avoids the morass of standards committees and allows cross-product-user interface design issues to be addressed quickly.

However, the most important lesson learned is not to create new procedures and process for bureaucracy's sake but to leverage existing management tools and systems such as the BTS that people were already using. This helps blend usability engineering into the existing engineering process without making it any harder or more complicated than it already is.

Trademarks

Microsoft Windows is a trademark of Microsoft Corporation. Macintosh is a trademark of Apple Corporation. OS/2 is a trademark of IBM corporation. Toolbook is a trademark of Asymetrix Quattro Pro, Paradox, dBase, Interbase and ObjectHelp are trademarks of Borland International.

Reference

Nielsen, Jakob. (1993). *Usability Engineering*, Academic Press, Boston.

CHAPTER 10

Usability Engineering for Lotus 1-2-3 Release 4™

Mary Beth Butler

Manager,
Spreadsheet Usability

Lotus Development
Corporation

Kate Ehrlich, Ph.D.

Research Scientist,
Workgroup Technologies

Lotus Development
Corporation

Mary Beth Butler is Manager of Spreadsheet Usability Testing at Lotus Development Corporation where she established the first usability lab. Butler has a BA in psychology from Brown University, and an MBA from Northeastern University. She serves on the editorial board of the Usability Professional's Association newsletter, Common Ground, *and is a member of* PC/Computing's *Usability Advisory Board.*

Kate Ehrlich is a Research Scientist in Workgroup Technologies, an applied research and development group at Lotus Development Corporation. Previously she managed UI design and usability testing at Sun Microsystems. She is a reviewer for ACM SIGCHI conferences and other professional journals and is currently Chair of local SIGCHI groups. She holds a Ph.D. in psychology from the University of Sussex, England.

Introduction

This chapter describes the usability testing for Lotus 1-2-3 Release 4™, a spreadsheet application running under Windows. Our case study begins in fall 1991 when the product was in an early planning phase and usability testing was just beginning. It ends shortly after the product was released, in the summer of 1993, when it was praised by customers and press alike for its ease of use.

Reviews such as the one below were commonplace:

> Lotus 1-2-3 for Windows has taken a quantum leap from release 1.1 to release 4. … While 1-2-3 power users will find numerous new features, all types of users will benefit because 1-2-3 Release 4 is considerably easier to use than its predecessors. Lotus has done extensive homework on usability testin.g (Miastkowski, 1993)

The product also received several awards for application software, including BYTE Magazine's Best of Spring COMDEX where it was recognized for major innovations in usability and workgroup capabilities. From InfoWorld, it received the highest rating for a Windows spreadsheet—a score of 7.8 (out of 10). The review specifically cited the product's ease of use: "Day-to-day usability shines" (Walkenbach, 1993). Customers have been similarly enthusiastic about the product; some even describing it as "fun."

We believe that the success of Lotus 1-2-3 Release 4 is indicative of what can happen when a product is developed from the start with a strong user focus reinforced through systematic usability testing and UI design. In this chapter we describe and reflect on our experiences of doing the usability testing for Lotus 1-2-3 Release 4, noting that a similar story could have been told from the vantage of the UI design.

Previous Research

Not all usability projects have enjoyed the same level of success. In a recent paper, Lundell and Notess (1991) report on a survey to investigate the critical factors that distinguish successful (as measured by demonstrable improvements in the product or higher customer satisfaction) from unsuccessful involvement of Human Factors. The critical factors were

- *Team focus*. The Human Factors (HF) engineer who was part of the team worked better than those who played the role of an on-call consultant.

- *Early involvement*. Projects in which the HF engineer was involved from the start were more likely to be successful than those in which the HF engineer came in later.

- *Management commitment.* Both Lundell and Notess (1991) and Grudin and Poltrock (1989) emphasize the importance of a management structure that understands and cares about Human Factors.

Of less significance were specific usability practices or methods. In particular, although it is frequently recommended that usability engineers set usability goals before starting a new user interface (e.g., Chapanis and Budurka, 1990, Nielsen, 1993), Lundell and Notess found a lack of agreement about the value of this exercise.

While we are not planning on debating these issues directly, it is useful to view the success of usability testing or other user-centered design activity as influenced by a combination of organizational factors and the outcomes associated with specific usability practices.

Data Collection

In presenting the history of usability testing for Lotus 1-2-3 Release 4, we drew on several sources:

- The direct experience of one of the authors (Mary Beth) in setting up and running the usability testing program.
- A series of in-depth interviews conducted by the second author (Kate), four months after the product shipped. Interviewees were recruited in approximately equal numbers from the spreadsheet and graphics product division; the latter having enjoyed a similar level of success for their presentation graphics product, Lotus Freelance ™.[1] Interviewees included software engineers, software architects, UI designers, usability engineers, product managers and senior managers.
- Archived designs from various stages of development.
- Archived reports on the final results of the usability tests, test plans and test logs of each subject.
- Videotaped recordings of testing sessions.

[1]PC/Computing gave Lotus an MVP award last year for producting Freelance Graphics 2.0, a product that "works the way we really work" (Bott, 1993).

Usability Testing at Lotus

In this section we describe Lotus in terms of its products, organization, and management. This context is important for understanding the role of usability testing in Lotus, as well as for understanding the rationale, decision making, and motivation behind the specific usability practices and procedures we developed.

Company Background

Lotus Development Corporation, founded in 1982, produces software products for individuals and workgroups. Its complete product line includes a variety of software applications, for a range of hardware platforms. The company's first product, a spreadsheet application commonly called 1-2-3, is the most popular personal computer software application in the world, with more than 20 million users, and it remains one of the company's most important products. Most product development is done in the Cambridge, Massachusetts, headquarters. Other development activities are located throughout the United States and internationally.

The spreadsheet market is characterized by close competition between Lotus and its two key rivals, Microsoft and Borland. In addition, the market for Windows products in general is increasingly focused on usability, as both trade press (e.g., Meyerson, 1993) and customers have begun to cite usability as a key differentiating factor when comparing leading applications.

Organization

At Lotus, individual product lines are managed by different corporate divisions. Each division has broad authority to structure its organization as appropriate for that product line. Therefore, product management (marketing), user interface design, and usability engineering, the three groups most responsible for the usability of a product at Lotus, are organized very differently in each division. For example, the usability testing group reports into product management in the spreadsheet division but is part of the UI design team in the graphics division. Other divisions have usability engineering reporting variously into product management, product development, documentation, or UI design. Almost all groups use outside consultants for at least some of their testing needs.

Product managers are responsible for defining customer requirements for a product and ensuring that these are met in the final product. UI designers are responsible for translating users' needs into specifications for overall screen layout and sequencing of operations. The development managers are responsible for the overall architecture of the product and for all implementation including the user interface. Usability engineers work cooperatively with these groups, as well as documentation and quality assurance, to determine what and how to test the product, to facilitate testing, and to ensure that test results are taken into account to improve the usability of the product.

In general, we have not found that a particular organizational placement of usability testing to have any inherent advantages. Success of the usability testing program has much more do to with a group's overall receptivity to testing, than to reporting structure.

Usability Lab

The usability labs function as a central facility for those products developed in Cambridge. Our first usability lab was completed in April 1992, well after we had successfully started usability testing. Previous to this, we had used offices or conference rooms or relied on outside consultants to test in their labs. However, neither of these made satisfactory long-term solutions. We wanted to demonstrate our commitment to usability to these groups, which meant we needed an official and permanent lab suitable for lab tours. Having some experience already with usability testing helped make the case. Having a lab also lends us a certain credibility with press, analysts, and savvy customers who know about usability labs and expect serious vendors to have at least one.

Lab Layout

Our lab is similar to most other usability labs, with one-way glass and multiple cameras to capture the computer screen and users' reactions. However, we designed our lab to support our goal of involving team members directly in usability testing. We felt that team involvement would ensure that we collected the right information and would teach team members about usability.

We placed emphasis on making the lab a place where team members could easily observe and participate in tests. This included making it easy for observers to drop in by locating the lab conveniently in the development building (and on the way to the cafeteria). Our floor plan (Figure 1) includes a slightly raised platform in the observation room with a large viewing monitor. This arrangement keeps team members in the lab, and close to the action, so that they can contribute questions or answers during the test. The raised platform provides a slight physical separation, so that team members' discussions do not disturb the test facilitator at work. The single biggest impact the lab had on the usability of our products was through this opportunity to involve team members directly in testing.

Figure 1   Usability lab floor plan

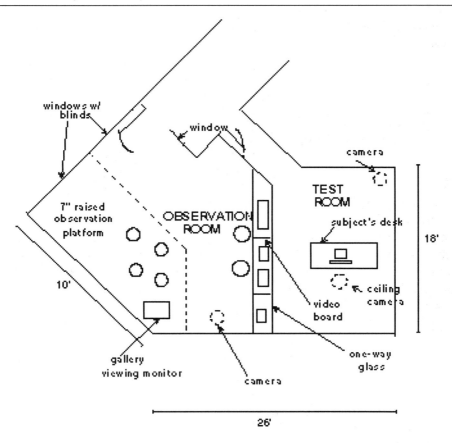

Advantages of a Permanent Lab

Capital investment in the lab demonstrated management commitment and helped convince product teams that management was serious about improving usability. This commitment, coupled with the fact that the lab was different, interesting, and fun, helped motivate team members to come and watch testing. Once we got them in the lab, we could generally get them "hooked" and signed up for subsequent participation.

Having a permanent lab had other important advantages. Using a traditional two-room lab meant we left users alone in the testing room. Users, if left alone, give important information about whether they think they are done with a task, which indicates whether a product provides enough feedback. Even skilled facilitators react in some way to a user completing a task; simply relaxing your natural tension as you observe the user is enough for them to sense they are done. When the user is seated alone in a room you are much more likely to hear, "Am I done? I can't tell if this did anything" than if you are seated next to the user.

Having a permanent facility also made it easier to schedule tests. It meant no hassles in locating rooms or equipment each time we wanted to test. Professional video equipment and a special effects generator meant we could record good quality videos that showed the action in the lab and the user's reactions; we could more easily analyze high quality videos, and they were more presentable to product team members or customers.

Lab funding

The lab was initially funded by one division (spreadsheets), but we made it available to other divisions in the company. This maximized the value of the investment made by the spreadsheet division, and helped support expansion of usability testing programs to other groups. Increasing the overall support of usability testing across the company was good for all the divisions, and helped establish testing as an accepted part of good product development. Subsequent demand for lab space has ensured funding for several additional labs in the company. The labs are geographically dispersed to support development groups located outside of Cambridge.

Software Development Process

Improving product usability begins with careful understanding of user needs translated into good basic designs. Product management and UI designers work together to define and specify customer requirements before any development begins.

We start usability testing in the lab on early prototypes developed by the UI designer using software prototyping tools or even just paper sketches. We try to maximize testing at this stage, iterating design on prototypes that are easier and less expensive to change than the real product. We also pay attention to how users' experience matches our understanding of customer requirements; testing at this stage also allows us to refine our product definition to better meet customer needs.

As the product passes through early code and alpha stages, we can increasingly test real code. This gives us a truer indication of the user's likely reaction to the final product. As time goes on, we can test more of the product, but changes are more expensive to make, because they may affect work already completed by development, quality assurance, and documentation. Once the product has been sent to beta testers the usability lab focuses on fine tuning the product.

New releases of products build on previous releases, so we make use of information from customer support calls to begin to identify areas of the product that can be improved in the next release. We often commission competitive analyses with outside consultants after the product has shipped, often in the form of comparative usability tests. Results from these tests are used to help us determine areas for improvement in the next release.

We turn now to describe a particular case: usability testing for Lotus 1-2-3 Release 4, recognizing that some of our experiences are shared with other groups at Lotus while others are unique to the spreadsheet group and this product. We also acknowledge our somewhat myopic view, which makes the usability testing appear exceedingly large in comparison with other functions. We especially note the centrality of UI design in designing the features to be easy to use.

Case Study: Lotus 1-2-3 Release 4

Getting Started

In 1991, while plans were underway to produce Lotus 1-2-3 Release 4, management in the spreadsheet division recognized that this release had to include major advances in usability. Customers and the trade press increasingly demanded that credible competitors produce highly usable products. Our competitors had started to take advantage of this growing interest in usability. The previous release of 1-2-3 was criticized in the trade press for lacking ease-of-use features that were available in competitive products. This competitive pressure helped management in the spreadsheet division make the decision to invest in usability testing.

Prior to 1991, there had been no formal usability testing on any spreadsheet products. However, the graphics division had demonstrated the value of usability testing by using it to initiate dramatic improvements in the usability of the Freelance product. The improvements resulted in laudatory reviews and increased market share.

Starting the Program

When the spreadsheet division began investigating options for a usability testing program, we were led to several consultants, who generously (and at no charge) introduced us to the field, showed us various labs, connected us to other usability professionals, and suggested options for our program.

We considered two proposals. One was to hire a usability consulting firm. In return for an annual retainer, it would test a certain number of users each month in a lab it would set up and staff near our offices. A second firm offered us a training course in usability testing, including an initial test as part of the training.

We decided to pursue the second option. While we believed the first firm had good intentions, we did not like the idea of having the lab separate from our main development building. Although this would have allowed us to do testing in which users would not know whose product they were testing, we felt that this slight advantage would be severely outweighed by the barrier this would add to getting developers into the lab to watch testing. In addition, this firm expected to use the lab for other customers, which would have limited how often and when we could test.

Most important, we felt that usability testing was a vital component in a process to educate the entire product team about usability. Any barrier between the testing and the product team would inhibit our effort to transfer this knowledge directly to the product team. We decided that doing the testing ourselves, with some initial consulting help, would be the best approach.

Initial Testing Efforts

We started testing even before we had completed our training course. We undertook a number of small projects, partially to get experience, and partially to demonstrate progress to management. Our initial tests were very informal, using semi-functional prototypes, involving key team members, and borrowing equipment and office space. These humble beginnings provided very useful information to the product team. Just as important, they helped us introduce the concept of testing to the product team, demonstrated the value of testing from the beginning of the project, and started building interest in the process.

Shortly after we started testing, we faced our biggest testing challenge. Our ability to successfully navigate the politics of this issue protected our place in the development process. The challenge was to decide whether the menus in Release 4 should look like those in the previous version, 1-2-3 for Windows 1.0, which was still faithful in important respects to the 1-2-3 "Classic" menu of our DOS version, or whether it could be changed substantially to a new structure. The proposed new menu would give 1-2-3 and all other Lotus products for Windows a similar interface, enabling us to create products for our customers that worked well together. This was an important decision, balancing the needs of customers migrating from DOS versions of 1-2-3, who were presumed to prefer the classic menu, with the possibility of sacrificing the usability of the whole suite of products. We wanted to satisfy our customers, be sensitive to the compatibility concerns of our huge installed base of current DOS users, and create an attractive suite of products that we expected to become an increasingly important requirement of customers. An incorrect decision on this issue would cost us customer satisfaction and, ultimately, revenue.

We tested 12 users on several iterations of the menus. Each user tried similar sets of tasks using both sets of menus. We counterbalanced presentation of the menus to prevent learning bias. We counted numbers of errors made by users looking for menu items. We also collected comments from the users' talking out loud, as well as from our probing questions of their experience using the menus. Typically, we asked the users to comment on whether menu items appeared where they expected or whether they felt frustrated trying to find menu items.

There were several problems with the way we did this test. The most important was that the two pieces of software we used to test the proposed menus did not work equally well. The prototype typically crashed several times during a test, which tended to distract users.

We drew criticism for our methodology from members of the product team on both sides of the debate, including concerns about the relatively small number of users tested and the possibility that the designers who acted as facilitators may have introduced bias during interviews with the users. The menu decision was an extremely controversial issue throughout the spreadsheet division. People could criticize methodology to help discredit results if they did not like the outcome.

Ultimately, the results did not show a clear preference for either menu. While the new menu seemed easier to use for most users, DOS users, as expected, expressed concern about any changes to the menu.

The lack of clear results helped us diffuse the controversy over the methodological approach. One of the points we argued in trying to explain usability testing was that it was not appropriate to think of it as a decision maker, but rather as a source of objective information on which to base decisions. Critics of the test had expressed concern that this major decision was going to be based on a statistically insignificant sample. Because the data did not clearly show a preference, management could not simply implement a result and point to usability results as the source of the decision. Instead, it used the tests to gain a better understanding of users before proceeding with a decision that had to be made quickly. The decision was ultimately made by management intelligently interpreting the outcome of the tests, rather than blindly relying on statistics.

As a result of this test, we were more careful about involving stakeholders in test planning, which improved the quality of the tests and reduced concerns from team members who felt left out of the process. In addition, we were more careful to explain the appropriate uses of usability information when presenting results. However, team members understood usability testing better as a result of this controversy, including both the benefits of testing and the degree to which management was inclined to rely on it for making decisions. These factors helped encourage more team members to participate in testing.

Role of Key Team Members

The support of key individuals from the product team who recognized the potential benefits of usability testing ensured that usability testing would become an accepted tool in the development process. In particular, the senior UI designer and the product manager initiated requests for most of the testing that occurred during 1-2-3 Release 4. The UI designer regularly rounded up developers to attend testing. The product manager was able to leverage his work with customers to assist in designing tasks that were relevant to the end user. Most important, both provided generous moral support through the initial rigors associated with starting up a new testing program.

Development participation was also important. The Development Manager for Data Query Assistant provided support by attending testing and encouraging his developers to attend. Developers for Data Query Assistant and Version Manager, two key product components, were among the first to ask for their work to be tested; their enthusiasm helped encourage other developers to participate.

The UI designer, product manager, and usability staff worked cooperatively to plan tests. We would decide together exactly what features, which users, and what tasks to test. These team members also helped by providing sample files, installing software in the lab, and encouraging other team members to attend testing. At least one or the other would attend all test sessions.

Getting Other Team Members Involved

For us, a very important factor in the success of usability testing was involving team members directly in the testing (see Ehrlich, Butler, and Pernice, 1994, for a more complete discussion of different ways to get team members involved). Our usability lab comfortably accommodates 10-12 team members during a test session. From the beginning, we wanted team members to have the opportunity to react to users' information by asking follow-up questions. This way we could be sure that all lines of inquiry were followed during a test, so that we would have the most complete information possible.

Initially, this process was a little hectic, with multiple team members feeding questions to the test facilitator, who was also trying to follow the user's activities, the test log, and manage the cameras. After some trial and error, we organized sessions with one team member (usually the UI designer or product manager) filtering questions from the rest of the team to the test facilitator. This process proved more workable and has remained in place.

Team members who participate in testing learn about usability. The most compelling experience for developers or designers is to see a user struggle with a carefully designed product; this quickly teaches them about the target users of a product and helps them understand what makes the product easy or hard to use. We feel our products will be better if we build usability in from the beginning; therefore, we see the educational role of the lab as equally important to the information it provides during a test.

By the time 1-2-3 Release 4 was released, most team members had participated in usability testing. Team leaders encouraged their staffs to attend tests. In final evaluations of the Release 4 development plan, many team members cited usability testing as one of the most effective components of the development effort.

Facilities

We started testing before our lab was constructed. Initially, we tested in the usability engineer's office, using her personal workstation. The usability engineer sat next to the users and logged each test session on a laptop. We also videotaped each session. One other observer was always present: either one of the developers or a UI designer. The UI designer or the usability engineer facilitated each session. Despite the cramped quarters, we were able to collect helpful information.

We next progressed to a slightly more elaborate temporary lab arrangement. We used a small conference room as the testing room. The usability engineer, designer, and user would all sit here. We videotaped the user's voice and the computer screen, with the camera positioned over the user's shoulder. We fed this video image to the usability engineer's office down the hall, which, once outfitted with a large viewing monitor, served as a workable observation room for five or six team members. This arrangement allowed us to achieve our goal of getting more product team members involved in testing by having them watch sessions live. The increased team participation helped us to collect the most relevant information for the team.

After several months of testing, we moved into our completed lab, where we could accommodate many team members (see Figure 2). Initial testing in less spacious surroundings had already stimulated team interest in the process; the addition of the more functional lab allowed us to fully involve all team members who wanted to participate.

Progression of the Product:
Results and Techniques

We focused our usability testing efforts throughout this project on the areas of the product where we thought that usability improvements would have the biggest impact on users. Many aspects of the product were tested, including user interface artifacts, specific features, feature choreography, terminology, and documentation. Some specific examples follow to illustrate our testing methods, show how usability testing changed our product development methods, and describe how usability testing differs for new features versus existing features.

Figure 2   Lotus Staff watching usability test

Data Query Assistant

Data Query Assistant (DQA) describes the tools available in 1-2-3 to access and work with databases. DQA was the first feature tested in 1-2-3 Release 4, and it was also the one most extensively tested and refined. We began work on DQA by testing software prototypes and continued past when the product had gone to beta testers. This process spanned more than a year and included about 10 different tests.

Our goal with DQA was to improve the usability of functionality that had always been in 1-2-3. We knew that many users clearly understood the value of database features and the advantages of using 1-2-3 to analyze and organize data. We wanted to provide tools to make this interaction easier than in previous versions.

The team started with general agreement about how customers would use these features and what they would do with them. The team quickly saw usability testing as an extremely valuable tool in perfecting their design and quickly incorporated it in their development plan. We adopted iterative testing from the beginning. Each time we reviewed results from one test, we immediately planned what and when to test next.

Understanding DQA

A typical task might be to create a list of all employees working in Cambridge from the worldwide corporate employee database. Here is a simplified description of the subtasks involved in using DQA.

1. Identify the database that might be in another file or somewhere in the same file.
2. Place a copy of the selected data in the worksheet as a "query table."
3. Create filters to select records from original database with desired characteristics (e.g., employees living in Cambridge) and show the results in the "query table."

Structuring User Tasks

When testing early, incomplete, or unstable versions of the product, we made the tests very specific in order to keep users from seeing the product crash too often during the test. At this stage, we created tests that asked the user to focus on each subtask individually. We communicated with the users almost continually through the session, prompting them to talk out loud, shepherding them away from buggy areas of the product, and asking questions that probed for additional information and reactions. A typical task of this type might be: "Select the employee database in preparation for creating a report."

As the product became more stable, we asked users to do more complete tasks, giving us a more realistic understanding of the kinds of problems users might have while trying to complete a job in their offices or a better understanding of the approach the user would take to try to complete a task. A typical task of this type might be, "You have been asked to use the employee database to produce a list of all employees who make more than $25,000." During this kind of test, we held questions until the end of the whole task, so that we did not distract users from their work.

After we had completed several rounds of iterative testing and redesign, we found that users could easily complete the subtasks, because we had greatly improved the usability of each subtask. However, as these subtasks became easier to do, we noticed that users had trouble navigating from subtask to subtask on their own. Therefore, we began to focus on helping the user understand the whole process of querying a database.

Evolution of DQA

In early versions, users had to make a series of selections. The first step was to select their database ("input") table by choosing New Query from the Tools menu. The next step took them through a series of choices on the Query menu. Users would get stuck after they chose New Query (see Figure 3).

Color Plate I The KODAK CREATE-A-PRINT 35 mm Enlargement Center (see Chapter 2, Figure 3).

Color Plate II The RCA DSS Digital Satellite System (see Chapter 3, Figure 3).

Color Plate III The Human Factors observation room at Compaq Computer Corporation (see Chapter 5, Figure 2).

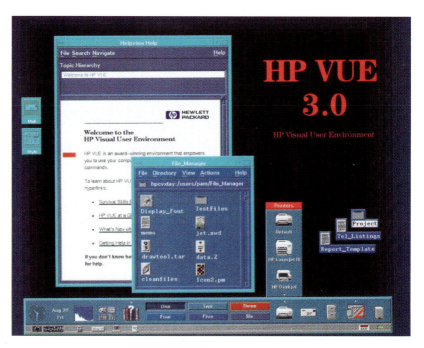

Color Plate IV HP VUE 3.0 (see Chapter 7, Figure 5).

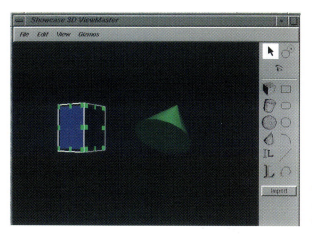

Color Plate V a. Silicon Graphics' Showcase 3D—a scene from an early prototype (see Chapter 8, Figure 4).

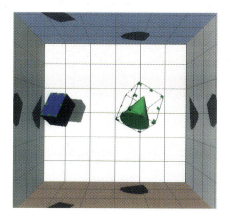

b. Showcase 3D—a scene from the finished product (see Chapter 8, Figure 5).

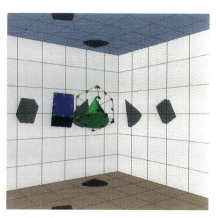

c. 3D scene rotated 45 degrees (see Chapter 8, Figure 6).

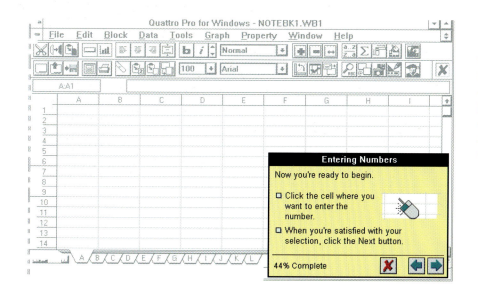

Color Plate VI
Borland International's computer-based tutorial design for interactive tutorial feature (see Chapter 9, Figure 11).

Color Plate VII American Airlines' Usability Lab (see Chapter 12, Figure 1).

a. Edit Suite

b. Control Room

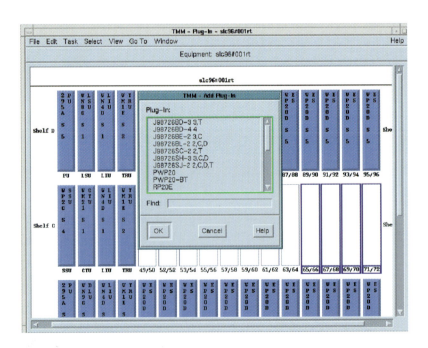

Color Plate VIII Bellcore's Technology Management Module: an example of a Plug-In window (see Chapter 16, Figure 3).

Figure 3   New Query dialog 1

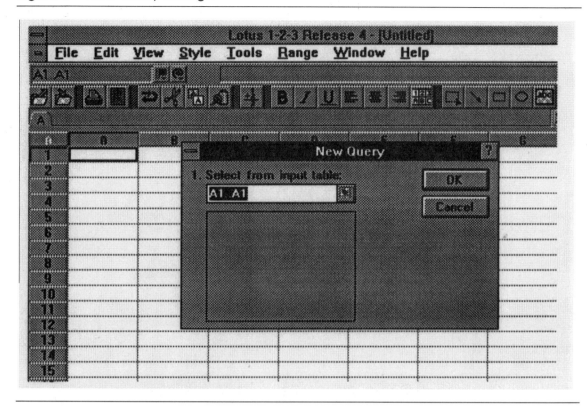

We decided to try to help the users by placing the necessary commands as options in a dialog box that appeared after the user made the initial selection from the Tools menu (Figure 4). Users had better results with this dialog box, but suggested that we number the steps to make the process clearer.

However, adding numbers to the dialog box was problematic. The problem was that the numbers implied that a particular order of commands is necessary. In fact, the user can choose these commands in any order and need not use all of these options. However, after testing this version and finding that users performed much more successfully, we decided to go with this design. This seemed like a good compromise between ease of learning and ease of use: the numbers would facilitate learning, but the dialog box would not force advanced users through steps they knew were unnecessary. This also helped the team learn that some less elegant software solutions can actually clarify the product for the user.

Finally, users suggested that we indent the text slightly to make the numbers stand out more (Figure 5). Users performed even better with this last design, which appears in the final product.

Figure 4   New Query dialog 2

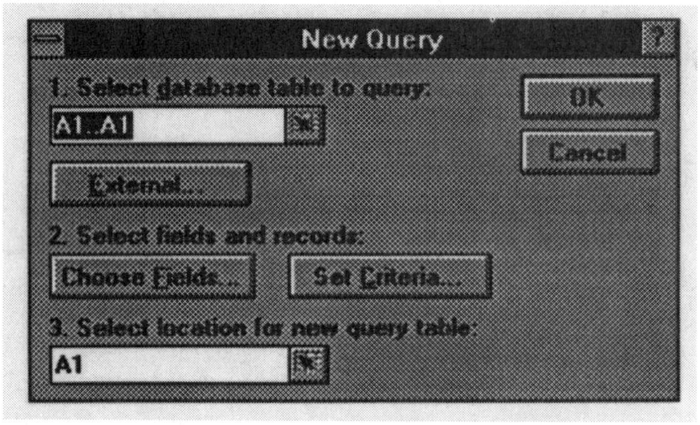

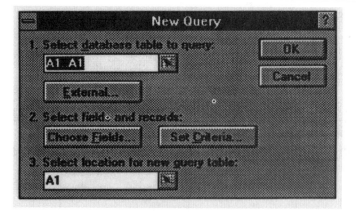

Figure 5   New Query dialog 3

Version Manager

Another example illustrates the role of usability testing in helping to resolve conflicts between UI designers and engineers. Lotus 1-2-3 Release 4 included a new feature known as Version Manager that allowed users to store multiple sets of data in the same cells. This feature required that users first name a range of cells (e.g., Expenses) and then assign names to the various versions stored in that range (e.g., Best Guess, Worst Case).

In an early iteration of Version Manager, the user had to first name the range of cells by choosing the Range Name command, before starting up Version Manager (which appears as a modeless dialog box) and then naming the version. The UI designers felt that users would have great difficulty understanding this sequence of actions and did not want the users to have to name ranges at all. Development agreed with this assumption, but felt that the limitation was too costly to correct. Design and development had repeated fruitless discussions on this issue and turned to usability testing to help shed some new light.

In testing an early version, users were unable to complete their tasks. We could clearly attribute the difficulties to users' confusion about when and how to name ranges. Initial testing drove home the point to development that users got really stuck with this sequence of steps, while also helping designers see that users were willing to name ranges, as long as doing this was made easier. Design and development worked together to produce a new approach in which users still had to name ranges, but could do this from within Version Manager. (See Figure 6 for final Version Manager). Testing showed that users were much more successful with this approach.

This initial change led to a new innovation: if there was text adjacent to a range of numbers, have Version Manager suggest that text as a range name, and save the users another step. Users found this approach even more helpful, and a new usability enhancement was added.

Testing Techniques

Basic Approach

Most of our tests involved thinking-aloud protocols. Generally we tested single users seated alone in the testing room. We instructed users to talk out loud to begin the test. The facilitator (almost always a member of the usability engineering staff) communicated with the user through an in-ceiling intercom. We generally tested three to five users over the course of one or two days. Each test lasted about two hours.

We paid users $100 for participating in the tests. Although this is on the high end of the scale of user compensation, we felt it was important to provide a strong incentive for users to attend testing. Because we were working against tight deadlines, we wanted to ensure that we never had to reschedule users and that we had sufficient attendance by users to produce enough data.

We also used "usability nights" as a way to vary our technique and collect information more rapidly. At these events, we invited groups of 10 users to our training facility. Each user was paired with a development team "buddy" for an evening session. We tested a variety of software, tasks, and users. For example, we tested 1-2-3 Release 4 with users of competitive products. One night we asked users to bring their own work to try on 1-2-3. And one night we even loaded a competitor's product and watched users work on that. This was an extremely flexible tool for trying new testing methods. The ability to accommodate larger groups of users and team members allowed us to collect a great deal of information very quickly.

Figure 6   Version manager

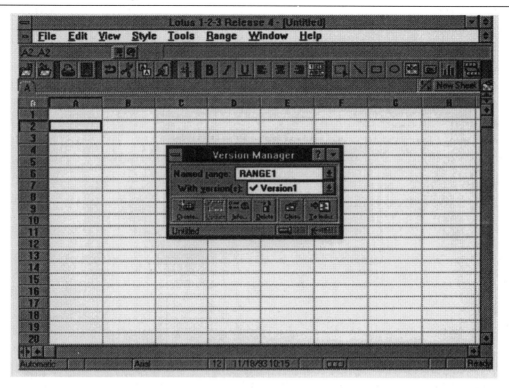

We found over time that we could iterate on any one feature only about once every three weeks, as the product team needed time to understand the results and implement changes. We could test different parts of the interface in different tests, so we were actually testing about once every other week. Table 1 shows the types of tests used.

Table 1   Some Methods Used During Testing of 1-2-3 Release 4

Method/Description	Advantages	Disadvantages
Prototype testing	Collect user reactions before investing in development	Does not work exactly like real product, so user reactions may not be accurate
Testing previous versions of 1-2-3 for Windows	Collect baseline data	
Testing very early, very buggy pre-alpha versions	Collect user reactions while changes can still be made	Have to talk users through the rough spots, limiting their real experience
Test alpha and beta version	Collect user reactions to the real product prior to ship while some changes can be made	Difficult and expensive to make significant UI changes at this stage
Competitive testing	Benchmark against competitors; sets implied usability goals	Time consuming and expensive

User selection

Users were selected based on how closely they matched our target user population for the feature being tested. They included current 1-2-3 users, users of competitors' products, DOS users, and Windows users. Each potential user was contacted by phone and screened for level of expertise on specific areas of the spreadsheet. We found that usability lab staff did not have time for time-consuming user screening interviews. Instead we used student interns from Tufts University majoring in human factors engineering to do the scheduling.

We tested few Lotus employees. We felt that Lotus employees were too sophisticated with technology, on the one hand, and too inexperienced with typical spreadsheet tasks, on the other, to accurately reflect our target market.

Some users were tested several times. Sometimes we tested the same user to see if he or she could remember how to use a feature or liked changes that we made. We did not find that users got "too good" at testing, or started to tell us what they thought we wanted to hear, even if they tested several times.

Data Collection

Before each test we decided which data collection method to use based on the kind of questions we had. We primarily used verbal protocols and qualitative data. Users' verbal reports of frustration showed us areas of the product we needed to change. We relied on user's descriptions of features to suggest new ways to represent the features in the interface. For example, we originally placed the feature to make text bold under the Style Fonts menu option. Users told us that they thought "fonts" only meant font size. When we changed the menu item to Style Fonts and Attributes, users easily found bold there.

We collected error rates primarily when attempting to determine the correct placement of a feature on a menu. We tried different menu placements, placing items where we found users had looked first for them.

We collected performance data primarily when we tested users on 1-2-3 Release 4 and our competitors. In those tests we asked users to complete tasks as quickly as possible, without talking out loud, and we did not interrupt them, to get truer measures of performance. We measured time to complete tasks, number of errors, and completion rate. Although this provided an interesting benchmark, we found that not having the users narrate their actions made it difficult to understand and diagnose problems. We concluded that this was not an effective testing technique.

Test observations were collected using data logging software. The data logger recorded user activities and comments and the times these occurred. Team members and student interns were pressed into service to act as data loggers. In addition, the test facilitator often kept handwritten notes during the test. Over time, we found the test logs kept by team members and interns did not capture enough information or contained too many typing errors. Eventually the test facilitator simply took over test logging, and the results were more satisfactory.

Communicating Results

The facilitator created final reports based on the test logs and handwritten notes. These reports were organized by topic and included summaries of what was seen, quotes from users about particular features, and recommendations as appropriate. The reports documented successes and problems. We distributed reports to relevant team members. These reports, along with all the test plans, scenarios, testing files, testing logs, and final reports, were stored in a centrally accessible Lotus Notes database so that any team member could review methods and results at any time. Throughout the project we found this to be an effective method to share information. It also allowed us to share information with staff throughout the company who regularly contributed advice and suggestions.

Few highlight videotapes were made, and videotapes were rarely reviewed except by team members who had missed important test sessions. We found that creating highlight videotapes was extremely time consuming. Since we were increasingly successful in getting team members to attend usability tests, we also found highlight tapes to be unnecessary. We continued to tape all sessions in case we wanted to review particular issues.

After awhile, we found the written reports almost superfluous. Team members who attended testing would hold quick discussion meetings immediately after testing and begin to implement changes. Since key team members increasingly attended testing, they checked final reports only to remind themselves of any issues they had not already addressed.

Sometimes, team members would meet to review the report and debrief about the test; however, we found that our report format did not particularly help the debriefing process. More often, the usability facilitator would meet with the designer or product manager to review areas that needed to be addressed. The designer typically took this list of issues up with development people who would negotiate changes based on their importance and the cost of the development solution. This method of direct communication among usability staff, designer, and product manager proved most effective for getting usability issues addressed during this project.

The reports were also of limited value because they took too long to produce and recorded only the opinions of the test facilitator. We continued to produce final reports because they helped us track issues and served as an archive for future changes. In addition, they were a helpful reference for Lotus staff working on related projects who did not normally attend our tests.

Because of this experience, we subsequently changed our reporting process to involve team members in assessing usability issues. This improved the utility and timeliness of the final reports.

Using Consultants vs. an In-House Testing Group

One of the issues that often comes up for people starting a new usability testing program is whether the work should be done by consultants who are trained and experienced in usability testing or by an in-house group who may start out with less experience. We have an opportunity to address this question since both the spreadsheet and the graphics groups used consultants before and after there was an in-house testing function. The advantages and disadvantages of using consultants are summarized in Table 2. We stress that the data in this table is based on the experiences from two particular groups and may not generalize to other situations.

Table 2   Advantages and Disadvantages of Using Consultants over an In-House Testing Group

Consultants	In-House Testing
Pro	
Good at jump starting the effort and getting some data quickly. May benefit from higher credibility given to external "expert."	Start-up time especially if it includes building a lab(s) can be many months. Criticism of product may be viewed as politically biased.
Can recruit a wide range of subjects, very useful for competitive analysis.	May be better at reaching own customers.
Good for doing competitve analyses because have broader perspective and less biased.[1]	Competitive analyses can take a lot of time to set up fairly and then to run if group lacks software and hardware in-house
Can free time for in-house test group to focus on more important tasks.	
Con	
Will have only a partial understanding of the product because not part of the team.	Will have a deep understanding of the product's goals and history because part of the team.
Good at identifying problems but less good at ranking them or developing solutions.	Can easily rank problems and offer initial solutions
Hard to maintain communication because may be located far away or working on other projects.	Person is very accessible.
Not strong follow-through because no overall responsibility for product.	Responsible for usability for the product, therefore motivated to follow through on decisions.

[*]There is considerable controversy over this issue. Many believe that consultants are no less biased than internal testers because they will want to please the person who pays them. On the other hand, at least one consultant (Seybold, 1988) believes that consultants are well placed to provide an objective, outsider's view of the product and gather a broader view of overall interface directions.

Developers and managers we spoke with expressed a consistent preference to use an in-house usability testing group over consultants. People's individual experiences with consultants varied. However, most agreed that it was useful to bring in consultants for certain specialized tasks such as competitive analyses or early testing before the usability lab has become established. The developers especially expressed a strong desire to keep the usability function within the group and were concerned that an overreliance on consultants, who have no allegiance to the Lotus product and may be far away, would adversely affect communication between usability and development.

All the people who had been involved in the early stages of usability testing had been happy to use consultants to "jump start" usability testing. For instance, a group of consultants hired by the graphics division had done a competitive analysis of the previous release of the product, which they presented to the team in the form of videotapes and extended presentations. The videotapes contained valuable data that helped the team identify key problem areas for their next release as well as give it a competitive benchmark of usability. When a new usability engineer was hired to do in-house testing for the group, she used the tapes as a quick learning tool. By reviewing both the questions and the responses from users she was able to gain a quick appreciation of interviewing techniques and data analysis. Thus the consultants provided valuable benchmarks for the next product and training for the new usability engineer.

Costs

There are some interesting cost comparisons between using consultants and creating an in-house testing facility. The start-up costs of the in-house facility can be quite high. We will use a ballpark estimate of $70,000, which was the cost of equipping a lab at Ford (Kitsuse, 1991), as representative of a well-equipped lab. In addition, the salary of a usability engineer is approximately $52,000 per year.[2] This brings the fixed cost for the first year to $122,000. Our incremental costs at Lotus (i.e., the cost of paying subjects) is $100 per session, which is high compared with the average of $60 (reported in Ehrlich and Rohn, 1994), but low compared to the start-up costs.

In contrast, consultants have no start-up costs to the vendor company but high incremental costs, averaging about $1000 per user. This amount includes lab and equipment rental and the consultant's time to design the study, find the subjects, do the hands-on testing, analyze the data, and deliver the results.

---

[2]This figure is based on the estimate of Nielsen (1994) of $200 per day.

Based on these numbers we can see that after five studies, each of which uses four subjects (the average number of subjects we ran[3]), the cost of using an in-house group is $122,000 + $2,000 = $124,000. By comparison, the accounting cost of using consultants alone to do these same five studies would have been $20,000[4]. However, after 100 studies[5] of four subjects each, the cost of using the in-house group is $122,000 + $40,000 = $162,00 whereas the cost of using consultants is $400,000.

What are the implications of these numbers? At one level they suggest that a company may wish to use consultants rather than fund an internal group if only a few studies are to be run or if the company is unsure about investing in usability testing (but note that usability labs can be a shared resource across groups). They also suggest that the cost of starting an in-house group can be cost effective in less than a year of regularly run studies.

But while these numbers tell an interesting story, they are often less important in making decisions about creating an internal group than factors such as those outlined in Table 2. There is no real cost associated with having someone be part of your team.

Lessons Learned

What lessons are to be learned from our experience of doing usability testing on Lotus 1-2-3 Release 4?

In the interviews with team members, conducted after the product shipped, we were struck by the high level of enthusiasm and support for usability testing. Yes, it had been hard at first to accept the evidence that features which had been carefully and thoughtfully crafted were not as obvious to the user as they were to the designer or developer. A few of the people even admitted that there was a tendency at first to deny the evidence by dismissing the results as being due to poor user selection or a poor choice of tasks. But even the most skeptical admitted that after seeing as few as two or three users all struggling, the problem lay with the software and not with the user.

These developers, UI designers, and product managers were committed to making the software easier to use even if it meant developing an interface that did not conform to the logic of the software or the logic behind the UI design. Developers paid

---

[3]Nielsen's discount usability approach (e.g., Nielsen, 1990, 1993, 1994) advocates three to five users per test. Virzi (1990) claims 80% of usability problems are found with four to five users.

[4]That is, we are not factoring in the hidden costs of training the consultant or the developer time and effort to get the right software to the consultant.

[5]Approximately 100 of these small (four subject) studies were run over the course of a year across, all the groups making use of the usability lab. That is, the 1-2-3 product group plus Freelance and several other smaller groups had the usability lab in constant use.

attention to minor details—sometimes as small as the placement of a single pixel—if they thought it would make a difference to the users.

Tracing usability testing for Lotus 1-2-3 Release 4 from fall 1991 to the present, we can see that the effort fell into three phases.

- In the first phase, Getting Started, the effort is directed at introducing usability testing, building a usability lab and getting support and buy-in from senior management and the rest of the team.
- The second phase, Testing, focuses on the operational side of testing. We implicitly measure our success at this stage by how much the product improves as a result of our effort.
- The third phase, Maintenance, occurs when usability testing has been successfully incorporated and is a routine part of software development.

The point of segmenting our effort this way is to emphasize that usability testing takes time to get introduced and incorporated into a group; frequently at least one or two complete product cycles.

Within these three phases, we attribute our success to a combination of **organizational factors** and **usability practices and procedures**. In Table 3, we list specific factors within these two categories and show their importance for each phase of our usability program.

Organizational Factors

One of the most important factors predicting the successful outcome of usability testing is when senior management understands and supports the effort (Lundell and Notess, 1991; Grudin and Poltrock, 1989). Based on our experiences we examine not only whether that is true but why it might be true.

Support by Senior Management

In both the spreadsheet and graphics divisions, senior management helped get the program rolling: by bringing in outside consultants until an internal group could be established, by making usability a focus and high priority of the project, and by demonstrating its commitment to usability in actions as well as words. For instance, senior managers frequently attended the live testing sessions.[6] They also made it clear

---

[6]In the Freelance group, videotape highlights were a common method for conveying test results. Senior managers were frequently in attendance at these meetings and sometimes even ran the meeting to convince their peers and the sales force of the benefit of usability testing.

to the development organization that they favored solutions that would make the product easier to use even if it made the engineering more challenging. More specifically, senior management's active support speeded the process of setting up the usability lab, which became a visible testament to usability testing and hence helped establish its importance.

Table 3   Importance of Each Factor at Different Phases of Usability Testing

	Getting Started	Testing	Maintenance
Organizational Factors			
Support by senior management	High	High	Moderate
External competition	High	High	Moderate
Team buy-in	High	High	High
Usability Practices			
Team participation in test sessions	High	High	Moderate
Timeliness of results	Moderate	High	High
Communication	High	High	High

This active, vocal support by senior management was one of the more powerful factors in making usability so successful. But why was that support important? If the team believed in making the product more usable, which it did, why was that belief not enough?

To find the answer we need to look at the history, reward structure, and culture of this group. People in the development group had been exposed to new ideas that did not necessarily work out. Many of the developers were therefore reluctant to incorporate usability testing into their process unless they were confident of a positive outcome, confident of being rewarded and confident that they would still feel proud of and successful in their own effort. Support from senior management signaled the importance of usability testing and instilled a level of confidence and courage into the effort.

We believe that strong support by senior management was especially critical when usability testing was first introduced. When a group first shifts to a user-centered development model, new criteria are used to make decisions and resolve conflicts, control over the UI shifts from the developers to the UI designers, and the development process itself is more iterative and less predictable. Senior management is in the best position to shepherd the development team through these fundamental and often painful changes. Once the team had seen the success of its effort, usability testing had built sufficient momentum to be able to continue with little or no intervention by senior management. But it was critical for senior management to keep the team focused on usability before there were any visible signs of success.

Competition

Another major influence came from the external pressure on Lotus from its competitors. In interviews it was clear that issues such as market share, competitive advantage, and the competitor's current product offering were all very much in people's consciousness. Lotus is a significant company in the arena of desktop applications, and there is very strong incentive to stay ahead of the competition. People at Lotus are highly sensitized to the tone of reviews in part because it reflects on their work but, more important, because the way a product is reviewed can have a major effect on sales. A positive review, such as the ones received for Lotus 1-2-3 Release 4, can influence people to buy the product.

The pressure that came from the marketplace provided the motivation for the product group to focus on usability and make it work. Once the decision was made to focus on improving the usability of its products, it was a simple matter of doing competitive analyses to see how well the usability of the Lotus product stacked up against the competition. The results of these tests indicated areas of weakness for Lotus and provided implicit usability goals.

Team Buy-In

Ehrlich and Rohn (1994) argued that product groups vary in their level of acceptance of usability testing from skeptical, through stages of curiosity and acceptance, to a stage where usability and UI designers are treated as true partners with the rest of the team. In a highly skeptical group, testing is treated as an outside "consulting" function with no clear relationship to the rest of the development organization. Usability testing is frequently done too late to make any substantive changes to the product. In contrast, groups that are more accepting of usability will schedule time for testing and for changes in the product based on the results of the testing. It was argued that groups that are more accepting of usability testing and UI design would also develop more usable products.

In the present case study, while the support of senior management paved the way for usability, it was really the individuals on the team who made the difference in the product. There were lots of cases where individual developers, product designers, and product managers went out of their way to ensure that the product would be usable. As we heard in one of the interviews, the developers were proud of their work and wanted users to like it and use it. They were therefore motivated to make changes when they were presented with evidence of users struggling. We will see later that seeing the users either in a live testing session or on videotape provided the necessary evidence to convince the team of the need for change.

In both the spreadsheet and graphics divisions, usability became the province of the whole team, not just the responsibility of the UI designer or the usability engineer.

Usability Practices and Procedures

The support of senior management, the competitive pressure, and the strong team buy-in all helped to create an environment in which there was a high level of support and motivation for usability testing. But what lessons have we learned about the testing itself from our case study? In reviewing previous research, it appeared that specific usability practices were not consistent indicators of whether usability testing had been able to make improvements to the product (Lundell and Notess, 1991). However, in our case study, several factors seemed to make a difference to the effectiveness of usability testing. We highlight three of these: (a) team participation in test sessions; (b) timeliness of results; (c) level of communication between the usability engineers and the rest of the team.

Team Participation in Test Sessions

The single most important part of the usability testing was having the members of the team themselves see the users by attending the live testing sessions.[7]

In our case, having people sit in on the live testing sessions (live video if you will) was very effective in conveying the real usability problems to the developers in a

---

[7]The people on the Freelance product team participated by attending a group presentation of videotaped highlights or by watching selected videotapes repeatedly to study particular problems in depth. As a result, it was often possible to pick up subtleties that were important to understanding the source of the user's problems. Whichever method was used (sitting in on live sessions or watching videotapes), the effect was the same. Everyone on the team understood and could internalize the user's problems.

much more graphic way than any report could have achieved. In the interviews, we heard how actually seeing a user struggle provided compelling evidence of the difficulty in using the product. As one of the developers explained, it was originally believed that the product would be okay because there were excellent UI designers on the team. But seeing people have difficulty using the product brought home the message that good UI by itself did not guarantee usability.

A lot of people in the interviews mentioned the impact of the user's nonverbal cues such as fidgeting, taking a long time to respond, or getting distracted as persuasive evidence of the user's difficulties. These nonverbal cues cannot be adequately described in a report. In fact, the graphics division adopted a deliberate policy of not intervening even when the user was clearly struggling and frustrated. The impact of seeing a user clearly agonizing carried far more weight than any written report of performance and sensitized developers to the user's point of view.

But there are less obvious reasons why it was important to view the test sessions. Team members found it far more persuasive to see users for themselves rather than just read the results of a test session. One of the developers, who had sat through many test sessions, confessed that she occasionally found herself making excuses for a user's performance when it was described to her in a report, even though she was extremely sympathetic to the user's point of view and had built up a huge repertoire of examples to draw from. When she saw the same behavior for herself she was much more likely to take it seriously and act on it.

After a time, the test sessions also took on a life and culture of their own and became a source of common knowledge throughout the team. In a group such as this one, where informal and frequent communication was important in the decision-making process, this common base of knowledge short-circuited any problems in convincing people of the need to change and was one of the factors that helped unify the group. This sense of community was not accidental. The lab was designed to be inviting and comfortable and conveniently located to encourage attendance.

One of the more interesting effects of having people view the test sessions was that there were always surprises. One of developers commented on how surprised he was to learn that users blamed themselves rather than the software for their problems. A number of people were struck by how much less users could accomplish than expected. In fact one person commented that you could tell the difference between people who had sat through several test sessions and those who had not by their belief in how much users could accomplish. People who had not sat through many test sessions routinely overestimated a user's ability. It was also interesting to note that it only took three or four viewings before a member of the team could distinguish between users who were having an unusually hard time and users whose problems were typical.

Timeliness of Results

Usability testing is a lot of work for product teams and has the potential to disrupt schedules by adding work to set up the software for the tests and by adding time to an already tight schedule to make changes based on the test results. If teams start regarding usability testing as too much work the effort is doomed. Therefore it is essential for the usability engineers to be flexible, to be able to respond quickly to requests for a usability test, and to deliver results of the test speedily.

The emphasis on timeliness means that verbal reports of results are far more effective than written reports, which are often superseded by changes to the product by the time the report is published. Written reports, annotated videotapes, and formal presentations do, however, form an important role as archival sources and for summarizing results for a large group.

One-on-one meetings between the test facilitator and either the UI designer or developer, held immediately after test sessions, were the most effective, timely way to communicate results. At these meetings, the implications of the user's behavior for changes in the design would be discussed. The UI designer would often then make the necessary changes, which would get passed on to the developer. The elapsed time between identifying a problem and getting a solution implemented could be as short as minutes. In one case, a developer was so struck by what he learned from a single test session that he immediately changed the code in time to still see the next test subject a few minutes later. Even though the test facilitators in the spreadsheet and graphics divisions differed in their use of videotapes and written reports, they both stressed the importance and value of this early, personal communication of results.

Communication

There was an extremely high level of communication and shared respect between the usability engineers and the others on the team. In addition there were other, more subtle signs of cohesion. First, the usability engineers, UI designers, and developers were all knowledgeable and in agreement about the target user population. This was especially true in the graphics group. During the interviews, each person gave a consistent, well-articulated description of the intended user. This is significant because a basic requirement of both usability testing and UI design is a well-thought-out description of the user. Disagreements about the target user population are high on the list of common sources of friction between the UI community and the developers. Second, in viewing the user's performance, the other people on the team typically agreed with the observations of the usability engineer. This is in contrast to groups that are much more doubtful of the role and value of usability testing, in which individuals may disagree—sometimes vehemently—with the usability engineer's observation and interpretation of the user's behavior.

It was very important for people to "trust" the usability engineer. Because users' behavior in the test sessions is open to interpretation, it is easy for the test facilitator to introduce some bias, intentional or not, in reporting the results. If the developers or designers believed that was the case they would either feel compelled to view all the test sessions personally or stop believing in the written reports. Since it is very time consuming to watch every session, many developers stopped participating after seeing three or four users unless it was directly relevant and instead waited for the summary reports. In the interviews, several people commented that they felt comfortable not viewing every session, even though they were missing the intangible benefit of seeing the user, because they could trust the accuracy of the reports. It is unlikely that the developers would have felt the same degree of trust if the test facilitator were less accessible, had any hidden agendas, or was less professional in conducting the test sessions.

Summary

We consider the usability testing on Lotus 1-2-3 Release 4 to have had a successful outcome. As a result of the testing many significant improvements were made to the product before it was shipped.

Organizational factors as well as specific usability practices and procedures contributed to making the product successful. From the senior manager to the individual engineer writing the code, everyone was committed to and believed in making the product as usable as possible. Within this context, the role of the usability engineer may be viewed as facilitator and mediator between the users and the product group (see Grudin, 1991, who talks of the importance of mediators in translating users' needs to developers as well as informing users of technological advances).

Many of the factors we consider to have been significant in determining the successful outcome confirm published practices and experiences (e.g., Lundell and Notess, 1991; Ehrlich and Rohn, 1994): notably the importance of support by senior management, "buy-in" by the team, a close relationship between the usability engineers and the rest of the team, and early involvement of usability and UI engineers. In addition, the strong competition among vendors of desktop application software provided a strong motivation as well as an implicit benchmark.

The predominant method we used to extract information about the weakness of a particular user interface was videotaped "thinking aloud" studies (see Nielsen, 1993, for a description of this methodology). While this is a common method in most software companies, our emphasis on getting everyone in the team involved in the testing, especially by attending the live sessions, made this method highly effective for communicating results in a timely, cost-effective manner. Usability testing, while recognized for highlighting serious usability problems, has also been considered an expensive and time consuming way to collect data (e.g., Jeffries et al, 1991; Karat, Campbell, and Fiegel, 1992; Desurvire, Kondziela, and Atwood, 1992; Muller, Dayton, and Root, 1993). Our contribution to this debate is to suggest that videotaped usability studies do not have to be expensive or time consuming and, moreover, can be highly effective in both finding problems and communicating them to the team.

There clearly are limitations to the data and insights we present in this chapter. As a case study, our experiences are not intended to provide any kind of general or systematic view of usability testing. Every situation has its own characteristics, which represent constraints as well as opportunities for successful incorporation of usability testing. There were several factors that made this case unique. However, we hope that some of our experiences are useful for other groups.

Acknowledgments

We would like to thank Bob Balaban, Matt Belge, Mary-Kate Foley, Jay Freed, Irene Greif, Kathy Howard, Ericca Lahti, Alice Meade, Kara Pernice, Larry Roshfeld, Hal Shubin, and Alexandra Trevelyan at Lotus for their careful reading of earlier versions of this chapter. Their thoughtful comments helped us to understand our users better. We are especially grateful to Mike Wiklund for giving us the opportunity to tell our story and for his extensive and helpful comments on an earlier draft.

References

Bott, Ed. (1993). "Who's Making the Best Windows Interfaces? Micro-Who? I Say Lotus," *PC/Computing* (August), 20.

Chapanis, A., and Budurka, W. J (1990). "Specifying Human-Computer Interface Requirements," *Behavior and Information Technology* 9 (6), 479-492.

Desurvire, H., Kondziela, J., and Atwood, M. E. (1992). "What Is Gained and Lost When Using Methods Other Than Empirical Testing," in *Posters and Short Talks CHI '92 Human Factors in Computing Systems*, pp. 125-126. ACM, New York.

Ehrlich, Kate, and Rohn, Janice A. (1994). "Cost Justification of usability Engineering: A Vendor's Perspective," in *Cost-Justifying Usability*, R. G. Bias and D. J. Mayhew, (eds.). Academic Press, Boston.

Ehrlich, Kate, Butler, Mary Beth, and Pernice, Kara. (1994). "Getting the Whole Team into Usability Testing," *IEEE Software* (January).

Grudin, J. (1991). "Interactive Systems: Bridging the Gaps Between Developers and Users," *Computer* (April), 59-69.

Grudin, J., and Poltrock, S. (1989). "User Interface Design in Large Corporations: Coordination and Communication Across Disciplines," in Proc. CHI '89 Human Factors in Computing Systems, pp. 197-203. ACM, New York.

Jeffries, R., Miller, J., Wharton, C., and Uyeda, K. (1991). "User Interface Evaluation in the Real World: A Comparison of Four Techniques," in Proc. CHI '91 *Human Factors in Computing Systems*, pp. 119-124. ACM, New York.

Karat, C.M., Campbell, R., and Fiegel, T. (1992). "Comparison of Empirical Testing and Walkthrough Methods in User Interface Evaluation," in *Proc. CHI '92 Human Factors in Computing Systems*, pp. 397-404. ACM, New York.

Kitsuse, A. (1991). "Why Aren't Computers . . ." *Across the Board* 28 (October), 44-48.

Lundell, Jay, and Notess, Mark. (1991). "Human Factors in Software Development: Models, Techniques and Outcomes," in *Proc. CHI '91 Human Factors in Computing Systems*, pp. 145-151. ACM, New York.

Meyerson, A. (1993). "A Usability Grand Tour," *PC/Computing*, (December), 326-335.

Miastkowski, Stan. (1993). "First Looks: Lotus 1-2-3 Release 4.0," *Windows Users*, (July), 48.

Muller, M. J., Dayton, T., and Root, R. (1992). "Comparing Studies That Compare Usability Assessment Methods: An Unsuccessful Search for Stable Criteria," in *Posters and Short Talks CHI '92 Human Factors in Computing Systems*, pp. 125-126. ACM, New York.

Nielsen, J. (1990). "Big paybacks from 'discount' usability engineering. *IEEE Software* 7, 3 (May), 107-108.

Nielsen, Jakob. (1993). *Usability Engineering*. Academic Press, Boston.

Nielsen, Jakob. (1994). "Guerilla HCI: Using Discount Usability engineering to Penetrate the Intimidation Barrier," in *Cost-Justifying Usability*, R. G. Bias and D. J. Mayhew (eds.). Academic Press, Boston.

Seybold, P. (1988). Panelist in Integrating Human Factors and Software Development, *Proc. CHI'88 Human Factors in Computing Systems*, pp. 157-159. ACM, New York.

Virzi, R. A. (1990). "Streamlining the Design Process: Running Fewer Subjects," in *Proceedings of the Human Factors Society 34th Annual Meeting* 1, 291-294.

Walkenbach, John. (1993). "1-2-3 for Windows Hits Stride with Release 4," *InfoWorld* (August 23), 75-78.

CHAPTER 11

The Microsoft Corporation Usability Group

**Mary Dieli,
Ken Dye,
Marshall McClintock,
and Mark Simpson**

Microsoft Corporation

Dr. Mary Dieli joined Microsoft in 1988 to found and run the Usability Group, a position she held through September 1993. Before joining Microsoft, Dieli worked at Adobe Systems Inc. as the Technical Publications Manager. She also worked at AT&T Bell Laboratories and at Apple Computer, and was an Assistant Professor at Santa Clara University. She has a B.A. degree in American Studies from the State University of New York at Binghamton, and a Ph.D. in Rhetoric with a specialization in Document Design from Carnegie Mellon University. Her Ph.D. dissertation study was a comparison of a variety of usability testing methods.

Ken Dye is usability manager for the desktop applications division at Microsoft. Dye holds an M.A. from the University of North Carolina-Charlotte and studied rhetoric at Carnegie-Mellon University. Before coming to Microsoft he was on the research faculty at North Carolina State University, worked for the American Institutes for Research, and SEI Information Services.

Marshall McClintock has been a manager in Microsoft's usability group for three years, where he has been responsible for usability activities in its desktop applications, workgroup, and systems divisions. Prior to joining Microsoft, he was a project manager at American Institutes for Research. Dr. McClintock holds a Ph.D. in the history and philosophy of social and behavioral sciences from the State University of New York at Binghamton as well as an M.A. in human factors psychology from George Mason University.

Mark Simpson has been a member of the Microsoft usability group since 1989 and a manager in the group since 1991. He became group manager in October 1993. Dr. Simpson has a Ph.D. in English with a concentration in rhetoric from Purdue University. His Ph.D. dissertation was an ethnographic study of the composing processes of computer documentation writers.

The Microsoft Corporation

Founded in 1975 by William H. Gates and Paul G. Allen, Microsoft[R] designs, develops, markets and supports a wide range of personal computer software systems, applications, development tools and languages, hardware peripherals and books. Based in Redmond, WA, the company employs more than 14,000 worldwide. The company has employees in 40 subsidiaries around the world and invests heavily in the international marketplace.

Best know for its MS-DOS[R] and Microsoft Windows[TM] operating systems, Microsoft also produces desktop office applications including Microsoft Word, Microsoft Excel, PowerPoint[R], Microsoft Mail and Microsoft Access[R] database management system. For the small business and home markets, Microsoft develops a full line of consumer products and multimedia titles that include such titles as Microsoft Works, Microsoft Money, Publisher, the Encarta[TM] multimedia encyclopedia and the Cinemania[TM] interactive movie guide. Microsoft also produces a family of development tools, including the Visual Basic™ programming system for the Windows and MS-DOS operating systems, the Visual C++™ development system, FORTRAN PowerStation, MASM, Delta Version Control and Test.

Microsoft has also recognized the need for service and support for a range of user needs, from the individual customer to large corporations. Many support services are provided directly from the company (one in every five Microsoft employees is dedicated to support) or through third-party partners that provide consulting, integration, customization, development, technical training and support or other services with Microsoft products. These companies are called *Solution Providers* because they apply technology and provide services to help solve customers' business problems.

A sample of the support and information services available from Microsoft and Microsoft solution providers includes the following:

Microsoft Product Support Service, which provides technical product support for all Microsoft software products and utilities. Customers contact product support services by phone or electronic inquiry.

Microsoft Education Services, which provides technical education and training courses on Microsoft products. This service is available in over 150 Microsoft Solution Provider Authorized Training Centers in the United States and from Microsoft subsidiaries worldwide.

Microsoft Consulting Services (MCS), which leverages and transfers its capabilities in Microsoft technology, methodologies, tools, training and experience to empower large numbers of corporate and government developers, independent software vendors (ISVs), value-added resellers (VARs) and other solution provider developers in making the transition to the Microsoft Solutions Platform.

Microsoft Press, which published 50 new titles last year. The books educate and provide product support solutions for users of Microsoft systems software, applications and languages. Microsoft Press titles are translated into 25 languages and are distributed to book and software stores worldwide.

In the early days of personal computing, software companies competed with each other primarily on the basis of features, seeing feature-packed products as likely to gain the most market share. But when personal computers and software became accessible, and necessary, tools for schools, businesses and homes, the target market changed from computer experts to "real people." This audience was interested not only in what it uses use the products to do, but in how easy it was going to be for to learn and use the software. "Today's computer users want to access and manipulate information without developing expertise in the underlying software and hardware.

In order to make software more usable, vendors must make software with the features that users want and need [and] implement those features in ways that make them easier to use" (Microsoft Corporation, 1991, p.1).

Because it produces software covering a variety of markets and different types of users, Microsoft was among the first software companies to realize that it needed to make ease of use as high a priority as a competitive feature set. Microsoft's Usability Group and its usability laboratories are evidence of a radical change in the company's product development process, a movement from feature-centered design to user-centered design.

To understand how this usability group works, we must first understand the context in which it works. Accordingly, in this chapter, we will first describe the organization and goals of a typical product team. Next we will describe the Usability Group's mission, its role in the organization and its "product." Then we will illustrate its product with three case studies. Finally, we will look to the future.

User-Centered Design: Building Consideration of the User into the Product Development Process

Microsoft product planning proceeds from information about how users work, think and solve problems. As mentioned previously, this was not always the case. However, it is the approach the teams take that has changed, not the structure of the teams. Microsoft defines *usability* as strategies for getting information about users into the development process in a timely way. Let us look at how the product development teams are typically structured and then at how they have modified their process to include consideration of usability data.

Product development teams at Microsoft are typically composed of several subteams, including Marketing, Program Management (interface design), Development, Testing (quality assurance, or QA), and User Education (documentation). Each of the subteams has goals specific to its role on the product team. For example, Marketing aims to define a new product, or a new release of an existing product, based on features that will compete and sell. Interface designers' primary goal is to design the interface, the part of the software program that the end-user sees. Development, the programmers, write the code to create the specified product, and QA ensures that the code performs as specified. As the programmers and testers work, they may propose refinements and alternatives to the interface. The User Education team's goal is to produce the print and on-line documentation and training that teaches users how to use the product and presents details about the product's features.

In pre-usability days, each sub-team based its work primarily on "traditional" sources of information about end users. Marketing often used demographic data based on feature-driven buyer profiles (e.g., surveys, focus groups, and customer feedback cards.) The Interface Design team often worked from marketing's data, and also from their "working" audience profile consisting of assumptions about when and how people would use the product. Development and QA built an audience profile from a number of sources: those listed above, instinct and experience, reviews in the trades, anecdotal information from the field, and information from other developers.

However, since the mid 1980s, software product teams have enhanced their working models of their audience with usability information, information about how easy the products are to learn and use. The extent to which Microsoft's teams changed their development process is reflected in the term they now describe that process with: user-centered design. Simply put, this means that the teams now include information about how users work, think and solve problems in their product planning. Not all of this information comes from the Usability Group. For example, program management has "... several data gathering techniques to help them focus on the user including instrumented versions[1], and beta testing" (Microsoft Corporation, 1991).

The Usability Group's role is to add to the team's user information by doing "formal" usability testing at all stages of product development. The table below lists the type of testing Usability Specialists might do at various phases in the development process, and the impact that testing might have on product development.[2]

To elaborate, we can simplify product development into three phases: product planning, which involves program managers and marketers most heavily; coding, which is done by developers and at which time the documentation team does most of its work; and testing, done by the quality assurance staff. During the planning phase, Usability Specialists can do at least several types of exploratory usability testing: with users only (to learn how they work), with competitors' products, on previous versions of the product, with documentation, and with prototype software. In this way, the usability data can impact the product specification that the program managers are writing, the marketing strategy, and the documentation plan. During development, the usability team can test iteratively with product prototypes and with documentation versions. This testing can impact the product as it evolves. And during the testing

---

[1]Instrumented versions of software are specially augmented versions that create a separate binary log file that records every mouse click and keystroke of a test user as well as the time it takes to complete each action. Analysts can then reconstruct and understand not only what tasks [0] a user accomplished, but how the user carried them out—i.e., when the user chose the keyboard instead of the menus or Toolbar to execute a given task.

[2]For a detailed diagram of the phases of usability testing as they correspond to the phases of product development, see M. Dieli, "The Usability Process: Working with Iterative Design Principles," *IEEE Transactions on Professional Communication*, Special Issue on Usability Testing (1989), 272-278.

phase, usability testing can confirm the ease-of-use of the "debug" versions of the software and documentation, impacting both the final product and future versions.

Table 1   Usability testing during product development

Phase in Product Development Process:	Planning	Coding	Testing
Type of Usability Testing:	Exploratory	Iterative	Confirmatory
What the Usability Data can Impact:	Product specification; documentation strategy.	Evolving new product (mock-ups; prototypes; code.)	Alpha, Beta and Final release versions; future versions

In sum, the shift to user-centered design means that product teams now consider their own usability data and that generated by the Usability Group through out the product development process. In the next section, we'll focus on Microsoft's Usability Group, looking at its history, philosophy, staff, facilities, and the types of services it can offer.

Microsoft's Usability Group

History

The Microsoft Usability Group was founded in May 1988 by Mary Dieli, who was hired by Microsoft to start a usability group, define its organizational stance, define staff positions and fill them, and build needed facilities. The original mission of the Microsoft Usability Group was to provide empirical data about people learning and using software to product teams in a timely way.

As was typical in the software industry, it was the technical writers at Microsoft who first saw the need for usability testing. Writers were often the first ones to use a running version of the product, so in that respect they may claim that the audience profile they work from is closest to the end user. So, in 1988 the Usability Group was located in the Applications Division's User Education Department, which also contained the Writing, Editing, Production, Computer-Based Training and Classroom Training groups as well as a Tools group which developed the software used by all the user education groups[3]. In the fall of 1988, when the Applications Division reorganized under the direction of Mike Maples, the Usability Group moved to the User Interface Architecture group.

Philosophy

From the beginning, we established ourselves as consultants to the development process. Our philosophy was that, rather than try to change an already successful development process, we would attach ourselves to it. This consulting philosophy also helped us, as user advocates, maintain an objective stance, something that the product teams tell us is important to them.

Staff

Our staff has roles that allow us to fulfill our consulting obligations, to offer full-service usability testing to any Microsoft team that wishes it. Over the past five years, the group has grown to 20 full-time, regular staff, fifteen of whom are directly involved in testing products (Figure 1 and Table 1).

In addition, this in-house staff is supplemented with several types of full- and part-time freelance staff: freelance usability testers and test coordinators to help us keep up with heavy demand, undergraduate and graduate student interns who work as usability specialists, and temporary staff to help with clerical tasks.

Table 2 Usability Group Staff

Position	Primary Responsibilities
Group Manager	Implement group mission; strategic planning
Usability Managers	Participate in strategic planning, maintain long-range test plans with product teams; supervise Usability Specialists
Usability Specialists	Plan and carry out tests; report data
Support Technician	Maintain lab equipment; develop lab tools.
Test Coordinators	Recruit and schedule test subjects.

---

[3]Susan Boeschen was the head of this user education team.

Figure 1   Usability group organization

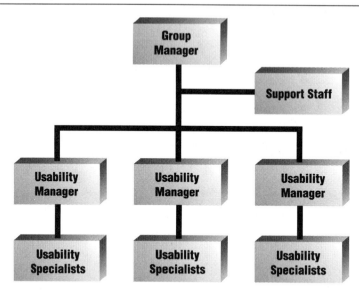

Initially, the staff worked on a demand basis, with usability specialists testing across groups. Criteria for selecting what we would test were (1) the impact the product had on the bottom line, and (2) how early it was in the product development process and, so, how much impact usability testing could have on the product. None of us predicted how quickly the product teams could respond to the demand for easier-to-use software and, how quickly these teams would want to incorporate usability into the design process at Microsoft. In response to that demand, we assigned specialists to product teams. Figure 2 illustrates how the managers work with the product teams and the usability specialists assigned to support them.

Facilities

In June 1989 we opened our first usability lab at Microsoft. Then, in response to increasing demand for usability lab testing, we opened a second in January 1992.[4] The

---

[4]The two usability labs are similar in design. We will describe the newer lab because it contains all the "best" features of both labs.

newer usability lab contains five separate self-contained rooms, each set up with a one-way mirror, cameras and other requisite equipment for observing and recording tests (Figure 3).

Figure 2   Working relationship between Usability Group and product teams

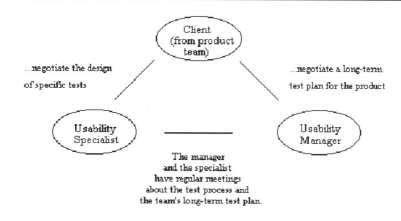

In designing the labs, we aimed to satisfy several goals:
- focus in the lab on cognitive process data,
- "open shop" philosophy; we wanted room for team members to observe and do problem-solving while watching the tests,
- "a picture is worth a thousand words"; we wanted use of video as a persuasion tool as well as a data source.

On the subjects' side of the lab, we installed a typical office desk and a small conference table. The conference table is particularly useful for tests that involve discussing low-fidelity prototypes or other paper mockups with subjects. The observers' areas are large enough to accommodate five people in addition to the usability specialist conducting the test, so that product team members can watch the tests. The gallery is essentially a long hallway separated from the observers' areas by sliding glass doors. The glass doors allow us to isolate each testing suite and make it possible to run up to five tests at one time without the noise from one test interfering with data collection in another.

Central to the usability lab operations is the on-line data collection software that the usability group has designed.

Figure 3   Usability Lab Diagram

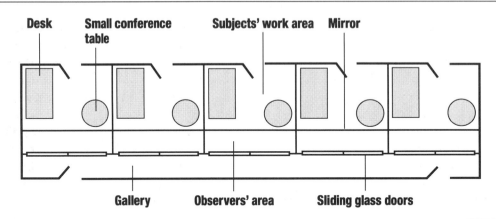

Figure 4   Usability lab

Services Offered

As detailed earlier, the goal of the Usability Group is to support product teams throughout the product cycle. This goal has required us to adopt a number of methods to address the particularities of each stage of the product cycle. Much of the work we do during product development takes place in the laboratories and focuses on features or smaller components of a product through several iterations. However, two of the primary usability activities during the planning and quality assurance stages take place outside the lab—field testing and field inquiry. Field testing examines stable versions of the product in the context of users' workplace or home, usually over a period of several weeks or months. Some aspects of product use are best studied in the field (such as installation) or over a longer period (such as learning). Field inquiry, on the other hand, focuses on users' work and work environment, rather than on their use of a particular software product. Its purpose is to inform designers' thinking about what the product should do and how it should look.

Obviously, laboratory and field work yield different types of data; considering data gained from each about the same product gives us a more complete picture of the end user. (See Table 3.)

Table 3   Comparison of Data from the Field and from the Lab

In the Laboratory	In the Field
artificial setting	"real" setting (workplace)
controlled	uncontrolled
measures task performance in hours	measures progress over time
process-tracing methods central	triangulation

In summary, with a large staff, state-of-the-art facilities, good links to our user community and the ability to test anywhere we can set up a portable lab, the Usability Group offers a wide variety of services to Microsoft's product teams (Table 4).

Table 4 Services Currently Offered by the Usability Group

Services currently offered by the Usability Group

- Conceptual model testing
- Ergonomic testing (for example, mouse testin.)
- Expert reviews
- Field inquiry (focuses on users' work)
- Field tests (focuses on product use in context)
- Human-Computer Interaction or Human Factors experimental research (the purpose of this research is to allow us to generalize behavior to a broad user population)
- Instrumented version tests (we'll review your plans, and help you analyze the results)
- Lab testing:
  - short, iterative tests focused on features
  - standard tests with more subjects than short tests
  - comparison tests (Microsoft product with a competitor's product)
  - out-of-box tests (looking at process from removing the shrink wrap through setup and tasks)
  - documentation/CBT tests (focused on documentation only rather than UI + documentation)
  - co-discovery tests (two or more people using the product together)
  - quick-turnaround tests
- Product specification reviews
- Task allocation testing (evaluating the distribution of work between the user and the computer)
- Task analysis
- Team training in informal usability testing
- Umbrella reports (summary of all usability test data on a product or feature)

Three Case Studies

In the following section we outline three examples of usability testing at Microsoft. The case studies are chosen to illustrate the variety of approaches we take in getting data about users into the product development process.

- *Testing Microsoft Word* overviews the testing process from the beginning of the development cycle through QA and describes in detail the iterative testing done in the usability lab to support the development of a major Microsoft product.

- *Field Testing Microsoft Publisher* focuses in on a longitudinal study conducted during the planning stage of a desktop publishing product and illustrates a method for field testing a released product to impact the design and development of a subsequent version of the product.

- *Designing a Tool to Collect Inexpensive Data* focuses more narrowly on a specific tool designed by the Microsoft Usability Group to facilitate collection of a particular kind of data, the terms users generate to characterize program functions.

The case studies exemplify two themes that run through all of the usability testing we do. The first theme is that of right timing: the character of the testing—purpose, methodology, etc.—depends on the point during the product development cycle at which we test. Both the Microsoft Word and Publisher testing, for example, support the particular needs of product teams encountered during the development and planning stages of the cycle. The second theme is that of right measure: all work that we do is constrained by the availability of time, money and human resources. The Term Tool, which we have used in the testing of Microsoft Excel, among other products, responds directly to those constraints.

Testing Microsoft Word

In this case study we describe the usability testing we did for a major release of Microsoft Word for Windows™. Microsoft Word for Windows is a high-end, full featured word processor designed for the business market. Over the development of Microsoft Word for Windows 6.0, we ran 43 usability tests with more than 250 subjects. Our focus here is to demonstrate the importance of getting usability information into each stage of the development process at a time and in a way that it is most effective.

For usability activities to have any impact, it must provide information that is appropriate to the stage of product development (Gould and Lewis, 1983). For example, usability studies of major conceptual issues late in a product's development are simply wasted effort unless you intend to use them to affect the next version. As we pointed out earlier, field studies, tests of basic concepts, and so on are appropriate during the planning phase with quick, iterative tests of prototypes and real code occurring during the development phase. Finally, testing with more complete scenarios are appropriate during the QA testing phase. A chart of usability activities over a project should show a relatively high level of activity during the planning phase, peaking toward the latter part of the development phase, and then tapering off rapidly during the QA testing phase. The usability activities we performed for Microsoft Word 6.0 illustrate these principles (Figures 5 & 6).

Figure 5   Level of activity during product development cycle

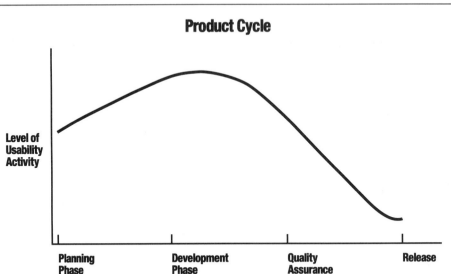

Within one month of Microsoft Word for Windows 2.0's release, we began a field study for the next version. We conducted the study over two months at several business locations in the Seattle area and involved users of various backgrounds. Rather than focusing on specific product features, this field study looked at the activities users perform with the product in their work environment. We combined data from this study with similar data from focus groups, customer visits and large-scale surveys. Our goal was to create an in-depth understanding of the work our customers were doing with our product and identify design opportunities for the next release.

As the team moved into high-level design, we began to conduct several detailed laboratory studies using the newly released version over the next four months. These studies looked in depth at specific issues that we targeted from the field data as well as other sources, such as product support calls and electronic bulletin boards. Some of the issues included print merge, tables, searching and easing the transition from other word processors to Microsoft Word for Windows. These laboratory studies were successful because they focused on questions that the team needed to decide before it could complete its product specification document. If our results were to have an effect, then the team needed the results as it was deciding those issues.

The Table feature is a good example of this detailed testing. Product support calls and site visits had told us that users encountered some difficulties using the Table feature

Figure 6   Product development cycle

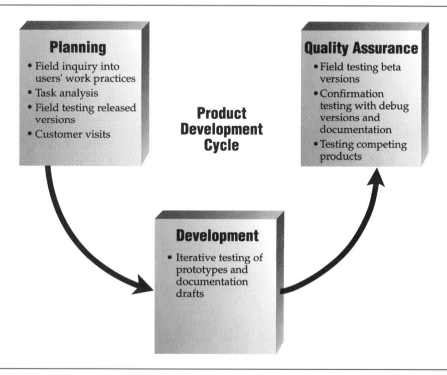

in Microsoft Word. However, this information did not allow us to pinpoint specific problems. We designed our laboratory study assuming that users were probably encountering a number of low-level difficulties, none of which were particularly great but that, when encountered together, created a less than satisfactory experience. By giving users a range of simple to complex tables to create in the lab, we provided the team with a priority list of difficulties that users encountered with the feature and explanations for why those difficulties occurred. For example, subjects could easily create simple tables, that is, tables with no merged cells. (Merging joins cells in adjacent columns together so that a heading can span two or more columns.) However, subjects quickly ran into difficulties when they modified tables that contain merged cells. The product defined columns as a logical relationship, but users used visual proximity. As a result some users encountered minor difficulties that tended to accumulate. By changing the way the product handled merged cells in columns, we eliminated those difficulties for users.

With the preliminary design specification complete, the team switched into detailed UI design, and again we changed our testing strategy. During this phase, we knew that the team required a great deal of low-level data on a feature-by-feature basis. If we waited until later in the process, the team would have less opportunity to use the data and we could not test features as thoroughly. Working closely with the development team, we created a detailed testing schedule, which mapped out when it would have specific features available for testing. Then, we ran iterative tests almost each week for the next 12 months.

Since we ran these tests quickly, we modified some procedures that we would ordinarily follow. First, we eliminated much of the formality we might otherwise follow, such as writing a proposal and team review of the task list and subject profile. Since we generally knew in advance what features we would test each week, we could eliminate the lead time that our subject recruiters typically needed. Second, we typically ran only five to six subjects (see Virzi, 1992; Nielsen, 1993). Third, two usability group members ran the subjects in parallel in one day.

We also developed a standard weekly process that after a few initial missteps ran like clockwork. On the Friday before the next test, we verified the status of the scheduled features at a team meeting. On Monday we developed tasks for the test that week. About midday Tuesday, we usually received the test prototype and began to check our proposed tasks with it. Since we typically tested with prototypes with little functionality, we needed to discover the limits of the prototype before the test. We also coordinated what assistance we would give subjects during the test and agreed on the data we would collect and how. On Wednesday, we ran the subjects. The five or six team members responsible for the features we were testing that week would run between the lab suites to watch subjects. Following the last subject, we held a quick debriefing meeting with team members to review our observations and discuss possible design alternatives. Over the next remaining two days we would collate our observation notes, review videotapes where our observations disagreed, and further develop recommendations. By Friday we summarized the test and our findings in a brief e-mail report for the rest of team, other interested development groups and our own archival purposes.

During these iterative tests, we focused on how well users understood a feature and where they had trouble using the feature. At this stage our goal was not to provide a well-developed model of user behavior but to identify and rank interface problems and their causes. Because we did these tests weekly, we retested some features as many as four or five times. While design changes often eliminated problems we found earlier, our retests of features often revealed lower level problems that were previously masked. In other cases, we tested solution after solution before finding a remedy for particularly intractable problems.

As the team moved into the quality assurance phase, we shifted to a cycle of broader testing. These tests focused on work scenarios that we identified in the planning phase. These scenarios involved using clusters of features to accomplish relatively complex, real-world tasks. For example, we might ask appropriate subjects to create a long business report including a table of contents, index, reference list and so on. Instead of a feature-by-feature focus, these tests looked at combining those features to accomplish real work. These tests verified the results of our iterative tests as well as making sure that we had taken advantage of the design opportunities identified during the research phase.

As the team moved on toward the final release of Microsoft Word for Windows 6.0, we began planning the next round of field studies and research issues. Even before that product was released to the public in November 1993, we were testing issues for the next release.

Our usability strategy had considerable impact on the final product. We attribute that success to providing the team with the type of information it needed at each point in the development cycle. It would have ignored anything else. When it focused on high-level design, we provided it with information from the field and on conceptual issues. When it focused on low-level design, we gave it quick feedback that addressed that level of design work. Equally important was the amount of testing we did through the product cycle as a whole. By conducting as many tests as we did, we could test more of the advanced, less frequently used features. Larger, less frequent tests often focus only on the most frequently used features. Our strategy allowed us to test virtually every feature in the product and often more than once.

Field Testing Microsoft Publisher

Microsoft Publisher for Windows™ is a desktop publishing program designed for the home and small business markets. In Publisher, users create objects or "frames" of several types—pictures and text, for example—which in turn form a desktop publishing (DTP) document. We completed our first test of Publisher several months before the first version was released, when we were asked to test a full-featured prototype to identify general problem areas before the product was code complete. Since we had become involved in testing late in the development cycle, we had minimal impact on the design of the product. We did, however, identify a number of problem areas that could be (and were) addressed before the product was released.

Despite our late involvement, our work on the pre V1.0 prototype allowed us to "get our foot in the door." We demonstrated the value of usability testing to the product team by providing usability data that the team could use even though they were far along in the development cycle. Our longer-term effort supporting Publisher began after the release of the first version.

Defining the Problem

To support the development of Publisher 2.0, we first walked through the projected development schedule with the Publisher team to identify potential usability issues and when they should be addressed to have impact on the product. During this process we identified several concerns:

- The designers wanted information about how users responded to the object-oriented metaphor that underlay the product. They were particularly concerned with the learning curve of less-experienced computer users who were familiar primarily with mainstream software applications like word processing and spreadsheets.

- The product team had little information about how users might use Publisher in a "real-world" setting. In particular, the team was interested in the kinds of tasks users accomplished, the influence of the context in which users worked and how well the product supported users' work.

- The team wanted to make the product more robust by adding features. However, the designers were also concerned about the impact on the product's overall usability that the addition of more complexity would bring.

Our approach to testing Publisher was to begin in the field by examining users' work and how well Publisher supported that work and then to move to the lab after program development got underway. We also wanted to look at the learning process issue in context over a longer period of time. A longer term field test was especially appropriate not only because it would provide answers to questions the Publisher team had, but also because we had a stable, released product (and a full set of documentation) to take into the field. In addition, we were at a point in the development process where we could take the time to do a longitudinal study.

We began planning the test by identifying users in the nearby community whom we could follow for several months (Figure 7). Our objective was to find users who represented the product's target market—small business owners and home users. We recognized also that a field test would allow us to gather useful data on the installation process—a process that can be difficult to test in the lab because it is difficult to predict (and simulate) the conditions users face in the real world (e.g., system configuration, environment, etc.). The team was also viewed installation as an important part of the user's learning process since it is during installation that users begin to form expectations about how to use a product.

Figure 7 Usability testing plan to support development of Publisher 2.0

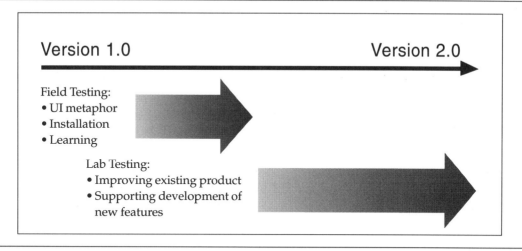

A problem for us, however, was to find users in the local community who had need of desktop publishing software (i.e., did tasks that could be supported by a DTP program) but who had not yet used or purchased DTP software. We did not want to work with computer enthusiasts whose main interest was experimenting with a new program. We wanted people who were currently doing tasks that Publisher could support—tasks like writing company or club newsletters, creating advertising materials, or designing business forms. To find these people, we queried our subject database to find users who were small business owners or managers (a large segment of the Publisher market) and who were currently relying on traditional word processing applications. We then screened a set of likely candidates to find out more about their work and selected six to participate in the study.

Designing the Test

The test design called for two phases. In the first, we brought Publisher to the field test subjects (still in the shrink-wrapped box) and watched them unpack the box, install the program, and begin using the program. We followed up with a second visit two weeks later, at which time we asked subjects to show us how they had been using the program. We also talked more generally with subjects about their work during this phase. We began the second phase six weeks later, so that subjects had time to learn and explore the program. Our focus during this phase was to measure how much of the program subjects had used and learned and the extent to which the program had been integrated into their work. Between the first and second phases, we did two short telephone interviews with subjects.

The test had two focuses, users' interaction with Publisher and users' work. We depended primarily on interviews and observations of subjects as they worked. We kept the interviews fairly unstructured, so that we could pursue topics of interest as they arose. In the early interviews, we were concerned primarily with describing subjects' work practices, particularly tasks that were or could be supported by a DTP program. The later interviews were what we called *guided tours*. We invited users to show us work that they had done with Publisher, and then asked them to walk us through the publication. We used the opportunity to collect data not only about the task but also about subjects' learning processes and problems they had had with the program.

A third source of data was artifacts from subjects' workplaces. These included routine work documents, documents they intended to turn into DTP publications, and actual publications created with Publisher. We also asked users to keep two logs—one a problem-wish list and the other a learning log. The problem-wish list was a collection of all the problems subjects had with Publisher as well as suggested "fixes" and ideas for improving the program. The learning log was a list of all documentation consulted, print and on-line. During the interviews we asked subjects to walk us through the logs and explain items they had listed.

In retrospect, the interviews provided us with the most valuable information. While keeping them loosely structured made it difficult to compare information across subjects, the open-endedness allowed us to collect much richer and suggestive data than if we had worked from a carefully scripted interview guide. The disadvantage was that we relied heavily on subjects' self-reports and seldom had the opportunity to corroborate subjects' comments either through observation or by talking with others at the site. The guided tours of subjects' documents were also valuable as a method for focusing talk about the program and their work. It was, however, very difficult to collect detailed data about subjects' environment, since we spent only two to three hours per visit with each subject and in most cases were restricted to the subjects' office or workspace. The artifacts—particularly the Publisher documents—were useful gauges of subjects' learning and use of the program as well as an index to problems. The logs, on the other hand, proved not be reliable sources of data. Subjects confessed that they did not always remember to write things down and sometimes complained that the log-keeping got in the way of using the program.

Impact

The impact of the field test was less on specific features and more on the team's understanding of how users learned and used the product, an understanding that influenced decisions the team had to make about Publisher's user-assistance model (print documentation, on-line help, templates, etc.) and the basic frame-based UI metaphor. We found, for example, that Publisher was seldom the users' "main" application (a role reserved for word processors or spreadsheet programs among most of the users tested). Instead, users relied on Publisher for periodic tasks like writing a company newsletter every two weeks or revising product information for seasonal sales. The implications for users was that they had to relearn Publisher to some extent each time they choose to use it. Moreover, we discovered that the features requiring the greatest relearning time were those not usually found in users' primary applications. The implication for the Publisher team was that it needed to focus predominantly on ease of learning (and relearning) those features.

We were also able to identify some unintended consequences of a Publisher help feature called PageWizards™. Essentially, Publisher PageWizards are interactive templates. Users are given a menu of publications (ranging from newsletters to business forms) and are allowed to customize the publications (such as choosing a particular newsletter style), after which Publisher "creates" the basic framework of the publication for them (Figure 8). Users were then able to fill out the framework by adding text or pictures of their choosing or further customizing the design. Users responded very well to the PageWizards, but they often ran into trouble when they tried to work with the more complex PageWizards.

The newsletter PageWizard, for example, was a two-column publication that contained many layered objects, including text frames, picture frames, fancy headlines, boxes composed of many line objects, and so on. When users began to work with this publication, they tended to get lost in the proliferation of objects. One user, for

Figure 8 A dialog from the customization process for the Publisher 2.0 newsletter PageWizard

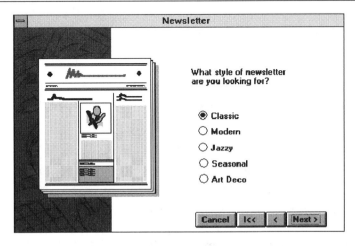

instance, painstakingly deconstructed the table of contents in order to customize it, realized it was too complicated to change, but could not reassemble it. The team's response was to reevaluate the complexity of PageWizards and to develop a set of "first-time help" demos that were automatically invoked when users began to work with compound objects (Figure 9).

Figure 9   Initial screen for the Publisher 2.0 Quick Demo of layering. The demo is presented to users automatically the first time they activated layered objects.

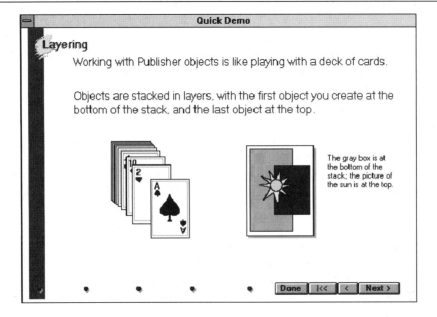

Designing a Tool to Collect Inexpensive Data

For any development cycle there is no shortage of useful data to collect, but there is a limit on the time and resources available to collect it. One of our goals is to create tools that provide us with useful data at little cost. We have created a number of useful data collection tools. One of them is Term Tool, an internal program developed by the Microsoft usability group. Term Tool helps us generate user vocabularies—lists of colloquial terms that users use to describe common tasks. By using Term Tool in conjunction with usability tests, we can provide additional data to the designer at little cost.

Generating User Vocabularies with Term Tool

Menus in graphical interfaces put a heavy burden on the designer to communicate the usefulness of a function in a very small amount of space—a single word or a short phrase. From usability testing it was clear that many users could not easily match some functions in Microsoft Excel for Windows™, such as Consolidate, Scenario Manager, or Parse, to tasks they wanted to perform. A user might want to combine several ranges, but not map that task to the Consolidate command. Nor could the user easily find information in Help without knowing the name of the command.

We reasoned that for each function there were a few words or phrases that most users might generate to describe a task. For example, users who wanted to consolidate several ranges in a spreadsheet might generate the terms "combine" or "totaling ranges" to describe the task. By eliciting these "colloquial" terms from users, we believed that we could significantly increase users' ability to match commands to tasks. We also reasoned that it would be very difficult for an indexer, particularly an indexer familiar with Microsoft Excel, to discover these terms without getting input from users.

Traditional usability tests are not a very good way to elicit colloquial terms from users. The words or phrases a user generates to represent a task are often a useful by-product of a usability test. But it is time consuming and expensive to test enough users to generate a representative sample of terms that would improve users performance with help in a meaningful way. So, our goal for this study was to develop a way of generating users' colloquial terms that was quick, inexpensive, and effective.[5]

The result of the study is an on-line tool called the Term Tool. Term Tool is a Visual Basic application that graphically represents tasks as before and after pictures. Users are asked to generate four terms in response to the question "If you were going to change this (Before) to this (After), what would you look up in help?" The responses from each user were written to a text delimited file and could be collected and collated in Microsoft Excel.

Term Tool has several advantages. Because it takes only 10 or 15 minutes to elicit response to 30 tasks, Term Tool can be "tacked on" to another, unrelated usability test. As a result, a large number of users from several usability tests can be tested without having to schedule many users for a single usability test. Term Tool can also be placed on diskette and mailed to any number of users. In one study, we mailed Term Tool to 77 users and received 68 responses.[6]

---

[5]Much of the work for this study was done by Leah Kaufman, a doctoral candidate in psychology at the University of Washington.

[6]Term Tool was originally coded with the help of Jonathan Cluts. Karl Melder of the MS usability group modified Term Tool to run from diskettes that could be mailed to users.

Designing Term Tool

Although we see many uses for Term Tool, we thought that on-line help indexes might be a useful place to start. If we could design a tool to improve indexes, we could use it for other tasks that require users to recognize or interpret terms. Indexes seemed like a good choice because in an index the proper term is the only cue users have to finding the right information.

When designing Term Tool we began by trying to devise the simplest model we could of how users might use an index to on-line help. Because we were interested in improving users' ability to discover functions in Microsoft Excel, we considered only users who knew what task they wanted to accomplish, but did not know what Microsoft Excel functionality to use to accomplish that task. We did not consider users who would have specific reference questions such as "What is the syntax for the IF function?" or "How do I use Scenario Manager to do what-if scenarios?"

We envisioned the user invoking three simple processes for using an index to map a real-world task to Microsoft Excel functions.

- Representing the task,
- Generating a term (or phrase),
- Searching the index for the term.

The user would then iterate the process until he or she found a hit in the index.

If this simple model were correct we could study the term generation process by providing a user with an appropriate representation of Microsoft Excel tasks. However, to do so we would have to represent the tasks nonverbally so as not to provide the user with verbal cues as to what an appropriate term might be. When considering how to represents the tasks, we thought of completing a task in Microsoft Excel as a classic example of problem solving. In order to successfully complete a task, a user must know the initial state of the problem, the goal state, and the right operators for transforming the initial state into the goal state.

The functions and commands in Microsoft Excel are the legal operators available to the user. By providing users with screen dumps representing the initial states and goal states of various spreadsheet problems we could prompt them to generate the terms they would use to describe those operators. To represent the states of the problem we designed the screen in Figure 10 for Term Tool.

To see how our design would work, we usability-tested Term Tool with 10 users who did not use spreadsheets. We selected non-spreadsheet users because they would have the least semantic knowledge of the tasks and were least likely to generate terms that corresponded to Microsoft Excel functions or commands. Also, because they have little background knowledge of Microsoft Excel, non-spreadsheet users are more likely to need to find information in help and are most likely to have difficulty using help indexes.

Figure 10 Screen from Term Tool

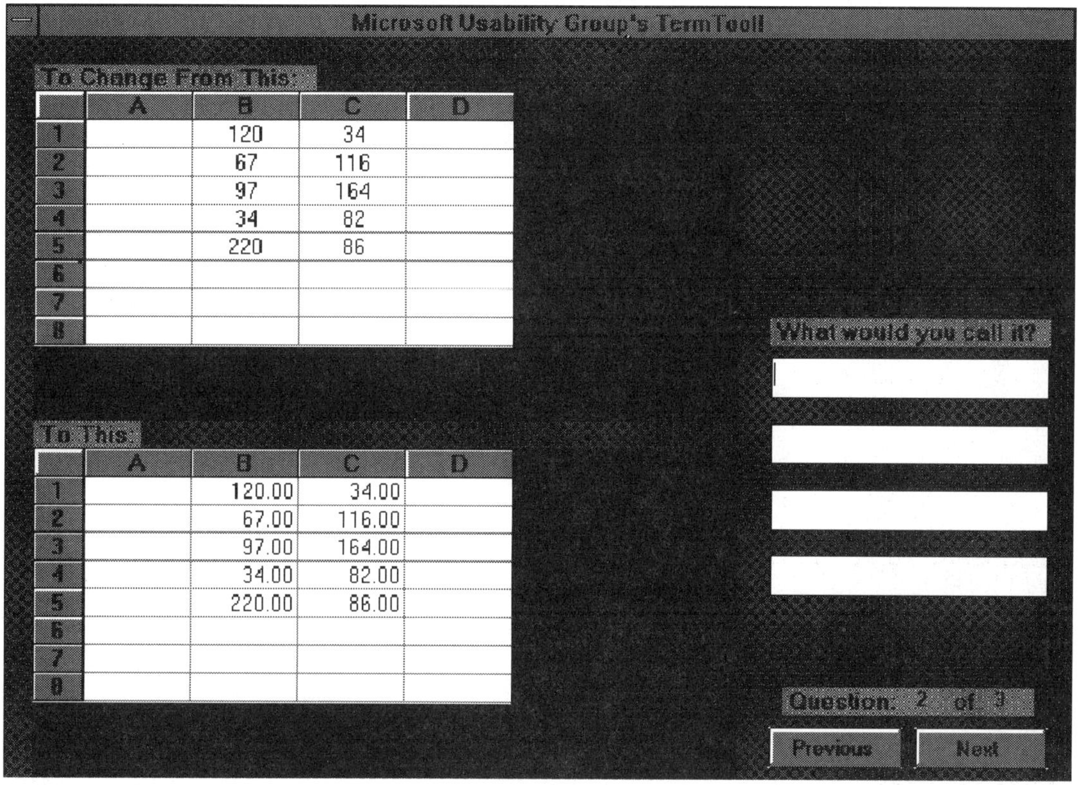

As a result of the usability test we discovered two things that helped us design the actual screens displayed to the user. The first is that some tasks are difficult to represent as before and after pictures, particularly problems that involve artifacts such as printing, print preview, or sending mail. Rather than change the design of the tool, we chose not to test tasks that involved creating output.

We also had difficulty with tasks for which the command was complex and accomplished several steps in a single step. Format Font, for example involves any number of possible changes including changing the style, weight, and size of text. Users tended to identify it as simply "changing the size of text." It is possible that the users confused the task, that they understood the concept "fonts," but failed to identify the change we represented as a font change. It is also possible that some new users represent a "font change" as a change in the characteristics (size, weight, and so on) of the characters.

We also discovered that if the before and after screens contained very much content, the users focused on the content rather than the task. For example, when they were asked to generate terms to describe the following task they tended to look for changes in the text rather than the position of the text.

Figure 11   Move column task presented in Term Tool

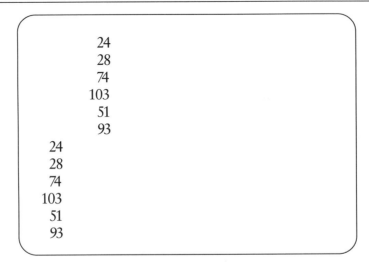

To solve this problem we made the screens as abstract as possible buy substituting Xs for numbers.

Testing Term Tool

It was not enough to simply generate a list of possible terms and include them in the index. We wanted to know whether including terms in an index would improve users' performance at finding information.

To test Term Tool we presented 25 Microsoft Excel tasks to 20 new spreadsheet users. The users were selected from the Microsoft usability database. All of the users reported that they used Windows, but had never used a spreadsheet.

We chose to test tasks involving the 30 most commonly used commands as collected by the instrumented version of Microsoft Excel 4.0 for Windows[TM] and eliminated tasks we did not feel we could adequately represent. The users in this part of the task generated 168 different "colloquial" terms. The highest number of terms for one command was 11 and the lowest number was 2. (Although users were asked to

Figure 12 Revised move column task presented in Term Tool

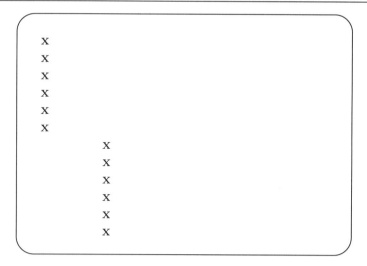

generate four terms, they were allowed to stop after one if they felt they could not generate additional terms.) If a term was generated by at least 5 users it was included in the index. The terms were included in a print index with the appropriate page number and a "see also" reference. For example, the colloquial term position was included in the index as

position
see also Alignment

We then tested 20 users in two conditions. Ten users were given the *Microsoft Excel 4.0 User's Guide* index. Ten users were given the Microsoft Excel 4.0 User's Guide Index with the user terms from Part I added to the index. Users were not given the text of the *User's Guide*, only the index. They were asked to find the page number where they would find information relating to a task displayed on the screen. When they chose the number of a page that did contain information about the task, we counted it as a success. When they chose the number of a page that did not contain information about the task, we counted it as an error. The results are shown in Figure 13.

Participants using the augmented index were successful 74.4% of the time while participants using the Microsoft Excel User's Guide index were successful 65% of the time. This difference is a reliable difference ($p < 0.05$ using a standard t-test).

Figure 13   Success rate on the index task

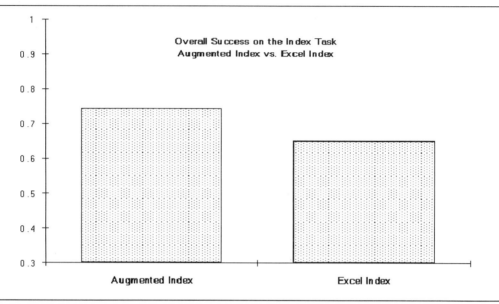

However, the difference was not as great as we expected, and we also found a reliable difference in the amount of time people spent searching for terms in the two indexes. Participants spent more time searching the augmented index, 26.029 seconds on average, versus the standard index, 21.818 seconds on average ($p < 0.05$ using a standard t-test). It seemed possible that participants were more successful simply because they spent more time searching for terms.

Despite the ambiguous results of the test we have concluded that Term Tool is an effective and inexpensive way of generating user vocabularies and a useful way to improve indexes, both print and on-line. We see a number of other uses for Term Tool. Two that seem promising are localization and improving indexes for users in specific domains such as accounting or engineering.

Lessons Learned

The success of the Usability Group at Microsoft has brought us increased visibility, increased demand for our usability services, and consequently, an increase in size. More important, perhaps, is a growth in our understanding of how we can best support product development within the company. Our experience has taught us that usability testing is essentially a rhetorical enterprise: its character depends on the nature of the problems the group addresses, the audience (or organization) it serves, our own skillset, and the usual (and sometimes not so usual) constraints like time, cost and availability of resources. Moreover, all of these parameters constantly change in a dynamic organization, requiring us to change to remain an effective advocate for usability. Our experience over the past five years has taught us a number of lessons that have affected our practice.

Centralization vs. Decentralization Is Not the Issue

Organizationally, the Microsoft Usability Group was created as a centralized service provider for teams across the company, and it continues to function in that capacity. Philosophically, the group began as centralized group distinct from product teams but has since become less a group apart and more a group connected with the work of the product teams. That is, we have found that to have a coherent impact on products we have to work closely with teams throughout the development process on a continual basis.

However, as a service provider, it makes sense for us to remain organizationally centralized, because our lab is in central location, our support staff works with the group as a whole, and, perhaps most important, centralization allows us to provide a consistent level of support across the company. Our group is in a position to see the interrelations of products, a perspective sometimes lost by members of individual product teams. In short, the challenge we face is to efficiently and effectively provide usability services to a large company with diverse needs. We have found the centralized-decentralized dichotomy to be inadequate for thinking about how we position ourselves in the company.

Promote Grassroots Usability

Despite the growth of the Usability Group over the past five years, we do not have enough people in the group to single-handedly support all of the company's products. The Microsoft Home series of products, for example, will grow to include over 100 products by the middle of the decade. To address this need we have developed a two-part strategy. The first is to develop a database of usability findings that can be searched and accessed by product teams throughout the company. Users of the database can search information about specific products, product features, and user profiles. The second is to create an in-house training program to teach product teams how to do their own usability testing. The training provides up-front classroom training to products teams as well as consulting support while the teams design and run their own tests. Our objective is to make data about users and usability testing a part of all product development efforts.

The Tool Is Not the Thing

One of the most important events in the history of usability testing at Microsoft, next to the founding of the usability group itself, was the creation of the usability lab. Unexpectedly, the lab has turned out to be somewhat of an organizational paradox. On one hand, the lab has clearly been a positive force. Not only has it supported the process of usability testing, it has been extremely important in establishing the identity of the usability group in the company (and, by extension, the importance of assessing usability). In effect, the lab has given a palpable, physical location to usability and has become a symbol of a corporate ideal. On the other hand, the tool has tended to become the thing: for many outside the usability group, the lab, and the kind of testing we do in the lab, sometimes is identified as usability. Since the early days of the usability group we have been developing contextual approaches to usability testing—as the Publisher field test illustrates. Nevertheless, when product teams think of users and usability, they often think of observing people using software in a usability lab.

One of our goals is to continue developing contextual approaches to usability testing and to make them a more visible part of our contribution to product development. For example, our efforts at supporting a user-centered design process take us—and the product teams themselves—out of the lab and into the community of users. Similarly, our work in promoting grassroots usability promises to bring the communities of users and product designers closer together. The lab has been a powerful change agent and will continue to be a useful tool for supporting incorporating user data into the development process. But a lesson we are learning is that we need to do better at communicating to product teams that the contributions of the Usability Group are not restricted to testing users in the lab.

Acknowledgments

Microsoft, MS-DOS, and PowerPoint are registered trademarks and Microsoft Windows, MS Access, Encarta, Cinemania, Visual Basic, and Visual C++ are trademarks of Microsoft Corporation.

References

Gould, J. D., and Lewis, C. H. (1983). "Designing for Usability—Key Principles and What Designers Think," in *Proceedings of the 1983 Computer-Human Interaction Conference*, pp. 50-53.

Microsoft Corporation. (1991). *Usability Backgrounder*. Authors, Redmond, WA.

Nielsen, J. (1993). *Usability Engineering*. Academic Press, Boston.

Virzi, R. (1992). "Refining the Test Phase of Usability Evaluation: How Many Subjects Is Enough?" *Human Factors 34*; 457-468.

CHAPTER 12

American Airlines

Janice S. James
American Airlines

Janice James has served as a Usability Specialist and Manager of the Usability Design Center and Automated Decision Support Center at American Airlines' SABRE Travel Information Network (STIN) for the past four years. Prior to joining American Airlines, she was a User Advocate for Computer Language Research, Inc., where she promoted and developed the company's usability testing process and facility. James cofounded the Usability Professionals' Association in 1991 and continues to serve as the chair for that organization. She was also the cofounder of the Kentuckiana Chapter of the Society for Technical Communication. She received a M.A. in technical communication from Bowling Green State University.

American Airlines SABRE Travel Information Network's Business

SABRE Travel Information Network (STIN), a division of American Airlines, Inc., markets SABRE, a privately owned, real-time computing network providing travel distribution and information services to nearly 26,000 travel agencies located in more than 64 countries on 6 continents. STIN employs 2,200 employees in the United States and Europe and is a part of the newly formed SABRE Group.

SABRE (Semi-Automated Business Research Environment), a sophisticated computerized reservations system, is used by travel agents worldwide to book airline, car

359

and hotel reservations, as well as to order theater tickets, bon voyage gifts, flowers and other travel-related goods and services. SABRE was released in 1959, and for the first time, SABRE enabled American Airlines to link a passenger name to a specific seat sold on an airplane. SABRE also made it possible to link passenger inventories in other airlines, which automated the way airlines handled interline reservations.

In 1974, American initiated a joint carrier feasibility study to explore the prospects for a jointly owned computer reservations system for travel agents. The project included several other airlines and was deemed economically practical by a study group in 1975. However, United Airlines withdrew from the project and announced its intentions to provide travel agents with its own computerized reservations system (CRS). Since United's system displayed schedules biased in favor of United, the installation of their computer reservation terminals posed a competitive threat to other airlines.

Consequently, American announced its intention to market its own reservation system. In 1976, American installed its first SABRE unit in a travel agency and formed STIN to market the system. Today, SABRE is installed on more than 103,900 computer terminals worldwide in travel agency offices.

How Usability Testing Started at AMR

The story I am going to tell you in this chapter moves along chronologically—from what it was like from the beginning of usability testing up to what it is today.

Our first experience with usability testing began in 1989. In conjunction with IBM through their multiples marketing program, we usability tested a product that had been in development for four months and was ready for release. Although with quite a bit of skepticism, a team of two developers, a representative from Customer Service, Training, and a couple of Product Development supervisors flew to Atlanta to use IBM's usability testing facility. One of the programmers of the product to be usability tested explained to me that prior to taking the trip, he thought the lab and the whole idea of usabiilty testing was just an expensive hoax—to put it mildly.

Upon arriving at IBM, the programmer was immediately impressed with the "normal" attitude of the staff. He explained that, in retrospect, it was the staff's confidence in what it was doing and the knowledge of the certain outcome of testing STIN's first user interface-intensive product that impressed him. He was also impressed, of course, with the level of technical equipment in the lab.

IBM recommended that the developers and support staff take the responsibility for conducting the test. The programmer thought to himself, after watching the first user, "what a dumb user." After watching the second user, he said it was pretty obvious that there were major usability problems with the software. By the time he finished watching the seventh user, he had changed his words from "what a dumb user" to "what a dumb program." He said that it became more and more painful to watch with each new user. The product, inaccurately named Intuitive SABRE, was not as intuitive as they thought it might be!

After returning to Dallas, the developers recommended that the product not be released, as scheduled. In fact, they felt that the results from the test were so poor that they asked for an additional eight months of development time. They were amazed when they got approval from the VP of Product Development to allow the extra development time to fix the problems.

As they began to look more deeply into their first usability experience, the developers became convinced that a usability lab was something STIN greatly needed, especially since more and more products in the future would have a real user interface. (SABRE, the host reservations system is strictly a command-driven product whose interface is a blank screen.) The challenge to convince upper management to invest the money in a usability lab ensued.

After fixing the first round of usability problems detected with Intuitive SABRE, we returned to another IBM site for more usability testing. The developers were stunned at the results. They were right on target with the design changes that they had made, and the outstanding issues were of a much more minute level. Peter Jansen, now Manager of SABRE Workstation Development, says he is convinced that this sealed the decision to invest the money to build AMR's own Usability Lab.

We Built It Big!

Invest money is what American Airlines did—over $700,000 to be exact—on a two test-bay, 3,000 sq. ft. facility (see Figure 1 and Color Plate VI). Even though a large sum of that money was spent on network communications to equip the lab for testing all products developed companywide, this is still a lot of money to spend on a usability lab. I do not hear of many corporations that invest that much money in a usability lab these days or even that invested that much money four years ago in 1989 when we had a stronger economy.

I was hired after the usability lab was completed the latter part of 1989. Since that time, usability testing at American Airlines has evolved into a program that includes more than just usability testing. Initially, however, the emphasis was only on usability testing, and the company did not officially include any other usability engineering processes in the product development cycle.

Figure 1   American Airlines' Usability Lab

Control Room and Test Room

Edit Suite

Why Such an Expensive Test Facility?

You have to be wondering why a corporation would spend so much money on an elaborate facility, but hire only one employee to implement a process and operate the lab. I had some difficulty understanding that as well. Although I do not know for sure, I have some thoughts about how it happened.

The most obvious explanation is that it always seems to be easier to gain approval for capital-related costs than it is to get approval for employee-associated costs. Second, I think management was convinced by outside consultants that we could build a succesful usability testing program with just one employee. The methodology American Airlines adopted is one based on a single person performing the day-to-day operation of the lab, while advising those who are actively involved in the development of a product how to develop, conduct, and evaluate the results of a test.

Consequently, during my first 3 ½ years at American Airlines, my responsibilities were quite different from those in my previous position at Computer Language Research, Inc. At CLR, I made myself responsible for all phases of usability testing— planning, conducting and analyzing the data and preparing a report of the results. The reason I say I made myself responsible is because since I had taken on the role of promoting usability testing, I automatically inherited the role of the sole usability testing practitioner for the company. At AA, however, I functioned more as an internal consultant, working with analysts in Product Development, Training and Marketing to guide them through the steps of usability testing.

What is important to note is that even though this method may not have been the most cost effective or one that instilled the highest quality of usability testing, it did work for 3½ years. Looking back, I think it actually enabled us to increase the awareness of more people in a shorter period of time than would have otherwise been possible. And that, in turn, actually contributed to us later being able to convince management to hire a dedicated staff.

Building Usability Testing into a Usability Engineering Program

When I first came to STIN, my primary goal was just to get people into the lab to test their products. The company had just spent a very large sum of money on a magnificent lab, so it was my job to get it into operation as quickly as possible. The last thing that AA wanted to happen was for a very expensive facililty to appear to be without business.

Amazingly, just about six weeks after I started working at American, we tested our first product in the new lab. I began getting phone calls probably my first week at STIN. Most people did not really understand what the Usability Lab was, but they had heard about it and had been encouraged by their managers to call and see how soon they could "get their products into the lab." I believe that we were able to make the lab operational in such a short time because of the excellent promotion of usability testing that took place while the lab was under construction.

In spite of getting started with the usability testing program so quickly, I was faced with some interesting challenges. For example, most people had a tendency to want to focus on the lab facility and its high-tech equipment instead of how to effectively develop a usability test. I found myself telling people repeatedly that learning to use the equipment should be the least of their worries and that there is much more to usability testing than operating the cameras, for example! It was also difficult keeping people out of the lab.

In most cases, I would not want to keep people out of the lab. However, some people were so excited to see the lab they had been hearing about that oftentimes they would just walk past my office straight into the lab and curiously start experimenting with the lab equipment. Several times, on their journeys to explore the lab, people would walk into a test room while a user was participating in a test. We soon had to put a sign on the door that discouraged people from entering the lab without first seeing me or my assistant.

The biggest challenge I had during my first year was to develop a way to educate the company about the usability testing process and the steps for planning, conducting and then analyzing-evaluating test data. As a first step toward accomplishing this task, I worked with Janice (Ginny) Redish and Joe Dumas with American Institutes for Research to develop a two-day usability testing workshop and handbook. The workshop was also intended to prepare those who would actually be doing usability testing so that when they attended their first meeting with me, I could assume that they had at least a basic understanding of the process.

The preconceived idea people had about usability testing before they attended the workshop was that you just brought your products into the lab, had some people (they thought just anyone could test the product—it did not matter who) use the applications and observe what happened. Many of the first groups to do usability testing were quite surprised, to say the least, when I began asking them to define the users of the product in terms of their skills, experiences and other relevant characteristics and to list any usability concerns they had about their software. Because of their belief that you just brought a product into the lab to see what happens and also because they were not used to defining usability concerns, they generally had a lot of difficulty with this exercise. In most cases, they just wanted to think about the tasks they would have the test evaluators do, without defining why the users should do those particular tasks.

This workshop saved me a tremendous amount of time. I avoided spending several hours that I previously spent during the initial meetings with each new group helping them understand the basic concepts and benefits of usability testing before we could even get started planning their test.

I met with each group once a week, beginning six weeks prior to the actual test date to guide them and review the tasks they had completed the prior week. Members from one or all the different departments conducting the test were responsible for completing all the tasks. I spent most of the hour to hour-and-a-half meetings each week making recommendations that would lead to a test that would provide the information they needed about their products.

My department offered the workshop once a month for the last six months of 1990. The workshop became a prerequisite for at least the team leader of the group responsible for conducting a usability test. In 1991, we filled the workshop again 11 times during the year, and in 1992, we reduced the workshop to 10 times, with further reductions this year to just 6 workshops. All in all, we have trained about 500 people throughout AMR at least the basics of usability testing.

Next Step—More In-House Training

Not long after I began work at American Airlines, I began feeling like the company was working backward in terms of its efforts to develop more usable products. It seemed to me that we had focused first on building the house before we had ever established its foundation.

We built this wonderful usability lab and were working very hard and energetically to implement a usability testing program and doing quite well at educating many people about usability testing. Those are huge accomplishments!

Unfortunately, we had not put enough effort into strengthening the skills of our user interface designers so that when they did usability test their products, they would not be shocked by some serious user interface design problems that turned up. I think that usability testing was a means by which we could fix the symptom of the real problem. The symptom was that some of our user interfaces were not designed to be easy to use or learn. The real problem, in my mind, was a lack of awareness, or perhaps even a bit of reluctance to admit, that it takes some special skills, knowledge, and experience to design usable interfaces.

All the usability testing in the world was not going to give the designers and developers of our software products the understanding and skills they needed to improve their designs. It would help, but it would take more time than we had available. We were risking the possibility of our competitors, such as Worldspan, catching up to us and perhaps even passing us by if we did not make some changes in the products we had to offer. STIN recognized that although we had been very comfortable for many years with SABRE being the number one computer reservations system, we could not rely on that always being the case.

I began formulating ideas about how to improve American's usability testing program. I knew that I probably would not be able to build a staff within the first couple of years of the start of our usability program. So, instead, I focused on helping to improve the existing user interface design skills within the company. We already had the usability testing workshop in place. That was the first step toward building a usability engineering program. As the second step, the usability lab sponsored a three-day workshop developed and conducted by Deborah Mayhew and Associates. The workshop teaches user interface design guidelines and principles. The following year we sponsored a three-day workshop specifically addressing the design of graphical user interfaces, and then this year, we offered another three-day advanced graphical user interface design workshop. All in all, we have provided graphical user interface design training to about 300 employees, primarily in STIN.

Third Step—Justifying a Staff

Although it had been somewhat of a nice change to be responsible only for consulting others while they did the work of planning, conducting and evaluating the results of a usability test, it did not take a genius to identify the disadvantages of this methodology. It was clear to me early on that it would be very difficult, if not impossible, to maintain any consistency in the way in which all STIN products would be tested, not to mention the quality and level of analysis and evaluation of problems that would take place. I also felt uncomfortable trying to teach the entire organization how to do usability testing while slipping in on the side as much human factors information as I possibly could.

I felt that we were operating a mediocre usability testing program instead of a good one. Looking back, I would guess that management probably viewed me as seeing the glass half empty instead of half full. Instead, I knew what could be and I was anxious to make it happen. So I kept pushing.

That is not to say that I couldn't see the advantages of the usability testing methodology STIN chose to implement. There were many advantages to and benefits we gained from the first 3 $\frac{1}{2}$ years of usability testing at American. For example, in too many instances, it was the first time that some developers had ever seen real users interact with their products. What an eye-opening experience for them! And it was not always just the developers who got their eyes opened. Many of the marketing staff, those people who often feel that they are closest to understanding the users, were often caught by surprise, and almost always immediately became converts of the usability testing process.

This may sound a bit odd, but some of the most successful experiences, in my mind, were the times when the analysts and developers had great difficulties watching a single user complete all the tasks of one test. To witness a user become totally frustrated at trying to use the application that the developers had put so much time and energy into developing was simply too painful for them to endure! It was not uncommon for a developer to walk out of the lab, commenting to me that they just could not stand to watch anymore. Or, they would try to convince me that we should not let the users try to use the product completely on their own without any help. There is no doubt that these experiences created for the developers and marketers an enhanced perspective on what makes a user interface easy to use and what does not, and a new enlightened view of the users and how they interact with STIN products.

Finally

It took 3½ years, which all happened to be 3½ financially difficult years for the airline industry, to finally increase the staff from two to six AND change our method of doing usability testing. What is important to mention is that it did not take that long to convince management and the ranks below management (they were the easiest to convince) that there were better ways of doing usability testing than the method we chose to implement. We were simply not given the luxury of increasing the number of employees within the company during those years. If anything, we were reducing the number of employees in many areas of the company.

This past year, STIN was still not allowed to increase the overall total number of employees in the organization. The only way I was going to get a staff was if other departments transferred their vacant employee slots to my department. That is exactly what happened. The product development department transferred four unfilled positions to the usability lab. What a breakthrough! After developing proposal after proposal and justification after justification over the last 3½ years on the cost benefits of having a trained and dedicated staff responsible for usability testing, I was finally successful. At last, management conceded that it would be a win-win situation to give up some employee slots so that I could build my staff. No longer would their product analysts and developers have to spend time learning the usability testing process and then invest the hours in planning and conducting a test when they could have been spending that valuable time developing products.

The time developers lost developing products so that they could do usability testing was one of the most influential pieces of information in my proposal for a dedicated usability staff. Luckily, I had some foresight during my first year with STIN and developed an evaluation/questionnaire for test teams to complete at the end of a product usability test. The questionnaire allowed me to collect information I knew I would later need to build my case for a staff.

On the questionnaire, I had each team leader identify the number of people who had been involved in the test, their job levels within the company, and the estimated number of hours each person had spent in each test phase (planning, conducting, analyzing/evaluating results). In the proposal, I provided the estimated cost of product development and other personnel doing a usability test, compared to the cost of dedicated usability professionals conducting usability tests. I proved that we could save 8% in salaries alone and over 23,000 hours of lost development time per year by hiring seven employees for a dedicated usability staff. (I didn't get seven additional employees.)

Another cost-reduction I cited in the proposal was the expense associated with the Usability Testing Workshop. If we hired a dedicated human factors staff responsible for usability testing, we would no longer have a need to teach the step-by-step process of usability testing. I proposed that we reduce the two-day hands-on Usability Testing Workshop to a new one-day workshop entitled Engineering Usability into AMR Products (AMR is the parent company of American Airlines). The one-day reduction would save STIN consultant costs as well as a full day's worth of time on the part of each analyst who attended the workshop. For each test a team of Product Development analysts previously conducted, we would save an estimated $11,000 by having a dedicated usability staff.

What is important to note here is that, many times, the people who made up a usability test team for a product usually were not the same people who conducted subsequent tests on the same product. Thus, we could not count on previous experience leading to reductions in a product development analyst's time spent planning and evaluating/analyzing test results of later tests. Whenever possible, we optimized any experience gained from previous tests, but we could not count on it due to personal time conflicts, change in responsibilities or positions, other commitments to the product, etc. Therefore, our costs associated with each test remained high.

More Training

Ginny Redish helped me see that there was still another gap in our development process somewhat unrelated to whether we increased the staff or not. That gap was a lack of understanding within STIN, and perhaps within all of AMR, of the importance of conducting user and task analysis as a critical part of product planning and development. So, we promoted and gained approval for a User and Task Analysis workshop for 1993, which turned out to be another successful workshop.

We announced the dates for the workshop one week, and by the end of the next week, all six classes scheduled throughout the year were booked, with many people signed up on a waiting list. I misjudged the number of workshops we would be able to fill during the year, but that was a really good misjudgment as far as I was concerned! We chose not to increase the class size to accommodate people on the waiting list, but maintained a limit of 20-25 attendees. Because the class includes many exercises, we wanted to allow for some individual attention from the instructor.

Fortunately, the Marketing Department sponsored an additional workshop for their Marketing Analysts and Product Managers, and the Product Development Department has also sponsored an additional two workshops to accommodate the many Development Analysts and Programmers who were not able to get into the original six workshops. The success of this step in building a Usability Engineering program is that over 215 people in just STIN alone are more aware of and sold on the importance of making user and task analysis a critical part of the development process.

I do not want to give the impression that STIN never did task analysis before. Of course we did. But it was not always routine. And not everyone understood the difference between just asking customers what they want from watching them do their jobs to better understand how they work and identify where their needs are not being met.

STIN is unlike most producers of software. STIN does not sell its products. The way STIN makes its money from the software product it develops and markets is through air reservations the travel agent makes. For this reason, it is absolutely critical that we deliver products that our customers want and will use to generate airline, car and hotel bookings. Otherwise, we reap no benefits whatsoever from the very products we invest a great deal in to develop.

Who Is on Board?

As you know by now, I had a lot of time to think about who I would want to make up my staff if I ever got approval to expand the department! Still, when it came time to recruit, it was difficult deciding what skills and backgrounds to look for in the people who would make up the long awaited and very-hard-worked-for staff. In the back of my mind, I had a very clear goal of continuing to build our usability testing program into a usability engineering program, so I needed people with a combination of skills, backgrounds and experiences.

American Airlines has a strong reputation for hiring within. It means that once you are in the company, the opportunities are almost endless. But it also means that at times we are short on people with very specialized skills and backgrounds. I knew that I wanted people who had human factors backgrounds, either through education or practical experience, and I knew that I needed people with strong user interface design skills, as well as people who were experienced and skilled in conducting user and task analysis, not to mention well trained in usability testing, with strong analytical and problem-solving skills. That very specific combination of skills did not exist within AMR, or at least those people were not looking for jobs when I was looking for them. So, I was able to hire from outside the company.

I hired four people who all have human factors backgrounds and experience. One employee is especially skilled in user interface design, two are most experienced in usability testing and one is most skilled in human factors work. If I had the opportunity to hire more people, which I will not for awhile, I would hire several more people with strong user interface design skills, perhaps a graphical designer or two, one or two technical communicators and most definitely a usability administrator. Since there are so many different types of usability processes to conduct and so many types of computer-related products to test, I believe that it is very important to have a very well-rounded staff.

In thinking about the qualities that I want in the people I hire, my list keeps growing and growing. Of course, I could probably not pay for the salary demanded by a person who has all the skills, experiences, and qualities that I feel are necessary, but I would make certain that I hired the person who came the closest to having all of the skills in Table 1.

My staff also includes a wonderful usability assistant who performs many of the day-to-day functions of keeping the lab operational. She schedules the usability tests, maintains our budget, orders equipment and handles all the administrative tasks involved with each of the workshops we sponsor.

Table 1 Qualities to look for

Education/Experience	Required Skills	Qualities or Attributes
Human factors	Marketing	Patient
Usability testing	Analytical	Tenacious
User interface design	Negotiation	Self motivated
	Listening	Detail oriented
	Interviewing	Analytical
	Motivation	Organized
	Communication–ability to report findings and tactfully communicate them to affected parties (oral and written)	Creative
		Desire to learn and experiment

My managerial responsibilities include running two operations that make up the Human Factors Department: the Usability Design Center and the Automated Decision Center (ADC). The ADC is an automated environment developed to improve the efficiency and effectiveness of traditional meetings. The Human Factors Department is organized in STIN under the Product Development/Training division. (However, STIN will be restructured in June 1994 into more of a matrixed organization. Figure 2 is an illustration of the current high-level structure of the Product Development organization. My department is currently a centralized group and will remain so in the reorganization. I happen to like how we are organized today under Product Development/Training. I report to a managing director who does not have direct development responsibility for any external software products, so there is no perceived bias of my department toward any one product line.

Usability Testing the First 3½ Years for AMR

For about the first year and a half of usability testing products at AMR, we conducted only what I call *formal usability tests*. Typically, for formal tests, we used between 9 and

12 test subjects, with each test ranging from 2 to 4 hours. Test evaluators performed tasks on their own while the test team behind the one-way mirror in a "control room" observed and logged all the events of the test.

As part of developing the usability test, we set measurement criteria. Since, in most cases in the past, Product Development or Marketing had not created usability objectives for each new product early in the Requirements Definition Phase, the products did not have any usability goals that they were being designed and developed to meet. To have some measurements against which we could measure the usability of the product, we set measurement criteria for the product as a step of developing the usability test. Needless to say, the measurement criteria were somewhat arbitrary, but we set the measurements based on how easy to use and learn we wanted the product to be and based on what we thought would be acceptable to our users. The standard set of criteria that we used (and still use) to measure the usability of all products included the following items.

Measurement Critieria Common to All Tests

- Number of errors (this might be broken down into more specifics like number of wrong menu choices, number of wrong key selections, number of wrong options selected, etc.)
- Number of help desk calls
- Number of references to documentation (if available)
- Number of references to on-line help (if available)
- Time to complete task
- Number of times user expresses frustration

We logged a frustration only if we could see or hear it verbally expressed (the user slammed his fist on the table, for example).

We used logging software during each test to track the occurrence of each of the items above. We also logged all user comments and team comments. Team comments included anything interesting the usability team observed about how the test subject used the product.

In addition to formal usability tests, last year we added *usability design walkthroughs* as another type of test more appropriate for products still early in the design phases. Many of the steps for developing a usability walkthrough are the same as those for developing a formal test. A comparison of the two types of tests is shown in Table 2.

In a usability design walkthrough, we informed the user that the product was not entirely functional, that there might be bugs in the software and that some things simply were not yet working. If we knew this was the case with a product in a formal test, we informed the user as well.

Figure 2 STIN Product Development/Training organization structure

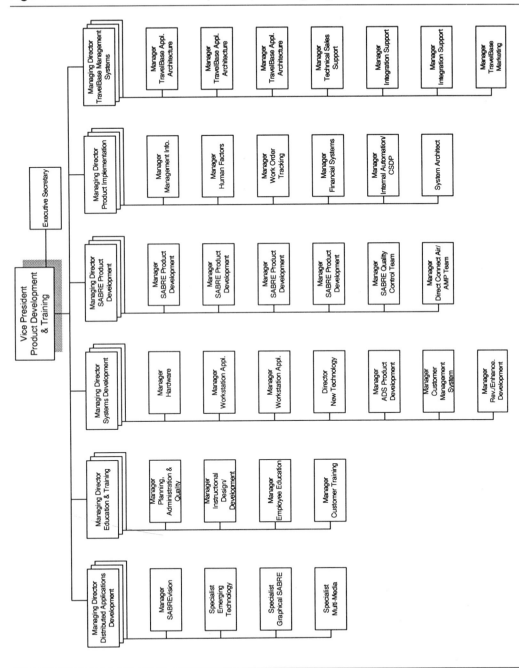

I think of a design walkthrough as a user's tour through an interface, with stops along the way to try out certain functions and to provide feedback about specific aspects of the interface as requested by the usability specialist based on the usability concern areas he or she has identified. Since a design walkthrough is conducted early in the product's design, the focus is usually on just one or a couple of areas of the product. We usually test only four to six users since that number can provide the feedback necessary to continue with the design of the product. And our intent is that those same areas of the product will be tested again throughout the product's lifecycle. Whether it is a design walkthrough or formal test, we test the real users of the product, usually with a range of experience levels. Of course this is dependent upon the purpose of the test.

Previous to hiring a dedicated usability staff, usability testing was the only type of usability process that was integrated into a product development cycle. And, it was simply on an as-requested basis, almost always too late and usually just one time during the product development cycle. I feel quite sure that these problems were due to the usability testing methodology that American chose to implement in the beginning. Remember, the product development teams were responsible primarily for all phases of testing. I was the only in-house consultant, and this meant a great deal of added responsibility on the developer's part, in the midst of also being responsible for developing the products and meeting timelines.

Since it was not a requirement for products to be usability tested, it was left up to each individual development group to decide whether or not to include usability testing in its timelines. The likelihood of this happening depended a great deal on several factors:

- the success of my encouragement and promotion of the process,
- through the encouragement of product development and marketing individuals who had successfully experienced usability testing and wanted to convince others to use the process (I call these people *usability champions*),
- the level of confidence that product managers (or higher level management) had in the process and their level of understanding the benefits gained from including usability testing in the product's development cycle.

During the past $3\frac{1}{2}$ years, we usability tested whatever and however many products we could possibly fit into the lab schedule. We usually operated at a 65% occupancy rate, but with a very high cancellation/rescheduling rate. We did not assign priorities to products by any criteria to determine which ones should definitely include usability testing. Many times it depended on how realistically the timelines had been created and if they allowed time for the process to be conducted.

Table 2   Walkthrough and Formal Tests Compared

Usability design walkthrough	Formal usability test
Conducted early in product development cycle—usually during the design phase. Product is usually in prototype form (interactive or static), on the computer on paper.	Conducted during later phases of product development cycle. The real product is tested.
No measurement criteria are developed as a part of the test planning, but measurements are tracked during the test.	Measurement criteria are developed for the product (if usability objectives were not set at the onset of the development cycle). Measurement criteria are logged during the test.
Tests 4–6 users	Tests 9–12 users
Duration of each test is about 2 hours.	Duration of test ranges 2–4 hours.
Test team develops usability concerns of product.	Test team develops usability concerns of product.
Tasks and scenarios are developed based on the usability concerns identified.	Tasks and scenarios are developed based on the usability concerns identifiied.
In the room with the user, the usability team member guides the user to parts of the product, sets the scene for the user and asks him or her to perform the task while the usability team member observes and asks predefined questions.	User works independently on the product to perform tasks and scenarios with no interaction with usability test team.
All events, both verbal and non-verbal, are logged during the walkthrough.	All events, both verbal and non-verbal, are logged during the walkthrough.
No posttest questionnaire. Questions are integrated into and asked during the walkthrough by a usability team member.	Includes a posttest questionnaire.

When product timelines did include time for usability testing, they usually planned for only one test during the entire cycle. Too many times, tests were scheduled too late in the cycle, meaning that the impact of changing the product was more drastic than if time had been invested in testing earlier in and throughout the cycle. Sometimes the changes to the product were not made until its next release. In contrast, certain product teams believed in the success that they had experienced with the process enough to schedule several tests during the product's lifecycle. Those were the individuals and projects that gave me confidence that more and more people were beginning to realize the value of usability testing.

What Is Different Today?

Today, I have a staff of five–four usability professionals and one usability lab assistant. My staff has assumed the responsibility for all usability testing, as well as other usability processes. The four Usability Design Analysts/Specialists in the Usability Design Center are responsible for working with a liaison from Product Development and, oftentimes, Marketing to plan and develop usability tests. They also provide user interface design consulting and conduct user and task analysis. Since this is our first year for having a staff, only six months into it, we are spending a great deal of time communicating to others in Product Development, Marketing and Training, as well as other AMR divisions, what we can contribute to help them create more usable products.

However, we are very careful with the "talk" we use. As I have learned during the last 10 years, it is incredibly easy to alienate that very person you so want to assist if you say the wrong thing or if you are insensitive to his or her ego. The one skill that I think I have had the greatest opportunity to improve since coming to American Airlines is my negotiation skills. But that goes with the territory of being hired from outside of the company to start a new program at any big corporation—especially those programs many people in the Product Development department might consider threatening to the integrity of their job performance.

I also hired all of my employees from outside of the company, so they are trying to be very careful about how, and how passionately, they market usability engineering. Even though the company has a four-year history of having had usability testing in-house, it still has some distance to go in terms of being commited to a true usability engineering program. My staff is making every attempt to become involved with a product as early as possible, they are marketing their skills and the processes they can perform to better define who our users are and how they perform their jobs, and they are literally bending over backwards in some cases to establish good working relationships with and the trust of those in the product development and marketing departments.

The department operates on the belief that usability is something engineered into a product, that it does not just happen, and it is not a result of only one type of process conducted one time during the product lifecyle. We focus our efforts on convincing those in any way involved in developing products that a user-centered design approach will ensure we deliver products that our customers and users need and want. We stress to everyone that usability is an iterative process and one that should be started as early in the development process as possible. These certainly are not novel concepts—only ones that all companies have not yet accepted fully, if at all.

To better reflect our department's philosophy about usability, we have made a couple of cosmetic changes. We changed the staff's job titles from Usability Analyst and Usabilility Specialist to Usability Design Analyst and Usability Design Specialist. The major difference between an analyst and a specialist position is in the level of experience. We have also changed the name of the Usability Lab to the Usability Design Center. With both of these name changes, we hope to convey the message that usability includes more than just usability testing and that the staff has skills and experiences that span beyond usability testing.

Soon after I hired staff members, we all realized we needed some tools to assist communications between them and other department members within the organization. We developed a handout and distributed it during large Product Development and Marketing department meetings to announce the department and title changes and to summarize the staff's skills and experiences. The handout also includes a product life-cyle wheel (Figure 3) that shows different usability processes in corresponding life-cyle development phases. Along with the wheel, we include in the handout a brief description of each of the processes. The information is not meant to overwhelm or confuse anyone with all the different types of usability processes or to imply that all processes must be conducted in each phase they appear in on the wheel. Instead, the wheel is meant to illustrate that usability is not just a one-time process.

Another change we made was to reduce the Usability Testing Workshop to a one-day class. The new usability workshop, Engineering Usability into AMR Products, outlines not only *when* in the Product Development Cycle (PDC) usability testing should be conducted, but it defines the whole concept of usability engineering/user-centered design. The workshop goes so far as to outline when within the PDC to fit all usability processes, including conducting task and user analysis, setting usability objectives and doing usability design walkthroughs. The workshop also makes a very strong point that none of these is a one-time task. It stresses that one process feeds into the other or that one process may mean having to go back to repeat a previous development phase to redefine some of the areas where we were not on target. This was the next step in building our Usability Engineering Program.

Figure 3   Product life-cycle wheel.

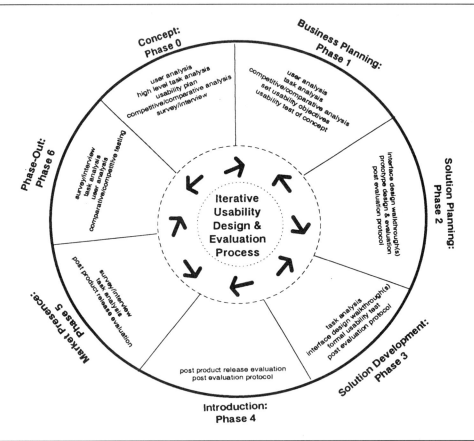

My staff still conducts usability design walkthroughs, as well as formal usability tests. The process is very much the same as before, but with some time commitment and, of course, responsibility changes. Formal usability tests also include comparitive or competitive tests of either our products vs. competitor's or sometimes two competitor's products that departments are reviewing for purchase and in-house use. My staff has an ongoing goal of discovering faster and more innovative ways of doing usability studies.

We have made all phases of the usability testing process participatory. Although we have drastically reduced the total number of hours product development or marketing analysts dedicate to the process, it is still very important that they are involved throughout, for several reasons. Their involvement prevents any negative repercussions at the completion of a test if the results are worse than were expected. I aslo see the developer's and analyst's (and often training and help-desk personnel's) involvement as critical to helping them understand and see for themselves what interface designs cause problems, why the problem designs are difficult to use, as well as which ones work well for the users.

Our Immediate Future

Taking over the usability testing responsibility is the easy task for my staff. Where we are required to put most of our efforts and energies is in getting involved with projects early on to help set usability objectives, provide user and task analysis, as well as user interface design consulting. We have already trained hundreds of people, through our Engineering Usability into AMR Products and User and Task Analysis workshops, about the importance of including all usability steps in the development of a product. However, getting people to realize the importance is the first step. The more important next step is getting them to follow through with that realization and do it.

Thus far, we have been successful in conducting task analysis for projects still in the early phases of development. And we have even been successful through joint efforts between members of my staff and a usability champion on the development team to convince some project teams to take a step back and reevaluate the users and their tasks.

Convincing Product Development that the task analysis process should drive the requirements of products is another one of our goals. Of course, we also hope this next year that we will be involved with some projects early enough to develop the usability objectives for them so that the products can be designed and developed specifically to meet those objectives.

We are also working to help the Marketing and Product Development Departments understand that sometimes there's a real difference between the customers and the users. As a company, we probably spend more time trying to please the customers instead of the actual users of our software products. STIN's Marketing Department spends a lot of time in focus groups and interviews and surveys and at conferences talking with our customers, who are not always the users. Of course we need to talk to the customers—they are the ones who we have to convince to place our products in their agencies. But, we also have to make sure we are spending time with the users. One of my group's goals is to help distinquish the customer from the user when they are indeed not the same person. This problem is one well understood now by the product development team of the product I discuss in the next section of this chapter!

One of the More Successful Product Efforts

I had a difficult time selecting a specific product that I could use to illustrate the success of our usability program. I kept looking for a product that reflected total success, and of course, I could not think of the perfect example. I finally realized that this is because there is no perfect product that has been a total success in any company!

The product, however, that has undergone the most changes as a result of task analysis and usability testing is a product currently under development, scheduled for release in 1994. The product will allow travel agents to select available cruises for a client based on all of the client's requirements. Today, the travel agent is forced to first collect information from the traveler, such as preferred travel time, price of the cruise, location and various other cruise ship criteria. Then, the agent who has collected that information, has to rely on a number of sources to put together a cruise package, including spending a great deal of time on the phone with cruise lines.

The product was originally intended to be a host-based product. After many hours spent in Joint Application Development (JAD) sessions, the development team began to question the appropriateness of a host-based product versus a PC application. Usability testing had already been scheduled for the product in its host-based state, shown in Figure 4. Even though the team felt certain, by the time the product was to go through usability testing, that it should not be a host-based product, the usability test was still conducted for three major reasons: to validate what the users expected from such an application, to show the cruise lines that progress was being made on the development of the product and to get input from the user—for the first time.

The product was being developed in conjuction with some major cruise lines, who, in JAD sessions, provided us input about their process (how they interact with the travel agent). Unfortunately, up to the point of usability testing, the development team had not involved the travel agents in the development process. Understandably so, they viewed the usability test as a possible critical turning point.

The test results did show that it was too difficult for agents to book a cruise on the host-based system. The new automated method did not buy the users any time, either. It was still faster for them to book cruises over the phone. The development team also found that about 5% of the terminology they used in the product did not match the travel agent's terminology. And we also found out that the travel agents performed bookings for groups in a completely different manner from that for an individual. Since we had considered the processes the same, the product was off target there, as well.

Following the usability test, the development team returned to the JAD process to convert the product to a PC Windows application. After the team completed about 80% of the design on paper, the product was put on hold. An outside consultant team was called in to evaluate the efforts that had already been dedicated to this product. While

Figure 4   The product in its host-based state

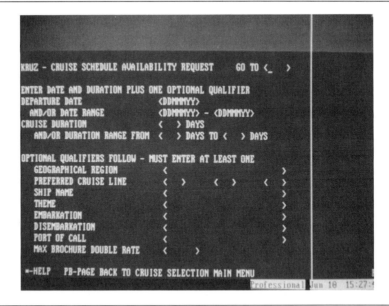

the consultants were conducting their study, the development team was also asked to ake a recommendation for the next step to take with the product. Their recommendation was to move forward with the development of a Windows-based product.

The development team's recommendation was accepted, and they expanded and restructured to develop the PC product. The new development team, which was a matrixed team of product development and marketing personnel, maintained the old product requirements established by the previous development team. They made only a few functionality changes, but completely overhauled the interface design of the product.

Three usability tests were scheduled for the product in 1993. The first usability design walkthrough (after design and functional specs had been frozen) tested the effectiveness and usability of icons, micro-help, menu titles, field labels and methods of access for varying levels of users with cruise-selling and graphical user interface experience. The product in that state is shown in Figure 5.

The usability design walkthrough uncovered some major problems. All users, regardless of level of expertise in either selling cruises or using graphical user interfaces, consistently experienced difficulties in all areas of the product targeted by the test. In general, the users (travel agents) were not technically adept at using traditional Windows application interfaces.

Figure 5   The product in its 1st PC version

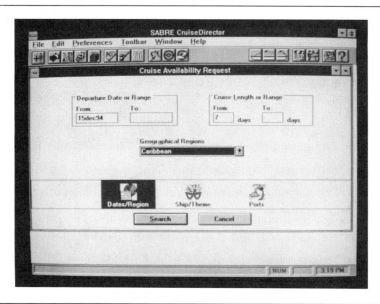

Another major problem users had was interacting with the multitude of icons. Participants were able to identify the correct meaning of only 15% of the icons and they identified some specific icons as representing functions other than what they were intended to represent. Since the icons represented one method of navigation to critical areas of the product, this turned out to be a major problem the product team could not ignore. Users also experienced serious difficulty in finding functions that were represented by menu options, as well as understanding the meanings and purpose of certain field labels.

Shortly after the team conducted their usability design walkthrough, the Usability Design Center began offering the new User and Task Analysis Workshop. Several members of the cruise application development team attended the workshop and became convinced that they should conduct a task analysis for their product. Again, it was already late in the development process, but the development team and manager were able to convince upper management that the time would be well spent, especially since very little time had been spent with the travel agents (real users) during the up-front design of the product.

Together, a member of my team and one of the Product Development team members conducted task analysis. It was another eye-opening experience. Although task analysis revealed that the product provided most of the functionality travel agents needed, it also revealed that some functions were more important to users than had been revealed in previously conducted focus groups and demonstrations. For example, in focus groups conducted with an advisory board (made up of travel agency owners, managers and agents), the board ranked the top five qualifiers they used to match a cruise to a customer's (traveler) need. The board rated the price of a cruise as number 5. The task analysis revealed, however, that almost all users (travel agents) rank the price of a cruise as the number 1 criterion they use to qualify a cruise for a customer. The Task Analysis also confirmed, like with the usability test, that the intended users of the product were not ready for a traditional Windows application.

Following the release of the Task Analysis results, the product development analysts and one of my usability design specialists completed a rough redesign of the user interface. Upon the recommendation of the usability design specialist, the new interface is much more graphical, has fewer icons and is absent of pulldown menus. The team was faced with asking management again to be able to rework the product. The good news is that everyone who saw the new design overwhelmingly accepted it. The bad news is that the development team was told that they could have no impact on the product's time to market. However, that was not entirely bad news since the product's functionality did not need to drastically change.

The cruise lines, who were partnering this project with us, however, were not convinced (putting it mildly) that the product's design should change. In reality, I think what was happening is that we were recommending yet more changes and they were not forgetting that PD had been working on this product since 1989. It did not matter to them that the product had been converted to a new platform and basically redesigned twice. In their minds, PD had been working on this product far too long, and we needed to finish it and release it. So, this also affected the final design changes that were made to the product.

Although the product has undergone major interface design changes, the changes primarily affect only the outer layer of the interface. A thorough redesign effort was not permitted because of the time to market constraints.

Another usability test is being conducted on the product as I write this chapter. But, my staff has been told that Product Development cannot make any changes to the product that would affect its functionality. The team is tied to the original release dates of the product. This is the reality of product development and usability! You win some, and you lose some.

At this point, you must be wondering why I chose this project, in particular, as a success story. It is simple.

- Without the first usability test with the product as a host-based product, it may never have been converted to a PC application.

- Without the usability design walkthrough of the first PC user interface, the development team would not have witnessed that the users had great difficulty interacting with and understanding the many icons used in the application. Or they would not have discovered that some of the terminology did not match that of the users. And, the development team might not have been convinced that if they continued to develop the product as a Windows product, that they would have to develop an interface that better accommodated the user's current inexperience with Windows applications.

- Without the task analysis workshop, we would not have easily convinced the development team that they should not have skipped this very important step in the development process, even if the impact of that lesson was them having to conduct the analysis late in the cycle.

All of these usability processes were performed too late in the cycle. That is without a doubt. However, I am delighted with the fact that the development team was willing to put forth the effort to identify the usability problems with the product and implement changes as much as they were permitted, *before* the product was released. No one would deny that the product is still not the best that it could be, but it is certainly much better, we think, than it might have been had Product Development not agreed to include these usability processes in their development cycle. And, as of the last meeting with the partners of this joint development, they were pleased with the most recent user interface changes. That, to many people involved with this project, is a huge success.

Lessons Learned

Just as with the cruise project I previously discussed, there are many many lessons to be learned in this business from every single project and at each different company involved in usability testing. What motivates me the most is that the lessons have been never-ending. I believe I have remained in this field and renewed my interest over and over because it has been such a dynamic field. There is always a new challenge. If you want to work in a field that remains constant, then usability engineering is not the one to get into.

Reflecting on my experiences with starting up usability programs for Computer Language Research, Inc., and American Airlines, it is easiest to compare those experiences within a small corporation to those within a large corporation. With both usability start-up projects, I spent an enormous amount of time marketing the benefits of usability engineering, sometimes to the point of thinking I was going to make myself physically sick if I had to repeat my speech one more time to win the trust of just one more skeptic. I have learned that the necessity of marketing usability testing and usability engineering never ends.

At both small and large companies, I spent a great deal of time and energy asking for and justifying more employees. No matter what size the organization, additional people seem to be very difficult to acquire for a process that does not immediately and without any uncertainty show the payback on that investment.

I found less difficulty in a small corporation than in a large corporation of actually implementing the usability process. In small corporations, you can often champion an idea and test it out much more easily than in a large organization. I had much more freedom working for a smaller company to research and try out new methods. The larger the company, the more people there are to convince and the more bureaucracy there is to work around.

I remember several years ago here at American Airlines when I took a Product Management course, we were told that, on the average, it takes three to five years to fully introduce and implement a new process into a large corporation. I thought to myself, "well, you've been pushing this usability stuff for almost two years now, so between 1 to three years from now, you should begin to see some results." It was not an encouraging thought at that moment, but now, looking back on that time, I am able to recognize that the company, especially STIN, has made enormous progress toward understanding and integrating at least pieces of usability engineering into the development of its products.

That does not mean that usability is a required process yet or that it is integrated early enough in the cycle of all products. But, progress is progress, and I keep telling myself to try to recongnize it for what it is, no matter how small it might be. It is much easier to look back and recognize the accomplishments that have been made in implementing any change than it is to recognize them while they are occuring. That very lesson is why I will always encourage new usability champions in corporations to just keep pushing for the changes they believe in and want to make a part of their companies. Most of all, I encourage them to try to see the accomplishments as they are being made.

I experienced much more difficulty in a small company acquiring the money needed to build a lab facility. At Computer Language Research, Inc., it seemed like we built the lab piece by piece. First, I found a space within the company that had two side-by-side rooms. The department the space belonged to just happened to have camera equipment that I could borrow. With one person from this group, I spent a lot of time talking about what I wanted to do with usability testing and what kind of lab setup I had in mind. I was able to generate enough of his interest to persuade him to help me set up a makeshift lab. Later, he was actually instrumental in helping me acquire the funds for building and equipping a small dedicated lab. He even assumed the responsibility of researching equipment to ensure the lab was set up with the required equipment.

I do not know if it is just that so much time has clouded my memory, but it seems like it was more fun starting up usability testing at the small corporation. Things seemed to happen much more quickly. With fewer people within the organization, the project had greater visibility and management seemed to be more excited by, accepting and supportive of the new process.

I remember one day I happened to run into our VP of Product Development in the hallway. He politely inquired about my progress with the usability testing project. I took full advantage of that opportune moment and told him we needed $600 to install a oneway mirror between the two rooms we had turned into our makeshift lab. He approved the money on the spot! Of course he was one of the management group I invited to observe the first usability test. It was also crititcal to get the support of our VP of Marketing, so I asked him to be a pilot evaluator. He accepted and was overwhelmed with what usability testing revealed about our product packaging.

The major points I want to stress through sharing the lessons I have learned in starting up usability programs are these:

- If you believe in usability testing, or user and task analysis, or rapid prototype development, or any other usability process and you want to bring it into your company, then just do it. Do not bother immediately with the formal proposal and request for special equipment or tools. Just put together a simple test with what you have, cameras or no cameras, and invite people to come. And they will! This is the best and easiest way to convince whomever you need to convince that usability testing, or whatever other process you want to implement, is a valuable tool. Once they see it for themselves, they will be on your side forever.

- The equipment you use to first do usability testing should be the least of your concerns. If you want to videotape, you can always borrow a camcorder or two from someone, if you have to. You can use a stopwatch if you need to time tasks and have no other way of doing it. You can even just take notes if you have no automated logging tool, or you can create a simple word processing file for test notes. You do not even need two rooms separated by a oneway mirror; you can sit in the room with the user if that is the only way you can do the test. The sophisticated and high-tech tools can come later, if you want them. Just do something.

- Get the support of the people in your organization who have purchasing power and who have the most influence over the primary organization you will support.

Pull them into what you are doing—invite them to presentations, ask them to participate in or observe a test. Let them witness for themselves the value of usability. You need them as your champions for obvious reasons!

- Keep talking! Get your message out to everyone who will listen. Share every success you have with as many people as will listen.

UE Issues of Special Concern to Me

During our first meeting of what is today the Usability Professionals' Association, we identified issues that were of concern to us and for which we needed answers. I think a large number of those issues will always remain issues. That is not to say that we are not finding solutions; it is just that we are continuously seeking better and more efficient ways of doing what we do. And each new company that starts a usability program will be faced with those same issues that all of us have dealt with sometime in our past. For example, I would say that the following are still hot issues for almost everyone in the field, including the very experienced to the less experienced professional. Luckily, the UPA is still focusing on these issues and its members address these issues through its newsletter, the *Common Ground*, and annual conferences.

- How do we do faster and more efficient usability testing (quick and dirty studies)?
- How do we convince management that usabilty will not increase time to market?
- What is the right mix of skills and experience for a human factors staff?
- What methods can we use to share evaluation results?
- What is the most effective way of evaluating complex systems?
- How do we get developers to make our recommended changes?
- Should we charge internal organizations for usability testing?

Chapters could probably be written on any one of these issues. But, the first step is to get usability testing started, and, I hope I have given you some ideas about that and the challenges that you can expect in that endeavor! Remember, just do it!

CHAPTER 13

Usability Engineering at Dun & Bradstreet Software

**Chauncey E. Wilson,
Beth A. Loring,
Len Conte, and
Karen Stanley**

*Dun & Bradstreet Software
Services, Inc.*

From left to right: Chauncey E. Wilson, Beth A. Loring, Len Conte, and Karen Stanley.

Chauncey E. Wilson is the manager of the Human Factors Team at D&B Software and senior architect for human-computer interaction. He holds a B.A. in physics from the University of Pittsburgh and has had extensive graduate training in social psychology and human factors engineering. Before joining D&B Software, Chauncey was a principal software usability engineer at Digital Equipment Corporation. Chauncey is the president of the Northern New England Chapter of the Society for Technical Communication and a member of the Usability Professionals' Association, the Association for Computing Machinery, and the Human Factors and Ergonomics Society. Chauncey has written articles on topics ranging from groupware to criminal victimization.

Beth A. Loring is a usability engineer at D&B Software. She holds a B.S. in engineering psychology from Tufts University, where she is currently an M.S. candidate in engineering design. Before joining D&B Software, Beth worked for six years as a usability specialist at the American Institutes for Research. Beth is currently the membership chair and newsletter editor for the New England Chapter of the Human Factors and Ergonomics Society. She is also a member of the Greater Boston Special

Interest Group for Computer-Human Interaction (SIGCHI) and the Usability Professionals' Association. Beth has written papers on diverse topics such as product safety, graphic design, vehicle navigation devices, and the usability of home electronics for older consumers.

Len Conte is a senior software architect at D&B Software. He graduated from Lafayette College with a B.A. in economics. He holds a masters degree in communications from Fairfield University and a certificate in knowledge engineering from Northeastern University. Len has worked in the software industry for 20 years, designing and implementing accounting software. His roles at D&B Software have included Project Leader, Systems Analyst, Knowledge Engineer, and Design Architect. He has spent the last five years in research and development and advanced technologies. His work in knowledge-based systems led him to the field of user interface design. He has designed user interfaces for knowledge-based systems and client-server applications within D&B Software. Len is a member of IEEE and AAAI.

Karen Stanley is a usability engineer at D&B Software. She has been working in the software industry for over eight years. She graduated from Fitchburg State College with a B.S. in computer science. Karen spent five years as a developer, concentrating primarily on the development of software user interfaces. Her interest in user interface design led her to specialize in human-computer interaction. She has taken courses at Tufts University, attended seminars, attended CHI conferences, and worked with experts in the field to gain a background in the design and testing of user interfaces. She worked as a user interface engineer at Bachman Information Systems, Inc., for over two years before joining D&B Software.

When this chapter was written, the Dun & Bradstreet (D&B) Software Human Factors Team had been together for about one year. D&B Software products run the financial, human resources, and manufacturing operations of large domestic and international companies. The mission of the team is to ensure that Dun & Bradstreet Software's new client-server products based on the Microsoft® Windows™ user interface are useful and usable; a formidable task given the number and scope of products being designed and developed simultaneously. To achieve our mission, we strove to embed the principles of usability engineering (know the users and their work, set goals, design early, and test often) into the development process. We introduced methods like contextual inquiry (Wixon, Jones, Tse, and Casaday, 1993), paper prototypes, usability goals (Gould, 1988), competitive analysis, and user interface design inspections (Nielsen, 1993). Some groups have embraced these methods; other groups are still skeptical. Our team wants to do proactive usability engineering (we have all seen it done wrong too many times). Doing usability engineering right in such a complex environment is a formidable challenge for our small team. This chapter describes our team, the scope of our work, our resources, illustrative case studies, and the lessons that we have learned over the last year.

The D&B Software Human Factors Team

In November 1993, four people made up the Human Factors Team. Chauncey Wilson, manager of the team, deliberately recruited individuals with varied backgrounds who could complement each other. A solid Human Factors Team requires a variety of different skills and interests. The background of each team member was described briefly at the beginning of the chapter.

Where We Fit in the Corporation

The Human Factors Team reports to the director of the Decision Support product group. Although we are based in one product group, we consult on usability issues with groups throughout D&B Software. We divide our main efforts among the four product areas: Decision Support, Financials, Manufacturing and Distribution, and Human Resources.

We act as internal consultants to the development teams for everything from isolated questions about design issues ("Should error dialog boxes have Help buttons?") to dedicated design efforts that stretch over months. Our team is funded by the director of the Decision Support organization and not from an overhead account. We write no formal proposals for our efforts nor bill funds to the appropriate project account. We do, however, keep track of approximately what percentage of time we spend working with the different teams. We like this method of funding since it means that we can spend more time actually doing design and usability work and less time writing detailed proposals.

HF Team Growth

A four-person team like ours is stretched thin supporting engineering, training, documentation, and product management groups and trying to get them to consider usability an integral part of development. The stretch is even greater when you consider that the current team members all live in the Boston area, but must provide support to our Atlanta office. Currently, at least one team member commutes to Atlanta every two or three weeks to provide consulting support. By the time this chapter is published, we should have a senior user interface designer in Atlanta to expand our team to five. If we suddenly had funding for more resources, we would like to see a usability specialist "assigned" to each major product group. If we followed this scheme, the HF team would have about 10 members, each of whom could get to understand the design issues with a particular product much better than our current band of four overachievers.

D&B Software—The Business

D&B Software is part of the Software Services segment of the Dun & Bradstreet Corporation. D&B Software is the largest company in this segment with revenues of about $500 million. D&B Software is a supplier of financial, human resources, manufacturing, and decision support software to large corporations. It was formed in 1991 with the merger of two companies who competed in the mainframe computer market: McCormack & Dodge Corporation and Management Science America, Inc. The company's major software development groups are split between Framingham, Massachusetts (near Boston); Atlanta, Georgia; and Tampa, Florida. Sales and support groups are found throughout the world. D&B Software employed about 1600 people at the end of 1993.

To meet the needs of a changing market, D&B Software began investing heavily in client-server technology in 1992. Client-server computing involves reengineering business practices to move management functions to divisional levels to capitalize on opportunities (managers can see product trends more quickly than if they have to wait for the report from corporate headquarters) and avoid bureaucratic gauntlets. This reengineering of business practices is done by moving from a mainframe architecture to a distributed computing architecture with three components: a host (a mainframe computer), a server (a powerful personal computer [PC] or minicomputer), and a client (a PC or workstation). Data on personnel, company finances, or manufacturing status are pulled down from a mainframe host and manipulated and organized by the server and client computers. Users interact with the client and use desktop productivity tools to query, analyze, summarize, and report on the state of their business in minutes or hours. The same analysis on a mainframe system might take days, weeks, or even months to produce unless you are good friends with the management information systems manager.

About D&B Software's Client–Server Products

The client–server products developed at D&B Software can be broken down into four basic categories:

- Decision Support Software for business analysis and reporting, which is the cornerstone for the other applications.
- Financial Applications, software to run the financial operations of a company, including accounts payable, accounts receivable, fixed assets, and general ledger applications.
- Manufacturing and Distribution Applications, software designed to run manufacturing plant operations such as production and distribution logistics.
- Human Resource Applications, software to manage payroll, personnel, and HR activities including recruitment, employee benefits, and employee record keeping.

These categories of products are all based on a common software architecture. The architecture defines common menu items, window styles, keyboard and mouse interactions, and data-entry methods. The goal of the architecture is to foster a common look and feel across all D&B Software applications. The architecture also defines a method for implementing workflow within a single application and between different applications. An example of workflow in our system is the approval process for purchasing new equipment. We can set up a workflow that will automatically route the information needed for approval to the appropriate people. One ramification of this technology is that we have to understand deeply the dynamics of our customers' business practices to design appropriate workflows.

Our software can be run on a variety of host and server platforms; however, the client components (e.g., financial reporting tools, financial data entry) of our applications run in the Microsoft® Windows™ graphical user interface (GUI) environment.

D&B Software products present strong challenges for our Human Factors Team. The products must be designed to accommodate diverse customers (both telephone companies and hospitals, for example) and users (data-entry clerks and chief financial officers). The GUI is gigantic—there are several thousand windows and dialog boxes, each with many fields. The interactions among the host, server, and client computers are complex and have subtle (and not so subtle) effects on design. Usability testing on our large-scale products is more difficult than it is with shrink-wrapped software because of the size of the system and the need to access data on host and server computers.

In addition to problems of customer diversity and size, we must deal with extremely short development cycles (six months for a minor release; one year for a major release) and therefore some resistance from development managers to the concept of iterative design and usability testing. To counter this resistance, we promote quick and efficient usability methods like user interface inspections, test drives, and paper prototypes.

D&B Software's Human Factors Program

This section describes the Human Factors program at D&B Software: how it was formed, who its members are, our roles in the company, and how we do our work.

How the Human Factors Team Was Formed

Management Sciences America (MSA), Inc., one of the two companies that merged to form D&B Software, was an early leader in usability testing. Ray Rupinski, formerly the manager of the usability lab and now a project manager in our Tampa office, managed the design of the MSA usability lab in Atlanta and ran it for about five years, starting in 1988. With the merger of MSA and McCormack & Dodge in 1991, the lab became a corporate D&B Software resource. Dun & Bradstreet Software, and other Dun & Bradstreet companies like A. C. Neilsen, Donnelley Directory, and Sales Technologies, take advantage of the usability lab. Ray's work with the usability lab was the precursor to the formation of the D&B Software Human Factors Team.

D&B Software began a wave of hiring in early 1992 to bolster its new client-server engineering teams. The company recognized that experience in human-computer interaction design was critical, since PC-based client-server technology was new to D&B Software. The first position recruited by D&B Software was that of Senior Architect for Human-Computer Interaction (HCI). The search took about four months (this was not an easy position to fill). Chauncey Wilson was hired in August 1992 as the company's HCI Architect. No time was lost getting Chauncey involved in design. After two hours with human resources personnel on his first day, Chauncey was ushered into a detailed design meeting with Dr. Tom Malone from MIT's Center for Coordination Science. Tom had collaborated with D&B Software developers on the design of the user interface for SmartStream® V1.0, the first client–sever product marketed by D&B Software.

On the third day at work as the D&B Software HCI architect, Chauncey met Ray Rupinski, the usability lab manager, and shortly thereafter the two of them formed the D&B Software Human Factors Team. The two members of the fledgling Human Factors Team focused on the development of GUI standards and guidelines, but within a few months their roles expanded from standard-bearers to that of evangelists, trainers, usability testers, and consistency czars; and the need for more than a two-person team was evident. Senior management showed strong support for human factors work by providing funds for three additional usability specialists in late 1992. Two people were hired from outside D&B Software, and one moved from another team at D&B Software. While the team gained three people, it also lost one as Ray decided to take a position as project manager in our Tampa office. Once the team was assembled, we had expertise in many areas: usability testing methods, programming architecture, user interface design, quality assurance, artificial intelligence, graphic design, and competitive product analysis.

We now have four full-time members on the Human Factors Team. We also draw support from other teams, college and internal interns, our graphic design department, and external consultants. The following sections describe how these people contribute to the usability efforts at D&B Software.

GUI Advocates on Development Teams

Our four-person team can not provide all the consulting that is expected, so we asked managers of each development team to appoint a person (developer, documenter, or application expert) as a usability advocate. The usability advocates from Framingham, MA and Atlanta meet periodically with our Human Factors Team by video conference, get extra training on user interface design topics, and let us know about issues that emerge from the design efforts of their respective teams.

The major benefit emerging from the meetings of the GUI advocates is communication of design ideas and consistency issues. GUI advocates can ask if anyone else has solved a vexing design problem and often find that someone else has a reasonable solution. Advocates also ask questions about consistency issues that are not easily answered from reading the Windows or D&B Software user interface style guide.

Intern Program

The Human Factors Team started a usability intern program in late 1992. The first intern was a D&B Software documentation manager with a strong interest in usability. Her job description was rewritten so that 50% of her time was dedicated to documentation usability issues. She conducted tests of on-line help, icons, and paper documentation. She left D&B Software in mid-1993, but before she left, she told us that her usability work was the most enjoyable part of her job.

During the summer of 1993, three students from the Human Factors program at Tufts University were hired as interns for the summer. The three college interns conducted usability studies on our software and documentation, participated in user interface inspections, and supported our quality assurance staff by looking for usability "bugs" during the last stages of development. An intern program is an excellent way to find talented employees. Two of the three interns were hired, one full time, the other part time, as a result of their work during the summer. The intern that we hired as a full-time employee works on a quality assurance team and will be responsible for finding and eliminating usability bugs. She will work closely with and be an extended member of our Human Factors Team. The intern program was a rousing success. We hope to continue it in the future.

Graphic Designers

Our team works closely with our graphic design department on icon design, color, and layout issues. A common activity of our two groups is to brainstorm on icons and graphics for our client–server products, then test the intuitiveness of our designs. We also involve our graphic designers in design meetings and consistency reviews so they get a better picture of how our products work.

Outside Consultants

We periodically hire consultants to teach courses on GUI design and usability evaluation methods. There are two main advantages in having outside consultants teach general courses rather than teaching them ourselves:

- It takes great effort to design good courses.

- External courses can make the work of the Human Factors Team more credible to developers (assuming that the course material supports the philosophy of the Human Factors Team).

During 1993, the Human Factors Team sponsored seven courses taught by consultants. Topics covered in the courses included user interface architectures, basic window styles, appropriate use of GUI controls, color and highlighting, error handling, and screen layout. The GUI courses had many exercises that reinforced the design principles. The reviews on these courses were generally good. A minor complaint was that the courses were sometimes too general and did not get at some of the issues specific to D&B Software. To rectify this complaint, the Human Factors Team put together a one-day follow-up course to cover design issues specific to our corporate user interface style.

We have not used consultants as partners in design or usability testing activities. Our large-scale applications require substantial background knowledge, and we feel that even the best consultants would have an overwhelming learning curve before they would be truly useful. Also, there is so much infrastructure with our products (databases, servers, LANs, etc.) that we cannot easily use an outside test lab. For example, the installation of one of our products requires detailed knowledge of multiple databases, products, and servers and takes much more time than the installation of word processing or spreadsheet applications. Usability testing of our products requires a much more serious commitment than the testing of a standalone product.

The ability to negotiate and understand the social psychology of the groups that we work with at D&B Software is essential for ensuring credibility and maintaining effectiveness. We enlisted the aid of John Bennett, formerly a human factors engineer at IBM and now a consultant specializing in the social and managerial aspects of the design process. John consulted with our group on ways to be effective in our interactions with individuals and groups who do not always share our goals. The emphasis was on the impact that language has on our credibility and persuasiveness. Some of the language rules followed by our team are these:

- Avoid the use of loaded words ("stupid design," "dumb developer") in memos and conversations.

- Ensure that we are clear on the type of conversation that we are having with our developers. Are we having a conversation about possibilities or a conversation about actions needed to solve problems?

- Praise the work of others. Sometimes we are so focused on design problems that we fail to give credit for good designs.

- Avoid personal blame. Try to solve problems rather than attach blame for designs that lead to usability problems.

We often review each other's memos to ensure that we use language that focuses on effective problem solving rather than the attribution of blame. Constant attention to the words that we use makes us more effective in our consulting efforts.

Our Daily Activities

The Human Factors Team works with development teams during all design phases, including project definition, analysis and design, construction, and approval and delivery. The extent to which we participate in each phase on a particular project depends upon the needs of the development team. Our daily activities may include the following:

- Gathering user feedback on our software products through usability testing (in-house and with customers, formal and informal), observation (during construction, during training, during beta testing, in the field), and individual interviews or focus groups (during customer visits, at beta sites, and at user conferences).

- Educating people in other disciplines about aspects of usability—its importance, user-centered design methodologies, and design trade-offs. We educate through one-on-one discussions, presentations to groups, contributing to a usability newsletter, monitoring an on-line GUI conference, and posting articles of interest on the wall near our offices.

- Promoting product consistency by attending design reviews, maintaining the company's user interface style guide, participating in interdisciplinary design teams, and reviewing design specifications.

- Communicating findings on usability issues to management and development teams through test reports, memos, discussions, and design meetings.

- Encouraging collaboration among the development, documentation, training, support, and marketing groups.

- Participating in the certification of products. Certification is the formal process used by D&B Software to determine if a product is ready for shipment to customers.

- Conducting competitive analyses and keeping up with the advances in technology. User interface technology is expanding rapidly. We need to keep up with new user interface technologies, including pen input, multimedia, virtual reality, data visualization, object-oriented design, and adaptive learning.

Other Roles

In addition to our daily activities, we participate in several company wide decision-making groups:

- The Interdisciplinary GUI Design Team has representatives from the four product areas, including writers, developers, trainers, and testers. It is led by the Human Factors Team. This group meets about once a month to discuss GUI issues. We use our video conference facilities to hold this meeting between Framingham and Atlanta.
- The Documentation and Education Standards Board includes writers, editors, and trainers, from Framingham; Atlanta; Tampa, Florida; Bristol, UK; and Brussels, Belgium. The Human Factors Team representative acts mostly as an observer, to keep up to date on documentation and training issues. This group meets about once every two months by teleconference.
- The D&B Software Product Team is a group of managers from development, support, packaging, training, documentation, and marketing that prepares final review material on a product's readiness to be released to the public. The Human Factors Team prepares a statement of the usability of products about to be released.
- The Dun & Bradstreet Corporate Consistency–Usability Task Force is composed of representatives from Dun & Bradstreet companies who are responsible for sharing technology on user interface consistency and usability issues. The Human Factors Team contributes to this group by passing on lessons that we have learned on how to design consistent and usable products.

Participation in these decision-making groups takes time away from the day-to-day design and usability activities that we listed earlier; however, this participation also has important benefits. First, the Human Factors Team has wide visibility and is seen as a valuable group within the company. Second, participation in these groups gives us a broad perspective on product development that we would not have working just with the engineering groups. And last, the Human Factors Team can use these groups as forums for implicit training on design issues.

The Skills and Knowledge We Need

We have discovered that certain core skills and knowledge are important in the D&B Software environment. If we were going to add a new member to our team, we would look for as many of the following attributes as possible:

- The ability to communicate with confidence and diplomacy.

- A wide repertoire of usability evaluation methods. We use formal and informal usability testing, paper prototypes, user interface inspections, questionnaires, brainstorming, and focus groups to gather information.

- Sensitivity to conflicting goals. Usability is important, but we must balance our work against the constraints of time to market , reliability, performance, and other criteria important to the company.

- Detailed knowledge of GUI design principles and the Microsoft Windows design guidelines.

- Technical background on relational database technology and transaction processing systems.

- The ability to move on after a setback. We need to be flexible enough to change our strategies when they are not effective.

How We Work with Development Teams

Distributed Design

At some software companies, a central design team creates a user interface design specification containing representations of product components and their interactions. Teams of developers then take this specification and implement it, with periodic input from the design team when problems arise. At D&B Software, user interface design is distributed among several hundred developers, application experts, and information designers. There is no central design team for each set of applications. Individual developers are responsible for implementing a particular set of functions and the GUI for these functions. This distributed design approach led the Human Factors Team to become a matrix organization, where we provide resources for all development groups at D&B Software and act as "design central." The role of design central is a difficult one for our small team. We struggle to keep up with all the requests that we get and worry that refusing requests for help will turn people away from our group. Success is gratifying, but also taxing for our team. We are still working on how best to set priorities.

Four Different Strategies

Our strategy for providing services varies depending on the criticality of requests, the duration of the project, and the background of team members. Although we work with different development teams, we meet weekly to assess our strategies and discuss how we can better support each other. We are also in constant contact by electronic mail and telephone.

Chauncey Wilson acts as the focal point for the team and is our representative at the corporate level. He focuses on company wide issues, such as creating user interface design standards; educating developers, writers, trainers, and managers about usability; organizing the work of the human factors team, and creating liaisons among people at the offices in Framingham, Atlanta, and abroad. He is involved with almost all the company's products, but does not participate start-to-finish on any one product.

Len Conte's background is in computer architecture and advanced technology, so he speaks the language of developers. He is a member of the Human Factors Team, but also reports to the manager of the Decision Support products. He has been with D&B Software the longest, so his history with the company and his rapport with the developers are assets to the team. Because he has a broad knowledge of the underlying system design, he addresses usability and technical issues with development teams and managers. He acts as a contact between the Human Factors Team and the Decision Support development team, promoting iterative design and usability testing as ways of verifying usability. His interest in new technology focuses him on the future of our client–server products, while also helping to guide the company toward solutions that are usable.

Beth Loring has a background in human factors and usability testing. She sometimes works closely with one development team and sometimes works on short-term projects, doing quick usability studies of important software components. During the development of the first version of D&B Software's client–server products, she tested many small pieces of the Decision Support software. During the design of the second versions of our products, she is working mostly with the Manufacturing and Distribution application team.

Karen Stanley has adopted a fourth strategy. She works closely within one specific design team—the team building the Decision Support reporting products. The advantage of this strategy is that she can become a real team member, rather than an "outside consultant" from the Human Factors Team. She is able to get at the nuts and bolds of the products, gain a greater understanding of the issues the developers face and the tasks users need to perform. The development team she works with happens to be colocated with the Human Factors Team, so impromptu discussions between Karen and the rest of the team are easy.

The Trade-off Between Being Consultants and Being Dedicated Resources

We have discussed the trade-off between working with a number of teams and working with only one team. Being part of the team allows us to have a deeper understanding of the design issues. We can discuss task flow, user expectations, functionality, and overall product integration. It is easier to make more informed recommendations for the user interface. Without this knowledge, we are often able to participate only at the user interface guideline level. Also, we become comfortable discussing issues with people on the team because we have a close relationship with them.

There are drawbacks to the dedicated resource approach, however. Karen Stanley's dedicated work with a single project made her feel removed from the rest of the Human Factors Team and out of touch with the larger set of D&B Software products. Since D&B Software is building a large set of integrated products, it is important that team members be aware of design issues beyond those of their specific products. We are keeping each other more aware by doing product design reviews that include the whole team rather than just one member, sending e-mail on consistency and usability issues to the whole team, and posting design issues in a Lotus Notes® conference that our team (and anyone else in the company) can access.

Human Factors Team Resources

Atlanta Usability Laboratory

The Human Factors Team has a formal usability test lab in Atlanta (Figure 1). The lab has three rooms: a participant room, an observation room, and an office. The participant room has a PC and three video cameras to provide a variety of views. The PC is connected to a video processor that converts the computer's video into a TV video signal. It is useful to have direct video signal because PC monitors have different scan rates than video cameras, so without direct signal you will see scan lines on your videotape. We have an intercom linking the participant room and the observation room so we can talk to the study participants. There is also a phone in the room that participants can use to call a simulated hotline if they experience problems during a testing session. Observers watch the proceedings through a large one-way mirror.

The observation room has four monitoring stations. Three monitoring stations have a set of headphones and camera controls. We can listen to participants and adjust the cameras to get the best view of the participant, computer screen, keyboard, or documentation. The fourth station has a video mixer that combines the views from the different cameras. With the mixer, we can superimpose the person's face over the image of the computer screen or get a small image of the keyboard. A VHS video recorder captures the mixed signal. We use a PC in the observation room to log events of interest,

Figure 1   D&B Software Atlanta usability laboratory

such as time to complete tasks, number of keying errors, and important comments. The customized logging software is synchronized with the videotape of the participant to facilitate data analysis.

The Framingham Discount Usability Laboratory

The usability laboratory in Framingham is a low-cost facility (Figure 2). It has only one room, a converted office. The equipment consists of a portable 8 mm video camera, an editing deck, and two PCs. The portable video camera sits on a movable tripod. The advantage of the "discount" laboratory is that it is portable, so we can take it on our customer visits. It is inexpensive (a video camera and editing deck cost about $3000) and only a few hours are required to learn how to use the equipment.

Figure 2   Setting up for a study in the Framingham discount laboratory

It is important to get the customer's permission before bringing a video camera to a customer site because many companies worry about security and trade secrets. If you fail to get permission you may be surrounded by burly guards and escorted to the security office. This happened to one of the authors several years ago when the head of security (who had approved the use of video for an interview at his site) went on vacation and forgot to let his second-in-command know about the videotaping. All was forgiven after the head of security was called at his vacation hideaway.

In addition to the 8 mm video camera, we use other portable equipment in our work. We use laptop computers to record usability issues at design meetings, at customer sites, and when we conduct usability studies outside the Atlanta lab. We sometimes use a portable tape recorder to record people's comments. When possible, we photograph the offices or work areas of our users to get a sense of their working environments. These photographs can reveal how much room there is for a mouse, whether any formal or informal documentation is nearby, what kind of hardware is used, and how much privacy the person has. We often ask users if they have any "homemade" documentation that they find useful. Some companies, for example, put together their own quick reference guide. If possible, we make a photocopy of the homemade documentation and use that as input for our user interface design activities.

Methods and Tools

A good user interface designer or usability engineer has a panoply of methods and tools that can be applied during the development process. We list some that we routinely use in our work.

Rapid Usability Testing

In addition to our formal testing in the Atlanta lab, we have had excellent payoff from quick usability tests with three to six participants sitting in their own offices. Our usability tests usually take about a day to plan, a day or two to conduct, and a day to get a brief report together. Our rapid usability testing is focused on a specific set of tasks and not on broad aspects of software usage. One of our team goals is to train some members of each development group to do rapid usability testing on their own.

Field interviews

Field interviews are an important source of usability data for our team. We use contextual inquiry methods (Whiteside, Bennett, and Holtzblatt, 1988) which involve understanding users in the context of their work environments. The results of field interviews provide data on individual and organizational usability issues. We often discover usability issues that would not have emerged in formal lab tests. For example, field interviews might indicate that inadequate computer memory creates a serious usability problem or that documentation is located in a manager's office and not accessible to all employees.

User Interface Reviews

We review our GUIs against Windows and internal D&B Software guidelines, and heuristics like those suggested by Nielsen (1993). User interface reviews are important since we cannot possibly conduct usability tests on every software component of our large-scale systems. Some reviews are formal, with facilitated meetings and assignments for reviewers. Others are done by a single member of the Human Factors Team. The goals of the reviews are to identify usability and consistency issues. These issues are tracked by the usability team usually by marking up a catalog of screen images. Subsequent reviews are used to determine the percentage of issues that have been addressed. User interface reviews are being formalized and made a part of our corporate development process.

Prototype Preparation Tools

Our team uses a variety of prototype preparation tools. Our tools range from scissors and paper to application builders like Visual Basic™ and PowerBuilder™. We encourage developers to do conceptual testing with paper prototypes (Figure 3) early in the process and then move into more detailed prototypes, using sophisticated software tools. Conceptual modeling with paper prototypes allows rapid testing of design ideas and does not lock in a developer to a particular implementation (Spool, 1993). Selling developers and managers on paper prototypes takes some work. Managers wonder why their engineers are using scissors, paper, and glue when they have $10,000 worth of hardware and software that can produce "real code." We counter these reactions by telling managers that a paper prototype takes almost no training (a few hours at most versus many hours for a tool like PowerBuilder), that other major (and profitable) vendors use paper prototypes as an integral part of their development process, and that paper prototyping is faster than prototyping with sophisticated tools. Paper prototypes are catching on at D&B Software.

Lotus Notes®

Most D&B Software client–server employees use a product called *Lotus Notes*. Lotus Notes is an important tool for us in several ways:

- It serves as our electronic mail system.
- It is a repository for design and development data.
- It is the mechanism for tracking software bugs.
- It is the repository for all icons used in our products.
- It is a forum for lively user interface design discussions.

Figure 3 Paper prototype of a dialog box for a database query tool

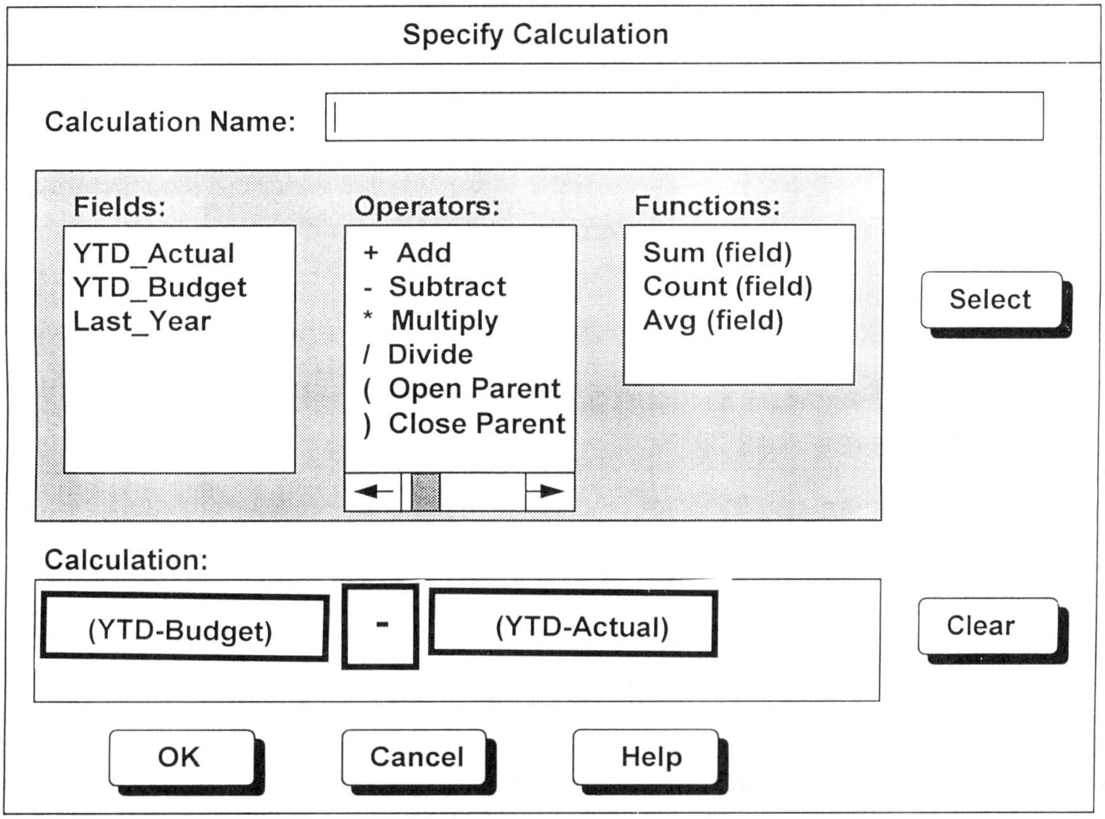

```
┌─────────────────────────────────────────────────────────────────┐
│                      Specify Calculation                           │
│                                                                    │
│   Calculation Name:  [                                      ]      │
│                                                                    │
│   ┌────────────────────────────────────────────────────┐         │
│   │  Fields:          Operators:        Functions:      │  ┌──────┐│
│   │  YTD_Actual       + Add             Sum (field)     │  │Select││
│   │  YTD_Budget       - Subtract        Count (field)   │  └──────┘│
│   │  Last_Year        * Multiply        Avg (field)     │         │
│   │                   / Divide                          │         │
│   │                   ( Open Parent                     │         │
│   │                   ) Close Parent                    │         │
│   │                   [◄]  [▓▓]  [►]                     │         │
│   └────────────────────────────────────────────────────┘         │
│                                                                    │
│   Calculation:                                                     │
│   ┌──────────────────────────────────────────────────┐  ┌──────┐ │
│   │  [(YTD-Budget)]  [-]  [(YTD-Actual)]              │  │Clear │ │
│   └──────────────────────────────────────────────────┘  └──────┘ │
│                                                                    │
│      [  OK  ]      [ Cancel ]      [  Help  ]                      │
└─────────────────────────────────────────────────────────────────┘
```

Lotus Notes is the glue that binds the entire D&B Software client–server community together. The Human Factors Team has set up a user interface design conference with Lotus Notes where anyone in the company can post a usability issue for discussion or a decision. This groupware tool allows our colleagues in Brussels and Australia to contribute to design ideas when we are sleeping. One of the problems with Lotus Notes and similar products is that the number of conferences can proliferate wildly. There can be product, GUI, architecture, training, support, and many other conferences for each product. When Lotus Notes overload occurs, developers, documentors, and designers limit their reading to a small set of conferences. On occasion, we remind developers to review entries in a particular conference or send e-mail on really important issues to all the product teams.

Remote Control Software

We sometimes do usability testing at a distance using remote control software. Remote control software lets us view what is happening on the screen of a computer at another site. When a user at the remote site chooses a menu item or navigates through on-line help, we can see the user's interaction with the software.

Remote control software allows people in Framingham access to a usability test going on in the Atlanta usability lab. The Framingham group can see how the usability participants interact with the test software and hear comments through a speaker phone. At the beginning of this remote usability testing, we typically introduce the group in Framingham to the participant and explain that we will be observing the participant's interaction with the test software. During the test session, the speaker phone in Framingham is set to mute so the user does not hear comments from the observers. At the conclusion of the usability test, observers in both locations can ask questions and hear answers firsthand. This saves the time and expense of copying or editing videotapes and asking people in Framingham to watch them.

We also use remote control software for training and demonstrations. Our customers in another city can see demonstrations of prototypes that are actually running on a PC in one of our development sites.

Remote control software is relatively easy to install and inexpensive ($150–$200 per copy). Five licenses for remote control software would cost less than a single round-trip business ticket between Chicago and Boston. Both computers must be running the remote control software and be connected by a high speed modem (9600 baud or faster), local area network (LAN), or a wide area network (WAN). Popular remote control applications for the PC are ReachOut™, pcANYWHERE for Windows™, and Close-Up®. Computer publications like *InfoWorld, Byte,* and *PC Magazine* are good sources of information on the advantages and disadvantages of the various remote control packages.

Competitive Analyses

We conduct competitive analyses by reviewing articles in trade journals, doing informal reviews of products against user interface guidelines, doing formal usability tests, and attending public demonstrations. Competitive analyses are useful for setting usability goals, for understanding how well a product supports a user's work, and for keeping up with innovations in GUI design. Many PC magazines conduct formal usability tests on products. The reviews of these tests can highlight usability issues to avoid during development of our own products.

Marketing Usability Within D&B Software

We market ourselves at D&B Software through several ongoing efforts. We conduct informal lunchtime usability seminars and more formal training courses. We also try to maintain a strong presence at management meetings, participate on key functional committees, create disciples in product groups, and foster connections with as many parts of the organization as possible.

Seminars

The Human Factors Team sponsors a lunchtime seminar series. The lunchtime usability seminars have been a success. Attendance ranges from 10 to 50 people. Sometimes a member of the Human Factors Team is the seminar speaker, and other times we have guest speakers from outside the company. On some occasions, we have a door prize, book giveaways, or homemade brownies for attendees. The goals of the seminars are to highlight new methodologies and GUI concepts, show the value of usability testing, teach our colleagues something about design, and have some fun. Seminar topics during 1993 included

- Usability for fun and profit
- The 10 most common usability problems
- Carpal tunnel syndrome
- Highlights from InterCHI (the international conference on human–computer interaction)
- Advances in human–computer interaction
- Discount usability testing
- Innovations in user interface design
- What makes on-line Help systems usable

Training in GUI Design

In the last year, about 30% of the D&B Software developers and writers attended courses in GUI design taught by outside consultants. This education is important because of the distributed nature of our product design—nearly every developer designs a portion of the GUI. This makes it imperative that each developer has some sense of good GUI design and knows when to ask us for help.

Visibility to Management

Visibility at management and development team meetings is critical to our team's success. Through we cannot possibly attend all meetings, we strive to attend important design meetings to lobby for usability, to be seen as an important part of the organization, and to understand development issues that might affect design trade-offs. This is a delicate balancing act given our current size of four people. If we go to too many meetings, our design work suffers; if we go to too few meetings, we lose the big picture and some visibility.

The Human Factors Team Philosophy

The philosophy of the Human Factors Team has several key principles:

- We are user advocates. This means that sometimes we will sometimes be at odds with management and developers.

- The user interface for our products consists of all aspects of users' interactions— the GUI, documentation, packaging, support, and training.

- Usability is not a simple concept. It must be considered in the context of the user's work.

- Standards and guidelines are necessary, but not sufficient, for designing usable products.

- Iterative design and testing are critical to the success of our products.

- Management support is a key to our success.

Adhering to these principles requires that we listen carefully to our users, developers, and managers. Practically speaking, our success depends as much on our communication skills as our technical skills. One thing our team considers very carefully is the impact of language on our colleagues. We aim to be strong in our user advocacy without inciting unnecessary friction.

The next section of this chapter will describe several case studies of user interface design at D&B Software.

D & B Software Case Studies in User Interface Design

We describe two case studies in this section. The first case study describes our experience developing Dun & Bradstreet Software GUI standards and guidelines. The development of a corporate user interface style guide is often one of the first and most difficult tasks for a new user interface designer. The second case study is a usability engineering success story. We describe how usability was an integral part of the design of a decision support tool called *Query&Reporter*™.

Case Study 1: D&B Software GUI Standards and Guidelines

The development of graphical user interface standards and guidelines was a high-priority task from the first day that our team was formed. Developers were desperate for standards because they wanted to do the right thing the first time and they believed that standards alone would yield a consistent and usable product. This case study describes our experience creating a style guide and getting developers to use it effectively.

Style Guide Development

Work on a D&B Software user interface style guide (formally called the *D&B Software Development Standards and Procedures Guide*) for the client–server architecture began in the fall of 1992. An earlier attempt at a D&B Software style guide, based on CUA guidelines (IBM, 1989), derailed when D&B Software acquired new software technology with its own user interface style guide. This new technology provided the basic architecture and workflow capabilities for all the D&B Software client–server products. Since we had two internal D&B Software user interface style guides, each of which contained valuable information, we decided to merge the two documents and create a unified D&B Software style guide. All the D&B Software applications were going to run in the Microsoft Windows environment, so we decided early that we would follow the Windows user interface style (Microsoft Press, 1992) as closely as possible. The D&B Software style guide would extend the Windows style guide to deal with basic window styles and transaction processing issues like security and workflow.

We created a single D&B Software user interface style guide, but it was a difficult task. D&B Software management asked a team of five people from human factors, documentation, and development to come up with the "definitive" D&B Software user interface style guide in three months—a challenging goal. The group merged the two D&B Software style guides, collected design issues from the rest of the company, and reviewed them with regard to compliance with the existing Windows guidelines, internationalization requirements, tool limitations, and architectural issues like security and database performance. For example, there is solid evidence that icons should be paired with text labels to make learning easier (Mayhew, 1992), but we decided to use only a graphic symbol because text labels would make internationalization more difficult. Some recommendations in the style guide (e.g., basic windows styles, basic search functions, locations of standard menu items) were tested in our usability lab.

We completed a draft of the D&B Software style guide in November 1992 and distributed it to the entire company. Developers provided feedback on the style guide in a Lotus Notes conference or through e-mail to one of the members of the style guide team. The final version of the D&B Software style guide was issued in January 1993. Shortly thereafter, we also published a 15-page user interface checklist as a supplement to the D&B Software style guide. The style guide and checklist were distributed to everyone in client–server development, about 275 people. The checklist was used during quality assurance testing as a consistency check. Examples of items from the checklist are shown in Table 1.

The checklist was popular among developers, many of whom felt that following the checklist would ensure consistency. The checklist did eliminate gross consistency problems, but was not a panacea.

Observations on the Use of the D&B Software Style Guide

The Human Factors Team, while agreeing that user interface standards were necessary, did not share the belief that standards alone would yield products that our users would applaud. We held to a metaphor that standards were like the foundation for a house; the foundation could provide a solid base on which to build, but would not guarantee that a product was consistent, aesthetically appealing, or usable. Our position was that iterative design and usability testing methods must accompany the use of standards and guidelines. This position was not popular since development managers for the new client–server products had not allocated time in their schedules for usability testing and iterative design.

The first complaint that we had about the D&B Software style guide was that it did not often provide yes–no answers to developers' design questions. In a casual survey of questions that came up during one phase of design, one member of the Human Factors Team found that fewer than 10% of the questions that came up during design meetings could be answered with a simple yes or no. A problem with all style guides

Table 1 Examples from the User Interface Checklist

GUI	✓ or NA	Verification List
Mouse input–basic operations		Pressing and holding mouse button 1 identifies selected object
		Pressing and holding mouse button 2 presents pop–up menu for window
		Clicking a control button causes operation to initiate or activate
		Double clicking initiates the defined double–click action as inidcated in the menu.
		Small objects have a "hot zone" around object to increase area where clicking will select the object
		Alternative to double–clicking is provided for essential operations
Keyboard input–navigation keys		Tab key navigates through each field on the screen in left–to–right, top–to–bottom order
		Tabbing after last field wraps to first
		Shift–tab navigates through screen in reverse order of tabbing

is that design principles sometimes conflict ("Put as much of the important information on one screen as possible" versus "Leave sufficient white space to allow for expansion of translated labels"), and resolutions to design questions require careful discussions of tradeoffs and possibly the collection of usability data. The internal and external user interface design classes sponsored by our team are making developers more aware of tradeoffs and the need to collect usability data to answer tough design questions.

Several months after the style guide was issued to all developers, the Human Factors Team was asked to review several hundred application windows from four different development groups for consistency. This was a Herculean task because of the sheer number of windows and the fact that consistency is not a simple concept

(Kellogg, 1989)—consistency has many dimensions. The review revealed numerous inconsistencies between windows within an application and between windows from different applications. Some of the inconsistencies were clear violations of the D&B Software user interface style; other inconsistencies arose because different application teams had chosen different ways to present information. One team, for example, chose to use a strip of icons to choose a set of attributes for customization while another team chose to use a dropdown menu for the same purpose. Both methods for choosing attributes followed the general Windows and D&B Software user interface styles, so in a sense, the developers were consistent with the style guides, but inconsistent between applications. Some of the larger inconsistencies were caused by the lack of communication among the different development teams.

The limited communication resulted from geography, time pressures to complete individual work, limited access to window designs (the code for prototype windows was scattered among a myriad network drives), and reluctance by developers to share their designs until "everything was perfect." The Human Factors Team encouraged different groups to work together, share their designs, and do consistency reviews. We are working on improving interapplication consistency in the next version of products by

- Having formal consistency inspections throughout the development cycle.
- Enforcing consistency through our tools.
- Having the equivalent of a trade fair where developers from different groups can see how others are designing their applications (Good, 1989).
- Creating a catalog of screen prints that can be distributed to all development teams.
- Publishing a user interface newsletter that would discuss consistency issues long before they could be included in the user interface style guide.
- Promoting management support for improving the consistency of our entire product suite.

Consistency of layout is a topic that the D&B Software style guide addresses at a general level. We give general guidance on the spacing and aligning of objects in our windows; however, in our review of application windows, we often found alignment and aesthetic problems. Many of these problems were easily correctable, but developers often considered them unimportant because they were not adding capabilities to the software. Any small set of alignment or aesthetic gaffes probably does not qualify as a significant problem; however, a large number of small problems can take the gloss off an interface and make it look amateurish. To improve the aesthetics of our application GUIs, we conducted half–day and one–day seminars where we critiqued the layout of a development teams' windows. The critique focused on alignment and grouping of controls, consistent spacing between objects, proper use of controls, and the flow of work within a screen (is there a smooth flow from left to right and top to bottom). These seminars worked better than we expected. When an entire team saw a set of screens designed by different people, the inconsistencies stood out clearly. The seminars provided a forum for explaining design principles in the context of the developers' actual products.

We continue to upgrade our D&B Software style guide and are currently evaluating a system for developing an online style guide that could be updated electronically with new user interface standards and recommendations.

Case Study 2: Design of the New Query&Reporter™ Tool

Query&Reporter, a component of D&B Software's SmartStream V2.0 Decision Support software, was a key to the success of our corporation's move into client–server computing. A member of our Human Factors Team played a significant role in the design and evaluation of the product. She used a variety of usability engineering methods throughout the development cycle. This case study chronicles her work. Sales of our SmartStream V2.0 Decision Support software in 1993 exceeded expectations.

About Query&Reporter

Query&Reporter retrieves unstructured data from database tables and presents that data in user–defined reports (Figure 4). Managers use Query&Reporter to support activities like business planning and forecasting. Decision support software is designed for rapid access to corporate data. We built Query&Reporter to be flexible for different types of users. It allows the "ad hoc" design of four types of objects: queries, reports, spreadsheets, and files that can be used by other analysis tools. We built Query&Reporter using a Windows product called Microsoft Access™.

Defining Requirements for Query&Reporter

The Human Factors Team started usability work on Query&Reporter after most of the functional requirements had been gathered. D&B Software determined that the users were people with a wide variety of technical and business backgrounds. The product had to accommodate the needs of both frequent users, such as Management

Figure 4   Query&Reporter main window

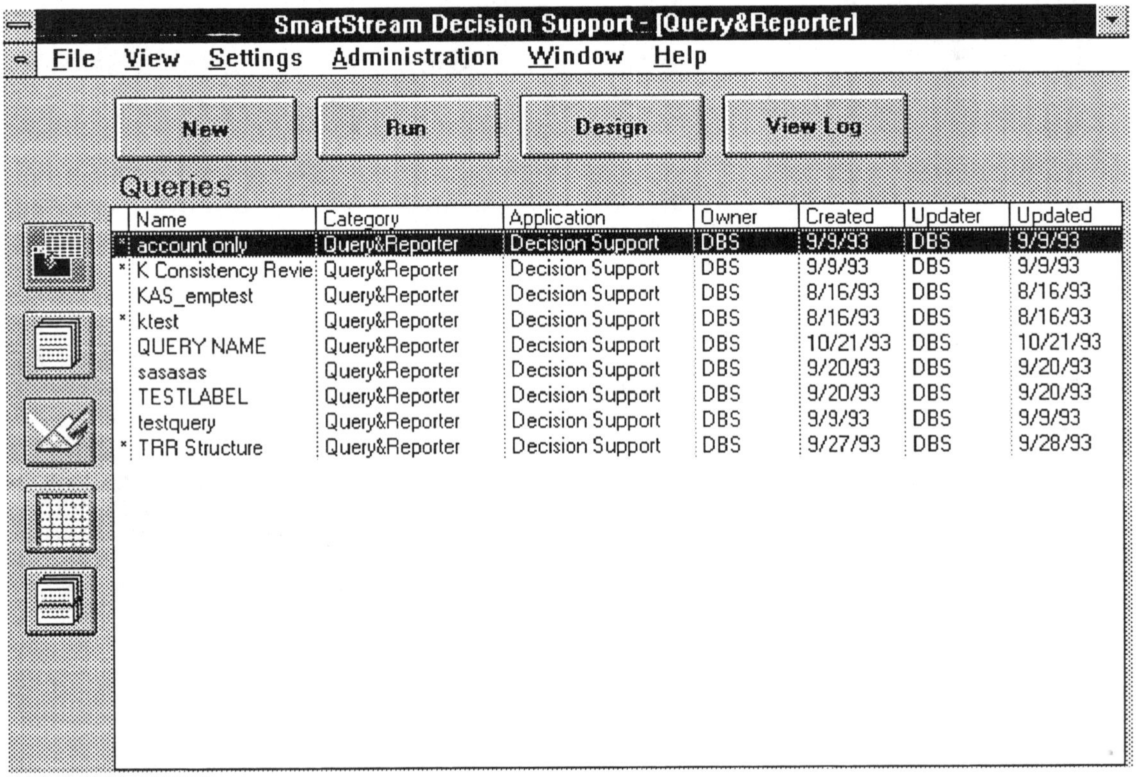

	SmartStream Decision Support - [Query&Reporter]						

File   View   Settings   Administration   Window   Help

New   Run   Design   View Log

Queries

Name	Category	Application	Owner	Created	Updater	Updated
ˣ account only	Query&Reporter	Decision Support	DBS	9/9/93	DBS	9/9/93
ˣ K Consistency Revie	Query&Reporter	Decision Support	DBS	9/9/93	DBS	9/9/93
KAS_emptest	Query&Reporter	Decision Support	DBS	8/16/93	DBS	8/16/93
ˣ ktest	Query&Reporter	Decision Support	DBS	8/16/93	DBS	8/16/93
QUERY NAME	Query&Reporter	Decision Support	DBS	10/21/93	DBS	10/21/93
sasasas	Query&Reporter	Decision Support	DBS	9/20/93	DBS	9/20/93
TESTLABEL	Query&Reporter	Decision Support	DBS	9/20/93	DBS	9/20/93
testquery	Query&Reporter	Decision Support	DBS	9/9/93	DBS	9/9/93
ˣ TRR Structure	Query&Reporter	Decision Support	DBS	9/27/93	DBS	9/28/93

Copyright © Dun and Bradstreet Software Services, Inc.

Information Systems specialists, and infrequent users, such as managers who simply wanted to examine specific sales data. Since Query&Reporter would be used by a wide range of users, product usability was especially important.

To facilitate learning for new and infrequent users, we provided a step–by–step, "wizard" feature (Figure 5). Wizards are tutorials that allow users to do actual work while they are learning. The wizard concept originated at Microsoft and is used in products like Excel, Microsoft Publisher, and Microsoft Access. To address the needs of more experienced users, Query&Reporter allows users to go directly to design screens where they can create database queries and reports without being led through a step–by–step process.

The Development Cycle

As mentioned earlier, some of the development cycles at D&B Software are extremely short. This was the case for Query&Reporter, which had a nine–month development–

Figure 5 The first in a set of eight Query&Reporter wizard windows used to create a database query

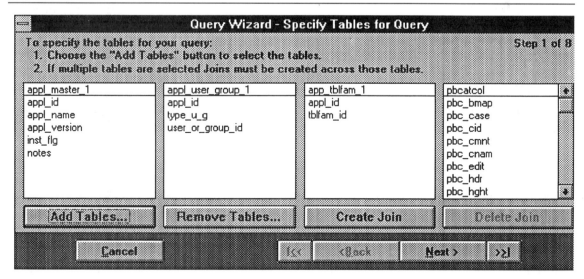

cycle. The product specification for Query&Reporter was packed with functional requirements with a strict deadline for final delivery. This made for a lot of work, but it created an exciting atmosphere for the members of the team and there was a great sense of accomplishment at the end of each week.

Usability Engineering Methods Used During the Development of Query&Reporter

To ensure that usability was built in from the beginning, the development manager for Query&Reporter requested that a usability specialist join her team as a dedicated resource. Karen Stanley worked with the Query&Reporter team as a dedicated usability engineer. During the course of the project, she used a variety of usability engineering techniques, including

- User interface flow diagrams
- Paper prototypes
- Usability testing
- Design reviews
- Consistency reviews
- Interviews and observations at beta test sites

The rest of this case study describes these techniques in more detail and highlights how effective they were in the overall context of product development.

How We Used User Interface Flow Diagrams

At the recommendation of her development manager, Karen and another colleague developed a set of user interface "flow diagrams" to describe the steps users would take to complete tasks using the wizard technology in Query&Reporter (Figure 6). The diagrams contained boxes representing windows. The Query&Reporter design team labeled the boxes with names describing each window's function at a high level. The team then linked the boxes together with lines and arrows indicating the flow of the windows in the step–by–step wizard portion of the product. These diagrams were on paper and low–tech, but crucial to the development of the product.

In early design meetings, the Query&Reporter team used the flow diagrams to drive both user interface and architectural decisions. After each design meeting, Karen altered the flows to reflect the decisions made in the meeting. The flow diagrams were the driving force for three phases of design over a period of about six months.

Karen's role as an integral member of the Query&Reporter design team gave her the ability to make sure usability issues were addressed during the design process. For example, because the system was designed to be very flexible, the user is given many options. Karen made sure that there would be a straightforward way for a user to determine what options were in effect for a given financial report. The product specification did not initially include this as a requirement but it became apparent that users would need this information as the product design progressed.

The flow diagrams made it possible to see the similarities and differences between different parts of the Query&Reporter application. This made it easier to uncover inconsistencies in the user interface, the functionality, and the process flow of the product.

Once the flows were in their final form, and the product design was complete, Karen used the flows as a starting point for detailed window design. The purpose for each window was defined, so now it was time to decide what user interface controls (e.g., list boxes, pushbuttons, dropdown lists, radio buttons) were needed to accomplish the goals of each window. Karen and the GUI developer on the project moved from conceptual design to detailed design by creating paper prototypes of the Query&Reporter windows.

How We Used Paper Prototypes

We used paper prototypes to test individual windows that required difficult design tradeoffs. Participants consisted of internal instructors, writers, the Human Factors Team, and personnel from other parts of the organization, representing a variety of potential users. Participants viewed paper prototypes of Query&Reporter windows and were asked how they would use the windows to complete several business tasks.

Figure 6 One of many flow diagrams used in the design of Query&Reporter

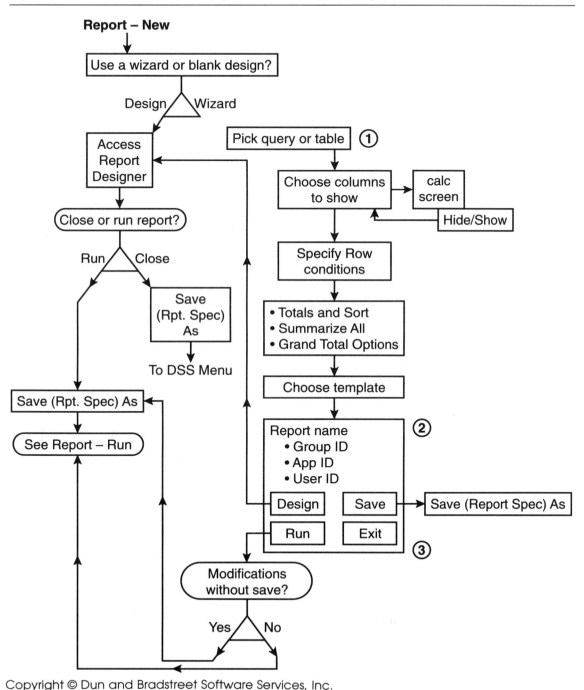

Copyright © Dun and Bradstreet Software Services, Inc.

The usability engineer recorded the participants' responses as they worked on the tasks and used the data to improve the next iteration of the prototype.

In one case, Karen tested different versions of the same window to see if users could create a calculation expression better with a set of buttons or a series of drop-down lists. The expression appeared in a multiline edit box as choices were selected. To make selections, Karen asked each participant to use his or her index finger as if it was a mouse pointer, move it to the button or list choice he or she wanted to select, and tap the paper to simulate a mouse click or double click. To populate the multiline edit box, Karen placed sticky paper cutouts containing the choice text in the edit box as the participant made selections.

The paper prototype sessions yielded valuable data for choosing among design alternatives. It was also fun to create the paper prototypes and use imaginative ways to simulate computer interaction.

Usability Testing

When the first software prototype of a wizard became available, we conducted "discount" usability tests with internal personnel. The usability test of the first wizard prototype had four participants: two internal trainers, one information designer, and one person who worked with financial data. All participants were familiar with database queries and reports. Their Windows' experience ranged from novice to expert.

We conducted the usability test at a workstation without the use of any video equipment. Karen and a documentation manager took notes as the participants stepped through the windows of the wizard to build a query. The test produced valuable feedback on error messages, terminology, interaction with certain controls, button names, and workflow.

We also conducted a usability test on a part of the Query&Reporter product that replaced an existing D&B Software product. The participants here were D&B Software customer support personnel who were familiar with the earlier product. One participant exclaimed that the user interface was "100 times better" than what was in the earlier product. Other participants voiced similar opinions. During testing we found that a critical piece of functionality had been missed in the design of the product. The design was then revised to include this functionality. The discovery of missing functionality was an unexpected benefit of usability testing.

Design Reviews

After testing the design of the first wizard (the product employed four different wizards for different tasks) and making design refinements, the second version of the wizard was reviewed by members of the Human Factors Team. Problem areas were pointed out and discussed among the group. Window designs were often reviewed by other members of the Human Factors Team. With only three months to design windows, this was a quick way to detect problems. Often, quick usability tests with the Human Factors Team members yielded critical feedback on the use of some windows.

Consistency Reviews

When most of the user interface had been constructed, we conducted a user interface consistency review. The purpose of the review was to have a team examine the product for inconsistencies with our user interface standards and guidelines. We also had to review the Query&Reporter interface for international design issues since our products are sold worldwide. A critical international design issue for these review sessions involved the space required for the text expansion that occurs when you translate English text. When English text is translated to European text, the length of the text expands from 30 to 300% with short words expanding the most (100 to 300%).

Table 2 Examples of Text Expansion

English	German	Percent Expansion
Edit	Bearbeiten	250
Move	Verschieben	275
Preferences	Bildschirmeinstellungen	209
Update	Aktualisieren	217

Table 2 illustrates the text expansion issue. If our user interface is not designed from the beginning for this text expansion, our budget for international engineering soars. The consistency reviews picked up numerous instances where room for text expansion was not sufficient.

The members of the Human Factors Team, several writers, and one of the Human Factors interns participated in the review. The people attending the review were all given printed screen shots of the windows in the product before the review. This gave them a chance to become familiar with the windows. We stepped through each menu and window. Members of the review team called out inconsistencies for each menu and window. Long discussions were not permitted because the goal was to review the entire user interface and not get hung up on any particular issue.

Exposing the product to a larger group of people was a great way to uncover design inconsistencies. We published a list of issues that resulted from the review. Examples of these issues are

- Keyboard navigation between fields in windows did not follow the standard left–to–right, top–to–bottom order.
- Menu items that displayed dialog boxes were missing ellipses.
- Different labels were used for the same control on different windows.
- Inconsistent spacing between controls.
- Error messages did not follow guidelines for clarity and helpfulness.

Karen worked with developers to address the consistency issues. Less formal reviews were held on subsequent updates of the product.

Interviews and Observations

When the design phase was complete, D&B Software installed Query&Reporter at four customer sites. Members of the Human Factors Team and the product development team visited test sites and observed customers using Query&Reporter and other D&B Software products. The field interviews confirmed the value of our usability work on the Query&Reporter Wizards, but also yielded many new insights on ways to make our products better.

During the D&B Software beta test for our client–server products, the Human Factors Team collaborated with our training group to get usability feedback during customer training sessions. Our team was introduced to customers at the beginning of training. The customers were told that we were interested in any feedback about our software, our documentation, or our training methods that we could use to improve our products. During hands–on exercises with our applications, customers were invited to call us over when they encountered things right or wrong with our products.

The training sessions provided an overwhelming amount of usability data. Customers pointed out everything from typos in the online help to shortcuts that would make them more productive. In one session, we collected more than 20 pages of feedback. At the end of each training day, we asked the trainer and all other D&B Software personnel to leave the room while we conducted a focus group with the customers. During the focus group, we asked about the day's highlights and lowlights, the training approach, and major usability issues. The daily focus groups were well received because customers could voice their opinions immediately, rather than waiting to fill out a questionnaire on the last day of class. We used the feedback from these sessions to make changes to the instructional methods, our documentation, and the user interface of our products. The feedback also revealed requirements that will be considered in the next version of the product.

Lessons Learned

We have learned some important lessons in our brief existence as a Human Factors Team. We hope they will be helpful to other fledgling teams.

- We found that it helps to have team members with varied backgrounds and experience. The four of us come from very different educational and employment backgrounds. We also have varied strengths and weaknesses. Our varied backgrounds allow us to share different perspectives, which is particularly effective during brainstorming and design sessions. We can think up innovative approaches based on a combination of what we have tried elsewhere.

- Group support is important in our environment. Off–site team meetings can be helpful. We get away from the office to discuss how we are doing, what challenges we face, and what we need to do on a companywide level. The meetings brought us closer together and helped us figure out how we can support each other better. This is an important issue for us, since we are such a small group supporting such large systems.

- Moving from a technology–focused design process to a user–centered design process does not happen overnight. It takes time to build credibility with management, account representatives, the field, and customers.

- Interpersonal skills are very important. We must be sensitive to the backgrounds, needs, and personalities of the people we interact with. The temperament of the people on the Human Factors Team can be more important than their credentials. We keep this in mind when interviewing potential hires. People who are candidates for user interface design work must have thick skins. The user interface for a complex product will get both kudos and boos, and user interface designers must be prepared for both.

- We wear many hats. We are GUI specialists, online help design experts, graphic designers, trainers, user advocates, testers, consultants, police officers, and advisors all rolled into one. This is what makes our job challenging and exciting, but it means we must always keep learning, and we must know where to go when we do not have answers.

- We spend a lot of time "evangelizing," or changing people's perceptions of human factors and usability. We teach people that usability is not just "making it pretty" or "cleaning up the windows."

- People often want yes or no answers to usability issues, but much of the time that is not possible. We continue to push for iterative design and usability testing, explaining that GUI design is an ongoing process.

- Geographic separation makes communication harder but not impossible. With our two largest facilities in Framingham and Atlanta, and many other sites around the world, we spend a lot of time in video conferences and teleconferences. One thing that we have learned is that it is critical to have some face–to–face meetings and not rely exclusively on electronic meetings. It is hard to build personal relationships when communication is purely electronic.

- Consistency and standards are important, particularly with systems this big. It is helpful to memorize the Windows GUI guidelines (Microsoft Press, 1992) and the internal standards. However, it is also important to recognize that standards can go only so far and to convey this to others.

- Customer training classes are rich sources of usability data. Usability specialists can benefit from collaboration with instructional designers and trainers.

- With systems this big, and schedules this tight, we never have time to do everything as thoroughly or as scientifically as we would like. We have to make trade-offs, such as sometimes using internal personnel for test participants instead of using customers and usability testing only the most critical or complex component. We have to keep in mind that any contribution we make will improve the product and not let the immensity of the project overwhelm us.

Acknowledgments

Thanks to Douglas Bayer, a truly supportive director at Dun & Bradstreet Software, and to Carol Govoni, the development manager of Query&Reporter who promoted usability engineering throughout development. Thanks to Michael Wicklund, the editor of this book for his patience, quick reviews, and understanding nature.

Microsoft and Microsoft Access are registered trademarks, and Windows and Visual Basic are trademarks of Microsoft Corporation.

Lotus and Lotus Notes are registered trademarks of Lotus Development Corporation.

Query&Reporter is a trademark of Dun & Bradstreet Software Services, Inc.

PowerBuilder is a trademark of Powersoft Corporation

ReachOut is a trademark of Ocean Isle Software

pcANYWHERE for Windows is a trademark of Symantec, Inc.

Close-Up is registered trademark of Norton-Lambert Corp.

SmartStream is a registered trademark of Dun & Bradstreet Software Services, Inc.

References

Good, M. (1989). "Developing the XUI Style," in J. Nielsen (ed.), *Coordinating User Interfaces for Consistency*, pp. 57–73, Academic Press, Boston.

Gould, J. (1988). "How to Design Usable Systems," in M. Helander (ed.), *Handbook of Human–Computer Interaction*, pp. 757–789, North–Holland, Amsterdam, The Netherlands.

IBM. (1989). Systems Application Architecture: Common User Access Advanced Interface Design Guide. Document Number: SY0328–300–R00–1089.

Kellog, W.A. (1989). "The Dimensions of Consistency," in J. Nielson (ed.), *Coordinating User Interfaces for Consistency*, pp. 9–20, Academic Press, Boston.

Mayhew, D.J. (1992). *Principles and Guidelines in Software User Interface Design*, pp. 312-315, PrenticeHall, Englewood Cliffs, NJ.

Microsoft Corporation. (1992). *The Windows Interface: An Application Design Guide*. Microsoft Press, Redmond, WA.

Nielsen, J. (1989). *Coordinating User Interfaces for Consistency*. Academic Press, Boston.

Nielsen, J. (1993). *Usability Engineering*. Academic Press, Boston.

Spool, J. (1993). Product Usability: Survival Techniques. Seminar presented to D&B Software.

Whiteside, J., Bennett, J., and Holtzblatt, K. (1988). "Usability Engineering: Our Experience and Evolution." In M. Helander (ed.), Handbook of Human–Computer Interaction, pp. 791–817, North–Holland, Amsterdam, The Netherlands.

Wixon, D., Jones, S., Tse, L., and Casaday, G. (1994). "Inspections and Design Reviews: Framework, History, and Reflection," in J. Nielsen and R. L. Mack (eds.), *Usability Inspection Methods*. Book in press.

CHAPTER 14

Interchange, an Online Service for People with Special Interests

Ron Perkins and David Rollert

Ziff-Davis Interactive Design Team

David Rollert   Ron Perkins

Ron Perkins is presently a senior interactive designer on the ZDI Design Team, where he directs the Customer Lab. He started a human interface group at The New England in 1990 and was a founding member of the Human Factors Laboratory at Wang in 1985. He holds a M.S. in experimental psychology from Tufts University.

David Rollert is ZDI Design Director. As a vice president at Citibank, in 1986, he helped to found the Humanware group to design systems for customers and staff and later directed that group. He began his career as a publication designer and started to work with interactive systems at Time, Inc., in 1981. He has a B.A. in the history of ideas from Williams College.

The authors can be reached at rperkins@zdi.ziff.com and drollert@zdi.ziff.com, respectively.

Designing Interchange™

A key theme for the Design Team at Ziff-Davis Interactive is *involvement*. The Design Team is involved in all aspects of product design, including usability, and it also works hard to involve all the other ZDI organizations in its efforts. Though we on the team have made plenty of mistakes along the way, the result is a pretty successful model for incorporating usability and design professionals and usability testing into the development of a very complex product. Before describing the Design Team in more detail, we should explain a little about Ziff-Davis as a whole and about Ziff-Davis Interactive.

Ziff-Davis Publishing

Ziff-Davis Publishing Company is the leading information provider for computer buyers, users, and marketers. An international media company, Ziff-Davis delivers high-quality information about computer products through magazines, newspapers, trade shows, conferences, newsletters, books, market research, training materials, electronic information products, and online services. Its magazines include *PC Magazine*, *PCWeek, PC/Computing, Computer Shopper, MacWeek, MacUser,* and *Computer Gaming World,* along with leading computing magazines in Germany, France, and the United Kingdom. The largest magazine, *PC Magazine,* had a circulation of over 1 million by 1992, making it the ninth largest U.S. magazine, just behind *Better Homes and Gardens* and just ahead of *Good Housekeeping.* Together, the magazines that year had a combined circulation of more than 3.6 million, with ad revenues of $661.9 million, up from $508.0 million the year before. Founded in 1927, Ziff-Davis has more than 4000 employees worldwide.

The company's specialty, besides computing, has been in publishing that is aimed at communities of readers with a special interest in one specific area. In earlier years (up until the mid-1980s), Ziff published such magazines as *Car and Driver, Popular Photography, Modern Bride,* and *Psychology Today.* Ziff is also a leader in electronic publishing, with subsidiaries such as Information Access Company (IAC) and Computer Library, among others.

Ziff-Davis Interactive, or ZDI, was formed in the summer of 1991. At the time, Ziff was already heavily involved in electronic publishing, with IAC a leader in developing and publishing large archival databases, Computer Library publishing the single most successful CD-ROM title (Computer Select), and a rapidly growing presence on the CompuServe Information Service (ZiffNet). ZDI was given the primary charter of doing for electronic publishing what Ziff had already done for magazines: to translate the special-interest model of publishing into its electronic form. In order to achieve this goal, the strategy was to build a new online service that provided customers with both powerful functionality and great ease of use, all in a beautiful package that delivered the highest quality editorial content available online.

The goal was to help busy people with a strong interest in a given subject to compress their time—to save time, not kill time—by making useful information both readily available and easily accessible. We decided not to dwell on the fact that a long line of companies and institutions, large and small, had tried before us and arguably failed at the goals we were setting out. And, of course, CompuServe, Prodigy, and America Online would all argue that they were in fact successful, and in any event they were not about to fold when confronted with the glory of our design, no matter how brilliant. We knew the design alone would never be enough to make the service a success: customers were going to pay their money not for the interface but rather to get at the body of content, tailored to their focused interests—starting with information about computing, where Ziff did have a significant competitive advantage. Of course, if the interface did not represent a major step ahead, that might be enough to doom the effort. So, we started with quite a challenge.

We considered many models for the new service. It could be represented as a library of files to download. It could be a highly packaged service—a sort of online magazine. Many metaphors were considered, as well: a library, a magazine, an online village, a digital pay-per-view cable TV service. After a lot of brainstorming and wrangling, we settled on, of all things, an information service, with the emphasis on *service*. We strove to create a service that offered our customers a way to access a vast storehouse of tens of gigabytes of information focused on special interests, initially concentrating on the computing information that Ziff knows so well (and to which we already own the rights). We half-jokingly dubbed this vast amount of information the Sea of Data. Our challenge was to present it all in a way that enabled customers to navigate and to find things easily and in which customers could comfortably contribute their own buckets of knowledge.

We wanted to build an interface that would add value to the information by culling and organizing it into packages of information that were built around both missions and interests. To do this, we created a structure in which editors assemble different views of our very large database into sections (Figure 1). The point of entry to each section would be a highlights screen that offered an index of all the available items, arranged in hierarchical folders, and featured items that would be of interest to people with an affinity or mission that matched the product's identity. Products would be collected by special interest, for example Computing or News, and laid out in groupings in directories that offered a broad map of the content available (Figure 2).

At the same time, it would be possible to search part or all of the service based on a large variety of criteria. Also, we would make it possible to use the service both online,

Figure 1   Main directory of Interchange

by dialing our host, or offline, by making it easy to mark areas that would be kept up-to-date on the customer's computer. The service would look and behave the same whether or not the customer were connected, though, of course, only the items the customer had marked to be kept would be available offline. We also wanted to make online bulletin boards easy to read and to contribute to in a meaningful way. Given the current expectations in the PC market, we would create a graphical user interface, exploiting direct manipulation techniques and using graphics and typography to present information attractively and effectively.

Interchange will come to market shortly after this is published. Readers will have to judge for themselves whether we met our goals.

Figure 2   Multiple windows, with product view on top

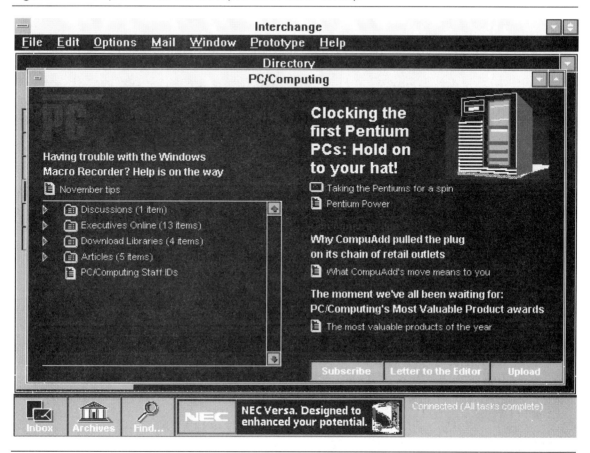

ZDI Design Team

The Design Team has the mission of making Interchange both easy to use and appealing.

Ease of use for us refers both to how easy it is to learn and understand a product and how smoothly and efficiently it can be used day after day. Creating such ease of use, we believe, comes from iterative refinement as much as from conceptual breakthrough. The trick is to constantly simplify both the conceptual model (the picture of the product that a customer forms in his or her mind) and the presentation (the visual appearance) without sacrificing the capabilities that customers will value. This design process simply takes time and invariably frustrates almost everybody involved long before the point of diminishing returns actually arrives. We have embraced the somewhat radical goal of a product that, no matter how functionally rich, requires *no* documentation in order to be used effectively. Our theory is that the cognitive and emotional investment you do not have to make in learning a product you then can put into *accepting it* and *using it effectively*. Many perfectly worthwhile products today do not meet this goal, but we believe that in the near future any great product design will have started out with this aim. Customers are less and less willing to do the work the designers should have done for them.

Appeal is even more elusive. Our customers must *want* the product. They have to be drawn to it, even just looking over a friend's shoulder; and they have to find it satisfying, month after month. With a subscription service in particular, customers have to like what we are doing each time, or they will soon be ex-customers. This may sound obvious, but we think much software design addresses the goal of customer appeal by loading up the product with features that can be advertised on the package. To some degree, this approach has worked for shrink-wrapped software until recently. Things are changing. For example, in the August 1993 issue of *PC/Computing*, a reader survey revealed that ease of learning and ease of use have become far more important than additional features for improving productivity.

True appeal means the product should be a continual joy to use. This is the difference not only between a car that breaks down a lot and one that is reliable, but also with a car that goes beyond reliability to be very safe and very exciting to drive and ride in, and even beautiful to look at. Why shouldn't an information service be something people covet?

We try never to speak of "users," but rather of "customers" or "members." Why bother with this distinction? Think of the common software design goal of "empowering the user." The way to do that, naturally, seems to be with added functions and widgets. Now think of empowering the *customer*. Well, customers are not buying widgets or features; customers are paying you to do something for them or help them in some way. Good design empowers customers by making it easy and pleasurable for them to go about their real business. Learning and using the product is never the real goal, except maybe for games.

There is another way of thinking about users and customers. Users are those annoying folks who hunger for more and better widgets but then never read the manual like they ought to. Customers are people who have needs to fill and should not have to bother reading a manual in the first place.

Designers tend to be drawn from the ranks of people who do, in fact, love new widgets. The Design Team wound up coining the term *widgethead* (as in, "Double scroll bars? What a widgethead idea!") and the widgethead salute (Figure 3) as a way of reminding each other that we are designing to meet customers' needs, not to amuse ourselves.

Figure 3   The widgethead salute

To achieve the goals of both ease of use and appeal, one group of about 10 people, the Design Team, is accountable for how satisfying the customer experience ultimately will turn out to be. The Design Team handles the design of the platform and its capabilities—the user interface design—as well as the design of the editorial content. We also conduct our own ongoing research, running an on-site customer research lab.

How It Started

We can boast of very enlightened management. The design director was one of the first people hired when ZDI was formed in 1991, and the importance of design to the success of the product has been consistently recognized. There has been a succession of doubters at all levels of the company, of course, but generally they in turn have become enthusiastic supporters as they have come to work with us.

Many efforts at usability design do not really influence the product sufficiently because of late involvement, indirect influence, or a subordinate position in the software development organizational hierarchy, among many other reasons (Grudin, Ehrlich, and Shriner, 1987). It has been said that the single most important aspect of any corporate usability organization is the position of its manager (Klemmer, 1989). At

Ziff-Davis Interactive, the Design Team is responsible for the total user experience and is led by a director whose peer is the software development director. Early involvement is assured because the interface design is prototyped and tested in parallel with the development effort. As we have said, designers are involved in every aspect of the product design, and members of other organizations are heavily involved in the design.

At first, our management was not demanding enough of us, being inclined to let us get away with designs that were too complex and off-putting, if well within the norms of PC applications. By now they expect us to come up with solutions that are self-revealing and attractive; so we have succeeded in making our lives harder.

The project represents a change of focus for just about everyone involved. Key people at ZDI have worked on the development of magazines and books, shrink-wrapped software for PCs, computer hardware, public-access terminals, and existing online services. For this project, we are trying to bring together the highest values of each of these worlds. Sometimes, instincts conflict.

For example, how much should we assume that our customers know about Windows standards? Well-mannered desktop applications like spreadsheets and word processors increasingly assume and reward higher levels of platform savvy. But what about when Windows standards are silly? Or just ugly? What if they are obscure? Different ZDIers from different backgrounds had opposite initial reactions to these questions; we wound up looking at our intended customers and saw a group of people who were not in love with the Windows aesthetic but resented having to learn new ways to do simple things they had already mastered. So we kept all the Windows basics—dialogs, key equivalents, scroll bars—while not feeling constrained by the exact appearance of a Windows button and able to reject the Windows system fonts as too hard to read and too unattractive, since people may largely read our content onscreen.

Our Place in the Organization

Like many development organizations, ZDI was both blessed and cursed by having on board a lot of smart people, all of them caring deeply about the quality of the finished product and filled with ideas on how to make it great. We were challenged to draw on the creativity and insight of so many diverse individuals without winding up with a committee-designed mess.

During the development phase, ZDI pursued a course of creating the user interface design and the platform architecture concurrently, with each effort heavily influencing the other. The user interface design was sketched by the Design Team and then tested with customers and discussed and debated with other organizations, particularly the rest of the Development Team—the people who were designing the architecture and programming the actual software. Each round of testing and discussion led to a new round of designs. Increasingly, the design became a collaboration involving the whole Development organization, with the Design Team driving the process and (almost always) with final decisions acceptable to the Design Team. The written specification from which the software was built was drafted partly by the designers, then edited and published by a third ZDI organization that had the specific charter of recording and then monitoring the progress of all requirements.

The customer research lab we built plays a key role in our design work and also in the creation of a corporate culture that considers ease of use and appealing design to be central to its efforts. We built the lab right in the midst of our office space, though accessible directly from what appears to be a public corridor, so respondents usually do not realize it is a Ziff facility. We also publish our testing schedules to the entire organization, and attendance is encouraged by management. People who have observed lab research—particularly on a product they have had a hand in designing—know what an exciting and humbling experience it is.

ZDIers outside the Design Team have attended our research sessions by the dozens and have a good sense of our method and the kind of feedback we get. This does not mean that we can dismiss issues away by saying, "The lab research shows that . . ." There is respect for the value of what can be learned by qualitative research combined with a healthy awareness that our findings cannot be quantified beyond a very gross level and are rarely absolute. We believe more in getting rich feedback from each respondent than in procuring numerical tabulations of errors and success rates. There are two basic reasons for this. First, we find the problems early in a series of respondents and correct or alter parts of the prototype between respondents. This practice would invalidate quantitative data collection. Also, because of the small sample sizes we work with, roughly a dozen respondents for each study, reporting many numbers would lead to justifiable skepticism among our statistics-savvy audience of developers and business people.

The Structure of the Design Team

There are 11 members of the Design Team at this writing (Figure 4), split into three groups: the user interface, content, and research teams. The user interface group takes care of the platform. In the case of Interchange, this covers all the commands and navigational structures, searching, the dialogs, the menus—all the widgets. The team's job is to make sure that the service does a lot with the fewest and simplest widgets. Members of this group tend to have come from other PC software development efforts. They also, as it happens, have often put in substantial time taking phone calls as customer sevice technical representatives.

Figure 4   The ZDI Design Team

The content design group handles the presentation of information. What does it all look like? How is information presented graphically, and how is it organized? Several of these designers also have software development backgrounds. All have substantial work experience as graphic designers, with both print and electronic experience. We have the bias that it is easier to turn a talented graphic designer into a good designer of interactive experiences than it is to turn a human factors engineer into a good graphic artist. Members of this team have worked for public broadcasting, multimedia publishers, banks, book publishers, and software publishers.

The research group is responsible partly for design and mostly for customer research. Design work focuses on issues such as searching tools, general consistency, and concepts as well as bringing literature on applied research to the group. For customer research, the identification of issues, planning, execution, and reporting are most important. This group also manages consultants and outside sources of specific expertise when they are needed. These consultants have major roles in analyzing problems and questioning assumptions.

Educational backgrounds of individual team members are all over the map. Some have graduate degrees; some have no college. Majors and graduate degrees have included psychology (the most common), fine arts, history of ideas, engineering, architecture, and film. The best training seems to be work experience, making real things for real people to use; the best preparation is an open mind and genuine empathy for customers. This may be why a number of these designers turn out to have trained and worked for a time as social workers, therapists, and teachers.

In general, individual designers are assigned to work as part of larger teams that include members of other organizations. The designers organize their own time and tasks to suit the needs of the larger team. For example, the designer who works with the team responsible for creating the News service on Interchange works with the editors directly, and jointly they develop work plans and schedules.

At the same time, an effort is made to move designers between projects periodically, both to promote cross-pollination and also to keep people fresh.

Marketing Our Services

Early on, we had to market our services, particularly with editors and newly hired programmers; both groups were accustomed to having to solve design issues for themselves. The most successful strategy for spreading acceptance of our role is for us to show results quickly; that is, to be a useful resource and a pleasure to work with. Arguing points in the abstract, especially where we did not yet have an established working relationship, led only to tension and mistrust. So we learned to build testable prototypes quickly—if necessary, building both what we felt was right and what the other group wanted. Though a trip to the lab was sometimes necessary, often just looking at the prototypes was enough to settle the matter.

Increasingly, we are approached even before an effort begins. Currently, we have more trouble avoiding unnecessary work than we do in attracting useful work.

Current Resources

We work on both Macintoshes and PCs. Partly, this is because Interchange is being developed for both platforms. Candidly, we also use both environments because, while most of our customers will use Interchange on PCs, we find Macintoshes much more efficient for early prototypes and graphics work, mostly because the available tools are better. Our early prototypes were created using SuperCard. Midway through the design process, we switched to prototyping on PCs using Microsoft's Visual Basic. VB had two advantages: it was capable of simulating most of what we wanted the product to do, and it ran on PCs instead of Macs, which made it easier to do lab testing with our largest customer base of PC users. The drawback to VB is that it requires real programming discipline, and preparing VB prototypes is a rarefied skill in its own right; so we wound up sacrificing most of the time of one of our best designers to making prototypes, as he became our VB expert.

We make substantial use of outside consultants, mostly human factors specialists, who help us by critiquing our work at various critical stages. No matter how good a designer might be, having a disinterested expert review one's work is enormously helpful. With hindsight, we would make even broader use of such resources.

Our on-site lab is our most visible and important resource. More about the lab follows.

Payback to the Organization

Having a staff design team and frequent customer testing at the center of the project helped in many ways. There was increased credibility with both our management and the outside organizations that will provide content and pay for advertising, in addition to increased confidence on the part of the whole development team that it was doing a good job that would succeed in the marketplace. On a practical level, the design team served as a conduit between the various internal organizations involved in development—not the only connection point, but a key one. The lab served both to raise issues that needed attention and to settle arguments that might otherwise have stalled progress. Because of their key role in the product definition, and thus familiarity with all the issues, the Design Team staff also became prime candidates to move into other roles at ZDI; three of the original eight members are now alumni, a trend that will surely continue.

Making Usability Useful to the Organization

Usability and Market Research

Our methodology for evaluating Interchange is a combination of market research and usability testing. Interchange must have appeal from the first impression, being usable, flexible, and meeting members' needs all at once. As noted, the challenge is that, as a service, Interchange must have appeal each time it is used.

The most important question is, "Do customers understand it and like it?" This cannot be answered until they have seen it and actually used it, especially for people who have never used an online service.

It is difficult to measure the appeal of a service for someone who may never have seen it before. Think of the telephone—no one could predict the appeal of it by asking if people liked the idea before they were exposed to its benefits. Since in an online service customers can simply stop using it at any time if they do not understand it, if it is not easy to use, or it they simply do not like it, customer appeal really drives the design of Interchange.

For an overall measurement of appeal, we use a methodology developed by marketers at packaged goods purveyors such as General Foods a few decades ago. A simple line scale allows us to gauge customer appeal by ranking three things relatively: the respondent's present experience, as a baseline; a written concept description, to set expectations and gauge interest; and the respondent's impression after experience with our prototype. We keep track of this one set of ratings on two different scales. First, we want to see if a respondent rates the concept description as better than current experience, and the prototype as better than the concept; we are looking for a two-way win. Second, we are interested to see whether the respondent rates the concept and prototype in the top two points (*very good* or *excellent*) of our six-point scale. Figure 5 shows an example of our line scale, marked the way we hope respondents will mark it.

Figure 5 Line scale with the prototype, concept, and competitor marked

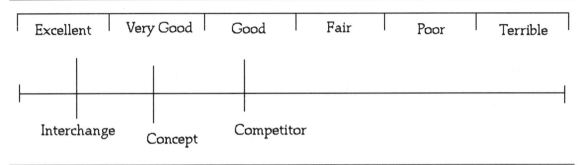

Both scores are useful, particularly the relative rankings. Over time, the relative rankings show less volatility than the absolute scores, since the relative rankings are not affected by whether a particular respondent happens to be a hard or easy grader—all that matters is that we are doing a better job than our competition and than the respondent expected. We still look at the top-box scores because we want to be sure that people like what we are doing and do not simply find it better than other stuff (the competition or the concept statement) they do not like in the first place. Figure 6 shows how our ratings have looked over time, up to the present. Note that the top-box scores bounce around, while the line-scale ratings represent a steady trend as we refine the design. These scores have been normalized to a sample size of 12, which is the typical number of respondents, though individual studies have had as few as 10 or as many as 15 respondents.

We also identify and study usability issues in the context of testing the appeal. Because of the rapidly changing design and the open-ended nature of tasks in an online service, we generally do not attempt to measure errors. Measuring time is also questionable, since we ask respondents to think out loud, discussing what they are

Figure 6   Ratings over time

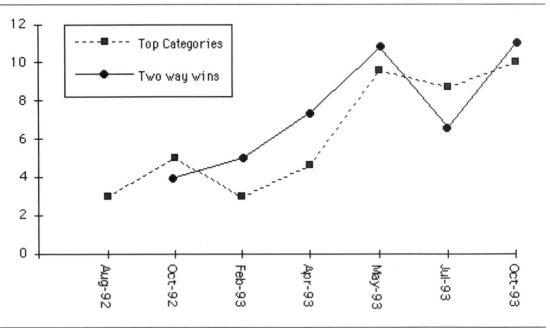

doing as they go. We do not believe in tallying the number of problems identified as an indicator of relative success, but rather look to the overall ratings as general measures of success over time. Generally, the problems are easily noticeable through observation and careful listening, and we just fix them and then test them again to see if the solution worked.

Usability Lab Facilities

As a small group concentrating mainly on Interchange and concerned about confidentiality, we first considered using outside facilities for testing. After surveying the local area and examining the costs, we decided to build our own on-site lab in Cambridge, Massachusetts. The lab, which cost about $60,000 to build and equip, paid for itself in the first year compared with the cost of formal studies in an outside facility. Importantly, the convenience of a lab in the building lowered the barriers to participation by everyone on the project. In an old part of a nicely renovated nineteenth-century factory building—the original Davenport sofa factory—the lab has some brick walls and an arched brick ceiling with skylights. It consists of a waiting room, a simulated office, and an observation room. A nearby conference room is wired for cameras, sound and video to serve as either an extended observation room or a focus group facility when needed (Figure 7). There are no one-way mirrors in the simulated office; we have two unobtrusive video cameras and a scan converter for the

PC or Macintosh display to cover all activities in the office cell. There are pictures on the walls, plants, and wood office furniture, which make a comfortable environment. Keeping the facilities simple is an important part of making usability engineering practical and affordable. We have the minimum amount of video and sound equipment to allow observation, production, and editing. The lab is both portable (on one wheeled cart) and easy to start up, with a single on-off switch. We deliberately did not invest in an elaborate and complex facility as some researchers have warned against [Klemmer, 1989], and we believe this helps in the perception of the lab as a cost-effective and indispensable tool for development.

Consultants as Session Moderators

Since we are involved and invested in the design process, we use consultants to serve as moderators for research. This keeps us honest by avoiding biased interview questions. We also get a reality check from their judgment, since we use seasoned professionals. There are some drawbacks to using someone from outside of our group, as we will explain.

Figure 7 The lab test cell and observation room

Interview Format

We have the interviewer sit in the room with the respondent. Although there may be some controversy in this method, we have found this approach is more likely to keep someone talking, to feel less intimidating, and to go more smoothly when things inevitably go wrong with the prototype.

Using an interviewer who is not intimately familiar with the prototype and the design has its problems: sometimes the interviewer does not know how the prototype works, how to field respondents' questions about the product, or how far to follow a line of questioning that we as designers are interested in. In fact, we have been keeping a list of all the fancy features that one moderator has falsely promised to various respondents. One solution we came up with is to connect the two rooms with Powerbooks via a network. Using the Announce software package, we can pass important information and questions to the moderator unobtrusively; the moderator's Powerbook lives on the floor under a plant by the side of the desk.

High Fidelity Prototypes

We believe in high fidelity prototypes for a number of reasons:

- With good people and the tools available today, a realistic simulation of the product is relatively easy to produce.
- It is the only way to show exactly what you mean in the design. People who have never seen the kind of product we are developing know by the end of a session what it is and whether they like it or not.
- Respondents think that it is real and so can focus on the details as well as the overall product concept and can give additional valuable feedback.
- Many parts of the prototype can be changed, even in the middle of a study, if a serious problem is found.
- Realistic prototypes provide real-world feedback from customers even at an early stage of development; we began testing long before the actual product coding began.

There are also some drawbacks to high fidelity prototypes:

- Respondents sometimes get stuck on details of the prototype and dwell on them. The moderator has to gently but firmly get them back on track.
- Getting a prototype working in the lab usually requires a lot of effort. Often, things will come together just before the first respondent walks in. When creating prototypes, work with trained professionals and, as the saying goes, do not try this at home.

- At very early stages, less than hi-fi prototypes make more sense, especially when trying out different ideas in parallel. Putting a lot of resources and effort into one prototype ironically can tend to lock in the design prematurely; the whole point of a prototype is to be able and willing to heavily modify or even discard the work.

Observing

Much of the design staff, along with developers, marketing staff, and management watch from the observation room when a study session is going on. We had to put an extra soundproofing wall between the two rooms to keep the loud outbursts from startling respondents. Sometimes the tension in the room is similar to that of the audience at a suspense movie, and every move of the mouse brings gasps and groans followed by uproarious laughter or applause depending on the outcome of the event.

There are trade-offs in encouraging such a high level of involvement. You cannot observe a participant's every move and be involved in a discussion about the session at the same time. Inside the observation room, another focus group is going on, where the design team members are analyzing problems and coming up with solutions while the session is still live. Observers can misinterpret behavior because they have not been listening carefully or have stepped in for just a couple of sessions and left. However, the researchers and designers responsible for the service see every single respondent.

This leads to a small dilemma for the scientist in the human factors engineer: you can observe and collect all the behavioral data for an entire study and compile it, analyze it, and prepare careful recommendations in a structured manner. Then you could be sure that no false assumptions were made about the observations and sit comfortably on your data. You must then communicate your recommendations and convince others to implement your solutions. Alternatively, you can involve everyone in the process and risk unstructured design decisions with the possibility that some of them will be wrong.

We believe in the latter approach for its richness, promotion of group cohesiveness, and efficiency of communication. We all can observe and agree on a problem exposed by the testing. Although there may be disagreement as to the actual cause, a new design is proposed and tested in the subsequent lab. If it proves to be the wrong solution, we can revise the design again for the next lab. The importance of everyone being involved is paramount.

Case Study: Testing Interchange

We will use the Interchange project as a case study and a laboratory session as an outline for the methodology we have used. First, some background information.

We are most concerned about the organization of a large amount of information (our Sea of Data), the visual appeal, and the ease-of-use.

By the time we come to market, we will have been iteratively testing evolving versions of prototypes for just over two years. As a case study, we will use the events surrounding a laboratory evaluation shortly before our we settled on the final design to illuminate some of the methodology, examine problems, tell some stories, and show some solutions.

Setup

In the days prior to testing we bring designers, editors, and the usability staff together to plan the scenarios and make sure the prototype supports them. We talk about a new windowing strategy that will be in the prototype; we cannot change it during the test and we are afraid of disastrous consequences. Window manipulation in software is a practical problem with some estimates that users spend much of their time and gestures just resizing and moving windows (Mayhew, 1992). We have had success with a cascading algorithm to prevent windows from piling up, but we wonder if we are solving the right problem. After success over the last few study sessions, it is risky to change something that appears to work. But we have introduced some new screen layouts based on a constant grid for positioning elements on the screen, and the presentation looks much better, with smoother transitions between windows. This calls for a new windowing scheme—bringing windows up in the same location to make screen elements line up seamlessly in the same places and also to behave more predictably. We hope that the new scheme keeps people oriented at least as well as our previous design, in which new windows cascaded from top left to bottom right in standard Windows fashion.

Preparation

For formal labs, we generally use 12 people, much as you would a jury. When a strong majority of them give consistent positive ratings and perform well, we have confidence that the product will make a favorable impression on release.

This time, as happens periodically, some of us have to work all weekend because the test starts on Tuesday and we need to use Monday for piloting. In piloting, we find problems with the evaluation protocol as well as the prototype. One aspect of the service that we are testing this time is the organization of the content. One of the editors, who has the job of choosing, organizing, and presenting content, writes a few new tasks to be included in the testing. She wants to make sure her content gets covered well.

Interviewing

As we discussed earlier, we want to know if the concept of Interchange sounds better than what people use now (they read a description) and then if those expectations are exceeded when they use the prototype.

The sessions we run last about 90 minutes. We verify the background and key information about respondents so we have a better idea of how to interpret what they do and say. Sometimes, the recruiting information turns out to be wrong. We have them read about the service in the concept statement, give them a set of tasks to complete, and then debrief them on any problems that they had. We use a simplified thinking-aloud method without elaborate protocol analysis (Neilson, 1993). During the course of a session, respondents are asked to rate overall their present experience with competitive products, then the written description of the new product, and finally the prototype they used.

Day One: It's Only a Prototype

The first day of testing reduces our anxieties as four people go through the tasks very quickly and give us high ratings, scoring the concept as better than their current experience and then rating the prototype even higher than their expectations. We are also getting higher absolute grades than earlier, with all four rating the prototype as very good or excellent. The new windowing scheme seems to make no difference in respondents' ability to stay oriented, while helping to get us higher marks for visual appearance and clarity. There is a key concept with which people are getting confused and some trouble with a dialog box that has been vexing us, but nothing significant is going wrong. The prototype does not even crash, despite its last-minute completion.

We make some changes to the prototype between respondents to try some new wording of dialogs and even the name of an icon. It seems foolish to waste respondents on facets of the design we already know need improvement. We feel comfortable changing the design in small ways during the course of a study since we are not tabulating our results, given the small sample sizes. Instead, we will analyze each respondent individually for clues on how to improve the interface.

Day Two: Seeing Dinosaurs

One respondent says, "I'm beginning to see how truly useful online services could be." We hope that if we are successful, no one will talk about the user interface, only find the content easy to access and appealing to use. The interface is free of obvious gee-whiz features, by design. This philosophy is not easy to sell to all software developers, but we think customers find value in clarity and simplicity more than in the semblance of power. We are looking for a successful session where at the end, when asked about the product, respondents will mention only content issues, essentially taking the interface for granted.

We forgot to tell John, the study moderator, that we changed a critical icon name. After the respondent fails to perform the task, John tells him to pick it by name, but it does not exist. This is hard enough on people as it is. We send John a message on the Powerbook, and he recovers.

All sorts of issues emerge in these studies. This time, respondents begin to see one carefully crafted icon as a Tyrannosaurus Rex eating a piece of paper (Figure 8). The concept we have been carefully goading respondents to understand is represented by an image of a hand proffering a document that also really does look like a dinosaur, now that they mention it.

Both days bring high ratings and lots of positive quotes. Everyone can feel the respondents' excitement, which is much more pronounced than in our previous studies, and it is particularly rewarding for us to see people actually using and enjoying this heavily evolved prototype.

Figure 8   The dinosaur icon

Ratings

On the single horizontal line, respondents rank each of the three reference points—current experience, concept statement, and experience with the prototype—either higher or lower than the previous and discuss the reasons why they chose that rank. One respondent says "This isn't as good as it sounds because I didn't see any Internet support." Knowing exactly what smaller decisions influence the overall scoring lets us know on what perception or dimension we need improvement; in this example, we do have Internet support, but that fact is not clear enough. Although this is qualitative research, the rating scale is used as a bottom line summary to track progress, as we explained earlier. Over time, we had seen our ratings go from basically neutral to very positive. In this study, for the first time, no one will rank the concept statement lower than his or her current experience, and no one will rank the prototype as falling short of the concept, though there will be one tie in each case. This is a far cry from the early days, when we were only seeing one-third of the respondents give us two-way wins, with the concept scoring better than current experience and the prototype exceeding expectations from the concept. We clearly are getting closer and closer to the mark.

Day Three: The Dialog Box from Hell

The last day of testing brings a standing-room-only audience to the lab, with up to 20 people crowded in at one time, due to the broadcast message we sent out to the project team about the success of the previous two days. At the same time, we are still watching the evidence mount against a particular dialog box.

Respondent number 11 has discovered a feature that we intentionally did not include in the task list because its appeal overshadows the other aspects of the service we are testing this time. This feature allows a customer to compose a search for specific information and then effectively to subscribe to that custom search, which can be run whenever desired to fish the Sea of Data for information that matches the criteria. This respondent sets it up to notify him each time a new article on notebook computers comes out. He clearly is thrilled by this feature, and his enthusiasm gives us all a sense of satisfaction.

One goal we have is to give the customer the experience that new discoveries are rewarded whenever they try something reasonable. Like on a good automobile, when you reach for where the drink cup holders should be and they fall readily to hand, you know someone was thinking of you. Wherever the customer goes, we want them to feel as though we have been there first.

A case in point is shown by a pattern that keeps getting clearer as we complete the testing. There is one dialog box where we have obvious problems: it stops cold everyone who sees it. Many have figured it out, but only under duress, and it truly appears to be the dialog box from hell. This is a serious problem, not only because it is not up to our usual standards, but also because it comes smack in the middle of using one of our most important features: the ability to maintain a list of items that will be automatically updated on the customer's computer each time he or she connects to the service. Respondents who use the command that updates items are confronted by the dialog box in Figure 9, which is intended to help them specify just what they want to update.

Figure 9 The dialog box from hell

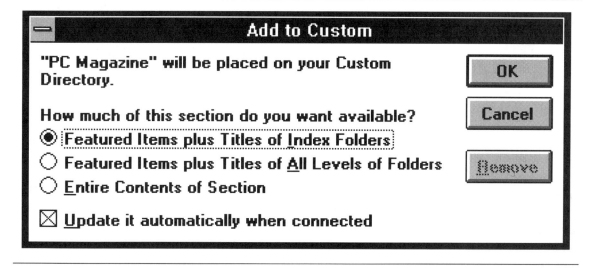

Notice the six different terms representing three concepts. There are four instances of jargon, diverse levels of obscure reference, and indirection. Some of the terms mentioned do not even appear in the interface for reference. We honestly can not believe that this got into our design. In subsequent weeks, we labor over the wording of this dialog box before concluding that the whole design is wrong, since it requires too many decisions to be made at once. Although it is very late in the development cycle, we propose a substantial redesign of the feature. The same capabilities remain, but are presented differently. The constructs addressed by the infernal dialog box are now handled by separate actions that combine to give the same capabilities. Now, no dialog box at all will confront our customers, but they will be able to do the same things. In the new design, they mark the specific items they want to update using a menu command. At this writing, we are busily building a prototype of the new solution for a quick test. Just because it is different does not mean it is better. We thought the old design was pretty wonderful until we built a prototype and tested it.

Showing Results

One of the goals of the research lab at ZDI is to make usability practical for the organization. We cannot afford to have a white-coated scientist's attitude. Senior managers do not read (or trust) lengthy reports, nor are they concerned with details of methodological rigor or brilliance. Developers, editors, and designers, our primary clients, also lack the time to check references for related research, interpret statistics, or learn theoretical principles of human cognition.

First, because of the intense involvement of the team members, less reporting is necessary than might otherwise be the case. We generally reach a consensus on the solution to key design issues on the merits of the arguments. Senior managers are willing and able to make the decisions, but generally do not need to.

Reporting to the larger organization of management, marketing, software development, and editorial staff is also reduced because of their direct observations of lab testing. Before each study, we use Lotus Notes to post a brief synopsis of the plan, recruitment screeners, and any test instruments or surveys into a database that anyone can access. During the study, we send out updates to keep team members posted on current successes and failures of the design. Soon after a study, we create a video highlights tape and give a brief presentation to which the entire ZDI organization is invited. About 15 to 20 minutes covering first impressions, a few successes, key design failures, and customer quotes gives a good overview of the process and results.

Some tips for getting large turnouts at presentations are to keep the data reporting succinct, the individual video clips reasonably short, and to be sure to include a little humor. We have found that presenting detailed charts about the population demographics and overall line scores for the prototype gets boring very fast. Seeing a set of video clips of two to four people exhibiting the same angst or delight is an effective way to tell the story of what it feels like to be a customer; anecdotes are very persuasive. Finally, respondents making very funny comments, designers parodying the testing process, or clips from your favorite movie or TV show can add entertainment value that holds the audience's attention. Some might think that showmanship is out of place in the presentation of research results, but we feel that all the careful studies in the world are useless if the important messages are not communicated effectively to the whole development organization. We also have found that people take us and our findings more seriously if we do not appear to take ourselves overly seriously.

Lessons Learned

A key lesson is organizational. We found it very difficult to keep all the other organizations sufficiently involved in the design while at the same time keeping them from dominating or bogging down the process. It seems that things went best when we solicited lots of early input through interviews and brainstorming, then formulated a well-thought-out proposal, and quickly invited key individuals from other organizations to discuss the proposals with us. Things went terribly when we failed to follow any of these steps. The worst times were when we attempted to lay out large parts of the design in isolation and then present this work in progress in formal reviews attended by large groups who had never before seen what was being presented.

Yin and Yang

Some things we did turned out to be both successes and failures. Doing the user interface design and the platform architecture simultaneously was one of the best things we did, and one of the most troublesome. The good news is that the product embodies the best concepts of both the Design Team and the Development Team. The bad news is that it took a long time (at least, what felt like a long time) for the vision to gel, and there were plenty of drawn-out arguments and frayed nerves along the way. One thing that helped was ZDI's heavy reliance on Lotus Notes. By conducting the bulk of our interorganizational design discussions in Notes databases and making those discussions open to the whole organization, we were able both to make everyone feel included and to avoid frequent large and lengthy meetings. We can also go back to see the reasoning behind design decisions, in case we (or respondents) change our minds again.

Organizational Memory

In an early version of the prototype, we tested a "channel changer" metaphor for the service directory (Figure 10). The design assumption was that people would use these buttons to scan across special interest areas quickly to see what was new and of interest. In the lab, it tested rather badly, with people getting completely confused; the experience sufficiently traumatized us that we regressed to a "file folder" metaphor for the service directory. Had we carefully analyzed why the channel changers failed, we would have progressed much faster.

Instead, for subsequent labs, the audience (designers, developers, management) all remembered how badly the channel changers worked and how easily people could use the file folder tabs, so it took us four months to get a viable design beyond the fall-back file folders—which almost no one really liked. The lesson we learned here was to analyze problems early and fix them immediately to keep the design fluid during early stages.

Figure 10   Early channel changers, file folders, and final channel changers

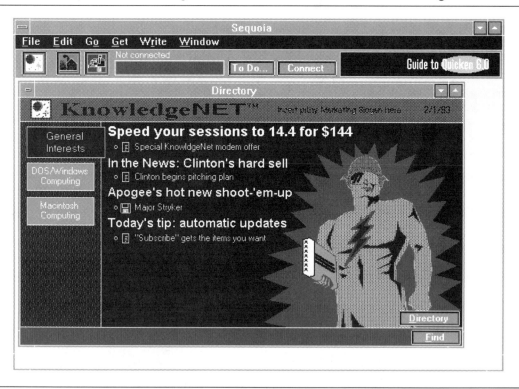

Figure 10   Early channel changers, file folders, and final channel changers (Continued)

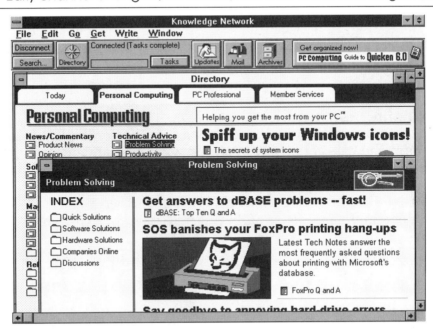

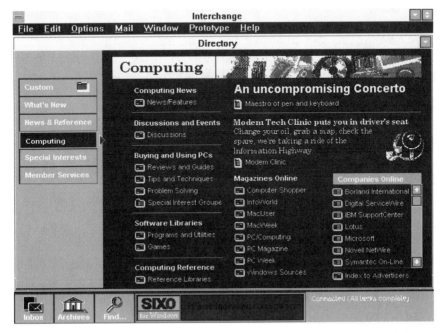

In the end, most of ZDI came to feel that the resulting design was largely their product, rather than the dictate of the Design Team. We like to think that we coopted everybody, but the truth is that we have a much better product than if we had defined the whole thing by ourselves, since developers and editors had many of the key creative insights based on their different experiences and knowledge.

Early Marketing Group Relationships

We have a warm and collaborative relationship with the Marketing group at ZDI. We share ideas and judgments, as well as data from our research efforts. We do not worry about turf when conducting research, but do make sure not to duplicate efforts. It would have been nice to develop the collaboration sooner. If we had, we probably would have done more and better early research about our customers' information habits and desires.

Healthy Suspicion of Early Consensus

While striving for consensus, at the same time we learned to be suspicious of ideas that were quickly popular with everyone on the ZDI team. The fact that such concepts appealed to the people who were intimately involved with every detail of the product tended to forecast that they would turn out to be too complicated for our customers. Not that our customers were simpletons: on the contrary, we were targeting sophisticated computing professionals. But even self-styled power users have neither the time nor energy to master needlessly complex constructs.

Understanding the Right Customer Population

We kept relearning the importance of recruiting lab respondents that accurately represented our intended customers. Recruiting questionnaires intended to screen out unlikely customers can turn out to be too porous, letting in people who are unlikely to ever want the product. By using lists of subscribers to Ziff publications, early on we recruited a lot of assistants and secretaries, since they answered the phone when we called the offices of the people who actually read the magazines. We have nothing against secretaries—as long as they happen to be interested enough in Interchange to subscribe to it and use it. Most of these folks were not. We then tightened the screening to the point that we only got engineers and technical support professionals, both groups that constitute an important part of our customer base, but cannot necessarily speak for all of our customers.

Keeping Research Confidential

We asked respondents to sign nondisclosure agreements before seeing the prototype, and none betrayed the confidence as far as we can tell. Still, judgment calls are necessary: even if you are inclined to trust someone's honesty, you still can not afford to show your business plans or your best ideas to a direct competitor. One respondent turned out to be a consultant to two of our competitors. We interviewed him for nearly an hour on general online issues, gave the person the standard honorarium, and sent him on his way—without showing him the prototype and without the respondent realizing that his session had been truncated.

Perfectionism

We found it hard to let go of a design element until we felt it was perfected and thoroughly tested. While this felt like a healthy and principled attitude, such perfectionism can have more to do with lack of courage than with creating the best possible product. There were times, especially early in the process while the product was still being defined, when our reluctance to map out proposals tried the patience of our colleagues and delayed progress. This was compounded by the natural tendency of developers to insist that all specifications be "final." In practice, progress came much faster and results were much better once we were willing to specify things as well as we could at that moment in time—being prepared both to live with our decisions if we had to and to revisit them if we could. Of course, this approach only works when there is a high level of trust and respect between organizations. Developers have to believe that designers will not attempt to change the specifications arbitrarily, and designers need to feel that developers care deeply about the quality and usability of the finished product and will strive to accommodate improvements.

Empathy and Leadership

Finally, even in a hospitable environment like ZDI's, design groups naturally slip into a service bureau mentality, reacting to deadlines and requests that come from other organizations. We have been no different. Partly, this service attitude is a deliberate strategy to influence thinking without appearing to be prima donnas from another planet, which is the other stereotypical stance for a design group. To some degree, it may be in the nature and personality of good, empathetic designers to strive to accommodate others' needs. Still, we hope that in the coming years design and usability professionals will increasingly feel confident and empowered to lead design efforts—not to the exclusion of other talent and disciplines, but without waiting for the go-ahead from developers and business people. This leadership calls for laying out visions and goals, to be sure, but it also involves the simple mechanics of purposefully and reliably producing workplans and schedules and specifications and prototypes and doing it better and faster than anyone expected. This takes some courage, and calls for overcoming perfectionism, but as a designer you just need to remind your empathic soul that you are doing it for the sake of those poor benighted customers who otherwise would not have the best possible products to brighten and improve their lives.

References

Grudin, J., S. F. Ehrlich, and R. Shriner. (1987). "Positioning Human Factors in the User Interface Development Chain," *Proceedings, CHI 1987*, pp. 125-131. Association for Computing Machinery.

Klemmer, Edmund T. (1989). *Ergonomics: Harness the Power of Human Factors in Your Business.* Ablex Publishing, Norwood, NJ.

Mayhew, Deborah H. (1992). *Principles and Guidelines in Software User Interface Design,* p. 447. Prentice-Hall, Englewood Cliffs, NJ.

Neilson, J. (1993). *Usability Engineering,* p. 18. Academic Press, Boston.

CHAPTER 15

The Evolution of Broadband Work in Ameritech's Customer Interface Systems and Human Factors Department

Arnold M. Lund
Ameritech

Arnold M. Lund received his B.A. degree in chemistry from the University of Chicago in 1972, his M.A. in psychology from California State University, Fullerton, in 1977, and his Ph.D. in experimental psychology from Northwestern University in 1980. From 1980 to 1989, he worked at AT&T Bell Laboratories where he supervised human factors and systems engineering groups. Since 1989, he has been with Ameritech, where he is manager of the Customer Interface Systems and Human Factors department. His department is responsible for multimedia applications, speech interfaces, graphical interfaces for network management, expert systems, and interfaces to new residential and business services. He is a member of the Human Factors and Ergonomics Society , ACM, and IEEE, a member of the HFES HCI Standards Committee, program-chair of the Communications Technical Group of the HFES, and past-president of the Chicago Metropolitan Chapter of the HFES. His publications have appeared in the SMPTE (Society of Motion Picture and Television Engineers) *Journal, the* IEEE Journal on Selected Areas in Communications, *the* International Teleconferencing Association Yearbook, *the* Journal of Experimental Child Psychology, *and the* Journal of Experimental Psychology: Human Learning and Memory.

On the first day of my new job at Ameritech, I sat in my apartment and thought about when I should show up for work. No one had told me when the workday begins, apparently assuming either that it did not matter or that I would know when to arrive. I decided that 8:30 was a good time to appear. I drove up to what seemed to be the front entrance of the new research and development building, walked up to the door, and found it locked. I tried the doorbell. It did not ring. I knocked. There was no sign of life. I then walked around the building and only found one door open. After entering, I wandered down hall after hall past empty rooms trying to find my way to the part of the building where the research and development center was located. I eventually came to a dead end, a glass wall through which I could see some activity in the research and development section. There was no way around the wall. Retracing my steps, I sat in the car for a while and noticed a delivery truck pull up to a shipping entrance. I quickly hopped out of my car, walked over to the shipping entrance, and followed the delivery people into the building. I tried to project the image that I was supervising them. Eventually I found someone who guided me to a bare office and I "started to work." As it happens, the research and development center had just moved to a new building, and this was the first official day in the new location. The challenge was not meant to be taken personally.

I tell this story as a parable for what many people feel as they start a new human factors group. The doors seem to be locked, sometimes progress is made only to be frustrated by hidden barriers, and finally a breakthrough is made (but apparently only by slipping in a back door). This chapter is intended to provide a personal account of building a new human factors department and dealing with these same challenges again and again. Following the evolution of a work program in the area of broadband services, it will describe typical decisions made and the reasons behind them, lessons learned, and how the work itself was shaped by the environment.

Corporate Context for Work

Ameritech provides full service communications and advanced information services to about 12 million customers in the midwestern United States. These services include traditional telephony services (local telephone service with enhancements such as call waiting and voice mail), cellular telephone service and support for new wireless portable computers, teleconferencing services, business communications services, and so on. It also provides services in New Zealand, Poland, and other international markets. Ameritech was founded in 1984 with the breakup of the AT&T Bell System and is one of the seven regional companies created by the divestiture.

When Ameritech was formed it inherited a monopoly culture that it took several years to overcome (Kleinfield, 1981). The company was not market oriented. It tended to view itself as a utility, with the goal of providing universal telephone service. Projects moved slowly, although the results were generally of high quality. Few risks were taken in introducing new products. The highest priority products tended to build on traditional telephone service (e.g., call waiting). It was assumed that internal systems did not require special efforts to be made usable, since employees would be around long enough to learn to use them no matter how they were designed.

The company had grown large and Ameritech was a company where the employees felt they would spend their entire working careers (as they had when Ameritech was part of AT&T). Ameritech was very hierarchical. The state telephone companies operated relatively autonomously, and distrust of centralized planning organizations and technical specialists from the "outside" persisted from predivestiture days. Careers were developed by moving through the hierarchy to gain a breadth of experience. Success was often defined as not making waves. Decisions were conservative and territory was protected.

In the late 1980s it became clear that the competition was entering the local telephone service market. Cost savings became important, and a goal of increasing network traffic was defined by management. It was in this environment that Ameritech began to build a research and development center. The focus of the center was on exploring technologies that would address Ameritech's priorities, and the new head of the center persuaded upper management that human factors needed to be integrated into the effort.

As a result, shortly after Ameritech began its research and development program, I was hired to build a human factors department for Ameritech (in March 1989). On the positive side of the ledger there was a general feeling from upper management and many people throughout the corporation that human factors had much to offer in increasing employee productivity and making products "user friendly." There was a commitment to provide the resources required to build a department and see if it would be effective. There was a long corporate tradition of striving for quality, at least in products offered to customers, into which human factors could be mapped.

On the negative side, the human factors department was placed in the central planning company (the Ameritech corporation is made up of several companies). The research and development center in general and the human factors department in particular were being built using people hired from outside the system, and those people were characterized by unique technical skills. Human factors people entered each project as outsiders and were distrusted as a result. Much of what human factors people had to contribute was viewed as bad news (there was no internal history of success stories to demonstrate the result of acting on the bad news). Human factors people identified problems with systems, and dealing with problems slowed system development and increased development costs. Human factors made waves in an environment where making waves was to be avoided. Finally, while many had the faith that human factors would help, almost none understood what it meant to actually do a human factors job.

The head of the research and development center was hired from outside Ameritech. He brought with him many years of experience managing research and development organizations, and at one point in his career he had managed a human factors department. His appreciation of the value of human factors and his understanding of what was required to support it was one of the characteristics that made the job of starting a human factors department at Ameritech attractive. His support has been an important factor in the ongoing success of the department.

Rather than having a human factors group report to a manager in a larger technology department, he created a center in which human factors was viewed as a technical core competency coequal with the other core competencies in the center such as expertise in information, switching, data, and transmission technologies. The authority that this brought became important in negotiating the role of human factors within Ameritech, setting work priorities (when more work was being requested than could be handled), and obtaining resources. It was expected during these early stages that as the research and development center grew, human factors would grow proportionally. Unfortunately, we forgot the corollary that as research and development changed and shrank, new pressures on the young human factors department would also have to be addressed.

Currently, like many companies in the 1990s, spurred on by competition and the need for greater productivity, Ameritech has been undergoing corporate reengineering. This reinvention of the company is attempting to define a new culture and new processes for operation. The focus in the company is moving away from the model of selling services to increase the number of calls on the telephone network and toward meeting each customer's communications and information needs. This fits well into our positioning of human factors as a discipline that helps those needs to be identified and ensures that products meet the needs effectively. The new focus on applications built with multimedia technologies to meet those customer needs has also raised the corporate sensitivity to the importance of human factors in achieving success in the marketplace another notch.

Organizationally (see Figure 1), the company is being restructured into business units (and the state operating companies have virtually been eliminated). Each business unit focuses on the needs of a class of customers, with a network business unit focusing on the needs of the other business units. Human factors is located in the engineering area within the network business unit. It is one of the four technology departments that support requests to implement new services and planning to evolve Ameritech's network and the products and services built using the network.

Figure 1   Organization chart

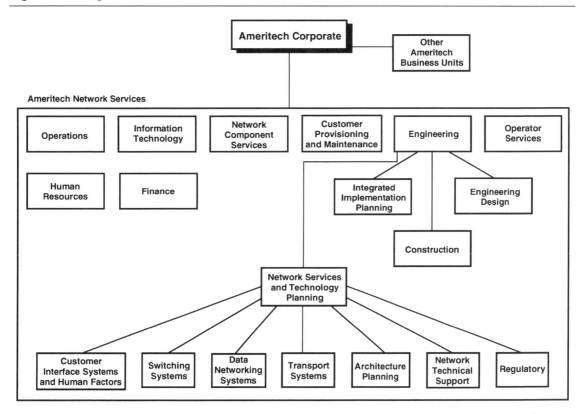

Culturally, the business units are beginning to hire people from the communities they serve to help better understand their customers (e.g., the unit responsible for the financial industry is bringing in people with a banking background). This is resulting in a change from viewing the human factors department as consisting of "outsiders" to one of viewing it as representing the hiring strategy of the future.

Finally, the restructuring process has provided new opportunities to educate the company about human factors. As each new business unit rolls out we have been able to work with the unit (from top executives down) and explain what human factors is and how we can support their business. We have done this by providing a generic description of what human factors is, a history of past successes that relate human factors work to the bottom line (allowing them to build cost and benefit estimates into business plans), and examples their business unit can relate to of how we might support each executive's business unit. We have case studies demonstrating anywhere from 20 to 100% increases in revenue after human factors involvement and 30 to 60% improvements in employee productivity. We still advise using a 10% estimate when building business cases, however, since that is a conservative number adequate to justify the value of human factors and guide the application of human factors to the most important projects. The goal is to position human factors as a solution to problems the units are just beginning to realize they have.

Ameritech's Human Factors Department

Charter

The charter of Ameritech's human factors department is to develop requirements for human interfaces to Ameritech products and services, and the network systems and platforms that support them; and to support the implementation of the requirements. This involves designing human interfaces for new and evolving Ameritech platforms, services, systems, and application concept demonstrations and iterative prototyping, testing, and redesign throughout the product–system development cycle. It also involves participating as a member of the development team (to resolve conflicts between requirements and implementation constraints), testing to ensure the final product meets Ameritech standards before deployment, and monitoring in the field to catch and fix problems arising only through high volume usage. As the only set of human factors people within Ameritech, the department supports (through appropriate charge-back formulas and other safeguards) the needs of all business units and even provides limited consulting to foreign ventures such as Ameritech's ownership of the telephone company in New Zealand (along with Bell Atlantic).

Some work of the department spans business units. This includes the development of an Ameritech "look and feel," internal design standards to bring consistency to a variety of interface types (e.g., telephony interfaces and graphical user interfaces). It includes representing Ameritech on appropriate national and international standards bodies (where the standards activity is viewed as directly affecting Ameritech's business and where Ameritech has a stake in the outcome). It also includes management of Ameritech's investment in academic research activities, Bellcore, and various consortia.

We have also defined a less formal role for ourselves, consistent with being a centralized human factors department. We believe we should strive to ensure that all of Ameritech's products and systems receive appropriate human factors support. One implication of this mission is that we view educating the corporation about usability and serving as human factors proselytizers as part of our responsibility. It is still not unusual to hear comments like

- What is it you do?
- We are shipping this new product tomorrow. We thought we would check to make sure its user friendly. It is, right?
- Are mice good?
- We took a two-day human factors course before we started, so we know our interface is usable.
- Why do you need to do a study? Is human factors not a science? Do you not know the right way to do it?
- The users do not know how to use our system properly. Can you figure out a way to train them?

We know we need to go beyond educating people about what human factors contributes and how it fits within the product realization process. We need to understand that developers, customers, and ourselves all use similar words to mean different things; and we need to carry much of the burden of translation. We need to convey a sense of the issues in usability. Simple questions can sometimes have complex answers. Further, except for those cases where the compelling feel of a product's interface provides much of the value of the product, the best user interface design is likely to be a design that is not noticed at all (because the users are able to concentrate on the tasks to be performed instead of the tools they are using to perform them).

Another implication of centralization is that as we look at the areas where we might provide support across the company we want to make sure we are supporting those projects that are the highest priority projects for the business units and the corporation while also making sure they are the projects where human factors efforts will have the greatest impact on either employee productivity or the customer.

For those projects that the human factors department cannot support directly (due to lack of resources), we work with project teams to help them understand what their human factors needs are, provide them with tools to address usability issues, and work with them to ensure they are able to find human factors support somewhere (e.g., from a consultant). If a business unit consistently has greater demands than we can support, we will help that unit grow its own human factors organization (none of the units have started human factors groups or departments, but we have developed plans for how we will work with them if they do). We are willing to matrix manage consultants or human factors people to ensure the business units receive the highest quality support possible, and we make our lab resources (including support staff) available to support their efforts.

In essence, we are "selling" human factors services within Ameritech. To the extent that we can grow our customer base and satisfy our customers, human factors will grow. Like a business, while stretching ourselves to deal with a growing demand, we have to be careful not to overextend. The expertise we have in specific product or system areas is like a product line and we work from these core competencies as we identify new areas to support. We also invest some effort in work that will allow us to develop new competencies in anticipation of a changing market for our services and to support a healthy department. For example, realizing that wireless communications is one of the technologies that is likely to be important for Ameritech in the future, we have sought the team responsible for this project inside Ameritech and have developed a program to identify the parameters customers use to evaluate the quality of wireless service. This, in turn, has given us the base on which to begin work on designing and evaluating services that will integrate wireless communications into the existing network.

Approach

Our approach to supporting projects is empirical, user centered, and assumes beginning-to-end involvement in the product realization process (see Lund and Tschirgi, 1991 for additional discussion and appropriate methodologies for each stage; Hawkins, 1991). We assume four stages in the process. The first stage is the analysis of the user needs to be met, and this is where task analysis, participation in focus groups, and ideation take place. The second stage is clarifying how the needs should be met and is the time when preliminary designs are prototyped and tested using potential users. The third stage is development and testing. During development support of detailed design activities and implementation tradeoffs is required. The final stage is deployment, when we follow the project to the field and determine whether it is working as planned, making changes when it is not. During each stage, human factors views its role as representing the user and as involving the user in the design process.

Usability in Ameritech means that a product or system is

- Easy to learn,
- Easy to use,
- Useful and effective,
- Satisfying and attractive,
- Safe.

Across projects, we believe it is important to accumulate knowledge that will increase our productivity from project to project (Figure 2). This knowledge might be in the form of generic conclusions drawn from specific studies, the results of studies addressing design issues spanning projects, or the development of design standards for Ameritech. While specific activities and stages at which human factors is involved may vary from project to project, this involvement throughout the process is the prototype we present to project teams.

Figure 2   Lab in use

One assumption we have made is that involvement at the beginning of the process allows larger changes to be made less expensively. Recently we developed a model based on our typical project costs and some assumptions drawn from the literature on continuous quality improvement (Karat, 1993; Nielsen, 1992; Perigord, 1987; and Virzi, 1990), and we now project that early involvement in projects typical of those we support in Ameritech saves approximately 15% in user interface development costs over late involvement in a project and results in significantly greater improvement. On the other hand, we have also found that the usability of a user interface design is highly situation specific. Things that work well in the lab may not work as well in the field. The closer a product is to deployment, the more closely the tests simulate the actual use of the product. The better the simulation, the better the prediction of how the product is going to fair in the field. Our goal on a project, therefore, is beginning-to-end involvement. We want to participate in refining the initial definition of a project, and stay with the project team until we have tested the project in the field and ensured that the final set of improvements needed are made.

Staffing Plan

We initially planned for a human factors department of 15 human factors people. This was an arbitrary number arrived at by my manager based on the expected final size of the research and development center (around 350). My initial sense was that this number was not too far off since early surveys of strategic corporate initiatives consistently resulted in estimates that between 14 and 18 human factors people would be needed to provide support for the most important projects.

Within a couple of years, however, demand for human factors work already required up to 15 to 20 people (and we were staffed at around 7), and we continued to hear about project teams that needed us but that knew nothing about us. At the time Ameritech began to reengineer itself the human factors staff was up to 11 people (including me as a technical manager personally supporting a limited number of projects, an office and lab administrator, and a technical support person for the lab). Approximately twice as much work was being requested as could be supported, and we no longer needed to generate new projects. In addition, a group of technology specialists (including computer scientists, experts in speech technologies, video, and artificial intelligence) was added to the human factors department to create a department with expertise addressing the complete human-system environment.

While growth was slow for a while, with reengineering it became important to develop a vision of what human factors in Ameritech could look like in the future. Questions were asked about where best to place human factors in the organizational structure of the corporation. It could be placed in a business unit (in a marketing organization), in the engineering area (a planning organization), or in information services (the development organization for systems that support business unit operations), for example. It could be organized as a centralized department, or it could be distributed throughout the company.

Ameritech's culture was changing (and continues to change) and each of the options seemed reasonable. The focus is now customers' needs, and with this change in focus is a broadening conviction that human factors will be playing a critical role in the future success of Ameritech. As the process of change began, therefore, several organizations began to vie for "ownership" of the human factors department. Ameritech's future CEO, on a trip to meet with the CEO of Apple, explicitly quizzed him on how many human factors people were needed in a company like Apple. Discussions flourished throughout the various planning teams about how human factors should be managed and how it should fit within the new structure. Every indication was that the demand for human factors support would increase.

To answer the question of how many human factors people would be needed in Ameritech, and to develop a plan for fitting them within the corporate organization, a "best of breed" study was conducted (Lund, 1994a). In this study 20 leading technology companies were surveyed and the relationship between the size of the company and the number of human factors people supporting the company was examined. The human factors programs in each of the companies was mature enough that I expected the number of human factors people would represent a balance of the cost of maintaining a program and the benefits gained from the program. A curve fitted to the data accounted for 76% of the variance. When X equals the number of human factors people that might be appropriate for a company of size Y (in thousands), the equation for the curve is:

$$X = 17.964 \times [10^{\wedge}(.0041606 \times Y)]$$

Using this equation, it was possible to predict that for a company the size of Ameritech approximately 35 to 40 human factors people would be needed. This was consistent with a structure based on a centralized department, with sizable groups in the business units with the greatest number of products requiring support (e.g., consumer and business). A reasonable transition plan, therefore, was to maintain the existing central department and, as the business units mature, to seed the units with people to start new groups as needed. This plan is compatible with published studies of organizational alternatives in the communications industry (Schwartz and Riley, 1988).

Schwartz and Riley, for example, describe the tension between centralized and decentralized human factors organizations. The argument is often made that decentralizing a human factors group, embedding the human factors professionals within project teams, allows individuals to have the greatest impact. Certainly as project teams drawing on a centralized resource become convinced of the value of the human factors group and find themselves in contention with other teams for support, they begin to demand "their own" human factors people. Schwartz and Riley note that, while it is possible to show that decentralized approaches to human factors have been successful, decentralization can cause human factors support to disappear in a company as the problem solving and people skills often possessed by human factors professionals are applied to project tasks that have nothing to do with the discipline.

Centralized groups and departments allow people supporting projects to draw on a variety of experiences, approaches, and ideas. They allow work to be managed more effectively, and as a result they allow for problems to be addressed that cross project boundaries (and as they are solved, organizational productivity increases). They provide a career path for professionals, a fertile ground for training new human factors employees, and an environment in which human factors contributions can be fairly evaluated. A centralized human factors department serves as a magnet for requests and is uniquely positioned to educate a company about how to use human factors resources effectively. For these and other reasons, a critical mass of human factors professionals often grows larger. Many of these advantages (and others) have been described in the literature (Hawkins, 1989).

Kotsonis and Lehder (1990) examined the experiences of human factors professionals themselves. They found that satisfaction with how human factors was organized and the perception of effectiveness increased significantly as the group size increased. They found no evidence of variations in how well people were integrated into projects as a function of type of organizational structure. Successful decentralization depended on individual professionals having a centralized group on which they could draw for professional support and resources. Finally, management support was identified as being critical for the success of human factors, and appropriate support was most likely to be associated with centralized rather than decentralized arrangements.

In large companies such as AT&T Bell Laboratories, human factors organizations seem to go through cycles. A new group is formed, and it grows into a department. Project demands eventually force the department to decentralize. Once decentralized, most of the human factors people disappear, but one or two groups begin to form the critical mass of human factors people that again form the basis of a future department.

Our expectation is that Ameritech will grow a centralized human factors department, with an extensive laboratory and prototyping infrastructure. Eventually several small groups of human factors people will appear within the largest business units. The centralized department can be used to seed new groups of human factors people, and it will be a place to which people can return when their unit's need for the resource declines. The centralized department will serve those business units unable to maintain their own groups and provide some supplemental staffing to the other groups. It will provide generic educational functions as well. This is, in essence, the model adopted by the executive task force in AT&T Bell Laboratories in the mid-1970s (Karlin, 1977; Schwartz and Riley, 1988). The goal will be to manage the relationships with the project teams to minimize the forces that will attempt to break up the centralized department, but to do so with the realization that history suggests these structures are dynamic rather than static and that as a result change should be managed (since it cannot be stopped). This will be new territory when it happens, and so we'll see how successful we are.

Since we are committed to ensuring that each Ameritech product is as usable as possible, while knowing resources for the foreseeable future will not be sufficient to meet the demand, we have developed a variety of supplemental sources of human factors help that we make available to projects. These include hiring graduate and undergraduate students as interns for limited periods of time, conducting joint projects with universities (sometimes using funding provided through corporate granting agencies), leveraging the human factors people working for our vendors, and hiring consultants. The consultants we have hired tend to fall into one of two categories. Some are human factors people between jobs, and others are members of larger firms.

The permanent human factors professionals in the department are all Ph.D. experimental psychologists from a variety of subdisciplines. This is something of a legacy from predivestiture Bell Laboratories and has been a requirement driven by executive traditions from those earlier days. Our intent is a transition to a more diverse employee pool by developing an interim program in which we hire exceptional Masters and Bachelors candidates, and support them while they attain a Ph.D. (splitting their time between graduate studies and project work at Ameritech). Ameritech employees in the past have obtained their Ph.D.s by working 20 to 30 hours a week at Ameritech and spending the remainder of the time on their studies. Other companies have sent people away to concentrate on their studies for 6 to 9 month stretches and have then had them work the remainder of the year on the job.

Since we were starting a human factors department, I initially looked specifically for people with experience in telecommunications. I also looked for people who had demonstrated the ability to successfully (and creatively) contribute to teams and who had demonstrated the ability to write professionally while working in an environment similar to Ameritech's. The former was important because the department's success depends on each individual's ability to be seen as a valued member of a team. The latter was important because I believe it demonstrates the ability to see and address broader issues that transcend projects, in spite of being driven by immediate project demands.

To increase the "energy" of the department as we reached critical mass we have explicitly worked to expand the diversity of the department. As the department grew beyond five human factors people, it also became clear that the addition of a lab support person would increase the productivity of the staff more than using the vacancy for another professional, and we added laboratory-related functions to the job description of what would otherwise have been a standard office administrator position.

Lab and Other Considerations

One challenge I attempted to address up front was career development. In a very large company, human factors people can move from group to group. In a company with a single department of human factors professionals, career options for people choosing to remain within the discipline are limited. I attempt to make it clear to people that there should not be a focus on management. Rather, the focus should be on growing a variety of technical skills and deepening skills. This increases the value Ameritech places on the person and the richness of the tasks that become available to the person, and it opens job opportunities for those that choose to develop their careers by moving to other companies. Dr. Kenneth Brousseau at the 1993 conference on Enterprise Integration at Purdue University described this as the expertise model of career development as opposed to the ladder model. The challenge, of course, is that the corporation is moving from a ladder model to a spiral model (in which expertise changes as business needs change), and so aspirations of the members of the department sometimes conflict with corporate values.

To support the staff, a human factors laboratory has been provided (Lund, 1994b). The core laboratory consists of three individual test rooms (two of which are linked with one-way mirrors), plus a large test room that can be used for focus groups or divided into several smaller units. The total area of the core laboratory is about 232 square meters (2496 square feet). Additional space available for laboratory testing is shared with other departments and covers approximately 260 square meters (2797 square feet). Studies of other laboratories suggest that the core laboratory should be capable of supporting approximately 15 researchers.

Usability laboratory work is supported by prototyping laboratories throughout the research and development wing of our new building. It is also linked to Ameritech's systems integration lab (SIL). The SIL is a microcosm of our telephone network, with representatives of each of the systems used in the network linked and supported as they are in the network. This allows us to test services in realistic environments before exposing them to millions of simultaneous users.

When we first began planning Ameritech's human factors department, we planned on a five-year "honeymoon" (based on the experiences of colleagues in groups and departments similar to ours). With corporate reengineering the honeymoon is ending a little earlier than expected, but fortunately the construction of our laboratory infrastructure also occurred faster than expected.

We also explicitly work to build an environment that supports creative activity. Part of a creative environment is a rich prototyping and laboratory environment, and a pleasant working environment. It also includes activities ranging from working to form the department into a coherent team (even though they rarely formally work together on projects) to supporting the professional activities and professional growth of members of the department. It includes founding a local chapter of the Human Factors and Ergonomics Society to increase regular contact with nearby colleagues (as well as increasing contact with potential job candidates and providing career opportunities for employees in other companies). Most important, a supportive work environment includes having a manager who can appreciate and acknowledge the value of unique human factors contributions.

General Work Plan

As mentioned earlier, the primary goal of the evolving work plan is to be supporting the highest priority projects for Ameritech and its business units, with a special focus on those projects where human factors efforts are highly leveraged in improving employee productivity or meeting customer needs. To grow the constituency for human factors work within the company and provide for changing corporate needs, however, we also manage our work much like a business might manage a portfolio of products.

We try to make sure that roughly 60% of the work in the department is devoted to projects with near-term benefits to the company. This might include designing a prompt for a collect calling service that uses speech recognition or a complete dialogue for Ameritech's new voice mail service. Another 30% of the work supports higher risk projects such as field trials and early concept prototypes. A large field trial of a new kind of display phone with a bar-code reader and the ability to read a credit card (supporting shopping and financial transactions) falls into this category. While the actual equipment and services were not used beyond the trial, the information we gained about user needs and design issues has been used in recent projects. Involvement in more forward looking activities ensures that for critical projects we are involved early enough to make significant changes to the direction of the projects, and we are building expertise that will allow us to be more effective in a wide range of specific projects in the future. The final 10% accounts for work that is as yet unsponsored (work that we believe enhances our productivity, risky projects that we undertake in anticipation of sponsors, and so on). Our earliest work on groupware falls into this category. We periodically conduct Delphi and Delphilike studies during which a group of people iteratively converges on a consensus view of a topic, internal surveys, and secondary research to project where we believe technologies and applications are evolving for our industry. We make sure we are building expertise in these areas.

To illustrate how work develops within the human factors department and the forces that shape it, it is useful to follow the development of the broadband work within the department. It began as forward looking work under the old corporate culture, and it began during the infancy of the department. It evolved through prototyping and field studies, and much of it entered the category of near-term impact. It also began as a cost-savings measure, but has evolved to where most of it is aimed at revenue production. Finally, it represents the development of a work plan that is directly associated with technologies critical to the future of Ameritech's business. The shape of the work plan is now firming even as the new corporate structure is defined and as the human factors department enters a new stage of its development.

Evolution of the Broadband Work Program

Video Conferencing

At the time the human factors department at Ameritech was formed, Ameritech was still focused largely on increasing revenues by increasing traffic on its traditional telephone network. There was a growing feeling among some marketing people and most of the people who had been hired to build a research and development center, however, that future prosperity for Ameritech was going to depend largely on the growth of broadband applications, applications such as video conferencing, entertainment, and others. To be ready when Marketing began to request services we felt we needed to have experience in the broadband area both with the technology and with how people use the technology. As a result, the Information Technologies department in research and development made a proposal to upper management that an internal video teleconferencing network be created.

The primary justification for the video teleconferencing network was based on the savings that would be realized by employees who would otherwise be traveling to corporate locations throughout the region. A secondary justification was that information gained through experience with the network would allow Ameritech to more effectively serve customers with broadband services in the future. Also included in the proposal was the construction of a video conferencing testbed to evaluate technologies and explore new applications and the future creation of a distance learning environment for internal training. Based on these arguments (and in particular the travel savings argument), the project was approved, and it became a high priority project.

For the human factors department it represented an internally focused project with future external revenue potential. It was beginning as a more forward looking project, but was likely to result in spin-off activities with near–term and forward looking implications. The project would build from a knowledge of the traditional communications needs of people, but would allow us to develop a background in technologies that we believed would be important for Ameritech in the future. It had a side benefit of being a project that was of high priority to the center in which we were placed (the organization that would be determining the resources we had available as we built the new human factors department). Further, the people with whom we would be working would be those we were likely to be working with on many related projects, and so building a strong team relationship with colleagues in close geographical proximity was laying the groundwork for years of future activity.

It should be noted that as we interviewed other companies (e.g., Sears) with extensive experience with video conferencing and reviewed the literature, a consistent pattern emerged. These networks are virtually always justified on the basis of savings in travel costs, and the cost savings are rarely found. Instead, people use their travel budgets in new ways and overall productivity increases. One area we believed needed to be investigated, therefore, was how an individual's mix of meetings was likely to be different with the introduction of the technology and what tools would be required to make an individual as productive as possible in each type of meeting. This posed a challenge. We did not believe the justification offered for the network, but we believed the network could be justified in other ways. We chose to try to broaden the expectations people had of the ways in which the network could benefit Ameritech and focus special attention on aspects of the network that we believed produced the most value.

The two projects human factors needed to support initially were the construction of a testbed and the construction of a network. A challenge for the human factors department was that the organization consisted of only three people: myself (the manager), a technical person (who specialized in telephony services using speech), and an office administrator. Neither I nor the technical person had expertise in the area, and the technical person's highest priority projects were those that marketing was currently requesting (consistent with our prioritization audits). Given the project's importance within the research and development center, I decided to support it myself until I could hire someone with appropriate expertise and interests.

Three primary deliverables were defined. These included

- The definition of critical usability issues in video conferencing, to be included in a white paper on video conferencing.
- The design of a video conferencing laboratory.
- The specification of performance characteristics, user interfaces, and functionality for the video conferencing network.

To produce these deliverables I knew a great deal of secondary research was going to be required. I decided to document that secondary research in the form of a guidelines document. This document would evolve as empirical work was conducted and would serve as a deliverable for transferring the knowledge obtained from the internal network to Marketing and to Ameritech's customers. Like other internal standards efforts, it would also allow us to "support" activities that we did not have people to support.

Another activity emerged as a byproduct of joining the teleconferencing team. Once one of the people on the project learned what human factors was about, he became a zealous advocate. He insisted in having a human factors person join him on trips throughout the region and make pronouncements on how local, previously autonomous project teams should fix their problems. Given the importance of building good relationships within an Ameritech where the states resented the intrusion of a central "authority" and the lack of knowledge about the topic during the early days of the project, this put us in a very difficult position. It also took a great deal of time away from work on the primary deliverables that were needed to conduct the analyses with authority. On the other hand, a zealous friend can be important to have when friends are few and far between, so we didn't want to disappoint him. I resolved the dilemma by avoiding presenting ourselves as omniscient authorities out to clean up other people's messes. Instead, we presented ourselves as coaches helping team members become more successful.

I began the design task by understanding the process of conducting meetings, both face-to-face and distributed (over a video conferencing network). I reviewed the social psychological literature on group dynamics, and I studied several face-to-face meetings held between Ameritech employees. While there has been little recent research in video teleconferencing, a great deal of research was conducted in the early 1980s; and I reviewed the literature to discover what is already known about distributed meetings. I also interviewed people who have been building successful video conferencing networks to learn how their networks are used, the functionality that has proven useful and why, and so on.

From this work I created a taxonomy of meeting types. For each type of meeting, I defined the kinds of functions that should be present on the network to support the goals of the meeting. We then worked with people throughout Ameritech who have been running small, local video conferencing applications to determine the types of meetings we needed to support. The highest frequency meetings were project reviews. Extended classroom sessions were projected to be the next most frequent type of meeting. While creative team meetings, where a group of people work on a problem solving or other creative task, were also expected to be frequent, the functions required to support them required desktop conferencing technology that was just beginning to emerge.

Upon interviewing people in Ameritech about how the network might be used, we discovered another important property the network needed to have. It needed to support multipoint meetings. Most teleconferencing research in the past had been based on point-to-point meetings (much like a video telephone call). Ameritech, however, is like many corporations today in that geographically it is widely distributed and meetings frequently involve representatives physically located in each of the five states Ameritech serves. The design problems for multipoint meetings were challenging and included determining protocols for who is "seen" by meeting locations, under what circumstances, and in what ways.

Conference control equipment was acquired that would allow us to program a variety of protocols for managing multipoint meetings. A system allowing the location "speaking" at the moment to capture the broadcast channel was implemented, but we also began to acquire equipment that would allow one location to "look around" a remote location if they chose to observe audience reactions in the way you might if you were in a face-to-face meeting around a table.

We then began creating guidelines for designing video conferencing rooms (Lund and Warren, 1992a), and about this time a second human factors person was hired for the project. Past research was used for the guidelines where it existed. Inferences were drawn from related design problems (e.g., drawing on guidelines from the design of conference rooms and from the design of television studios). Other guidelines were simply based on tables of anthropometric data and quick surveys of existing environments (e.g., the space taken up by papers and other materials during meetings). We conducted research to fill in gaps and update critical design elements (Lund, 1991; Lund, 1992; Lund and Warren, 1992b). We also found internal documents describing guidelines for building rooms, and we worked with the authors so they understood (and bought into) how we were incorporating their work into ours. This partnership helped enroll them in owning the final document, since they were among the people who would need to implement it. Finally, we combined the guidelines to produce a design tool that could be used to lay out new video conferencing rooms based on the space available, and to guide the choice of equipment and choice and placement of furniture. We then made the guidelines available as working drafts to room design coordinators throughout the region. We traveled around the company to brief the teams building the rooms on how to interpret and implement the guidelines in their various situations.

A preliminary test of the guidelines was the design of the video conferencing lab (Figure 3). In addition, a sense of where the guidelines were soft (where little data were available for design elements we felt were likely to be important for meeting effectiveness) led us to design in specific physical elements in the environment in such a way that they could be manipulated for testing. This included a movable wall, tables that could be reconfigured in a variety of ways, and mounts that allowed speakers and cameras to be placed in positions throughout the room.

Figure 3   Video conferencing lab

Since so much of the guidelines document was based on reasonable guesses, several steps were taken to ensure continuous improvement. First, all early users of the network were asked to complete a survey. The survey identified the strengths and weaknesses of the design and resulted in data that would help rank hypotheses about how the design affected meeting effectiveness. As the improvements were made and the network evolved from laboratory environment to delivered, stable service, we designed a new questionnaire.

To increase the percentage of attendees completing the quality improvement questionnaire, a small feedback card was created that only took a matter of seconds to complete and that was easy to place in video conferencing rooms around the region (see Figure 4). The logistics of collecting the data and returning it to us for analysis were also worked out. The focus of the questionnaire was also changed from the gross issues of optimizing the local environment from a local perspective, to the more subtle diagnostic problem of identifying room problems from the perspective of distant rooms. In addition, issues that the new network administrators were becoming concerned about were included.

Figure 4   Rating card

Multi-Point Video Conference Rating Card

Please fill out this card for each video conference in which you participate that has more than two locations in the conference (a multi-point conference). Return it to your room coordinator or to the address on the reverse side.

Conference Date: _____ Duration of Conference (in Hours): _____

Conference Purpose: _____

Location List

Your Location (1): _____ Location 2: _____

Location 3: _____ Location 4: _____

Location 5: _____ Location 6: _____

	No. of People at Location	% of Time Talked
Your Location		
Location 2		
Location 3		
Location 4		
Location 5		
Location 6		

TOTAL: 100%

Overall quality of the video transmission. *(High = 10, Low = 0)* ...._____

Overall quality of the audio transmission. *(High = 10, Low = 0)* ...._____

Overall quality of the transitions between locations.
(High = 10, Low = 0) ...._____

Rate your overall satisfaction with the video conference.
(High = 10, Low = 0) ...._____

Did the conference reservation process go smoothly?
(Very Smooth = 10, Not Smooth At All = 0) ...._____

Were all site connections made promptly and on time? *(Yes or No)* ...._____

Were there any service interruptions
during your conference?
(If Yes, give number and duration) _____

Point-to-Point Video Conference Rating Card

Please fill out this card for each video conference in which you participate that involved only two locations (a point-to-point conference). Return it to your room coordinator or to the address on the reverse side.

Conference Date: _____ Duration of Conference (in Hours): _____

Conference Purpose: _____

Location List   Your Location (1): _____ Location 2: _____

	No. of People at Location	% of Time Talked
Your Location		
Location 2		

TOTAL: 100%

How true of your video conference transmission was each of the following (Circle one number for each description):

		Very		Some What		Not at All
Video was...	Natural	1	2	3	4	5
	Blurry	1	2	3	4	5
	Sharp	1	2	3	4	5
	Smooth	1	2	3	4	5
	Incomplete	1	2	3	4	5
	Detailed	1	2	3	4	5
Audio was...	Distorted	1	2	3	4	5
	Audible	1	2	3	4	5
	Echo Free	1	2	3	4	5
	Natural	1	2	3	4	5
	Inconsistant	1	2	3	4	5
	Crisp	1	2	3	4	5

Rate your overall satisfaction with the video conference.
(High = 10, Low = 0) ...._____

Did the conference reservation process go smoothly?
(Very Smooth = 10, Not Smooth At All = 0) ...._____

Were all site connections made promptly and on time? *(Yes or No)* ____

Were there any service interruptions
during your conference?
(If Yes, give number and duration) _____

A second step to ensure continuous improvement included looking for opportunities to have the guidelines published in such a way that they would stimulate debate and additional research by others in the field that might result in improvements in the guidelines. This included presenting the guidelines in professional forums (e.g., the International Symposium on Human Factors in Telecommunications, the Bellcore/BCC Symposium on User-Centered Design, and others), working with Bellcore to incorporate the guidelines into internal documents circulated to other regions entering the area, and submitting the guidelines for publication in journals where readers were most likely to make use of them (Lund and Warren, 1992a).

Besides designing the functions required to support meetings of various types and the physical requirements of the video conferencing environment, we were also concerned with specifying the appropriate level of video quality for each meeting type. The decision about the appropriate level of video quality on the network was problematic. The technology is changing very rapidly. Costs are coming down for a given bandwidth, and the quality of compression and decompression technologies is improving. These changes are the energy behind the recent growth in video conferencing. Still, opinions about the minimum bandwidth required for acceptable quality for a given application remain strong among many decision makers. The decision about the bandwidth that would be used on Ameritech's network, therefore, was made more for political reasons than good human factors reasons.

One group of people was convinced that 45Mb transmission was required, and for many years educators insisted that, while they could not afford it, 45Mb quality was going to be required for effective distance education. The team with which we were working believed that 1.5Mb quality was going to be what the market could afford and therefore that is what we should use on our network. Research at Bellcore was suggesting that bit rates even lower than 1.5Mb would be adequate, and the experience of companies like Apple was confirming the data through practice; so we did not feel it necessary to "push back" on our partners in building the network during these early stages. We also knew that the network would grow slowly, and the early questionnaire data we collected would provide clues as to whether we were providing adequate video quality to support effective meetings.

We did note two things, however. One was that we had the hypothesis that different kinds of meetings could require different levels of video quality. For example, a collaborative meeting during which the focus of participants was on a shared document and not on the video probably would not require a very high bandwidth for live video. On the other hand, for a broadcast by the CEO to the corporation to convey important information and build corporate consensus, high bandwidth and large images might be important. Second, the debate had been around the bit rate that was appropriate for a given application. This was a mistake, since the quality available at a given bit rate is getting better and better as compression–decompression technologies improve.

What was needed was a set of scales that were capable of describing the quality requirements of video in a given application and a technique for predicting viewer reactions to a given video stream using these scales. We succeeded in persuading the project manager of the importance of this work and initiating a line of work to create these scales, techniques, and associated tools. We were indeed able to obtain a set of scales that captured important elements viewers use to evaluate video quality and to begin to tease out classes of video content (into which video streams could be automatically categorized) requiring different bit rates (Lund and Warren, 1992b). The impact of this work, however, has been felt less in the design of the video conference network itself than in spin-off activities that arose later.

When the network first went into operation it had six rooms. When the network was turned over to the department supporting this area of internal communications it consisted of 12 rooms. It has grown continuously until it now consists of 44 rooms, not counting the 6 distance learning rooms. A recent survey showed nearly all the rooms were reserved at least 90% of the time.

As noted earlier, the evolution of this project has coincided with the evolution of the corporation. The corporation moved through an intense cost savings initiative to reengineering. Part of the spirit of the reengineering effort is to hold costs down by using technology when available and building high performance teams that may be geographically widely distributed. Both the cost savings and the emphasis on teaming generate an internal demand for the video conferencing network. These needs are similar to those being experienced by many other companies to whom we sell video conferencing services.

One unexpected problem is that the network became so popular that our ability to "test" alternative designs was squeezed out. Meetings were regularly scheduled in the experimental test room, and users of the network (especially executives) had little tolerance for parametric studies that might result in reduced service. Even local management, sensitive to the fact that research and development was still in its infancy, did not want to jeopardize the positive feelings of participants with research that would be intrusive. Further, for briefings on sensitive topics, users of the network were not enamored with having "observation" cameras in the room that might allow people to see and hear sensitive information (although their sense was that the video conference network itself was adequately secure). As a result, we transitioned the network from the research and development center to the information systems center to maintain as a stable internal resource. To support experimental work, however, we added to the new laboratory two rooms that could be connected to study key video conferencing parameters (and provided for potential, albeit intermittent, connections to the backbone network) and equipped them for use in laboratory studies.

Distance Learning

Working on a successful video conferencing network clearly established our credibility with project teams inside Ameritech working in the broadband area. We began receiving requests to represent Ameritech's interests on national and international standards committees; and once the internal video conferencing network was operating, we began to receive an increasing number of requests from marketing people throughout the company who were beginning to sell teleconferencing facilities to schools in the region. The challenge was that training was one of the categories of conferences that the existing network had not yet specifically been engineered to support. We expanded our efforts, therefore, into distance education.

As before, an early step was to identify the guidelines that should apply to the new environment, and we provided consulting on how to adapt them to this new application (Lund and Warren, 1992b). We also began talking with people experienced in a variety of distance education projects (e.g., Ball State and the University of Wisconsin) about their experiences. We joined a team extending the internal video conferencing network to support distance learning and helped design and build rooms in which to work out effective distance learning classroom (Figure 5) designs.

Figure 5   Video classroom

It was clear, however, that for growth in the work to be sustained we needed to be actively supporting revenue generating activities as well. As a result we proposed specific joint projects identifying and addressing behavioral issues that we believed were important for product success to marketing. We began to help both marketing and schools in Northern Michigan evaluate the effectiveness of distance education, for example. We began to evaluate how teaching and learning changes with different distance education technologies and to identify elements that will be important for future distance education projects.

Other Applications

The next step in the evolution of the work was a growth in marketing interest beyond traditional applications of broadband technologies to video conferencing and distance learning. Marketing began to move in the direction we had predicted when we began the teleconferencing effort, and it moved in that direction because the corporate culture was beginning to change from a focus on the traditional communications business to meeting customers' needs to reach people and information.

Corporate interest in broadband services evolved even as individual marketing people had begun to dabble in the area. They began by looking at how multimedia was growing. They concluded that business was moving in the direction of desktop video, and they created a task force to look specifically at residential services. As part of the effort to promote human factors within Ameritech, I look for opportunities to influence corporate directions with human factors input. Seeing a memo on the task force, I offered a few opinions electronically to the vice president who was chairing the task force about the human factors issues that they needed to consider. These observations were made based largely on the experiences we had gained from the video conferencing work and some of the early distance education work. The vice president, in turn, invited me to join the task force, where people seemed to recognize immediately that the success of residential services were going to be heavily dependent on the successful resolution of human factors challenges such as the ease of using interfaces to shopping and entertainment. They asked us to support a consumer testing lab inside the usability lab specifically designed to test residential broadband services. We helped shape the business plans (defining the nature of the services that might be supported, barriers to be overcome, socio-technical issues, and other issues), and we helped screen competitive products in terms of their human factors characteristics that might give us a competitive advantage or place us at a disadvantage.

This work is still evolving, but application work and the identification of critical performance issues in the design of the network itself continue to depend heavily on human factors analyses. A new corporate organization devoted to broadband applications has been exploring how to ensure they have a full-time human factors staff to work on the issues that are arising in this new application area (and they have concluded that a dotted line reporting relationship out of my department will meet their needs). We are again building a design guidelines document, again filling in gaps with research on specific design elements (e.g., testing alternative input devices and defining design changes based on their properties), and again working on application designs.

Our work on the teleconferencing project led us to attempt to understand the nature of collaborative activity and how technology might affect collaboration. We did small internal tests of new groupware packages and generated requirements for software supporting certain kinds of collaborative activities. We began a partnership with the University of Michigan to develop a NSF proposal for the study of distributed groupware applications. We began working with Bellcore on developing an Ameritech application of their desktop video technology (Figure 6) and working with Bellcore and a vendor on testing video walls for casual collaboration (e.g., linking coffee rooms in two locations). This work fit the category of forward looking and was designed to build expertise and allow us to more effectively support project requests we might receive. Each project, however, was evaluated and undertaken based on the criterion that there had to be a plausible chain of events by which it would actually benefit the business (recognizing that projects undertaken in relative ignorance are fairly risky).

Because of the expertise we had been developing in the area, we began to get pulled into the marketing examination of applications for desktop video conferencing. We participated by helping them understand where social needs might arise that these technologies could address and issues that would need to be resolved (especially design issues) before the technologies could successfully be deployed. For example, telecommuting was seen as an exciting opportunity for applying the technology, especially the opportunity to increase the number of knowledge workers telecommuting.

We argued, however, that desktop video conferencing for telecommuting probably needed to be paired with collaborative software to allow home workers to participate in geographically distributed teams. We expected several barriers. One was the difficulty managers have in dealing with remote workers, and so we wanted to see if we could develop tools that would allow managers and reportees to feel they were "in touch" with one another (managers should feel they know what their reportees are doing, and the reportees should feel they are being fairly evaluated and can obtain advice when needed). Another was the need for the home worker to obtain support information when needed, either by contacting experts or reaching into large information databases. A third was ensuring that the home worker feels "part" of the company for which he or she works, and that connectedness was expected to come from

Figure 6   Desktop video conference

feeling linked to the social environment of colleagues and friends at work. Marketing was persuaded that we should plan a trial to begin exploring methods for overcoming these barriers and to obtain usage data that would allow a business case to be built.

As the company changed, it has turned more and more into what is sometimes known as the virtual corporation. It is building joint ventures with a variety of major companies, with expertise in areas that complement the core competencies of Ameritech. One of these activities is the recently announced partnership with INTEL. The goal is to build a desktop workstation environment that combines telephony, workstation, and collaborative tools. Because of the growing background in desktop collaboration and the close partnership we had developed with the marketing people working in the area, marketing involved us in negotiating the partnership arrangements with INTEL. Joint design and testing activities are underway.

This work, in turn, has led to initiatives in medicine and education. Some of these have been in partnership with vendors, such as creating collaborative medical workstations that allow radiological images and vital signs to be shared. Others have been partnerships with universities, such as the CoVis project. CoVis allows geographically distributed high school students to collaborate while conducting experiments across the country and using high-end computer simulations. The broadband workplan continues to build on itself, and the relationships developed ensure true beginning-to-end involvement in the product realization process (Figure 7).

Lessons Learned

The most important lessons we have learned so far have been the following.

First, it is important to have friends. Work grows on a person-by-person basis. When people believe their project was more successful because of human factors

Figure 7   Geneology of broadband work

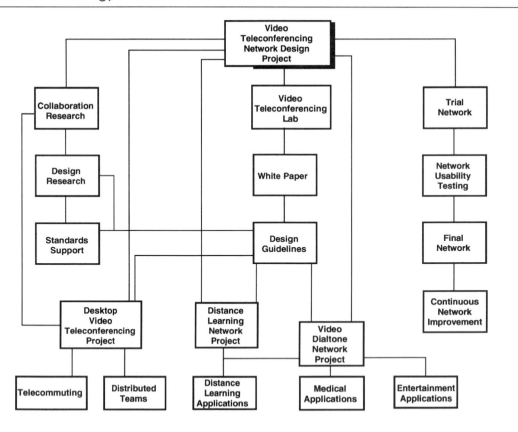

involvement, and they have found they can work with a human factors partner, they come back for support on new projects. Indeed, the relationship becomes one of ongoing teaming and human factors is able to get involved at the earliest stages of the product development process and to ensure that process accommodates human factors methodologies. Further, much of the new work we receive is a result of referrals from these friends, and the friends serve as an excellent window into their respective organizations when we are seeking to develop work.

Second, selling the work never stops. The corporation continually changes and there is little organizational memory for human factors contributions. The memory is in individuals with whom we have worked. There are few "standardized" processes in product development inside Ameritech, and so how human factors is going to be involved needs to be negotiated for almost every project undertaken with new people. The corporation is a large one (70,000 employees and $11 billion in revenue), and with the limited number of human factors people we have the probability that the key projects in which we should be involved will find us without effort on our part is smaller than it should be. The pressures are increasingly on developers to "shorten cycle time." When they view human factors activities as slowing the process, they want to reduce the role. Education about the benefits of human factors for the customer and thereby for Ameritech, how it should be involved to obtain those benefits, and how corporate resources can actually be saved when human factors is properly engaged (like quality, human factors in some sense is free since a dollar invested to improve usability is more than returned in decreased cost or increased revenue) is critical.

Third, the strength of our work is its empirical nature. It is easy to fall into the trap of running fewer and fewer subjects, until design is based entirely on the expertise of the human factors people, and thinking you have lost nothing. While the resulting design has a reasonable probability of being better than no involvement at all, there are several important consequences.

- It is not as good as it would be when appropriate studies are done.
- Thirty seconds of a subject struggling with an interface when viewed by the project team, often has more weight than hours of logical argument about a design problem.
- When growing and maintaining a human factors group or department, it is important to show the value the effort brings to the company. Objective measures of that value can be directly derived from appropriate studies.
- Once project teams believe that empirical work is not required for good design, the value of "special training" comes into question.

Fourth, beware of being too nice. As noted, keeping and growing friends is critical to success. Friends frequently ask for special favors ("I know you're busy, but can't you just look at this?"). When the process is compromised for a friend, a friend understands it as a favor and is open about expressing concerns about what is being done and negotiating alternative approaches that better meet her or his needs. However, we have learned that when we have compromised the process for people we do not know well, they confuse the compromise as the normal process and are either dissatisfied with the result or come to the mistaken belief that "that is all there is." Further, juggling lots of these favors also means there is less time to achieve excellence on the high priority projects. There are times, therefore, when human factors is helped most when we learn to say "no" in a nice, but effective, way.

Fifth, in today's corporate environment change is the norm. Plan for it. This means not remaining passive waiting for work to be requested. Risks need to be taken. A vision (continuously updated) of where the human factors group should be in the future (what work it wants to be doing) should be developed, and education, negotiation, and preparation should be undertaken to move the group toward that vision. With change, there needs to be a continual recrafting of how the goal of human factors work contributes to new corporate goals (e.g., the shift from being a "quality" activity to an "assessing customer needs" activity). To keep the corporation valuing human factors, the corporation needs to see how human factors contributes to what it believes will lead to success. The past is not nearly as important to a corporation as whether existing resources are contributing to its future. With changing corporate directions and priorities, the company is less interested in providing tenure, and employees are more interested in finding the best position to be working in the near term. This implies that change of personnel is the norm. The change contract should be, "You give me your best while you are with me, and I'll help you grow and become more valuable to any employer. When we part, we'll part as friends."

Acknowledgments

I would like to thank Judy Tschirgi for the many fruitful discussions we had in preparing an earlier paper together, that helped crystallize the thoughts recorded in this chapter.

References

Hawkins, W. H. (1989). "Where Does Human Factors Fit in R&D organizations?" *Proceedings of the 1989 IEEE International Conference on Systems, Man, and Cybernetics*, Cambridge, MA.

Hawkins, W. H. (1991). "The Role of User Interface Professionals in Large Software Projects," *IEEE Transactions on Professional Communication* 34 (2), 94–100.

Karat, C. (1993). "Cost-Benefit and Business Case Analysis of Usability Engineering." Tutorial Notes from INTERCHI '93 (obtained from author).

Karlan, J. E. (1977). "The Changing and Expanding Role of Human Factors in Telecommunications Engineering at Bell Laboratories," *Proceedings of the Eighth International Symposium of Human Factors in Telecommunications*, Cambridge, England.

Kleinfield, S. (1981). *The Biggest Company on Earth: A Profile of AT&T*. Holt, Rinehart and Winston, New York.

Kotsonis, M. E., and Lehder, D. Z. (1990). Poster given at the Human Factors Society Convention in Orlando, FL (paper available from the authors).

Lund, A. M. (1991). "User Needs and the Subjective Measurement of Video Quality." Paper presented at the IEEE International Workshop on the Quality of Telecommunications Services and Products, Quebec, Canada.

Lund, A. M. (1992). "The influence of Video Image Size and Resolution on Viewing-Distance Preferences," SMPTE Journal (May,) 406–415.

Lund, A. M. (1994a). "How Many Human Factors People Is Enough?" *Ergonomics in Design*.

Lund, A. M. (1994b). "Ameritech's Usability Laboratory," *Behavior and Information Technology* 13 (1).

Lund, A. M., and Tschirgi, J. E. (1991). "Designing for People: Integrating Human Factors into the Product Realization Process," *IEEE Journal on Selected Areas in Communications* 9 (4), 496–500.

Lund, A. M., and Warren, R. E. (1992a). "Human Factors Design Guidelines for Video Teleconferencing," *ITCA (International Teleconferencing Association) Yearbook: 1992*, pp. 25–36. ITCA, Washington, DC.

Lund, A. M., and Warren, R. E. (1992b). "Guidelines for the Design of Video Teleconferencing Applications," *Proceedings of the 14th International Symposium on Human Factors in Telecommunications*, in press.

Nielsen, J. (1992). "Finding Usability Problems Through Heuristic Evaluation," *Proceedings of ACM CHI '92*, Monterey, CA, pp. 373–380.

Perigord, M. (1987). *Achieving Total Quality Management: A Program for Action*. Productivity Press; Cambridge, MA.

Schwartz, B. K., and Riley, C. A. (1988). "Evolution or Extinction? A Case Study of Decentralized Human Factors in a Telecommunications R&D Company," *Proceedings of the 12th International Symposium on Human Factors in Telecommunications*, The Hague, The Netherlands, pp. 1–11.

Virzi, R. A. (1990). "Streamlining the Design Process: Running Fewer Subjects.,"*Proceedings of the Human Factors Society 34th Annual Meeting*, Orlando, FL.

CHAPTER 16

Bellcore's User-Centered Design Approach

**Aita Salasoo,
Ellen A. White,
Tom Dayton,
Brenda J. Burkhart, and
Robert W. Root**

Bellcore

left to right: Ellen A. White, Robert W. Root, Brenda J. Burkhart, Tom Dayton, and Aita Salasoo

Aita Salasoo directs the Usability Engineering and Technology Group at Bellcore, where she has seven years of software and usability experience. Previous to this, she earned a Ph.D. from Indiana University, taught, and conducted research in cognitive psychology and psycholinguistics.

Ellen White joined Bellcore in 1986 after completing a Ph.D. in experimental psychology from Johns Hopkins University. Her expertise includes graphical user interface design, telecommunications software requirements, and teaching user-centered design methods.

Tom Dayton develops methods for user-centered design and ways to transfer those methods to others. Before joining Bellcore in 1990, he supplemented his Ph.D. in experimental psychology with a research postdoctoral position at IBM's Watson Research Center.

Brenda Burkhart joined Bellcore in 1990 with eight years of user interface experience at JPL and TRW. She has an MA from California State, Northridge, in human factors-applied experimental psychology and is currently working on graphical user interface consistency and design for telecommunications software.

Bob Root has worked on graphical user interface design guidelines, introduction of information technology into organizations, and business process reengineering. He joined Bellcore after finishing his Ph.D. in social psychology at the University of California, San Diego.

Our story deals with large, specialized software products in the changing world of communications and computing. Some of the changes have been opportunities for increasing the usability of these products. We share our experiences here, not any corporate policy or image. We do so believing there are lessons you may take and apply as you see fit. First, we provide an overview of Bellcore and user-centered design at Bellcore. Then, we zoom into two contrasting cases of user-centered design successes.

Bellcore's Business

Bellcore (Bell Communications Research) is a 10-year-old telecommunications research and development consortium with an annual revenue stream of $1.1 billion, based in northern New Jersey. Our approximately 7000 employees provide research, engineering, and other technical services for the telephone operating companies of Ameritech Corporation, Bell Atlantic Corporation, BellSouth Corporation, NYNEX Corporation, Pacific Telesis Group, Southwestern Bell Corporation, and U S WEST, Inc.—and other client companies. Specifically, we support the ability of our clients to provide local telephone services and care for the underlying telecommunications network. This includes two major components:

- Research on fundamental network technologies, as well as formal definitions of generic requirements and contributions to industrywide standards for network hardware and software components,

- Software systems to support planning, engineering, managing, and maintaining the telecommunications network, as well as provisioning services on that network.

Luckily, you need not know how a phone works to use one. In that spirit, we will try to not dwell on the inner workings of telephone operating companies in explaining user-centered design at Bellcore. First, we will clarify some important terms and make a few general observations about this business and Bellcore.

We shall be using the term *user-centered design* to signify systematic activities that involve users in the endeavor of building usable products. To us, *usability engineering* is more encompassing in scope, while having the same goal. Some usability engineering techniques, such as heuristic evaluation, may exclude users. Finally, we use the term *human factors* to cover knowledge associated with human physical and mental capabilities that can be applied to the same goal of building usable products. We also differentiate between specialists and practitioners; the former is a subset of the latter. In many instances we interchange *user-centered design* and *usability practitioner or specialist*; this is because in reality we cannot always involve users and sometimes use other means to improve the usability of products.

Technology and Competition

Two related trends keep the telecommunications business exciting. First, network and computing technology innovations are increasing rapidly, leading to more powerful and varied technical solutions and possible services. New services are a lot more sophisticated than "plain old telephone service," or POTS, as the prevalent telecommunications service of previous decades is affectionately known in the industry. These days, we can send voice, as well as additional forms of data like fax and video, via the phone. A phone is no longer a predictable device in a known location with a small number of possible functions. Instead, answering machines, alarms, and computers are all within the grasp of the mobile telecommunications consumer.

Second, the number of players in all sectors of the telecommunications business is growing fast. This means that pressures to provide new or better service to customers faster and cheaper are rampant. A consequence of the competition is that what was once a frill may now be an important marketing opportunity for telecommunications companies trying to meet the needs of sophisticated users of telecommunications services for the exchange of information. This is extremely relevant for usability issues. Together, these trends keep Bellcore's clients and Bellcore's work vital and challenging. As our case studies will demonstrate, they also have influenced the course of user-centered design work at Bellcore.

Culture

The telecommunications industry has exhibited both user-friendly and user-unfriendly sides to the public. In general it is still true that phones in the United States are easy to use; this is more true for older, simpler payphones, which had substantial human factors contributions to their design. In contrast, ordering telephone service can be a foreign language experience for a consumer. You may well be bombarded with incomprehensible technology-based choices that involve historical jargon and acronyms, being presented quite unabashedly by the service representative, despite your confusion.

Bellcore's culture has grown from this mixed tradition. It was inherited from its roots at AT&T, Bell Laboratories, Western Electric, and the Bell Operating Companies. Formal training in computer science and electrical engineering and experience in telephone operating companies are the dominant backgrounds of our work force.

Our Systems and Operations line of business deals with consultation, integration, and development of software solutions for supporting telecommunications operations. Like other large software companies, we face the challenges of faster development cycles, platform diversity in the marketplace, and the need to reduce costs. In addition, our customers' businesses are data intensive and based in part on older software systems that cannot be discounted in planning for the future.

User-Centered Design at Bellcore

When created, Bellcore inherited several groups of behavioral and cognitive scientists from Bell Labs, as well as a small number of human factors engineers scattered among software projects. Bellcore software products and research efforts had variable and largely hidden coverage of user interface and behavioral science issues. Some software products had more focus on user interface design than others and there were research successes attributed to behavioral science, but these were not perceived as important issues by the company's management.

The decade of our existence has happily coincided with a rediscovery of human factors in the guise of usability engineering (and user-centered design) in the software and manufacturing industries. At Bellcore, user-centered design gained visibility with senior management at a time when usability concepts and methods were viewed as contributing to the corporate emphasis on quality defined as customer satisfaction. Previously informal efforts were organized into a corporate strategy, culminating in 1991 in a user-centered design policy (Figure 1). Another major factor in getting corporate support for user-centered design came from the observation that companies, including Bellcore's owners and software industry leaders, were embracing the user-centered design approach.

Figure 1   Core of Bellcore's user-centered design policy

Policy	**All producers of software products will apply user-centered design methods:** • **task analysis,** • **usability objectives,** • **early prototyping,** • **usability testing, and** • **iterative design.**
Reason	The purpose of this policy is to ensure that Bellcore products meet documented objectives for usability and usefulness and that there is an early and continuous focus on users throughout the analysis, design, and development process.
Responsibility	Product and development managers
When	Throughout the software development life cycle

User-centered design, human factors, and behavioral science research efforts at Bellcore are directed at benefiting our clients in the areas of new service development, operations support, software development, marketing, and research. Some benefits are more direct than others. Obviously, user-tested and subsequently improved software has immediate benefits for users in our client companies and the associated business functions. These benefits include easier, faster, and more error-free task performance, as well as decreased end user training costs. Improved methods in early task analysis and the development of graphical user interface architectures and style guides also improve Bellcore's productivity. Finally, behavioral research of new technologies (e.g., screen-assisted telephone displays, video services) leads to improved understanding of applications that is an essential part of creating revenue-generating services for our client companies.

Not surprisingly, changes in the telecommunications industry have led to questions about the future of Bellcore by its owners. The last two years have witnessed major internal reengineering and an ongoing examination of viable options for the future role of Bellcore. There have been several consequences for user-centered design work.

Today there are about 80 recognized user-centered design practitioners, user interface designers, and behavioral scientists at Bellcore. Most are members of groups containing three or more people with a similar background; approximately one-third are in groups dedicated to usability or behavioral sciences issues. The number of specialists has decreased slightly, in keeping with the overall company work force changes. At the same time, however, we have increased awareness by software developers and managers, and a larger number of new user-centered design practitioners.

Periods of companywide coordinated management of user-centered design work existed for two years before being overtaken by other internal reengineering and planning umbrellas. Nevertheless, other informal activities have endured. They include regular informal lunch meetings with speakers presenting work in computer-human interaction and user-centered design, and practitioners and researchers from many fields have productive information exchanges. In addition, bulletin boards for electronic communication about user-centered design and related topics have been in use for three years, with some sustained longer, local efforts. Educational efforts include renewed attention to a human factors curriculum in our training organization and the active participation in four three-day user-centered design symposia held in the last seven years for our clients and Bellcore employees.

The sustained managerial visibility and continuing demand for user-centered design work are accompanied by new challenges. In 1991 we listed three ubiquitous needs for user-centered design to become a successful Bellcore-wide approach (Salasoo et al., 1991a). The needs were in the areas of user-centered design resources, recognition of user-centered design results, and integration into the product development process. Let us assess the current state of user-centered design at Bellcore relative to these needs.

User-Centered Design Resources

The resource issue can be addressed in terms of overall shortages, growth of expertise, and changing needs for the staffing of software projects.

There is still a resource shortage, but this problem is not unique to user-centered design or to Bellcore. Resource allocation was helped by the user-centered design policy, which required user-centered design responsibility to be assigned to a manager and a technical team member on every software project. Also, recent internal restructuring has allowed human performance analysts to participate in the early definition of customer needs and has also placed usability engineering responsibilities early in the software life cycle and on equal footing with other kinds of systems engineering. One consequence has been slight clumping of usability practitioners into groups directed by managers with a usability or behavioral sciences background in the systems engineering organization. From his or her home group, an individual is assigned to work on specific product needs. An additional group of usability specialists exists in a software support lab, providing internal consultation on broader issues. This trend toward some centralization is an attempt to optimize the application of scarce resources.

Despite overall shrinkage of our work force in the last three years, the number of user-centered design practitioners (not specialists) is growing. This growth is from hiring people with user-centered design expertise, as well as from successful technology transfer and internal training efforts for software analysts and developers to reach intermediate levels of user-centered design expertise. Thus, the current challenge is to create more specialists from beginning- and intermediate-level practitioners.

Resource allocation is also affected by the model of software development in use. Graphical user interfaces and an increased emphasis on software reuse require different resources than those needed for more traditional software development. Estimates of 6% of project staffing or 2-4 staff-years per project for usability engineering work (Nielsen, 1993) do not account for the greater demands of graphical user interface (GUI) design and testing. Especially when product teams are still on a learning curve in GUI experience, we have observed benefits from applying more user-centered design expertise (see the TMM case later) and detriments in their absence. With significant reuse, software is assembled rather than built. Thus, user interface consistency issues inevitably emerge later in the development life cycle and may seem too difficult to solve in the available time. In most cases, the older and more established a reused software component, the less likely its user interface will be changed, even if usability efforts identify the need. Thus, we have learned that we need to be flexible as we plan how to staff and schedule reuse-based software projects effectively from a user-centered design perspective.

User-Centered Design Results and Recognition

We see progress in terms of user-centered design results in many ways. Bellcore publications in the last few years have regularly linked software and network product successes to user-centered design efforts. This is particularly true for workstation- and PC-based new software products employing graphical user interfaces to provide support for increasingly complex network engineering tasks or more generic online browsing tasks (e.g., the SuperBook™ System), as well as for new network service capabilities (e.g., video, screen-assisted telephony.) The company has acknowledged outstanding contributions with formal performance evaluations, corporate and peer awards, and promotions. Closer to the trenches, however, some user-centered design struggles, such as getting in the door (see the LSS case later) and in other cases to be on equal footing with other team activities, still occur on a product or individual basis. We anticipate continuing educational efforts before we can safely say our culture is infused with a truly user-centered design approach.

Integration in the Product Development Process

Integration is multifaceted and, we believe, the key to successful user-centered design at Bellcore. Our second case study addresses this in detail. Here, we will briefly mention one important integration issue we are addressing.

Bellcore has an evolving set of guidelines for the design of graphical user interfaces, known as the GUI style guide (Bellcore, 1993).[1] Creating and using the style guide has united user-centered design practitioners and product teams. The style guide is a central part of Bellcore's software reuse strategy for developing workstation-based systems. The specific integration issue we are currently tackling is how to integrate use of the style guide into the Bellcore software life cycle. Beyond the style guide document, we are providing a three-pronged conformance process to achieve a common look and feel in our new software products. This includes consultation and mentoring by style guide champions and user-centered design specialists early in a product's life cycle. In addition, we have created a short style guide conformance checklist to help designers, developers, and testers begin to assess user interface consistency issues. Our plan is to operationalize parts of the checklist as generic test scripts and to ultimately transfer responsibility for some user interface consistency testing to product testing organizations. This will help consistency modification requests to be accorded the priority they deserve during the system test phase of a product. We see this style guide conformance process as supplementing, not replacing, the important GUI design and user involvement contributions, early in the software development life cycle, as well as during the testing phase. Our experiences to date suggest that integration and buy-in by product managers and teams are important for user-centered design successes, not just for effective use of the style guide.

---

[1]To obtain copies of the style guide (LP-CSP-000023), call 1-800-521-CORE in the United States and Canada and 1-908-699-5800 in other countries.

SuperBook is a trademark of Bellcore.

In all, the three issues we identified in 1991 are still relevant. The details of resources and integration may differ, showing change and maybe progress. Most important, the current climate allows public pride over user-centered design contributions to successful Bellcore software products.

Two User-Centered Design Success Stories

Next, we describe two case studies of user-centered design at Bellcore. Together, they cover the continuum of resource scenarios faced in our software development efforts. They also provide a flavor of the variety of benefits, both potential and realized, that our user-centered design approach to software product development can bring; there are many other examples that due to space constraints cannot be presented here.

LSS: Small Project, Big Impact

We already noted that, like the vast majority of software development organizations around the world, ours has too few usability and human factors specialists. To cope, there is some centralization of user-centered design expertise, which is aimed at enabling better management of the scarce resources. One such group has been involved in adapting, innovating, and transferring user-centered design techniques to Bellcore software product teams. The idea is to help development teams learn to do user-centered design *themselves* and so to grow the base of usability practitioners in the organization. To be most effective, a user-centered approach must be practiced in some way by everyone from marketers to programmers to trainers, in ways appropriate to their particular jobs. The LSS case study illustrates this hands-on consultation-training approach for spreading user-centered design expertise.

LSS—Reengineering the Production of Directories

The Listing Services System (LSS) is an evolving software system that manages telecommunications customer information and helps telephone operating company database administrators, directory analysts, and clerical workers design and produce information products such as white pages directories. This business function is being reengineered and partially automated by our customer companies. Today about 600 users of the mainframe LSS product spend a lot of effort to integrate information with a variety of formats from different sources. Some of these workers manually lay out the text and graphics, combining them into directories. The need for greater efficiency and flexibility of these information management and publishing functions is driven by increased competition in the local telephone business; the type of solution LSS is providing is enabled by computing technology advances. The work we describe here was part of an ongoing attempt to integrate existing user activities from manual, batch, and real-time components into a seamless work flow in one medium—a WYSI-WYG[2] real-time software system. Ultimately the directory pages will appear to their composers in their final forms on a computer screen, the page components directly manipulable.

The LSS case study describes how two internal usability consultants helped a small development team that had no such specialists of its own. The consultants spent only a little time on the projects and dove into them with little knowledge of the users' tasks or the product, yet they improved the software product and left the team able to use the techniques without assistance. Two separate user-centered design consultations were provided to the same development group, but with different software developers and different circumstances (Table 1). In the first case the interface was already designed and the product was almost completely coded, so there was little time for user-centered design or for code changes. Although the specialists' consultation at this stage had only a little influence on the released product, the benefits of user-centered design impressed the development group and their customers enough for them to call in the consultants again. The opportunity for the second consultation was a drastic expansion of the product's functional scope, with plenty of time to explore users' fundamental needs in a series of participatory sessions.

Table 1   User-Centered Design Techniques Used for the LSS Product

Stage of Development	General Technique	Particular Technique
Early	Business process analysis Gross task analysis	Brown paper modeling CARD
Late	Detailed task analysis Screen layout and behavior analysis Usability testing	CARD PICTIVE Semi-formal user testing of computerized software prototype

---

[2]"What you see is what you get."

Requirements Validation and Design Refinement

The requirements manager and software designer of a 20-person team of a major LSS release wanted to ensure that the product, which had a prototype and was in the midst of being coded, was actually aligned with the way users work. Conformance to Bellcore's graphical user interface design guidelines (Bellcore, 1993) was also an issue for the product management. They had no human factors specialists on the product team, the person who had originally generated the user interface requirements was no longer available even to answer questions, and no current team members had discussed the design in any detail with potential users. Little time was left before the product was to be shipped, the budget covered only one session of user feedback, and the telephone operating company administrators and clerks who use LSS were 1500 miles away. For help, the LSS team turned to Bellcore's own consultants from an internal usability engineering group. Three usability specialists were able to help two members of the LSS product team learn how to practice user-centered design themselves. All the activities described here were done by the internal mentor-consultants and the LSS product team members.

Methods and Training

We chose a participatory approach over formal usability testing. The goal was to review the user's task flow and, if necessary, redesign the interface. We chose the CARD method (Tudor et al., 1993) to quickly make the task flow more explicit, so that users could understand the new way their work would flow when they were using the new software product. One way we used CARD was by pasting screen dumps from the LSS prototype onto index cards and using the cards to simulate use of the software. Then, we laid the cards out on the table around which design participants sat. As a result they could manipulate the cards as a means of expressing their ideas about how the interface should be used. Another use of CARD to capture ideas about the task flow is shown in Figure 2.

We planned to make low-technology prototypes of potential computer screens with PICTIVE (Muller, Wildman, and White, 1993), to help users criticize and redesign the screens' implementations of the task flow that they just helped design. PICTIVE involves using paper and pen materials for making prototype screens; its major advantages are that several people can work at once (collaboratively) and that users have as much access to the prototyping medium as product team members. Video is used in PICTIVE to capture informal "design walkthroughs" and record rationales and dynamic aspects of the prototype for future use or communication.

During training, information exchange occurred in two directions: User-centered design techniques were transferred from the internal consultants to the product team members, and product and domain knowledge were transferred in the other direction.

Figure 2 Example of CARD method with blank index cards used for identifying task components (left panel) and then capturing the task flow (right panel). The table is covered with brown paper, on which notations can be made.

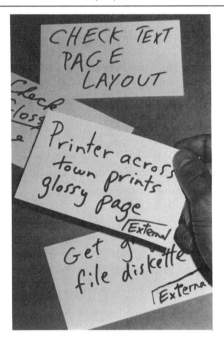 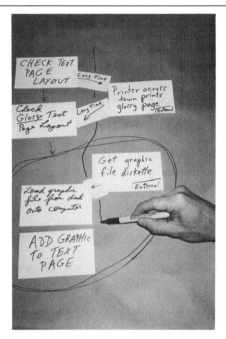

This involved two hours for the usability specialists to learn about the software, users, and tasks; two hours of lecture, video, and demonstration of the specific methods (CARD and PICTIVE); and finally, a practice session in which the LSS developer tried out the task analysis and screen prototyping activities on a friendly user, receiving feedback from the user-centered design specialists. The practice session was the heart of the tutorial-consultation, providing guided practice in applying the user-centered design methods appropriate to the developers' circumstance, using their own product, in a friendly learning-conducive environment.

Field Experience

After this preparation, we made two visits to users in the field. In addition to two LSS team members, a user-centered design consultant went on the first visit, which was aimed at refining the product design. The LSS developers, newly trained in user-centered design practices, ran this session, receiving support from the specialist as needed. As in all live performances, there were surprises and midstream shifts during the design session with users. Attendees were not the anticipated three users and one manager, but three users and four managers. This meant more work to empower the users in the design session. Our intended focus on screen appearance and the behavior of the interface was resisted by the participants, who kept turning to the underlying tasks and work flow. This, in fact, supported the advice given originally by the usability consultants to the LSS product team about the value of feedback about fundamental task organization issues. The results were very encouraging, both in terms of the ability to apply the activities so soon and in terms of identified issues for the LSS product—of 20 items, 16 were usability concerns that otherwise would not have been discovered.

Several months later, the two LSS developers went back to the field to test the usability of the software. One of the usability consultants helped plan the activities. Constraints included the fact that the available users were two who had already been involved in the design session. Informal methods were used including a usability questionnaire and task-based user observation and discussions. The new LSS usability practitioners returned with a handful of important usability problems that were fixed before the product was shipped. Six months after this release went to the field, there have been no usability modification requests, which is a significant accomplishment for the LSS product.

Hands-on mentoring by the usability consultants was very effective for the LSS product team, despite other restrictions on the potential effectiveness of applying user-centered design techniques. Learning by doing, rather than by reading and listening, helped with the transfer of techniques. The practice was particularly valuable in preparing new user-centered design practitioners to be flexible and to facilitate interactions in a participatory design session. Customer satisfaction with the LSS and the development team was enhanced, and therefore the value of user-centered design activities to Bellcore's Systems and Operations organizations was increased. In fact, this experience led the LSS manager to call in the same usability consultants right at the start of the next product release. The manager wrote:

> Although our experience with developer-led user-centered design was both limited in scope and very late in the development cycle, it gave us a feeling for the types of issues that might be raised in such an activity. We also were able to see the potential benefits of considering user input in designing work flows and screens, particularly on the level of acceptance by the users once the software was deployed.

Concept Exploration: Business Needs

LSS management had dedicated a five-person team, including a new human factors specialist with little hands-on user-centered design experience, to understanding the long-term vision for a fully automated LSS product. Helping customers reengineer the existing process was a key part of this assignment. Several internal usability consultants were brought in at the start of this effort at the request of the manager who had witnessed the benefits of user-centered design for the previous release of the product (described previously). The immediate goal of the development team was to create a software prototype to be used for marketing purposes. Only if customers liked the vision of the solution for directory information management and publishing would a new software product be funded. Time and budget had been allocated for user involvement, and there was an opportunity to make substantial changes to the existing product.

The internal user-centered design consultants worked with the LSS usability practitioner and the prototype developers, much as for the earlier release. That is, the consultants learned about the prototype context and constraints, and the product team members learned about, and practiced, the techniques to be applied. We used business process analysis to establish the broader context in which workers did their jobs. Then we used task analysis to get at the moderate-level details of workers' activities at their desks and the CARD technique (described previously) to elicit task and work flow information from the customer participants. Participants wrote major steps of the flows on index cards and laid them out spatially on the table to represent the flows. The resulting information was then organized into a model drawn on a big piece of paper on the wall. This brown-paper model was the focus of analysis and discussion of problem areas involving both the work process itself and the multiple software systems that support it. Once problem areas were defined, we returned to the index cards that represented the major task steps to decompose those steps into their constituents (see Figure 2 for a sample of this task).

Three field trips to seek user involvement were undertaken; some of them included one or two usability consultants.[3] Customers reported increased satisfaction with the requirements generation process, because they felt that the product team better understood the realities of their work environment. Asking customers to identify problems and opportunities for improvement strengthened their sense of involvement in the process and relieved designers of some of the burden of making decisions on their behalf. The business process analysis was valuable, over and above the detailed task analysis usually associated with requirements. The business process analysis established the broad framework within which separate tasks were embedded. This is particularly important when business functions are being reengineered. In our case it

---

[3]LSS users are employees of telephone operating companies with very specialized responsibilities associated with the production of telephone directories. It is not always easy to get access to these people, and we try to make every effort to minimize their time away from normal responsibilities. Also, we need to sample users from a range of companies,which may differ in their specific procedures. As a result, we may spend more time traveling to and from users than if we were supporting mass-market products.

facilitated problem solving. For example, one problem a customer had previously identified as being due to one task turned out to be due to another task, when the problem was examined in the context of the general work flow.

Key to User-Centered Design Consultation Success with LSS

Whether early or late in a product release cycle, user-centered design activities can help if they are done with an eye toward maximizing the benefit within the resources available. Mentor-consultants can help a product team that lacks usability expertise, if the help is wanted and if it is transferred in a way that involves and empowers the product team.

TMM: The Power of Integrated User-Centered Design

This case study highlights the evolution of a new software product in which usability expertise was applied during all phases. User-centered design specialists (who also served as domain experts and systems engineers) were involved early and continuously as full product team members. They brought task-based user input, prototype techniques and an appreciation for common interface design to the product team, gaining credibility from their domain and software expertise, over and above their user interface design and usability testing contributions.

TMM—Software to Help Engineers Manage Technology

The Technology Management Module (TMM) software system is a second-generation software product that supports telephone operating company engineers and provides maintenance of an inventory of telephone equipment. The telecommunications network is composed of interconnected pieces of equipment that transmit voice and data across a geographical area. TMM keeps track of this equipment, locations where the equipment is placed, and the connectivity between equipment and locations. Also maintained are details such as equipment configurations and plug-in electronic components that can provide different types of services. Approximately 2000 employees of the U.S. Bell Operating Companies will use TMM when it is fully deployed in 1996.

While the telecommunications network has been engineered and inventoried since its inception, both the rapid technology and competition changes in this industry have led to increasing complexity and importance of these functions. The knowledge required of telephone company engineers and engineering clerks, the users of TMM, and the time pressures they face led to the need to improve on existing procedures, which in many cases included use of LEIM (Loop Electronics Inventory Module) software. Computing technology advances enabled TMM to provide more powerful and efficient solutions to this business problem.

TMM is a graphical, workstation-based software product centered around five major engineering and inventory functions, e.g., placing equipment, placing network connections between equipment. Each function, comprising a number of user tasks, is performed in its own window (Figure 3 and Color Plate VIII). Each window is designed according to an object-action paradigm. That is, objects are represented in the main area of the window and must be selected to enable users to carry out appropriate actions from the menu bar.

TMM was born in 1991, evolving from an 8 staff-year research project and developing into the released software product over the next two years. Staffing levels increased to the current total of 23 people, 3 of whom are user-centered design practitioners.[4] The first product release was in mid-1993, and subsequent releases are planned through 1995 and beyond. The product life cycle consisted of concept exploration, proof of concept, product definition, product development, and product test phases. For each phase we will highlight how user-centered design contributed to the effort.

Concept Exploration: User Needs and a Research Prototype

The vision for the TMM product was born out of a teaming approach with our Applied Research and software organizations to apply state-of-the-art database and interface technologies to telecommunications engineering problems. We had also identified the need to change an existing engineering software system (LEIM) that was reaching its limits for handling data in a relational database. The research prototype provided the vision that enabled allocation of resources for significant new work on a software system. Using high-end software and hardware, we demonstrated the benefits of combining object technology with flexible graphics to users and potential customers.

One of the four team members was a user-centered design practitioner and another was a user representative. Significant user-centered contributions to the prototype included field trips to determine user needs (Salasoo, Rosenstein, and Collier, 1991b), high-level task analysis and scenario generation, usability testing and generation of key equipment icons (Salasoo, 1990), and collection of engineers' concerns with the current methods and tools available to them. Our usability lab was used for several usability testing tasks, to share video clips of engineers' problems in the field with the product team, as well as to produce a task-based video of the research prototype, which was critical to its successful socialization with customers and internal development managers.

---

[4]These staffing levels do not include people responsible for designing and incorporating TMM's extensive learning support (including documentation, training, and online help) and deployment staff, both of which are centralized functions at Bellcore. Although learning support is an acknowledged and essential aspect of TMM's user-centered design approach, in this case study we focus on the role of usability practitioners in the design of TMM's user interface software.

Figure 3 An example of the TMM Plug-In window. This window shows the layout of modular electronic components or "plug-ins" arranged onto shelves in a large piece of telecommunications equipment. The empty spaces into which plug-ins are placed are called "slots." In this example, slots 65-72 have been selected. Superimposed on the window is a dialog box listing the possible choices of plug-ins the engineer may place into the selected slots.

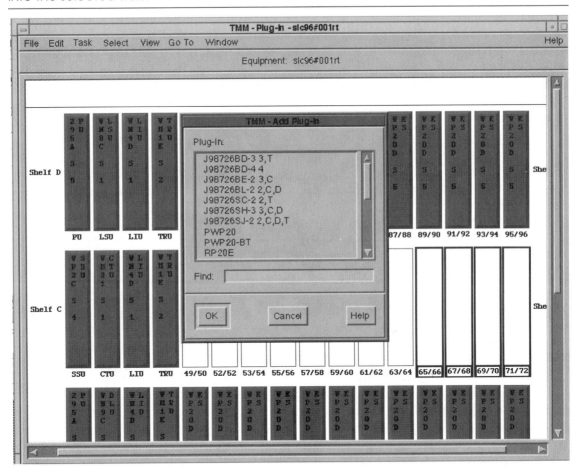

Proof of Concept: Task Focus and Technology Port

Excited by the possibilities afforded by the research prototype, customers asked us to determine both the specific engineering task to be supported first and the feasibility of the demonstrated capabilities on UNIX® workstations.[5] Thus, one usability practitioner prepared a prototype of a specific equipment editing task using a low-end prototyping tool, while other team members began porting to the Sun workstation platform, using C++ and determining which object-oriented database, look-and-feel, and graphical interface toolkit should be used for the TMM product. Early user input came from tests with the low-end prototype in the usability lab, while GUI technology issues were being ironed out. Users talked aloud about what they expected and desired from a support system, while trying out the low-end prototype. This input, earlier research results, and informal usability tests with incrementally available software product prototypes were used by user-centered design practitioners to write specifications for more details of TMM's user interface.

As early versions of TMM software became available for use, technological feasibility was assumed and users were brought in to the usability lab to exercise all aspects of the interface. These sessions were driven by representative scenarios, but were informal in the sense that no performance measures were recorded. Slightly more structured usability testing included task-based performance by users and a usability questionnaire. This user input served as a tool for detailed functional analysis of the job and how the system supports the job. Because the users involved in the testing were previously unfamiliar with graphical user interfaces, this testing provided a valuable opportunity for them to visualize how their work tasks could be supported using GUI technology. Once exposed to the vast potential of GUIs, these users were quick to suggest design alternatives and point out additional product features that would help them perform their job tasks. The major result of this usability testing effort was a list of over 100 potential changes to the product that was used in later phases.

Product Definition: Common and Task GUI Teams

Given that the platform and component tools for the TMM product were determined, it was clear that more extensive specification of the user interface was needed to make the progress necessary to deliver the software product. User testing had identified changes needed by early versions of the software and additional critical functions not yet designed.

The first step was to provide detailed specification for one of the user tasks that had already been evaluated in the previous phase. The first draft of the specification radically changed the product to accommodate most of the listed changes and increase the focus on industry (Open Software Foundation, 1991) and corporate GUI design guidelines (Bellcore, 1993). The first draft was written rapidly by a usability practitioner

---

[5]UNIX is a registered trademark of UNIX System Laboratories, Inc.

who had just joined the product team. It was based on user input but with little consultation with software developers. This led to an important lesson about the benefits of integration in graphical user interface design: GUI design cannot be done in isolation. Not only is user input required, but the development perspective must be represented as well. Thus, an interdisciplinary team approach was proposed and adopted.

A design team was assembled for each of the five primary functions, and an additional design team was assembled to address common functions and the product as a whole. The interdisciplinary design teams had members with clearly defined roles: systems engineer, GUI designer, GUI developer, database designer-developer, and end user representative. The systems engineer handled the fundamental model that drove the software, as well as detailed data requirements. The user-centered design practitioner served as the GUI designer and in most cases was the team leader. Database designer developer input was important because the processing methods needed for some user actions in the GUI were developed and stored in an object-oriented database. End user representatives were Bellcore employees who had previously performed the engineering function in a Bell Operating Company.

The functions and responsibilities of the common GUI team and the five function GUI teams follow. Additional details about specifying common components and their reuse in TMM can be found in Burkhart, Leland, and Shalmon (1993).

Common GUI Team's Goals.

- Understand the user interface software environment (e.g., X Windows[TM],[6] OSF[TM] Motif[TM] [7]) in enough detail so that design constraints are known
- Design common functions that can be used across GUI tasks (e.g., the user interaction sequence required to add an object to the database)
- Develop common user interface software that implements the common GUI functions
- Develop standards to address areas that cannot be covered by a common software tool and are not covered by other standards documents
- Provide a standardized specification template for GUI requirements and design
- Provide concrete *examples* to demonstrate the use of common components using actual designed TMM tasks

Single-Function GUI Teams' Goals.

- Understand common GUI functions and guidelines or standards

---

[6]X Windows is a trademark of the Massachusetts Institute of Technology.
[7]OSF and Motif are trademarks of the Open Software Foundation, Inc

- Have GUI designers committed to designing with the common GUI software and to commercial and corporate standards, to maximize design reuse, consistency, and code reuse
- Propose design solutions, outlining alternatives or compromises that are necessary. Iterate based on team input
- Describe the resulting designs using a standardized specification template to organize the GUI documentation and specify the interface at the same level of detail for all windows, including
  - menu bar items
  - menu options that are accessible from each menu bar item
  - a definition of any nonstandard menu option function
  - dialog boxes generated by the menu option (including actions generated based on input or control buttons)
  - conditions for item availability (e.g., if object x and object y are selected, then gray out "Add")
  - data validation (if necessary)

Communication both within and across teams was extremely important in assuring a common user interface for the product as a whole. Most teams had members that were on at least one other team and this helped to facilitate the information dissemination.
   The best functioning teams effectively

- Trusted the skills and expertise of team members
- Allowed overlap of roles as appropriate to individual skills and motivation
- Provided constructive input and worked through design issues
- Were flexible and incorporated change readily

These teams existed mostly during product definition, whereas later decisions regarding GUI design fell primarily into the hands of the GUI designer. Because of the designer's knowledge of both the users' domain and the software implementation environment (thanks partially to participation in an interdisciplinary team), this person was in the best position to make design decisions. As needed, the GUI designer consulted fellow team members on specific issues.

Product Development: Design Iteration

At the start of product development, the user interface design specifications had been agreed upon by the entire product team. Design iteration characterized the major user-centered design activity performed during this phase, occupying approximately half of the time of three usability practitioners over an eight-month period. Usually the developers initiated a design iteration, although this often resulted in a valuable synergistic effect that ultimately produced a better product. Typical triggers for changes in the design specifications included the need for additional details, inability to implement an item or tool as specified, and resource constraints. These changes included, for example, converting a paned area of a larger window into a separate window.

Trade-offs, which are inevitable during product development, were typically made by the GUI designer based on knowledge of user needs and development capabilities. During design iteration, the usability practitioners split their time equally between negotiation-conflict resolution and actual (re)design work. The value of the significant involvement of usability practitioners during product development was that design changes were addressed as a matter of course, rather than being escalated to crises later during testing. Changes were documented so that the interface could be appropriately tested.

Product Test: Comparative Usability Testing

Product testing included both traditional system testing and separate usability testing. The primary purpose of system testing was to ensure that the system functioned as specified in requirements and design documents. Typically, those conducting the tests were software professionals in a system test organization or domain experts who also had a background in software-related issues. In contrast, end users of TMM—telephone operating company employees who daily perform the engineering tasks TMM supports—participated in usability testing to test the adequacy of the GUI design in supporting their work tasks.

System Testing

The software was delivered to system test incrementally, as coherent units (e.g., a single window) became available. Some of the system testers were Bellcore employees who were software professionals with little knowledge of the engineering domain. Others, however, were "guest testers," telephone operating company employees who came to Bellcore for approximately two weeks to work with the Bellcore system testers.

The guest testers were chosen not only because of their expertise in the engineering process TMM supports, but also for their previous experience in testing, deploying, or supporting software. Although perhaps not prospective end users of TMM themselves, the guest testers served as user representatives and brought a user's perspective to the testing. As part of TMM's user-centered approach, the guest testers' participation in system testing allowed user interface and usability problems to be discovered and reported early (up to six months before product shipment). Some of these problems or "bugs" were addressed before the final product was shipped, and even before end-user usability testing occurred.

System testers and guest testers kept the GUI designers informed about reported problems. For those problems requiring GUI design changes, the GUI designers for the specific TMM function involved took responsibility for determining the solution, documenting the change, and ensuring it was implemented correctly.

Usability Testing

To demonstrate the impact that the UCD effort had on the design of TMM, a comparative usability test was conducted. This decision to pursue usability testing entailed a commitment from TMM managers to obtain additional usability resources, over and above the three full-time usability practitioners already on the project. To prepare for and carry out the testing and to analyze the data, five additional usability practitioners were used on a part-time basis, as well as a summer intern. Clearly, the importance of usability data was reflected in this dedication of supplemental resources.

Usability testing compared TMM to its predecessor product, LEIM (Loop Electronics Inventory Module), which had a character-based user interface. One of the primary reasons for conducting the usability test was to collect baseline data from LEIM, which would be used to help determine realistic usability goals for TMM. Prior to conducting the test, we set the minimum usability goal for TMM to the same level as the existing LEIM system. Also, based on our extensive use of graphical displays designed with consistency as a foremost principle, we set our target usability goal at a 50% improvement over comparable tasks in the older product.

The usability test participants, eight telephone company engineers or staff personnel who support the engineers, were given an engineering scenario of providing service to a new location. The scenario consisted of 22 tasks that were performed using both TMM and LEIM (Burkhart, Hemphill, and Jones, 1994). An example of one of the testing task scenarios was adding a plug-in component to an empty slot within a piece of equipment (see Figure 3). To carry out each task using TMM or LEIM, multiple user actions were required (e.g., select slot, choose Add menu option, etc.). Additionally, after completing the scenario with each system, participants filled out a questionnaire asking them to rate the ease-of-use for each component task.

The usability test revealed that TMM was significantly better than LEIM: Users performed the tasks more quickly, they made fewer errors, and they found it easier to use. Analysis of the task time data indicated that across all 22 tasks, the average percentage savings in time was 56%. A few changes were made to the first release of TMM, based on this usability testing. Informal round-table discussions with testing participants and the product team were useful. When other team members heard user concerns about specific items, they were inspired to make them before the product was shipped. One example of a software change made as a result of usability testing concerned automatic assignment of cursor focus to windows and dialog boxes. In the version of TMM used for testing, when a window was given input focus, the cursor was automatically available for the user to type data, but for dialog boxes the user had to click with the mouse before typing was allowed. Based on persistent user complaints about the differences between windows and dialog boxes in this regard, dialog box input focus was changed so that it worked consistently with that for windows.

By conducting a comparative usability test, we were able to quantify the benefits of the new interface. The comparative usability analysis showed that by designing for usability and consistency we were effective in producing a considerably more usable system. More detailed analyses will let us set reasonable usability objectives and target improvements to GUI design components of future TMM releases.

Key to User-Centered Design Impact for TMM

The task analysis work from early phases of TMM, in conjunction with use of object-oriented technologies, contributed to the significant decision to design TMM based on a large common graphical user interface foundation. The successful implementation of this decision made the biggest single difference for the TMM software product. Three usability specialists played a key role on that product team. Appropriate staffing with usability specialists as well as the focus on reuse and consistency in TMM were bolstered by a corporate climate encouraging such activities. TMM stands out as a shining example of what *can* be achieved as a result of good user-centered design. Engineers have said of their task with TMM: ". . . this is a very difficult task, but TMM handles it in a logical and intuitive way" and "Mistakes and changes can be done very quickly. Even deleting a complete system and reconfiguring becomes very easy."

Lessons Learned

From the title of this chapter—"Bellcore's User-Centered Design Approach"—you might have assumed that we advocate *one* approach to user-centered design for all our products. We hope that the case studies we presented dispelled this notion and gave you an appreciation for the variety of projects and user-centered activities and solutions ongoing as part of Bellcore's Systems and Operations way of doing business.

To summarize some of the most important lessons we have learned about helping ensure that user-centered design has a positive impact on software products, we paraphrase a few well-known aphorisms.

If You Can't Beat 'Em, Join 'Em

Usability practitioners and specialists should dispense with the idea of *beating* anyone and just *join up*! The ideal product development situation involves usability practitioners from the outset as full participants in a multidisciplinary design team. Instead of serving only a specialized function (e.g., usability testing) and darting in and out of the product life cycle at specific points, we feel that usability practitioners should be integrated throughout the life cycle. The TMM case is representative of many success stories at Bellcore in which user-centered design specialists were key participants from the product's inception through its deployment. They are responsible for *designing* the product's user interface, not just for providing guidance or suggesting alternatives or quoting usability metrics. To perform this design function well, trade-offs and negotiations are imperative. It is our experience that the best usability practitioners are those who learn as much as they can to help bridge the gap between the users' world and the software developers' world. They learn the jargon, the issues, the needs, and the constraints so that they are better equipped to ask the right questions and make the right trade-off decisions.

Better Late Than Never

We do not, alas, live in an ideal world. Resources are scarce, and product managers are still discovering the merits of user-centered design. Our motto of "better late than never," and its corollary "something is better than nothing," stress the importance of injecting user-centered design practices into a product development process no matter what stage has been reached. The LSS case study showed that usability consultants entering a project when the coding was nearly completed could not only improve that release of the product and the users' perception of it but, more important, could help ensure that user-centered design issues were considered from the outset of subsequent work on that product. If time, staffing, or attitudes do not permit full integration of usability practitioners into the product team, then do what you can with what you do have and make a positive impact even if it is just a small one. In addition, make sure that key stakeholders (e.g., users, managers, developers) realize that the impact of user-centered design on the product could be even greater if appropriate resources are devoted to it.

Reach out and Touch Someone®8

Usability practitioners are thought of as those who come into contact with users, and we agree that this is one of the essential aspects of good user-centered design. We also understand that design is multidisciplinary and that there are many stakeholders in addition to users (e.g., systems engineers, managers, developers, testers, trainers, documenters). We often find usability practitioners serving the role of facilitator within product teams, bringing together the diverse perspectives of the stakeholders. In the TMM case, the usability specialist was typically the leader of each design team—responsible for making sure that all voices were heard and that decisions were negotiated. In the LSS case, the internal usability consultants spent most of their time helping developers learn and practice the meeting facilitation skills necessary to elicit needs and solution ideas from users. The participatory design methods themselves (e.g., PICTIVE, CARD) work because they allow individuals with different backgrounds to express their own design ideas in small groups and collaborate with others to achieve a common vision.

Don't Sweat the Small Stuff

We focus user-centered design efforts on the early phases of the software development life cycle because that is where the biggest payoff is. If the software product is not being designed with the right capabilities or if it does not fit in with the users' business processes, no amount of "window dressing" will make it a useful and usable solution. As shown in the LSS case, users who are given a chance and the appropriate techniques will focus on essential aspects such as business needs and task flows. Taking a broad business perspective helped ensure that resources were devoted to building software that solved the users' most pressing needs. As the product life cycle continues into requirements, design, and implementation, the maxim of "don't sweat the small stuff" still holds. Assuming that the correct product features have been targeted, then thousands of decisions remain to be made when designing and building a software product with those features. The TMM case shows one good way of focusing resources on the most important design issues; namely, by forming a team responsible for common elements of design across the subsystems of the software. Team organization allowed more resources to be devoted to issues that affected larger aspects of the software, and fewer resources to issues that affected more limited aspects of the software.

---

[8]Reach out and touch someone is a registered trademark of AT&T.

Finally . . .

Our experiences have taught us as usability practitioners and managers to be well armed, to persevere, and to be ready for anything. We encourage you likewise, no matter where you and your work setting are in terms of user-centeredness. Tackle the hard problems head on and you will be rewarded by satisfied users and customers. In particular, none of these solutions comes for free. Organizational investment is needed for successful infusion of user-centered design into a product line. The investment may take the form of high-quality internal or external mentor-consultants or of a pool of usability specialists who can participate in integrated product teams effectively.

Acknowledgments

We thank John Bennett, Steve Huling, and Dave Imhoff for comments on an earlier draft of this chapter, and our colleagues and participants in user-centered design work for continual challenges and opportunities to learn.

References

Bellcore. (1993). *Graphical User Interface Design Guidelines for Bellcore Software Products*, LP-CSP-000023, Issue 1.

Burkhart, Brenda. J., Hemphill, Darold D., and Jones, Scott. (1994). "The Value of a Baseline in Determining Design Success". *CHI'94 Proceedings*, ACM Press, New York.

Burkhart, Brenda J., Leland, Mary D. P., and Shalmon, Doron. (1993). "Large Scale Reuse and User Interface Consistency on the TMM Project," *BOOST'93 Proceedings*, pp. 102-111. Bellcore, Livingston, NJ.

Muller, Michael J., Wildman, Daniel M., and White, Ellen A. (1993). "Equal Opportunity PD Using PICTIVE," *Communications of the ACM 36*, 64-66.

Nielsen, Jakob. (1993). *Usability Engineering*. Academic Press, Boston.

Open Software Foundation. (1991). *OSF/Motif Style Guide, Release 1.1.* Prentice Hall, Englewood Cliffs, NJ.

Salasoo, Aita. (1990). "Towards Usable Icon Sets: A Case Study from Telecommunications Engineering," *Proceedings of the 34th Meeting of the Human Factors Society*, pp. 203-207. Human Factors Society, Santa Monica.

Salasoo, Aita, Brunner, Hans, Flamm, Lois E., Glynn, Judith, Morch, Andres, Reyna, Rudy, Silver, Edward, and Warren, Robert E. (1991a). "The State of User-Centered Design in the Regions and at Bellcore," *Proceedings of the Bellcore/BCC Symposium on User-Centered Design: Making It Happen* (Bellcore Special Report SR-OPT-002130), pp. 1-20.

Salasoo, Aita, Rosenstein, Mark, and Collier, George H. (1991b). "Insight from Situated Action Analysis: The Case of Telephone Operating Company Engineers," *SIGCHI Bulletin 23*, 76.

Schuler, Douglas S., and Namioka, Aki N. (eds.) (1993). *Participatory Design: Principles and Practices* Lawrence Erlbaum Associates, Hillsdale, NJ.

Tudor, Leslie G., Muller, Michael J., Dayton, Tom, and Root, Robert W. (1993). "A Participatory Design Technique for High-Level Task Analysis, Critique, and Redesign: The CARD Method," *Proceedings of the Human Factors and Ergonomic Society 37th Annual Meeting*, Human Factors and Ergonomic Society, Santa Monica.

CHAPTER 17

GE Information Services

Reynold P. Stimart
GE Information Services,
Rockville, Maryland

Ren Stimart manages the User Interface Group at GE Information Services, which he formed three years ago. Since he joined GE Information Services 10 years ago, he has also managed other groups such as those responsible for computer-based training, end-user training and documentation, and technical consulting for improving product design. Prior to joining GE, he lead projects at the Xerox's International Center for Training and Management Development for four years. There he developed computer-based training systems and worked on high technology instructional applications. He worked for three years with Education Turnkey Systems, a consulting firm, establishing and assessing effective educational programs and for two years with the Virginia State Department of Education supervising experimental educational programs. Previously he was an assistant professor at the University of Miami and a research associate in the Bureau of Educational Research of the University of Virginia. For the last five years, he has also been teaching graduate courses in research design and measurement at Marymount University.
Stimart graduated in mathematics from the University of Minnesota. He received his Master's and did Ph.D. work in educational research at the University of Virginia.

GE Information Services' Business

GE Information Services is one of 13 key business units of General Electric Company. It was established in 1965 when GE commercialized the concept of timesharing, developed at Dartmouth College. GE Information Services' headquarters is located in Rockville, Maryland. It has offices worldwide, including field offices in United States, Europe, Africa, Asia and Australia. The field offices have sales and technical support personnel. Each of the international regions has it's own sales headquarters and some marketing functions. The field offices concentrate on custom solutions to client needs generally using the software applications developed in headquarters engineering.

With 2,500 employees worldwide, approximately 40% outside the United States, there is a worldwide client support staff of over 200 trained specialists who provide skilled local, in-country support. The GE Information Services Global Support Services group provides support in countries where there is no local presence.

This unit is one of the world's largest providers of network-based information services—including electronic data interchange (EDI), electronic messaging and networking management—for the conduct of global electronic commerce. Revenue from Europe and Asia accounts for approximately 40% of total revenue. Its key business segments are growing 30% annually. It has a client base of more than 15,000 corporations and associates. GE Information Services has nearly 13,000 EDI trading partners and is growing at 40% annually. It has more than 350,000 mailboxes and is the recognized leader in worldwide EDI network services market. GE Information Services has approximately 21% of the electronic-mail (E-mail) market and is growing this area at 11% annually. In addition, there are currently over 30 X.400 interconnections to other service providers and the number is steadily increasing.

The GE Information Services infrastructure is composed of four supercenters (Cleveland, Rockville, Amsterdam and Tokyo) with 22 network control centers. There is direct, local network access from 750 cities in 35 countries. Users in an additional 75 countries have access via PDNs and IRC interconnections. GE Information Services is the operator of the largest private packet-switched network in the world, accessible from more than 100 countries, supporting 8,000 simultaneous users. It has over 200 clients with SNI connections and has 25 SNA nodes deployed around the world.

GE Information Services' Usability Engineering Program

GE Information Services began as a computer timesharing business and has slowly evolved into its present state. In its earlier days, most of the applications were for use by the data processing department or people who were highly skilled in programming and program operations. As such, the user interface of the applications was not of high priority, the developers had near complete control of how it should look. This made perfect sense as the developer was frequently very much like the user of the services. They both had similar training and experiences. They both valued interfaces that talked their language. This scenario is an old story. I mention it only because it describes the atmosphere that in some ways was still in place at the conception and birth of the usability and engineering program at GE Information Services.

The user interface group as an identifiable unit has existed for about three years at this point. It has varied in size with a growing base of six people and a flux of an additional two to four people. The growth of the base has been slow and steady. The additional people are supervised by the base staff. They come to the group as interns who have completed their doctoral degree requirements in human factors and have yet to undertake their dissertations, coop students in a related field, GE Information Services people who are completing a master's degree program while working full time, and others in the company who are looking for some experience working with clients. The additional people make up an essential component of the group. Without them, it could not provide user interface support for many of the projects. The adjunct staff members are typically less experienced than the user interface staff, so they provide an infusion of some nontraditional ways to do things. In addition, the affiliations with universities keep the group abreast of current interface thoughts.

Overview of User Interface Group in the Software Development Process

The User Interface Group's involvement in the software development process varies from application to application, but ideally the Group is involved early and throughout the process. In the case study section of this chapter, I describe a specific example of the involvement. Here I will discuss the User Interface Group at a general level.

We have found the key user interface processes that make the largest difference for success include defining the user characteristics, performing a task analysis, developing a prototype, and performing a usability test. To define the user characteristics we survey the users, interview our field sales organizations, collect input from our client services organization and talk with the users. Task analyses vary from following clients around as they do their job to creating process flows through discussions with them or people who are very familiar with their job. We worry about not only the isolated part of the job that we are supporting, but also how it fits into the total job, such as what other software applications may also be used. Prototypes are put together as early as possible, frequently in conjunction with a requirements document, and continually refined throughout the design process. Since usability testing is the substantiation of the ease of use of the design, it happens in piecemeal on major components and near the end so the total impact can be assessed. The idea is to do it before a great deal of development has taken place.

History of the Group's Beginning

The usability engineering program began as part of the End-User Support group, which had end-user training and documentation functions. The lion's share of the activities of the group at that time seemed to be in response to correcting problems the user was having with the application interfaces. So the third function of the group was born with the objective of putting the other two out of business. It started modestly, with no personnel except those who were borrowed from time to time from the training and documentation functions.

That was seven years ago. It gradually became a group of its own within the training and documentation function. Resistance for including a user interface component on any project was great at the start. There were few in the marketing or engineering function who thought it was worthwhile. They had been developing software without the purported expertise and thought they were doing fine. In fact to say there was some resistance is an understatement. The marketing people viewed many of the things like surveying the user, task analysis, and determining the look and feel of the product as their proprietary domain. The engineering people thought they developed the interface based on the requirements brought to them by marketing. They also thought that this was the fun part of developing the software, at which they prided themselves as being very good.

One of my first attempts at improving the software was when I tackled trying to improve EDI*PC, which is a PC front-end to GE Information Services' offering that moves business documents like invoices and purchase orders between companies. GE Information Services recognized the potential for EDI earlier than most companies. They hurried EDI*PC out to the clients. While it did the job, it suffered from some severe user interface problems as did most companies' applications in those days. I gathered a small group of people at the request of the Vice President in charge of the emerging EDI market. We called it *HEAT*, which stood for Human Engineering Action Team. We wanted to turn up the "heat" on the usability engineering problems. A documentation writer who supported the product, a client service person who answered the calls from clients in need of help, a couple of people from sales in the technical support area, and a few marketing people formed the group. We met and brainstormed to gain consensus on the areas of the product in which the clients were having difficulty. We identified 188 distinct issues that we felt should be dealt with.

Shortly after this, I was part of a group that visited a third party seller of business software. The seller was interested in adding EDI*PC to its offerings and had reviewed a copy of the software. The decision was to not take on EDI*PC because every product it took on it supported through its own client service organization. The assessment was that the product would be too big a drain on the firm's resources. The seller described what it thought would be problems to the user of the product that could potentially result in a call to its support organization. From the description, I compiled an additional list of 89 items beyond the original 188 from HEAT. I then took that information and built a prototype with Bricklin's Demo program to demonstrate how the application might be improved so that it accounted for some of the issues. Here I had a slight setback. My mistake was I distributed the prototype to the marketing organization with a courtesy copy to the engineering organization responsible for building the original. The explosions began with the developers and continued on through the vice president of engineering. Who was I to be fooling around in the engineering domain building prototypes? As a matter of fact, EDI*PC was really only a prototype that was turned into a product. Not only was I building prototypes, but I was in the training organization that reported to sales of all places. It took weeks of apologizing for stepping on toes and explaining that it was not a prototype as they meant it but only a visual representation of how it might look. This set off another round of debates over whether vaporware could be considered a prototype. We finally agreed to call what I was doing a _visual description._

When the User Interface Group was finally formed, one of the first things it did was to tackle the redesign of EDI*PC . EDI*PC was one of the first products of its type in the industry and was beginning to look its age. The interface design had its roots in older technology. It was menu driven and system oriented without much concern for grouping similar things together. Figure 1 shows before and after pictures of the main screen of the two versions, Version 6.0 compared to Version 7.0. Prior to Version 7.0 there had been six major and many partial releases that focused on functionality expansions. Mostly these were requested by clients or anticipated needs GE was trying to fulfill. Version 7.0 was the first to focus on the usability as part of that functionality. The objective of EDI*PC 7.0 was to give it a more modern appearance, (i.e., replace the menus and its organization with icons and a restructuring) and to make it a more intuitive program to use.

Figure 1a Before User Interface Group involvement, EDI*PC, Version 6.0

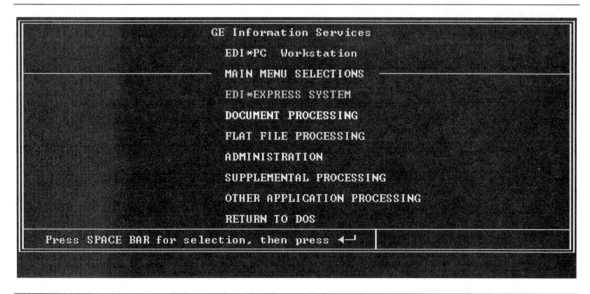

Figure 1b After User Interface Group involvement, EDI*PC, Version 7.0

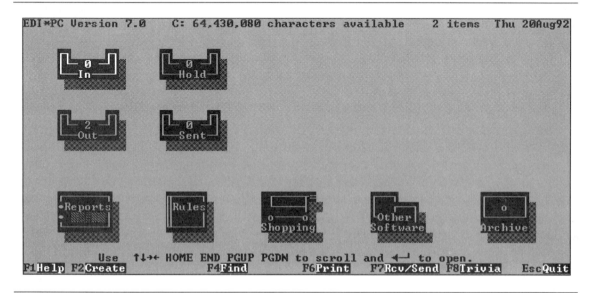

What was achieved as evidenced from the main screen was a movement away from a menu driven approach to a character graphic representation of objects with accompanying actions. The hierarchy of this new design was flatter, requiring less menu navigation. There was some original resistance to the design from internal groups because of its departure from the previous version and the perceived potential problems this would create for our current users. It was clear from talking to potential clients that there was better acceptance of this redesign, but clients comfortable with previous versions were thought to have more trouble orienting to the new look. In fact what happened was that the support levels dropped to about a third of the normal amount during the upgrade to the existing clients. This really proved the worth of the User Interface Group.

Being placed in the training and documentation group was convenient because of some of the shared values of the members of all the components, but the User Interface Group lacked training and documentation's charter. So I began looking for a home more suitable for its function. The marketing and engineering organizations were interested in creating a group. Both vice presidents were supporters and thought the group fit in their organizations. Marketing viewed it as part of the products requirement definition and engineering viewed it as part of the software development process. My original thought was that marketing was the better place for it, because it set the requirements for the product and ultimately made decisions on the product's existence. Ultimately, engineering was where the group ended up. It was able to allocate the initial three positions from engineering personnel, while marketing was having problems covering its existing operational needs. Engineering turned out to be the better fit because of support we got from above and unanticipated influence that could be exerted on product outcome.

Where the User Interface Group Fits in the Organization

Overview of GE Information Services

The members of the User Interface Group have consulting responsibilities that are aligned with specific marketing areas, such as business communication, electronic document interchange, managed network services, and GEnie. They are a centralized group that serve all of GE Information Services's units. Some of the benefits of this approach are that resources can be shifted around as the demands shift in organizations, it promotes a single user interface style for all of GE Information Services interfaces, and it enables members of the user interface group to confer with each other on difficult issues.

Software development is divided into two areas: core engineering and client customization. Core engineering has the responsibility for generic product development. It develops products with broad generic applicability, products that are designed for use by large market segments. It reports to either the Vice President of Information Delivery Services (IDS) or the Vice President of Electronic Commerce Services (ECS), both of whom also have a marketing function. The core engineering groups are located in Rockville, Maryland, Brentwood, Tennessee, and Dublin, Ireland, each having distinct product development responsibility.

There are five times as many software developers in the client customization area as the core engineering area. The developers in the client customization area have the responsibility of dealing directly with GE Information Services' clients. They form the technical part of the sales organization, who respond to a specific client need with a specific client solution. They typically modify products developed by the core engineering groups to satisfy the client needs, but they also develop smaller niche products from scratch when there are no generic products to build from. Sometimes these niche products become generic products when they fit a broader client need and then development and refinement typically transfers back to the core engineering area. The client customization groups report to the three Vice Presidents of Sales, who have responsibilities for the United States, Europe and Asia Pacific. They are located worldwide in the GE Information Services sales offices.

Organization Chart and Reporting

The User Interface Group's charter is to make GE Information Services software easier to use. While it is true the group cannot support all the software, it has at least some involvement in all major applications. The User Interface Group reports to the VP of IDS. It is part of a marketing and development group that provides services and support for many parts of the organization (see Figure 2). The rationale for the placement of the group is because it serves engineering, marketing and sales across the company and so do the other components of that marketing and development group. The majority of the products it supports are in the ECS organization, because it is this organization that develops most of the products that have some user frontend. The next biggest area that it supports is the sales organizations for the same reasons.

Primary Initiatives

The User Interface Group focuses on five initiatives that represent most of the activities of the group: consulting, evaluation, tools, training and standards. The overall goal or mission of the group is simply to improve the usability of GE Information Services

Figure 2   Conceptual organization chart

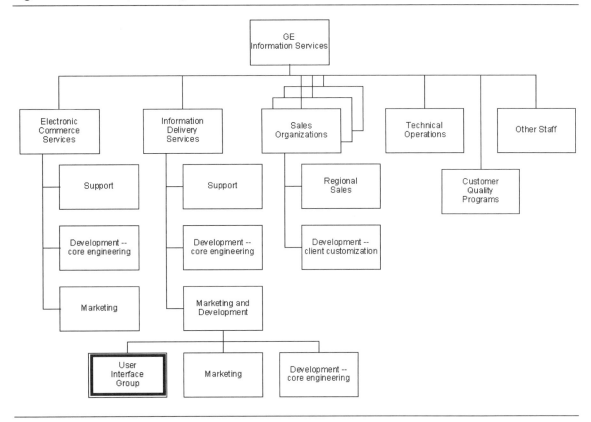

applications. Each of the initiatives contribute to that goal. In some years there is more emphasis on one initiative than another, but for the most part consulting and evaluation take the most time and require the most resources. They focus on short term aspects of the goal and so show the most immediate result. The other three are important for their lasting effect and the potential to reduce resource needs from the User Interface Group. These initiatives transfer some of the burden to the software developers and they are instrumental in the improvement of the software development process.

Figure 3   When to prepare a prototype and test

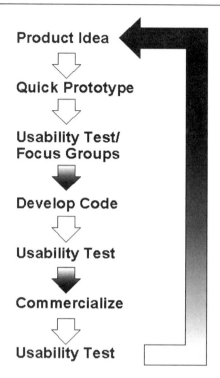

Product Idea

Quick Prototype

Usability Test/
Focus Groups

Develop Code

Usability Test

Commercialize

Usability Test

Consulting

The consulting initiative includes providing assistance to the developers and marketing groups to design the best possible human–machine interface for an application. Some of the activities of the consulting initiative include user surveys to define the targeted user, task analysis, prototyping, focus groups, and negotiating user interface issues between the groups.

We like to prepare a prototype early and often through the process (see Figure 3). Because of the prototype's visual nature, it ends up to be the lightning rod for collecting user interface and product issues. The prototypes first phase is usually done with the product marketing manager. It is then shown to other members of the marketing organization to ensure it fits the overall vision of where the product should go. Frequently about this same time, the developers are shown the prototype as a validity check to see if the concept can be built. Along the way the prototype gets expanded to include more of the functionality and then it is shown to clients in focus groups to get reactions to the design and features. This prototype ends up to be about half of the functional specification. It describes in pictures the visual and navigational parts of the product that used to be impossible with words alone so that everyone had a common understanding.

The user interface consultant is a full member of any product development team. He or she participates in planning, design, and progress review meetings and is viewed as the final arbitrator of user interface issues. The consultant's desire is not to make arbitrary decisions, but to garner enough information to provide an informed consultation. And when there appears to be no compelling rational for one approach over another, the consultant's experience and knowledge of related products become the deciding factor.

Evaluation

The evaluation initiative takes several different forms. If the application in need of evaluating will have little exposure or the risk of an incorrect design is small, then the evaluation may merely be an expert review. One of the human factor specialists reviews the product or a prototype of the product and provides feedback on how easy it will be for the user to use it. This expert review provides a quick user interface assessment for products where the user interface group may not have been involved with its design.

If the group is after a detailed understanding of how well the user interface communicates and where the problems may be, it will do a full-scale usability test in the usability lab. Typical users are asked to perform typical tasks they would do with the product. The users are either hired specifically for the usability test or are clients who would be using the product. The tasks are always written in the jargon of the users and are outgrowths of the conversations with the users earlier in the process.

For a more surface-level review of the interface, done in a hurry, the group will do a modified usability test. Here six to eight typical users are put together in a classroom and asked to do the typical tasks. The difference here is that the users are given self-paced forms to allow them to do self-reporting of the problems they encounter. While the users are going through the test, monitors are roaming around and taking notes. Testers who run into a problem, can signal for assistance. This approach to usability testing is an inexpensive way to get a quick look at the user interface problems, but suffers from an incomplete understanding of the problems.

Standards

The User Interface Group is responsible for developing and maintaining the guidelines that specify how the GE Information Services' applications should look and feel. As members provide advice in the consulting initiative, part of what we are doing is providing an oral guideline. We are in the process of turning those oral directions into written guidelines. The standards initiative should be thought of as a number of standards as each platform requires a specific guideline. The guideline for Microsoft Windows is completed. Guidelines are still needed for Macintosh, Motif and DOS. Product-specific guidelines are in place for DOS products like the Sales Force Automation project, but the general guideline is still to be developed. All the standards, those developed or to be developed, are subsets of the industry standards. The group is not rewriting, for example, *The Windows Interface: An Application Design Guide* written by Microsoft, but it forms the basis for the GE Information Services specific guidelines.

Tools

The tools initiative worries about standardizing the software development approach. It has the goal of making it easier to develop a user interface correctly than it is to do it incorrectly. The User Interface Group reviews and tests commercially available development tools to see how they fit the GE Information Services development environment and culture. Prototyping tools, GUI builders, form design tools, cross-platform development tools, etc. are examined. If it is appropriate, the tool is selected for inclusion in the GE Information Services toolset. It may also be expanded to include any peculiarities in the GE Information Service's approach. For example, if a forms design tool was selected, sample layouts or templates would be included for the development team's use.

Training

The User Interface Group is also responsible for disseminating information and techniques to the software development staffs for improving the GE Information Services' user interfaces. The goal is not to make the development people human factors experts, but to make them aware of general issues, make them self sufficient for general things like adherence to standards, and alert them to when the User Interface Group should be called into the development process and when they can help with a specific issue.

Composition of the Group

The User Interface Group has been steadily growing since its formation as a group in 1990. Identifying and hiring folks with the right skills and motivations was difficult at the start. I put ads in the newspapers, attended and recruited at professional conferences, put out requests through head hunters, had our internal recruiting staff looking for people, networked with all those who I knew might have a source, and advertised through on-line bulletin boards. It still took me over a year to find the nucleus of the staff. I wanted people who, as the saying goes, could hit the ground running. I wanted people who were already trained in human–computer interaction and had some experience doing the kinds of user interface tasks I had in mind.

Just three years later, I now think that task would be easier. There are now more colleges graduating people with the appropriate degrees, and I have changed the approach. I now look for interns who have as part of their degree requirement a real-world experience. This approach means I get six to eight months to look at a potential employee, who in turn gets that same time period to examine GE Information Services. If there is a position after or during the internship, the intern can then make the transition to a full-time employee. I get someone who I am quite sure will fit in and who will do things the GE Information Services way. If not, I have extended my network of associates, and there is always a potential for a later position. The interns, in turn, have gotten real-world experience to put on their resumes.

Human Factors and Computer Science Expertise

There are nine people in the group, six permanent and three temporary. Five of the nine are Ph.D.-level people trained in human factors, some of whom have not received the degree yet. Two are masters-level people who are trained in computer science, psychology or human factors. The last two are very skilled programmers and system analysts.

Culture of the Group

To get a sense of the culture of the group (Figure 4), you should have a sense of how we work together. We are a centrally organized group with responsibilities to all marketing and engineering functions. We work primarily with the groups that have responsibility for software that resides on the users' personal computers. We do very little for those groups responsible for applications that run totally on our remote computers except for occassional help to improve documentation. Perhaps part of the reason it took so long to hire the staff was because I was looking for people who would get along and work well together. We interact on a continual basis, bouncing ideas off each other to test reality. It is common in the group to see two or more members in small impromptu meetings discussing a particularly difficult problem. Each has his or her own responsibilities to particular marketing and engineering organizations. All have their current programs they are working on. But, each also has responsibility as part of the User Interface Group to gain consistency in look and feel across the product lines.

This very team-oriented approach is supported and encouraged from Jack Welsh, CEO of General Electric, on down. Welsh, in trying to rid General Electric of some of the bureaucracy, wants to break down barriers of hierarchy, function and geography and empower cross-functional teams. He pushes for shared values within GE. He says, "companies can't afford to tell employees what to do. It takes too long. Instead, values are meant to guide people and , in turn, to drive the organization continually toward profitability and other benchmarks." The User Interface Group has twice as much work to do as staff to do it. We members need to make the best use of our time that we can. We do this through shared values.

Figure 4   The UI Group. Back: Deirdre Hannon, Deborah Magid, Cathy O'Donnell. Front: David White, Ren Stimart, Marta Miller.

M&Ms in the Afternoon

I would not want to leave the reader with the idea that all we do is sit around in meetings and converse. The group is extremely busy, and in fact we have to work at getting together at times when we can relax. We all get caught up in what we are doing and have to be reminded to check with each other to see if what we each are doing has impact on or help for the other members of the team. Staff meetings are usually to take care of the more mundane administrivia. We try to get away for lunch at least once every other week. We will use just about any excuse, birthday, anniversary with the company, hunger. If those things do not work, there is always M&Ms in the afternoon. On my desk I have a jar filled with M&Ms or some other candy. M&Ms are the preferred because they are chocolate and tinkle when the jar is poured. Its like a Pavlovian dog's response. Before the jar is set down, the saliva is flowing and the group is in my office. That takes some doing as we are spread out on a fairly large floor. We take our "five" standing up around the jar. Its a great opportunity to keep the group in touch with each other . The dogs that show up at the door for a chocolate are not all in the User Interface Group. I usually get a good mix of breeds: programmers, secretaries, marketing people, managers from other organizations, etc.

Use of External Resources

To supplement the efforts of the group, we involve at lot of other people from outside the organization.

Consultants

Over the years, we have used a number of different types of consultants to help offset the shortfall of resources within the User Interface Group. Initially we did not have a usability testing laboratory. We dealt with it in two ways, by either doing a modified, self-administered test or by contracting for testing in a third party lab. The third party lab extended our resources and provided us with facilities we could not justify initially. Now that we have a lab we still use third party labs when we either have a very sensitive test to be performed or we need an impartial assessment for something we were all involved in designing. We also occasionally use outside consultants to help with product design and development. We do not do this often because it takes too long to bring the consultant up to speed on GE Information Services and our product areas. It works when we have a long standing relationship, so we gain efficiency from project to project.

We also use consultants to supplement the skills of the group. For example, we have no graphic artist on staff and would probably never have one. For icons, graphic buttons, or other screen beautifications, we look for skilled professionals, but it is not something that would keep somebody busy full time.

Universities

Partnerships between industry and academia are frequently strained relationships. They have different motivations and internal measurements of success. Their missions are different, but in that difference lies the reason for partnering with a university. GE Information Services does not do research and development except in very limited ways, while that is the business of universities. Over the last several years GE Information Services has been contributing to basic research and exploration of ideas that could effect the look and feel some of our products. While we expect no immediate payoff, we are already getting some from the studies we have funded. Of course we also work with universities with the rotation of interns through the organization, but that benefits the individual more than the university.

Extended Family and the Man on the Street

Our test subjects are seldom GE Information Services employees. Such employees just do not look like the clients for whom we are trying to develop applications. Typically GE Information Services employees are too technical with too much knowledge of GE's products. The only exception is when we are actually building an application for our own use. Therefore, we look to clients, spouses, children, neighbors, people who answer an ad in the grocery store, and temporary agencies. We use clients when we are doing focus groups, surveys, task analyses and usability tests. Most are more than willing to participate and help define the products. For the person on the street, we pay for participation when we find people who match our predefined profile of the potential user of the product.

Relationship with Other Functions

As I have indicated earlier, the User Interface Group is built around a teamwork approach. The same can be said for the groups formed to develop applications. The approach within GE Information Services is to empower a cross-functional group that is well positioned to understand the product, its components, and how it fits into the business world–and then stand back and get out of the way so they can get the job done. This is a team that makes its own decisions as to what features it should have, the development approach and all aspects of the product. This does not mean it does it in isolation, because each knows when to confer with others. The User Interface Group's members are part of these empowered groups along with representatives from engineering, marketing, sales, documentation and training. These groups are formed at the very start of a project. An idea might be thought of by marketing and requirements begin to be written. It is at this time that the group would be formed.

Input would be sought from sales to get its perception of the marketplace and access to potential clients. Engineering would begin working the internal processing issues, and the User Interface Group would start working the product's look and feel. Documentation, training and client support would deal with issues of how to support the product.

Case Study: BusinessTalk System 2000

The following case study is presented to provide a sense of how the User Interface Group works within GE Information Services. It illustrates most aspects of the support that the user interface group provides. In some cases, it is involved only in pre-design concepts, in others asked to make the product user friendly just prior to commercialization, and in others still asked to do just a usability test to "confirm" that the user interface is designed well. While the majority of the products it is involved with today are ones that it takes an active role in from the start to the end, its resources limit the degree of involvement at each level. This case study focuses on a product that was a long time in development and had many false starts. Ultimately it included the full user interface development process as done at GE Information Services. It also represents a product to which the group devoted the required amount of resources and did not compromise the effort.

The Product

BusinessTalk System 2000 is a family of products that is one of GE Information Services's offerings from a wide portfolio of electronic commerce services. This family of electronic messaging and related business communications services link a customer's geographically dispersed locations with GE Information Services' worldwide network to provide a unique set of business communications and information management solutions.

BusinessTalk 2000 is a flexible, powerful and robust communications system designed to retrieve and distribute information to members of a geographically dispersed business community. It is an umbrella of products and services that combines electronic mail, third party industry-specific databases, private bulletin boards and electronic news clipping services into an easy-to-use icon and menu driven communications and information management tool. BusinessTalk 2000 is available for PC DOS, Microsoft Windows and the Macintosh environments.

The look and feel of BusinessTalk 2000 on the three environments is similar, but each is unique. There were separate engineering and marketing teams for each, and each went through a different user interface process as a result. The case study could have been about any of the versions as each represents a different user interface challenge and solution. For this case study, I will be focusing on the Microsoft Windows version and so every time I talk about BusinessTalk 2000 I will be referring to that version. Also note that BusinessTalk 2000 is the frontend to GE Information Services' network and processing capabilities. While there are certainly user interface issues and implications with a distributed system, for the most part the discussion will be about the frontend.

Setting the Stage

BusinessTalk 2000 Windows version has its origins on the DOS platform. The concept of BusinessTalk 2000 was to extend the functionality of its predecessor and make it a replacement for a number of electronic mail and bulletin board products to consolidate GE Information Services' product offerings. It was originally going to be another DOS product with an improved user interface that had a more object-oriented feel to it.

The self-contained User Interface Group was just beginning when this effort began. It was still feeling its way through how to work with the development groups. It had very limited resources as it was only partially staffed. Acceptance of the User Interface Group was a slight problem with the Windows team as it is with all teams when you initially begin working with them. With the Windows team it went smoother than most because the Marketing and Product Managers were looking for assistance. Usually, there is initial resistance as the UI Group is viewed as taking away the "fun" stuff. After it works with a team for a while this perception changes. Much of what is perceived as the fun stuff is only a small part of what the User Interface Group does, and there is a discovery that there is enough fun to go around. Many of the developers are very good at user interface design, but they have a conflict of interest. They want the code to be as elegant as possible and that frequently is at odds with user interface effort. It is difficult to be fair minded about each and it is healthy for each to have an advocate.

Initial Steps

Next to Last Try

A series of development groups worked on a design for this product, four in all. It was not intended that way, but happened as a result of normal reorganizations and changes in GE Information Services priorities. Each took its turn at designing the product and its interface, thinking it would be commercialized. Some groups got further than others. The effort prior to its real commercialization was essentially finished when the user interface group first became involved, and the role here was as an internal reviewer.

Mixed Acceptance

Internal reviews, GE Information Services' alpha tests, tend to be excruciating events for those involved. We are much harder on ourselves than any outside reviewers ever could be. We look at the product first with our own set of prejudices of how it should look and perform. Most people at GE Information Services are highly technical, even those in positions that might merely be consumers of the product have far more background in the inner workings of the equipment and how it has to communicate and share processing with our host computer. So those prejudices are not those normal to our client groups in general. They also look at a product from a collective view of our clients. They do not see a product as it would fit one client, but as they would suppose it would satisfy the unique set of requirements of all of our clients. Most of our clients do not agree on which features are important nor how they should look. In an alpha test, these all become a wanted feature, even though they may be in conflict. And because we are so client satisfaction focused that want is a demand and the result is hand-to-hand conflict between the testers and the developers.

Acceptance was mixed. One client who was using this version of BusinessTalk 2000 extensively was relatively satisfied with its look and feel. This client viewed it as an improvement over previous electronic mail packages it used. When the product was released to a large alpha testing group within GE Information Services, the response was not as positive. It should be noted though that an alpha test is frequently used as a gripe session to vent not only on the product, but also with related products or the process for rolling out a product. You have people who are passionately interested in getting their specific needs satisfied without regard for other interests. So some discontent was to be expected.

The alpha test for this version of BusinessTalk 2000 was a group of approximately 100 people with varying interests in the product. Some were sales folks who would have to sell it, so they viewed it as they thought their clients would. Some were client support folks whose job it is to worry about how many people it would take to support the product. Frequently, this group is the most valuable as its healthy paranoia acts as a defensive shield for the expected onslaught of telephone calls. Some were marketing folks with an interest in how this product fit into the family of products. Some were international folks who have an interest in markets of non-native American English speakers with complex communication problems.

Alpha testers are typically selected because they are a vocal group who will give an honest opinion of a product that is in a pre-release state. This BusinessTalk 2000 version group was no exception. Responses to this version filled the development teams' hard disks with electronic mail on what was wrong with it and suggestions on how to improve it so it would fill just the niche in which they were interested. How much of the discontent was just the normal reaction to a first look at a product and how much was an indication of how potential clients would view it was not fully understood.

This was the first development effort of a major product being developed in Microsoft Windows. Hence, the development team had little Microsoft Windows experience. Some developers were learning as they went on how to develop an application in this environment. Microsoft was also not clear at this point on what an application should look like in this environment. They originally released the IBM CUA guidelines as part of the developer's kit. It was obvious from looking at the applications being developed at Microsoft, i.e. Word, Excel, Powerpoint, etc., that their different development teams were starting from different points of view.

Death of the Next to Last Try

The alpha test generated a great deal of concern about the product with the user interface receiving a lot of that attention. As a result, the BusinessTalk 2000 marketing team asked the User Interface Group to contract with external human factors specialists to perform an expert review while the marketing team went on to explore its business options.

The external specialists found many things that they suspected would cause users problems. The impact of the news, while not totally unexpected because of feedback from the alpha testers, was nonetheless felt. The business directions that came out of the marketing exploration were to

- have a single interface for each operating environment,
- provide a means for custom development on top the core product, and
- to have an application program interface as the ultimate goal.

The marketing team began negotiating with companies who had products that seemed to fit the business needs and had an acceptable user interface.

Death Greatly Exaggerated

As Mark Twain responded to the editor of the *New York Journal* when shown a cable inquiring if he were dead or dying, "report of my death greatly exaggerated," so too was the death of BusinessTalk 2000. I am focusing here on the user interface, but its rebirth was really the result of underlying processing on both the host and the PC that turned out to be more irreplaceable than originally thought. So this time we started with a concern for the interface as it was one of the factors that provided so much trouble on the previous effort.

The Engineering Project Manager of the Microsoft Windows development team took the initiative and asked for User Interface Group input as they began a redesign. There were some in the engineering group who thought it was a waste of time. In fact they pointed to one successful sale of the beta version of BusinessTalk 2000 in its pre-death state. While it was true there was a happy customer, the happiness was probably due to a unique set of circumstances. The customer had been using a previous DOS version that was even more difficult to use and there was a very good relationship with this client. The manager's objective was to avoid the hailstorm of complaints that arose from our internal reviews and to develop a product that was not only acceptable, but exceptional with regard to the user interface. He had been with GE Information Services for 18 years, coding and managing development groups. His was the first group to tackle Microsoft Windows applications, and so it went through a trial by fire learning of how to do it when it took on BusinessTalk 2000.

The Plan

In May 1991 the Product Marketing Manager, with input from others and the advantage of an untold number of meetings, put out an outline of the key features that would be in BusinessTalk 2000 for Windows. The platform would have

- a Microsoft Windows interface: using multiple document interface (MDI);
- applications represented as stand-alone icons on MDI desktop;
- help fully integrated, using standard Microsoft/Windows Help engine;
- full file transfer support;
- hierarchical icons;
- complete supports for the transaction set being used;
- multitasking support for other Windows applications.

The first application on the platform would be electronic mail. It would contain

- all features of GE Information Services mail products;
- full attach file support;
- addressing both ad-hoc and address book methods;
- integrated Mail filing system: with folders and search capability;
- support for the host interactive features;
- mail scheduler.

Steps in the Process

Assessment of the Problems

A typical effort would include a great deal of time gathering client input before the design effort began. Clients or potential clients would be surveyed. Sales groups would be asked what they needed. The client services organization would provide input on the problems with the current products. This project was atypical because of all the past history through previous versions. We already had a very solid understanding of what was needed. We had already spoken to many clients and people who deal with clients. We did not necessarily know how it should be accomplished or the specifics of the solution, but we were very clear on what features it should include and that it needed to be user friendly as determined by our users.

The marketing and engineering team wanted to develop a world class user interface. While specific usability engineering goals were not articulated, as we now try to do, there was a clear notion of a need to perform better than what had been previously demonstrated with the past effort. We wanted performance in the usability test significantly improved. We wanted shorter installation times and shorter times to do the reading and creation of the first e-mail items. We wanted acceptance from our internal reviewers and very positive reaction from our clients. The one target that we never really stated, but that was on everyone's mind, was the desire to build something we could be proud of.

Product Manager Pushed for More User Interface Involvement

The marketing product manager was a strong advocate for improved usability. This was not easy in a time when there were a lot of people saying "just do it". Performance targets and success was in terms of getting the product to market in order to meet revenue and cost targets. In addition, the market pressure to get a Microsoft Windows product out and to just improve our product line was great. Our competition was in the process of developing similar capabilities, and our sales people were demanding fast action. This was also the early stages of the User Interface Group existence, and so the process we were trying to put in place was pretty much unknown and required a great deal of trust on the part of the team. The product manager had seen and been part of past efforts. He had seen the effect of pushing a product out before it was ready from a user interface perspective. He worked very hard to resist the pressure and provide the time and support to do the user interface design right.

Paper Prototype by the Team

The engineering team was no less dedicated to getting it right this time. A couple of the team members started by sketching out on paper a prototype of what the interface might ideally look like before the User Interface Group got involved. They were anticipating the need and the solution before there was an official go ahead to modify the previous design. When we actually did start the design effort, we started by looking at this paper prototype and then put it away only to re-examine it later in the cycle. The paper prototype was a good example of the richness of the design process when you have developers with user interface sensitivity.

Locked in a Room or the Project Manager and Me

For the next several weeks the engineering project manager and I locked ourselves in a room to lay out the general design. We sketched ideas, we argued, we rehashed things that did not work, we kept telling people to stay away until we were ready for them. We started from the technical problems and the loosely articulated usability engineering goals at the same time. The project manager had spent a great deal of time thinking through what was wrong with the previous version and obstacles to building a successful product that would be accepted by our internal people and clients. In his mind there were two driving forces: being able to compete with local area network (LAN)–based e-mail systems and being able to provide sufficient levels of customization for our integrated solutions approach.

Bear in mind that the BusinessTalk 2000 product connects through a wide area network. Most of our clients make that connection through modems. The user's PC dials GE Information Services Network, and then users send or receive mail, retrieve information from a database or bulletin board, etc. A competing method to do this is to have everything on a LAN, where everyone is always connected. The user does not initiate a connection, and no delay is experienced before communication can flow. The down side to the LAN approach is that people who are geographically dispersed or not on a LAN are not interconnected.

Our potential users may be of all types. Those who have used services on LAN systems have certain expectations. They want things to be instantaneous. So one of the challenges was to manage users' expectations and interactions so that the delayed, user initiated actions were more palatable. This was partly a technical issue and partly a usability issue. No matter what we did the user's computer still needs to dial a number, the PC and remote computer have to establish communication links and the PC and the host computer have to exchange information–all of which takes time.

One of the design issues then became whether or not to make it obvious that the user is connected or that a connection was even required. We opted to not make it very obtrusive. One of the ways we did this was by providing indicators of when a connection was necessary to perform the function. See the drawing in Figure 5. On the pulldown menus, lightning bolts were used and the lower righthand corner of the screen had a lightning bolt that would turn from gray to yellow when there was a connection. To manage the users' waiting time, status messages were provided at the bottom of the screen to indicate that progress toward connection was still progressing.

We also worried about adhering to user interface standards. We wanted to be consistent with what the industry was saying and doing. At the time however, Microsoft was taking liberties in their following of the CUA guidelines. Our guidelines became the examples and instancies found in the applications Microsoft was developing, including Windows itself.

The room we locked ourselves into had a white board on the wall. We filled it many times over as we mapped use patterns and made comparisons to make sure we were consistent from one area of the design to another. When the design started to have some shape and form, we would take occasional breaks by asking a member of the engineering or marketing team to confirm that it was possible to develop as we designed or that our assumptions on required functionality conformed to the marketing plan. We also had the occasional visit from upper management checking our progress and wondering when we would be done. Finally we were satisfied that we had enough specified and we were done with the initial design.

Figure 5   Screen with connection indicators

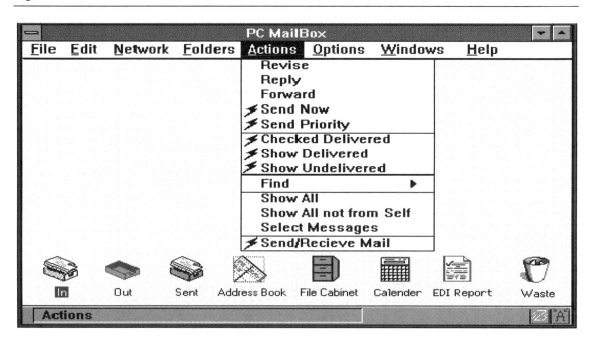

Prototypes

For other design efforts, we always used a prototype to test the look and feel. Unfortunately in May 1991 there were few tools that satisfied our needs. We wanted a Dan Bricklin Demo II kind of product that would allow us to lay out screens and navigate between them for Microsoft Windows. This is what we show all the interested parties so they can have a clear idea of what we have in mind and they can react to its inadequacies. Since this was so critical an activity, we had to come up with demo tool ourselves. One of the developers in the Windows group built it. The screen shown in Figure 6 below is an example screen of that early prototype.

Team Review and Negotiations

Once the initial design was completed and the prototype was at least underway, we began the negotiation process. We knew when we started that schedules and technical issues would influence the outcome. The team was being pushed hard to produce a product quickly. We sat down with the team and began getting estimates on how long

Figure 6   First prototype of Business Talk System 2000 for Windows

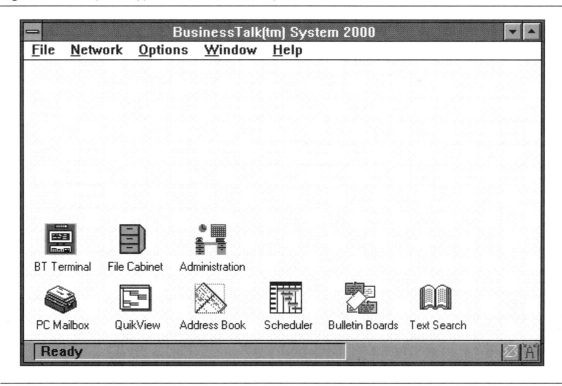

it would take to build the product according to the ideas we had come up with. In some areas we bumped up against the inadequacies of our development environment. So our choice became this, is it worth it to find a way around the problem or do we find another way that is directly doable. It came down to how important was that aspect of the product. For some, we added calendar time to be able to do it and for others it did not appear to be worth it.

We wanted everyone's input so we brought people into the room singularly or in small groups to discuss their areas of responsibility. We revised the design based on the input and then brought them all together to clarify and negotiate what we defined to be BusinessTalk 2000.

The schedule became compressed. When Marketing and Sales wanted to demonstrate BusinessTalk 2000, it made the Documentation group nervous because it did not think it could be ready in time. Virtually all our effort went into the development of BusinessTalk 2000 with no time for much else. The Documentation group had to rely on the prototype and discussions with User Interface Group, Engineering and Marketing instead of the more traditional method of working from specifications.

Resolving User Interface Problems During Coding

As with most complex development efforts, you miss things during the design phase. Once coding began on the BusinessTalk 2000 interface, what we could gloss over in a prototype became a hole or a problem in the code. Some were inconsistencies, highlighted when real processes were started. Some were differences in opinion on the best word choice or best structure. Some were the result of completing a design thought in a related area.

The process for resolving the user interface problems was clarified as we worked our way through breathing life into the code. The notion of who was responsible for what became operational as we began implementing. Marketing worried about and made decisions on what functionality would be included in each of the phases, how it fit into the family of products and cost issues affecting price. Engineering worried about and made decisions on all the aspects of development. The User Interface Group had the final call on the look and feel, and because everyone has an opinion on the user interface, we received a great deal of advice. Where it may not have been true at the beginning of the process, it was certainly true by the time we reached this point in the development, each team member had his or her role. We learned that if we didn't abide by the decision making division, we would perseverate and churn on the issue, loosing our focus on delivery.

All that sounds like the right thing to do, and one might ask, "why would you do it any differently?" I think the answer is not that we choose to do it differently, but rather we forget that the people with the appropriate expertise should make the decisions in their area. When everyone wants to build the best product possible, all have some of their self-worth tied up in its success. So no one wants to sit by idly while someone messes it up. It comes down to trust, which has to be developed between the team members. Probably the toughest place to gain this trust is at the user interface, because it is the most visible.

An Eye on the Future

BusinessTalk 2000 was an extremely important product. The product team viewed it as the heart of all our future products. It represented new territory in that we had built no significant Microsoft Windows product yet. It was the place at which we would establish the style for all the products that followed. It was also where we would lay the foundation for a more integrated application environment. Our view was that BusinessTalk 2000 would be glue for all the messaging activities of our clients. Two of our major marketing thrusts, EDI and business communications were separate and the teams' grand vision was the merger. So as we kept our eye on the product, we kept our eye on how it would handle other product areas. EDI for example required more complex addressing, scheduling, and file management. We wanted to make sure we did nothing to preclude BusinessTalk 2000 extension into these other areas.

As a footnote, the diligence paid off. BusinessTalk 2000 has influenced other Microsoft Windows development efforts by being the example style guide and by becoming our application integrator.

The Usability Test and Its Impact

This section is not on how to do a usability test, but rather a discussion of how it fits into the GE Information Services development process. I want to emphasize here the impact of testing. It should also be noted that at the time of this product development effort, we did not have usability lab and had to rely on outside sources when we wanted to do a formal product testing. We had been doing our testing in a less formal setting. A more complete description of the less formal approach has been described elsewhere.[1]

I did not have to push for the usability testing. The Marketing Product Manager did it for me. He called the initial planning meeting, where he wanted to discuss

- timing of the test,
- host and frontend software to be used,

- testbed applications,
- help and documentation support,
- preparation of the testers.

We pushed for usability testing as early as possible. With that we gave up having documentation. The help system had only limited review before testing and lacked graphics, a browse function and completeness in areas that were not going to be tested.

Setting

This usability test was conducted on pre-alpha software at the American Institute for Research (AIR). *Pre-alpha* means that we were getting close to release for testing by internal users, but the software was still as buggy as a Minnesota swamp in June. We worked very closely with AIR on the type of subjects to use, the tasks and structure of the test, and observed and kibbitzed through the entire test. They administered the test and wrote up the results. GE Information Services' testing process in our lab looks very similar, except we have written our own data logging software and have improved on lab layout and equipment.

Figure 7 Users profile

Sex	Age	Occupation	Hrs/week using Windows	Windows applications used	Communications applications used
F	26	Research Analyst	5-10	Microsoft Word	Microsoft Mail 2.1C
M	40	Systems Operator	4-6	WordPerfect 5.1, Solitaire	Bulletin Board, World, Compuserve, MCI mail
M	35	Acquisitions Engineer	10	Microsoft Excel & Project Ami Pro	Vax-based electronic mail
.	.	.	.	.	.
.	.	.	.	.	.
.	.	.	.	.	.
F	40	Exec Sec/Off Mgr (temp)	20	Microsoft Word, WordPerfect 5.1	GE PC Mailbox
F	43	Comp. Consult /Trainer	1.3	Windows3.0	Procomm, Prodigy Primenet
F	46	Budget Analyst	10	Microsoft Excel, Word & PowerPoint	none

Sixteen subjects tested BusinessTalk 2000. They represented the profile of our typical users. We had approximately equal numbers of males and females with an age spread from 26 to 48. We were not interested in testing Microsoft Windows, so we required the subjects to have knowledge of Windows and experience using it. The background survey they filled out before the test confirmed we had a match on our requirements. We also selected our subjects so they represented the type of experiences that our users were likely to have had with e-mail and retrieval of information from a data base. Our users are divided into those who have had and those who have not had experience using similar products. The ones who have had experience were further divided into those who have used it on wide area networks and local area networks.

Figure 8   Tasks used in test and scenario

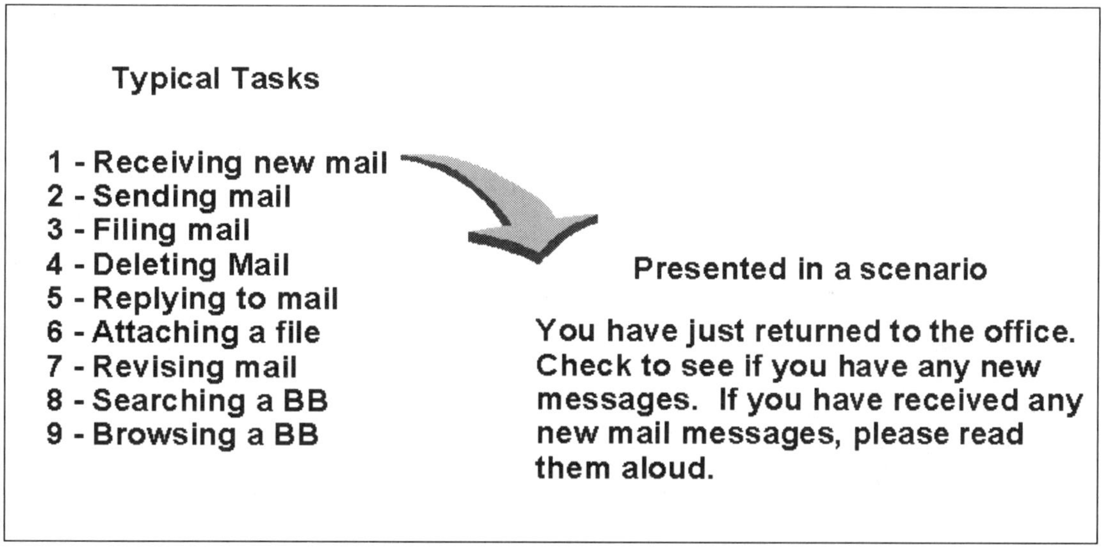

Typical Tasks

1 - Receiving new mail
2 - Sending mail
3 - Filing mail
4 - Deleting Mail
5 - Replying to mail
6 - Attaching a file
7 - Revising mail
8 - Searching a BB
9 - Browsing a BB

Presented in a scenario

You have just returned to the office. Check to see if you have any new messages. If you have received any new mail messages, please read them aloud.

In the usability test we used nine tasks to guide the subjects through the typical activities for which the users would use the product. They had some on-line help. The first seven tasks, as shown in Figure 8, related to the e-mail portion of BusinessTalk 2000 and the last two focused on information retrieval. In deciding which tasks would be included, we wanted those things that would represent about 80% of the user's normal activities. We wrote the tasks as scenarios they might see at work so they were easier to relate to. Each subject was tested for a half-day, which spread the testing over three weeks.

Each day in the early parts of the testing I did a telephone review with the Engineering Project Manager. We discussed those things that were being identified as problems. Some of them were merely bugs that were unintentional and not really part of the usability problems we were trying to uncover in the usability testing. Some were refinements to the user interface approach and some were more significant issues that we gained a full appreciation for as we watched more subjects.

We invited guests to observe what was going on in the test. Marketing, Engineering and other folks involved in the product were encouraged to come and watch how BusinessTalk 2000 performed. Marketing was too busy, but the Engineering Project Manager and the person responsible for documentation came for a day. There is nothing more convincing that a problem exists than to watch a typical user struggle with a portion of the product. You cannot dismiss the issue that it is merely an atypical user who probably would not be a user anyway, when you watch somebody who is articulate and tells you he or she cannot find something despite looking in all the likely places. Its often more agonizing for the observers than the subject, because it is like the real world in that you cannot be there to help each one through the problem. The Engineering Project Manager wanted us to provide more help as the user he was observing was struggling with the Task 5, replying to mail. The task identified a bug in the software so it was not performing as it was suppose to. I believe he called it cruel and unusual punishment, for him and the subject, but we allowed the subject to continue as we did with most to gain an understanding of what users expected and how the interface shaped their thinking.

Problems Identified

Figure 9   Task times from the usability test

Usability task	Subject task times (in minutes)						Avg.
	1	2	3	4	5	...	
Task 1 - Receiving new mail	17.5 *	13.5	6.5	13.0 *	8.5	...	15.5
Task 2 - Sending mail	10.5	36.0	3.5	36.5 **	3.0	...	16.0
. . .	. . .	. . .	. . .	. . .	. . .	...	. . .
Task 9 - Browsing the bulletin boards	16.0	11.0	39.0	18.0	28.0	...	22.0

* = subject needed assistance to complete the task

** = subject could not complete the task and was led through the steps

The full report followed a month after the completion of the usability test. We tracked times to complete a task, errors encountered, how the subjects felt about it, comments they made, etc. The results indicated we still were not done with the user interface. Figure 9 shows how long it took to complete the tasks. For example, Task 1, receiving new mail, had an average time that was three times greater than what we would target for an ideal system. For an electronic mail product, getting your mail should be so obvious that it should reach out off the screen and say "here I am." Not only was the time to execute too long, but almost two-thirds of the subjects needed some assistance on the task. Not a good thing, if you think in terms of how they would get that assistance or what disruption it might cause in their use of BusinessTalk 2000. Remember our primary business is not the sale of the software, but movement of information through the software and our network. Problems equate to telephone calls to our client services desk or an impediment to its use.

Figure 10 Perceptions of ease of use

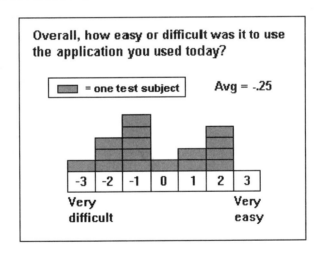

Sixteen subjects do not equate to a heavy duty research study, but the pattern was very clear. There was no doubt in our minds that we needed to fix some things. We also were aware that many of the problems would go away on subsequent uses because the user would have learned how to do things. We focused on first time users because of the problems they encounter and because we were aware that those first impressions make a difference on how users felt about the product. The attitudinal data we collected reinforced the other findings. We used several questions with a Likert scale to ferret out impressions of BusinessTalk 2000 (Figure 10). The question asking, how easy or difficult the product was to use had an average rating below neutral. Our current objective for this item is a score near the top of the positive scale. Our experience indicates that subjects are usually extremely polite and do not like to give poor ratings. When the rating drops below a point from the top, it is a general indication that a fix is needed.

Figure 11   Errors made by subjects when receiving new mail

Usability Problem	Task 1 - Receiving new mail																Total
	1	2	3	4	5	6	7	8	9	10	11	12	13	14	15	16	
Chose a Display Mail option from Post Office	X	X		X	X	X	X	X		X	X	X	X	X	X	X	14
Opened in basket before getting mail	X	X	X	X		X	X	X	X		X	X	X			X	12
Said there is no new mail	X	X		X	X	X		X	X	X		X	X			X	11
Read mail from Mailbag	X			X	X		X			X	X	X		X	X	X	10
Chose Search Mail from Mail						X	X		X					X	X		5
. . .	.	.	.	.	.	.	.	.	.	.	.	.	.	.	.	.	.
Tried Forward to view next message									X								1

X = subject experienced this problem

We also examined the errors the subjects made for each task. To highlight Task 1 again, we found a clear pattern of difficulty and formed some ideas on how to fix the problem (Figure 11). To display their mail, they should have gone to the Mail menu and selected Send and Receive Mail. Their mail would have been retrieved and put in their In basket. Instead, the subjects got lost in the Post Office. Fourteen out of the 16 subjects chose the Post Office as the way to get their mail. In the design, the Post Office was meant as a metaphor to separate remote functionality from things to be done on the user's PC. We intended it as a sort of advanced set of functions. Those things that would be used often we put as pulldown menu options or buttons. The Post Office ended up to be too seductive. The subjects were drawn to it because it was prominent as an icon on the screen. Those that got trapped in the Post Office ended up trying to do everything there.

The other common error for Task 1 occurred as the subjects drew conclusions from the basket icons. The baskets have two states: empty and with letters in them. Most looked at the In basket icon and concluded that they had no mail because it was empty. Even those subjects with remote mail services experience did not immediately think in terms of going on-line to retrieve their mail and there were no queues to lead them in that direction. When they opened the basket, it tended to substantiate their conclusion because there was nothing in it. Many had to be prompted and told that indeed they did have mail and they should try to get it.

Of course we identified many other things and in many ways the examples I have provided represented some of the most severe problems. The next step in the process though was to try to do something about the issues before we released it as a commercial product. Armed with the completed report and the support of the Engineering Project Manager we went to the engineering team to talk about what would or would not be done.

Much of the conversation was convincing the team that a problem existed and that the solution we had in mind to correct the issue was viable and had the potential to fix the problem. Having had the Engineering Project Manager observe during the test was a tremendous asset. The only thing better would have been to have the entire team watch the testing. It is extremely convincing that a problem exists when you see a typical person struggling with a task. Some members of the team resisted because they had trouble seeing an item as an issue that seemed so natural to them. They accepted on a trust level, but it just took a little time for them to believe it. The team had a high desire to create an exceptional product and so the discussions were lively.

Figure 12 summarizes the plan. There were about 100 suggestions that came out of the usability test. We classified them in two ways: by priority of when it should be done and by the level of effort it was going to take to implement it. The priority of when to do it was important, as it had potential for delaying milestones in the development process. Some things we wanted to be sure got into the product before our internal reviewers saw it so we did not have to repair their reactions and expectations for the product. Others had to be done before clients saw it, and some things we rejected. Eighty-five percent of the suggestions were included in the plan, and for the 15% we chose not to do, it was because it was not clear that the suggestions would make a difference or they were alternatives to suggestions being implemented.

Some of the suggestions we determined could be implemented in a few hours, some would require substantial amounts of time and still others would take work just to determine how long it would take to implement. More than one-fifth of the suggestions were completed before the usability test was completed. They were the result of my daily telephone calls during the usability test with the Engineering Project Manager.

Figure 12 Planned actions from the usability test

Priority	Level of Effort to Implement	finished while testing	a few hours	a few days	a few weeks	more than a month	not known	% Total
Priority	do before Alpha test	13	11	11	1	-	1	**38**
	do before CR	7	9	19	7	6	-	**47**
	don't do it	1	-	2	-	-	11	**15**
	% Total	**21**	**20**	**33**	**8**	**6**	**12**	**100**

Our next step was review and agreement from the Marketing Product Manager. The decision here was how much impact would there be on the development schedule. For the most part the Marketing Product Manager agreed with the team's plan. The agreement was struck that we should proceed with the first step to implement those things that had to be completed before the internal review.

We did not get everything into the first internal or commercial releases. We did get the items that we believed would make the biggest differences though. They accounted for about 80% of the things we had planned. The changes ranged from cosmetic to major restructuring. The cosmetic changes designed to ease retrieving mail included simple things like changes in wording. Figure 13 shows how it looked during the usability test. New Mail was changed on the File pulldown menu to Create Mail to avoid the misconception that New Mail meant to retrieve it. For similar reasons, Import ... and Export ... were changed to Import Text ... and Export Text .... Users were confused, thinking that Import ... would retrieve their mail.

An example of the bigger changes was the removal of the Post Office (Figure 14). Even though the effort was more substantial, it was deemed as necessary because of all the problems it created. The functionality was placed as an Advanced ... item on

Summary of Impact

Figure 13   Minor changes make a difference

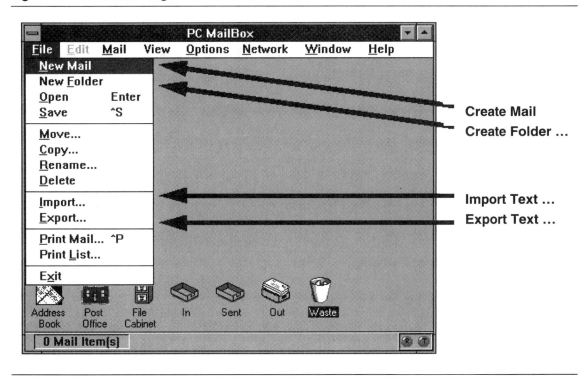

the Mail pulldown menu. The idea was to give it less visibility, and hence only those users who would really need it then might find it. Certainly, the most of our users would seldom if ever use the functionality.

We know from subsequent usability tests on later versions of the product that the changes we made in that first version were worthwhile. We have decreased time to perform tasks from 30% to 40% in critical areas, and the attitudinal ratings have substantially improved. We are not done improving BusinessTalk 2000. Each time we test we find more areas worthy of tweaking. Even suggestions from that first usability test remain on the list for future enhancements. They tend to be those things that had lower priority because the impact on the client was more questionable.

Figure 14   Removal of the Post Office

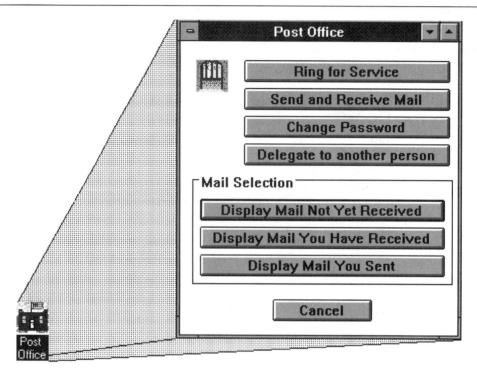

Field and Client Interest Is High for GUI

As we got closer to the release date, the field and client interest increased. More pressure began to build. The sales reps were eagerly demonstrating the first prototypes and early releases as they tend to do to gain a competitive advantage. They were saying things like their clients' primary interest was in the new Graphical User Interface. Several clients even began contacting their GE Information Services sales representatives as they heard of the coming product. They wanted to be beta site candidates. One client wanted "to 'touch and feel' an early copy of BusinessTalk 2000 on the Windows platform." Hence the client later became a candidate for the beta test.

Some of the sales reps and clients began lobbying for features they thought would not make it into the first release. A phased approach is difficult if you try to please all the people interested in a new product. In some cases we made some minor additions, but for the most part we tried to stay to the original intent of the first release. It meant in some cases that we had to either delay a potential client or assume we even lost some clients. With our varied client base, if you try to do it all at once, no one is happy because you cannot complete it.

When Are You Done?

Upper management continued to push for the release of the product. The list of items uncovered in the usability test tended to make them a bit nervous. In fact, one manager with some responsibility for delivering the product, received very positive feedback from a sales representative after it was demonstrated to a client. The sales rep's response was do not bother changing the Post Office, just fix the bugs and get it out. This prompted the higher level manager to say "we are/have become obsessed with the GUI being perfect." He wanted to make sure we were balancing continued work on the interface with the potential of lost business.

The Engineering Project Manager responded by reiterating we were working towards a plan agreed to by Marketing, User Interface, Engineering and Documentation. It was to

- get the usability test done ASAP,
- select most important items that are small,
- make those changes for the alpha version,
- select any changes needed (if any) for commercial release,
- document all changes for commercial release,
- have documentation focus on the commercial release,
- execute the plan.

The Marketing Product Manager also supported staying the course, which was the deciding factor that allowed us to continue with the improvements. While it was not clear whether the Post Office would be removed before the alpha test, many of the smaller items would be fixed. Critical user interface items would be reworked. The decision was made to postpone going to the field until the development team reworked the software by implementing the most critical user interface changes that the usability test highlighted.

Finishing Touches

We contracted with a graphic artist to develop the icons for BusinessTalk 2000. As I stated earlier, we have no one on staff who has that kind of background or training. The icons used in the early prototypes were either drawn from the Microsoft library of icons or were sketched by one of the development team members. The intent of using a graphical artist was to end up with icons that had a professional presentation and looked like they were part of a family of icons.

In February 1992, the alpha version was released for internal review. Fear that field personnel would not like it did not materialize. In preparation for commercialization of BusinessTalk 2000, sales blitzes were conducted at the field offices. The reception was very positive. The concerns that were raised centered on missing features that were delayed in the phased release approach. The sales folks wanted to immediately convert everyone, but their clients would not have access to their current bulletin boards and databases until the next release.

Just prior to commercialization, we reviewed BusinessTalk 2000 to see how we had done against the recommended changes for the user interface and to document those items that we still considered to be outstanding issues. The list had many items on it that would have to be taken care of in future releases, but we had all done quite well and were comfortable with it for a first release. There was room for improvement, but there always would be. BusinessTalk 2000 was commercialized in the second quarter of 1992. It continues to be enhanced and improved with each subsequent release.

Lessons Learned

Starting a User Interface Group

If you are starting a User Interface Group, do the following:

- Look for a godfather—you need support from as high up in the organization as you can get it. You are going to need budgetary considerations that can be solved only as a trade-off with existing organizations.
- PR never hurts—work on selling the group and the benefits that can be realized. Remember most people have not got the foggiest idea what you do. Most think that all you have to do is beautify the product and you should be able to do that at your desk without talking to clients.

- Start anywhere—the organization in which you begin is not that important. To be successful you have to be a cross-functional group, so as long as you can do that in the organization in which you are placed, you will be fine.

- It takes time—be patient. In most cases there will be distrust and a lot of misunderstanding that has to be overcome. You are an agent of change in the development process, which is a scary thing for those who have done it a different way.

- Start small and focused—you need early successes. What you would like is for people to say "wow" after you have completed your first project. Keep the numbers of staff small so you are not worrying about coordination and justification of your existence, until you have proven your worth.

Teaming Is the Key to Success

By *teaming* I mean, open communications across functional groups with everyone striving toward the same goal. In the GE Information Services environment, it usually includes marketing, engineering and support services like documentation, training and client services. It may also mean others who play a smaller role but are interested in the product like pricing, legal and distribution. The goal may be to create the "best" product and thereby make a profit. But, to Marketing that may mean a product chuck full of features, to Engineering that may mean a product that is very efficient and to Client Services that may mean a product where the number of support telephone calls is low. I have found that the User Interface Group is frequently the focus of the design and development process because what it produces is so visible. This puts the User Interface Group in the position of negotiator between organizations that have opposing views of the world. Everyone has an opinion of how the user interface should be designed. They are all legitimate opinions because they are all users. The challenge is to design the product for your client users and convince the team members that they may not be typical.

Each Product Effort is Different

Be prepared to approach each new product as if you had no previous track record. At least the initial projects after the creation of a User Interface Group will see a lot of new faces or the product itself will be unique in total or part. The User Interface Group as an identifiable entity at GE Information Services has been in existence for over three years, however we are still making inroads into organizations and product areas that we had not touched before. When you begin on the new product area do not assume that everyone knows your role or what you do. Take time in one of the early meetings to go through the activities you will doing to ensure the success of the user interface. Make sure that key user interface items like task analysis, focus groups, prototyping, usability testing, etc. get on the schedule as milestones with dates for delivery. Try to avoid the frequent trap of identifying the user interface problems with no time to implement the solutions before commercialization. It is much more difficult to fix the problem after you have already sold it to a large number of clients.

Continually Work on Improving the User Interface Process

It is easy to get stuck in a rut and assume that your approach is the correct one. Build in time to your schedule and make it a part of normal operations to check on how you are doing. Go back to your clients, the marketing and engineering teams, and ask them how you have done. Was the support level about right? Did the write-up from the usability testing serve the desired purpose? Is there anything else that the user interface group could have done to make it flow better? If you do not ask you cannot improve the process, all you can do is change it.

The Five Minute Brainstorms

Adherence to standards, applying the right techniques, doing the politically correct things and all the other things you read in books is only part of the answer to creating an effective user interface. The inspiration for making the substantial improvements comes from looking at the problem in a variety of ways. Our greatest successes come from using a collaborative approach within the user interface group. We use frequent brainstorming sessions to test out ideas and to grow and expand germs of ideas into full blown solutions. The sum of the members is greater than the parts.

Be Careful How You Position Yourself

You should not act as a policeman, but you have to make your presence known. As I have indicated already, the team approach is the most successful. If you take an authoritarian approach and try to dictate the user interface very rigidly, you break down the strength of the team approach. In a lot of cases, there is no one right way to design it. If you pretend as if there is, you loose credibility and the collaborative spirit.

On the other hand, you cannot be wishy-washy on issues that clearly should have one way. Just because there is no best way to perform a certain function, does not mean you should violate principles of consistency and handle each incidence differently throughout the product.

Approach It Like a Business

My final thought is to approach the user interface function like a business. You should worry about having clearly defined business objectives. Whether or not you are a profit and loss center, you will be looked at from the rest of the organization as to the benefits you are bringing to the product. It is not enough to have testimonials indicating how user friendly the products are that you have worked on. First, I am not sure what user friendly is or at least I am sure that I can get no agreement to a definition. Measure it. Find ways to quantify the increase in sales, improved user satisfaction, reduced calls for support, faster ramp times—whatever is a meaningful number for those who make decisions on the existence and growth of the user interface function. After you measure it, publicize it. Make it part of your annual performance review. Send summary letters on how you are doing to upper management. You need to establish baseline data on how users are performing with products and constantly notch up improvements. If you are going to be successful, you have to own what you produce and have a passion for improvement.

Reference

1. Miller, M., and O'Donnell, C. "Usability Testing on a Shoe String", Chi 1993.

CHAPTER 18

GTE Laboratories
Incorporated: The
Evolution of Usability
Within New
Service Design

Robert A. Virzi and
James F. Sorce

Robert Virzi joined the technical staff at GTE Laboratories in 1987, after a short stint at Bellcore. His primary research interest has been to improve the usability testing and design processes, but he has also explored new interaction techniques suited for telephony-based user interfaces. Bob received his B.A. from S.U.N.Y Buffalo in 1980 and his Ph.D. in cognitive psychology from Johns Hopkins University in 1984. He can be reached by electronic mail at rvirzi@gte.com.

James Sorce has been managing the Service Concept Design department at GTE Laboratories since its inception in 1986. Previously, he spent seven years in academic settings conducting research on human cognition and emotional development. He then spent four years at AT&T Bell Labs and Bellcore providing service descriptions, designing and evaluating user interfaces, and specifying functional requirements for new network services. Jim received his B.S. from Canisius College, his M.S. from the University of Denver, and his Ph.D.in developmental psychology from S.U.N.Y Buffalo.

Introduction

GTE has always been interested in the usability of its products and services. However, over the past few years, emphasis on the user interface has increased tremendously in light of the growing body of evidence that highlights the importance of usability for both our *customers*, contributing to their service usage and satisfaction, and for our *employees*, contributing to their effectiveness and productivity.

In this chapter we will first introduce GTE and the role of GTE Laboratories Incorporated (GTE Labs) within the corporation. Then, so that you can understand the context in which our usability program is embedded, we describe our Service Concept Design department. Our general mission is to develop and apply a state-of-the-art design process that can improve GTE's ability to offer innovative telecommunications services. To do this we explore a variety of design tools and techniques that allow us to define value from the customers' perspective. From these new service design roots, our usability component has grown in size and influence and is now actively supporting a wide variety of user interface design activities for GTE businesses. We still design and evaluate user interfaces for new revenue-generating services, but our usability specialists are now experiencing increased requests for help in developing applications aimed at reducing business operating costs (e.g., automating routine aspects of customer contact such as call routing, account inquiry, repair status, and directory assistance).

We have learned a great deal about the advantages and disadvantages of being a centralized R&D organization with two distinct goals—to improve the state of the art in user interface design and evaluation and to provide practical application-specific support to product managers and internal operations personnel. By providing readers with the rationale behind our approach to usability, coupled with an actual case study, we hope to convey not only how we think about design, but what we actually do to create a user interface that achieves high scores on measures of user performance and satisfaction. We also hope to provide some insights into the practical obstacles we have faced trying to conduct high quality user interface design. We have attempted to overcome these obstacles by improving our design process (e.g., refining the relationships between Marketing, Engineering, and Finance), and through research (e.g., developing more efficient and effective design and evaluation tools and techniques).

What Is GTE?

GTE, founded in 1918, is a worldwide provider of telecommunications products and services. With an annual revenue in 1992 of $20 billion and 130,000 employees, the corporation is one of the largest publicly owned telecommunications companies in the world. It is organized into the following separate strategic businesses:

- GTE Telephone Operations, a division of GTE Service Corporation, is the largest U.S.-based local exchange carrier. Operating on a national basis, it provides local telephone service to residential, business, government, and interexchange carriers through 21.4 million access lines, covering portions of 40 states. GTE also provides telephone service internationally in Canada, the Dominican Republic, and Venezuela.

- GTE Mobilnet/Contel Cellular is the second-largest cellular service provider in the United States, offering mobile–cellular products and network services to over 1 million customers in 77 metropolitan and 41 rural areas.

- GTE Directories Corporation is one of the world's largest publishers of Yellow Pages telephone directories. It annually produces almost 1,100 telephone directories for GTE and other telephone companies in 43 states and 13 other countries, with a total circulation of 54 million copies.

- GTE Airfone pioneered in-flight telecommunications services for passengers on commercial aircraft. Currently, over 2,000 U.S.-based aircraft are equipped with Airfone service and over 33 million calls have been completed. It also operates Railfone service on Amtrak passenger trains. Currently, about 140 railcars are equipped and over 1.87 million calls have been completed.

- GTE Spacenet provides satellite-based telecommunications services and systems for businesses, news organizations, and government agencies worldwide. It also provides private networks for domestic and international data, video, and voice communications.

- GTE Government Systems provides advanced-technology command, control, communications, intelligence,and information systems designed to meet the high performance requirements of its government and defense customers.

With the recent technological advances in digital communications and changes in the regulatory environment, GTE, like the rest of the telecommunications industry, is rethinking all of its businesses. It must prepare to defend its current telecommunications businesses from a wide variety of new and aggressive competitors. At the same time, it must prepare to take advantage of exciting new business opportunities never before open to it. GTE Labs is a critical resource that is helping GTE meet these challenges.

The Role of GTE Labs

GTE Labs is the central R&D facility for GTE Corporation. Its mission is to conduct research and development that will enable GTE's businesses to take greater advantage of existing and emerging technologies and provide the technical expertise required to support the exploration, evaluation, and decisions relating to new business opportunities. GTE Labs currently has approximately 500 employees, with over 75% of the technical staff holding advanced degrees.

Each year the corporation assigns GTE Labs an operating budget funded by contributions it extracts from each of its businesses. GTE 's businesses annually review their technology requirements and submit their high priority R&D needs to GTE Labs. From these requests, the various technical groups within GTE Labs develop formal work plans that attempt to match our technical skills to their highest priority business requests. The businesses review our proposals and, if necessary, negotiate modifications until both parties agree upon the work plan. As one might expect, especially with the telecommunications industry in such turmoil, many of the businesses' recent requests have been for near-term development support rather than longer-term exploratory research. Add to this their aggressive completion schedules, and the negotiated work plans frequently constrain us to apply well-known technologies and methods to their business problem rather than encouraging us to advance the state of the art in new technologies and methods. To counterbalance this, GTE Labs can dedicate some of its yearly budget to research topics that have not been requested by any business, but that GTE Labs' investigators believe may become valuable to them in the future. In this way, GTE Labs' management tries to *anticipate* critical business needs, launching new research programs and developing technological expertise far in advance of specific business requests. One such program that GTE Labs initiated in anticipation of critical requests from multiple businesses was the Service Concept Design department.

Service Concept Design Department

In 1986, GTE Laboratories initiated a long-term research program aimed at supporting GTE's telecommunications businesses as they strategically prepare to compete in the telecommunications industry of the future. Our desire was to help make GTE's current services more competitive and help them develop successful new services.

New Service Development Is High Risk

Our starting point was an awareness that many new services fail in the marketplace. To determine why this is the case, we turned to results from industry studies, which suggest that, while many factors can contribute to the failure of a new service, one factor was common to many failures—services that are well engineered and use state of the art technology fail when they do not provide benefits that users appreciate. Services that fail either provide unique features that no one really wants or they do not provide anything superior to the competition that would motivate customers to switch.

Users Demand Value

Our assertion was that customers do not buy features, they buy *value*. A new service becomes valuable to users to the extent that it provides *useful* and *usable* solutions to their important needs and problems. Thus, our newly formed department determined that our mission should be to complement the technology-oriented research already being conducted at GTE Labs by focusing our research program on a user-centered approach to new service development. Our aim was to understand customers' needs and preferences, then use this knowledge to guide feature definition, user interface design, and system implementation, while incorporating periodic utility and usability testing to ensure that our developing service concept continued to be valued by our target customers. Thus, as will be described later, consumer researchers and human factors experts would play critical roles within our newly formed department.

GTE Requires Profitability

While GTE's customers judge the success of our services by their value, we recognized that GTE must judge the success of a service by many factors, an important one being *profitability*. Utility and usability are not sufficient to ensure profits for GTE, although the chances are clearly better with them than without them. GTE can seriously consider offering only those new service concepts that appear capable of successfully competing against alternatives and generating sufficient profit to warrant their development effort and expense.

If any of these three key ingredients (utility, usability, or profitability) is deficient, the proposed service offering is at risk. At this point we concluded that our research program would first need to consider how other industries develop new products and services in a competitive environment, then absorb the best of that knowledge into an approach of our own that would be uniquely suited to the telecommunications industry and to the strengths of GTE.

Focus on Design

We quickly learned that attempting to operationally define an entire new service development process and customize it for GTE was too large an undertaking for our small, start-up research program. We elected to focus our efforts on the *design* stage of new service development. After investigating successful new product development processes (especially in the consumer products industry), we became convinced that the best way to ensure that a new service will be valued highly by customers and profitable for GTE once it is launched is to guarantee that service designers know, up front, what customers need or desire and what it will take to satisfy these needs. All subsequent design, development and launch decisions should be made in light of these critical customer requirements. We were convinced that relatively small amounts of extra time and effort spent during design could create disproportionately large benefits in later stages of the process. Thus, we concluded that the design stage provides the best leverage point for ensuring that innovation, value, and profitability are built into a new service.

Our Research Objective

Our research objective was becoming clearer. We would create a GTE paradigm for designing innovative new services that would be highly valued by customers, while returning profits to GTE. To meet this objective we launched a two-pronged attack:

- We defined a *step-by-step design process* that is customer centered, service oriented, and customized for GTE's telecommunications businesses.
- We identified *state-of-the-art methods and tools* that can increase efficiency and decrease risk at each step in the process—modifying existing techniques where weaknesses are discovered, and creating new ones as required.

Our Service Design Process:
An Iterative Experiment

Our initial step-by-step process incorporated elements from successful consumer and industrial design processes. However, their formal descriptions were too general to guide our implementation activities. We needed to define our own process in detail, describing team makeup, specific tasks, work flows, methods, procedures, expected outputs, etc. Our approach involved

- Generating our "best guess" hypothesis about how to operationally define each process step,

- Testing our hypothesis by actually designing a new service in collaboration with a GTE business,
- Noting where and how the process could be improved,
- Revising our hypothesis and applying it in the next new service project.

Thus, by successive approximation, we hoped to significantly improve our design process, making it a better fit with GTE businesses.

Makeup of Service Concept Design Department

We recognized that new service design is fundamentally a multidisciplinary process. The disciplines depicted in Figure 1 represent those we believe are necessary to design telecommunications services; e.g., industry analysis, market research, systems engineering, industrial design, human factors, software engineering, hardware engineering, and new business planning.

Figure 1 Team participants in the new service design process

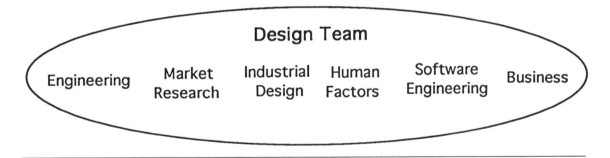

We also acknowledged that it would be impractical to have all of the desired design expertise resident within our department. The ideal design team would include *technology* experts with indepth knowledge of the hardware, software, and system alternatives that seemed most promising for the chosen service category. However, since our design team needs to support multiple GTE businesses with quite diverse new business opportunities, we would require a large and evolving mix of technology experts. Fortunately, an extremely diverse range of technology expertise exists within GTE Labs, although the individuals are distributed across departments. We needed to involve them as project "consultants." Also, the ideal design team would include *subject matter* experts in a particular service category (e.g., industry and market analysts; network, operations, legal and financial experts). Again, we have found that such expertise frequently exists within GTE's businesses, although the individuals are scattered throughout various organizations. We needed to involve them as project "consultants" as well. Thus, we elected to staff our department with a core group of service designers whose expertise was not typically available elsewhere in GTE Labs or GTE's businesses—*utility and usability experts*. We hired individuals who could (a) take a leadership role in coordinating multidisciplinary, multiorganizational design teams, (b) actively participate as user advocates in a user-centered design process, and (c) carry out applied research to improve the state of the art in utility and usability methods and tools.

The department currently has twelve members. Six hold Ph.D. degrees in various aspects of psychology (e.g., cognitive, experimental, linguistics). Collectively, they had extensive prior experience working as human factors and market research experts in industry, identifying and quantifying user needs, generating and screening service concepts, designing user interfaces, assessing user performance and preference, and forecasting customer demand. Some were more familiar with audio interfaces, others with text and graphics interfaces. One came to us from a market research consulting firm that specialized in new product design. Two additional members (with MS and BS degrees in psychology) provide critical research support, including the production of experimental stimuli, subject recruiting, data collection, and statistical analyses for our laboratory and field activities.

Since concept prototyping is a critical tool for both our utility and usability experts, three members (with MS degrees in communications or computer science) specialize in prototype design and production. Collectively, they had extensive prior experience in audio and video media production, multimedia application design and development, interactive computer applications, and rapid prototyping of user interface designs. The final member of the department provides technical laboratory support for the department. He orders, installs, reconfigures, and troubleshoots all of the equipment we use in our laboratory for building computerized prototypes, creating and editing multimedia content, and for collecting and documenting subject's behavioral and verbal responses during our experiments.

In the initial years, the department also benefited from the contributions of additional members. Members with an MS in market research and an MBA (with an emphasis on new business startups) played key roles in helping us formulate our "strawman" service concept design process. Two MS software engineers helped us define, acquire, and integrate various prototyping capabilities for our laboratory.

Summary of Major Design Activities

The ultimate goal of the service design stage is to specify the design for a profitable service that a GTE business could offer in a chosen service category. The input to this stage can be minimal—the identification of the new service category in which the GTE business is interested. The output from the design stage includes the specification of the most profitable service found, its positioning among the current and future competition, the best technology for implementing the service, and a financial model detailing the projected cash flows.

In this section, for each step of our current new service design process we state the major tasks that must be accomplished by the design team. We expect that the design participants will be drawn from multiple organizations within GTE Labs and the GTE business. We specifically highlight the roles played by our customer advocates—the service concept design team members responsible for "building in" utility and usability.

Figure 2 is a somewhat simplified and idealized summary of our new service design process. We still consider it a "working hypothesis" since we continually revise it based on our additional application experiences and by incorporating the results from our research aimed at creating new tools and techniques.

Technical and Market Background

Our first task is to gain enough understanding about the service domain of interest to be able to identify promising new business opportunities that support the strategic goals of a GTE business. While we already know a great deal about the service domains of our existing businesses, many new opportunities are surfacing in areas other than traditional telephony. The team's activities center around gathering, analyzing, and synthesizing information in order to characterize the current industry (e.g., identifying who the current and future competitors are; finding out what kind of profits are being generated in the service area; surveying the technology used by the current competition, the substitutes, and by analogs to identify existing and new technology options) and identify trends in these areas.

Activities in this background step typically involve extensive reviews of the literature (e.g., journals, trade magazines, industry reports), monitoring conferences and trade shows, and interviewing industry experts and competitors. Team members from the business play a major role here.

Our own utility and usability experts also play a critical role in this step. We are responsible for:

Figure 2   Core steps in the new service design process

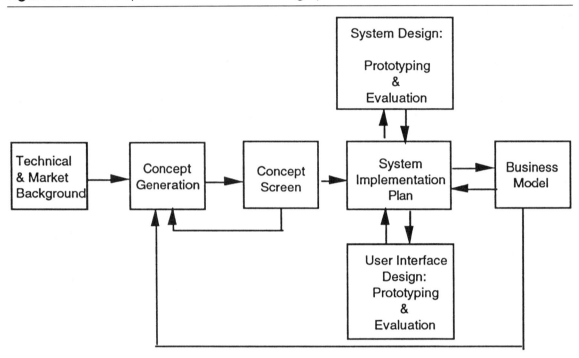

- Identifying the core benefits that customers are looking for,
- Assessing the extent to which customers are (dis)satisfied with current competitive alternatives,
- Understanding when, where, why and how customers are using current alternatives,
- Measuring customers' current performance with and preference for various service features and user interface characteristics,
- Tracking customers' changing needs and preferences,
- Assessing the potential usability advantages of emerging user interface technologies.

A key technique we apply here is currently referred to in business as the "voice of the customer." Beginning with a qualitative study (usually personal interviews involving consumers from the service domain of interest), we develop lists of relevant service attributes and benefits. We also compile a list of potential competitors to our yet unspecified new service concept. In a subsequent quantitative study (usually paper-and-pencil or computerized questionnaires), we determine consumers' priorities for these attributes and benefits. Finally, we obtain customers' evaluations (via structured rating questions) of how well each potential competitor satisfies each of the key attributes and benefits. Our goal is to uncover those attributes and benefits of the service domain that are very important to consumers but are not being satisfied by existing services. These areas of consumer disappointment provide us with new service opportunities.

Generating Concepts

Armed with knowledge about customers' unfulfilled needs, strengths and weaknesses of current and potential competitors, and technology options, the team now generates a wide variety of possible service solutions that take advantage of the identified trends. All team members, regardless of their particular organization or disciplinary expertise, participate in this activity. Their goal is to think strategically and creatively. To facilitate this, we frame the activity as a problem-solving task and apply common brainstorming techniques. The desired output is a collection of significantly different innovative service concepts that address some constellation of important customer-identified needs, while taking into account likely competitor, technology, and legal or regulatory conditions.

We are currently experimenting with various methods of improving our concept generation step. For example, some GTE employees would be valuable participants but are either not formally assigned to the design team or are physically located thousands of miles away. It is extremely difficult for them to travel to a central site and dedicate a week to generating concepts with us. Therefore, we are piloting a technique for providing "electronic brainstorming." We hope we can tap the creativity of individuals throughout the corporation by enabling them to participate asynchronously whenever they have 30–60 minutes to devote to the task. The software allows them to introduce their own innovative ideas and also to review and build upon the ideas contributed by others. Our early pilot results are encouraging, so we are continuing to experiment with this tool.

Our utility and usability experts not only serve as customer advocates during team brainstorming and discussion sessions, but, because of their interpersonal and experimental testing skills, they typically serve as group facilitators and discussion moderators. Once interesting concepts are produced, their key role is to figure out how to convey the essence of the service (e.g., its benefits, features, user interface, mode of delivery, price) clearly and concisely in a form that can be readily understood and appreciated by the rest of the team, business management, and potential customers. Typically, concepts at the end of this step are represented as short written descriptions with graphics or rough storyboards.

Screening Concepts

From the set of concepts generated in the previous step, the team must now decide which of the proposed solutions is most likely to succeed and warrants the continued investment of scarce design resources. The team considers a promising concept to be one that passes various screening criteria (e.g., potential market demand, technical feasibility, cost, fit with the company, length of time required for introduction).

In this step, the team's engineering experts have primary responsibility for investigating the technology options and tradeoffs involved in implementing the various concept descriptions. They also project the costs of the components of each service and identify aspects of the service that may not be possible to implement at all.

Our utility experts are responsible for gauging consumer acceptance of the various concepts. The technique we apply to estimate the market potential of new service ideas is called a concept test. This format for representing the concepts that consumers will evaluate is narrowly defined and standardized. It consists of a half page illustration that depicts someone using the service, accompanied by two or three paragraphs of text describing the benefits of the service (who would use it, when, and why), how the service is delivered, and its price. Potential consumers are presented with each concept statement and asked a standard battery of questions that address purchase Interest (e.g., their likelihood to buy), purchase diagnostics (e.g., perceived value and uniqueness), price sensitivity, and demographics. While consumers' answers to these questions cannot be taken at face value, they are quite useful as a relative measure of purchase intent, especially if we add benchmark services to the concept test—those that have already been commercialized and for which we have an established purchase history.

Our usability experts have no major task responsibilities during this step. The concepts in this form are still at such a high level of abstraction that usability evaluations are not yet appropriate.

Unfortunately, a concept that seems promising from the consumer–revenue perspective is not always promising from the technology–cost perspective (and the reverse case is also true). Such contradictory findings are common at this early stage of design, and indicate that the concepts must undergo further redesign. Thus, based on these results, the team begins to make difficult tradeoffs between functionality and cost. Features may be added or dropped. Sometimes, entirely new concepts are formed by combining the best aspects from different concepts. This step is successfully completed when the team agrees upon a *single* compromise service—one we believe will provide consumers with most of what they want, will be competitively viable, and will provide GTE with a handsome profit.

Detailed Design: System Implementation Plan

Now, the team fleshes out all of the design details for the selected concept. At this point written descriptions are not adequate to ensure that the proposed system will perform satisfactorily from both the engineering and usability perspectives. Thus, operational models of the service (i.e., working prototypes) are built and tested from each expertise's perspective. Theoretically, a single working model could support the iterative design-test-redesign activities of both perspectives. However, we have not found a single prototyping environment that can adequately support the needs of both perspectives. In addition, the two perspectives typically have different priorities for deciding what service functionality needs to be developed first and at what level of completeness and precision. There is also contention for the shared equipment. Thus, in practice, we have found that these two design activities are accomplished more efficiently when separate prototypes are employed to support system design and user interface design. As a consequence, two separate teams form. They are typically composed of people from different disciplines, employ different prototyping tools, and apply different evaluation methods.

As suggested in Figure 2, these two design efforts can occur in parallel. However, there must be a high degree of ongoing communication and interaction between the two, since design decisions made in one group will necessarily affect and be affected by design decisions made in the other. Communication is not a problem when the two activities share the same laboratory facilities so that each group has ready access to the other and their prototypes. This facilitates frequent and informal demonstrations, discussions, and status updates. The final system implementation plan will reflect the practical compromises negotiated between these two design teams.

The *system design* team focuses on the performance of specific hardware and software components as well as the overall system. Frequently, results from initial system prototype evaluations fail to meet their expectations for performance, cost, or engineering feasibility. The team engages in iterative design–build–test cycles until the prototype performs satisfactorily.

The *user interface design* team focuses on consumer performance and preference. Our utility and usability experts are core members of this team. Utility experts are responsible for refining the specific feature set so that consumers will highly value it over competitive alternatives, while usability experts are responsible for designing the user interface to support rapid learning and effective operation of these features.

The major challenge in trying to involve consumers during this detailed user interface design step is that services are intangible—especially innovative services with which customers have no prior experience. In order for our utility and usability experts to accurately measure customer performance and preference and to obtain valuable diagnostic feedback, customers need to be able to experience the proposed concept—in a very concrete way. Thus, *rapid prototyping* serves as a critical design tool. The inclusion of "look and feel" prototypes allows user interface designers to take advantage of iterative design-prototype-test cycles whereby the interface evolves over time, guided by user feedback, as it is fleshed out with increasing precision and detail. This same prototype also serves as an excellent vehicle for utility experts, allowing them to obtain increasingly accurate measures of customer preference and purchase intent.

Business Model

As the two prototype design teams negotiate tentative decisions about the system and user interface specifications, they feed information about the potential costs and revenue associated with the design into a business model that produces an estimate of profitability. This business model serves as an additional diagnostic design tool since sensitivity analyses can point out those aspects of the system implementation plan that most strongly affect profitability. Armed with this knowledge, another design iteration begins. System designers attempt to reduce the cost of particularly expensive system components, while utility experts modify or drop features that fail to deliver adequate benefits, and usability experts refine troublesome aspects of the user interface. Such design iterations continue until the business model results suggest that the concept (a) is promising enough to take to development, (b) has serious enough flaws to be returned to an earlier step in the design process, or (c) should be terminated.

These Go–No Go decision points are a critical aspect of our design process. The decision maker must review the "facts," judge their accuracy, weigh their importance, resolve contradictions, recognize gaps, and finally make a Go–No Go investment decision based on this set of incomplete and imprecise data. We believe that the new service *champion* from within the business unit should serve as the decision maker for the team. The rest of the team play the role of an expert decision-support system. We help to gather, analyze, organize, interpret, and present the relevant design information to the decision maker. If the decision maker concludes that the risk is too high for a "Go" decision, we help identify the source of the risk, recommend ways to modify the design to reduce the risk, and gather follow-up evidence indicating when the level of risk has been reduced enough to justify a "Go" decision.

While this decision-support approach sounds good in theory, it has proven to be difficult in practice. Sometimes the decision-makers are so conservative that our design team simply does not have sufficient time or resources to gather evidence that is convincing enough to lead them to make a "Go" decision. At other times, the decision makers are so liberal that they are willing to invest in further development even though the current evidence suggests it is a very risky venture. Another practical problem we have faced is that it is sometimes difficult to find an ideal decision maker within the business unit—someone who is willing to champion the new service idea, is committed enough to stay involved at a detailed design level, and is capable of garnering the necessary investment funding when "Go" decisions are made. We have not yet found an obvious solution to these decision-making problems. However, we strongly believe that the decision maker must be someone from the business and not a team member from GTE Labs. We also know from experience that the process works best when the decision maker is not just willing to manage the design process, but is also a strong champion of the service concept.

Research Issues: Utility and Usability

Proposing a new service design process was one thing. Applying it to real GTE business opportunities was another. As our business partners presented us with ambitious schedules and limited resources, we found that many of the methods and tools we had relied upon to conduct scientific research were ill-suited for our current design tasks. We were continually faced with having to complete a particular design activity more quickly and cheaply than our current tools and techniques would allow. Thus, we initiated a research program aimed at creating more efficient design tools and techniques. Here, we describe a few items on our current research agenda aimed at supporting our detailed user interface design and evaluation activities.

First, we questioned how we should present our novel new service ideas to customers so they can provide us with valid and useful feedback concerning utility, usability, and purchase intent. Our past experiences led us to observe that while *high fidelity* prototypes (i.e., where the person using the prototype cannot distinguish it from the final service) solve this problem quite well, building in high fidelity is costly—typically consuming too much of our precious design time and money. Thus, we are studying the conditions under which prototype fidelity can be significantly reduced without compromising the quality of customer feedback.

A second research topic surfaced as we implemented iterative design-build-test cycles. We observed that we were spending too much time in the testing phase—gathering and analyzing customers' performance data. Thus, we are pursuing two complementary means of increasing iterative design efficiency. We are evaluating the cost–benefit tradeoffs associated with substituting alternative usability techniques (e.g., enactment, heuristic analysis, think-aloud protocol) for traditional performance testing. We are also empirically investigating how few subjects we can test during a single design-build-test iteration without sacrificing quality.

Third, we have frequently observed that customers do not choose one service over its competitor based solely on the design of their user interfaces. Rather, the user interface is only one of a number of service characteristics that influence customers' choice behavior. So, given limited design time and funds, how much of it should be spent optimizing usability vs. seeking improvements in other features or price characteristics? We are developing methods for measuring the relative importance of specific user interface characteristics compared to other service features in determining customers' preference for a new service. This information will help us spend our design resources wisely, optimizing those aspects of the service that will have the greatest impact on user acceptance.

Fourth, we are experimenting with alternative ways of documenting and communicating our final user interface specifications. Our objective is to be able to provide developers with a specification language that is easy for them to understand, and that captures system behaviors accurately and comprehensively.

Finally, we continually explore ways to improve user interface designs, either by creating new techniques for current technologies (e.g., devising new interaction techniques for navigating through audio menus and forms), by evaluating the relative usability advantages and disavantages of emerging technologies (e.g., keypad input vs. automatic speech recognition) or by exploring the usability potential of new in-home devices (e.g., how to integrate sound and text in screen-based telephones).

Utility and Usability Take On a Life of Their Own

Our initial motivation for developing utility and usability expertise at GTE Labs was to be ready to support GTE businesses in their search for new revenue-producing services for residential and business customers. To date, our R&D program has produced a handful of successful new service designs, as well as practical tools and techniques that support customer-centered user interface design and testing.

Recently, however, we have received many requests for usability consulting from GTE businesses where the design objective is to introduce technology to help reduce operations costs and increase employee productivity. Typically, in these cases we are invited to participate as the project is developing its system implementation plan—after concept generation and screening have already been completed. Referring back to Figure 2, we enter at the box labeled *System Implementation Plan*. We typically have lead responsibility for the user interface design and play a supporting role in system design activities. Fortunately, we have found that many of the methods and tools we developed as part of the new service design process are directly applicable to this more restricted kind of usability consulting assignment.

The following case study exemplifies how our usability experts have applied the lessons learned from new service design to successfully support an operations application.

Case Study: Automating Call Handling at a Customer Contact Center

The case study we have chosen illustrates an effort that was confined to the later stages of the new service design process, when usability issues predominate. Our client had already selected an application, obviating the need for up-front market research activities. The application was loosely defined and our role was to identify the specific functionality of the system, design and test the user interface, and oversee its implementation.

Problem Statement

One of GTE's service businesses maintains several customer service centers around the country. These centers are staffed with highly trained personnel who can answer subscribers' questions and resolve service problems. They field telephone calls from a diverse user population, perhaps slightly more technically-savvy than the general population. Nationwide these centers field about 4 million calls per year, ranging from simple account balance enquiries to complicated calls requiring the operator to diagnose and fix problems.

This business enlisted our help because they faced a critical problem: costs associated with these customer service centers were growing at a faster rate than revenues.

They feared that, if left unchecked, these costs would erode the overall profitability of the business. Containing and managing these increasing costs became a company priority.

Managers in the business felt that interactive voice response (IVR) technology might help them solve this problem. IVR systems allow callers to hear recorded announcements by pressing keys on a telephone keypad. These managers reasoned that some of the simpler calls could be handled completely within the IVR system, so that the caller would not need to speak with an operator, thus lessening the need for increased staffing in the centers. One of these managers was familiar with our expertise in IVR technology from an earlier project, and he contacted us asking if we would join this effort.

After talking with headquarters staff and visiting a customer service center, we felt that we should take on this project for a variety of reasons. First, we had worked with the client before, and felt that we had established good working relations and mutual respect. Second, the business was very serious about the project, and was committed to a pilot of IVR technology. Both of these conditions were good indicators that work our group did on the project would be both welcomed and used. Finally, we had personal interest in exploring IVR technology since it is a part of an ongoing research program in our department. We felt that this would be a good opportunity to put this expertise to a practical test.

Forming the Project Team

Early on, we tried to identify the people that would be involved in the project and the roles they would play (see Figure 3). We felt that this step was particularly important for this project because the organizations involved are hundreds of miles apart. Several people from GTE Labs participated in this project. Lydia Volaitis joined the authors on a full-time basis as a codesigner of the user interface. Ramesh Chandak, Jim Paschetto, and Sandra Teare assisted in several phases of the project, predominately associated with building prototypes of the service. GTE Labs' role was to lead the design effort and to produce a written specification of the user interface.

Upper management appointed a project manager from the marketing organization of the business. She was charged with guiding the overall project and locating the resources necessary within her business. About one-third of the way into the project, four subject matter experts from the business joined the team. They played two roles in the design process. At times, they served as surrogates for the customer, having spent extensive time talking with them on the telephone. At other times, they provided input regarding the "company view," helping to ensure that the system we built fit with the accepted methods of operation and procedures within the business.

Two additional players joined the project part way through: a manager at the pilot location and a development vendor. The pilot-site manager wielded considerable clout, as her organization actually funded the trial. The development vendor was responsible for building the system based on specifications generated by GTE Labs. This vendor was the only non-GTE company involved in the project.

Figure 3 The organizations involved in the project, along with their major responsibilities. Arrows indicate major lines of communications.

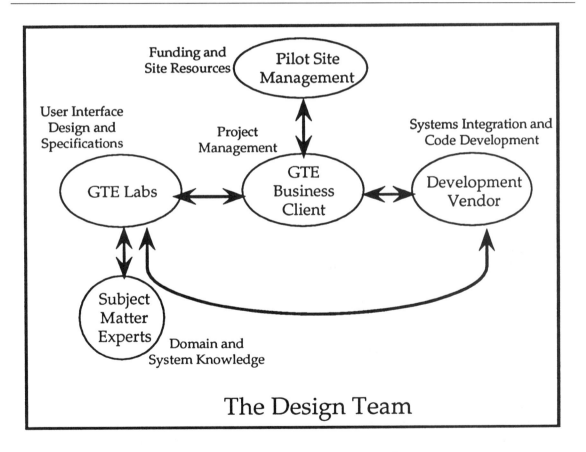

Understanding the Problem

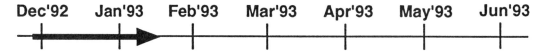

As indicated in the preceding timeline, our involvement began in late November 1992. The background work we did to understand the nuances of the problem ran until mid-January. When we started, our clients had already collected some survey data that identified the proportion of people calling with various types of problems. This information was valuable because it allowed us to focus our efforts on those areas that appeared likely to have the greatest impact. Armed with this, we visited a service center to obtain more detail on this subset of the problems. We conducted structured interviews with service representatives, monitored and categorized about 100 customer calls, and analyzed the overall work flow. By the time we left the service center, we had a fairly clear idea of the scope and complexity of call center operations. We were also able to generate a list of potential candidates for automation. Our strategy was to choose areas that were simple enough to automate, but that would also have a big impact on operations.

IVR technology is already widely used in call centers. Insurance companies, banks, technical support centers, and airlines, to name just a few, use this technology. In this case, we were fortunate in that several of our client's direct competitors also used IVR's for similar types of applications. This gave us the opportunity to exercise a large number of systems, listening to what seemed to work well so that we could incorporate these aspects into our own design.

Based on this background work, we sketched out the features that we felt the system should eventually have and indicated the candidates we felt should be implemented first. Our thinking at this time was very high level, lacking all the details needed to implement a service. This "high-level systems requirement" (see Example 1) was presented to the manager in charge of the project in a face-to-face meeting. She agreed with the overall plan and asked us to continue working in that vein.

Selecting a Vendor and a Pilot Site

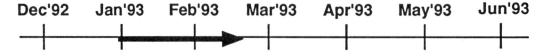

During this phase of the project, which lasted about six weeks, we worked with our client to clarify the system requirements. There are many voice processing vendors,

Example 1 Our initial view of the functionality desired in the final system is shown here, in generic form. Items followed by an asterisk were proposed for immediate implementation; other items were expected to be added at a later date.

Bill Related Functions
- Account Balances*
- Payment Information*
- Late Payments*
- Current Usage*
- Bill Explanations

Sales Office Transfer*

Service Features
- Review Current Options*
- Purchase New Options

Fax Back Functions
- Maps
- Manuals
- Instructions

Tutorials
- Topic A*
- Topic B*

and each offers a unique set of capabilities and liabilities. For example, some vendors can integrate very tightly with the telephone network, while others provide less flexibility in call handling. The degree of flexibility in handling calls, in turn, affects the kind of user interface options we would be able to design into the system. Eventually, the project manager chose a vendor based on a combination of what they could offer and their price. User interface concerns were weighed in the decision making process, but cost concerns were considered more important for the pilot. The business managers viewed this project as a test of the technology, and they wanted to limit their financial risk. Consequently, some user interface options we had been considering were ruled out because they would have been too expensive to implement (e.g., giving callers the option of receiving complex information by facsimile rather than by voice).

Because we were the most technically oriented members of the design team, we found ourselves responsible for evaluating the system design and implementation plans presented by vendors. Ideally, people with systems engineering and computer science backgrounds would have been brought in to assist with these evaluations. We did not have time to do that on this project, so we acted as technology consultants, assuring that our client's concerns were adequately and completely addressed by the solutions presented by the vendors. In effect, we were translators, expressing our client's needs in terms the vendors could understand, while explaining the vendor's solutions in our client's language.

During this phase a suitable pilot site needed to be selected. Our clients have numerous call centers scattered throughout the country. We needed to choose one that met a number of technical constraints (e.g., market size that was neither too big nor too small, correct hardware and software available at location, and room for the installation) and management constraints (e.g., level of on-site commitment, staffing, viewed as an important test market, and need for relief promised by IVR). After some false starts, we were able to choose a site, but not before we relaxed some of the technical constraints. As is often the case with a pilot project like this, management concerns often influence the technical aspects of the project. We did our best to influence the outcomes when it mattered to the user interface and lived within the constraints imposed regardless.

Initial Design Effort

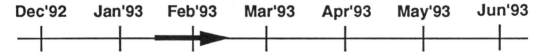

Based on what we had learned in our background research and with our understanding of system capabilities, we created our initial user interface design. In order to make the design concrete, something that is difficult with speech-based applications, we built a crude HyperCard™ simulation of the IVR system. As Figure 4 shows, a telephone keypad was displayed on a computer screen. Users pressed the buttons by positioning a cursor over them with the mouse. Digitized messages were played through the computer's speaker. A text window shows the wording of the prompt spoken by the computer. This window was hidden during subject testing but was valuable when reviewing the design with our clients.

This simulation was crude in that it performed no error checking, was recorded in one of the author's voices, and was not optimized for speed. Using this method, however, we could mimic the intended telephone-based user interface quickly and use the prototype to help define the user interface requirements.

Part of our department's research agenda is to study alternative user interface styles for IVR (work done in collaboration with Paul Resnick, at the MIT Center for Coordination Science). We had completed several laboratory studies that suggested one of these new techniques, which we called the *skip and scan* style, might make IVR

Figure 4   A screen from the simulated IVR system is shown. Users interacted with it by using a mouse to press buttons on the telephone keypad displayed on the screen. They heard the system response over the computer's speaker. Thus the important aspects of a telephone-based user interface were preserved while development time was dramatically reduced. The window at the left of the screen presents the words that are spoken by the recorded voice.

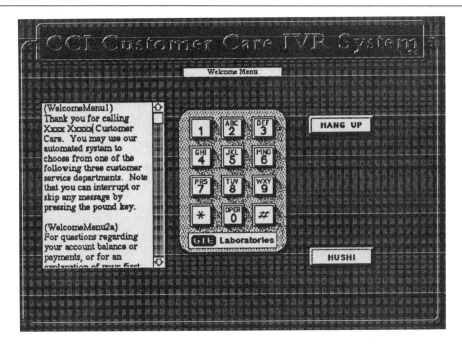

applications more usable. However, we were hesitant to apply the skip and scan style to this pilot system. Although we had considerable laboratory evidence that the style was advantageous, it had not yet been used in the "real world." Rather than make that decision at the Labs, we chose to build two versions of our prototype: a standard version and one that demonstrated the skip and scan style. That way, we reasoned, we could demonstrate the two styles to our client and to her management and let them decide if they wanted to move ahead with the new interaction technique.

We built both prototypes, packed them onto an Apple PowerBook™, and brought them to our client's location. We presented our experimental results and demonstrated both versions of the system to a management team, explaining the benefits of the new style while pointing out that it had not been used in a commercial system.

We were gratified that the client decided to use the skip and scan style. What we found interesting was that it was not our laboratory data that convinced them. Actually interacting with the two versions of the prototype persuaded them the new style was best for their application. We suspect that if the team had not actually interacted with the prototypes, their natural inclination would have been to choose the standard version.

We also used the prototype to focus discussion on the requirements for the IVR system. At the end of the meeting we had agreed that some of the functionality demonstrated in the prototype was required and should be carried over into the trial system. The management team, particularly the site manager, felt we had excluded some options that were required because they would have a major impact on operations efficiency. We agreed to include these functions, even though we were concerned that the functions would be difficult for users to access using IVR technology. Finally, some of the functions we demonstrated were excluded from the system. This was either because the managers did not perceive them as valuable or because they would be technically difficult to deliver from a systems perspective.

By the end of the meeting we had agreed on what the system requirements should be. The business managers were concerned that the IVR system would negatively influence customer perceptions of service quality. To minimize this impact, we jointly agreed that the caller should be given ample opportunity to drop out of the IVR system to speak with a call center representative. Our clients stated that they would consider the project successful if the IVR system was used by 10% of all callers. In addition to this overriding concern, we agreed on four basic functions that the pilot system would support:

- **Account balance** and payment information for the particular caller's account,
- **Sales office locator** that gives the caller information regarding the sales office nearest their location,
- **City and town database** providing information callers may need to use the service in over 2000 specific geographic regions,
- **Tutorial information** on a series of frequently asked questions.

We stated that we would revise the prototype and begin work on the detailed user interface specification. We asked that a small group of subject matter experts be assigned to work with us on the design. Four people with extensive experience in the call center were assigned on the spot.

Starting All Over

We met with the subject matter experts to redesign the call flows based on what we now believed would be the features in the pilot system. Working together, we started from what customers would hear when they first called the system, and we worked our way down each of the decision paths. The efforts were still fairly high level, emphasizing the general flow of the application and some of the key phrasing that would be needed, while avoiding getting bogged down in discussion of the details. We explained that we would take responsibility for most of the detailed wording, and asked the subject matter experts to take responsibility for the wording of the tutorials that were to be included in the application.

These design meetings lasted two days. At the end of the meetings we had a pretty good idea of the way the system would work, but all the information was in our heads—little had been committed to paper. The total written output of our meetings were 10 handwritten pages. We went home and undertook two tasks: (1) writing a formal specification of the system using a state description language that we have been evolving over the past several years; and (2) building a prototype of the service.

The state notation we use to describe IVR systems is a very precise way to specify the behavior we want the system to exhibit. Each page of the description constitutes a state in the system. Loosely speaking, this translates into a single menu on the system. All of the events that can occur are listed sequentially down the page (see Example 2). Most of these are user events, such as pressing a particular key on the telephone keypad, but some events are system events, for example, a timer expiring. Associated with each event is the action that the system will perform if that event occurs in that state. In Example 2, a state that describes a three-item menu, the actions associated with the user pressing 1, 2, or 3 on his or her telephone show transitions to other states, but the action associated with the user pressing any of the keys 4 through 9 is to play an error message.

This format, though tedious and time consuming to produce, can precisely specify the behavior expected of the system. We have found that most developers appreciate specifications to this level of detail, as it tends to make it easier to plan and execute development.

Example 2   This shows what a hypothetical page from our state specification might look like. It is an example of a three-item menu. Events appear on the left. Actions associated with events appear as pseudo-code. Comments appear at the end of lines, marked by a backslash, \. Message text appears at the end of the state.

Startup	Put ANI number into *caller_id*	\ save ID in variable
	set timeout = 3 seconds	\ set the timer
	play message 1:skip 2, 3, 4	\ indicates skip sequence with #
1	Go to **Sales** state	\ transfer to another state
2	if *caller_id* number is valid	\ conditional test of variable
	Go to **Balance Enquiry** state	\ if yes, transfer here
	else	
	Go to **Get Caller ID Number** state	\ if no, transfer here
3	Go to Billing Descriptions state	\ transfer to another state
4–9, *	play message 5	\ play error message
	play message 2: skip 3, 4	\ repeat menu choices
#	play next message in skip sequence	\ key used to skip messages
0	play message 6	\ caller opts out to live rep
	transfer call to operator	
Timeout	play message 2: skip 3, 4	\ repeat menu on no user action
Message 1	Please select from the following list of three choices. Note that you can interrupt any message, and skip to the next one, by pressing the pound key in the lower righthand corner.	
Message 2	For a list of sales locations near you, press 1. Remember, you can skip to the next option by pressing pound.	
Message 3	To review your account balance, including last payment date, press 2.	
Message 4	For descriptions of the various billing plans we have available, press 3.	
Message 5	<beep><key pressed by caller> is not accepted right now.	
Message 6	Please hold while your call is transferred to a representative.	

At the end of this phase of the project we had completed our first draft of the formal specifications. Most of the system behavior was captured in this 38-page document, although we knew we had not addressed the details in some of the more complicated aspects of the interface. We planned to return to these areas after we had updated the prototype and conducted user tests.

Building and Testing the Prototype

We built a robust prototype of the service, again using HyperCard™. We needed this prototype to be realistic enough to use to test the details of the user interface, as this was our next step. Much of the earlier prototype code was recycled, but we needed to make this version more comprehensive. For example, error handling was accomplished as we expected it to occur in the real system, and we used a better sounding voice for the recordings. Because we needed to have the prototype ready for testing as quickly as possible, an intensive effort was given to its development.

We tested the prototype with three different populations: (1) naive subjects likely to use a similar service were tested using the think-aloud testing methodology; (2) human factors experts that had experience with IVR design conducted a heuristic analysis; and (3) employees of the business unit were asked to provide comments on the prototype. Populations (1) and (2) provided us with a great deal of information regarding how the user interface should be restructured. We uncovered several navigation problems (callers were unable to find some kinds of information) and identified prompt wording that was confusing. The other group, the subject matter experts, gave us qualitatively different information. These evaluators focused on the veracity and value of the statements the prototype played to callers. For example, the facts in several of the tutorials sections were questioned.

Working Out the Details

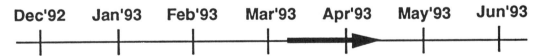

We sifted through all the comments and criticisms and used them to guide our next design iteration. Although we made many changes, they tended to be small refinements rather than more dramatic alterations of the user interface. For example, considerable effort was given to writing and rewriting the tutorial portions of the service to make sure it was both accurate from the company's perspective and understandable to callers.

All of the changes were incorporated into the specification document we were preparing. This document had grown considerably, to about 70 pages, representing a large proportion of the time taken in this phase. We do not yet have tools that help us to write the specifications (other than word processors), so checking the work for completeness and syntax is very laborious. One way we uncover specification errors is by building the prototype. On many occasions the prototyping team found mistakes in the specifications, which we then fixed.

To our surprise, our clients asked us to update the prototype so that they could use it for training and socializing the concept within their company. Our previous clients have typically viewed the prototype as something designers needed to carry out the design, without any real value in itself. Here was a client that viewed the prototype as a valuable tool that they intended to use for purposes we had never intended.

We agreed to update the prototype, even though we had not planned to do so. Because this version was associated with our department and we expected it to get wide exposure, we polished out the rough edges that were not important when we controlled the prototype. Prompts were rerecorded and a cleaner graphical treatment was applied to the screens. The entire prototype was bullet proofed, so that it could not be inadvertently broken by a casual user.

We delivered our final specifications to our client who, in turn, delivered them to the development vendor. We expected our involvement in the project to taper off at this point, but this turned out not to be the case.

Getting the System Built

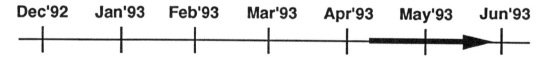

As mentioned earlier, the system used a new interaction technique, skip and scan menus, which depart from the standard menu style. Implementing this technique with an IVR scripting language that does not have the proper primitives is cumbersome, although it can be done. The scripting language our developers were using suffered from this problem.

After reviewing the specifications, the vendor tried to convince us that the technique was not really a good idea. After all, they had never really built a system quite like the one we proposed, and they rightly claimed some expertise at building IVR systems. We explained our rationale and offered the evidence we had from the laboratory, without much success at convincing the developer.

At this point our client stepped in, with the weight of one who is paying the bills. She gave us her full support and told the vendor that the system must use the new style. This closed the matter, and the developer resolved to build the system as specified. We appreciated the strength of our client's support, but question if it would have been so strong if she had not directly experienced the difference between the two approaches through the prototype. Our sense was that if she had not had this experience, she may well have been persuaded by the vendor's comments.

We had expected to interact with the developer periodically to explain or clarify the specifications to be sure that they were being implemented accurately. Unfortunately, we were disappointed by the unusually large effort we had to devote to this phase of the project. Perhaps it was because the developer had never built a system like this one before, or perhaps it was because they were understaffed for the complexity of the effort, but it quickly became clear that the system they were delivering was going to be severely deficient. As a result, this turned out to be much more than a background task for us. Two people were consumed full-time reviewing the system as pieces were rewritten, comparing it to the specifications, and negotiating solutions with the developer. Other people from GTE labs helped with testing during this critical phase as well.

The reason we became so involved in the development effort is that we realized that we had much more to lose than the developer if the pilot system failed. Our reputations in the company were at stake. We felt we had designed a very good system and were frustrated that all our work would be lost if the implementation failed. We were quite fortunate that we had the luxury of reassigning staff to meet the needs of this project without seriously disrupting other efforts.

Turning It On—and Making Sure It Works

Finally, after about six months of effort, involving three designers, two prototypers, some voice talent, a vendor's development team, and myriad people in the business, the system was ready and we took our first caller at 7 AM on May 25. Despite all our testing and design work, we anxiously awaited confirmation that the system was working as planned.

For the first few hours, the only feedback we had regarding system operation came from the call center representatives who handled callers once they opted out of the IVR (the system was designed so that callers could get to a representative at any point in the call). While the representatives reported that some callers complained about the introduction of IVR technology (an anticipated outcome), this number was no higher than expected. The feeling among the representatives was that the system was working, and at least was not making their jobs any harder. Information regarding call volumes and hold times (which we obtained later that first day) supported this perception.

A part of the system specification included a definition of call logs, identifying what individual callers did during their phone calls. The log contained each of the states that the caller had entered, along with the time. We analyzed these files as soon as they were available so that we could determine how callers were using the system. These analyses gave us our first hard evidence that callers were using the system as anticipated, nearly two days after the system had been turned live.

At first, we compiled call-log reports on a daily basis, but after about a month we changed to weekly reporting on the system. These reports were presented by the project manager to upper management in the business. They included data on how many people were choosing to use the IVR system (about 40%), how many were using it effectively to obtain information (75% of those who used it), and where some problem areas lay. These problems suggested both changes to make to the user interface and ways to expand and improve the databases that underlay some features.

Overall, our clients were very happy with the performance of the system, perhaps even more so than us. We had tried to obtain clear criteria for determining the success or failure of the pilot, but in the end perception was more important than data. Plans for rolling out the service to the rest of the call centers in the business were made. While this was a gratifying result, we lobbied for GTE Labs participation in an ongoing effort to evaluate and refine the system based on field data. They agreed and we plan to continue our work on this system, modifying and improving it, as it is turned up across the country.

Lessons Learned

In retrospect, our most powerful tool in the creation of this service was undoubtedly our ability to quickly build interactive prototypes of the design ideas we were considering. The prototype allowed us to socialize our ideas and solicit input from a large number of people in our client's organization. There were two effects from this: (1) the actual features in the service differed considerably from those in our initial design and (2) people throughout the organization felt they owned at least a part of the project, predisposing them to support it.

We have used the state notation discussed in this chapter before and since this project as a specification technique. It works exceptionally well for IVR systems, which are inherently state based. Although the format can become cumbersome and unwieldy, particularly as changes are made to the design, it does a very good job of defining the behavior expected of the service in detail. Our experience shows that developers actually prefer very detailed and precise specifications over those that are open to interpretation because it makes their job *easier*. We hope to refine this technique in the future, including building tools to support designers in using the notation to create designs.

We learned a considerable amount regarding how to be viewed as a contributor on a team even though we were 1000 miles away from our clients. We were on the phone with them almost daily and met with them face-to-face several times during the project. Interestingly, even though our help was acknowledged by team members, much of the upper management in the business unit was unaware of the extent of our work. This raises the issue of how a consulting organization can effectively make its work known and spread its reputation throughout the company. We are still trying to answer this question.

Finally, this project drove home the point that we, as user interface designers, are vulnerable to poor implementation. In the case reported here, had we not filled-in for the deficiencies of the development organization, we are certain the entire system would have been killed based on poor performance. Not only would this have reflected poorly on us, the business would have missed a cost-containment opportunity.

RESOURCES

This section of the book presents lists of resources for usability planners, practitioners, and students. The lists cover

- books
- periodicals, proceedings, and newsletters
- professional societies
- academic programs
- usability consultants

In some cases, you are referred to other documents that provide an updated list of resources, such as the Human Factors and Ergonomics Society's Directory of Graduate Human Factors Programs in the U.S.A.

Books

Bailey, R. (1982). *Human performance engineering: A guide for system designers.* Engelwood Cliffs, NJ: Prentice-Hall.

Bass, J., and Prasun, D. (1993). *User interface software.* New York: John Wiley and Sons.

Brown, C. M. (1988). *Human–computer interface guidelines.* Norwood, NJ: Ablex Publishing Corporation.

Bullinger, H., and Gunzenhauser, R. (eds). (1988). *Software ergonomics: Advances and applications.* New York: Halsted Press.

Casey, S. (1993). *Set phasers on stun: And other true tales of design, technology, and human error.* Santa Barbara, CA: Aegean Publishing Company.

Cushman, W., and Rosenberg, D. (1991). *Human factors in product design, Advances in human factors/ergonomics,* 14. New York: Elsevier Science Publishers B.V.

Dreyfuss, H. (1967). *Designing for people.* New York: Grossman Publishers; a division of Viking Press.

Dumas, J. (1988). *Designing user interfaces for software.* Englewood Cliffs, NJ: Prentice-Hall.

Dumas, J., and Redish, J. (1993). *A practical guide to usability testing.* Norwood, NJ: Ablex Publishing Corporation.

Edmonds, E. (ed.). (1992). *The seperable user interface.* New York: Academic Press.

Ehrich, R., and Williges, R. (eds.). (1986). *Human–computer dialog design, Advances in human factors/ergonomics,* New York: Elsevier Science Publishers B. V.

Golman, A., and McDonald, S. (1987). *The group depth interview: Principles and practice.* Englewood Cliffs, NJ: Prentice-Hall.

Hix, D., and Hartson, R. (1993). *Developing user interfaces: Ensuring usability through product and process.* New York: John Wiley and Sons.

Hix, D., and Hartson, R. (1988). *Advances in human–computer interaction,* Norwood, NJ: Ablex Publishing Corporation.

Horton, W. (19—). *Designing and writing online documentation.* New York, NY: John Wiley and Sons.

Klemmer, E. (ed.). (1989). *Ergonomics: Harness the power of human factors in your business.* Norwood, NJ: Ablex Publishing Corporation.

Larson, J. (1992). *Interactive software: Tools for building interactive user interfaces.* Englewood Cliffs, NJ: Yourdon Press.

Lorenz, C. (1990). *The design dimension: The new competitive weapon for product strategy and global marketing.* Cambridge, MA: Basil Blackwell.

Marcus A. (1992), *Graphic design for electronic documents and user interfaces.* New York: ACM Press.

Martin, C. (1988). *User-centered requirements analysis.* Engelwood Cliffs, NJ: Prentice-Hall.

Mayhew, D. (1992). *Principles and guidelines in software user interface design.* Engelwood Cliffs, NJ: Prentice-Hall.

McCormick, E., and Sanders, M. (1982). *Human factors in engineering and design*, 5th ed. New York: McGraw-Hill Book Company.

Nielsen, J. (1993). *Usability engineering*. Boston: Academic Press.

Norman, D. (1988). *The design of everyday things*. New York: Basic Books.

Peters, T., and Waterman, R. (1982). *In search of excellence*. New York: Warner Books.

Peters, T. (1987). *Thriving on chaos*. New York: Harper Perennial.

Powell, J. (1990). *Designing user interfaces*. San Marcos, CA: Microtrend Books, Slawson Communications.

Rubinstein, R., and Hersh, H. (1984). *The human factor: Designing computer systems for people*. Burlington, MA: Digital Press.

Salvendy, G. (ed.). (1987). *Handbook of human factors*. New York: John Wiley and Sons.

Simpson, H. (1985). *Design of user-friendly programs for small computers*. New York: McGraw-Hill Book Company.

Schneiderman, B. (1992). *Designing the user interface: Strategies for effective human–computer interaction*, 2nd ed. Reading, MA: Addison-Wesley Publishing Company.

Smith S., and Mosier, J. (1986). *Guidelines for designing uuser interface software*. (Technical Report ESD-TR-86-278). Bedford, MA: MITRE Corporation.

Tognazzini, B. (1992). *Tog on interface*. Reading, MA: Addison-Wesley Publishing Company, Inc.

Tufte, E. (1990). *Envisioning information*. Cheshire, CT: Graphics Press.

Tufte, E. (1983). *The visual design of quantitative information*. Cheshire, CT: Graphics Press.

Van Cott, H., and Kinkade, R. (1972). *Human engineering guide to equipment design*. Washington, DC: U.S. Government Printing Office.

Vassiliou, Y. (1984). *Human factors and interactive computer systems*. Norwood, NJ: Ablex Publishing Corporation.

Woodson, W. (ed.). (1981). *Human factors design handbook*. New York: McGraw-Hill Book Company.

Periodicals, proceedings, and newsletters

Applied ergonomics. Oxford: Butterworth–Heinemann Ltd.

Before and after: How to design cool stuff. Roseville, CA: John McWade.

Behaviour and information technology. Bristol, PA: Taylor and Francis.

Common ground: The newletter of usability professionals. Usability Professionals Association.

Communications of the ACM. New York: Association for Computing Machinery.

Computers in human behavior. Elmsford: Pergamon Press.

Ergonomics. Bristol, PA: Taylor & Francis.

Ergonomics in design. Santa Monica, CA: Human Factors and Ergonomics Society.

Human–computer interaction. Hillsdale, NJ: Lawrence Erlbaum Associates

Human factors and ergonomics society bulletin. Santa Monica, CA: Human Factors and Ergonomics Society.

IEEE computer graphics and applications. Los Alamitos, CA.

I.D. Magazine. New York.

Interacting with computers. Oxford: Butterworth-Heinemann Ltd.

Journal of the human factors and ergonomics society. Santa Monica, CA: Human Factors and Ergonomics Society.

Proceedings of the ACM special interest group on computer and human interaction. Baltimore: Association for Computing Machinery.

Proceedings of the human factors and ergonomics society. Santa Monica, CA: Human Factors and Ergonomics Society.

Proceedings of the national computer graphics association. Fairfax, VA: National Computer Graphics Association.

Proceedings of the society for information display. Playa Del Rey, CA: Society for Information Display.

Proceedings of the society for technical communication. Arlington, VA: Society for Technical Communication.

Proceedings of INTERACT. New York: Elsevier Science Publishing Company B.V.

SIGGRAPH (special interest group on computer graphics) bulletin. New York: Association for Computing Machinery.

Professional Societies

The following societies address the interests and needs of people involved in user-centered design. For cases where the society has no central office, the name of an organizer or officer is given.

- Ergonomics Society
  Rod Graves, Secretary
  University of Technology
  Loughborough, LEIC LE11 3TU
  England

- Human Factors and Ergonomics Society (HFES)
  P.O. Box 1369
  Santa Monica, CA 90406

- IEEE Systems, Man, and Cybernetics Society
  345 East 47th Street
  New York, NY 10017

- Industrial Designers Society of America (IDSA)
  1142-E Walker Road
  Great Falls, VA 22066

- Society for Information Display
  8055 W. Manchester Avenue
  Suite 615
  Playa del Rey, CA 90293

- Society for Technical Communication (STC)
  Suite 904
  901 North Stuart Street
  Arlington, VA 22203

- Special Interest Group on Computer and Human Interaction (SIGCHI)
  Association for Computing Machinery
  P.O. Box 12115
  Church Street Station
  New York, NY 10249

- Usability Professionals Association (UPA)
  Janice James, Chairperson
  American Airlines / STIN
  P.O. Box 619616 MD 4230
  DFW Airport, TX 75261-9616

A more extensive listing of societies, including many established outside the United States, is provided in K. Pelsma (ed.). (1987). *Ergonomics sourcebook* (Lawrence, Kansas: The Report Store).

Academic Programs

The Human Factors and Ergonomic Society publishes the *Directory of graduate human factors programs in the U.S.A.* For each academic program, the directory describes the graduate program, the application procedure, admission requirements, tuition and fee amounts, financial assistance terms, degree requirements, the curriculum, research and teaching opportunities, student statistics, and the background of faculty members. For a copy of the directory, contact

The Human Factors and Ergonomics Society
P.O Box 1369
Santa Monica, CA 90406-1369
(310) 394-1811

Sometimes, you will find short courses and seminars advertised or announced in the bulletins and newsletters published by the professional societies listed earlier.

Consultants

The Human Factors and Ergonomic Society also publishes: *Directory of human factors/ergonomics consultants*. This directory lists consultants individually and by company.

You can also find consultants listed in membership directories published by the professional associations listed earlier.

INDEX